A GOOD AND WISE MEASURE
The Search for the Canadian–American Boundary, 1783–1842

In this detailed and fascinating book, Francis Carroll tells the story of the attempts to settle the original boundary between British North America and the United States. Though established by the Treaty of Paris in 1783, the boundary was plagued by ambiguities and errors in the document. The border stretched over twenty-five hundred miles, from New Brunswick and Maine to the St Lawrence River, through the Great Lakes, and from Lake Superior to the Lake of the Woods. It was steadily filling with people of competing interests – Loyalists and Yankees, fur traders and soldiers, Europeans and First Nations peoples – and became a major focus of Anglo–Canadian–American relations for almost sixty years.

The author's extensive research draws on manuscript materials never used for the subject before. The book is the first to explain thoroughly the Herculean efforts of the surveyors and crews working for the four boundary commissions set up by the Treaty of Ghent (1814). It reveals the network of geopolitical intrigue underlying the failed arbitration (1830–1) of King William I of the Netherlands. It deals with the Rebellions of 1837 and the border skirmishes that complicated the search for a settlement. And it shows how rapid political change in the North Atlantic world in 1840–1 allowed Daniel Webster and Lord Ashburton to negotiate a reasonable compromise settlement – 'A good and wise measure,' as Ashburton called it.

Filled with the politics and intrigues of the time, the book brings to life a remarkable, rambunctious period in the diplomatic and political history of both Canada and the United States, which led, almost miraculously, to establishment of the longest undefended border in the world.

FRANCIS M. CARROLL is Senior Scholar of History at the University of Manitoba and a Fellow of St John's College.

A Good and Wise Measure

The Search for the
Canadian–American Boundary,
1783–1842

FRANCIS M. CARROLL

UNIVERSITY OF TORONTO PRESS
Toronto Buffalo London

© University of Toronto Press Incorporated 2001
Toronto Buffalo London
Printed in Canada
Reprinted 2003

ISBN 0-8020-4829-3 (cloth)
ISBN 0-8020-8358-7 (paper)

Printed on acid-free paper

National Library of Canada Cataloguing in Publication Data

Carroll, Francis M
  A good and wise measure : the search for the Canadian–American boundary,
  1783–1842

  Includes bibliographical references and index.
  ISBN 0-8020-4829-3 (bound)   ISBN 0-8020-8358-7 (pbk.)

  1. Northeast boundary of the United States.   2. Canada – Boundaries –
  Northeastern States.   3. Northeastern States – Boundaries – Canada.
  4. United States – Foreign relations – Great Britain.   5. Great Britain –
  Foreign relations – United States.   6. Canada – History – 1763–1867.
  7. United States – History – 1783–1865.   I. Title.

  FC183.C37 2001   327.73041   C00-933039-9
  E398.C37 2001

The poem by Edward Winslow on page xxiii is from W.O. Raymond, ed.,
The Winslow Papers (Saint John: New Brunswick Historical Society, 1901), 425–6.

University of Toronto Press acknowledges the financial assistance to its
publishing program of the Canada Council for the Arts and the Ontario Arts
Council.

This book has been published with the help of a grant from the Humanities
and Social Sciences Federation of Canada, using funds provided by the Social
Sciences and Humanities Research Council of Canada.

University of Toronto Press acknowledges the financial support for its
publishing activities of the Government of Canada through the Book
Publishing Industry Development Program (BPIDP).

FOR ABSENT FRIENDS

David Butler
  1940–1989

Don Murphy
  1934–1986

Charles L. Odoroff
  1938–1987

The discussion of these questions, now pretty nearly exhausted, leave the universal impression that the treaty was a good and wise measure, and good and wise because it was fair.

Baron Ashburton (Alexander Baring) to Daniel Webster, 28 April 1843

Contents

x Contents

List of Maps

Preface

An undetermined frontier is a fertile source of trouble, not so much because of the value of the disputed territory as of the claim that it is national property. What the nation has it will hold; sentiment adds strength to the grasp; even to sell may appear an unworthy compromise in a young country. As long, therefore, as the boundaries between the United States and Canada were anywhere in dispute, a local irritation might have quickly developed into widespread inflammatory disorder. So dangerous were many of these unresolved problems that Americans and Canadians may well be thankful that they have been honourably settled, and are to-day incidents of history which rarely excite hostile comment on either side.[1]

Sir Robert Falconer, 1925

The Canadian–American boundary is one of the most stable and open in the world. For all practical purposes the border is undefended. There is a certain amount of public-relations 'hype' to this notion, but there is also more than a grain of truth. Throughout the twentieth century the undefended Canadian–American boundary, and all that it implies, was a model to the rest of the world of how reasonable people in neighbouring countries have been able to resolve their difficulties and live together in the international community without reverting to war, intimidation, or bickering.

This happy state of affairs was not always the case. The Canadian–American boundary was a source of serious irritation, threats of violence, and endless bad feeling within the Anglo–Canadian–American world from the end of the War for American Independence until almost the middle of the nineteenth century. 'Blood is no guaranty against bloodshed,' Percy Corbett, the distinguished international lawyer, noted in commenting on Canadian–American disputes.[2] Even after the boundary was finally settled by diplomacy in the 1840s, the decisions rankled many people for several generations. To be sure, many of these passions had their origins in deeper emotional or philosophical differences between the nations rather than in merely the location of a boundary line on the ground, but these feelings were powerful and significant none the less.

This book attempts to explain the struggle to find an acceptable boundary between Canada and the United States in the eastern half of the continent – specifically, the boundary between British North America and the United States of America as defined by the Treaty of Paris of 1783, which ended the Revolutionary War. This was not an easy task. It proved almost impossible in the two decades after 1783, and it did not get any easier in the early nineteenth century as populations moved into the contested border regions and as political communities evolved along the border areas with competing claims and ambitions. One study of Canadian–American relations called the boundary terms in the treaty of 1783 'a very Pandora's box, whence issued problems and perplexities that more than once led Britain and America to the verge of war and were for many years a constant source of irritation to the peoples of the United States and Canada.'[3] Herculean efforts in terms of human energy and financial commitment were made time after time through the Boundary Commissions and through the diplomatic process. The results were incomplete. As late as the 1830s only separated segments of the boundary had been agreed on, and it looked as if new crises along the frontier would explode into a third Anglo–Canadian–American war. Only with great difficulty was a settlement reached in the Webster–Ashburton Treaty of 1842, and then, as mentioned, a long heritage of bitterness and a sense of betrayal echoed right into the twentieth century.

A realistic view of human nature and political dynamics helps us to understand these rivalries and this process. The placement of a permanent boundary was sure to have serious consequences for many people, and not always to their individual satisfaction. Sir Francis Hincks, one of the most important Canadian politicians of the mid-nineteenth century and a distinguished servant of the Crown, understood perfectly both the process of reaching a boundary agreement and the resentments arising out of a final settlement. In 1885 Hincks explained this to a Montreal audience:

International treaties are in most cases entered into, either with the object of terminating an existing war, or of preventing a resort to hostilities, by the amicable settlement of questions in controversy. As a rule I believe that international treaties are almost invariably condemned by the people on whose behalf they have been negotiated. This is not surprising. In order to effect the object, which both parties must have in view, as they would not otherwise enter into the negotiation, mutual concessions must be made, and in countries where public opinion has its due weight, as it has both in Great Britain and the United States, those in opposition to the Government which is responsible for the treaty, will be sure to be dissatisfied. In the case of a dependency like Canada, the strong probability is that all parties will unite in denouncing a treaty which, however fair and reasonable under existing circumstances, is not precisely what they would desire.[4]

Here was a clear statement of the many pitfalls and the scope for resentment. In keeping with Hincks's sentiments, I do not intend to assign blame or to allege betrayal – to show who was sacrificed for whom. The people who worked on the boundary were hard-headed and practical. They struggled earnestly to obtain the best boundary for their countries, and, thanks to the ambiguities of the treaty of 1783 and the absence of treaty maps, no side had a perfect case. '"Right" and "wrong" are large terms to apply to claims in an unsurveyed wilderness,' wrote two commentators over fifty years ago, 'and neither side is entitled to "the white gloves,"' and the participants used every resource at their disposal, be that diplomacy, legal argument, bluff, intrigue, or whatever.[5] The object was to get the best boundary to protect their interests. The fact that Englishmen and Canadians, on one side, and Americans, on the other, tended to see each other in the most unfavourable light did not make things any simpler. The British and Canadians held the 'Yankees' to be wily, devious, grasping, and always increasing their demands. The Americans in turn thought them arrogant, domineering, bullying, and likely to insist on having things their own way. The memory of the two wars, the skirmishing with Indians along the frontier, and the periodic conflicts in the border region kept alive these stereotypical images. Figures do emerge who were heroes or villains. However, as the decades passed and crisis after crisis was met, it became increasingly apparent that a deadlock had been reached over key sections of the boundary. By the 1830s the sequence of incidents seemed to promise another Anglo–Canadian–American war.

What is remarkable is that the boundary was gradually worked out and agreed on. This result came in stages and through great effort. Indeed, it was not completed until the major diplomatic negotiations in 1842, but it *was* done. How much the final boundary fulfilled the precise terms of the treaty of 1783, and how much it represented a reasonable compromise with political reality, are major themes in this book. In the controversy surrounding the Webster–Ashburton Treaty in 1842, Lord Ashburton declared that the boundary settlement 'was a good and wise measure, and good and wise because it was fair. ...'[6] That this same boundary is so often praised today is probably a fair testimonial to Ashburton's judgment.

An often-neglected element in the boundary settlement, and in fact in Anglo–American relations generally, is the innovative use of arbitration. Arbitration as a means of settling disputes between nation-states had fallen into disuse in Europe in the aftermath of the ideological schisms of the Reformation. The creation of commissions, as in the Jay–Grenville Treaty of 1794 (a 'mixed' commission) to determine the St Croix River boundary, was innovative and, in this case, successful. These commissions marked a turning point in the practice of modern international law and diplomacy. The advantage of the settlement of disputes by some form of arbitral machinery was that it offered a judicial decision rather than a diplomatic or political agreement. Furthermore, the decision was binding and final. For the U.S. government there was the additional advantage that having once agreed by treaty to arbitrate a dispute, it did not need to submit the award itself to the Senate for ratification.

Several forms of arbitral machinery were used in the attempts to settle the boundary between the United States and British North America – mixed commissions, joint commissions, and single arbitrators. However, there were pitfalls. The joint commissions created by articles 4–7 of the Treaty of Ghent in 1814 required unanimity that was impossible to attain in the two most controversial sections of the border, and even the 'friendly sovereign' chosen as single arbitrator or umpire avoided a clear decision, recommending instead a compromise solution. Nevertheless, arbitration became an increasingly favoured means of settling disputes during the nineteenth century, culminating perhaps in the award of the Tribunal of Arbitration in Geneva in 1872 and in support for the Hague Peace Conferences in 1899 and 1907. Arbitration as a method of settling international disputes was one of the legacies of the boundary question.

In addition to the matter of the diplomatic and political settlement, the search for the boundary was also one of the epic stories of North American history. It is a story of exploration and survey, of hardship and the struggle against nature, of both death and triumph. Oddly enough, it has never been fully told. Western North American exploration, the fur trade, the Lewis and Clark expedition, and the Oregon question have all had their spokesmen. Such has not been the case with the exploration, survey, and mapping of the eastern Canadian–American boundary. Nevertheless, from the selection of the St Croix River between New Brunswick and Maine in 1798 to the determination of the northwesternmost point on the Lake of the Woods in 1842 separating what is now Minnesota, Ontario, and Manitoba, this is one of the great stories of exploration and adventure in North American history. The boundary commissions arising variously out of the Jay–Grenville Treaty of 1794 (the St Croix Commission) and the Treaty of Ghent of 1814 (commissions for each of articles 4–7) carried out their work over many years, cost thousands of dollars, involved hundreds of people (some of them quite important), and represented major efforts by the countries involved. A third theme of this book is the physical struggle to traverse and master this vast borderland, as well as the process through which a settlement was reached.

The cover of the book attempts to illustrate both the scope of the story and the nature of the exploration and mapping. The 1806 map of North America represents a version of the contested boundary while the photograph, albeit from a later period, about 1869, shows something of the camps and instruments of the surveyors.

Francis M. Carroll

Acknowledgments

I grew up in northern Minnesota within miles of the Canadian–American border. As a boy I listened to the CBC broadcasts of *Hockey Night in Canada* and cheered loudly for the Toronto Maple Leafs. Later I canoed along the border, through Basswood Lake and Crooked Lake and on the edge of Hunter Island – the old fur trade routes. I had been twice to Winnipeg and once to Thunder Bay (or Port Arthur and Fort William, as they were then) before I saw Minneapolis and St Paul. Many of my schoolmates and neighbours had French-Canadian names; their families had followed the lumber trade west from Quebec and Maine to the pineries of Minnesota two generations before. After leaving Minnesota I married a young woman from Detroit with a Canadian father and neighbours from Ontario, Alberta, and New Brunswick. So I saw myself as a border person and part of a border community.

Nevertheless, it was not until I began to teach, first the history of American foreign policy, then the history of the North Atlantic community, and finally the history of Canadian–American relations, that I began to understand the prolonged search for the Canadian–American boundary. To my surprise, I found that my hometown, which was along the St Louis River, might well have been a border town if the British surveyor David Thompson and the British boundary commissioner Anthony Barclay had prevailed in 1826.

I may have been a child of the border, but I knew very little about it. Nor did anyone else. I discovered that the many stories about the settlement of the boundary were to be found only in manuscript collections in London, Ottawa, and Washington or in forgotten books and memoirs published in the nineteenth century. Bits and pieces of the history had been written, but the eastern boundary has never attracted interest comparable to that of the Oregon settlement or even of the Florida or Mexican boundaries. Yet the boundary set out in 1783 at the end of the American War of Independence defined the shape of both the new United States and British North America. The location of that boundary, which ran through what became the very heartland, as well as the frontier, of much of the two jurisdictions, remained a matter of confusion and tension for almost sixty years. It seemed odd to me that no general work attempted to tell the story of the great struggle to settle this frontier.

My first research efforts on the boundary started in the 1970s with a focus on the Webster–Ashburton Treaty of 1842. It had not really been examined since E.D. Adams's long article in the *American Historical Review* in 1912. Midway through my research, however, Howard Jones published his excellent book, *To the Webster–Ashburton Treaty* (1977). Jones explained so well the problems of the treaty and the confusion of the maps that further work on the treaty seemed pointless. I turned to other projects. However, in my teaching I continued to be confronted by other problems that Jones had not touched.

Therefore, in 1995 when I was invited by Professor Gary McDowell to be the first John Adams Fellow at the Institute of United States Studies at the University of London, I had a wonderful opportunity to resume work on the boundary by looking at the almost completely forgotten boundary commissions created by the Treaty of Ghent, which had ended the War of 1812. These four commissions decided two segments of the boundary but failed to agree on two others. One of those segments – the New Brunswick–Maine boundary – was submitted to the arbitration of the king of the Netherlands, who proposed a compromise line. This compromise was rejected as exceeding the powers of the arbitrator. While the story of the commissions – their explorations, surveys, mapping, and negotiations – was a fascinating chapter of the history of North American and British–American relations, it left the matter of the actual settlement of the boundary unresolved. Clearly, to make sense of things and to bring the story to its logical conclusion, I had to take the story through the turmoil of the 1830s and the fresh surveys to the Webster–Ashburton Treaty in 1842. Similarly, the early attempts to deal with the boundary in the 1790s and the years before the War of 1812 needed some explanation, as did the important negotiations about the boundary at the peace talks at Ghent in 1814. Thus, gradually the whole eastern Canadian–American boundary – from the islands in Passamaquoddy Bay to the northwesternmost point of the

Lake of the Woods – came into focus. This book is the result of these efforts, and it tells the epic story of the nearly sixty years of struggle to determine the boundary once and for all.

A book of this kind depends on the good will and help of many people. The University of Manitoba supported me generously with both sabbatical leaves and research grants. These gave me the tools with which to work and the time to research and write. The librarians and archivists of the many resource collections consulted were invariably helpful and thoughtful. It is a particular pleasure to acknowledge the assistance of Patricia Kennedy of the National Archives of Canada, in Ottawa, Nicholas Noyes, the librarian of the Maine Historical Society, in Portland, Maine, and Julia F. Wallace, the head of government publications at the Wilson Library at the University of Minnesota, in Minneapolis. At the Elizabeth Dafoe Library of the University of Manitoba in Winnipeg, I owe a special debt to Barbara Bennell and her staff in the Document Delivery Department.

A great door was opened to me in 1995 by Professor Gary McDowell when he offered me a fellowship at the Institute of United States Studies at the University of London. An office in the Senate Building and access to the University of London Library, the riches of the Institute of Historical Research Library in the same building, and the extraordinary materials in the British Library, then still across the street, made work on this project easy and convenient. Once a draft of the book was written I benefited from the advice and encouragement of my graduate student, John Fierst, who took time from work on his own thesis, and his project to compile a definitive edition of the John Tanner narrative, to read the manuscript.

As the book reached publication stage I received very good advice from Ann Regan of the Minnesota Historical Society Press in St Paul, Linda Oberholtz Davis of Dorling Kindersley in London, and George Nicholson of Sterling Lord Literistics in New York. The complications of the preparation of the manuscript were skilfully handled by Sandra Ferguson, secretary to the History Department of the University of Manitoba. Once in the hands of the University of Toronto Press the manuscript was improved by the brilliant copy editing of John S. Parry. Finally, the reader may benefit from the maps distributed throughout the book. I worried for months as to how I might go about making my own maps; with the help and direction of my colleague Professor Michael Kinnear in the History Department of the University of Manitoba, I was able to do this.

Boundary Line

First find out the River Saint Croix, from whose source
A line that's extended due north in its course
Thro' the country will strike on the highlands which test
Of fam'd Nova Scotia the angle northwest –
Then westward along the said highland extend it
To south of what streams with St. Lawrence are blended.
Thus let it proceed, till it meet in its course,
Connecticut's River's northwesternmost source –
Then down the said river until it arrive
At degrees of north latitude forty & five.
Due west in a line now its course it must take,
And strike a great stream from Ontario's Lake;
This bold rapid stream Cataraqui they call,
Which loses its name at the town Montreal.
This line then its progress far westerly makes
Thro' four very famous & fresh water lakes,
These lakes with each other by streights are connected
All which by the line must be duly bisected –
Ontario, Erie and Huron – these name –
And wide spread Superior, west of the same,
The last mentioned lake the said line passes thro'
To north of Isle Royale and Phelipeaux too –
Proceeding still farther the same must be traced
Thro' Long Lake and Wood's Lake that lies to north west.
Still westward it goes Mississippi to find,
Then down its great stream far to south let it wind
To latitude thirty and one it extends,
The leaving this river to eastward it tends
Till Apalachicola meeting it winds
To the north, till the mouth of Flint-river it finds,
Thence east to the river St. Mary's they name,
And winds as it winds to the mouth of the same.
Next thro' the Atlantic northward it goes
All Isles sixty miles from the coast to inclose,
Excepting those Islands which now and of yore
Of the province first named e'er belong'd to the shore.
That Great River St. Croix then points out its course
Through its centre from Fundy-Bay up to its source.

– Edward Winslow, c. 1797

A GOOD AND WISE MEASURE
The Search for the Canadian–American Boundary, 1783–1842

Chapter One

Introduction: Working out a Method, 1783–1814

Baron Ashburton (Alexander Baring) came out of retirement in December 1841 at the urgent request of the new foreign secretary, Lord Aberdeen, in order to deal quickly and decisively with the growing danger of a third Anglo–Canadian–American war. Such a conflict threatened to be the inevitable consequence of a series of explosive crises that had erupted in the previous few years along the unresolved boundary between the United States and British North America. Ashburton had already turned down a cabinet position in the new Tory government formed by Sir Robert Peel in September 1841. Ashburton had served as president of the Board of Trade in Peel's first government in 1834, and he had been an active member of Parliament from 1806 to 1835 before being elevated to the peerage. However, his fame and position were the result of his years as the head of the banking firm of Baring Brothers & Company. Arguably Ashburton, or Alexander Baring as he then was, had been one of the most powerful people in the world, or at least the bank was held to be so influential in international money matters as to be described by the duc de Richelieu as one 'of the six great powers in Europe.'[1] When the United States acquired the Louisiana territory from France in 1803, Alexander Baring helped to arrange the financing whereby the bank (together with the Dutch firm of Hope & Company) effectively bought Louisiana and sold it back to the United States.

Certainly one of the leading bankers of his day, with excellent political connections with the Tory government, Ashburton had other attributes that made him seem the perfect choice to negotiate a settlement of the troublesome boundary problems. As a young man in the 1790s, Baring had lived in the United States, managing the affairs of the bank, making investments, and ultimately marrying the wealthy

Philadelphia débutante, Anne Bingham. On returning to Britain, he became a knowledgeable speaker in the House of Commons on American affairs. He never lost those interests. On the eve of Peel's forming a government in 1841, Baring, created Baron Ashburton in 1835, was writing letters to him advising courses of action in dealing with the Americans. When asked by Lord Aberdeen in December, Ashburton, then aged sixty-seven, was willing for the sake of peace to leave his ailing wife and his Greek-revival country house in Devon, 'The Grange,' to travel to Washington. The greatest problems of the boundary had defied solution for almost sixty years, but a rare opportunity had presented itself that made the efforts by Ashburton and Aberdeen worthwhile.

There had been a change of government in the United States also. In late 1840 the people had turned out the Democrats of Andrew Jackson and Martin Van Buren and elected a new Whig administration led by a hero of the War of 1812, General William Henry Harrison. The new president, sworn in on 4 March, appointed Daniel Webster of Massachusetts as his secretary of state, and Webster remained in the cabinet when John Tyler of Virginia succeeded to the Presidency following Harrison's death from pneumonia after just over a month in office. Webster was one of the towering figures of pre–Civil War American history. One of the most successful lawyers and persuasive advocates in the country, Webster had made a lasting reputation by arguing cases before the U.S. Supreme Court. Webster, who served in the Senate 1827–41 and 1845–50, had emerged as a dominant figure in that branch of Congress, where his powers of oratory made him a force in the Whig party and a leading spokesman for the national interest, the federal Union, in the growing sectional crisis between the north and the south. Even his physical appearance – a prominent high forehead, deeply set dark eyes, and a firm, squarely set jaw – was so striking as to earn him the description of the 'god-like Daniel.' More to the point, however, both before and after his appointment as secretary of state, Webster had urged a settlement of the boundary question on the basis of a sensible compromise, rather than continuing the attempt to decipher the original treaty of 1783 and obtain agreement on which land formations along the disputed borderlands that document might have been intended to demarcate.

Why had the boundary been such a source of confusion and disagreement for all of those years since the American War of Independence? The Treaty of Paris, ending the war in 1783, specifically attempted to prevent misunderstandings and disagreements when dividing the continent. 'And that all Disputes which might arise in future on the Subject of the Boundaries of the said United States, may be prevented,' the second article began, but these noble aspirations were doomed to failure. The actual descriptions of the boundary, in slightly archaic language, posed great problems: 'From the North West Angle of Nova Scotia, viz. That Angle which is formed by a Line drawn due North from the Source of the Saint Croix River to the Highlands along the said Highlands which divide those Rivers that empty themselves into the River St. Lawrence, from those which fall into the Atlantic Ocean, to the North-western-most Head of Connecticut River.' The boundary was to proceed along that river to the forty-fifth parallel of latitude, along that parallel west to the St Lawrence River, and then along the middle of the St Lawrence into Lake Ontario. The boundary was to pass through the middle of each of Lakes Ontario, Erie, and Huron into Lake Superior. The final reaches of the northern border were to extend 'thence through Lake Superior Northward of the Isles Royal & Phelipeaux to the Long Lake; Thence through the Middle of said Long-Lake, and the Water Communication between it & the Lake of the Woods, to the said Lake of the Woods; Thence through the said Lake to the most North-western Point thereof, and from thence on a due West Course to the River Mississippi,' thus south along the Mississippi to the northern border of what was then Spanish Florida, and east to the Atlantic again.[2] This was to be the boundary of the thirteen original United States of America.

But what did all these terms mean? Where was the 'North West Angle of Nova Scotia'? Did it exist as a place? Which river was the St Croix? What were the 'Highlands' that divided the waters that flowed into the St Lawrence River from those that flowed into the Atlantic Ocean? Did the term 'Highlands' mean mountains or merely watersheds? Numerous other problems arose as well. Reference points were wrong; specific river sources were debatable; islands in rivers could be validly claimed by either side. In the west there proved to be no Isle Phelipeaux and no Long Lake in Lake Superior. The Mississippi River was south and east of Lake of the Woods, not west. How could all of this be untangled?

These confused or competing landmarks were further complicated by the intervention of people and their needs. Into the border region there appeared over time groups of Loyalists, settlers, Indians, fur traders, soldiers, lumbermen, land speculators, fishermen, merchant sailors, steamboat operators, and of course politicians – all of whom had special needs and interests and ambitions that competed with those of their counterparts on the other side of the increasingly disputed border. Human frailty played no small part in rendering a difficult problem almost insoluble. But how did all of this happen? How did 'the world's longest undefended border' have such a muddled and confrontational beginning?

The negotiation of the Treaty of Paris in the summer and autumn of 1782 forms a fascinating story that is long and complicated. Not merely did Britain and the new United States have to divide the continent to define their territories in North America, but they had to do so in the context of French and Spanish interests, especially in the river valleys of the Ohio and the Mississippi. France and Spain had themselves been rivals in parts of this western frontier country in the eighteenth century. However, after France lost the Seven Years' War, it ceded its colony of New France to Britain in 1763. This territory included all of the St Lawrence River valley and the Great Lakes basin east and south of the Hudson's Bay watershed (already British) and claims to the Ohio River valley west to the Mississippi. Through force of arms the British had also acquired the Spanish colony of Florida. The result was the Britain held almost all of the eastern half of the North American continent from Hudson Bay in the north to Florida in the south, from the Atlantic to the Mississippi, although France did retain the islands of St Pierre and Miquelon off the coast of Newfoundland. France voluntarily transferred the west bank of the Mississippi to Spain in 1763. It had lost or given up its major North American continental possessions.

Thus, as a result of the Seven Years' War, Britain and its seaboard colonies in North America found themselves in a commanding position, but it was a position that soon revealed some serious contradictions. The Seven Years' War had begun when young Major George Washington of the Virginia militia was sent in 1753 by Governor Dinwiddie to serve notice to the French, who had just built a fort at the confluence of the Allegheny and Monongahela rivers near the present city of Pittsburgh, Pennsylvania, that they were trespassing on territory claimed in the charter of Virginia and granted to several land companies under the authority of the British Crown. The outcome of the war that unfolded appeared to validate the British and colonial claims to these upper Ohio valley lands, but the British acquisition of New France made things more complicated. Britain acquired all French claims to the lands south of the Great Lakes as well as the settlement along the St Lawrence River and north of the Great Lakes. Britain also took on responsibilities for the Native people in those regions, whose sense of indignation and alien-

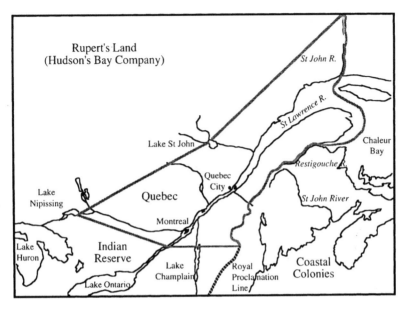

Map 1A. Boundaries created by the Royal Proclamation of 1763

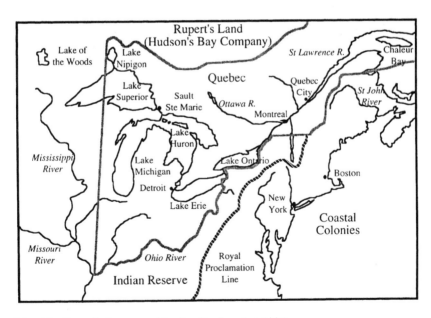

Map 1B. Boundaries created by the Quebec Act, 1774

ation at their transfer to British colonial status boiled over into what is remembered as Pontiac's Rebellion. Furthermore, British subjects quickly stepped into the workings of a very lucrative fur trade operating out of Montreal, which, while French in origin, was quickly taken over, at least at the top, by a combination of Yankees and Scots. These British fur traders rapidly adopted an attitude towards the possession of the Ohio River valley that was similar to that of their French predecessors. Thus the new possessions of Montreal and Quebec shifted Britain's perspective on North American affairs, in addition to merely augmenting Britain's North American territories. The seaboard colonies now quarrelled with British authorities about their claims to the Ohio–Great Lakes basin, in much the same way as they had with the old French regime. These quarrels themselves contributed to the events that led to the outbreak of the American Revolution, and not surprisingly the question of dividing the continent emerged again at the peace talks ending the war.[3]

How best to form the boundaries, once Britain had accepted American independence? Benjamin Franklin's proposal at Paris that it cede all the Canadian possessions to the United States was quickly dismissed. So was the suggestion that the forty-fifth degree of latitude, which separated New York from the province of Quebec, be extended west to the Mississippi River, as was a proposed diagonal line to be drawn from the forty-fifth parallel northwest to Lake Superior. To the American offer that the St John River be the eastern boundary, the British objected that this would place new Loyalist settlements within U.S. jurisdiction. Eventually, a boundary was negotiated in Paris that combined historic borders and what were hoped were workable natural frontiers. In the relatively settled east, the old colonies of Massachusetts, Nova Scotia, Quebec, and New York had had their boundaries described for over a hundred years. Elements of those historic boundaries were made part of the 1783 treaty. In the west, the main channels of the water courses of the Great Lakes and their connecting rivers as far as the Lake of the Woods and then west, as it was believed, to the Mississippi were thought to provide natural frontiers. This package seemed reasonable and clear enough to those looking at the great map of North America by John Mitchell.[4]

While the arrangements appeared simple and clear, numerous problems emerged to cloud the intentions of the negotiators. Although Mitchell's map of 1755, and perhaps several other maps, had been used in the negotiations, Mitchell's contained some serious geographical errors. For example, although the northeastern boundary was to begin at the St Croix River, which was fully labelled on the map, there was no river flowing into Passamaquoddy Bay that was commonly known by that name. Thus the first step in dealing with the eastern boundary was to determine which of the several possible rivers the negotiations intended to be the St Croix. Similarly, the treaty declared that the western border was to be created by a line extending from the northwestern-most point of the Lake of the Woods to the Mississippi and then south along that river. Mitchell's map had a large rectangular inset west of Lake of the Woods, out from under which the Mississippi River appeared to be fully formed and flowing south. In fact, the source of the Mississippi was eventually located well south and slightly east of the Lake of the Woods. Even these cartographic failings would have been less serious if there had been a copy of a map, with the intended boundaries clearly marked on it, attached to the peace treaty. In fact, there was no treaty map – an omission that further complicated and confused the whole question right up to the present time.

Still another problem bedevilled the peace settlement generally and boundary matters specifically. This was the erratic nature of British politics and interests in the years that included the end of the American war and the next decade. The war had gone very badly for Britain. By 1780 it was fighting not merely the American colonists, but France, Spain, and the Dutch as well. Furthermore, the British were pretty much isolated by unfriendly neutrals in Europe and by a growing threat of independence in Ireland. When Lord Rockingham formed a government in 1782 after the resignation of the discredited Lord North, there was considerable urgency to end the war as quickly as possible. Other British policy objectives at the peace conference were to undermine French leadership in the coalition against it. France's own complicated political agenda meant that the British diplomats were able to sow the seeds of discord at the peace conference, not the least of which was their attempt, successful in the event, to woo the Americans away from the French alliance despite all the assistance that the French had given them in the War of Independence. A generous boundary settlement, even if based only on the pre-Revolution colonial boundaries, was part of the British enticement to the Americans to step away from the protection of the French. In later years the effort to court the Americans looked to many Canadian and British commentators to have been the work of stupidity or incompetence, but in the circumstances of the early 1780s the British were dealing with a strategic crisis.[5]

In addition to these international considerations, there was the instability of British domestic politics. A key element was the unpopularity of the Whigs, which led to the defeat of Lord Shelburne (he had succeeded Lord Rockingham, who died in July 1782) in March 1783. The new government was an unlikely coalition led by Lord North and Charles James Fox, but it was no more successful in domestic terms than Shelburne's, and it fell in December 1783. Only with the creation of a government under William Pitt, the younger, which stayed in power until 1801, was stability restored to British domestic politics. Throughout all of this turmoil, although the international situation changed rapidly, neither the North–Fox nor the Pitt government repudiated the Treaty of Paris negotiated by Lord Shelburne, but neither was sympathetic to Shelburne's delicate strategic objectives. Not surprisingly, they both looked at many of the provisions of the treaty from a different perspective – particularly as the crisis atmosphere of the early 1780s receded.[6]

Other North American elements of the post-war situation changed also. During the war the population of Britain's province of Quebec was overwhelmingly French, and although the citizens of that province had not rallied to the American cause in the war, they had been quite restrained in their support for Britain. Where their ultimate sympathies might lie was something of an open question. However, in the aftermath of the opening of peace talks, Loyalists from the rebelling colonies began moving in considerable numbers into both the maritime colony of Nova Scotia, including the border region that in 1784 became the colony of New Brunswick, and the province of Quebec, particularly North of Lake Ontario and Lake Erie. In short, the Loyalists settled several of the very areas where the boundary would be contested within a decade of the treaty's signing. Thus by 1783 and 1784 there was a British 'interest' in those border regions that could not be said to have existed in so clearly defined a form in 1780 and 1782.

Arguably one British interest that did precede the end of the war was that of the defence of the Native people and the Montreal fur trade that depended on the Native people. At the peace conference in 1782 the French had shown considerable solicitude for the Indians of the Ohio River valley, but clearly they wanted to deny that region to the Americans, to establish the Spanish more strongly there, and generally to encourage instability and rivalry among the Americans, the British, the Spanish, and the Indians, which might work to the long-term interests of France. In the circumstances of 1782 the British abandoned any obli-

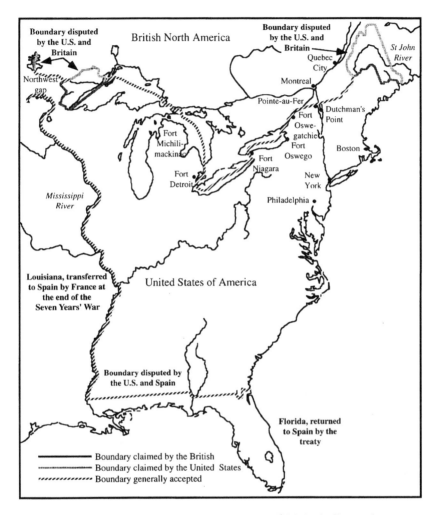

Map 2. Boundaries created by the Treaty of Paris, 1783, including major boundary disputes

gation to the Native people, at least south of the Great Lakes, in order to draw the Americans out of the French orbit and to frustrate any further expansion of Spanish power in North America.[7] After the peace treaty was signed in 1783, however, Britain ordered its troops to remain in the seven major garrisons well within the northern territory over which the

United States had been given sovereignty from Lake Champlain to the Straits of Mackinac. This military presence reassured the Indians, provided a means through which the Montreal fur traders could continue to operate south of the Great Lakes as if the War of Independence had never taken place, and left British forces poised to pick up the pieces of the new American republic before the Spanish if the United States collapsed during the mid-1780s. It also kept alive the idea of an Indian buffer state between the Great Lakes and the Ohio River.[8]

Had the United States disintegrated in the 1780s, during the fragile period of the Articles of Confederation, the history of the North American continent and the British empire would have been very different from the one we know today. In the event, the new U.S. constitution of 1787 created a structure of central government capable of making policy decisions, financing them, and implementing them. That George Washington became the first president no doubt contributed significantly to making the system work, but the new regime also provided remarkable continuity to the struggles along the western borderland dating back to the 1750s, specifically in the region between Lake Erie and the Ohio River. The victory of General Anthony Wayne at Fallen Timbers on 20 August 1794 over Indian forces supported by British troops in Fort Detroit and along the Maumee River also came close to provoking a clash between British and American soldiers. These events were simply the most dramatic of a series of crises that had developed between Britain and the United States in the decade following the end of the War of Independence. Some of these difficulties arose out of the pre-war colonial debts and issues concerning the Loyalists, some over trade relations between the two countries, but others were the result of border problems in both the east and the west arising out of the terms of the treaty of 1783.

Even before the battle of Fallen Timbers in 1794, John Jay had been sent to London to negotiate a treaty with Great Britain that would resolve these difficulties. The result was the Jay–Grenville Treaty of 1794. It was extremely unpopular at the time, dividing George Washington's government into two factions. Indeed, historians still disagree about the merits of the document. As for the boundary, the treaty constituted a major accomplishment. The British agreed to withdraw from the seven forts along the western border, allowing the United States to take possession of the border region from Lake Champlain, in upstate New York, to Fort Michilimackinac, controlling the straits between Lake Huron and Lake

Michigan. The price for this withdrawal was the U.S. grant of concessions to British fur traders to operate in American territory and to enjoy free access to the Mississippi River and the extension of new guarantees to Native people that they could move without restriction across the border in the pursuit of their affairs.[9]

The two most obscure parts of the boundary (today's Maine–New Brunswick and Minnesota–Ontario borders) were to be determined by two joint efforts. The western section was to be surveyed from St Anthony Falls to the source of the Mississippi and then to the Lake of the Woods, although this provision was never acted on. The eastern boundary presented a more pressing problem. As early as the summer of 1783, Governor John Parr of Nova Scotia had urged the settlement of discharged soldiers on the eastern side of what he called the St Croix River (the Schoodiac) at what became the town of St Andrews, which had about 600 houses by the end of the decade. In 1784, authorities in Massachusetts (which included the district of Maine until 1820) – who held that the Magaguadavic River, several miles to the east, was the true St Croix River – complained to John Jay, then secretary for foreign affairs for the U.S. Congress. By November 1785 Jay requested the American minister in London to bring the matter of these encroachments to the attention of the British government.[10] However, no attempt was made to deal with the question, and early in 1790 Congress proposed a commission to establish the boundary at the St Croix River intended in the treaty of 1783. Nevertheless, it was left to the Jay–Grenville negotiations to make specific provisions to deal with the disputed claims. The location of the St Croix River and the due-north line were to be decided by three commissioners, one chosen by Britain, one by the United States, and one agreed on by the two commissioners or chosen by lot – i.e., a 'mixed' commission. A decision required only a majority agreement and would be binding. This process was itself significant and marked the first time since the Reformation that two sovereign states had attempted to settle a dispute by arbitration.[11]

Colonel Thomas Barclay was appointed British commissioner in March 1796 at the urging of Governor Sir John Wentworth of Nova Scotia, and he was to have a key role in the history of the boundary for the next twenty-five years. Barclay was a prominent New York Loyalist. His father had been rector of Trinity Church in lower Manhattan, and as a young man he had in 1772 graduated from King's College (which became Columbia University) and then read law in the office of John Jay. When the War for Independence broke out, Barclay saw active service in the King's forces, leaving New York in 1784 as a colonel to go to Annapolis, Nova Scotia. There he had a new career both in law and in politics, becoming Speaker of the legislative assembly and an effective ally of Governor Wentworth. This appointment as commissioner in 1796 led to his return to New York, where, except in the latter stages of the War of 1812, he was to spend the rest of his life either as British consul, appointed in 1799, or as a boundary commissioner.[12]

President Washington first appointed as American commissioner General Henry Knox of Massachusetts, who refused to serve, and then David Howell of Providence, Rhode Island. Howell was a lawyer, who had studied at the College of New Jersey (later Princeton University). He had been a member of the Continental Congress from Rhode Island and a professor at Rhode Island College (later Brown University) and he had held several offices in his state, including attorney general and justice of the supreme court. The matter of the third commissioner was proposed at a preliminary meeting between Barclay and Howell. Several names were discussed, but when Howell nominated Judge Egbert Benson of New York, the matter was settled. Although Benson was an American, he was also a cousin of Barclay's and, as a result, enjoyed a degree of Barclay's confidence that he would act impartially. Benson, who had graduated from King's College in 1765, was a lawyer who had been the first attorney general for the state of New York and some time later was appointed a judge on the U.S. circuit court.[13] The two commissioners agreed to accept Benson at the first meeting in Halifax in August 1796.[14]

The board of three commissioners was to make its decisions on the questions before it on the basis of evidence submitted by agents of the two countries. Although the Duke of Kent suggested for agent the name of an old friend to the governor, Thomas Carleton, the British agent appointed was Ward Chipman, a Loyalist originally from Marblehead, Massachusetts. Chipman had graduated from Harvard with honours in 1770 and had also completed a master's degree, after which he read law in the office of Jonathan Sewell, following in his father's footsteps as a barrister. Chipman also supported the Crown in the Revolution and subsequently removed to England and then to New Brunswick. He has been described as an 'amiable' man, with 'a sharp, calculating intelligence and a driving, imperious will.' Chipman became one of the founders of Saint John and a key figure in the legal profession and eventually solicitor general and advocate general of the province.[15] The American agent was James Sullivan, a lawyer and Congressman, later attorney general and supreme court judge for Massachusetts and governor in 1807 and 1808. Sullivan was the author of *History of the District of Maine*, published in 1795, and also president of the Historical Society of Massachusetts.[16]

Howell, Sullivan, Samuel Webber, the astronomer from Harvard College who was to be a surveyor for the St Croix Commission, and several people who were part of the American contingent sailed on 12 August from Boston to Halifax on the chartered sloop *Portland Packet*. The Americans arrived on the sixteenth and were well entertained by the Loyalists of Halifax. Colonel Barclay arrived from Annapolis, Nova Scotia, on the twenty-first, and Chipman from Saint John on 24 August 1796. The two commissioners agreed on the selection of Benson as the third commissioner, instructed the surveyors to begin their work, and adjourned the meeting to reconvene with Benson in St Andrews, New Brunswick, on 4 October 1796, when the oaths of office were sworn and a secretary was appointed. Edward Winslow, a Loyalist descended from the first governor of the Plymouth Colony, then living in Fredericton, New Brunswick, was made secretary. He had graduated from Harvard in 1765 and had served in the British army during the revolution, emerging as a colonel.[17] At this meeting James Sullivan, on behalf of the United States, claimed the Magaguadavic River, on the eastern side of Passamaquoddy Bay, as the St Croix intended by the treaty of 1783, and Ward Chipman, for Britain, claimed the Schoodiac River, which flowed past St Andrews on the northwest side of the bay. The commissioners themselves visited the mouth of the Schoodiac and Magaguadavic rivers by boat. Two parties of boatmen and chainmen, each led by British and American surveyors, spent September and October exploring and mapping the two rivers; these operations resumed again the following summer.[18]

The board of commissioners reconvened in Boston in July 1797 and listened to witnesses and received depositions taken in St Andrews from numerous local people, including several Natives from the Passamaquoddy and Machias bands. On 15 August the commissioners travelled to Quincy, Massachusetts, to take the testimony of President John Adams, who had been one of the negotiators of the Treaty of Paris in 1782–3. A written deposition from John Jay, who had also been a negotiator, was received.[19]

The board received reports from the surveying parties and the arguments from the two agents. James Sullivan based his claim to the Magaguadavic on the argument that the diplomats in Paris had used Mitchell's map of North America during the treaty negotiations. On

Mitchell's map the St Croix was the largest of the three streams shown flowing into Passamaquoddy Bay and was well east of the second largest stream, the Passamaquoddy River, which Sullivan concluded was the Schoodiac, although Mitchell's map was particularly inaccurate in the northern regions. Sullivan's view was reinforced by the testimony of several Indians who claimed that the Magaguadavic had been called the St Croix River in years past.[20] On the other side, Chipman based his argument on the exploration and survey work done at the mouth of the Schoodiac. The name St Croix came from the settlement of the French explorers Samuel de Champlain and Pierre De Gua de Mont established on the Ile de St Croix in 1604.[21]

The discovery in 1772 by Robert Pagan, from St Andrews, and Thomas Wright, who were surveying the river that year, of the remains of de Mont's fortifications on an island near the mouth of the Schoodiac convinced the board of commissioners that this was the river understood in the treaty of 1783 to be the St Croix. Through Pagan's influence, Chipman also got supporting testimony from local Indians identifying the sites of the first landings of French explorers in the bay. This proved conclusive, and it was a great victory for Ward Chipman.[22] Sullivan attempted to find similar landmarks at the mouth of the Magaguadavic, but to 'his great mortification and disappointment ... he could find no island there.'[23]

This agreement in itself, however, was not sufficient to end the labours of the commission. The lower Schoodiac was formed by two major tributaries: the Schoodiac Lakes, which flowed in from the west, and the Chiputneticook, a more conventional stream flowing in from the north. As the subsequent boundary was to run due north from the source of the St Croix, the source of these two water systems, miles apart, represented a considerable difference. The board met again at Providence, Rhode Island, briefly in June 1798 and then more extensively in October, to consider the various documents, survey reports, and arguments of the two agents. All three commissioners came to different conclusions about the proper source of the river intended in the treaty of 1783, and reaching agreement seemed very difficult. Howell first favoured the Magaguadavic, but he then shifted to the lower Chiputneticook. Benson had agreed with Barclay and Chipman in identifying the Schoodiac as the St Croix, but not with Barclay's conclusion that its source lay at the western end of the Schoodiac Lakes. Benson said that a chain of lakes could not be understood to be a river and was prepared to follow Barclay's claim only to the place where the Schoodiac broadened out into Genesagaragumsis Lake. A line drawn due north from this point, however, would have been inconvenient both to the Americans, who had granted land between there and the Chiputneticook, and to the British and New Brunswickers, because it would place their military posts, which were further north at Presque Isle and Grand Falls, on the American side of the boundary. A unanimous decision seemed impossible.[24]

Chipman shifted his support to the Chiputneticook and obtained the agreement of Robert Liston, the British minister to the United States, who arrived fortuitously in Providence. After listening to the arguments before the board on 23 October 1798, Liston said that Britain would accept the Chiputneticook if the source were agreed to be the western head.[25] Such an agreement would secure for the United States the land that it had already granted north of the Schoodiac Lakes and west of the Chiputneticook and, for British North America, a due-north line west of the fortress at Presque Isle and intersecting with the St John River four miles west of the Grand Falls – a major stage in river transportation for the region. To this proposal the three commissioners then agreed, and the source of the St Croix River in the treaty was said to be the western headwaters of the Chiputneticook. They signed a declaration to this effect on 25 October 1798. A map was prepared, and a marker placed at the site. The St Croix Commission had successfully completed its task by securing almost 130 miles of boundary.[26]

In the immediate aftermath of the decision both sides expressed satisfaction, and perhaps felt relief, that a potentially dangerous issue had been resolved. The U.S. secretary of state, Timothy Pickering, wrote to James Sullivan to congratulate him. The St Croix decision, he shrewdly observed, 'without gratifying either party in the extreme, will I persuade myself render both parties contented.'[27] Thomas Barclay reported to Lord Grenville that the results of the decision had been 'very favorable' and would produce an 'infinitely preferable national boundary to [that of] the upper Scoudiac.'[28] Sir John Wentworth, the lieutenant-governor of Nova Scotia, wrote to Edward Winslow to praise Barclay and Chipman. 'All candid, judicious men, must give them great credit,' he said. Winslow himself wrote to Edward Lutwyche, Nova Scotia's agent in London, to describe the boundary settlement as being 'favorable to Great Britain.' The American claim to the Magaguadavic would have cost the province both St Andrews and Fredericton. 'As it is, we lose not a single British settlement,' and he noted that only 'a few miserable Frenchmen at Madawaska on the route to Canada will fall within their territory.'

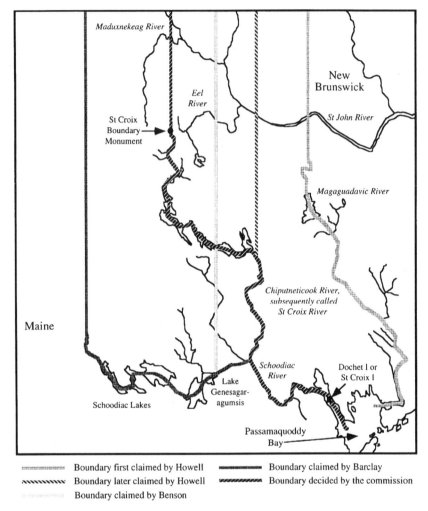

Map 3. St Croix Commission, 1796–8, to determine the correct river and the due-north line: claims and final boundary

Winslow added that he was certain that the land route to Canada would be improved on at some later negotiation.[29]

While James Sullivan was not delighted with all the proceedings of the commission, he did nevertheless comment to Ward Chipman midway through their work, 'Why shall not all the nations on earth determine their disputes in this mode, rather than choke the rivers with their carcasses, and stain the soil of continents with their slain? The whole business has been proceeded upon with great ease, candor, and good humor.'[30] This was the sort of testimonial, together with the successful decision concerning the St Croix River, that led Britain and the United States to return later to the mechanism of a commission as a means of settling other boundary problems. However, the comfortable satisfaction with this commission and its result would not last long. Within a generation, spokesmen for both sides would complain about how subsequent claims along the border had been rendered more difficult by mistakes made by the St Croix Commission.

Although the determination of the St Croix River in 1798 was a major accomplishment, it represented the settlement of only a tiny segment of the entire boundary between British possessions and the United States. The St Croix Commission had concluded that it did not have the authority to make decisions about the boundary among the islands in Passamaquoddy Bay, and the provisions of the Jay–Grenville Treaty for a survey of the upper Mississippi were never implemented.[31] By 1801, therefore, James Madison, secretary of state in the new Jefferson administration, consulted with James Sullivan about the eastern border. As a result of these discussions, Rufus King, the American minister in London, was instructed to open negotiations on these several problems.

Rufus King and Foreign Secretary Lord Hawkesbury signed a treaty on 12 May 1803, placing the coastal boundary on a line running from the mouth of the St Croix south and west of Deer Island and then north around Campobello Island and thence on into the Bay of Fundy (but making no mention of Grand Manan Island, which seems to have been originally inhabited by Americans). The due-north line from the source of the St Croix was to be marked by a board of three commissioners, which was also to determine the northwestern head of the Connecticut River. While the actual line from the 'northwest Angle of Nova Scotia' to the northwesternmost head of the Connecticut was still left to be determined, it is reasonable to conclude that the King–Hawkesbury agreement would have contributed to an ultimate decision that was closer to that claimed by the United States.[32] Further provisions in the treaty created a western boundary from the northwesternmost point of the Lake of the Woods to the source of the Mississippi, which was thought likely to be found somewhere south and east of the northwesternmost point of Lake of the Woods.

The King–Hawkesbury convention was certainly favourable to U.S. interests, particularly those of Maine. However, in the interval between the opening of talks and the arrival of the signed treaty in Washington, DC, the circumstances of the United States changed substantially with its acquisition of a vast territory west of the Mississippi through the purchase of Louisiana. The French did not spell out in any detail the boundaries of the territory that they sold to the United States. This ambiguity, whether deliberate or not, led to decades of disagreement between the United States and its southern neighbours, Spain and later Mexico, over the extent of land acquired in the purchase – namely, about West Florida and Texas. The ambiguities about the northern extent of the territory acquired led the U.S. Senate, after considerable debate, to ratify the King–Hawkesbury convention with a reservation effectively nullifying the fifth article dealing with the northwest boundary. The British in turn refused to accept the modifications, as was their right, and the whole treaty therefore died.[33]

These same issues arose again in fresh talks in 1806 and 1807 led by James Monroe and William Pinckney. The Passamaquoddy Bay border was run southeast from the mouth of the St Croix River, west of Deer Island, through the narrow channel west of Campobello Island and out into the Bay of Fundy. Campobello Island was to remain British, but the United States was to be granted access to the more navigable waters between it and Deer Island. Both parties claimed Grand Manan but left its status undecided. These talks eventually broke down again over problems in the northwest. In this instance, the British proposed that the forty-ninth parallel of latitude (which had been an informal boundary between British and French fur trade interests since 1713) be joined to a line drawn either north or south from the northwesternmost point of the Lake of the Woods. This of course was exactly the proposition to which both sides agreed in 1818 and could just as well have been put in place in 1807.

The Americans objected to language in 1807 that implied western limits to the boundary that might have closed the door to its claims in Oregon. Another key issue was the right of British subjects to move freely in the United States. The Jay–Grenville Treaty of 1794 had given them access to the Mississippi River. This provision had been very irksome to Americans in the west, particularly fur traders, because it had the effect of giving Canadian fur traders the opportunity to dominate both trade and territory in the upper Great Lakes region and beyond. The public issue in the talks was the tariff duties that traders might be expected to pay, although clearly the intention was to eliminate the fur traders altogether. American authorities had also prohibited British traders from access to the Missouri River basin. The British claimed that such a restriction violated Jay–Grenville; the Americans argued that such privileges did not apply in territory acquired in 1803. These were the obstacles that prevented the signing of any agreement in 1807.[34]

In truth, the climate for British–American cooperation had reached its high point in the years of the undeclared naval war with France between 1798 and 1800. The election of Thomas Jefferson to the presidency in 1800 began a process of deteriorating relations that ended in the outbreak of the War of 1812. This decline was aggravated by the American acquisition of Louisiana and particularly by the resumption of war in Europe, with all of its attendant problems of trade restrictions imposed by British orders-in-council and British impressment of U.S. citizens. The clash between HMS *Leopard* and USS *Chesapeake* in late 1807, and the revival of Indian warfare along the frontier of the Ohio and Indiana regions, made negotiation and compromise on boundary issues less likely. Most such questions remained unsettled, therefore, as Britain and the United States descended into war in 1812.[35] The success of the arms of either side stood to change the boundary radically. Only the irony of neither side's being able to achieve a decisive victory produced a peace settlement based on a return to the pre-war boundaries.

The War of 1812 was fought in the borderlands between the United States and British North America as well as at sea. Early in the war American forces crossed the Detroit River and invaded Upper Canada (now southern Ontario), only to retreat back to Fort Detroit and to surrender much of the northwest territory. The United States lost much of the region, from Ohio to the Mississippi River, including Fort Mackinac in the north. With U.S. Commodore Oliver Hazard Perry's naval victory at Put-in-Bay on Lake Erie in September 1813, the U.S. army under Major-General William Henry Harrison was able to re-establish a presence in the northwest and reoccupy parts of Upper Canada. Control of the Niagara region went back and forth during the war; the 1813 American seizure of York (Toronto) in Upper Canada was abandoned, and U.S. forces withdrew after burning the capital's public buildings. American attempts to capture Montreal in 1813 failed to threaten that city. Combined British naval and land forces from Halifax occupied parts of the coast of Maine in 1814 as far as the Penobscot River, capturing both Castine and Belfast. British troops landed in Maryland in the late summer of 1814, captured Washington, DC, burned the public buildings, and then attacked the city of Baltimore. However, after an unsuccessful bombardment of its fortifications, the force withdrew from Chesapeake Bay.

Nevertheless, both sides still held bits of the other's territory along the border, although neither British nor U.S. forces had been able to mount a successful and decisive offensive campaign against the other. Perhaps because of the lack of spectacular military success, the war was not popular in either country, and after the defeat of Napoleon in April 1814 the British prime minister, Lord Liverpool, concluded that 'it was our decided Interest to bring the War with America to a termination as speedily as possible.'[36] Although the British turned down a Russian offer of mediation in September 1813, late in that year Lord Castlereagh, the foreign secretary, invited President James Madison to open peace talks 'upon principles of perfect reciprocity.'[37] Therefore, after extended preliminaries, peace negotiations started at Ghent, in Flanders, on 8 August 1814.[38]

The Americans sent five peace commissioners to represent them. John Quincy Adams, son of former President John Adams, was the nominal leader. Raised in part in Europe, educated at Leyden and Harvard, trained as both a lawyer and a diplomat, he also served in the U.S. Senate from Massachusetts. Adams was irritable and difficult, but he was able and determined as well. Furthermore, his connection with boundary matters would follow him when he was secretary of state and later president.[39] Albert Gallatin emerged as the facilitator in the delegation. A brilliant Swiss-born émigré to the United States, Gallatin had enjoyed a remarkable political career as a Jeffersonian and specifically as secretary of the treasury. He too remained linked to the boundary question as a diplomat, negotiating with the British in 1818 and 1827 and preparing the arguments for the arbitration of King William I of the Netherlands in 1830. Indeed, as a young man in 1780, newly arrived in the United States, Gallatin had very briefly commanded militia on Passamaquoddy Bay.[40] The U.S. opposition Federalist party was represented by James A. Bayard, a senator from Delaware who had opposed the war, although, like Gallatin, he was something of a moderate at Ghent.[41] President Madison later also appointed two other delegates. Henry Clay of Kentucky, Speaker of the House of Representatives, had been one of the 'War Hawks' who had favoured going to war in 1811 and 1812, and he also spoke for western interests. When Clay became secretary of state under John Quincy Adams in the 1820s he was immersed in boundary issues again.[42] Jonathan Russell, a merchant from Rhode Island, had also been a 'War Hawk,' but he also had some diplomatic experience. He had served in both Paris and London as chargé d'affaires and had remained in England during the war.[43]

The British were represented by three negotiators. Vice-Admiral Lord Gambier served as chairman of the delegation and represented both naval interests and British military might at the talks. An elderly gentleman, Lord Gambier had been forty-two years in the Royal Navy and had commanded the British fleet at the Battle of Copenhagen in 1807; he was also prominent in the English Bible Society.[44] The key political figure in the British delegation was Henry Goulburn, a member of Parliament and undersecretary for war and colonies, and as such he was to look after military and Canadian affairs for the British. Only thirty-one years old, Goulburn was a promising politician. He was later appointed to the privy council in 1821 and served as chancellor of the exchequer under the Duke of Wellington and Sir Robert Peel and was also home secretary under the latter.[45] Dr William Adams was a legal scholar, appointed in part on the assumption that the Americans were particularly legalistic in their reasoning and argumentation.[46] Lord Castlereagh, the foreign secretary, passed through Ghent in August to confer with the three-man delegation while on his way to Austria, but he and many of the officials of the Foreign Office were preoccupied with the affairs of Europe at the Congress of Vienna. In Castlereagh's absence, Lord Bathurst, secretary for war and colonies, took charge of the Foreign Office. In fact, the British delegation kept in close touch with both London and Vienna during the talks.[47]

The British opened the talks on 8, 9, and 10 August 1814 with dramatic proposals for redrawing the map of North America. Taking the position that protection of the interests of their Indian allies must be a *sine qua non* in the treaty, the British insisted that an Indian buffer state be created between the Ohio River and the upper Great Lakes. They also argued that, to redress the unfavourable military balance along the eastern Great Lakes, as they saw it, the United States must have no naval vessels on Lake Ontario and Lake Erie and no land fortifications near their shores. To give British subjects access to the Mississippi River (expressly permitted under both the Treaty of Paris of 1783 and the Jay–Grenville Treaty of 1794), they proposed the cession to Britain of territory west of Lake Superior as far as the Mississippi and the Lake of the Woods. Finally, to provide more secure communications between New Brunswick and Lower Canada, the British proposed that the eastern boundary be substantially revised. Later the British commissioners also mentioned that they regarded the fishing privileges in the treaty of 1783 to have been cancelled by the war.[48]

The Americans were shocked and angered at these wide-reaching demands, which assumed complete British military victory, rather than a war that had become more or less a stalemate. John Quincy Adams thought the British attitude 'peremptory' and 'overbearing.'[49] However, the U.S. delegation returned meticulous replies to the British commissioners. The Indian buffer state constituted the most serious threat to the United States and would have cost the country the region that later became the states of Illinois, Indiana, Michigan, Ohio, and Wisconsin. This idea had been put forward first by the French in 1782 and then again by the British from time to time in the 1790s. In the words of the British commissioners, this Indian state was to be a 'barrier' to the United States, but in the context of the War of 1812 the Americans saw this proposal as an attempt to create a puppet state that would allow Britain in effect to acquire U.S. territory between the Great Lakes and the Ohio River. The Americans argued that they were not authorized in their instructions to deal with Indian affairs and that the earlier invitation to open talks had made no mention of these matters. Indeed, Adams compared the Indians in the United States to Britain's periodically rebellious Irish subjects. Furthermore, the Americans pointed out that their government had already negotiated peace settlements with many of the Native Peoples in the region, and that in several instances the Indians had changed sides in the war and were now opposing the British. Moreover, they said, there were as many as one hundred thousand American citizens living in the territory north of the Ohio. The British blandly suggested that these settlers in the proposed Indian state could 'shift for themselves.'[50] As for British acquisition of territory west of Lake Superior (much of northern Minnesota) and in the district of Maine (between the Penobscot and the St Croix rivers), the Americans said once again that their instructions did not authorize them to cede territory. Altogether the British were demanding that the United States give up almost one-third of its territory.

On the military questions in the eastern Great Lakes, the Americans disagreed with the British about the balance of power in the region and argued that the fortunes of war in no way justified a surrender of their right to defend their own soil. The Americans argued that these terms were in no respect consistent with the invitation to negotiations from Lord Castlereagh, with the issues out of which the war arose, or with the principles of *uti possidetis* (peace based on territory held at the time of negotiations) or *status quo ante bellum* (peace based on circumstances before the war).

On 24 August the Americans rejected the British terms. 'A Treaty concluded on such terms would be but an armistice,' they said. 'It is impossible in the natural course of events, that she should not at the first favourable opportunity recur to arms, for the recovery of her territory, of her rights, of her honour. Instead of settling existing differences, such a peace would only create new Causes of war, sow the seeds of a permanent hatred, and lay the foundation of hostilities for an indefinite period.'[51] In these circumstances, Gallatin wrote to Secretary of State Monroe that it was clear that the British had extensive military plans for the northern states, the Chesapeake Bay area, and New Orleans. He thought that the talks would end within two weeks. Goulburn informed Castlereagh, then in Paris, that a 'rupture in effect has taken place by the answer of the American commissioners.'[52] Neither side wanted to be responsible for breaking off the talks, however, so a very elaborate correspondence followed for many weeks.

In defence of their demands, the British commissioners replied that their provisions for the Indians and their territorial demands arose out of a need to defend British North America from American aggression. It was, they said, 'notorious to the whole world that the conquest of Canada and its permanent annexation to the United States was the declared object of the American Government.'[53] Although this may have been an obvious assumption to make, in stating the rationale for their demands in such terms the British commissioners may have overplayed their hand. The Americans were able to argue that the annexation of the Canadas had not been the declared objective of their government, whatever individual citizens might be quoted as saying. The British took on themselves the burden of appearing to want to prolong the war for territorial gains. When Madison published the British correspondence in October, public opposition to the British position began to build in England, not to mention in the United States.[54]

On the instructions of Lords Liverpool and Bathurst, the British subsequently said on 19 September that military control of the eastern Great Lakes was negotiable but that they could not sign a peace treaty 'unless the Indian nations are included in it, and restored to all the rights, privileges, and territories which they enjoyed in the year 1811.'[55] This admission offered the Americans some room for negotiations on this threatening issue. They replied on 25 September, using much the same language as the British in regard to the post-war circumstances of the Indian nations – there was no apparent 'difference with respect to the object in view.' The British responded with a draft article stating that after hostilities with the Indians had ceased the Americans would restore to them 'all the possessions, rights, and privileges, which they may have enjoyed or been entitled to in 1811, previous to such hostilities.' The Americans accepted this draft article on 13 October, ending the impasse over Britain's major treaty requirement.[56]

The Americans also proposed in their letter of 25 September that the treaty of 1783's border between New Brunswick and Quebec and the district of Maine be determined by a boundary commission. This idea was not immediately pursued. Rather, the British commissioners said on 8 October that the cession of all of the district of Maine had never been proposed, but only those portions that would provide access to Quebec from New Brunswick. When the British offered on 21 October to end the war and settle the boundary on the basis of *uti possidetis* (the territory held by both sides at the moment), the Americans rejected the proposal on the same argument as before – namely, that they had no authority to surrender territory.[57]

Although British staff officers had in April 1814 talked confidently about the determination to 'give Jonathan [i.e., the United States] a good drubbing,' by September and October time was not running in favour of Britain.[58] Despite the success of British forces during the summer, with operations seizing about one hundred miles of the eastern coastline of Maine, from Eastport on Moose Island in July to Castine and Bangor on the Penobscot River in September, news of the capture of Washington in August was followed by its subsequent abandonment and the British defeat at Baltimore the next month. This left the Chesapeake Bay campaign inconclusive. More important still, the defeat of British naval forces at the Battle of Plattsburg Bay, also in September, resulted in the withdrawal of the British troops under Lieutenant-General Sir George Prevost and the general realization that there would be no decisive action in the New York area in 1814. By this time as well, quarrels with the Russians at Vienna and anxieties about the stability of France made the peace in Europe appear more fragile than it had in the summer. Moreover, domestic demands in Britain for revenge to be extracted from the Americans had shifted by autumn to complaints over the enormous public debt and the burden on the taxpayers of continued warfare.

It was in this context that Lord Liverpool consulted the Duke of Wellington about taking command of British forces in North America.

Wellington replied on 9 November that he was willing to go to America, but he raised several serious concerns. First, he thought that circumstances in Europe were so unpredictable that he was indispensable there, and so events proved when Napoleon returned to France from Elba in March 1815. Second, he was not confident that his leadership of the army would change the situation in America. Wellington observed that naval supremacy on the Great Lakes and Lake Champlain was crucial. 'I shall do you but little good in America,' he said, 'and I shall go there only to prove the truth of [General] Prevost's defence, and to sign a peace which might as well be signed now.' As for the peace talks at Ghent, he made an important observation. 'In regard to your present negotiations, I confess that I think you have no right, from the state of the war, to demand any concessions of territory from America.' In short, he told Liverpool that while British forces in America had not done badly, the state of the military situation was not such that Britain could demand territory on the basis of *uti possidetis*. Even the occupation of eastern Maine was not militarily secure enough to be confidently held. These demands, Wellington said, simply had the effect of uniting the Americans and encouraging them to avoid making peace.[59] The historian Bradford Perkins has suggested that the original British demands may have been a 'probe-and-delay strategy' that the government was not willing to pursue if the Americans resisted. Resist they did.[60]

Gradually the British commissioners drew back from their first extraordinary demands. The impasse over the Indian question broke in mid-October when the Americans agreed to provisions in the treaty that the Indians be extended the rights and privileges that they had enjoyed before the outbreak of the war and that no punitive measures be taken against anyone who had supported the opposite side in the war. On 10 November the Americans submitted a draft treaty, or *projet*, following British reluctance to do so. The text included several articles dealing with impressment, blockade, and indemnity for property that the British refused to consider. However, the most important passage was in article 1, where both parties agreed that 'All Territory, Places and Possessions' be restored to their original owners. This would end the war on the basis of *status quo ante bellum*, and the British agreed, with only some slight change to the text. First, the islands in Passamaquoddy Bay, claimed by both sides but occupied by British forces during the war, would remain in British hands until the boundary was decided. Second, the treaty would not go into force until it had been ratified and exchanged – a reaction to the failed treaties of 1803 and 1806. According to the draft,

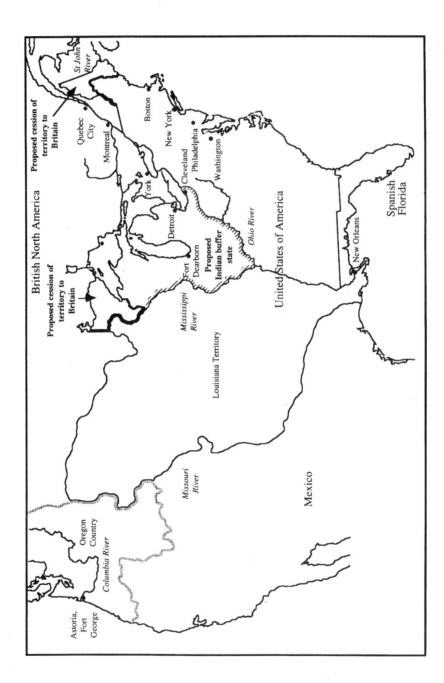

Map 4. British boundary proposals during peace talks at Ghent, 1814

all fighting was to cease, prisoners of war were to be returned, and the Indians were to accept peace and to be extended all the rights they had enjoyed in 1811. Private property was to be restored to its owners, although the matter of slaves created controversies later, and the international slave trade was to be abolished. There were several other problems to be worked out, the most difficult being Britain's insistence that its subjects retain the right to use the Mississippi (which had been part of the treaties of 1783 and 1794) and the American desire to retain the right to fish in certain inshore British North American waters and to cure their catches on certain areas of coastline (part of the treaty of 1783). Failure to reach an agreement about these matters was resolved by silence on them in the text of the treaty and a decision to leave them for later negotiations.[61]

In the earlier correspondence between the commissioners, the boundary created by the treaty of 1783 had not been seriously discussed. The various British proposals contemplated entirely new boundaries throughout much of the frontier region. Only in the American draft treaty did the old unresolved boundaries come back into focus. Here the Americans submitted five draft articles, which revived the idea of boundary commissions. The final text of the treaty outlined the particulars of the four commissions as follows:

- **article 4:** for the disputed islands in Passamaquoddy Bay, including Moose Island and Grand Manan, which the British had earlier insisted were theirs
- **article 5:** for the boundary from the source of the St Croix River to the highlands separating the waters flowing into the Atlantic from those flowing into the St Lawrence River and on to the head of the Connecticut River and then along the forty-fifth degree of north latitude to the St Lawrence
- **article 6:** for the boundary from the St Lawrence through the Great Lakes to Sault Ste Marie
- **article 7:** for the boundary from the Sault through Lake Superior to the Lake of the Woods
- **article 8:** authorized the appointment of a secretary, agents, surveyors, and other staff to carry out the work of each of the commissions and for the sharing of expenses

Each of these articles assigned the task of determining these boundaries to a three-person 'mixed' commission, based on the model used in the

St Croix Commission. Two commissioners each appointed by a government, the Americans suggested, would themselves select the third, either by agreement or by lot. The British accepted the general idea but objected to the three-person, mixed commission. They recommended a joint commission made up of two commissioners, one appointed by each government. In the event of the commissioners' failure to reach unanimous agreement, the matter would be referred to a 'friendly Sovereign or State,' as a single arbitrator or umpire, for a final decision.[62]

The Americans agreed to this change, and the details were worked out about where and when the boundary commissions would first meet to began their deliberations.[63] Thus the commissions became elaborate machinery for the settlement of a boundary, but the relevant provisions of the old treaty of 1783 had already proven so difficult that extraordinary precautions did not seem unwarranted. But would even these be sufficient?

The last meeting took place on 23 December 1814 at four o'clock in the afternoon at the residence of the British commissioners in Ghent. Clear copies of the treaty had been hurriedly prepared overnight for reading and signing. While exchanging copies of the documents, Lord Gambier said that he hoped that the peace would be permanent. Adams replied, 'I hoped it would be the last treaty of peace between Great Britain and the United States.'[64] And so it was. The Treaty of Ghent, ending the War of 1812, was signed and sealed the next day, on the afternoon of Christmas Eve 1814.

It is often remarked that the document avoided mention of the issues that brought on the war and that in effect it settled nothing. This judgment, however, is too simplistic. British North America – Canada – was secured, and no American soldier ever invaded it again. Many people, including Henry Goulburn, would not in 1814 have believed that possible. For the Americans, their nation was saved with no loss of territory. For the boundary, a process was set in motion that divided the continent; the Rush–Gallatin Convention of 1818 determined that the forty-ninth parallel would divide British territory in North America from the United States west from the Lake of the Woods to the Rocky Mountains, with joint occupancy to be the rule for the Oregon territory.

This book deals with the twenty-eight-year struggle that emerged from the Treaty of Ghent, as the British and the Americans, with increasing input from colonial authorities in British North America, sought to determine the boundaries. Part I (chapters 2–6) examines the work of four boundary commissions that emerged from articles 4–7 of the Treaty of Ghent. Chapter 2 looks at the commission implementing article 4, which dealt with the islands in Passamaquoddy Bay. The next two chapters study the work of the commission for article 5, on the northeastern boundary, which sought the source of the St Croix and the elusive 'highlands' (chapter 3) and the forty-fifth parallel and the source of the Connecticut (chapter 4). Chapter 5 describes the workings of the commission under article 6, for the St Lawrence and the Great Lakes. As those three bodies were winding down in the early 1820s, work began on article 7, from Lake Superior to the Lake of the Woods (chapter 6).

Part II (chapters 7–10) deals with the complex aftermath of the work of the commissions and the general uncertainty as the United States and the British colonies in North America sought during the 1820s and 1830s to work out their mutual relations. It looks at preparations during the mid- and late 1820s for arbitration by a friendly foreign sovereign on the unresolved article 5, concerning the northeastern border (chapter 7), and then at the arbitration award itself in 1831 and its attendant problems (chapter 8). The troubles in the late 1820s and the early to mid-1830s along the still-problematic frontier between British North America and the United States are considered (chapter 9) and the crises and further boundary work of the late 1830s are examined (chapter 10).

After decades of uncertainty, the unresolved issues surrounding the boundary and relations between Britain, British North America, and the United States came to a head and found a resolution, all in a short span of time; this startling series of events is the theme of part III (chapters 11–13). In 1840–1 new governments came to power in Britain, the United States, and the recently united Province of Canada, as is shown in chapter 11, facilitating re-examination of old issues with new eyes. The year 1842 saw the complex, almost-byzantine negotiations led by Lord Ashburton and U.S. Secretary of State Daniel Webster, analysed in chapter 12, that led to the resolution of most of the outstanding issues surrounding the boundary. Chapter 13 considers the shadow that soon emerged over the hard-won treaty and over the two remarkable figures who put it together – a shadow that still hangs over this none the less 'good and wise measure.'

PART ONE

Commissions under the Treaty of Ghent: 1816–1827

Chapter 2

Article 4: Islands in the Bay

'As to my colleague Col. Barclay, he has *appeared* very well,' U.S. Commissioner John Holmes wrote to U.S. Secretary of State James Monroe on 20 October 1816, following the first meetings of the commission under article 4 of the Treaty of Ghent, charged with determining the boundary among the islands of Passamaquoddy Bay. 'But that this gentleman,' Holmes went on to say, 'who has investigated this subject *once before*, should not, in some measure, have *prejudged* the case, is perhaps more to be *wished*, than *expected*.'[1]

The British constituted a formidable presence at St Andrews, New Brunswick, in that early autumn of 1816. Colonel Thomas Barclay had been one of the most prominent Loyalists to stay in North America, and his subsequent career in law and politics in Nova Scotia (where he had been Speaker of the colonial assembly), and as a crown representative and eventually British consul in New York, further enhanced his prestige. That he was also distinguished in New York social circles, and had married his children into powerful families on both sides of the Atlantic, improved his position in the workings of the border commission. Moreover, the fact that Barclay had been officially engaged in the boundary question since the St Croix Commission in 1796 definitely gave him an edge in dealing with the Americans.

British Agent Ward Chipman also benefited from a similar status – a prominent Loyalist from Massachusetts, a brilliant student at Harvard, a founder of New Brunswick, but most importantly the masterful British agent in the St Croix Commission whose researches determined the outcome in 1798. His work as British agent for these boundary commissions (articles 4 and 5) would be the greatest test of his skill as a lawyer and advocate. Sir John Wentworth, the former governor of New Hamp-

shire and retired lieutenant-governor of Nova Scotia, sent his congratulations to Ward Chipman. 'I learn that you are again soon to be
employed with our good & very able friend Col. Barclay' to settle both
parts of the easternmost boundary, and he expressed his full confidence
in their 'experience & ability,' although he worried that the Americans
would be unyielding in the negotiations.[2]

The two Americans were not insignificant figures, but they were definitely of a younger generation. Now aged forty-three, John Holmes, the
commissioner, had graduated from Rhode Island College (later Brown
University), when the St Croix Commission was making preparations for
its first meeting in 1796. Holmes was admitted to the Massachusetts bar
in 1799 and was active in local politics in the Maine district. Indeed his
election to Congress in the autumn of 1816 eventually complicated and
perhaps undermined his position as commissioner. He was later prominent in the creation of Maine as a separate state in 1820, and he was
elected to the U.S. Senate by the new Maine legislature that year.[3] James
T. Austin, the U.S. agent, was even younger, at thirty-two. Having gone to
both Andover and Boston Latin School, Austin had graduated from
Harvard third in his class of 1802. He was admitted to the Massachusetts
bar in 1805, and the following year he married the daughter of the
prominent Massachusetts Federalist, Elbridge Gerry. He held a number
of minor appointments and sat in the state legislature from 1812 to
1832. Later Austin was state attorney general from 1832 to 1843 and
made a reputation for himself as a strong opponent of the anti-slavery
movement.[4] These were able young men, to be sure, with promising
careers in state politics, but would they be out of their depth working
with the seasoned Barclay and Chipman? Events over the next fourteen
months would show.

Barclay returned to the United States from England in August 1815.
Although he had served as commissioner of prisoners during the early
stages of the War of 1812, he had spent 1814 and 1815 in London. He
resumed his position as British consul in New York, but gave up those
duties a year later with the first meetings of the boundary commission.[5]
In company with several others involved in boundary matters, Barclay
sailed from New York for St Andrews, New Brunswick, in early September, putting in at Portland on 12 September to pick up more members
of the party. At Portland, the weather turned against them, and,
becalmed for six days, they eventually put to sea and were able to reach
St Andrews on the twenty-second to begin work.[6]

The first meeting took place on 23 September 1816. Barclay and Holmes exchanged commissions and took their oaths of office before a local justice of the peace, Hugh Mackay, Esq. They swore 'impartially to examine and decide the claims to be submitted ... according to such evidence as shall be laid before [them] on the part of his said Britannic Majesty, and of the said United States respectively'[7] The agents, Chipman and Austin, also exchanged commissions, although at the meeting the next day Holmes protested that Chipman's was simply a letter signed by Lord Bathurst, secretary for war and colonies, not an official document with seals and titles. The commissioners, however, agreed to accept Chipman as British agent, subject to the eventual appearance of correctly formed documents. The commission dated 24 January 1817 and properly issued by the king, finally reached Chipman, naming him and his son Ward Chipman, Jr, jointly as agents. On 23 September 1816 Anthony Barclay, the commissioner's youngest son, a mere twenty-four years old, was appointed secretary of the commission at a princely salary of £500 per year.[8]

The following day, Barclay and Holmes, sitting as the board of commissioners, heard the two agents put forward their claims. On behalf of the United States, Austin claimed 'all the Islands in the Bay of Passamaquoddy and the Island of Grand Manan in the Bay of Fundy.' Chipman asserted the British claim that all the islands of the bay had traditionally been part of Nova Scotia and had not passed into U.S. possession under the terms of the Treaty of Paris of 1783.[9] After this presentation the commissioners agreed that the agents would require time to assemble the evidence to support their claims and therefore that the board would reconvene in Boston on 28 May 1817. As well, various maps and surveys of Passamaquoddy Bay that had been prepared for the St Croix Commission would also be made available to the agents, arrangements were accepted about depositions from witnesses, and the schooner *Jefferson* was hired to facilitate a brief survey of parts of Passamaquoddy Bay. The board then adjourned until the following spring.[10]

The participants were a bit wary of each other. Ward Chipman had written to a friend in March 1816 of his anxiety about presumed American insistence on 'an unqualified cession of all they claim.'[11] Holmes's misgivings about the possibility of Barclay's having 'prejudged' the question have been mentioned above. Barclay made no specific comment on the Americans this early in the proceedings, but in his report to Lord Castlereagh, the foreign secretary, he made it clear that he regarded the objections raised about the credentials of the British agent as overly legalistic. It was the commissioners themselves who were to act impartially as a tribunal to determine the boundary question, not the agents, who were the advocates hired by each country to represent their interests before the board. In fact, the commissioners, at least outside the meetings of the board, took a much more partisan role in finding evidence and marshalling arguments.

The issue before this commission was superficially simple – determining the boundary from the mouth of the already agreed-on St Croix River out through Passamaquoddy Bay into the open waters of the Bay of Fundy. However, the text of the treaty of 1783 was not altogether clear in its description of what was to be the boundary. The border was to be a line 'comprehending all Islands within twenty Leagues of any Part of the Shores of the United States, & lying between Lines to be drawn due East from the points where the aforesaid Boundaries between Nova Scotia on the one Part [the St Croix River] and East Florida on the other, shall respectively touch the Bay of Fundy and the Atlantic Ocean, excepting such Islands as now are or heretofore have been within the Limits of the said Province of Nova Scotia.'[12] There were two contradictory descriptions in this passage. In one the United States was to possess 'all Islands within twenty Leagues' of its own shores, especially south and west of a line drawn 'East' from the mouth of the St Croix. By contrast, the latter part of the passage states that the border will include only those islands 'excepting such Islands as now or heretofore have been within the Limits of the said Province of Nova Scotia.' Either argument would depend on pre-Revolutionary definitions of Nova Scotia. Did its old boundaries encompass the islands in question, or had those islands always been possessed by Massachusetts?

If the historic boundaries of Nova Scotia and Massachusetts were the key to the problem, how might they be determined? This was not as simple a task as it might appear. James I created the colony of Nova Scotia in 1621 by grant of a charter to Sir William Alexander, and the territory included all the modern landmass of Nova Scotia, New Brunswick, and the Gaspé peninsula. The relevant passage of the English version of the Latin charter described Cape Sable, the southwestern peninsula of the modern Nova Scotia, and then said that the boundary ran around that headland to St Mary's Bay, on the Bay of Fundy side of the peninsula, 'and thence toward the north by a straight line crossing the entrance or mouth of that great ship road [the Bay of Fundy] which runs into the eastern track of land between the countries of the *Souriqueis* and the

Etchemins [terms for the Acadian regions of Nova Scotia and what is now Maine] to the river commonly called St. Croix ... including and comprehending within the aforesaid seashores and their circumferences from sea to sea, all lands and continents with the rivers, streams, bays, shores, islands or seas lying near or within six leagues of any part of the same on the western, northern or eastern parts of the said shores and precincts.'[13]

This was a very expansive description, but much of the territory mentioned was then in French hands and did not come fully into British possession until the end of the Seven Years' War in 1763. However, in 1691 Massachusetts received a new charter that included all of Nova Scotia and that might be seen to supersede the charter of 1621. As for the line drawn from St Mary's Bay to the St Croix, it did not actually touch Grand Manan, but what of the terms 'circumferences from sea to sea, all lands and continents with the rivers, streams, bays, shores, islands or seas lying near or within six leagues of any part of the same on the western, northern or eastern parts of the said shores and precincts'? Did this description establish a parallel line that included all the islands within six leagues of the St Mary's Bay–St Croix River line; and, even if it did, was this 1621 charter not nullified by subsequent events within the British empire? In fact Barclay confided to Castlereagh that he was 'apprehensive' that it would not be possible to 'support with equal evidence His Majesty's claim to the Island of Grand Manan ... an island of far more national importance, than any of the others.'[14] Nevertheless, it was on this 1621 document that the legal claims of the British case rested.

With the end of the Seven Years' War the whole of the region had come into British possession, and a description of the colony and the territory under his jurisdiction was included in the commission of Lieutenant-Governor Montagu Wilmot in 1763. This document said that in former times the boundary of Nova Scotia had extended as far west as the Penobscot River, but for practical purposes the colony 'shall be bounded by Line drawn from Cape Sable across the entrance of the Bay of Fundy to the mouth of the River St. Croix.'[15] The commissions of several subsequent governors of Nova Scotia used the same terms. The line mentioned in that context was slightly farther south than that of 1621, and, while it touched the northern shore of Grand Manan, the text omitted any reference to the inclusive 'circumference' used in the earlier charter. These commissions weakened the British claim to this island and became the basis of the legal claims of the American agent, who argued that the omission of 'circumference' had been deliberate, if indeed the 1621 charter were still relevant at all. Furthermore, he noted that people from Massachusetts had settled key parts of Nova Scotia and, more important, Massachusetts militias had captured strategic areas such as Port Royal and Louisbourg and other parts of the region for the British in 1704, 1707, 1710, 1745, and 1755.

It was on these issues that the agents, Chipman and Austin, worked indefatigably over the winter of 1816–17, collecting documentation. Barclay himself, although he had complete confidence in Chipman, was fully involved in accumulating evidence. Even before the commission had met in September 1816, Barclay had written to the Foreign Office in London asking for documents that could be used in building the British case. By January 1817 these materials were arriving, and Barclay was ordering more.[16] On the U.S. side, James T. Austin wrote on 8 February 1817 to President-elect James Monroe, still secretary of state, that his case would be 'a full exposition of the rights of the American Government' based on careful reading of the colonial charters and grants. The task, however, Austin admitted 'has extended the labor far beyond what I had originally contemplated.'[17] So it was a busy winter.

The spring meeting of the board of commissioners was to take place in Boston on 28 May 1817. Ward Chipman, who had to sail from New Brunswick, did not arrive until 2 June as a result of an attack of gout at home and then contrary winds at sea. This delay had prevented Barclay, as he told Castlereagh, from meeting with Chipman on 20 May in order to examine the British evidence and argument, perhaps with a view to making some suggestions in order to strengthen the case.[18] However, the board began its work on 3 June. The agents read their arguments for the next several days and submitted to the board their formal statements, together with the colonial charters, letters of commission, maps, and other materials. The commissioners then instructed the agents to examine these materials and prepare official replies for the autumn session of the board to be held on 25 September, also in Boston. Several more days were spent receiving depositions from private citizens, and on 12 June the board adjourned.[19]

Barclay confided to Castlereagh, midway through the June meetings, that he was not hopeful that agreement could be reached on the islands. He said that he had encouraged Chipman to introduce certain documents before the board not to facilitate a unanimous decision, but to influence a foreign sovereign in the event of arbitration.[20] Just prior to the autumn meeting, Austin wrote to the new secretary of state, John Quincy Adams, warning similarly that there was every probability that the commissioners would be unable to agree, and eventually he requested another session of the board so that he could reply to the British case, largely for the presumed benefit of an arbitrator.[21]

By late June 1817 the American commissioner, John Holmes, was having worries of a different sort. In November 1816 Holmes had been elected to the House of Representatives from the district of Alfred, Massachusetts (now Maine), and he was expected to take his seat in the new congress in early December 1817. Because the agents would at the very least make formal replies to each other at the September meetings, and because there was no clear end in sight for the board's work, Holmes was under a serious time constraint, inasmuch as the U.S. constitution forbade a member of Congress from holding another government appointment. Thus he could not take his seat in Congress while still a commissioner for the United States. Time was not in his favour, or perhaps that of the United States. Holmes wrote to the secretary of state on 26 June 1817 to alert him to his worries. Furthermore, in late August he received a letter from Colonel Barclay that said that if he resigned his position Barclay would feel empowered by the terms of the Treaty of Ghent to act singly in reaching a decision for the board. Holmes had immediately protested Barclay's right to act singly; very probably this suggestion was only a bluff on Barclay's part, but it created more alarm for Holmes and brought home to him the awkwardness of his position.[22]

The board of commissioners reconvened on 25 September 1817 in Boston. At the first session the commissioners examined accounts and disbursed monies, and the following day they began hearing the official responses of the two agents to the arguments and evidence submitted in June. For six daily sessions the board heard the debate of the two agents. The British argument was based largely on the 1621 grant by James I to Sir William Alexander, which drew a line from St Mary's Bay on the south side of the Bay of Fundy to the St Croix River on the north side and included all islands within six leagues of that line (including Grand Manan). The American argument discredited the 1621 charter by pointing out that it was nullified in 1691 by a new charter for Massachusetts that included all of 1621 Nova Scotia and the Gulf of St Lawrence. The modern Nova Scotia dated from 1713, when a portion of Massachusetts was made into a new colony. These boundaries were to be found in the commissions to various governors of the province, and they did not include islands west of the line across the Bay of Fundy, which remained part of Massachusetts right up to and after the treaty of 1783.[23]

Having exhausted this debate (the American brief alone ran to over 2,000 folio pages), the two agents asked the commissioners for time to prepare new evidence and counter-arguments to be presented in the spring of 1818. Such a request was most unwelcome to Holmes, who would have to resign his position as commissioner or his seat in Congress if the issue were not decided in the autumn of 1817. For his part Barclay said that he had heard enough to make a decision, but he did not want to take on himself responsibility for denying the agents a full opportunity to say all that they wanted to on the subject. Holmes thought this 'a willful refusal to act' and wrote to Secretary of State Adams asking what he should do. Holmes also urged that President Monroe and the new British minister to the United States, Charles Bagot, instruct both Austin and Chipman not to insist on another sitting of the board. (Adams had already urged Austin to expedite matters so that Holmes could complete his duties.) All of this created what Austin considered the only unpleasantness of the whole proceeding.[24]

In this tense situation, Barclay played his hand carefully, as he showed in a letter to Castlereagh. Were Holmes to resign, a new commissioner would have to be appointed, necessitating a considerable prolongation of the proceedings while the cases were reargued (no further mention of Barclay acting unilaterally). Furthermore, in language open to several interpretations, he said that he did not expect that a successor to Holmes 'would possess that candor and Discrimination, I had in every instance experienced in this Gentleman.' Unquestionably no new American commissioner would be under so much pressure to bring the proceedings to a close as Holmes then was. Nor was the prospect of referring the question to a friendly sovereign attractive to Barclay. In the rejected King–Hawkesbury Convention of 1803 and the unfinished treaty of 1807, both Britain and the United States had indicated a willingness to accept a boundary in which the United States got Moose, Dudley, and Frederick islands. An arbitrator was likely to confirm this position. The British claim to Grand Manan was, in Barclay's view, the weakest part of the British case, and an arbitrator would probably either split the island or grant all of it to the United States. Barclay concluded that Britain had little to gain by allowing the matter to go to arbitration. After consulting with Chipman, who agreed with him, Barclay decided to negotiate.[25]

Meeting with Holmes in private on 6 October, Barclay presented him with what he called an ultimatum. Britain would give up all claims to Moose, Dudley, and Frederick islands in exchange for the United States, doing the same for the rest of the islands in Passamaquoddy Bay and for Grand Manan. Moose, Dudley, and Frederick were of little value to New Brunswick, and Moose had been settled by Americans, whereas Grand Manan was of great importance to Britain and had been recently settled by Loyalists. Holmes was 'astonished' that Barclay or Chipman 'had ever been serious' in claiming Grand Manan, but Barclay told him that the United States could choose either this offer or arbitration. Holmes tried to bargain for Campobello Island in exchange for Grand Manan, but 'I told him he had my ultimatum,' Barclay said, 'an ultimatum I had brought myself with much difficulty to offer.' These talks went on at some length, and not until the morning of 9 October was Holmes persuaded to give in. He accepted Barclay's offer 'with great reluctance and apparent hesitation.' The one concession that Barclay made was to write a personal agreement that American vessels could use the ship channel north around Campobello Island through Passamaquoddy Bay (the channel between Campobello and the mainland having exposed rocks at low tide). An interim agreement was signed on 10 October. It was a brilliant triumph for Barclay and Chipman.[26]

All these talks and decisions took place in secret. On 11 October James T. Austin wrote to John Quincy Adams that he understood that the commissioners had reached a decision, although the terms of 'the arrangement made by the Comsrs. is unknown to me.'[27] He did say that the board would meet again on 24 November in New York to announce its decision. Holmes himself wrote to Adams a few days later to say that the commissioners had 'proceeded amicably, and [had] been able to come to a *decision*.' However, he admitted, 'the decision, though not perhaps so favorable to the United States as it ought to be, yet it is, I trust, better than to disagree, and such as comports with the honor as well as interest of the United States.'[28]

In New York on 24 November both commissioners were able to sign the documents setting forth the decision of the board that Moose, Dudley, and Frederick islands would go to the United States and all the other islands, including Grand Manan, to Britain. Holmes sent off a copy of the document to Adams, along with his letter of resignation. Castlereagh later wrote to Barclay to express the approval of the government over the terms of the award. President Monroe mentioned the decision in his annual message to Congress on 2 December 1817. Monroe, who had worked on the same boundary question in 1806 and 1807, expressed his 'satisfaction' that the 'islands in the possession of each party before the late war have been decreed to it.' No mention was made of Grand Manan.[29] The Boston *Gazette* reported that the questions before the commission had been settled 'in a most amicable and satisfactory manner.'[30]

Shortly after the decision, John Quincy Adams wrote to the British minister to Washington, Charles Bagot, to inquire whether he was empowered to transfer the three islands to the United States. Bagot did not have any instructions in this matter, but he wrote immediately to Castlereagh and to the governor general of British North America and the lieutenant-governor of Nova Scotia. Neither of the latter two officials had any power to act, but Castlereagh sent a warrant to Bagot dated 4 February 1818 that officially authorized the transfer of Moose, Dudley, and Frederick islands to the United States. When this document arrived in Washington in May, Bagot gave it to Adams with instructions that it be forwarded to the lieutenant-governor of Nova Scotia, Earl Dalhousie, in Halifax, to be carried out. On 30 June 1818 the transfer took place at Fort Sullivan on Moose Island, with bands, flags, and cannon salutes. Several days before, the citizens of Eastport thanked the British commandant, officers, and soldiers for their kindnesses and moderation while occupying parts of Maine during and after the war.[31]

The commission under the fourth article of the Treaty of Ghent was the first of the four bodies to complete its work and resolve the questions before it. It was also charged with the least-complicated question. That it reached a decision and made an award in late 1817 was important, both for itself and for the possible precedent that it might set. Was its decision a good one? In many ways it was a good compromise, which is not quite the same thing. It gave the United States Moose Island, which had a substantial number of American citizens, together with the nearby islands of Dudley and Frederick. Likewise, American ships received free passage through New Brunswick waters, around Campobello Island and into the main channels of Passamaquoddy Bay and the Bay of Fundy. New Brunswick got Campobello and the more important Grand Manan, both of which had Loyalist settlements. Strictly speaking, New Brunswick had a better claim, under either the 1621 or the 1763 documents, to the islands awarded to the United States, although they had less value to New Brunswick than to Maine. Grand Manan, in contrast, was more clearly off the coast of Maine, and only a special reading of the documents of 1621 and 1763 might make it British territory. How-

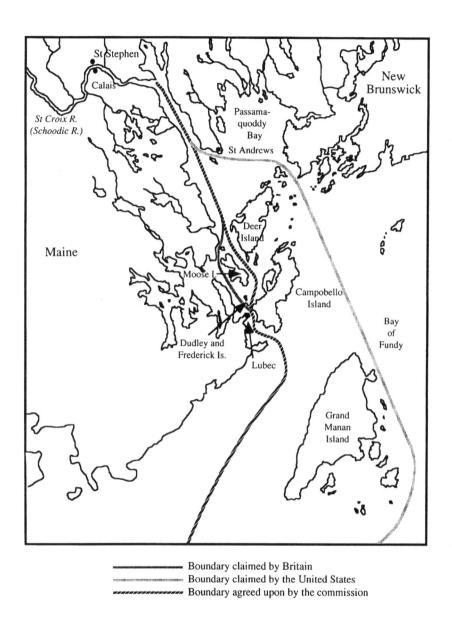

St Stephen

Calais

St Croix R.
(Schoodic R.)

New
Brunswick

Passama-
quoddy
Bay

St Andrews

Maine

Deer
Island

Moose I

Campobello
Island

Dudley and
Frederick Is.

Lubec

Bay
of
Fundy

Grand
Manan
Island

━━━━━━━ Boundary claimed by Britain
░░░░░░░ Boundary claimed by the United States
▬▬▬▬▬▬ Boundary agreed upon by the commission

Map 5. Islands in Passamaquoddy Bay: claims and final line

ever, with its Loyalist population and *de facto* governance by New Brunswick, it was of very great value to that province. Had either side held rigidly to its strict legal claims, an element of injustice would have resulted. The compromise sacrificed the legal claims for a more reasonable and practical agreement. In early 1816 Chipman had agreed with former Nova Scotia lieutenant-governor Sir John Wentworth that the Americans were unlikely to agree to any settlement that was not 'an unqualified cession of all they claim.'[32] In fact, the Americans had been much more accommodating.

William F. Ganong, in his major study of the boundaries of New Brunswick, says that the province was fortunate in the Passamaquoddy Bay settlement. He placed much more value on Campobello and Grand Manan than on the three smaller islands awarded to the United States.[33] A.L. Burt felt that Barclay 'could have beaten Holmes in a game of chess.' Holmes did not think several moves ahead, Burt concluded, and therefore was outmanoeuvred by Barclay's ultimatum of 6 October in such a way as to give up both Campobello and Grand Manan.[34] Holmes had reached the conclusion that the United States could hardly do worse by allowing the question to go to arbitration than by accepting Barclay's offer, but he accepted it anyway. He emphasized the benefits of an immediate and inexpensive settlement. Certainly Holmes did let his need to see the work of the commission completed before 1 December, so that he could take his seat in Congress, influence his actions in reaching a decision. Whether the United States suffered serious loss as a result of Holmes's being hurried along by Barclay is less clear. In any case, in closing his report to Castlereagh, Barclay paid generous tribute to Chipman's skills in making a masterful presentation of the British case. Ganong went further and said that New Brunswick owed a great debt to both Chipman and Barclay.[35] It would remain to be seen whether the other commissions would be so flexible and so successful.

Chapter Three

Article 5: Highlands and the Source of the St Croix

The border commission under the fifth article of the Treaty of Ghent met at St Andrews, New Brunswick, on 23 September 1816, together with the commission under the fourth article. British Commissioner Colonel Thomas Barclay (articles 4 and 5) had joined Cornelius P. Van Ness, U.S. commissioner for article 5, in Portland and along with U.S. Commissioner John Holmes (article 4) and others sailed to their meeting on the twenty-third. Although the two somewhat-overlapping bodies met in conjunction with each other, they followed very different paths. The islands of Passamaquoddy Bay were all well known, and the commissioners of article 4 were to decide which claims were stronger, based on historical charters and documents.

The work of the article-5 commission – on the northeastern boundary, from the Bay of Fundy to the St Lawrence River – was much broader in scope and much more difficult. Its task was to identify the five landmarks mentioned in the Treaty of Paris of 1783:

- the due-north line from the source of the St Croix River (already decided in 1798)
- the Northwest Angle of Nova Scotia
- the highlands separating the waters that flowed into the St Lawrence from those that drained into the Atlantic Ocean
- the northwesternmost head of the Connecticut River
- the forty-fifth parallel of latitude from the Connecticut River to the St Lawrence River

This was a very large task. Surveying work on the first three landmarks (examined in this chapter) and on the last two (chapter 4) spanned four surveying seasons, 1817–20, and research and complex negotiations took place during that work and afterwards.

The most obviously important and controversial of all these assignments involved the Northwest Angle of Nova Scotia and the highlands separating the St Lawrence and the Atlantic watersheds. Parts of this border country had never been explored, much less surveyed and accurately mapped. The region was thickly forested with pine, spruce, and cedar, together with maple, birch, beech, ash, and elm, and it was thinly populated, with about 600 people, mostly French-speaking Acadians, living in the Aroostook and Madawaska areas by 1808. The landmarks mentioned in the treaty – the Northwest Angle and the highlands – were not generally well known and certainly not already agreed on. The maps used in the negotiation of the treaty of 1783 were as inaccurate and unhelpful on this part of the boundary as elsewhere, and no map had been attached to the treaty. This commission had not only to consider the information contained in all the old documents, together with the text of the treaty, but also to try to match the negotiators' presumed intentions with the expressed needs and desires of the communities involved. The Americans, buttressed by maps published in London in the 1790s, assumed that the due-north line extended beyond the St John River to the brow of the St Lawrence. This understanding brought into the controversy possession of the upper St John River valley, a 26,000-square-mile watershed that was the largest along the east coast between the St Lawrence and the Susquehanna in Pennsylvania and Maryland. Foremost, however, was the matter of determining what territory was being discussed, and because of the incomplete knowledge of the country the first task was authorizing the exploration, survey, and mapping of much of the contested New Brunswick–Maine wilderness. Thus began one of the epic stories of North American history.[1]

Colonel Thomas Barclay was again to be the British commissioner, and the British agents again were Ward Chipman and Ward Chipman, Jr. The American commissioner was Cornelius P. Van Ness of Burlington, Vermont. Van Ness had been born into a prominent Dutch family in Kinderhook, New York. His father had been a general in the War of Independence and later a congressman, and one uncle had been a second to Aaron Burr in his tragic duel with Alexander Hamilton. Van Ness himself read law and was called to the bar in 1803 together with his neighbour Martin Van Buren. Van Ness left New York for Vermont in

1806 and settled in Burlington in 1809, accepting the post of U.S. district attorney the following year and that of collector of customs in 1813. He cultivated good relations with the Madison administration, and his appointment as commissioner arose from that connection. Later he served in Vermont's legislature, was briefly chief justice of the state's supreme court, and was twice elected governor. In 1816, at age thirty-four, however, Van Ness was just starting his career. Born the year the Treaty of Paris was negotiated, he, like Holmes, was a generation younger than Barclay and Chipman.[2]

Van Ness's meetings with Barclay and Chipman were more brief and superficial than those of the other commission. Credentials were exchanged, and the secretary was appointed – Henry H. Orne from Massachusetts. However, the United States had not yet appointed an agent, so no functions at that level, particularly given Ward Chipman's defective documents, could be carried out. Furthermore, neither of the surveyors attended the meetings. Even so, the two commissioners decided that the most pressing need was for a survey of various parts of the borderland. It was too late in the season to begin surveying, so they made plans to meet again in the spring of 1817 to give instructions to the agents and the surveyors for the work to be done that summer.

Over the winter President James Madison appointed William C. Bradley as the U.S. agent. Bradley was also from Vermont, born in Westminster in 1782. A very precocious youth, he was sent to Yale at age thirteen but was expelled for involvement in a prank and went home to his enraged father, Stephen Row Bradley, who was a Yale graduate and a U.S. senator. After several difficult years, he was able to read law, and he was called to the Vermont bar in 1802. He had a modest political career, being elected to the state legislature in 1806 and serving in Congress from 1813 to 1815 and again from 1823 to 1827. Although his brief experience at Yale was unhappy, Bradley became something of a linguist, if not a scholar, knowing Latin, Greek, Hebrew, and Arabic, as well as French and German.[3]

Snow, ice, and spring flooding usually continued in the woods of the Maine–New Brunswick borderland until May or June, the commission was advised, and 1816 had had one of the coldest summers on record, so there was no need for it to have an early meeting in 1817. Thus it convened in Boston only on 4 June, to assemble key participants and to plan the program of work. Both commissioners and both agents attended, with William C. Bradley being administered his oath and the new, correct documents for the Chipmans being officially filed. The

British surveyor was Colonel Joseph Bouchette, from Montreal, who had succeeded his uncle, Samuel J. Holland, as surveyor general of Lower Canada. Bouchette had received great praise for his hydrographic surveys of York and wrote several books on the geography of British North America. During the War of 1812 he raised a company of volunteers, for which he was given the rank of lieutenant-colonel. By the end of the war Bouchette was promoting one of his books in England, where he renewed his friendship with the Duke of Kent. Though obviously well qualified for the position of surveyor for the commission, Bouchette may have owed his appointment to influence in London.[4] The American surveyor, John Johnson, had had some academic training and had settled near Burlington, Vermont, working as a surveyor and engineer. As well as building dams, bridges (he invented a truss for long bridges), and mills, he worked as a surveyor in both Vermont and Lower Canada. When the War of 1812 broke out he became a captain in the militia, and he later served for many years as state surveyor. Johnson's biographer described his character in terms of 'uprightness' and 'probity' and his appointment to the commission as being a result of his reputation for surveying skill and mathematical knowledge, although the British assistant surveyor, Colin Campbell, later remembered Johnson as 'a vulgar and uneducated Man,' 'an unprincipled Scoundrel,' and 'a shrewd intelligent Yankee.'[5]

Commissioner Van Ness proposed that the work of the surveyors begin at the point where the forty-fifth parallel met the St Lawrence River, so that the efforts of the commissions under both the fifth and sixth articles of the Treaty of Ghent would be coordinated at that common point. However, Barclay had been informed that a scientist was being sent from Britain to take the sightings in that region, and he had not yet arrived in North America. The commissioners decided therefore that the survey should start in the east and should be conducted in two phases. Both an American party, led by Johnson, and a British, under Bouchette, would attempt to find the highlands mentioned in the treaty, while two other groups, headed by Colin Campbell, the British assistant surveyor, and by Charles Turner, his American counterpart, would survey and mark the line due north from the source of the St Croix.[6]

The agents spent several days drafting suitable instructions for the surveyors, finishing by 11 June. They instructed the surveyors where to carry out their expeditions and spelled out many of their tasks in minute detail. They devoted particular attention to the methods of operation and the keeping of records. Each party, consisting of the surveyors, chainmen, instrument bearers, blazers, and axemen, was to consist entirely of citizens of its own country. The two teams were to carry out parallel surveys and to keep field books and journals, recording all data, distances, elevations, and other details. At the beginning of each day the two parties were to compare notes, and if any differences were found the variant work was to be resurveyed until the findings were identical. If disagreement still existed, this variation was to be noted down in the presence of both parties, entered on the maps, and made part of the public record. The parties were to mark the due-north line by cutting trees and brush for eight feet on either side of the line and to indicate the line with durable markers placed no further than a mile apart. The surveyors were to prepare accurate maps at a prescribed scale, keep careful accounts of all expenditures, and maintain strict discipline among the crews.[7]

Although the crews were recruited and operated on the basis of nationality, the surveyors and the men all took oaths before magistrates agreeing to follow orders from either of the two agents and to carry out their duties 'to the best of [their] skill and ability without any regard to the interest of either party,' and it was emphasized that their work was to be a 'true and impartial representation of the rivers, waters, land, hills and mountains which [they] shall survey.'[8] Every precaution was taken to ensure that national partisanship did not colour the work of the surveys. The board of commissioners finished its work on 12 June 1817, with an examination of expenses incurred so far. It then adjourned to meet again in early May of the following year.

The agents and surveyors were left to look after the recruiting and equipping of their crews in Massachusetts and New Brunswick, and men enlisted had to take their oaths before a magistrate. All this was to have been done by 22 June, but oaths were still being recorded on the twenty-eighth. John Johnson came down to Boston from his home in Burlington on 25 June and, together with Colonel Charles Turner and their crew of twenty-nine, sailed for Saint John, New Brunswick, on the thirtieth. At Saint John the Americans were met by Chipman, Bouchette, and Campbell, who had made arrangements for them, and on 9 July the two parties left by steamboat up the St John River for the overnight trip to Fredericton. There they arranged boats and supplies and looked after last-minute details: 'grinding axes, caulking the Batteaux, and sundry small jobs as necessary.'[9] The amount of supplies and equipment needed was enormous. Campbell reported to Chipman the supplies he had acquired, including a large log canoe, a small log canoe, birch-bark canoes, tents and poles, cases, straps, canvas, stretchers, axes, pikes, tools, kegs, tin work, stationery, and candles. Vast amounts of food had to be taken along (some stored along the route), such as bread, ham, pork, tongue, pease, rice, molasses, sugar, tea, and rum. Various charges for freight and storage had to be met. Chainmen and instrument bearers were to receive U.S. $1.50 per day, and axemen and labourers $1.00. Payments to the men alone might total almost $5,000 per year. The secretary was given a salary of $1,111 per year, and the surveyors $1,500. However, both the commissioners and the agents received $4,444.44, or £1,000 sterling, per year. The commissions were an expensive way to determine the border. American disbursements alone were $22,651.03 in 1817 and $24,337.58 in 1818; British costs would have been similar.[10]

By 15 July 1817 the advance parties left Fredericton, followed by a smaller group, in birch-bark canoes, that included Bouchette and Johnson. They proceeded up the St John River, poling their boats or being towed, and then entered the Maduxnekeag Creek, where they were able to store some of their supplies with a local settler. At this point also, they split their forces, with Johnson's party travelling by land to Houlton Plantation and Bouchette's continuing by boat and canoe up the Maduxnekeag towards the monument of 1797 at the source of the St Croix. Everything became unpleasant as rain settled in. Nevertheless, by 25 July both parties arrived at the 1797 monument – Johnson at noon and Bouchette some time earlier.[11]

The source of the St Croix had been fixed in a swamp, and the 'monument' there consisted of a yellow birch with iron hoops around it and a stake, on which was marked 'S.T. 1797.'[12] The two parties set up separate camps nearby, the Canadians to the east, on a bit of high ground rising above the swamp, and the Americans to the southwest, on some dry ground. The surveyors spent the next several days taking astronomical sightings in order to determine latitude and longitude and also to calculate the compass variation for plotting the due-north line from that point. Only with painstaking work were Johnson and Bouchette able to sort out the peculiarities of their instruments and come up with identical results. In the meantime, the weather got worse. Several days of rain prohibited work altogether and also translated into colds and fever. Campbell functioned as camp doctor: he 'administer'd a dose of Salts to Simon David, Wm. Manley, Dewar McKenzie, dress'd A. Campbell's ankle, Dewar's knee, and McKenzie's foot and gave Tuffs a dose of Sallop,' while his own hand was 'much swelled.'[13]

The crews had been clearing trees and brush at the site and preparing a new marker. This was a huge cedar log, hewn into a long square beam that would stand ten to twelve feet high. On the east side was carved 'NEW BRUNSWICK JULY 31, 1817,' and on the west side, 'UNITED STATES JULY 31 1817.' The names of the two surveyors were carved on the north and south sides. Stones were also placed on the east and west sides, on which abbreviated versions were chiselled. After completion of work on 31 July, both parties 'gave three cheers & all had a glass of grog.'[14] The formalities were not ignored.

After some further checking of instruments and more preparations, campsites were moved further north, all the more difficult in the constant rain. The work of surveying the due-north line from the new monument began on 2 August. Crews used both theodolites and circumferentors to sight the line north and placed posts and stones as markers indicating the distance from the source of the St Croix. They cleared brush and trees in a swath sixteen feet wide. This was dense, mixed forest of pine, spruce, and fir, broken by clumps of hardwoods such as birch and maple. The men completed roughly two-and-a-half miles the first day. However, almost immediately a problem surfaced between Johnson and the assistant surveyors, who claimed that careful sighting of stakes allowed making of an accurate line without continual use of instruments. Nevertheless, at the end of the second day Johnson checked the stakes with the telescope on his theodolite and found a distinct curve to the west in the line. Bouchette and the assistants were shown the error and agreed to use an instrument that would allow, as Johnson put it, 'back and forward observations' that would be more accurate. Another theodolite had to be obtained from Chipman in Saint John.[15]

Although this issue was in fact a technical problem, there was some degree of wariness, if not suspicion, between the two crews. Captain Montgomery Cairnes, an engineer from the 81st Regiment of Foot, and a member of the British party, described the relationship between the two chief surveyors: 'Squire Johnson and Colonel Bouchette both think they have got to windward of each other, at least both say so and seem perfectly content with what has been done, each also thinking the other a fool, a fact that remains also hereafter to be proved.'[16] Bouchette had reported to Chipman a week earlier, 'So far I agree perfectly with Mr. Johnson who appears (to say the least of him) an excellent meaning man,' and he expected continued 'harmony & good understanding' between them. However, by 4 August Bouchette was complaining that Johnson had 'attempted to play a Yankee trick' on him.[17]

Cairnes gave the younger Ward Chipman a colourful description of the U.S. surveying party and its peculiarities that calls to mind a painting by the nineteenth-century frontier artist George Caleb Bingham. 'The Americans have no kind of order or system in their camp but live Jack fellows alike, and whatever is done is only done as a matter of favor from the head to the foot, Each member considering himself equally worthy. Squire Turner being too hardened in his vulgar habits ever to leave them off, and Squire Johnson too soft to make them jump as he might under proper authority. They frequently decide their affairs of honor with the fist, and then it is over. They have a great many writers among them and no doubt there will be famous accounts given to the New World of this Exploring Survey.' Cairnes did not think very highly of the level of education or skill of the Americans, who were essentially 'woodsmen ... Mechanics, scribes, and Pharisees,' as he put it. Nevertheless, they were 'ready and anxious' to 'oblige "the Captain,"' as he was called, because he supplied both parties with fresh trout that he caught in the streams. Whatever the faults of the Americans, they were able to take care of themselves. 'The Americans get on tenfold better than we do,' Cairnes noted, 'because they "look before they leap,"' whereas the British seemed to be constantly running short of food and supplies.[18]

If Cairnes was critical of the Americans, he eventually had some misgivings about the British party also. By mid-September he was reporting that supplies were running out, 'the men are covered with Boils & filled with discontent and we have no Medicines with the party owing to lack of forethought.' Part of the discontent, he thought, concerned Bouchette's leadership. 'The men of our party look pale & ill & will only move when they get their "Bitters" [ale] as usual, which is too much (being a pint per day) when this is done, I don't know what will be the consequences, as they have no confidence in their Chief & curse him openly, which we cannot prevent.'[19] Cairnes certainly had increasingly critical views of Bouchette. On 18 August he commented that the surveyor's behaviour 'grows daily & hourly more & more that of a Madman,' and he described his berating and beating his son, an assistant surveyor, in front of the whole party. Later in the month Cairnes reported a similar incident when, before all the men, Bouchette kicked a Black crew member in the ribs.[20]

With the work of surveying the due-north line safely under way by early August, Johnson and Bouchette turned to other matters. Both went to Houlton Plantation to arrange for supplies and to work on their accounts. They also moved some thirteen miles ahead of the work parties, for taking sightings to determine the accurate location of the due-north line and marking it with temporary stakes, to be replaced when the surveying crews caught up. Illness and injury continued to plague the crews, and on any given day several men would be unable to work. On 12 August, British Assistant Surveyor Campbell reported that the day 'commenced raining heavy at sunrise and continued without intermission during the Day, so that neither party could leave their Camps.' Furthermore, he was 'still very feverish & vomiting frequently,' although he 'gave Medicine to three of the Am. Party, also some Plasters, Lint & Salves, their Med. Chest being out at the settlement.'[21] Miserable circumstances improved modestly when Cairnes caught some fish or shot a partridge for meals. Logistics remained a constant problem – bringing in preserved foods, acquiring some fresh food, moving all the supplies to new campsites. Periodic shortages of food, together with the unauthorized consumption of rum, gave rise to complaints by both the crews and by the agents. The following year the commissioners ordered that each man on the survey was to get 'one pound of pork, one pound and a half of hard bread, half a pint of pease or white beans, one ounce of Musourado Sugar, a quarter of a pint of tea per day ... one gill of rum per day, and in addition thereto a gill of Rice on each succeeding Sunday to each man.'[22] By 18 August Johnson and Bouchette had rejoined the assistant surveyors, now some four miles north of the monument, and then they prepared to return to the St John River to search for the highlands mentioned in the treaty of 1783. The weather having been consistently bad, Bouchette's health also began to decline.

Throughout early September, Johnson and Bouchette proceeded to make their way north, past Presque Isle River and the Aroostook River, to emerge near Grand Falls on the St John River, some seventy-seven miles and twenty-seven chains from the source of the St Croix. At this point, with Bouchette ill again, Johnson lame, and all the men tired and in need of a chance to wash their clothes, the parties stayed at the British barracks, where they were 'very civilly treated by the commanding officer.' They had explored Mars Hill and presumed that a range of highlands ran west to Katahdin Mountain, many miles west, which Bouchette asserted was 'highly conspicuous for its height.' Between the Aroostook and the St John they climbed another 'line of Land' that Bouchette found 'extremely high.'[23] Writing a few years later, Peter Fisher described Mars Hill as 'majestically towering above the adjacent country.' Fisher noted that the hill afforded a good view in all directions: to Mount Katahdin to the west, the Aroostook watershed to the

north, Moose Mountain beyond the St John valley to the east, and Houlton Plantation to the south.[24]

At the encampment on the St John River, Cairnes had some misgivings about how much further north the parties might go. He had
already complained at length about the weather and, particularly about
the lack of blankets and clothing for coping with temperatures that fell
below freezing at night. Now he worried about the direction of the
expedition. Bouchette had said that he intended to carry on to 'the first
waters ever so small that descend to the Restigouche' and that at that
point 'he will stop and prove that they empty into the St. Lawrence, or
the Bay of Chaleur, which is the same thing.'[25] This goal represented a
major objective, and although it involved a boundary different from
that hoped for by the Americans, it revealed that the British surveying
party accepted the principle that the highlands of the treaty of 1783 lay
north of the St John.

North beyond the St John the ridges were high, though swampy as
well. The surveyors reached the Restigouche portage, which was formed
by a ridge originating in the Sugar Mountains. Johnson found the prom-
ontory 'evidently the highest land we passed over on the line during the
season.' The extent of the highland was not known, but it appeared to
run both northwest and east 'sufficiently to divide the waters of the
above said rivers [St John and Restigouche].'[26] From that height of land
the men descended on 8 October to the Little Wagansis River, some
ninety-nine miles and four chains from the St Croix. The Little Wagansis
was a tributary of the Restigouche, and so the parties were out of the
Bay of Fundy watershed and into the streams draining into the Bay of
Chaleurs. As Bouchette described the discovery of the Little Wagansis,
'Mr. Johnson the United States Surveyor & myself having perfectly
agreed on its being the first water connected with the St. Lawrence and
which is particularly alluded to in the Sixth Article of our Instructions,
We concluded thereon as being the Extreme point defined for the Sus-
pension of the Explorations.'[27] This agreement confirmed that the
boundary indeed lay north of the St John River, although Bouchette
and Johnson differed as to the role of the Wagansis. Had they discovered the Northwest Angle of Nova Scotia, referred to in the treaty of
1783? Were they on the slope of the treaty's highlands? For Bouchette
this stream was the end of the search, because it originated in the highlands that, he asserted, divided the waters flowing into the St Lawrence
(actually the Gulf) from those flowing into the Atlantic (the St John
draining into the Bay of Fundy). For Johnson the Wagansis represented

a shift in watersheds from the Bay of Fundy to the gulf, although the actual watershed of the St Lawrence *River* had yet to be discovered. Whatever the immediate conclusions, these surveyors had reached a turning point.

The weather was deteriorating, and so Bouchette and Johnson, having carried out a major part of their mission, turned back. Anticipating the discovery of the Little Wagansis, Cairnes had written to Ward Chipman, Jr, on 25 September that a favourable resolution of the boundary was in sight. 'I may venture to say that so far no Highlands of any consequence have escaped our notice, and that when the various Ridges (particularly the one at this post which almost will connect with the Restigouche Highlands) come to be represented upon the Plan of Survey, these general features will be pleasing to your Father's & your sight, affording abundant argument against that dreadful jump which Yankee seems resolved on trying toward the Walls of Quebec.' Cairnes, Bouchette, and probably others in the British surveying party clearly regarded a possible boundary north of the St John along the Restigouche watershed to be a satisfactory settlement. 'A little more toil,' Cairnes concluded, 'and I trust we shall come to an honorable conclusion of our labors for this season.'[28]

Meanwhile, the parties clearing brush and marking off the due-north line had progressed some twenty miles from the source of the St Croix River before damage to their theodolite and other instruments halted operations in October. It was time to end the season.

When Bouchette and Johnson reached the Little Wagansis River on 8 October 1817, they seemed to agree that they had found the point close to that described in the treaty of 1783 where the waters flowed into the St Lawrence. Of course this stream flowed into the Restigouche and thence into the Bay of Chaleurs and the Gulf, rather than into the St Lawrence River itself. Nevertheless, it was part of a different watershed and not part of those rivers flowing into the Bay of Fundy and the Atlantic Ocean directly. On 11 October, Bouchette, then on the Grand River near the St John, wrote to Chipman that the exploration parties had reached the Restigouche portage and the Little Wagansis. Although he did not want to make any hasty conclusions, he did assert that 'it is therefore evident that by this intersection [of the due-north line with the Little Wagansis] we do not only participate in all the advantages of the Portage ..., but by the sketch I shall send you, you will be convinced that the Commanding Ground would also appertain to His Majesty's

Government.' Bouchette held that this was important from a military point of view and would give Britain control of the Restigouche and the country north and west of it for 100 miles (presuming, as he did, that the Americans would not be awarded the Temiscouata Portage).[29]

In his correspondence with Chipman about this news in November, Barclay commented that Bouchette's letter to Chipman had strongly suggested that the Wagansis watershed was the highlands and that it was 'advantageous to His Majesty, as Great Britain will partake in all the advantages of the Portage.' He asked if this was indeed the case and said that he would rely on Chipman in this matter. However, he added, 'On this Article we must exert ourselves,' although he stated that it was 'unnecessary' to make such an admonition to the two Chipmans.[30] Barclay wrote again to Chipman about a month later that he was not sufficiently familiar with the region to have a clear sense of the matter and was prepared to accept Chipman's advice. 'This point ...' Barclay wrote, 'I leave wholly to your better information and judgement, with this one remark, that if adopting this river will tend to His Majesty's Interest there can be no objection to falling in with the wishes of the American Surveyor.' It would be possible to repudiate this solution, however, because the river flowed into the Gulf rather than into the St Lawrence River.[31]

When Barclay wrote to Lord Castlereagh less than a month later he sounded more willing to accept the Little Wagansis as the highlands. Bouchette and Johnson, he said, 'concluded their exploring survey for the season, on the supposition that the stream comported with the description in the second Article of the Treaty of 1783, respecting the Highlands and the waters running into the River St. Lawrence.' While he also noted that it would be possible to object to this proposal because the river flowed into the Gulf of St Lawrence, he suggested: 'At present it is impossible to determine whether the assuming of this stream will comport with His Majesty's interest.'[32] In short, both Chipman and Barclay had accepted Bouchette's conclusion that the highlands sought in the treaty were north of the St John near the source of the Little Wagansis, and that this finding was advantageous to British North America because it would not actually bring the border as far north as the streams flowing into the St Lawrence River itself.

The board of commissioners had adjourned in June 1817 with the intention of meeting again in New York on 5 May 1818. However, the pressing work along the forty-fifth parallel, in conjunction with the commission under Ghent's sixth article, made it expedient to shift the meeting place to Burlington, Vermont, nearer the forty-fifth parallel, on 15 May. What unfolded was a series of meetings in Burlington, in Montreal, and in St Regis.[33] Given the substantial amount of work remaining on the survey of the due-north line, on the explorations for the Northwest Angle of Nova Scotia, and on the highlands, this redirection of focus did not matter very much. However, over the winter of 1817–18 Barclay and Chipman changed their opinions about the eastern boundary, and three developments, examined in detail below, dramatically affected the commission – Colonel Bouchette was relieved of his duties as surveyor and replaced by a more reliable man, Ward Chipman submitted a memorial to the board urging it to change the surveyors' instructions, and Colonel Barclay wrote to Lord Castlereagh informing him of the need to protect British interests by denying the Americans territory north of the St John.

First, Bouchette was to be replaced as British surveyor. Barclay had never approved of his appointment and on learning of it had complained to the Colonial Office on 14 June 1815 that Bouchette was essentially a draftsman, while what was needed was an astronomer and surveyor. During the summer of 1817, in the course of the first survey, there were numerous complaints about Bouchette's behaviour by members of the British surveying party. The most damning came from Ward Chipman, Jr, who persuaded his father and Barclay that Bouchette was 'unequal to this duty' and 'unfit for his office.' However, Bouchette was also accused of being 'bullied by the American Surveyor.'[34] Furthermore, Bouchette was constantly ill throughout the summer. He attended the meeting in Burlington in May 1818 but came down with a fever and had to be taken back to Montreal.[35] However, historians such as W.S. MacNutt and Henry S. Burrage have concluded that Bouchette was relieved because he had been 'gulled' by the American surveyor about the identification of the 'highlands' in the treaty of 1783 and 'for his willingness to accept defeat,' even though Barclay, Chipman, and others had also done so as recently as the autumn.[36] Bouchette had described the boundary along the same St Lawrence watershed in his 1815 book on the geography of Lower Canada, so that his work with the American surveyor did not constitute a retreat on his part.[37] Clearly by early 1818 Bouchette had to be replaced, because Barclay and Chipman had conceived a new vision of what the boundary might be. They were also alert to the fact that a demarcation north of the St John would not serve British and British North American needs and interests. Thus several considerations entered into the decision to replace him. When Barclay wrote to Castlereagh on 1 January 1818, he emphasized the dissatisfaction felt with Bouchette and proposed a successor nominated by Chipman.[38]

William F. Odell replaced Bouchette. Born in 1774 the son of a Loyalist clergyman in New Jersey, he was taken to New Brunswick as a child. Odell's father seems to have left the service of the church and was appointed secretary of the province of New Brunswick in 1781. However, as a result of his family's modest resources Odell did not receive higher education and at eighteen became deputy clerk of pleas. He subsequently read law under Ward Chipman and was called to the bar in 1806. Odell practised law and held several minor offices, but he also taught himself surveying and became deputy surveyor of the province.[39] Although he performed his job for the commission satisfactorily, it is clear that he was no better qualified in either astronomy or surveying than Bouchette, but he was a New Brunswicker and a protégé of the Chipmans'. They had approached him as early as November 1817, and by February of the following year he was appointed.[40]

Second, Ward Chipman submitted a memorial to the board on 23 May 1817 requesting new instructions ordering the surveyors to abandon work on the due-north line and explorations north of the St John River and to concentrate on the search for the highlands in the region to the south, between the Aroostook and the Des Chutes rivers and in the area west of Mars Hill. This crucial strategic move strongly implied that he thought that the Northwest Angle and the highlands were well south of the St John, not to mention the St Lawrence.[41] One of his goals as he explained to Henry Goulburn at the Colonial Office in a letter in late March, was to minimize expense and speed up the procedure by having the two agents make claims to specific boundary lines, which would then be explored, surveyed, and mapped. The evidence for the claims of each would then be presented to the board of commissioners for it to decide which claim conformed to the treaty of 1783.[42] There was certainly merit in this method, but the British were also reorienting their hopes and expectations for a border line.

The American agent, William C. Bradley, responded immediately and vigorously that Chipman's proposal would be a violation of the procedures agreed to the previous year and a deliberate limiting of the territory to be explored. It would inevitably use up more time and money, rather than less. The board ordered that the work of surveying and marking the due-north line, together with explorations north of the St John River, continue for another season, but also that the area from the

Aroostook and Des Chutes rivers as far west as the Chaudière and the Kennebec rivers be explored.[43]

Third and finally, on 23 May 1818, the same day in which Chipman had submitted to the board his memorial about instructions for the survey, Barclay wrote to Castlereagh. Any American claim north of the St John, he said, would 'by this means cut off all rightful communication between His Majesty's Provinces of Nova Scotia and New Brunswick with Canada, a measure ruinous to His Majesty's interests, and unquestionably never intended by either of the Parties at the time of the execution of the Treaty of 1783.'[44] This was very much a reversal of Barclay's comments to Castlereagh in December. Thus, between the beginning of 1818 and the meeting of the board in May, the British inclination to accept the Little Wagansis watershed as the highlands referred to in the treaty of 1783 evaporated, largely as a result of Chipman's efforts.

The work for the 1818 season took the surveying parties back into the wilderness across some of the territory traversed the previous summer. Colin Campbell assembled the British crews in late June and sent them first to Fredericton and then by small boats on to Grand Falls, but he was feeling ill and taking medicine even before work started. All along the way up the St John River the parties were plagued by rain and lightning. William F. Odell and John Johnson met at the Madawaska settlements on the St John on 11 July and, after making some arrangements for supplies and equipment, and following delay caused by heavy rain, they proceeded up the Grand River and then overland to the Little Wagansis to the tree that marked the point ninety-nine miles due north of the source of the St Croix where the exploration had stopped the previous October. It was a struggle to get supplies up the Grand River. Indeed on 17 July the crews spent much of the day in the water carrying cargo on their backs. Odell ordered an extra ration of grog for the men because of the 'exposure and fatigues of the day.'[45] The work was very slow, with sickness and injuries constantly reducing the workforce. Although the ridges forming the Wagansis watershed had been described by Johnson the previous year as the highest encountered, Odell argued that the land, 'with the exception of a few insignificant rises near the River, is low, flat and swampy, and chiefly covered with Spruce and Cedar.'[46]

The parties pressed on from this point exploring the tributaries of the Restigouche – the Petite Fourche and the Grande Fourche – while generally travelling north. In these regions they found what Odell described as a 'luxuriant growth of Timber.' Birch, ash, and maple were in abundance, with evidence that the maples had been tapped for sugar. As they progressed north they passed through stands of large pine, spruce, and fir, and Odell noted finding the largest cedars seen by the surveyors. After passing numerous streams flowing east into the Restigouche, the parties at last on 2 September found a small river draining to the west. This was about fifteen miles north of the Grande Fourche, or about forty-five miles from the St John River. They had crossed a high ridge, 'the highest Point intersected by the Line run this year,' Odell noted. They then descended into more moderate country with 'no appearance of Highlands.'[47] The small stream ran through a meadow flooded by waters backed up from beaver dams, so they named it the Beaver River. They were 143 miles from the monument at the source of the St Croix.

Campbell was sent on to explore this river to be certain that it did not turn east to join the Restigouche. He and his party laboured through shallow water and around more beaver dams. After following its 'serpentine' course they found that the Beaver River entered a lake some four or five miles long. Around the lake and along the river that flowed out from the lake at the north end, they found substantial evidence of recent human activity in the form of paths, campsites, and logs laid across streams for crossing. They presumed this to be Métis Lake, and although they did not see the St Lawrence or trace further the stream flowing north, they concluded that these waters would empty into the St Lawrence River. They had in fact found the St Lawrence watershed. After four days on this expedition, Campbell's group returned to the main party on 8 September.[48] By 18 September they were all back on the St John River.

The surveying parties then proceeded to Mars Hill, which they reached on 28 September. Mars Hill was the first high landmass north of the source of the St Croix. The highest of its two peaks was about 1,660 feet; it was just over a mile west of the due-north line and forty miles north of the monument. It was such a landmark that it is not surprising that the New Brunswickers looked to it as the topographical formation that must be the highlands of the 1783 treaty. Moreover, for practical reasons it was attractive because it was well south of the St John River, not to mention the St Lawrence. Unfortunately, the rivers flowing directly from both sides of its slopes ran into the St John, and therefore Mars Hill did not form a major watershed. In fact, it stands something of an isolated peak, with east-flowing streams actually rising on its west side.

Mars Hill being heavily wooded, the surveying parties spent several days cutting trees in order to clear sufficient space to get a good view of the surrounding country. Odell's party worked on the north peak, and Johnson's on the south peak. When weather permitted over the next week or so, both parties took sightings on other landmarks to be seen from the summits. Odell reported 'a range of mountains very high, and apparently bald,' running to the west, Spencer Mountain and Katahdin Mountain being the most distant and most prominent. Odell concluded that this range constituted a clear highlands running more or less east and west and forming the watershed for the Penobscot and Kennebec rivers, which flowed south into the Atlantic, and for the St John River, which flowed mostly north in this sector and eventually emptied into the Bay of Fundy. Looking to the northeast, beyond the St John, Odell saw 'very high land,' whereas to the north 'there appears to be less inequality in the Face of the country than in any other.'[49] In short, the highlands were to be seen west of Mars Hill, not north, in Odell's opinion.

Johnson, in contrast, noted that Mars Hill, rather than being part of a continuous highlands stretching to the west, was something of an isolated peak, 'surrounded on all sides by the same glade of low land.' Johnson, taking sightings mainly to the north, argued that the land generally fell away for many miles until, beyond the St John River, it could be seen to rise again to some height, where ridge after ridge could be observed. From these slopes rose the Madawaska, the Green, and the Temiscouata rivers, on the south side flowing into the St John, and the Beaver River and numerous others on the north, flowing into the St Lawrence. Johnson also commented on the Green River Mountain (in the regions just north of the St John River), which he said was slightly higher than Mars Hill.[50] In other words, Johnson saw Mars Hill as of no topographical significance (being unconnected with any range of highlands whatsoever) and noted higher mountains further north, in the St Lawrence watershed.

By 12 October the two parties left Mars Hill. Odell took his crews into the Meduxnekeag River valley, where he, Campbell, and several others followed one of the tributaries that ran south towards the Houlton Plantation to Park's Place. Looking west, he confirmed his impression of a ridge to the north and west of him running from Mars Hill to the Spencer Mountains.[51] Johnson took his men back up the St John River west of Grand Falls and the due-north line to the Madawaska and Green rivers. There he ascended the Green River Mountain, which he estimated to be 1,074 feet high. From there he could see many of the landmarks that he had observed from Mars Hill, and he felt reassured that the highlands to the north were higher than any others in the region and clearly discernible all the way west to Lake Temiscouata.[52] By the end of the season in October 1818 the surveying parties, and subsequently the agents as well, were further apart in their assessment of the way in which the topography of the land conformed to the provisions of the treaty of 1783 than they had been a year earlier. This was a gap that was never closed. The new British surveyor, together with the more aggressive approach by Ward Chipman, infused new vigour into the group's attitude.

Chipman wrote to Barclay as the year closed. The British had not yet solved the problem of the northern boundary, but they had created some alternatives. Though still worried that he did not perceive the situation clearly enough, he saw the crucial issue as being

> whether the due north line is to cross the River St. John, or in other words, whether the North West Angle of Nova Scotia is to be found and decided to be the highlands lying to the northwards, or in highlands lying to the southward of the river St. John; for if this angle should be decided to be at any point in highlands northward of this river, our cause will be virtually lost, and it will in such case be of little consequence where this point of highlands shall be found, or in what direction the line along the highlands shall be *from thence* traced to the Connecticut; and in the other hand if the angle should be decided to be at any point in the highlands southward of the river, it will be comparatively of little consequence to the United States, where this point of highlands shall be found, whether at Mars Hill or at the river Restook [Aroostook] or at any other spot to the southward of the River St. John, or in what direction the line along the highlands shall be *from thence* traced to the Connecticut.[53]

This, in Chipman's elaborate eighteenth-century prose, was a profound observation. He had understood and articulated the problem of the northeastern boundary in the form that it would be considered for the next twenty-five years.

The board of commissioners was to have met in November 1818, but the surveyors had not had time to complete their reports, so the meetings were rescheduled for 3 May 1819 in New York, but another delay followed when contrary winds detained the British agent while he was sailing from New Brunswick. In the interval, accounts were looked after and the reports of the astronomers and surveyors were submitted. By 13 May, Ward Chipman submitted a memorial arguing that continued work on the due-north line had prevented the complete survey of the Mars Hill area authorized the previous year, and he also complained the American agent, William C. Bradley, had based his report on conversations with people who were not under oath to give impartial information. Two days later Bradley replied, saying that both parties had seen from Mars Hill the range of highlands mentioned in his report and that they had explored the eastern sector while in the vicinity of the Beaver River. Therefore, it did not seem to him unreasonable to accept the observations of local people that waters further west and on the north side of the watershed also flowed into the St Lawrence. Bradley said also that Bouchette had referred to these same hills in his 1817 report, and he asserted that the current British surveyor had changed his opinion about the topography between leaving the field in 1817 and submitting his report in 1818. The following day Chipman argued that the objectionable report of the American surveyor had not been part of the joint reports of both surveyors submitted to the agents in advance of the board's meeting and therefore was not part of the consultative process expected. In common law, Chipman charged, evidence could not be arbitrarily presented, and he said that the honour and dignity of the two countries was too much involved to permit any irregular procedures. He urged Bradley to withdraw the report and the map in question. After dealing with still more financial matters, the board gave the agents and surveyors instructions for the coming season and then closed their proceedings for the year.[54]

The 1819 season saw a much greater diversity of exploration than the previous two summers, as both sides looked in the more remote countryside for the topographical features that would reinforce their arguments for the cases that they were building. William F. Odell and the newly appointed American surveyor, Captain Alden Partridge, met on 6 July on the River Des Chutes in the hope of making sightings of Mars Hill. However, the atmosphere was too hazy to permit it, and they therefore shifted to the Aroostook River. The parties ascended that stream expecting to reach the headwaters of the St John or the Penobscot. Partridge went on ahead while Odell made a survey of the river. Partridge, Odell concluded, intended to make only a very 'slight' exploration of this region, later 'bending their whole attention north of the River St. John.'[55] The American returned to report that, because of extraordinarily low water that summer, he had not been able to get as far up the North Branch of the Aroostook as he had planned and that he had not found the lakes from which he hoped to gain access to either of the other rivers. He then left the Aroostook to explore the upper St John. Odell, having learned from a local that it had been possible in 1789, tried with the British party, to go up the Aroostook, following one of its tributaries in the hope of finding the headwaters of the St John and the Penobscot. Water levels in the streams were even lower than when Partridge had attempted the same mission several weeks earlier. Furthermore, the Britons' barometer began to leak and was rendered useless, reducing their ability to determine altitudes. They returned to the Aroostook and took sightings on Mars Hill to the south and recorded what they saw as a chain of ridges running west and east. 'This view of the country,' Odell reported, 'fully confirms the remarks made last year.'[56]

British Assistant Surveyor Colin Campbell took his party to Mount Katahdin in what is now central Maine, by portaging from the Schoodiac River (part of the St Croix) to the Matawamkeag River, which is a tributary of the Penobscot. He was looking for the watersheds for the Penobscot and the Kennebec rivers flowing south into the Atlantic Ocean and for the Chaudière River running northwest into the St Lawrence opposite Quebec City. As Campbell put it, 'conceiving it clearly proved that we are thus far on the real high lands dividing the waters, and having seen that height stretching to the northeast for many miles, continued to trace it.' Furthermore, Campbell asserted that 'there are no high lands North of the sources of the Chaudiere and Kennebec.'[57] He was convinced that Mount Katahdin was part of the highlands running more or less east and west, dividing the waters flowing into the St Lawrence from those that emptied into the Atlantic – namely, the highlands intended in the treaty of 1783. Campbell was unable to complete his explorations in October 1819, so in March 1820, as the ice was going out of the rivers in Maine, he and his party returned for further explorations at the height of land between the Kennebec and Chaudière rivers.

The new U.S. surveyor, Alden Partridge, took his party first to Quebec in mid-June 1819 and across the Temiscouata Portage into Lake Temiscouata; they then made their way south to the River Des Chutes, where they met the British party on 6 July. Above the Des Chutes valley, together with the British party, they took sightings on Mars Hill and the land configurations to the west. In Partridge's view, 'To the West are some eminences of less elevation,' whereas to the 'North-west and North the country appears to rise pretty uniformly.'[58] By early September the American surveyors under Partridge also explored the upper

Chaudière River. W.G. Hunter, an assistant surveyor, took an American party up the Allagash River, a tributary of the upper St John, around Mount Katahdin and into Umbasucsus Lake, which eventually flowed south into the Penobscot and the Matawamkeag, more or less reversing the route that Campbell had taken earlier.

The board of commissioners met again in Boston on 11 May 1820. Both Odell and Partridge submitted reports. Some disagreements emerged about parties going off independently to make surveys, rather than working in conjunction. New instructions gave the American surveyor authority to determine where the explorations would take place north of the St John River and the British surveyor the power to decide where the parties should work south of the St John. The summer surveying of 1820 would be the last chance to find the topographical evidence that would build each case. The Commissioners also scheduled a board meeting in New York on 22 November 1820.

The explorations of the 1820 season were ambitious. This would be the last chance to discover in the field convincing evidence for each side, and major efforts were put forward. Odell and a new U.S. surveyor, N.H. Loring, set off with parties to examine once again Mount Katahdin and the Allagash and Penobscot watersheds. In early July, Odell went up the Penobscot by way of the Schoodiac Lakes, plagued by rain and insects. On 15 July he complained in his journal, 'Raining most of the night, our Encampment very uncomfortable, neither cedars nor dry wood – & the Musquitoes very numerous – frequent showers during the night.'[60] Odell met Loring on 18 July, and they worked their way along the upper Penobscot until they were able to climb Mount Katahdin. There they attempted to take sightings on such landmarks as Mars Hill, although the weather was hazy. Loring reported, 'In that section of the country I could see no mountains, neither were there any hills of uncommon heights, nor any elevated ground which might be termed a ridge or Spur of Highlands.'[61] They then proceeded across a two-mile portage and into one of the western tributaries of the St John River. Campbell, who had also ascended the Penobscot, crossed into one of the sources of the Allagash River. W.G. Hunter, an American assistant surveyor, and Charles Loss, a British assistant surveyor, explored the upper reaches of the St John – its West Branch and its South or Main Branch. These they followed to the portages into the Penobscot. They also looked at several tributaries on the northwest side of the St John, such as the Black River.[62]

Several other expeditions looked at the various rivers further north that drained into the St Lawrence. Thomas Carlile, a British assistant surveyor, and H. Burnham, an American assistant surveyor, explored the Ouellé River, which emptied into the St Lawrence and had its source in a swamp close to the source of the Black River and the Little St John, which flowed southeast into the St John River. Dr. Tiarks, the British astronomer, and H. Burnham ascended the Green River, north from the St John, and, exploring at its headwaters, found the source of the Rimouski River, which also flows northwest into the St Lawrence. They then proceeded across the portage into the Tuladi River, which also flowed into Temiscouata Lake and thence into the Madawaska River, a tributary of the St John. While at the watershed they also explored north into Lake Métis and the Beaver River, first explored in 1818. Late in December Carlile and Burnham returned to this area to look at the Metgermatti portage and Rivière du Loup, which also flowed northwest into the St Lawrence.

Most of the 1820 season (and a few days in 1821 as well) were spent exploring along the northern and western perimeter of the St John watershed in an attempt to authenticate claims for the treaty highlands. By mid-October, with ice forming along the edges of the streams, Tiarks proceeded to Mars Hill for several days, while just a few days later Odell sent his crews down the St John River. On 11 October the season finished for Odell and his men. Starting in the morning at 7, with a southeast wind steadily rising, they approached Fredericton. 'When we reached Paul's Creek it began to rain & I landed and walked home,' he noted in the last entry of his journal, 'where I arrived a little before two.'[63]

The board of commissioners for article 5 met in New York on 23 November 1820. It was immediately clear that neither the surveyors nor the agents were ready to make their official presentations (Ward Chipman, in fact, did not attend). The commissioners instructed the agents that further surveys would not be productive: 'It is therefore ordered that the Agents come prepared to the next meeting of the board with their arguments.'[64] Even then, however, the agents were still not fully prepared. Neither the secretary nor the agents appeared at the opening session on 15 May 1821, Chipman being delayed by adverse winds once again.

Not until 24 May could work begin. At that session William C. Bradley, the American agent, protested that he had not received an advance copy of the British argument, which focused entirely on the location of the Northwest Angle of Nova Scotia (to the exclusion of the source of the Connecticut River and the matter of the forty-fifth parallel of latitude), nor had he received all the necessary data from the British surveyors. Therefore he was not able to present the whole American argument. He said that neither side could make its arguments until there had been a full exchange of data and evidence. Chipman felt that each side had abundant evidence. He also complained that he had been accused by the governor of Maine of delaying the proceedings (not altogether preposterous in view of the near-agreement of 1817). In the end, both agents read their opening arguments, but more time was allowed to enable them to study each other's full statements. The board adjourned to meet again in New York on 1 August 1821, as will be shown below in chapter 4, on page 85. This then would be the real beginning of the decision-making process. The board would at last function as a tribunal, hearing both the arguments and the evidence submitted to it for the whole of its part of the border – from the source of the St Croix River, all across the contested Maine–New Brunswick–Lower Canada border, to the point where the forty-fifth parallel met the St Lawrence River.[65] Meanwhile it had been busy on other parts of its mandate.

Chapter Four

Article 5: The Forty-Fifth Parallel, the Connecticut, and Deadlock

Assessing the various elements of the boundary between New Brunswick, Lower Canada (Quebec), and Maine – the subject of chapter 3 – has generally been understood to be the most important task of the commission under the fifth article of the Treaty of Ghent. The commission was also responsible, however, for marking out the forty-fifth degree of latitude from the Connecticut River to the St Lawrence River (or the Iroquois or Cataraquy, as it was called in the Treaty of Paris of 1783) and for determining the northwesternmost source of the Connecticut River. The forty-fifth parallel had been surveyed before the Revolutionary War in the 1770s by John Collins and Thomas Valentine to mark the boundary of the British colony of New York and the new province of Quebec.[1] These two tasks sounded quite straightforward and simple, but, as with all aspects of the boundary, they were not as simple as they seemed. They took up four surveying seasons, beginning in 1817, as the first part of this chapter shows. When they finally ended in 1820, the board of commissioners for article 5 could address the totality of its work, dealing with the Maine–New Brunswick boundary and Lower Canada's boundary with Maine, New Hampshire, Vermont, and New York.

To begin with, the Americans wanted to begin the survey at the point where the forty-fifth parallel struck the St Lawrence. Because the commission under the *sixth* article of the Treaty of Ghent was to *begin* its work at that point, it was logical, as well as important, that the two commissions agree about the location of the forty-fifth degree of north latitude.[2] In fact, as early as 18 January 1817 the British commissioner under article 6 sent the British astronomical surveyor, David Thompson, to the little settlement of St Regis on the south bank of the St Lawrence to take sightings to determine the exact location of the line of latitude.[3] The Americans carried on correspondence during the winter of 1817 to decide on an astronomer to take the sightings for them. Cornelius Van Ness suggested to president-elect James Monroe Major Andrew Ellicott, a professor of mathematics at the U.S. Military Academy at West Point, and Ellicott, when approached, seemed willing.[4]

The British government, however, had an opinion on the subject and informed Colonel Thomas Barclay that it would appoint an astronomer and send him to North America to take the sightings. Clearly, the government did not have complete confidence in the scientific training of such self-taught men as David Thompson or the Americans. Barclay therefore had to disagree with Van Ness when the latter proposed that the survey parties begin on the St Lawrence and work their way east marking the forty-fifth parallel. At the meetings of the commission in Boston in June 1817, Barclay said that work on the forty-fifth parallel could not begin until the British astronomer arrived from England. As a result, the survey work of the commission under the fifth article began in July on the due-north line from the source of the St Croix River rather than on the St Lawrence.[5] Barclay assumed that the scientist from Britain would arrive by midsummer and that he and Van Ness would be able to join the commissioners under the sixth article at St Regis to observe the sightings of the forty-fifth parallel. That, however, was not to be.[6]

Who were these scientists whose skills were to determine the location of the forty-fifth parallel? Neither of the two British commissioners was fully confident in Colonel Joseph Bouchette, so they were happy to rely on an appointment from England.[7] The British government selected Dr Johann Ludwig Tiarks. a German-born scientist educated at the University of Gottingen, who was serving as assistant librarian to the celebrated scientist Sir Joseph Banks. Very probably proposed to the government by Banks, Tiarks was twenty-eight years old in 1817 and well trained in the navigational and surveying skills needed to make the accurate sightings to determine the geographical position of landmarks along the contested border. Tiarks may well have played a more important role than anyone expected at the time. Not only was he for several years a critical figure in surveying the parallel, but he also was active in the parties that worked along the headwaters of the Connecticut and the watershed of the St John River. In 1825 he returned to North America to join in the survey of the Lake of the Woods, and in 1829 and 1830 he assisted in the preparation of arguments for the arbitration by the king of the

Netherlands.[8] Tiarks sailed for New York in the summer of 1817, but he did not arrive until late August, too late for the planned joint meeting of both commissions and almost too late to accomplish much during that season.

The American government first appointed Major Andrew Ellicott as astronomer. Then sixty-three years old, Ellicott had enjoyed an interesting career and was sometimes described as the leading American astronomer and mathematician. In addition to serving in the Revolutionary War, Ellicott had helped his father found Ellicott City in Maryland in 1774, published the first *United States Almanac* beginning in 1782, completed the surveying in 1784 of the Mason–Dixon line between western Maryland and Pennsylvania, and worked on the boundaries between several other states. Highly regarded by Thomas Jefferson, Ellicott was asked to train Meriwether Lewis to take astronomical observations before his great expedition. In 1813 Ellicott was appointed professor of mathematics at West Point.[9] He did little work for the commission during the 1817 season and suggested to the government that it appoint Ferdinand R. Hassler instead as astronomer. Hassler was from Switzerland and had studied at the University of Bern. He immigrated to the United States in 1805 and quickly found a place in the American scientific community, serving first as a professor of mathematics at West Point, where he met Ellicott, and then at Union College in New York. Sent abroad to obtain scientific instruments for mapping the coastline, Hassler was stranded in England during the War of 1812. Ironically, during his stay in England Hassler became friends with Tiarks. On his return to the United States, Hassler became first superintendent of the U.S. Coastal Survey. However, subsequent legislation restricted that post to officers holding U.S. military commissions. It was following his release from the Coastal Survey that Hassler was appointed astronomer to the commission in 1818.[10] Thus both the United States and Britain hired German-language scientists to solve the technical problems of the boundary.

When Tiarks arrived at the British party's camp on the St Lawrence in September 1817, work had been going on for some time. David Thompson and David P. Adams, an American surveyor, had taken sightings earlier in the year, and Major Ellicott had joined them by 15 June, although both parties were by September pursuing other tasks. Ellicott had found the location of the forty-fifth degree of latitude at the St Lawrence River to be 'within two or three feet' of the place marked in 1768 by Samuel

Holland, the surveyor general of Canada.[11] However, Ellicott had no official standing in the eyes of the sixth-article commission. Nevertheless, he concluded that the survey of the line of latitude would be a simple matter of marking minor adjustments to that old colonial boundary. Thompson, in contrast, had calculated the forty-fifth parallel to be considerably further south – some 1,200 feet south.

Tiarks joined the British camp and was warmly greeted by the commissioner. He found that the previous survey had been made with sextants only, although the Americans had a more sophisticated reflecting circle theodolite built by Troughton and Simm of London. Tiarks was taken to the American camp, near the point were the line had been estimated. The British astronomer took sightings and made calculations that placed the forty-fifth degree of latitude within 130 feet of Ellicott's calculation. This reading was divided in half, so that the line was determined to be within sixty feet of the British and American astronomers' sightings.[12] Thompson's variant sighting was simply ignored. Work then went on towards the east, with more sightings taken to lay out the parallel and the results marked on the ground and in field books. The deterioration of the weather in early November ended Tiarks's efforts. The sky was consistently overcast, and the cold affected the accuracy of the instruments. The British commissioner left for Montreal and advised Tiarks to quit also. The German scientist complained to Sir Joseph Banks in England that he had not been able to work as efficiently as he had expected because of the 'terrible cold.'[13]

Although there was much more work to be done, the American agent, William C. Bradley, wrote to Secretary of State John Quincy Adams in May 1818 that it looked as if the results of the two astronomers would be quite close to the old survey of the provincial boundary of the 1770s.[14] This conclusion perhaps generated illusory confidence that the positioning of the forty-fifth parallel would be a simple matter.

Everyone assumed that the June 1818 meeting at St Regis of the board of commissioners would go smoothly regarding the survey of the forty-fifth parallel west to the Connecticut River. The new American astronomer, Ferdinand Hassler, was ill, however, and did not arrive for some days. Nevertheless, the commissioners instructed the astronomers to work with the agents in determining the line as quickly as possible.[15] Work got underway in July, and by 4 August Tiarks was able to report that the parties had reached Fort Covington Village, several miles east of the St Lawrence. There were troubles with the crews. It was impossible to have oaths properly sworn because there were no magistrates in the area. Several crew members were lazy and drunk and had to be dismissed, and so there were not enough men. While the crews were sitting at dinner on 21 July, a great storm blew up. 'Our tent blew over, the dishes were overturned and tables carried almost over my head to a great distance,' Tiarks recounted. But there was much worse. 'Mr. Hassler had the misfortune of losing on this occasion his repeating [circle theodolite] which was entirely destroyed by the tent which covered it falling over it.' Hassler also lost two barometers. These were the scientific instruments that he had acquired in London, and alternatives now had to be borrowed from the surveyors working on the St Lawrence.[16] Tiarks's observatory was buffeted by the 'hurricane,' but nothing was damaged. The two astronomers vowed henceforth to build wooden observatories for their instruments rather than keeping them in canvas tents. More trouble was to follow.

As the season was drawing to a close the two parties reached the area of Lake Champlain and specifically Rouse's Point. This is the northern end of the lake, where the body of water narrows and from which the Richelieu River flows north towards Montreal. These narrows form a strategic area, because whoever held Rouse's Point could control the passage of men and vessels north or south on the lake. The significance of the military control of the lake and the waterways would have been in everyone's mind, with the decisive Battle of Plattsburgh only four years behind them. The American government had constructed a stone fort on one side of the passage after the War of 1812 and was working on a second one. It was therefore with some amazement and disbelief that Tiarks and the American assistant surveyor, Lieutenant Vinton, found that their sightings showed the true forty-fifth line of latitude to lie considerably south of the old line surveyed in the 1770s by Collins and Valentine. Several more sightings produced the same results. The two men then left the lake to go to Odell Town, a short distance north and west. Sightings there again revealed the true forty-fifth parallel to be between 3,000 and 3,535 feet south of the Collins–Valentine line. When Hassler himself took a sighting, he placed the old line 4,646 feet north of the true line. The conclusion was clear. Using the reflecting-circle theodolite, the three astronomers found the old line to be way off, placing the two U.S. forts well within British territory.[17]

This situation raised several problems, not least the potential wrath of local Americans were they to learn that the forts and sections of their property were now part of British North America. The astronomers told no one about their findings, not even their crews. Tiarks wrote to Barclay, and Barclay wrote to Charles Bagot in Washington, urging him to inform the U.S. government and to request that it safeguard the forts from a possible destructive outburst by the local people so that the fortification would pass into British hands in good repair.[18] Bagot went immediately to see Secretary of State John Quincy Adams to explain the situation. Adams, however, refused to be rushed. He said that he had no knowledge of the matter, but when shown a copy of Tiarks's letter to Barclay he agreed to take up the problem with the president and let Bagot know when anything was decided. Adams sent a bland note to Bagot assuring him that the destruction of the forts by the local inhabitants was not likely. Bagot then explained the situation to Castlereagh, by which time Barclay had already written to Joseph Planta, the undersecretary of the Foreign Office.[19]

Adams was not officially informed of these matters by the American agent until November. William C. Bradley wrote to him from Burlington, Vermont, on 2 November to say that he had 'unpleasant information from Mr. Hassler' – the old Collins–Valentine surveys appeared to be seriously incorrect, and, 'if the *observed* latitude is to be adopted by the Commissioners,' there would be an 'alarming result.' He added, 'From these observations such latitude will fall from 40 to 45 seconds south of the existing line while the important fortress near Rouse's point is south only 14 seconds.'[20] Although both the British and the American parties had suspected that the old line had errors, no one expected such dramatic findings.[21]

The board of commissioners met in New York on 3 May 1819. The surveyors and astronomers said that they were unable to submit final reports and opinions about the whole of the boundary, but on 11 May Tiarks and Hassler both presented their findings on the location of the forty-fifth degree of latitude. They confirmed the alarming news of the previous autumn. A clearly jubilant Barclay wrote to Castlereagh, 'It is with satisfaction that I acquaint your Lordship, that the mean result of astronomical observations, during the last season, of the astronomers of both Nations accord, each with the other, to mathematical nicety.' As a result, 'the American fortifications consequently fall within the limits of His Majesty's Province of Canada.'[22] The agreement of the two astronomers did not actually resolve the issue of where the parallel was to be drawn, but rather it created a whole new controversy to com-

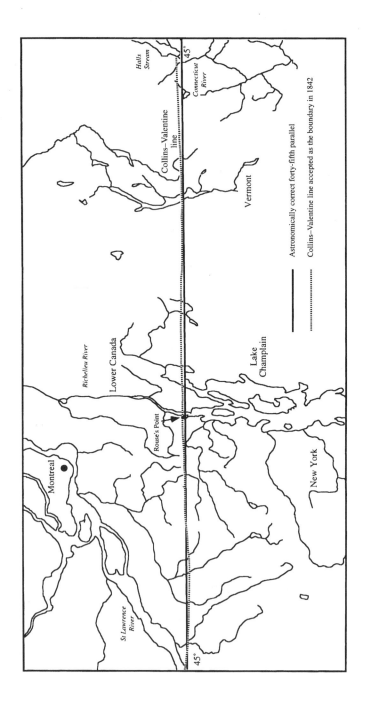

Map 6. Forty-fifth parallel and final boundary (Collins–Valentine line), 1842

Halls Stream

45°

Collins–Valentine line

Connecticut River

Vermont

Astronomically correct forty-fifth parallel

Collins–Valentine line accepted as the boundary in 1842

Richelieu River

Lower Canada

Lake Champlain

Rouse's Point

Montreal

New York

St Lawrence River

45°

plicate any boundary settlement under the fifth article of the Treaty of Ghent.

Over the winter of 1818–19 another problem began to unfold as well. In December Tiarks wrote Thomas Barclay to inform the commissioner that he had taken up winter residence in Newark, New Jersey. He became the next-door neighbour of Ferdinand Hassler, and presumably the two of them could work together on their data. In fact, they seemed to have agreed between them that they were not sufficiently well paid for their important work. Tiarks had accepted his appointment for a fee of £200 per year. (approximately $922 in U.S. dollars), plus expenses. This, he had pointed out to Barclay shortly after he arrived, was much less than the surveyors (£500 to £600 per year) or their assistants (£300). It was substantially less, he later told Joseph Planta, the undersecretary at the Foreign Office, than the American surveyor, who he said, quite erroneously, earned $5,000 per year. Tiarks proposed that £700 per year, as well as expenses, would be a more equitable payment. Failing some favourable adjustment, Tiarks asked that he be given his fare back to England and be permitted to resign his duties as astronomer.[23] After some consultation with Barclay, the Foreign Office agreed to raise Tiarks's stipend to £700 per year, as requested.[24]

For his part, Hassler had been superintendent of the U.S. Coastal Survey at a salary of $5,000 per year until Congress ruled that position available only to military officers. Hassler's appointment as astronomer was something of a compensation for the other job, but the president was able to offer him an annual salary of only $2,000. During the winter of 1819 Hassler corresponded with Commissioner Van Ness demanding $5,000 per year, as in his previous office. Van Ness offered Hassler first $3,000 and then $4,000, together with expenses, but Hassler would not budge. Hassler also rejected Van Ness's suggestion that the matter go to the president, who had originally hired him. Following the board's meeting in May, Van Ness wrote to Adams explaining the situation and expressing incredulity that Hassler was 'so insensible to both his own interest, and that of the United States, as to persist in his determination' to hold out for his full demand.[25]

Adams responded to Van Ness that, although both the president and the secretary of war were out of town, he was taking the initiative to engage Major Ellicott again as astronomer and that, as for Hassler, 'I have come to the conclusion, that in no event, recourse should be had with him again, if it is possible to have the service performed by another person.'[26] Ellicott, sixty-five years old and not in very good health, declined, despite being released from his duties at West Point by the superintendent of the academy. However, some persuasion was clearly attempted, because by 16 July Van Ness was able to inform the secretary of state that Ellicott had agreed to accept the task.[27]

Of course, while these negotiations were going on, the summer surveying season was slipping by. Barclay complained of this to Castlereagh in May but noted that Tiarks had been instructed to continue taking observations of the forty-fifth parallel with the British party and the American surveyors. Not surprisingly, the British could subsequently point to the United States whenever there were further complaints of delays.[28] By late July, Ellicott was able to get up to Lake Champlain, where he found that Hassler had taken all the instruments provided by the U.S. government. Fortunately, he had brought his own and his health remained good. 'So far I have experienced no fatigue whatever,' he reported to his wife, Sara, although, 'my young men cannot say as much, and it appears to me that they could perform the laborious duty of sleeping eighteen hours out of 24, if not interrupted.'[29]

A more serious discovery of Ellicott's was that he did not quite understand Tiarks's methods of calculation. Hassler and Tiarks had enjoyed similar training, they were good friends, and they had complete confidence in each other. Between Tiarks and Ellicott, however, there was a large gap in both age and training. Ellicott wrote to his wife that he 'candidly confess[ed] that I do not yet comprehend the method pursued by the British astronomer and Mr. Hassler, it is different from anything I have yet seen or heard of – not more than one observation in ten can possibly be applied to the boundary,' but he did affirm that 'those that can are probably good, but their mode of calculation is laborious in the extreme.'[30] For his part, the British astronomer was not comfortable with Ellicott either. First, there had been confusion about the meeting place on Lake Champlain. When they got together Ellicott was cordial enough but was evasive about the work, both past and future. Second, Ellicott and the West Point cadets whom he brought with him did not appear to have taken the proper oaths. Queries about this to Van Ness did not yield answers. Third, Ellicott also delegated much of his work to members of his staff and either stayed in camp or went to Burlington, Vermont, to conserve his health. In short, the survey was 'as much disjointed as it possibly can be,' Tiarks felt.[31] None the less, when Ellicott began to take sightings to locate the forty-fifth parallel, they were within 100 feet of Tiarks's.[32] So the British findings were confirmed.

Further observations were planned for the following summer of 1820. However, Ellicott's health began a serious decline by this time. He reached Lake Champlain in July but took ill very quickly and returned to his family at West Point, delegating his duties to his associates. Barclay wrote to Van Ness on 21 August 1820 that he had encountered Ellicott on the street in New York and demanded to know why he was not on the frontier. In a week the American was dead; he collapsed while boarding a steamboat for the north.[33] The United States was left with the inescapable fact that all the new calculations located the forty-fifth parallel sufficiently south of the old Collins–Valentine line that the fortifications at Rouse's Point were within British territory. The British agent described the 'great disappointment and mortification expressed on the part of the United States' at these events. He concluded that the American agent would 'resist any further demarcation of this part of the boundary however clearly ascertained.'[34]

Bradley attempted to develop an argument that the treaty of 1783 intended the boundary to be the 'geocentric' rather than the 'observed' latitude, thus calculating the angle of the sun or relevant star from the axis at the centre of the earth, rather than from the earth's surface. 'Geocentric latitude' would place the forty-fifth parallel several miles north of the old line. However, Bradley developed serious misgivings about this idea when all the scientists whom he consulted rejected it; one even refused to assist him in making the calculations, lest public knowledge of his involvement be 'injurious to his character as a mathematician.'[35]

The last major issue to be decided by the commission under article five of the Treaty of Ghent was to determine the northwesternmost head of the Connecticut River, which would form the border between Lower Canada and New Hampshire. This region was as much in dispute as other parts of the boundary. The Collins–Valentine survey of the forty-fifth parallel had been marked with a cedar post on the banks of the Connecticut River in 1771. New Hampshire authorized a commission to identify the northwestern head of the Connecticut in 1789, selecting Hall's Stream in the process, and Samuel Hall, the surveyor general of Lower Canada, sent a party into the area to delineate the township of Drayton, east of Hall's Stream, but there was no official agreement to this project from the two governments. Although the War of 1812 had led to widespread smuggling and ambivalent loyalties, national sentiments developed steadily afterwards, and tensions began to grow as pro-Canadian and pro-American factions crystallized within the populations. By the time the commission for article 5 reached the Connecticut River, the New Hampshire settlers were distinctly anxious about Barclay's reputation as a wily negotiator.[36]

The work on the Connecticut River was to be done during the 1820 surveying season. One party, under Thomas Carlile, the British assistant surveyor, approached the river from the north, along the Margallaway River, and then passed overland to the headwaters of the Arnold River, an upper tributary of the Chaudière River, which flows into the St Lawrence. It found a swamp that drained south into the middle lake of the Connecticut River, the surrounding country being mountainous and covered in hardwoods. It descended the Connecticut, exploring both Indian Stream and Hall's Stream in the process. It found the sources of these two rivers only a short distance ('a few yards') from the source of the St Francis River, which drained into the St Lawrence. Carlile concluded that the 'main branch of Indian Stream is the most northerly by nearly two miles, if the information I have received be correct.'[37]

In November 1820 Tiarks led a party into those same rivers. He found the Connecticut, though the most easterly of the three, wider and more swiftly flowing than the two other tributaries. Three substantial lakes formed in the course of the upper river, with many small streams adding to the volume of water in its course. It was now so late in the season that the weather was making work and movement increasingly difficult: fairly deep snow covered the ground, thin sheets of ice had formed on many small streams, and there were regular periods of cold rain. Several members of the party, including a young boy, were sent to Montreal. At one point the main group entered what Tiarks called a 'windfall.' – an extensive area where trees had been blown over, almost blocking passage. Tiarks acknowledged that the source of Indian Stream was north of that of the Connecticut and its lakes, but he maintained that the larger stream flowing through the Connecticut Lakes was the river intended for the boundary. However, supplies were running out, and the party was forced to make tea out of the bark of grey birches; Tiarks had run out of paper and was keeping his journal on strips of birch-bark. By 13 November the party had descended Hall's Stream to the vicinity of the Vermont border and a settlement, where they got some assistance from the inhabitants and the use of horses. This ended the expedition, but the men were not able to get to Montreal until 17 November.[38] Time had run out before a fully satisfactory survey of the headwaters of the Connecticut could be completed. The

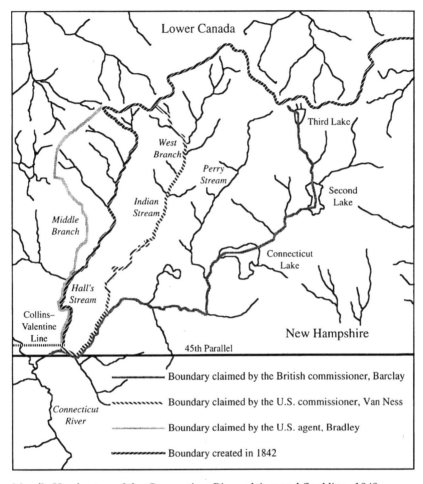

Map 7. Headwaters of the Connecticut River: claims and final line, 1842

maps drawn relied on the work of the survey and on previously prepared maps.[39]

The surveying work of 1820 completed an extensive exploration of
four of the areas under the fifth article of the Treaty of Ghent, east
and west. Through four summers, from 1817 to 1820, as chapter 3
recounted, parties had surveyed and marked the due-north line from

the source of the St Croix River and had searched for the 'highlands' of the treaty of 1783 west from Mars Hill and west from the Métis River. As this chapter has shown, the marking of the forty-fifth parallel, which had been assumed to require only a minimum of effort, had similarly used up parts of four seasons, and the search for the northwesternmost head of the Connecticut River had taken place mostly in 1820, although exploration of the regions of the upper St John, the Chaudière, and the Kennebec had taken the parties into some of the watersheds of the Connecticut. This was the only region in which the American agent retained a lingering desire to work further, despite the decision to stop.[40]

The British were confident that they had seen all the terrain needed to establish a case to justify their claims. However, they had had their own anxieties. On 12 August 1816, even before the commissions on articles 4 and 5 convened, Colonel Barclay had observed to Lord Castlereagh that it was 'very doubtful' whether the highlands of the treaty of 1783 could be found, and he expressed similar anxiety about which source of the Connecticut might be the treaty's northwesternmost head. He feared that these questions would have to be referred to a friendly sovereign for arbitration.[41] In September 1817 Barclay had written to Castlereagh again to tell him that he was confident that the commissioners would reach a decision 'favorable to the Claims of His Majesty.' Fourteen months later, however, Barclay again wrote that it was unlikely that the commissioners would agree – his view for the next several years.[42] In 1819 and 1820 he was particularly anxious not to oppose any American procedural requests out of fear that the Americans would use any refusal on his part to break off the commission's work.[43] Barclay and Castlereagh corresponded at some length, beginning in early 1818, also about possible U.S. willingness to negotiate a new boundary rather than continuing the expensive and time-consuming surveys and commission work. Barclay urged caution about taking the lead on this question – any suggestion to negotiate a boundary before the commission had finished its work would signal Britain's lack of confidence in the strength of its case, Barclay felt. Better to wait until the Americans themselves proposed negotiations or until the possibility of the commission reaching a decision collapsed.[44]

Also worrying for both sides were complaints by the U.S. Congress that the work of the commissions was too lengthy and too costly. In 1820 Congress refused for some time to appropriate funds for the salary of the U.S. agent. Commissioner Van Ness wrote immediately to Secretary of State Adams to point out that, in the absence of an agent, U.S. interests – claims to disputed territory along the border – would not be represented before the commission, which had to make its decision on the basis of the evidence presented to it.[45] Certainly the commissions' work was expensive, and there were four of them. The accounts seem to vary considerably, but for the commission under the fifth article alone, American expenses submitted for 1817 amounted to $27,854.00 and for 1820, $69,718.57. The total of available figures (and some data are missing) showed that $135,664.38 (or £29,298) had been spent by 1820 on just this one of the four commissions.[46]

Van Ness wrote to John Quincy Adams in January 1821 noting that President Monroe had omitted any reference to the progress of the boundary commission in his annual message to Congress. The work, he said, was completed. 'The obstacles to be encountered in making these surveys have been great and numerous. The whole extent of the country from the source of the St. Croix north to the river St. Lawrence, and between that line and the head of the Connecticut river, is one vast and entire wilderness, inhabited by no human being, except a few savages, and in one spot a few Frenchmen. The services performed here have been extremely arduous, and the difficulty and expense of transportation, and of subsisting the persons engaged in the work, have necessarily been considerable.'[47] The commissions' work was monumental indeed, but would Congress be impressed? Would the Americans attempt to cut their expenses by negotiating a new boundary settlement along landmarks that were sufficiently well known to eliminate disagreements about where the border might be? The British wondered.[48]

With completion of the survey expeditions and the astronomical sightings came the task of compiling all the data, drawing maps of the regions explored, and preparing the arguments to present before the board of commissioners for article 5. Throughout the winter of 1820–21 this work proceeded. The board's meeting in New York in May 1821 was not as productive as had been hoped. Disagreements developed about the appropriate exchange of data prior to the presentation of the formal arguments. Nevertheless, the two agents established the claims on behalf of the two countries and presented their first formal arguments. The British agent claimed that the Northwest Angle of Nova Scotia was the point where the line due north from the source of the St Croix River reached Mars Hill, some forty miles distant, and then followed a chain of hills west that formed on the north the watershed of the St John and on the south the watershed of the Penobscot and the Kennebec rivers, which flowed into the Atlantic. This line of hills eventually reached the watershed of the Chaudière River, which flowed into the St

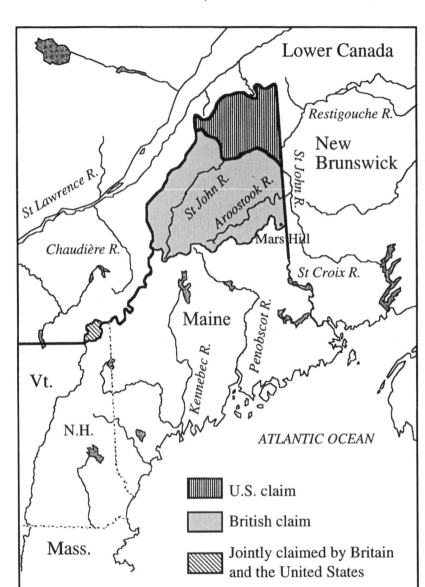

Map 8. Claims of the boundary commissioners (article 5), 1822

Lawrence. The British also claimed a small brook that ran into the Third Lake at the headwaters of the Connecticut River and the forty-fifth degree of latitude as surveyed in the previous seasons as the western boundary.[49]

The American agent claimed that the Northwest Angle of Nova Scotia was the point where the due-north line from the source of the St Croix River reached the watershed of the Beaver River, which flowed into Métis Lake and River and on into the St Lawrence. The boundary was then to follow the watershed of the St Lawrence west and southwest until it reached the Middle Branch of Hall's Stream, which flowed into the Connecticut River. The American agent claimed that the old Collins–Valentine line had been the intended forty-fifth parallel mentioned in the treaty of 1783; if this were not the line, it should be determined by the principles of geocentric, rather than observed, latitude (which would have placed the line about thirteen miles north of the Collins–Valentine line).[50]

The board did not sit for its crucial meeting in New York until 1 August 1821. The U.S. agent failed to appear that day but attended on the sixth. On that day the U.S. commissioner was sick, although at least papers were filed with the secretary. On 10 August, at the fifth session, the agents began reading their formal answers to the claims and arguments presented to the board in May and June. The British agent, Ward Chipman, spoke to the board for two and a half days, while his American counterpart, William C. Bradley, read his answer on 14 August. By this time the differences between the two agents were well understood, and both sides spent much time in objecting to various documents or maps submitted and by raising procedural questions.[51]

The British agent wrote to Henry Goulburn at the Foreign Office giving his opinion of the American argument. He stated that it was 'swelled to a very voluminous size,' together with a great deal of irrelevant material that tended 'to perplex and confound every just view of the points in discussion.' He was particularly dismissive of Bradley's arguments concerning the boundary at the forty-fifth parallel. The presumption that the negotiators in 1783 intended the old Collins–Valentine line to be perpetuated, whatever the accuracy of that work, stood in the face of complaints over the years from both Vermont and Quebec about its inaccuracies. That Bradley reverted in the end to a secondary argument of insisting on the geocentric instead of the observed latitude was simply 'extraordinary.' Certainly, this was the weakest point in the American argument. Chipman disapproved of the fact that the American materials totalled almost 400 folio pages. He also concluded that the commissioners were unlikely to agree on a boundary line, which would force the two governments to seek the arbitration of a friendly sovereign. At the same time he was increasingly alarmed at what he saw as encroachments by people from the new state of Maine in territories along the Aroostook River and as far north as the Madawaska settlements along the south bank of the St John.[52]

Bradley, for his part, was just as disgusted with Chipman, who, he felt, had failed to co-ordinate the British work with the Americans during the past year. Furthermore, Chipman had insisted on introducing maps that were not made jointly, but were wholly supplied by the British surveyors and were, as he put it, 'extremely partial' to the British case. The British argument, Bradley believed, had 'never been stated with any great precision' but ran from Mars Hill to near the source of the Chaudière and thence to a brook draining into the northeasternmost source of the Connecticut rather than the northwesternmost. Bradley complained to Secretary of State John Quincy Adams that the steady employment of an experienced American astronomer would have helped him marshall his arguments. 'It is certain that the British Agent has received great assistance from Dr. Tiarks, whose officious zeal in their behalf has been manifest on more that one occasion.'[53] Obviously the British received better value from their surveyors than had the Americans. Bradley clearly disliked Tiarks and claimed, oddly, that he possessed 'a share of small intrigue uncommon for an astronomer.' However, he reserved his greatest criticism for Chipman: 'The spirit with which the business has been of late conducted on the part of the British Agent and of the British Commissioner and the disingenuous, not to say dishonorable, course which they have pursued on several occasions has been somewhat perplexing.' He had attempted to restrain himself in order to preserve the dignity of the proceedings, he said, especially because the British seemed keen to provoke the Americans, having nothing to lose from an incident and something to gain. Bradley thought his own efforts seriously undermined by the fact that Commissioner Van Ness seemed to maintain judicial objectivity while Commissioner Barclay had 'displayed much more of the feeling of a party than those of a judge and this inequality of principle has in some measure increased my difficulties.'[54] Relations had clearly deteriorated greatly since that first summer of 1817 at the source of the St Croix River.

The commissioners – as the agents and probably everyone connected with the commissions now realized – were unable to agree on a boundary line. Indeed, they disagreed on every aspect of the boundary, even over which maps to include with the documents. After the adjournment of the August meeting on the fourteenth, the board convened again on 20 September 1821 in New York to bring matters to a close. The agents submitted some final materials and memorials and made some last replies. Various accounts were settled. All members of the board were now clear in their minds about the boundary. Bradley wrote that Barclay had stated that he intended to support the British claim 'to its utmost extent.'[55] Barclay informed Lord Castlereagh, now Marquis of Londonderry: 'After repeated conferences we have not been able to come to a decision; and therefore have resolved, as directed by the Treaty, separately, to make our reports to both Governments, detailing the points on which we differ, and the grounds on which our respective opinions have been formed.'[56] The final proceedings were deferred until spring, by which time the paper work and accounts could be completed.

Each commissioner had two objectives in his reports – to make the best possible arguments for the claims of his own government and to discredit as far as possible those of the opposite side. The intention was not only to explain to the two governments why the commission had been unable to reach agreement but also, and perhaps more important, to impress the friendly sovereign who would probably arbitrate the whole question. In making their arguments, the commissioners not only used the formal statements that the agents had prepared, together with the work of the astronomers and surveyors, but they also introduced some opinions and conclusions of their own.

The key to Barclay's argument was a careful and legalistic reading of the relevant passages of the treaty of 1783 in regard to what it actually said and what it did not say. First Barclay declared that the Northwest Angle of Nova Scotia referred to in the treaty was not actually a known landmark in 1783, as the American agent in 1798, James Sullivan, had admitted. 'Who has seen and can point [out] that place?' Sullivan had submitted: 'Nova Scotia had no North West Angle prior to the Treaty of 1782.'[57] Twenty-three years later, Chipman and Barclay had not forgotten. The treaty provided for its finding, Barclay claimed, as Sullivan had tried before, rather than identifying it, and it could be found by two processes. First, one could look at the text of the Royal Proclamation of 1763, in which language very similar to the treaty of 1783 described the boundaries between the new province of Quebec and the older British colonies. However, in the 1763 proclamation the description began at the forty-fifth parallel, ran to the northwesternmost head of the Connecticut River, and then continued along the highlands dividing the waters flowing into the St Lawrence from those flowing into the sea. This description ran from west to east. If one started from that western position, Barclay reasoned, the highlands to be first encountered were those dividing the Chaudière (which flowed into the St Lawrence) from the Androscoggin, Kennebec, and Penobscot rivers (which flowed into the Atlantic). Thus the provision of the treaty was fulfilled. This highland subsequently ran east and could be said to terminate at Mars Hill, and it also formed the watershed of the south bank of the St John River. The Northwest Angle was found where this line of highlands intersected with the due-north line from the source of the St Croix River. The Americans went wrong in their reading of the treaty of 1783, Barclay declared, because that document described the boundary from east to west, wherein the logic of the description in the Proclamation of 1763 was not so clear.[58]

Second, one could attempt a careful reading of the text of the 1783 treaty itself. In the first reference to the Northwest Angle, the treaty said 'due north from the source of the St. Croix River to the Highland, along the said Highlands which divide those Rivers.' Barclay insisted that this meant the *first* highlands encountered due north of the St Croix. These were formed by Mars Hill, and they constituted the watershed that he had previously described, which separated the St John from the Penobscot, the Kennebec, and the Angroscoggin rivers until it reached the source of the Chaudière. Thus at that point it could be said to divide the waters flowing into the St Lawrence from those flowing into the Atlantic. The Americans misconstrued the passage, Barclay claimed, as if it read that the line were to be extended due north from the St Croix 'until it arrives at Highlands which divide the Rivers, etc.'[59] However, even if one accepted the American reading, other problems immediately arose. Those involved the due-north line crossing the St John River, which flowed into the Bay of Fundy, and the Restigouche River, which flowed into the Gulf of St Lawrence. Within the text of the treaty of 1783 neither of those bodies of water could be considered the Atlantic Ocean, because other parts of the document referred to them as discrete bodies of water. The drafters could not have intended specifically to identify the Bay of Fundy and the Gulf for one purpose and then assumed that they were also encompassed in the Atlantic for another purpose, as the Americans asserted. An example, Barclay pointed out, was that article 3 allowed the Americans to fish specifically in the Gulf but made no corresponding provision for them to use the lower St John River. Therefore the treaty had never intended, Barclay concluded, for the Americans to have access to the upper St John.[60]

Barclay also discussed the recently published minutes of the U.S. Continental Congress, in which instructions for a more limited boundary were proposed. Barclay used the testimony of John Adams before the commissioners – to the effect that the Americans had suggested a line from the St John River to its source as a boundary and then abandoned it in favour of the St Croix because it had been more clearly mentioned in colonial charters – to indicate that the Americans in Paris in 1782 had given up any expectation of extending their territory as far north as the St John, much less beyond it.[61]

As for the northwesternmost head of the Connecticut, Barclay argued that the only logical river was the one universally known as the Connecticut, not possibly any of the other northern tributaries. He declared that the relevant source was a small brook entering the Third Lake from the northwest – Hall's Stream, he noted, entered the Connecticut south of the forty-fifth parallel, and Indian Stream, though rising north of the main branch of the Connecticut, was a river of half the volume of the Connecticut where they joined. On the forty-fifth parallel itself, the Treaty of Ghent was unambiguous: the commissioners were to 'cause the boundary aforesaid ... to be surveyed and marked according to the provisions of the said treaty of Peace.' Application of conventional geographical principles could accurately fulfil the treaty.[62]

The report of the American commissioner worked as much to challenge the British arguments as to establish the U.S. case, perhaps because many felt that the American argument was more obvious. Van Ness questioned the soundness of the British commissioner's reliance on the wording of the first reference in the treaty of 1783 to the highlands by turning to the second reference, where the text did say that, the boundary was to run from the source of the St Croix 'directly north to the aforesaid Highlands which divide the Rivers,' and he asserted that neither passage gave any indication that the *first* highlands were to be the identifying point.[63] As for reading the description from west to east, as Barclay had suggested, Van Ness pointed out that there were two watersheds or highlands beyond the source of the Chaudière and that the northern one, which contained numerous rivers running into the St Lawrence and into the north bank of the St John, was as compelling as the southern. The flaw in Barclay's thinking, Van Ness asserted, was that the rivers rising in the southern highlands, on the north or south side, all flowed into the Atlantic, which did not conform to the language of the treaty, which described a highlands dividing waters that flowed into the St Lawrence from those running into the Atlantic. As for the due-north line from the St Croix crossing the St John and other rivers, Van Ness noted that in various of the geographical lines – the forty-fifth parallel, for example – the line intersected streams flowing in several directions. The controlling feature was the correct highlands, with rivers flowing into the St Lawrence, and extending the line north of the St John and the Restigouche was not a problem. The language of the treaty of 1783 indicated that the highlands were to be found to the north and not to the west, as the British agent had inferred. Looking at a copy of Mitchell's map uncovered the intentions of the negotiators; they would have understood any line running north to cross several rivers, including the St John. As for the proposition that rivers emptying into the Bay of Fundy and the Gulf did not flow into the Atlantic, this was absurd. All the major rivers along the coast emptied into bays of one kind or another, rather than directly into the ocean. The Bay of Fundy and the Gulf of St Lawrence had to be understood to be part of the Atlantic Ocean.[64]

Van Ness then turned to the historical context of the description in the treaty, which was a major part of the American argument. The charter of 1621 to Sir William Alexander described the western border of Nova Scotia from the St Croix 'by an imaginary line conceived to run through the land northward to the next Road of ships, river, or spring, discharging itself into the great River of Canada [the St Lawrence].' This line was struck north through all intervening rivers to the St Lawrence itself. The Royal Proclamation of 1763 – which, as Barclay had pointed out, described the border from west to east – said that it was to pass 'along the Highlands which divide the Rivers that empty themselves into the said River St. Lawrence from those which fall into the sea,' but Van Ness also quoted the next line, 'and also along the north coast of the Baye de Chaleurs and the Gulph of St. Lawrence.' This last phrase described a much more northerly line than suggested by Barclay. The final text that he drew on was that of the Quebec Act of 1774. In defining the boundaries of Quebec, the text read, 'a line from the Bay of Chaleurs, along the Highlands which divide the Rivers which empty themselves into the River St. Lawrence from those which fall into the sea, to a point in the forty-fifth degree of north latitude.' In both the 1763 and the 1774 documents, the Quebec–Massachusetts–Nova Scotia boundaries were to be formed by a line determined primarily by the St

Lawrence watershed, with western Nova Scotia (later New Brunswick) and eastern Massachusetts (later Maine) being separated along their common frontier by the line due north from the St Croix River. The Northwest Angle of Nova Scotia was the point, Van Ness argued, where the northern Massachusetts–Nova Scotia border met the Quebec boundary. The treaty of 1783 simply copied this text, with all its historical relevance, albeit changing 'sea' to 'Atlantic Ocean.' For Van Ness this change was insignificant and 'could have no effect.'[65] For the British, it broke any link with the older charters and proclamations. However, Van Ness asked further whether, if the pre-Revolution colonial boundaries were determined by a watershed along the St Lawrence, the treaty of 1783 expanded the boundaries of Quebec or Nova Scotia by shifting the boundary to a more southerly watershed. Impossible, he concluded.

Van Ness attempted to show that the British agent, Chipman, while working on the St Croix Commission in 1798, had himself admitted much of the American claim when he wrote 'that this north line must of necessity cross the River St. John,' and that he had done so again, while serving as agent on the commission under article 4 of the Treaty of Ghent, when he said that 'the northwest angle of Nova Scotia, mentioned in the treaty as the commencing point of the boundary of the United States, is the north-west angle of the said Province of Nova Scotia designated in the said grant to Sir William Alexander.'[66] As for John Adams's presumed abandonment of the St John River in the 1782 negotiations, Van Ness said that the dropping of claims to the St John meant that the Americans merely reverted to the old colonial boundaries (described above). In short, the present line was to be the old colonial border.[67]

The northwesternmost head of the Connecticut presented a problem to the American commissioner. He was in the awkward position of differing with both his own agent and the British on its location. William C. Bradley, the U.S. agent, had proposed the Middle Branch of Hall's Stream; Van Ness agreed with the British objection that Hall's Stream entered the Connecticut below the forty-fifth parallel and therefore was probably not intended. However, he disputed the British exclusion of rivers that did not bear the name Connecticut. The language of the treaty implied, Van Ness said, that there were several heads to the river. Furthermore, the brook identified by the British was too small (only seventy rods long), draining into the Third Lake on the main branch of the upper Connecticut, to be the source of anything. Van Ness proposed instead the Indian Stream – while smaller than the main branch of the Connecticut, it was east of Hall's Stream and west of the main branch. Thus it, not only had its source further north than any of the other tributaries, but it was also west of the main branch of the Connecticut.[68]

The new survey of the forty-fifth parallel created a major problem for the Americans, and Van Ness was clearly perplexed. The passages in the agent's arguments dealing with the subject were certainly the weakest parts of the Americans' brief, although in the aftermath of the War of 1812 possession of the forts at the head of Lake Champlain was crucial to them. Van Ness's objective in his report was to avoid committing the United States one way or another on the question. Thus, instead of supporting the admittedly weak arguments of the American agent (that the Collins–Valentine line had been intended by the treaty of 1783 or that a geocentric latitude be calculated to determine the forty-fifth parallel), Van Ness simply wrote to Barclay on 22 October 1821 that 'it will not be necessary for me to report any opinion on the questions which have been made relative to the boundary line from Connecticut River to the Iroquois.'[69] This statement had the effect of forcing the politicians or diplomats to settle the issue. Perhaps that was all that was necessary. The work of the commission had reached an impasse, with the two commissioners unable to agree on any important issue. However, as one of the most careful students of the boundary question noted, no subsequent discussion of the issues ever went beyond the arguments expressed here.[70]

A final meeting of the board of commissioners was convened in New York on 1 April 1822. There accounts were settled, copies of the reports were exchanged, and official letters were sent to the two governments informing them of the failure to reach a decision.

In the aftermath of the October 1821 meetings of the board and the failure of the commissioners to reach an agreement, the British concluded that the Americans would attempt to negotiate a treaty that would create a new commission to draw up a new boundary along the frontier from the St Croix River both north and west to the St Lawrence. Thomas Barclay and Stratford Canning, the new British minister to the United States, both wrote to alert the British government.[71] This information proved correct. Early in the new year Secretary of State Adams wrote to Richard Rush, the American minister in London, that because of the difficulty in selecting a sovereign in whom both governments could 'repose equal confidence' to arbitrate the boundary, he should approach Lord Londonderry about whether the British government would be willing to 'adjust the difference, by direct communication between the two Governments.'[72] Before any progress could be made on this suggestion, the board of commissioners met for its final sessions in New York in April 1822 and submitted its reports. On 16 April Barclay and Ward Chipman, Jr, sailed for England to present to the Foreign Office the papers, maps, and reports of the commission.[73] Barclay had to return home in late July, but before he left he urged the British government to reject this proposal of negotiations for a new boundary and to seek a solution through arbitration. The British arguments for the boundary were 'irresistible,' Barclay wrote confidently, and British interests were likely to be better served by an impartial arbitrator than by negotiation. He did admit that the Northwest Angle of Nova Scotia 'opened a very wide field of discussion,' but he was satisfied that the testimony of John Adams and the recently published *Secret Journals of the Continental Congress* showed that the United States had not aspired at the Paris peace negotiations to establish a boundary as far north as the St John River.[74]

Confident in the British case, Barclay was very wary of seeking a compromise solution through negotiations, and he gave an insightful explanation to the foreign secretary. The question of the northeastern boundary touched the vital territorial interests of Maine, Massachusetts, New Hampshire, New York, and Vermont, he pointed out. A negotiated compromise could be achieved only through a process of give and take, in which one U.S. state gave up something in exchange for something from another state. No state was likely to accept the loss of any of its territory in exchange for territory granted to another state, even if it were in the national interest, and the federal government did not have the power to coerce the states and force them to accept such a loss. Therefore negotiation and compromise were impossible, Barclay reasoned. 'There is not the slightest chance of any new Commission or negotiation coming to a more satisfactory result than the present with regard to the rights in dispute, and the very nature of the political institutions of the United States seem to forbid a compromise of territorial rights.'[75] The treaty of 1783, in contrast, was part of the supreme law of the land, and all states must accept it. The Treaty of Ghent was also already accepted and in force. The execution of these treaties, as in the arbitration of a friendly sovereign, was possible because it presumed only to define a boundary already existing, whereas a compromise solution, however reasonable generally, would constitute the drawing of a new boundary and therefore was extremely unlikely to be acceptable. This was a shrewd insight by this old Loyalist and New Yorker into the political workings of the United States and the constitutional relationship between the federal and state governments. Barclay's analysis contained an element of prophecy in its anticipation of events the next twenty years.

Barclay was confident in the British case by 1821. In his letter to Londonderry, he outlined the dangers to Quebec and the British position in North America generally if the United States were to secure a boundary on the St Lawrence watershed north of the St John River (within eleven to twenty miles of the river and Quebec City itself in some places, Barclay said) and be in possession of the forts on Lake Champlain. Much had changed in Barclay's mind since 1817, when at the end of the first season of exploration and survey he, Chipman, and the British surveyor had seemed prepared to acquiesce in the presumption that the Northwest Angle of Nova Scotia and the relevant highlands were north of the St John on the watershed of the Little Wagansis flowing into the Restigouche River.[76] Indeed, those supporting the British case over the next few years became increasingly confident and dogmatic about the merits of a line running west of Mars Hill to the Chaudière watershed.

This story resumes in chapter 7, after the rest of part I describes the epic stuggles of surveyors to sketch out the rest of the border as far west as the Lake of the Woods.

Chapter Five

Article 6: The St Lawrence and the Great Lakes

Article 6 of the Treaty of Ghent of 1814 created a commission authorized to determine the Great Lakes boundary between the United States and British North America. This part of the boundary stretched almost a thousand miles and would require four seasons (1817–20) for the surveying alone. The northeastern boundary may well have attracted more attention, because lumbermen and settlers were steadily encroaching on the contested borderlands, but the boundary for the Great Lakes involved enormous expanses of territory, numerous physical problems, and conflicting interests as well. Even more than in Maine and New Brunswick, in the Great Lakes basin the French and British Canadians, as fur traders, had been a dominant presence for years. Indeed, the alliances between both the fur traders and the British army and the Native people in the region had led to one of the major tensions that finally led to the War of 1812. In that conflict the United States lost all of the upper Great Lakes. While U.S. General William Henry Harrison recaptured Detroit, only the Treaty of Ghent restored much of the rest of the region to the United States. The American hold in the area remained tenuous, despite the efforts of the American Fur Company and later probings by the U.S. army and various governmental officials. Thus much was at stake in the boundary proceedings, under article 6.

President James Madison offered General Peter B. Porter the appointment as commissioner under both the sixth and seventh articles of the Treaty of Ghent in November 1815, and the Senate confirmed him in January 1816.[1] Porter was born in Connecticut in 1773, graduated from Yale in 1791, and studied law with Judge Tapping Reeve in Litchfield, Connecticut. He moved to upstate New York in 1795, settling eventually in Black Rock (now part of Buffalo), where he practised law, participated in a transportation company that moved goods around Niagara Falls, and served in Congress. During the War of 1812 Porter joined the New York militia, raised a brigade, and saw service at Chippawa, Lundy's Lane, and Fort Erie. British troops operating in New York burned his large house at Black Rock – an event about which 'the affluent American general could speak ... with the greatest good-humor,' one of his British colleagues recorded.[2] He was a major-general by the time the war ended. Porter was re-elected to Congress but resigned to become American commissioner. He later became involved in the Erie Canal project in New York, and in 1828 President John Quincy Adams appointed him secretary of war. Porter was regarded as a strong personality and a good speaker, but he was also seen as ambitious.

John Ogilvy was appointed British commissioner. Ogilvy was born in Scotland about 1769 and moved to Montreal in 1790, engaging in the fur trade. By 1792 he was sending traders out to Michilimackinac and the Mississippi, and in 1796 he became a partner in the firm Parker, Gerrard and Ogilvy. This company was not only successful in the fur trade, making Alexander Mackenzie a partner in 1803, but also entered transatlantic shipping and passenger service. The fur trade was in a very turbulent and competitive state; Ogilvy kept trading south of the Great Lakes, in American territory, but worked for a merger of the several competing firms with the North West Company in 1804. Within ten years, a wealthy man, he sold out his major interests in the fur trade. In October 1816 Ogilvy received documents from Lord Castlereagh dated 30 June appointing him commissioner under the sixth and seventh articles of the Treaty of Ghent.[3] A shrewd businessman, he was also something of a conciliator. One critic said of him that he was 'apt to be obstinate in trifles, and immediately afterwards too pliant in matters of importance,' but the American assistant surveyor, William A. Bird remembered him out in his own canoe checking on the work daily, 'a man of indomitable energy and perseverance.'[4] Certainly, a career in the fur trade in the upper Great Lakes gave Ogilvy extraordinary qualifications to represent British interests in determining the boundary in that region.

As set forth in the treaty under the sixth article, the commission was to meet in Albany, New York. No date had been determined, and some confusion ensued, but on 18 November 1816 the first meeting began, to exchange credentials, to work out procedures, and to identify required personnel. As well as the two agents, only one of them yet appointed, the commission wanted a secretary and an assistant secretary. Each party was to have a surveyor, an assistant surveyor, a trigonometric surveyor, a draftsman, a steward, a cook, a waiter, chainbearers, axe-men, and boatmen, numbering about twenty-five personnel in total. The commissioners and the agents were each to receive U.S.$4,444 per year, the equivalent of £1,000 sterling; the secretaries, $2,200, the chief surveyors, $2,000; the draftsmen, $600; and the boatmen, $960. The cooks and stewards, earned only $96 per year for their services. In total the salaries during 1817 for the U.S. commission cost the federal government $19,109, along with numerous other expenses for food, equipment, and services.[5]

The commissioners concluded their proceedings by deciding to meet again on 10 May 1817 at St Regis, on the St Lawrence River, which they understood from earlier surveys to be the point at which the forty-fifth parallel intersected with the river and where their mapping of the boundary on the river should begin.[6]

Colonel Ogilvy, so styled because of his years in the militia, left Montreal for St Regis on 7 May 1817. Members of his party, perhaps as many as nine, departed over the next several days; with men, supplies, and baggage being moved by boat up the St Lawrence. By the thirteenth they were all put up in houses in the settlements near St Regis. Stephen Sewell described the area: 'St. Regis is a poor village, although surrounded by an excellent country of land. It has the advantage of being beautifully situated, occupying a small part of a point of land formed by the noble St. Lawrence on one side & the river St. Regis on the other.'[7] Sewell's father, born in Cambridge, Massachusetts, was the Loyalist Jonathan Sewell, then chief justice of Lower Canada. Stephen Sewell had been raised in England but had read law with Ward Chipman in Saint John, New Brunswick. He had moved to Montreal in 1791 and held numerous public offices. His quarrels with the government during the War of 1812 led to his dismissal, but he became secretary to the commission in 1817, signalling his restoration to official favour.[8]

The Americans had not yet appeared, because of the spring weather and the state of the roads, and Sewell's diary notes the movement of Loyalists, fur traders, soldiers, and Native people along the river. The recent War of 1812 was still on people's minds, but, a certain tranquility prevailed. 'In the St. Lawrence lay a cluster of large and delightful islands,' Sewell observed, 'and looking down the river you see a sheet of water extending eight or ten miles.' Commissioner Ogilvy organized church services for the party on Sunday, 18 May, sending the Catholics to the church at St Regis and producing prayer books with which to conduct a Protestant service himself. On the afternoon of Tuesday, 10 May, General Porter arrived, together with Colonel Samuel Hawkins, the American agent, and several other men. The Americans set up camp on St Regis Island, a short distance away, the centre piece of which was a magnificent marquee, provided by Major Joseph Delafield's family. There also arrived with Porter two packing cases sent by the Foreign Office to the British commission, through Colonel Barclay in New York. These contained a variety of scientific instruments, including two 30-inch transits, one sextant, an artificial horizon, two theodolites, two compasses, a plane table, a land chain, and other pieces of equipment.[9]

Visits were exchanged the following day, and Ogilvy invited the American party to dinner. On Friday, 23 May, the two commissioners met to exchange documents and to record and file the credentials and oaths of the various officials and members of the two parties. Both officials submitted nominees for secretary, who were chosen by lot. Sewell was named secretary, and Major Donald Fraser, of Albany, assistant secretary. For the next several days credentials and oaths were filed. Ogilvy reported that during the winter he had instructed David Thompson, the British surveyor, to begin taking observations to determine where the forty-fifth parallel intersected the St Lawrence. David Adams, from Boston, the American surveyor, was now instructed to repeat the sightings by himself, and Thompson, to begin the survey up the St Lawrence. These men were officially designated astronomical surveyors, and each had an assistant surveyor as well.[10]

David Thompson had only a few years earlier retired from the fur trade, in which he had enjoyed a brilliant career exploring much of western Canada. Born in London in 1770, he had been apprenticed to the Hudson's Bay Company in 1784 and had been trained in the field as an astronomer and surveyor. Thompson joined the North West Company in 1794 and spent most of that season exploring and mapping the western Great Lakes borderland between British North America and the United States. By the time he left the fur trade and settled in Quebec in 1811, he had completed the most accurate map in existence of western Canada and the northern United States, from Lake Superior to the Pacific. This map hung at one end of the great hall in the fur post at Fort William. Thus Thompson, like Ogilvy, brought to the commission a great deal of experience in the Great Lakes region. Furthermore, he was a man of mark. His American counterpart in 1817, David P. Adams, described him as 'a gentleman, whom for his rectitude of heart, honesty of disposition, integrity of character and abilities in his profession, I shall ever hold in the highest estimation.'[11] In March Thompson had been at St Regis taking sightings to locate the forty-fifth parallel.

Surveying parties were sent out to begin work immediately, travelling by boat and canoe and sleeping in tents, although there was still snow in mid-May. Their task was to survey and map the rivers and lakes by the elaborate method of theodolite triangulation. Survey crews created a measured baseline between two points along one shore and then took careful sightings through a theodolite from each end of the baseline to a single object on the opposite shore. This created a triangle, the length of one side of which was known, together with the measurement of the three angles. Simple geometry allowed calculation of the other two legs of the triangle and hence determination of the distance to the other shore. The repetition of this process carefully measured the rivers or lakes, each party working on separate sections of the shoreline. Astronomical sightings also identified the latitude and longitude and fixed the location of the sequence of triangles.

Both British and American army officers along the frontier were directed to be of assistance to the surveying parties, although this support could not always be counted on. Major Andrew Ellicott arrived from West Point on 27 May to assist in determining the forty-fifth parallel. Ellicott brought with him a large 'Zenith Sector,' with a seven-foot radius, that he and David Rittenhouse of Pennsylvania had made some years earlier. Ellicott worked with the surveying parties for about six weeks. Sewell found him 'full of anecdotes' and of 'great vigor of mind for his age which is between 60 and 70.' Within a month's time Major Delafield noted from Ellicott's work that the United States would lose territory through the new survey of the forty-fifth parallel. On 4 June the British party moved up river to Cornwall Island and got its tents put up and baggage stored just before a cloudburst opened up. The two commissioners and the gentlemen in the parties went in to Cornwall to celebrate the King's birthday, which 'gave the highest satisfaction to all the party,' Sewell recorded with pleasure.[12]

The board of commissioners convened officially for the first time on Monday, 9 June 1817. It determined procedural matters such as keeping of records and management of the commission's affairs, and it gave instructions to the surveying parties. As the board attempted to plan the work, the American agent, Colonel Hawkins, registered objections. Acting Secretary of State Richard Rush had instructed him that the commissioners would have the power to make decisions and that his 'duty will therefore naturally direct itself towards aiding them in all appropriate ways, with a view to leading their judgement upon all points to just and satisfactory conclusions.'[13] Hawkins understood this to mean that the agents would direct the work of the surveying parties and would subsequently submit the results to the board, which would sit as a panel of judges. The commissioners understood that they were to direct the surveying work and that the agents were to see that the work got done and to advise them. Nevertheless, in a letter to the board on 29 May, Hawkins asserted that the agents should '*manage the business* of their respective governments' as lawyers or advocates and present the result of the labours of the surveyors to the board, which was then to function as a judicial body to decide the matter.[14] The commissioners disagreed and asked for the advice of the acting secretary of state. Rush consulted with President Monroe but came down strongly on the side of the commissioners, stating plainly, 'I have carefully examined Colonel Hawkins's paper in connection with the Treaty, and think that he is wrong.' The agents were to be 'altogether ancillary to the Board' and therefore 'must necessarily be under its direction.'[15] The president agreed and told Porter so when he met with the commissioners in Ogdensburg in August, during his tour of the northern states. Hawkins later received official notification of this decision by letter on 5 May 1818.[16]

By the end of June 1817, the commissioners moved their encampment further up river to Barnhart's Island. Ogilvy obtained from the army a large marquee thirty feet long and fifteen feet wide, forming a 'large dining room' and two smaller rooms. The British officials could thus live in some comfort in the wilderness. Porter and Ogilvy conferred every other week, supervising the surveying parties in the intervals. Above Barnhart's Island, near the rapids in the St Lawrence, they were unable to find bottom with their eighty-foot line. The current was so strong – ten miles an hour, Major Fraser calculated – that they had to abandon the lead weight for fear of capsizing the canoe. By mid-July they moved to Long Sault, where the British party was able to camp on farmland owned by Ogilvy.[17]

The cold of May and June gave way to the heat of July. One morning Sewell recorded that the party found the thermometer broken on the ground – the wax holding the glass to the brass had melted. Mosquitoes and other insects were a plague. Sewell also commented on the settlers from England, Scotland, and Ireland passing up river for Perth and the west. 'Although not dressed in rags, there is an appearance of great want amongst them, and they frequently lament having quitted their own country.' Sewell thought it unfortunate that the government did not assist such settlers with rations of some kind. Delafield was fascinated by the Catholic priests and the Indians encountered along the St Lawrence, the extent of settlement on the Upper Canadian side of the river, and the post-war recovery. He described the Mohawk women at St Regis, dressed in dark clothes and very devout. However, he thought that the Catholic priest, trained in Quebec, together with the British soldiers who supplied the Indians with guns and powder, served to prejudice the Native people against the Americans. Delafield concluded that he could win their devotion to the United States with $50 worth of gifts. Nevertheless, the Mohawks and Oneidas along the St Lawrence worked for the surveying parties as guides and boatmen. Delafield made constant notes about them.[18] On 31 July, Porter, Ogilvy, Hawkins, Delafield, and Sewell went to Ogden's Island and Hamilton, New York (soon to be renamed Waddington), to be presented to President Monroe. Sewell thought that the president 'looked much worn' for a man of sixty but found that his 'manners are very affable' and that 'he is a man of superior mind.'[19] This was a generous compliment from Sewell, a Loyalist whose public life had predisposed him strongly against a Jeffersonian Democrat such as Monroe.

By mid-August 1817 the commissioners moved camp further up the St Lawrence to Isle aux Chats and convened a board in General Porter's marquee. Porter and Delafield left the work parties for almost a month, in late August and early September, to travel to the Niagara River. The surveying parties kept hard at work and by 1 September moved still further up the St Lawrence to Williamsburg. On 6 September Dr Tiarks, sent out by the Foreign Office by way of New York, reached the camp. He was put right to work taking sightings to ascertain the forty-fifth parallel. Even Delafield was impressed by his scientific instruments. Tiarks confirmed the position that Ellicott had marked with a stone monument on the shores of the St Lawrence.[20] Work carried on until 2 November, by which time the weather had closed in and there was a foot of snow on the ground. The board met again at St Regis, instructed the astronomers to prepare maps from their data over the winter, and decided to convene again at Hamilton, New York, on 15 May 1818.[21]

Porter reported to Secretary of State Adams that he was pleased with the work accomplished. There were, he said, no good maps of the St Lawrence River area, and this survey would generate an excellent set of charts 'containing (as we propose that ours shall do) all the information necessary to the safe navigation of these extensive waters' which would 'be of immense practical use to the commerce of the western people.'[22]

Arrangements were confirmed during the winter of 1817–18 for the joint meeting at St Regis of the commissioners under Ghent's article 6 and those for article 5 to determine where the forty-fifth parallel intersected with the St Lawrence River.[23] A joint meeting had been proposed the previous June but had been held off so that the British astronomer, Tiarks, could assist.[24] Britain's failure to appoint an agent during the past season had concerned both Ogilvy and Porter. At Ogilvy's request, the governor-in-chief of British North America, Sir John Sherbrooke, had been asked to select a suitable candidate, and he suggested Colonel John Hale, a Quebec lawyer, whom William Bird described as 'a fine old English gentleman.' Hale presented himself at the board at Hamilton on 1 June 1818.[25] Ogilvy was not quite sure how to work with him, as he confessed to Lord Castlereagh. During the previous season he had himself directed the British party in the absence of an agent, while the American agent had had rather more independence than Ogilvy was prepared to accept.[26]

On 6 June the two boards met at St Regis. Unfortunately, illness kept away Ferdinand Hassler, the American astronomer. The commissioners decided that Hassler should confer with the other surveyors when he arrived and that the commission under the fifth article would determine the sighting of the forty-fifth parallel at the St Lawrence River.[27] The two groups of commissioners then departed, Porter and Ogilvy leaving for Hamilton. By 15 June David Thompson was fully engaged surveying the upper St Lawrence. By the end of the summer the parties had made their way through the St Lawrence and the tangled maze of the Thousand Islands. As Porter described it, the work was 'extremely intricate & laborious, but, at the same time, indispensable to an intelligent execution of our commission.'[28] The parties had surveyed nearly fifteen hundred islands. They then entered Lake Ontario, with David P. Adams directing the survey on the south shore and David Thompson leading the party on the north shore. At the end of the season they were ready to begin work on the Niagara River at the western end of Lake Ontario.[29]

The Americans were troubled throughout the summer of 1818 by the continued disagreements between Commissioner Porter and Agent Hawkins. When the joint board had convened in the spring, both Cornelius Van Ness and William C. Bradley had attempted to bring about a 'reconciliation,' but without success. During the summer Porter delegated a large measure of responsibility to Hawkins and his assistant, Delafield, but Hawkins was not satisfied and became increasingly difficult and distant from the commissioner. In the meantime, bad feeling erupted between the American surveyor, Adams, and his assistant, William Darby. Adams insisted that certain of Darby's work was inaccurate and had to be redone, which charge Darby greatly resented. By the end of July, Darby had also antagonized Porter, who fired him. Delafield found himself in the middle of this controversy, as he had in the earlier one.[30]

The commissioners planned their first meeting for 1819 at Niagara Falls. Colonel Ogilvy was late in arriving, but he camped on Navy Island (to be made famous during the Rebellion of 1837), and by 4 June work could commence. The secretary, Stephen Sewell, had resigned in March and had been succeeded by Donald Fraser, formerly associate secretary. American Surveyor David P. Adams had resigned during the winter, to return to the Navy, and had recommended as his replacement his assistant, William A. Bird, who, he felt, was reasonably familiar with fixing latitude and longitude. Experts could be hired as needed, or perhaps David Thompson could take the astronomical sightings for the Americans, Adams naively suggested. Three trigonometrical surveyors were hired, including Captain David Bates Douglass, late a member of the 1820 expedition to the headwaters of the Mississippi led by Governor Lewis Cass of the Michigan Territory, James Ferguson, who remained with the commission until its conclusion. Also taken on were two draftsmen and several crew members.[31] Douglass, a Yale graduate, taught at West Point and was the son-in-law of Andrew Ellicott, while Ferguson, originally from Scotland, had worked as an engineer on the Erie Canal.

The commissioners gave instructions that when the two surveyors, then completing work from the previous year, joined the board, they were to carry out the survey of the Niagara River and then proceed into Lake Erie. The surveying parties worked throughout June and most of July on the Niagara River, a region that was rapidly being settled and would soon expand dramatically with the completion of the Erie Canal in 1825. Although the great Niagara Falls did not detain the surveyors, Delafield passed them repeatedly and never lost his 'sensation of awe' and his feeling of 'wonder, gratitude & delight' at their sight.[32] By 19 July, arrangements were complete to transport the surveyors and their equipment to the islands on Lake Erie off Sandusky, Ohio, site of the naval battle of Put-in-Bay during the War of 1812. The commissioners decided that they did not need to accompany the surveying parties throughout the whole summer but that they would 'occasionally visit them, to observe the progress, supply their wants, and furnish such instructions as may from time to time be necessary.'[33] Ogilvy sailed west with the surveying parties, and Porter stayed for the moment in Black Rock, while Delafield returned to New York City to present to Hawkins the records of the board's June meeting. Hawkins communicated with the commission only through Delafield during the summer, and his connection with it became more remote.[34]

Lake Erie was to be charted in the same way as Lake Ontario – with parties surveying separately on both sides of the lake. Indeed, work seemed to be going so well that late in the summer the parties had made their way into the Detroit River. Then disaster struck. 'I have the painful duty of informing you of the death of my Colleague, Col. Ogilvy, the British Commissioner under the 6th & 7th articles of the Treaty of Ghent.' So wrote General Porter to John Quincy Adams from Sugar Island on the Detroit River on 30 September 1819. 'The loss of this Gentleman, so greatly distinguished for his intelligence and vigor in the discharge of his official duties, and for his correct and honorable deportment in his private relations of life, will be felt by the American as well as the British Government. He died after a fortnights illness, on Tuesday last at the British town of Amherstburg, near the mouth of the River, of a bilious fever, which has prevailed to an alarming extent in this part of the country, and has visited our surveying parties with particular exposure amongst the Islands, and the marshes at the west end of Lake Erie.'[35] Ogilvy and two other members of the British party died, and all the other people, including Porter, had been sick. Described as bilious fever, or sometimes ague, these afflictions were probably malaria. Porter had just returned from his home in Black Rock, New York, to find both camps laid waste by illness and several men already sent back east to recover. Porter said, 'There is now in the British camp, but one Surveyor and one man fit for duty, and the condition of our own is but little better.'[36] By late summer Donald Fraser had reported growing sickness within the American camp at Put-in-Bay Island. On 30 August he wrote that Douglass and Ferguson were improving, but Bird, who had come down with fever and ague that day, was 'shaking like an aspen leaf.' As the men fell ill, he gave them tartar emetic, to induce vomiting; Glauber salts, as a purgative, and whisky with lake water, possibly to cheer them up. All of this, he thought, would be 'conducive to the health of the men,' but perhaps more practically Fraser also gave them a concoction made of quinine bark.[37]

The two commissioners had earlier hoped that the surveying parties would complete Lake Huron and move into Sault Ste Marie, but this calamity made such plans impossible for 1819. Porter, assuming command of the British party, halted work, sent all the men home, and instructed the surveyors and draftsmen to proceed with converting their sightings and calculations to maps. If the British were to appoint a new commissioner quickly, Porter felt, it might still be possible to reach Lake Superior in the next season.[38]

Ogilvy's death created a pressing problem for the British. All the commissions had experienced numerous resignations or dismissals of senior officials – agents, surveyors, secretaries – but the commissioners had always made the decisions, kept the business going, and brought in new people. The loss of a commissioner threatened to be much more disruptive – even Ogilvy's papers and scientific instruments could not be extracted from his executors until February 1820. Indeed, the prospect that John Holmes, American commissioner for article 4 of Ghent, might have to resign to take his seat in Congress had clearly influenced decision-making on the islands in Passamaquoddy Bay in 1817. So the British government had to appoint a new commissioner quickly. To this end, John Hale, the British agent newly appointed in 1819, put his own name forward. Colonel Barclay, however, had already proposed his son Anthony.[39]

Anthony Barclay was born on 27 September 1792, the tenth of the Barclays' twelve children and the youngest son. He was born in Annapolis, Nova Scotia, but was brought up largely in New York City. He was trained in law and studied at the Inns of Court in London. He had been appointed secretary to article 4's commission in 1816 and so was familiar with the work; that commission had already reached a decision. Castlereagh agreed to his nomination, and Anthony Barclay was sent a letter of appointment on 10 January 1820, along with instructions and copies of the Foreign Office correspondence with Ogilvy. One colleague praised young Barclay's 'great diligence, ability, and firmness of purpose' and said that 'he of all men was enabled, by previous education and quiet amenity of manner, to cope with the eager and exacting temper of American diplomatists, and to make good the right thing.'[40] On 3 June 1820 Barclay presented his credentials at the board's meeting at Grosse Île, Michigan, on the Detroit River, almost within sight of the place where Ogilvy had died. John Hale was to remain the British agent and was to render Barclay all possible assistance.

There were several other important posts to be filled in 1820. At the suggestion of Anthony Barclay, Dr John Bigsby became the board's assistant secretary (eventually secretary and assistant were combined to provide a more attractive salary). After the terrible experience of the previous summer, it was thought essential to have on hand someone who could deal with sickness and disease. As Barclay wrote to Porter, 'the strong conviction of the necessity of such professional assistance in the unhealthy marshes to which the Surveyors will be exposed' prompted the appointment of Bigsby.[41] John Bigsby was born in Nottingham in 1792 and had trained at the University of Edinburgh. He became an army surgeon in 1816 and was sent to Quebec two years later. He developed an interest in geology and went off to look for rock samples in Upper Canada, where he encountered Major Joseph Delafield, also an amateur geologist, who may also have had a hand in his appointment. Henry Rowe Schoolcraft, the American Indian agent at Sault Ste Marie, described Bigsby as having 'a very bustling, clerk-like manner, which does not impress one with the quiet and repose of a philosopher,' although Schoolcraft also shared and appreciated Bigsby's knowledge of geology.[42]

The U.S. agent, Samuel Hawkins, had functioned only minimally in 1819 and then left the commission altogether at the end of the season; Porter and several compatriots had managed the U.S. survey. As the 1820 season approached the vacuum remained unaddressed, but in May Delafield travelled to Washington, DC, to confer with John Quincy Adams about the commission's accounts, especially those concerning Hawkins. Delafield, having been with the commission since 1817, offered his services. Adams asked him to prepare a memorandum to show the president explaining the circumstances. As a result, on 19 May 1820 Adams was able to appoint Delafield 'Acting' agent.[43] Delafield had been attached to the surveying parties for the previous two years as secretary or clerk of the American agent and knew the work well (his brother, a young career army officer, had resigned as draftsman to the commission in 1819). Delafield was born in New York in 1790, graduated from Yale in 1808, and was admitted to the bar in 1811. He had also joined the militia and served during the War of 1812, emerging with the rank of major. He had joined the commission in 1817, and, like Bigsby, he was also interested in geology and minerals. (While working for the commission, Delafield began what became one of the best private collections of minerals in the country.) By the end of the 1820 season General Porter wrote to Adams that he was 'gratified in having ... the assistance of Major Delafield, whose intelligence, habits of business, and correct deportment have rendered him very useful.' After all of the disputes with Hawkins, Delafield must have been a relief to Porter. 'The ease and repose of the major's manners contrast rather favorably with the fussiness of the British subs,' wrote one admirer. The commissioner urged Adams to give him the full appointment.[44]

By the summer of 1820 the commissions under articles 6 and 7 had begun to run into difficulties in the United States. In part as a result of his quarrel with Hawkins, Porter had been accused of benefiting through land speculation from his knowledge of the placement of the boundary line. He was able to demonstrate that he had not purchased any lands near the border, thus laying those charges to rest. However, the general expense of the western commissions was troubling Congress, as had the cost of the commission for article 5. Congress asked to see the accounts, and in December Adams sent it a list of the expenditures from 1817 to 1820.

By this time the total of salaries, equipment, supplies, transportation (chartering vessels such as the newly constructed *Red Jacket* out of Black Rock), preserved food for the surveying parties, and various other expenses had run to about $161,548 – a huge sum – for the four years.[45] There was general recognition as well that the work would require several more years, but no one would have imagined in 1820 that the survey from Sault Ste Marie to the Lake of the Woods would continue until 1826. Congress responded to these costs by cutting the salaries of the American commissioner and agent. Initially Delafield was not paid at the same rate as Hawkins, his predecessor, but in 1821 Porter's salary was reduced from $4,444.44 (the equivalent of the £1,000 sterling paid to the British commissioner) to $2,500. Porter wrote to Adams that he thought this congressional action insulting to him personally and somewhat demeaning for U.S. prestige. As in the past, he was certain that he would 'outlive the temporary odium which it is calculated to throw upon me.' Porter was clearly not happy with the hostility of Congress towards himself and the work of the commission.[46]

Commissioners Anthony Barclay and General Porter were able to meet in New York City in March 1820 to plan operations for the season; the British party would join the Americans at Black Rock on the Niagara River, and they would proceed together to the Detroit River. Although the two men established a working relationship, they never seemed to have the cordiality and respect that had existed between Porter and Ogilvy. However, Bigsby, who joined the commission at this point, thought that 'good feeling, caution, ingenuity, knowledge of various kinds, were required from time to time in both parts of the Commission, to avoid apparently insurmountable obstruction ... and to decide wisely in doubtful cases,' and he felt that the American members were 'men of strict honour, and frank and friendly to all – to myself personally most kind.' He noted that the commission's work was made more difficult by a lack of precedents in international law and practice and that the language of the treaty of 1783 was often so vague and uncertain that agreement on the boundary was not a simple matter.[47]

The board of commissioners met on 3 June at Grosse Île in the Detroit River, where Barclay officially presented his credentials. The British party had left Montreal on 9 May, as soon as the ice went out of the St Lawrence, but huge ice floes in Lake Erie and the Niagara River detained both groups at Black Rock. By 13 May they all boarded a steamer, and they made their way along the south shore of Lake Erie and up the Detroit River to Amherstburg, then a town of about five hundred people. The British agent, John Hale, submitted a memorial urging that the surveying parties be left to carry out their duties without the commissioners, agents, and secretaries remaining in the field to supervise them. As he put it, the surveying work to be done 'cannot be ascertained by ocular observations; they must be established by men of science, and by them laid down on paper.'[48] The results would emerge only after processing of the scientific and mathematical data during the winter and submission of them to the commissioners in the form of finished maps. The commissioners were not altogether convinced and kept both the agents and Secretary Bigsby in the field, although they themselves felt less need to stay this summer.[49]

The Americans celebrated Independence Day with a festive excursion on the first paddle-wheel steamboat on the upper Great Lakes, *Walk in the Water,* in the company of men and women from the garrison at Detroit. Later they sat down to an 'excellent dinner' and danced to the music of the army band. Major Delafield recorded numerous dinner parties and dances while they were in Detroit, including several social occasions with Governor Lewis Cass and Mrs Cass.[50]

Detroit, which had changed hands several times during the War of 1812, then had a population of about 1,400. However, its distinctiveness as a colourful French-Canadian fur trade centre and garrison town

would disappear with the influx of settlers from the east following opening of the Erie Canal in 1825 and introduction of steamships on the
Great Lakes. 'The Rivers Detroit and St. Clair have a lively fringe of comfortable and even pretty dwellings, embowered in pear, apple, and
peach orchards, with here and there a church-tower or a clump of wych-
elms shadowing an advanced bank of the river,' Bigsby remembered.
'Productive farms stretch out of sight into the woods behind.' Although
the region was apparently beautiful and verdant, its extreme heat,
Bigsby found, produced a kind of lethargy. Even in 1820 there was a surprising variety of people in the Detroit–Fort Malden–Amherstburg area.
Bigsby described meeting the Reverend Jedidiah Morse, a New England
clergyman now remembered as the father of American geography as
well as the father of the artist and inventor Samuel F.B. Morse. Bigsby
found Morse dressed in an old-fashioned long black coat, black knee-
breeches and silk stockings, and a white neck cloth and broad-brimmed
hat. The following year Bigsby encountered Captain Charles Stewart,
the famous British abolitionist, then residing in Amherstburg. Various
French and English noblemen turned up, but Bigsby was most impressed by a chance meeting in the woods with the new governor general of British North America, Lord Dalhousie, who was inspecting the
lands under his jurisdiction.[51]

   In the summer season of 1820 the parties were to survey the eastern
end of Lake Erie, the remainder of the Detroit River, Lake St Clair, and
the St Clair River. The fear of fever in the later summer prompted them
to leave sections of Lake St Clair unfinished and to move north into
Lake Huron. As Barclay put it in his report to Lord Castlereagh, they
had done so 'in order that the Shores and Islands of that tempestuous
Lake might be surveyed during the mildest months, and also because
the most fatal diseases prevailed during that season on the River and
Lake St. Clair.'[52] Bigsby described the several channels of the St Clair
River where it emptied into the lake. 'Marshy islands' in the delta gave
way to a shoreline made up of 'a savannah of long, bright green grass,
with woods in the rear disposed in capes, islands, and devious avenues.'
The doctor stepped into this green grass to find himself in six inches or
more of water. As the temperature rose over the next few days, the water
turned bad and illnesses returned. Those stricken with fever were bled
and given quinine by the physician. This year everyone survived.[53]

   Later in the summer work focused on Lake Huron, around the Neebish Rapids and Channel, St Joseph's Island, Drummond's Island, and
Manitoulin Island. David Thompson was the only member at the time

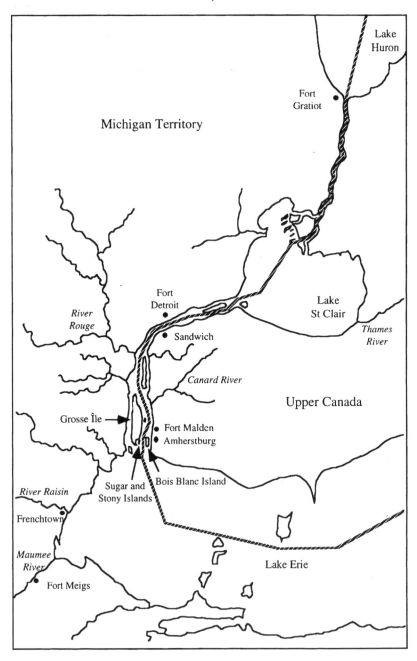

Map 9. Detroit River–Lake St Clair boundary

who could take accurate astronomical readings, which he did for both the British and the American parties. The Royal Navy made its small ship, HMS *Confiance*, captured from the Americans at Fort St Joseph in 1814, available to the commission and moved men and supplies through Lake Huron. Even so, the weather made work difficult. Despite calm frequently in the mornings, winds were very strong and very changeable by midday. Mosquitoes were a constant irritant, and the food was monotonous.

Bigsby complained to Barclay that British officers at Fort Willington on Drummond Island at the mouth of the St Mary's River had refused to provide supplies, although the parties had been able to get some sugar, beets, and fresh lamb at Michilimackinac. They also bought white fish, something of a delicacy, although Bigsby ate so much of it that summer that 'for ten years afterward [he] could not see fish on the dinner table without a shudder.'[54] Admittedly, Drummond Island was rocky and did not grow agricultural produce. After the Treaty of Ghent, British forces had abandoned the fort on Mackinac Island and built a new military post on Drummond Island, which dominated the approaches to the St Mary's River and the Sault. There the British army continued to receive American Indians and give presents to them. By 1820 there was a settlement of some fifteen whitewashed log houses, a crowded Indian village, and the fort with all its buildings. In 1828, several years after the commission had allocated the island to the United States, the British garrison moved to Penetanguishine, at the southern end of Georgian Bay.[55]

The Americans had divided into two parties. One, led by James Ferguson, explored and surveyed the mouth of the St Mary's River; the other, under Delafield, worked among the islands between the Sault and Georgian Bay. Delafield was able to live on board the schooner *Red Jacket* provided for them, but the surveyors and their crews had to do their work on shore. Bad weather and rough seas would often isolate the crews for several days, resulting in short rations and exposure to the elements. Someone was almost always sick with bilious fever or ague. Life on the *Red Jacket* had its perils also. One man fell into Lake Huron while attempting to jump from the schooner to a small boat; he could not swim, so Delafield leaped into the water to rescue him. The poor man 'was sinking for the third time when I caught him,' Delafield wrote in his journal. The Americans found the surveying as difficult as the British. Rain, cloud, fog, and smoke from forest fires made it difficult to take astronomical bearings to establish base lines. Gradually, however, the work got done. Delafield was constantly occupied with his own geological explorations and search for unusual mineral specimens, but he was also delighted by the company of a remarkable Jewish woman, a Mrs Solomon, who invited him to tea on Drummond's Island.[56]

Though isolated, the parties got mail periodically, saw Indians regularly, and occasionally exchanged greetings and news with fur traders returning to Montreal from the west. The surveying parties had seen Indians from time to time as early as St Regis in 1817, but along the north shore of Lake Huron they worked close to several Indian encampments. Delafield described a visit to one settlement near Drummond's Island, where at first the women hid at their approach. Through the assistance of a French Canadian living among the Indians, the Americans traded pork for potatoes and squashes. There seemed to be no deer or large game on the islands, and bad weather had prevented fishing, so the pork was gratefully received. Delafield described the Indian process of drying and roasting corn over a low fire and also the making of canoes, both activities going on when they arrived. Delafield and Major Fraser both admired the canoes, which were 'handsome and well made' by the women. True tourists, the two men ordered some model canoes and bark baskets to take home as souvenirs. From time to time they met other Indians on the water and through similar visits to settlements were generally able to buy fresh food from them.[57] Periodically they met fur traders moving rapidly in large canoes. Delafield stopped to talk with a Lake Winnipeg trader in a birch canoe, 'Eight paddlers and a trader seated like a Nabob in their center composed their party.' Now independent, the man had previously worked for Lord Selkirk and was returning to Montreal after thirty years in the country. When the Americans noticed that the canoe was named *Prêt-a-Bryre*, 'ready to drink,' a keg of rum was broken out and toasts were drunk all round. The voyageurs parted for the east under full song.[58] Surprisingly, Delafield missed seeing Governor Cass's large Mississippi expedition, which passed through the Straits of Mackinac in early September 1820.

By the end of the season only parts of the St Clair area remained to be done to complete the work under article 6. Barclay wrote, with some satisfaction, 'I am happy to state ... from Mr. Surveyor Thompson's communication, for your Lordship's information, that he thinks far more progress has been made in the late summer, than during any preceding year.'[59] Barclay ascribed this success to the more streamlined procedures of sending the two surveying parties off to work on assigned sections of the boundary waters without duplicating all of the work for purposes of verification. Barclay expected completion of the survey of this part of the boundary in the next season. He made only one qualified statement about the country: 'The whole country above alluded to is but little inhabited, very rough, and wild, being still for the most part in its pristine state: consequently it presents every obstacle which can be encountered, with little means of subduing any.'[60]

The board of commissioners met early in the spring of 1821 at Black Rock to examine the work done on the maps over the winter and to authorize completion of work in the region. Barclay wrote a cautious letter to the foreign secretary, now succeeded to the title Lord Londonderry, predicting 'difficulty and delay' but concluding that 'ultimately a satisfactory decision may be obtained.'[61] In fact, David Thompson had been sent off in midwinter to take sightings at Point Pelee and on the Detroit River. Parts of Lake St Clair, the several rivers that flowed into it, and the several channels of the St Clair River entering the lake were surveyed by May and June, before the temperatures could create a health problem in the marshes. This process corrected earlier errors and completed unfinished work from the previous season. By June some of the parties had gone back to work further north among the islands leading into the St Mary's River and the Neebish Rapids and Channel. Surveying parties also worked as far east in Lake Huron as the French River, a major canoe route for the fur trade to Lake Nippissing and the Ottawa River, and as far west as the Straits of Mackinac. By late July the American party had finished its assignments around Point Pelee and Put-in-Bay, having determined base lines and triangulation by taking bearings on bonfires set as beacons. The British were pretty well finished by September. This season thus completed the whole one thousand–mile section of the boundary from the point where the forty-fifth parallel struck the St Lawrence River to the Neebish Channel in the St Mary's River near Sault Ste Marie.[62]

After most of the data had been compiled, the commissioners met in New York City on 12 November 1821. They remained in conference for almost four weeks, sorting out the islands to be assigned to each country and the direction of the line. Four informal principles shaped their decisions: the boundary would always be a water line and not divide any islands; that where there were several channels, the most navigable would be the line; where there were several navigable channels, the line would follow the largest body of water; and where there were several channels, the line closest to the centre of the waterway would be chosen, provided that good navigation was left to both parties.[63] There was also an informal process of balancing the portioning out of islands, particularly strategic ones. (Examples of strategic islands would be Wolfe Island opposite Kingston, Upper Canada, and Grosse Île off Detroit.) Through this kind of process, the commissioners reached agreement about most of the boundary from the St Lawrence through Lakes Ontario, Erie, and Huron, all the way to the Sault.

However, by mid-December the commissioners had come to something of an impasse. They disagreed about the section of the Detroit River opposite Amherstburg and Fort Malden. They conceded to the Americans a large island on their side of the Detroit River, Grosse Isle. There were several smaller islands in various channels in the middle or on the Upper Canadian side of the river. Bois Blanc Island was directly opposite Amherstburg. General Porter had claimed it, but was prepared to relinquish claims to it for possession of three still-smaller islands close to Grosse Île – Sugar, Fox, and Stoney Islands. Anthony Barclay claimed these three but was willing to relinquish them if the United States agreed not to fortify them. Porter had no authority to make such a commitment, and he told Barclay 'that he dare not show his face in Washington, if he should resign the United States claim to the same.' After a great deal of discussion, with no solution in sight, the two commissioners wrote to John Quincy Adams and to the British minister in Washington, Stratford Canning, to ask them to make a decision or to advise the commissioners how to resolve the impasse over three very insignificant islands.[64]

Neither Canning nor Adams was quick to respond. Porter went to Washington to confer with Adams and to draft a report on the question. Canning took the opportunity to write to Lord Londonderry for advice, but he also wrote to Barclay indicating that he did not think that the general settlement was sufficiently favourable to Britain to allow him to make a decision on the three islands.[65] Adams's view, as expressed to Richard Rush, the American minister to Britain, was that the commissioners had no authority to make limitations about fortifications. Such a matter would have to be negotiated in a separate treaty and submitted to the U.S. Senate. While the U.S. government was not prepared to negotiate a special treaty for these three islands, Adams instructed Rush to sound out the British about a treaty that provided for the 'disarming of the Islands as well as the waters, provided the stipulation is made reciprocal, and the application to all the Islands at the mouth of the Detroit River.'[66] There seemed little prospect of this proposal's being accepted, despite the recent Rush–Bagot agreement of 1817 limiting naval ships in the Great Lakes.

On 29 January 1822 the board of commissioners met in Philadelphia, where both commissioners presented statements of their positions. They also drafted a joint statement of their differences.[67] Barclay's letters to Londonderry of both 18 January and 9 February emphasized the merits of the otherwise completely agreed on boundary. 'Your Lordship will excuse me in remarking, that the Line, so far as it has been conditionally agreed upon, is perfectly satisfactory to His Majesty's Agent, as he informs me, and to the claim made by him on behalf of His Majesty.'[68] Meanwhile, Governor General Lord Dalhousie, who had been consulted by Canning about the military importance of the three small islands, wrote on 23 February that he had no objection in principle to the Americans holding them unless they were to be used for 'hostile and offensive intentions, in which point of view I consider them of the highest importance to the safety and security of His Majesty's Frontier, and as effectively commanding that branch of the Detroit River.'[69] No fortifications of the islands ever took place, and indeed no British naval base was ever built at Amherstburg. We should view this tempest in a teapot, however, in the context of the suspicions engendered by the War of 1812.[70]

In any case, these alarms were too late to affect British decision. On 9 March 1822 the foreign secretary wrote to Canning that His Majesty's Government agreed to 'consent to concede to the U. States the possession of the three small islands which at present appear to constitute the only point of difference between the two Commissioners' but predicated this concession on the immediate ratification of the whole of the rest of the border.[71] Barclay was taking his winter holidays in Savannah, Georgia, but Canning wrote to Londonderry that he had talked with Secretary of State Adams about the cession of the three islands and that Adams had appreciated the conciliatory gesture.[72]

After some postponements at the request of General Porter that raised Canning's suspicion, the last session of the board of commissioners under article 6 took place on 18 June 1822 at Utica, New York. Barclay gave Porter a written proposal for the adjustment of previous differences concerning the three islands in the Detroit River. Porter in return gave his acceptance of the offer 'without delay' and also in writing. Both statements were then entered in the journal of the board. The two men then signed the joint report that they had earlier drafted. A minor flurry occurred when Barclay insisted that, as the representative of Britain, he sign all the documents first and above Porter's name. Porter could not agree but suggested that they each sign first and above the other on those copies of the documents that they were to keep for their own countries.[73] Sign they did, thus formally settling a major section of the boundary, almost one thousand miles in length.

This was a significant settlement. It was not without controversy at the time. Anthony Barclay and David Thompson came under criticism for allowing Barnhart's Island in the St Lawrence to go to the Americans.[74] However, in terms of serious vital interests, both British North America and the United States protected their security and provided for workable transportation routes along the water boundary. Just as important, the commission in this section of the border proved successful. The Passamaquoddy Bay commission (article 4) had been successful, the New Brunswick–Maine commission (article 5) had just reached an impasse, and the Lake Superior–Lake of the Woods commission (article 7) was yet to start its work. It was still possible to be optimistic about a settlement for the whole of the boundary.

Chapter Six

Article 7: From Lake Superior to the Lake of the Woods

The commission under the seventh article of the Treaty of Ghent was to decide the border from Sault Ste Marie across Lake Superior, through the water communication to the Lake of the Woods, to the northwest-ernmost point of that lake. In the words of the Treaty of Paris of 1783, the line was to go from the Sault, 'thence through Lake Superior North-ward of Isles Royal & Phelipeaux to the Long Lake; Thence through the Middle of said Long Lake, and the Water Communication between it & the Lake of the Woods, ... Thence through the said Lake to the most Northwestern Point thereof.'[1] The boundary from that point was origi-nally to extend west to the Mississippi; however, that river was actually to the south. Furthermore, the American acquisition of Louisiana from France in 1803 and the Convention of 1818, which established the forty-ninth parallel as the boundary from the Lake of the Woods west to the Rocky Mountains, had rendered that provision of the treaty obsolete. Indeed, the commission's task would be to link the northwesternmost point of the Lake of the Woods by a straight line with the forty-ninth parallel, be it north or south.

This part of the boundary, which now separates Ontario and Minne-sota, was certainly the most remote, for both the British and the Ameri-cans. There had been fur traders out of Montreal, and even out of Hudson Bay, in the Lake Superior region since perhaps the 1740s. David Thompson, the British astronomical surveyor, had explored the area of western Lake Superior in the late eighteenth century for the North West Company. John Jacob Astor's American Fur Company had ventured into Lake Superior in the first decade of the nineteenth century, but only in alliance with the Nor'westers. Official American presence was almost non-existent. Major Zebulon Pike had undertaken an exploratory mis-sion in 1806 to find the source of the Mississippi, and the U.S. army had attempted some raiding parties at the Sault late in the War of 1812. In 1820 Lewis Cass, governor of the Michigan Territory, led a large expedition into Lake Superior, up the St Louis River, and west to what was thought to be the source of the Mississippi; and in 1823 Major Stephen H. Long travelled with a party from the Mississippi north into Lake Winnipeg and then east along the canoe route to Fort William and Lake Superior. However, the U.S. position in the region was very fragile, and the loyalties of the Native people were very doubtful.

The commission under article 7 had entirely the same senior personnel as that under article 6, unlike the earlier commissions for articles 4 and 5, which had officials and appointees independent of each other. Thus as the commissioners and agents were coming to a decision in the winter of 1822 about the boundary under article 6 from St Regis on the St Lawrence River through Lakes Ontario, Erie, and Huron, preparations were beginning to send the same parties of surveyors up the St Mary's River at the Sault and on into Lake Superior. Surveying for article 7 would continue until 1825, but unresolved issues would extend the life of the commission into 1827.

The commissioners looking ahead in 1822 at the work of surveying the last stretch of the boundary were under no illusions. Anthony Barclay wrote to the undersecretary at the Foreign Office that 'the country through which the boundary line must pass, is, and will continue, for the most part unknown, until surveyed.'[2] The area was not inhabited, he said, except by Native people. He estimated that work could be completed by the end of the season in 1823. General Porter had a similar view of the region, describing it as 'a totally wild & uninhabited country, affording no means for the comfort or even subsistence of persons engaged in this service, and a climate so cold and inhospitable that a small portion only of the year can be employed in active duties.'[3] Dr John Bigsby described the land west of Lake Superior as 'sterility itself, an assemblage of rocky mounds, with small intervals of marsh.' As for the weather, Bigsby noted that at the end of June there were still small blocks of ice on the lake, not to mention fogs and storms.[4] However, for Native people, though few in number, this country may have been an eden. Bigsby described an idyllic scene near what is now Basswood Lake: 'We saw, sitting before a conical wigwam, a handsome, comfortably-dressed young Indian and his wife at work, a child playing with pebbles on the shore, and a fox-like dog keeping watch. There they sat, fearless and secure. It occurred to me that many an Englishman might envy them.'[5]

Porter wrote to Secretary of State John Quincy Adams that the parties would not use the exacting procedures of trigonometrical surveying – the triangulation employed earlier – but would need precise methods for determining the northwesternmost corner of the Lake of the Woods. He said that the language describing the boundary in the treaty of 1783 was as inaccurate in this region as elsewhere along the border, although he did not expect great difficulties in reaching an accommodation with the British on 'where it [the boundary] ought to be established, to comport best with the views of the parties at the time of making the Treaty.'[6] He too thought that the work would need but two seasons.

Major Joseph Delafield, the American agent, also wrote to Adams outlining the tasks at hand. The Grand Portage route along the Pigeon River had been abandoned by the fur traders after the treaty of 1783 in favour of a more northern route along the Kamanistiquia River, at Fort William, and these two routes would be fully examined. The southern route at Fond du Lac up the St Louis River 'does not seem to be in question, altho it has by some persons been rather improvidently suggested.'[7] Delafield was presumably referring to Henry Rowe Schoolcraft's mention in his 1821 book about his travels to the area of 'two grand routes pursued by the north west traders' from Lake Superior west – the Grand Portage trail and the Fond du Lac–St Louis River–Lake Vermillion chain.[8] Ramsay Crooks, general manager of the American Fur Company, had assured Delafield that the Pigeon River–Grand Portage passage west was 'the known and direct route.'[9] While political considerations did not seem to him to pose much of a problem, Delafield did think that the harshness of the terrain would increase the time needed for the survey. He also thought it important to establish an American presence: 'Our Indian relations, the competition in the Fur Trade, and the increase of a lawless population in that quarter, are amongst the claims for a definite limit of jurisdiction between the two Countries, even if it were not a Treaty obligation,' he concluded.[10]

The June 1822 meeting of the board of commissioners in Utica, New York, that settled the boundary under article 6 also issued instructions to the new surveying parties. These noted landmarks from St Joseph's Island at the Sault to 'the most north western point of Lake of the Woods' and instructed the parties to report regularly.[11] Delafield recruited twenty-one-year-old George W. Whistler, an army engineer at West Point commissioned just three years earlier, as a draftsman to assist twenty-four-year-old James Ferguson, who had become the principal U.S. surveyor. As the historian William E. Lass has pointed out, both

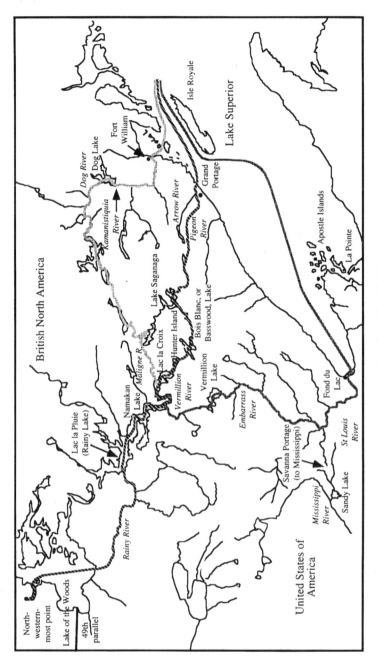

Map 10. Boundary from Lake Superior to the Lake of the Woods: claims and final, 1842

men were much younger then and had no experience comparable to that of the British surveyor, David Thompson (then fifty-two). Whistler, the father of the famous painter, was born in Fort Wayne the son of Captain James Whistler, and he had spent at least part of his youth in early Detroit.

Delafield joined the American party sailing to Mackinac Island on the schooner *Red Jacket*, and it arrived on 3 June after a trip of only eleven days. Delafield received detailed advice from Ramsay Crooks about the kinds of equipment and supplies that would be needed for an expedition so far beyond convenient resupply from commercial sources – boats, for example, to cross Lake Superior; canoes for the rivers and lakes beyond Superior; pork packed in small kegs and flour in carefully prepared cloth sacks. Beyond Mackinac Island the expedition would have to carry almost everything that it needed. The American Fur Company's manager at Mackinac Island, Robert Stuart, was hired to perform any services that the surveying party might need in the next year. Following Crooks's practical instructions, Delafield oversaw the outfitting of the surveying parties and the hiring of more work crews and then returned east at the end of the month. The surveying parties would be left pretty much to themselves, with both the commissioners and the agents remaining in the east and a meeting at the Sault tentatively planned for the following spring of 1823.[12]

Ferguson and Whistler and their crews made their way into Lake Superior, the largest and most forbidding of the Great Lakes. French explorers had first entered the lake in the early seventeenth century. Missionaries, cartographers, and fur traders had followed. By the late eighteenth century the lake was a sufficiently important waterway for the fur trade to figure in the boundary provisions of the treaty of 1783. Therefore, during the summer of 1822 the American surveyors canoed along the eastern edge to the North West Company's fur post, Fort William, on Thunder Bay. They then paddled forty miles southwest to the Pigeon River and the site of the old fur trade post Grand Portage – the Great Carrying Place – abandoned since 1804. There they identified what they regarded as the Long Lake of the treaty of 1783, and they proceeded inland along the old canoe route. The Pigeon River and the eight-mile portage itself Ferguson found extremely difficult. He also noted two waterways west: the Pigeon River–Fowl Lakes–Moose Lake route and also the Arrow River–Arrow Lake route.

The rest of the summer was spent surveying and mapping along the lakes and rivers as far west as Lake Saganaga. The Americans were surprised to find that the water routes west from Lake Superior did not simply follow a single river but extended from lake to lake, connected by impassible waterfalls or rapids that required repeated land portages. In fact, the height of land was discovered to be only about fifty miles inland from Lake Superior, after which the water drained west and north, eventually into the Lake of the Woods and Hudson Bay, respectively. Ferguson said that he made trigonometrical surveys of the larger lakes but recorded by log and compass the distances and directions of the portages.[13]

Thompson and his British party left Lower Canada by June 1822, passing through Lake Simcoe on 9 June and entering the rapids at Sault Ste Marie by 24 June. Over the winter Thompson had constructed to his design a special boat for the western survey. It was to be clinker-built, of cedar planks, in order to be both light and strong.[14] The St Mary's River at the Sault had been mapped the previous season. The surveyors made their way along the south coast of Lake Superior, stopping on 14 July at Chequamegon Bay and the community at La Pointe on Madeline Island – still a major Ojibwa settlement and a valuable fur trade centre. They proceeded on to Fond du Lac, site of the modern cities of Duluth and Superior, and to the St Louis River, then the site of a large Ojibwa village and a major American Fur Company post. Only six years earlier, in 1816, Lord Selkirk had captured Fond du Lac, along with Fort William, in retaliation for the North West Company's involvement in the 'Seven Oaks Massacre,' in which the governor and twenty-two settlers of Selkirk's Hudson's Bay Company settlement in Red River were killed. While the post at Fond du Lac at the time was officially American (actually owned jointly by John Jacob Astor and the Nor'westers), Selkirk had seized the goods and arrested the Métis traders anyway. The volatility of the undefined border region was therefore fresh in everyone's minds.[15]

The surveyors, with the assistance of John Charles Sayer, a North West Company fur trader, proceeded northeast, along the north shore of Lake Superior, reaching Grand Portage by 22 July. They went on to Fort William, then the main North West Company post in the region, returning to Pigeon River at Grand Portage to proceed inland along the old canoe route as far as Lake Namakan by mid-August. They later returned to Lake Superior and surveyed the coastal waters along its northern side. Part of Thompson's success in the wilderness rested on his ability to deal fairly with Native people and on his concern for the welfare of his men. Dr Bigsby described Thompson's giving Indians gifts of tobacco and blue cloth and explaining the mission of the surveyors to worried

Natives. The documents do not tell much about what Native people thought about the question of the boundary. Bigsby gave a hint of their anxiety along with his description of Thompson's character and ability. 'What is your purpose in rambling over our waters, and putting them into your books?' asked Two-hearts, of the Rainy Lake Ojibwa. Thompson answered that the surveyors meant the Indians no harm but were merely measuring how far north fell the 'shadow' of the United States and how far south extended 'the shadow of their great father, King George.' The Indians, Bigsby said, 'expressed content.' Thompson had a wealth of knowledge of the wilderness, but he also looked after his men in a variety of other ways. On Sundays he read to his French Catholic crews, 'in most extraordinarily pronounced French, three chapters out of the Old Testament, and as many out of the New, adding such explanations as seemed to him suitable.' The men appreciated his concern, Bigsby observed. By 21 October Thompson was into Lake Huron on his way back to his home in Williamstown in Lower Canada to work on the maps over the winter.[16]

Joseph Delafield reported to John Quincy Adams in the autumn of 1822 that he had been in touch with the American surveyors and was confident that the historic Pigeon River–Grand Portage route would be agreed on as the water communication intended in the treaty of 1783. He was pleased to say that 'there is no longer any serious question open as to the general course that the Line is intended to be run; and because it is now more certain, that upon the return of the Surveyors, the next season, the Board will be possessed of the necessary information to determine the doubts under the seventh article of the Treaty, and designate the line.'[17] It seemed reasonable in 1822, but he could not have been more wrong.

Because of the great distances travelled to reach the region beyond Lake Superior, James Ferguson, George W. Whistler, and most of their crews were actually to spend the winter of 1822–3 at Fort William, rather than returning to the east and then journeying out again for the 1823 season. It was hoped that this process would allow completion of the project in two years. Indeed, wintering at Fort William did enable the crews to work right up to mid-October, when the small lakes began to freeze. Moreover, Ferguson was able to survey Isle Royale from the ice after Lake Superior froze. He established base lines by driving pins into the ice and taking his bearings from them. In the following spring the ice went out of Thunder Bay by 6 May, but ice flows could be found on Lake Superior as late as 28 June.[18]

Though of less importance since the merger of the Hudson's Bay Company and the North West Company in 1821, Fort William, built in 1804, was still a large and formidable establishment, with palisades on four sides and block houses on each corner. Delafield said that the gate had been strengthened since Selkirk's capture of the fort in 1816. Carpenters, coopers, tinsmiths, blacksmiths, armourers, tailors, and canoe-builders supported the fur trade establishment. There were about thirty women and children and a similar number of fur traders and surveyors. A large farm helped provide food for the settlement. As recently as 1818 some 800 men had together camped there, both 'North Men' who wintered at fur posts in the interior and 'Pork Eaters' who took cargoes to and from Montreal.

The fort had offices, storehouses, dwellings, and a great hall large enough to feed 100 at once. Portraits lined the walls, including one of Admiral Lord Nelson, and David Thompson's large and celebrated map of western British North America dominated one end of the great hall. At the table men sat according to rank, the seniors at the head, 'clerks and guides, &c. of respectable but humbler grade, ranged down the table in order due,' Bigsby noted. Fish and game were served, including delicacies such as buffalo tongue and beaver tail, on fine china brought from Europe. Although both Bigsby and Delafield agreed that the 'palmy days were gone' for Fort William, there were still numerous clerks, voyageurs, and Indians staying there.[19] However, the winter was long, and the men found it boring. Ferguson said that there were only three 'gentlemen' at the fort, and all topics of conversation were eventually exhausted.

The Hudson's Bay Company, which had operated Fort William since the merger, organized dances every two weeks to keep the fur traders from becoming 'morose and savage,' as Ferguson put it. They danced Scottish reels to the music of two fiddles and a triangle. The dances seemed to cheer everyone but Ferguson. 'I don't dance,' he reported wistfully, although he did his duty by sponsoring one evening's entertainment. 'Our men from Black Rock [New York] are dandies here and do us honor,' he added.[20]

Anthony Barclay wrote in May 1823 to the new foreign secretary, George Canning, that David Thompson was to return to Lake Superior as soon as the ice broke up in the St Lawrence and canoe traffic was again possible. Thompson, who had worked on maps over the winter in Williamstown, had assured Barclay that it would not be possible to finish the work of the survey until the end of the 1824 season – three summers of work instead of two.[21] Thompson, his son Samuel, and nine others on their way west passed through Kingston on 12 May, Bigsby reported, having left Montreal ten days earlier.[22] They went down Lake Ontario to York (Toronto) and then north to Lake Simcoe and Georgian Bay. The surveyors had some work to do among the islands in the western end of Lake Huron, but they then turned north, passing through the Sault.

Like Mackinac Island, Sault Ste Marie was a vital crossroads for the fur trade, for Indian affairs, and for transportation between the eastern cities and the northwest frontier. Both the Americans and the British had fur trading operations at the Sault, and the Americans, through the efforts of Governor Lewis Cass, purchased land from the Indians at the Sault during the summer of 1820 to build Fort Brady. By 1822 the fort had a complement of two companies of infantry. This was the northernmost American fort in the west and was intended to impress both Native people and fur traders and to diminish British influence. To further these objectives, the United States also appointed Henry Rowe Schoolcraft as Indian agent at the Sault; he took up residence in 1821.[23]

The surveyors passing through the Sault always stopped for supplies and information. The village on the American side of the Sault was small, with a few houses, both large and small, and some Indian wigwams, while the British settlement included about fifteen log houses and the substantial North West Company post. The surveyors generally visited the fur traders John Johnston on the American side and Charles Oakes Ermatinger on the British. Johnston had worked for the North West Company as a young man of twenty-nine straight from Ireland, but by the 1820s he was in the service of John Jacob Astor's company. Although his house had been destroyed in the war, it had been rebuilt and included a library of over one thousand well-bound books in English and French. He lived as a country gentleman with his Ojibwa wife and family. Bigsby commented on him as 'a much-respected Indian trader,' who lived 'most hospitably in a house, whose neatness is in striking contrast with the careless dilapidation reigning around,' and he gave generous compliments to Mrs Johnston. Delafield also described Johnston as a 'gentleman' who had 'seen much of the polite world,' and he too gave warm praise to Johnston's wife and children. In 1820 Mrs Johnston had intervened in a dispute between Governor Cass and the local Ojibwa, preventing a conflict and persuading the Indians not to fly the British flag on the American side of the river and to sell the land to build Fort Brady.[24]

On the British side, Ermatinger had a large, comfortable stone house, built at a cost of £2,000, in which he entertained members of the surveying parties. He built a windmill at the Sault, hoping, Bigsby said, to encourage local people to grow grain. His main task, however, was to manage the North West Company's fur trade operations in the region, including a post on Drummond Island which he maintained until 1828. Bigsby described him as 'every inch a trader, public-spirited, skilful, sanguine, and indefatigable.' Despite the genteel ambiance cultivated by Johnston and Ermatinger, Bigsby noted that the general conversation at the Sault focused on the availability of furs, the success of the winter hunt, the raiding parties of the Sioux, and the recent 'Seven Oaks Massacre' at Red River. The violence of the frontier was brought home to him when he met an attractive white woman who had a silver plate in her head to cover the scar where she had been scalped.[25]

Bigsby described Lake Superior as 'beautifully wild,' and 'it becomes magnificent when we reflect on the size, celebrity, and remoteness of this body of fresh water.' It had 'no parallel in America' for geological interest.[26] Bigsby and Thompson reached Grand Portage by 29 June and led the crews on into the canoe routes west from Lake Superior. By 11 July they were passing through Lac la Croix, where Bigsby noted wild rice so thick that 'we sometimes could hardly push our canoes through it,' and the water-lilies were beautiful: 'much the finest I have ever seen.' They were by 15 July on the Rainy River, where 'all is serenity and beauty,' and by the nineteenth into the Lake of the Woods.

Bigsby stated that they spent nine days surveying the 'very large and intricate Lake,' taking sightings to determine its northwesternmost corner. The lake as perceived by the surveyors bears little resemblance to the huge expanse of water to be found on modern maps. Because of the known use of the lake as a water course into the Hudson Bay watershed, only its central portions were of interest. Bigsby described three parts: the southern area into which the Rainy River flowed, called Parpequawungar Sakahagan or Lake of the Sand Hills; the northern area from which the Winnipeg River exited, called Kaminitik Sakahagan or Lake of the Woods; and an eastern area that was not surveyed, called Whitefish Lake. The surveyors first explored the shallow and sometimes marshy waters of the southwestern part, then turned north and worked their way towards Rat Portage at the northern end. The country was increasingly picturesque. Near Rat Portage, Bigsby recounted, 'the scene becomes precisely that of the Thousand Islands on the St.

Lawrence below Kingston, so exquisitely beautiful when seen on a calm evening when the shadows are long.'[27]

Bigsby acknowledged that the party abandoned the more exacting trigonometrical surveying method for a more rapid process of taking astronomical sightings at fixed points of approximately equal distances and then 'filling up the intervals by compass and log or estimates.' Thompson later recalled using Massey's Patent Log, which the crew towed from one of the canoes to determine accurate distance on the water. By that process the men could move along at about four miles an hour and still get what was held to be a fairly accurate map of the lake. However, Bigsby admitted that they must have 'passed unnoticed several small rivers, because, in a low woody country, it is not easy to see an entering stream, unless we catch sight of it when fully opposite, or are very near.'[28] This was true, and in fact they had sacrificed precision for the sake of time, and this rapid survey would result in a serious potential threat to British interests in the west.

During the course of these labours, one member of the crew became so ill that he had to be left with friendly Natives, and David Thompson himself became sick at Rainy Lake.[29] The rest of that month the crew worked along the Rainy River route. It ran out of food and arrived, weak and exhausted, at Fort William on 23 August. As the men passed Sheep Island, opposite Fort William, after weeks in the wilderness, Bigsby recounted, they saw 'lines of haycocks, and four haymakers in white shirt sleeves and straw hats. This sudden coming upon one of the prettiest sights of Christendom, which we had left far away, and long ago, made us quite tender, as the Indians say.' By 1 September, Thompson was back on Lake Superior working his way along the shore. He and his party did some surveying among the islands of the St Mary's River and on 16 October entered Lake Huron on the way home.[30]

Entering the Thousand Islands in the St Lawrence River in mid-November, Thompson and two canoes loaded with men and equipment were challenged in mid-river by an Upper Canadian customs assistant and two searchers, who ordered them ashore at the Cedars. Never having been stopped before, the surveyors were unwilling to be detained. Bigsby explained, 'The three canoes drifted down to the lower end of the village and near shore, when a combat, with paddles, poles, etc., commenced between our Bark Canoe and five custom house officers, which ended in both parties being considerably hurt and in the seizure of our property – even to the daily provisions of the men.' Language difficulties and a certain amount of drink contributed to the disorder.

Mr Simpson, the collector of customs, whose son-in-law had been beaten, bloodied, and nearly drowned and had his finger bitten, wanted charges pressed. Bigsby was able to smooth these troubled waters by paying a $5 fine for the release of the men.[31]

Major Delafield meanwhile had left New York on 3 May 1823 to consult with Ferguson on the work of 1822 and 1823. Although steamboats had been in operation on the Hudson River for some years, Delafield was able to take the still-unfinished Erie Canal from Albany as far west as Rochester. From Black Rock and Buffalo he travelled again by steamboat to Detroit, where he held meetings with Governor Lewis Cass and numerous army officers before boarding a schooner for Mackinac Island. The whole trip from New York took forty-two days. At the Straits, Delafield bought supplies from the American Fur Company, purchased a large canoe, and engaged a crew of French Canadians. While he was at Mackinac Island a parcel arrived from Fort William with Ferguson's maps and accounts from the previous summer's work. Delafield left Mackinac on 17 June, passing up through Sault Ste Marie and into Lake Superior bound for Fort William. He saw Lieutenant Henry W. Bayfield sail for Fort William on 20 June in the lake survey vessel, HMS *Recover.* He himself left by canoe on the twenty-nineth.[32]

At Fort William the American party obtained two smaller 'North canoes' and then embarked for Grand Portage and the Pigeon River. The passage along Lake Superior took three days in thick fog, but, with the help of Ferguson's maps, careful compass work by Delafield, and a certain amount of luck, the canoes made Pigeon Point and the site of the old Grand Portage. Then began the arduous eight-mile portage around the Pigeon River falls. Delafield described the muddy portage trail, steep and overgrown, and the process of carrying the canoes and baggage. The men fastened a strap, or tumpline, which he called a 'portage collar,' to the goods. The goods were then placed on a voyageur's back and held by the strap that ran across the man's forehead. More goods piled on top filled 'up the load to the back of his head, [and] bending forward, he takes it over his post on a slow trot, a very fast walk with bended knees.' Two bundles were carried more easily than one, but some men carried three. 'The Canadians surpass all others upon the portage,' Delafield noted. It took three days to reach navigable water, but once back in the canoes Delafield found the scenery of lakes and rocks increasingly striking. He described one lake as 'a beautiful sheet of water much like the last, surrounded by similar highlands.'[33] Once at the height of land, the party could progress west along the chain of lakes and portages leading to Lac la Pluie (Rainy Lake). On 29 July Delafield met David Thompson and his friend Dr Bigsby on the Rainy River and was disconcerted to learn that the British party had not seen or heard of Ferguson and the American party on the Lake of the Woods. The next day, however, Delafield met four fur canoes coming down from the Athabasca country to the west. They had been moving fast and had seen Ferguson and the U.S. party in the Lake of the Woods. Late on the afternoon of 31 July, after almost three months of steady travel, Delafield found the American surveyors along the north shore of the Lake of the Woods.[34]

Ferguson was in the process of taking sightings with his sextant to determine the position of Rat Portage near the head of the Winnipeg River. He concluded, as Thompson had earlier in the summer, that the northwesternmost point of Lake of the Woods was near Rat Portage. Given the lake's tangle of twisting shorelines, numerous peninsulas, and countless islands, Delafield was not so confident. 'The truth is that the N.W. end of the lake is indented by very deep bays,' he worried, and these should probably be explored. He further queried, 'A question too may be raised, by what rule is the most N.W. point to be ascertained?'[35] It was a relevant question. None the less Ferguson thought that he had completed his survey of the lake and needed only to do some additional work at the height of land between the Lake Superior and Rainy River watersheds and along the shoreline between Grand Portage and Fort William. The party started back on Monday, 4 August. At the Hudson's Bay Company's Fort La Pluie, on the Rainy River, Delafield met John Tanner, about whom he had heard on the way out. Tanner was a white man who had been kidnapped as a child and raised by Indians. He was recovering from gunshot wounds but would eventually make his way to Michigan and his old home in Kentucky. Delafield left some supplies for him and urged the fur trader to look after him, which Tanner later generously acknowledged.[36] Opposite Fort La Pluie was an American Fur Company post built the previous year to discourage British fur traders from operating further south in U.S. territory. However, it was not prospering. Delafield thought it abandoned, and Bigsby, who also stopped there, quoted the Hudson's Bay Company factor, Simon McGillivray, Jr, as saying, 'We are starving them out, and have nearly succeeded.'[37]

Ferguson and Delafield split up, the surveyor going to Grand Portage and the agent taking the new British canoe route to Fort William by way of the Kamanistiquia River. Once both groups were together at Fort William, they said farewell to Thompson and Bigsby and left for the Sault on 28 August. Major Delafield and George W. Whistler travelled in the agent's large 'Mackinac' canoe, and Ferguson and several others took the rather larger barge of the surveyor. The unsettled weather of September gave them problems on Lake Superior from time to time, but they arrived at the Sault on 14 September and commented to Schoolcraft that the boundary survey was 'completed to the contemplated point on the Lake of the Woods, as called for by the Treaty of Ghent.'[38] Delafield sailed out of Mackinac Island on 3 October bound for Buffalo. By 24 October 1823, he was back in New York City, but the work of the commission was far from completed.

The Americans reported to John Quincy Adams in the autumn of 1823. General Porter said that it was with some disappointment that he informed the secretary of state that 'although I have reason to believe that they have prosecuted their labors with great industry and perseverance, during an absence of seventeen months, and have met with no serious accident, yet I regret to find their surveys are not sufficiently advanced to enable us to close the Commission ... as we had expected.'[39] The country was more rugged than could be imagined, but too much time had been spent during the 1822 season exploring at the insistence of the British. 'Mr. Thompson the principal British Surveyor, who has long been well acquainted with the interior of North America, has heretofore entertained a belief that a boundary best according with the description of the Treaty, and the supposed view of the parties at the time of making it, could be traced through the bay at the South West extremity of Lake Superior, called *Fond du Lac*, and thence up the River St. Louis, in a direction towards Lake of the Woods; and I find that, on some of the printed maps, the boundary is laid along this route; while others represent it (no doubt correctly) as passing along the chain of land and water communication, on what is called the *Grand Portage* route.'[40] However, although the two parties had spent part of 1822 pursuing Fond du Lac, Porter concluded that they had reached a general agreement that the Pigeon River–Grand Portage route was the 'correct one.'

Delafield, who wrote first from Detroit on his return back, and then from New York, said much the same thing. He too recognized that the work had not been completed in the two seasons and explained that the land was quite formidable. It was 'mountains and valleys, or rock and water, to the exclusion of plains, and of earth,' he said, and 'the islands are entirely of rock, supporting in their fissures a stunted growth of trees, and are of no value in any sense.'[41] The old canoe route did not follow 'direct water'; there was not a single navigable river that could be followed to the Lake of the Woods, further complicating the surveying process. Delafield described the northern route west from Lake Superior by way of Fort William and the Kamanistiquia River, which was now used by the traders of the North West Company and the Hudson's Bay Company. American traders worked out of Fond du Lac, to the south. However, Delafield was confident that the Pigeon River route was the intended boundary. He also noted that the first examination of the Lake of the Woods had placed its northwesternmost point at Rat Portage, near the present town of Keewatin.[42]

The board of commissioners met in February 1824 in Albany, and the agents and surveyors submitted reports. David Thompson asserted that Fond du Lac was the longest lake (some fifteen to seventeen miles) adjacent to Lake Superior, that the St Louis River was the largest stream to empty into the western half of Superior, and that therefore both must be surveyed more closely. Furthermore, thirteen 'considerable' rivers that emptied into Superior along its northern shore between the St Louis and the Pigeon rivers needed examination too. Thompson also reported to the board that the circumnavigation of Lake Superior had revealed no island conforming to the Isle Phelipeaux mentioned in the treaty of 1783.[43] Delafield's report said that if the Pigeon River–Grand Portage route were not so obviously the water communication intended in the treaty of 1783, he would have proposed the Kamanistiquia River– Fort William route. The British agent, John Hale, refused to abandon any possible route from Lake Superior to the Lake of the Woods until further surveys had been made and more information accumulated. The commissioners gave instructions to explore first the Pigeon River route and then the Fond du Lac route, as well as to search for Isle Phelipeaux, which did not exist, and to determine the position of Caribou Island, which did. The crucial issue for Hale was to find the true 'Long Lake' mentioned in the treaty. He also noted that parts of the St Mary's River needed further work, which should take place in the 1824 season.[44]

In the aftermath of the Albany meetings, a discouraged General Porter wrote to Secretary of State Adams. 'It is a matter of much regret with Major Delafield and myself, that the British Commissioner and Agent should have differed so widely from us in regard to the extent of the examinations and surveys necessary to a decision under this article of the Treaty.' Porter did not actually say that a decision was no longer possible, and he may have deluded himself to some degree, but he clearly understood that the British were putting much more pressure on the Americans to broaden the exploration than he thought justified. The British – driven, Porter concluded, by public opinion – seemed determined to find a southern water route to the Lake of the Woods. 'Such a result appears to have been expected by the people of Canada if not by the British Government.'[45] As a result, the surveyors would be heading west again in April for another full season of work.

Although the British had got their way on the question of expanding the survey, all was not perfect for them either. The American and British surveyors had attempted to determine the northwesternmost point of the Lake of the Woods the previous summer. The tentative location was near Rat Portage, which was at the beginning of the Winnipeg River. This was the canoe route to Lake Winnipeg and the Red River settlement, and it was vital for communications with eastern Canada. Because of a large landmass or peninsula on the east side of the Lake of the Woods, a line drawn south from Rat Portage to the forty-ninth parallel would cross this peninsula. Canoe and boat traffic between Rainy River and the Red River settlement would thus have to pass through American waters and wouldbe subject to tariff duties and American regulation. This turn of events was regarded as calamitous by the British, and it was the cause of considerable anxiety in the highest circles in Britain during the next several years.[46]

David Thompson headed out from Williamstown in early May 1824, up the Ottawa River and across Lake Nipissing, following the old voyageur route along the French River into Georgian Bay. He entered Lake Superior by June 12 and travelled to Fort William, before returning to Pigeon River and the Grand Portage route to begin surveying on 1 July. The summer work covered those lakes and rivers from Lake Superior to the Lake of the Woods. By 11 July Thompson was working at Lac la Croix, by mid-month he was on the Rainy River, and by the end of the month he was in the Lake of the Woods, exploring the western side from Buffalo Bay to determine the position of the forty-ninth parallel. For a week and a half, to that end, he made astronomical sightings. He set in place small monuments of stone cairns or wooden stakes at each major sighting. He saw no need to return again to Rat Portage. By 4 August he was heading east up the Rainy River, completing surveying work along the canoe route, and exactly a month later he returned to Lake Superior.[47] The American surveyors worked west of Lake Superior along the Arrow River, the north side of 'Hunter Island,' and as far west as Namakan Lake. They then returned to Sault Ste Marie, where they did further surveys of St Mary's River around St George's Island.[48] Both the British and the Americans returned to Montreal by the old voyageur route up the French River to Lake Nipissing and down the Ottawa River, arriving in late October.

All this traffic along the fur trade routes was cause for alarm among at least some traders. Simon McGillivray, for some years the factor at the Hudson's Bay Company post at Rainy Lake, simply mentioned in his annual reports the passage of the American survey crews or such figures as Major Stephen H. Long in 1823. The new factor, John Duncan Cameron, saw the U.S. parties as a threat, however. 'The Americans are endeavouring to get possession of all our hunting grounds,' he wrote in his 1824–5 report. In fact, as a result of David Thompson's claim for the St Louis River route, the Americans had shifted their claim from the old Pigeon River trail to that of the new Kamanistiquia River route. If 'Jonathan' – the Americans – should succeed in this claim, Cameron complained, the Hudson's Bay Company would have to abandon 'the whole [Rainy River] department' because it would not be 'worthwhile' maintaining a post with so limited a territory.[49] This was perhaps an unforeseen consequence of the British push to Fond du Lac in the south.

The board of commissioners met in Montreal in October 1824 in what must have been strained, if not heated, circumstances. Delafield presented a memorial in which he urged the commissioners to decide then and there the point on Lake Superior from which the boundary line would proceed west towards the Lake of the Woods. The British agent, John Hale, requested the complete survey of the water route from Fond du Lac to the Lake of the Woods (or at least to the Vermillion River, which was known from Crane Lake on the Grand Portage route).[50]

These two proposals represented a substantial area of disagreement. Even the British commissioner, reporting on the board's meeting to the foreign secretary, said that only fifteen miles of river at the Sault and Caribou Island in Lake Superior needed to be surveyed to complete the section from Lake Huron through Lake Superior. However, 'in addition to the several communications already surveyed between Lake Superior and Lake of the Woods, it should be deemed expedient to examine another not yet explored, as constituting more probably the true course of the Boundary in consequence (besides other reasons) of its being the most practicable, easy, and expeditious route to the interior.' This was the Fond du Lac–St Louis River route, and Barclay, over the objections of General Porter, insisted on its exploration as a 'necessary preliminary to my consenting to confer with him respecting the final decision of the line.'[51] Barclay assured Canning that he fully expected completion of all remaining surveying work during the summer of 1825 and a decision in the autumn.

This turn of events dismayed the Americans. Largely because they felt that the Pigeon River–Grand Portage route was so clearly what the treaty of 1783 had intended and because they thought it so easily discernible on Mitchell's map, even without a boundary marked, they believed that serious efforts to consider alternatives were an expensive waste of time. General Porter explained to Secretary of State Adams that he and the American agent had been of the opinion that the boundary line could have been decided at this meeting of the board but that the British commissioner had insisted on a survey of the St Louis River region. In the end, Porter had to agree or 'break up the commission without effecting the objects of the two Governments in instituting it.'[52] His price for agreement, however, was a clear understanding that the commission would finish its work at the meeting the next year. Major Delafield echoed Porter's statements but insisted that the exploration of the St Louis River follow the completion of the other remaining work at the Sault and on Lake Superior. As for the southern St Louis River route, he said that the British agent had not actually made a claim for it, but he concluded that British insistence on exploration of the area 'renders it probable that he may eventually do so.'[53] Delafield said that if such were the case, he would claim the northern Kamanistiquia River–Fort William route, but he was so confident that the logic of the Pigeon River route would prevail that such a counter-claim did not seem essential.

While events were unfolding at the board meeting in Montreal in October 1824, Britain was trying to secure its interests at the Lake of the Woods. The Colonial Office had asked Nicholas Garry, deputy governor of the Hudson's Bay Company, about the consequences of a boundary line that extended to Rat Portage on the lake. The Hudson's Bay Company and the North West Company had merged in 1821, so the powerful London-based firm now had an interest in safe water passage to and from eastern Canada. During his trip through Lake of the Woods in 1821, Garry had noted in his diary, 'It is from this Portage that the Line which was to divide the United States from British Possessions was to run.' By 1824, however, he believed that Britain must retain control of the water communications on the Lake of the Woods so as not to jeopardize contact between the Red River settlement and the rest of British North America. U.S. tariffs and regulations would also injure the economic base of the colony. He urged that American territory near Rat Portage 'ought not, under any circumstances, be admitted to by His Majesty's Government,' and he further advised that, whatever the boundary might be, the natural water channels be left free to all traffic.[54]

Garry's letter and others were conveyed to Commissioner Barclay by Joseph Planta, undersecretary at the Foreign Office, together with the proposal that the Lake of the Woods be resurveyed, possibly privately, in the hope of a more favourable result.[55] Henry Rolleston, a senior clerk in the Foreign Office, wrote to Barclay within a few days of Planta, to say that he had talked with Dr Tiarks, who had suggested how to recalculate the northwesternmost point of the Lake of the Woods: 'On applying this principle to the Chart which you enclosed in your Dispatch of 10 March ... you will not fail to observe that the Rat Portage is, in a trifling degree, a more N.W. point than the spot pointed out by you. The difference, however, is so trifling, that Dr. Tiarks thinks it very probable a survey made for the express purpose, might produce a different result.'[56] In short, a deliberate effort could be made to produce a favourable boundary in the Lake of the Woods. No wonder that Rolleston warned Barclay to keep 'this communication as private and confidential.'

The British government clearly regarded this whole question with increasing concern. In early February 1825, Planta wrote again to Barclay telling him that by the foreign secretary's 'direction' he was not to reach a decision with the American commissioner about the boundary 'until after you shall have communicated to this Department the result of the survey directed by my letter of 11th December to be privately made, with the view of more accurately determining, on scientific principles, the most North Western point of the Lake of the Woods.'[57] These plans were quite agreeable to Barclay, who had already written to Planta that he would have David Thompson resurvey the area, although it might prolong the commission's work by two years. Indeed, Barclay anticipated the Foreign Office's eventual decision to send Tiarks out to do the job himself when he urged that if it did so Tiarks should not attempt to disguise his mission. 'It will be impossible to conceal his visit; the Americans are notoriously inquisitive, not without reason,' he candidly warned.[58] Barclay anticipated correctly. On 2 April 1825, Foreign

Secretary Canning ordered Tiarks to sail immediately for New York to put himself in touch with Barclay and to proceed west to 'assist in determining, upon scientific principles, the most North Western point of the Lake of the Woods.'[59]

Tiarks arrived in New York on 12 May and left with Barclay for Lake Superior and the west three days later.[60] Thompson himself had left Montreal in late April and proceeded west by way of the Ottawa River route in order to do some further surveys in the St. Mary's River before Barclay and his entourage arrived at the Sault. Once at Fort William, however, Thompson was struck with dysentery and forced to return to the Sault. Thompson's son Samuel, the assistant surveyor, took a small party southwest to Fond du Lac to explore and map the St Louis River route north to the Vermillion River and its connection with Crane Lake and Rainy Lake.[61] Tiarks and Barclay reached the Lake of the Woods by 24 July. Tiarks examined the sites of previous astronomical observations identified by David Thompson, where he took new sightings to determine more precisely the position of the western bays and inlets of the lake. The most promising exploration was along a finger of water (now called Angle Inlet) that ran west and north of the site where the La Vérendryes had built a fur trade post, Fort St Charles, in the 1730s. There Tiarks got the results that he wanted and pushed the lake's northwesternmost point well west of the route from Rainy River to Rat Portage. Barclay, Tiarks, and Samuel Thompson and their parties returned to the Sault by 4 September. Barclay and Tiarks left for Montreal and New York, while the Thompsons remained to complete the last of the work and auction off the equipment, returning home in late October to prepare the final reports and maps.[62]

On his return to New York in October 1825, Barclay wrote immediately to the Foreign Office to say that, although all the calculations had not yet been completed, Tiarks had assured him that the new site 'unquestionably corresponds with the interests which His Majesty's Government is desirous of preserving in these parts; although the difference in our favour is very minute, being but less than a fraction of a mile.'[63] Tiarks completed his formal report to the commissioners and sent a notarized copy to the secretary, Donald Fraser, on 18 November 1825.[64] Barclay had earlier made provision for evidence to be presented to the board that would allow Tiarks to make a report on his findings, after which he would be able to return to England. Tiarks himself wrote to Planta in January 1826 to assure him that the new positioning would place the boundary line where it would 'in no wise interfere with the route of the Hudson's Bay Co. through the lake.'[65] When Tiarks returned to Britain, Henry Rolleston wrote to Barclay that it was 'very satisfactory to find that it [the results of the survey] has been such as was anticipated.'[66]

Commenting on all these developments to U.S. Secretary of State Henry Clay, General Porter seemed unaware of what had actually happened. Still preoccupied with the possible British claim to the St Louis River route west, he told Clay that both Barclay and Tiarks had been exploring this route during the summer. Moreover, after talking to both of them he added: 'I apprehend no serious difficulty in our amicable adjustment of the boundary at our next meeting.'[67]

The board of commissioners met in Albany, New York, in early November 1825. The maps and astronomical calculations were by no means ready for presentation, and neither the British agent nor the British surveyor was able to attend, so the meeting was adjourned until the following May.[68] However, discussions between the two commissioners gave them both some indication of the prospects for a satisfactory decision. General Porter was still hopeful about an 'amicable adjustment,' but he was clearly worried about Barclay's determination to make a spurious claim to the St Louis River route.[69] Barclay had already identified the three areas of likely disagreement in a letter to the foreign secretary. The northwesternmost corner of the Lake of the Woods was a possible problem, but Barclay asserted that 'it can scarcely be conceived that they will attempt to overthrow the testimony of Dr. Tiarks.' The water communication from Lake Superior to the Lake of the Woods was a matter over which Barclay that expected 'there will probably arise much difficulty.' Finally, the three Neebish channels at the southern end of the St Mary's River at the Sault presented a disagreement with serious implications.[70]

For its part the British government was anxious that the northwesternmost point of the Lake of the Woods, having now been identified to its satisfaction, be agreed on and marked without regard to the fate of the overall decision of the commission. London instructed Barclay to invite the American commissioner to make a joint statement to authorize its immediate marking. If Porter were to insist on Rat Portage, Barclay was to protest and report to the British government for further instructions.[71] Barclay wrote to Porter suggesting that a marker be placed, but Porter replied that he did not feel authorized to take such action under the terms of his commission. However, he would consult with Secretary of State Clay.

As the summer of 1826 wore on, the British clearly became increasingly uncomfortable about the American silence. The Foreign Office seemed willing to ignore the question of locating the forty-ninth parallel if that were the problem, in order to obtain agreement on the marker at the Lake of the Woods.[72] Not until late September did Clay get around to seeking President John Quincy Adams's views on the question. Clay's first inclination was to let this matter be determined by the overall decision of the commission, but he nevertheless proposed it to the president. Adams in turn gave his agreement that the northwesternmost point of the Lake of the Woods be determined and marked and that a line be extended to the forty-ninth parallel, in conformity with the Convention of 1818. The president agreed 'from the considerations that much harmony has hitherto happily prevailed between Mr. Barclay and yourself, in the discharge of your arduous duties.'[73] Barclay reported to the Foreign Office on 27 October that a 'decision' had been reached at the point identified by Tiarks and that this had been entered into the journal of the commission, but not signed.[74]

The board had not met in May 1826 as planned. First, Thompson announced that he would need much longer to complete the maps of the region, and then the British agent, John Hale, said that he would be unable to leave his dying wife. The meeting was moved back to late June and then deferred until 21 September.[75] In the meantime, the Foreign Office advised Barclay on the Neebish Channel in the St Mary's River. Canning was insistent that – in parallel with the decision about Barnhart's Island in the St Lawrence, taken in 1822 by the commission under article 6 – Britain should receive St George's Island (Sugar Island) and the East Neebish Channel. He urged Barclay to stand firm on this matter, although he suggested that he would agree to allow the Americans use of the Eastern Neebish Channel in exchange for British use of the south channel around Barnhart's Island.[76]

When the board did convene in New York on 4 October 1826, the astronomers and surveyors submitted their maps (David Thompson himself had completed four sets of eighteen maps), and the agents presented their claims and arguments. John Hale, the British agent, argued for the Middle Neebish Channel in the St. Mary's River, for the St Louis River–Fond du Lac route from Lake Superior to the Lake of the Woods, and the site that Tiarks had identified as the northwesternmost point of the Lake of the Woods. He objected to the introduction of historical maps as evidence in the arguments of the Americans. Major Joseph Delafield, the American agent, claimed the Eastern Neebish Channel

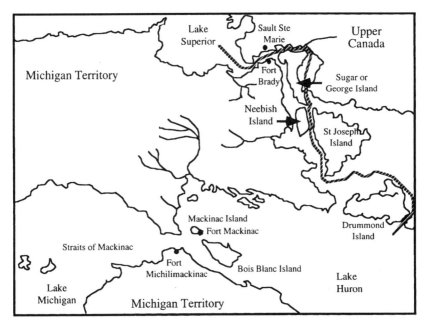

Map 11. Sault Ste Marie: final boundary

and St George's Island in the St. Mary's River, the Kamanistiquia River–Fort William route from Lake Superior to the Lake of the Woods, and Rat Portage as the northwesternmost corner of the Lake of the Woods. He objected to the introduction of letters from fur traders, such as William McGillivray, and scientific data, such as Tiarks's report and maps by Lieutenant Henry W. Bayfield, RN, because that material had not been produced under the oaths required of all persons working for the commission.[77]

The commissioners then deliberated for almost three weeks, attempting to reach an agreement on the three major issues. When the arguments between the two men had crystallized, but before their discussions had reached a conclusion, Porter wrote to the secretary of state. The circumstances of a likely disagreement were as 'unexpected as it is unpleasant,' he said, and he suspected that Barclay was acting 'under specific instructions from his government,' which had been influenced by British fur trade interests. Porter further surmised that when the commissioners actually came down to drafting their final joint report Barclay would either agree with the American arguments or he would request a postponement of a decision, as he had in the case of the decision of the commission under article 6 in 1822, in order to consult with his government in London. This procedure would allow Barclay 'to obtain from them in the name of *friendly cessions,* what he professes that his own judgement will not permit him to yield as a *right.*' Although Porter was reluctant to prolong the life of the commission for the several months that this process would take, he was convinced, he said, that once officials in London compared the arguments of the two agents they would 'instruct him [Barclay] to agree, substantially if not *in toto,* to the boundary I have assumed.'[78] Delafield also signed the letter, associating himself with Porter's views.

Events unfolded as Porter had anticipated, and he wrote to Clay informing him. Barclay reported the same circumstances to the Foreign Office on 28 October 1826. He pointed out that the commissioners had agreed on the boundary from the upper St Mary's River across Lake Superior to Isle Royal, and they agreed on the line from Rainy Lake to the northwesternmost corner of the Lake of the Woods (with Porter accepting Tiarks's identification, over Delafield's objections), but they disagreed on the Neebish Channel in the lower St Mary's River and on the boundary from Lake Superior to Rainy Lake. They had rejected the compromise that the foreign secretary had authorized in February – that the Americans be allowed to use the East Neebish Channel in exchange for British use of the channel south of Barnhart's Island in the St Lawrence. Similarly, although Porter had been prepared to abandon the Kamanistiquia route for the Pigeon River route, he would not agree to running the boundary for eight miles along the old land trail south of the Pigeon River at Grand Portage.

Barclay hoped that negotiations directly between the new British minister, Charles Vaughan, and the U.S. State Department might lead to a settlement on the Neebish Channel, but he asked if the Foreign Office would be willing to see the commission break down over the old eight-mile portage south of the Pigeon River. The fur companies had not used Pigeon River for over twenty years and had a perfectly good route from Fort William through the Kamanistiquia River and Dog Lake. Were the question to go to an arbitrator, Barclay thought it most probable that the two claims for the St Louis River and the Kamanistiquia River would be rejected in favour of the Pigeon River. However, 'as natural Boundaries are preferred on account of their certainty, I should apprehend that the Question of Portages might be decided against us on that ground.'[79] Should he terminate the commission on the basis of this minor advantage, which was almost certain to be lost in an arbitration anyway?

The initiatives taken through the British minister in Washington did not succeed. The Secretary of State wrote to Charles Vaughan on 15 November 1826 explaining in detail the merits of the American claim to St George's Island and the East Neebish Channel and pointing out that neither Commissioner Porter, under the terms of the Treaty of Ghent, nor the president, under the U.S. constitution, had the authority to negotiate the exchange of freedom of passage through the East Neebish Channel for that south of Barnhart's Island. This would require a separately negotiated treaty. Vaughan informed both Canning and Barclay that this initiative had failed.[80] President Adams, in his annual message to Congress in December, made a pessimistic reference to the commission: 'Nor can we renounce the expectation, enfeebled as it is, that they may agree upon their report to the satisfaction or acquiescence of both parties.'[81]

Hopes for compromise on the eight-mile Grand Portage at Pigeon River faltered as well. Porter was informed by Henry Clay that, as with the Neebish Channel, there could be no special concessions to allow British subjects free use of the trails on the U.S. side of the border under the authority of the Treaty of Ghent. This conclusion was not communicated to Barclay until 20 April 1827 – an added irritation to both him and the Foreign Office.[82] However, in the meantime, Barclay was waiting for a satisfactory reply from London for instructions as to whether to compromise with the Americans or break off the work of the commission. In January 1827 the undersecretary advised Barclay that if the compromise that the commissioner had earlier alluded to was not achieved, he should 'close your Commission' in order 'to have recourse to the ultimate mode of settlement prescribed by the Treaty of Ghent, namely, reference to a Third Power.'[83] This advice did not address the question that Barclay had posed.

Meanwhile the British government was in a state of crisis. On 17 February 1827 the prime minister, Lord Liverpool, had a paralytic stroke, and it was unclear for some weeks whether he would recover sufficiently to carry on as head of the government. The foreign secretary, George Canning, in declining health himself, was a leading candidate to replace Liverpool, and on 12 April he was asked to form a government. This he did, splitting the Tory party in the process. Lord Dudley was made foreign secretary, but Canning attempted to continue to control foreign affairs. The strain of all this was too great, and Canning himself died on 8 August 1827, giving rise to the short-lived cabinet of Lord Goderich, which gave way in turn in January 1828 to a more stable government headed by the Duke of Wellington.[84] What role North American affairs may have played during these months is difficult to assess. The vague and cautious instructions that Barclay received in 1827 are certainly a reflection of an unwillingness by anyone to take a bold step in dealing with the boundary question, as Lord Castlereagh had done in 1822 in similar circumstances.

Barclay wrote again in April 1827 to the Foreign Office in language similar to that which he had addressed to Castlereagh in 1822. He outlined the areas in agreement as well as the issues in contention. Although he stood by the right to claim St George's Island in all justice, he pointed out that he did not regard it as intrinsically valuable. 'I am not aware, however, that in any other light St. George's Island is worthy of contention,' he wrote, 'except as so much soil, which is not scarce in these regions.'[85] As for the portage place at the Pigeon River, the merits of this concession, as a favour to the fur companies, hardly outweighed jeopardizing the settlement of the whole section of boundary, particularly with the current placement of the northwesternmost corner of the Lake of the Woods so favourable to British interests. Barclay asked for Canning's views as to whether he should concede these two controversial bits of territory or close the commission.

The Foreign Office responded on 5 July, informing Barclay that in view of the Americans' unwillingness to accept either of the compromise solutions proposed for the Neebish Channel and the Grand Portage, there was no need for Lord Dudley, the foreign secretary, to send any fresh instructions. 'It therefore only remains for you agreeably to [follow] instructions you have already received, to close your Commission with as little delay as possible, & to make your Report in the manner provided by Treaty, on the points of disagreement.'[86]

Was Prime Minister Canning uncompromising as a matter of principle? Were the boundary questions pushed to one side during the British political turmoil of the summer of 1827? Or did the Foreign Office, contrary to Barclay's tentative suggestion, hold the Neebish Channel and the obsolete canoe route at Grand Portage to be too valuable to be left to the Americans? The records give no indication, but Commissioner Barclay was allowed no choice in the matter.

This meant the termination of the proceedings, and Porter and Delafield were informed that Barclay would be able to join them for a meeting of the board of commissioners in October 1827.[87] It also meant the end of the projected attempt to mark the northwesternmost corner of the Lake of the Woods with a proposed monument (although a small stone cairn had been left there by the surveyors in 1825) and to survey the forty-ninth parallel from the Lake of the Woods to the Red River. The British had requested that this be done while the expertise of the survey crews was still available. In the long delay through the spring and summer of 1827 the crews, which had been held in readiness, were dismissed on orders from London.[88]

This result did not come altogether as a surprise to the Americans. Porter had revealed to Secretary of State Clay in December 1826 his growing pessimism about a favourable decision. Delafield reported to Clay in early April 1827 that he had talked in New York to Colonel Thomas Barclay, through whom dispatches from the Foreign Office had been sent to his son, Anthony, and that 'it was Canning's wish to refer the subject to a friendly power.' Delafield said that it had not been Colonel Barclay's intention to say that the letters instructed his son to terminate the discussions, but that was Delafield's conclusion none the less.[89]

The board met in New York on 26 October 1827. Porter and Barclay agreed to submit separate reports, exchange maps, discharge the remaining members of their staff, and terminate the commission. They met again on 24 December to settle their financial accounts and exchange copies of their final reports.[90] Delafield was outraged over the British report, only one copy of which had been delivered before Barclay left New York for Savannah. He wrote to Porter that the document embodied 'as much disingenuousness, craftiness, false extraction, and bold assertion, as I can ever remember to have read.' Not only did he complain that the report included maps by Thompson that had never been submitted to the board, but he also questioned whether Thompson had drawn fresh maps to justify the British claim. Delafield, very angry about the matter, felt that he or Porter, or both, should write a further report refuting the arguments of the British report.[91]

In effect over a year had been wasted. The last surveying work had been completed in 1825. Much of 1826 had been spent completing the maps. Most of 1827 had been spent waiting for a specific reply from the Foreign Office about the Neebish Channel and the Grand Portage. In the absence of new instructions, the decision to terminate could just as well have been made the previous year. The effort to get a decision had been worthwhile, but in the end it failed. Although the surveying and the map work of the commission were of great value, the search for the

boundary from Lake Huron to the Lake of the Woods remained unresolved.[92]

The boundary question languished for over ten years. In late July 1839
U.S. Secretary of State John Forsyth proposed to the British minister in
Washington, Henry S. Fox, that a convention be negotiated to make
arrangements for a friendly sovereign to arbitrate the boundary dispute
in the western region, as provided for in the Treaty of Ghent. Fox wrote
to Lord Palmerston, then foreign secretary, that the American government anticipated that Wisconsin would become a state within a few
years and hoped to settle the border before representatives from the
new state entered Congress as interested parties, complicating the
whole question, as representatives from Maine had done for the northeastern boundary after 1820. The British government never responded
to this initiative.[93]

PART TWO

Arbitration and Uncertainty:
The 1820s and 1830s

Chapter Seven

Preparing for Arbitration

Even before surveying work started in 1822 on the region from Lake Superior to the Lake of the Woods under article 7 of the Treaty of Ghent, efforts resumed to deal with the failure of the commission under article 5 – the northeastern boundary. By 1822 no Anglo–American boundary commission had failed to produce a reasonably satisfactory result, and indeed the arbitral process, had worked well in the past in settling joint problems with political dimensions. So there was room for hope that the whole of the boundary in eastern North America would be amicably decided by this process. The difficulties that emerged on the New Brunswick–Quebec–Maine boundary, however, presented serious problems, and the unwelcome news of the earlier errors in the Quebec–New York boundary only escalated the crisis for the Americans and emphasized the increasingly unbridgeable gap between the two main parties. Preparation for arbitration of these problems by a single arbitrator would finally begin late in the decade.

While spokesmen for both governments had voiced their misgivings about arbitration, this was the method provided by the Treaty of Ghent to resolve matters, in the event that commissions failed to reach a decision. Secretary of State John Quincy Adams noted in his diary in late 1821 a letter from Christopher Hughes, an American diplomat in Europe, stating that Henry Goulburn had made a disparaging remark about the arbitration of War of 1812 claims only recently concluded by the tsar of Russia. Adams commented that it would be unlikely that any European sovereign could be expected to master the voluminous material accumulated in regard to the boundary question.[1] Questioning whether a foreigner would be better able to sort out the many facets of this complex controversy than the two commissioners, Adams had on 29 October 1822, proposed to the British minister in Washington, Stratford Canning, an attempt at a compromise, which would grant Britain the security of a military road linking Quebec and New Brunswick and satisfy American needs and aspirations. 'I then asked him whether it was probable we could negotiate for a successful adjustment of that line. Why, what were we disposed to do? "Then," said I, "you want a road between your two provinces, do you not?" "Yes." "Well," said I, "we will treat on this basis. You shall have the road, and give us an equivalent accommodation in territory."'[2]

As reasonable as that sounded, the British were wary. Commissioner Thomas Barclay had pointed out the extreme difficulty of ratifying a genuine compromise treaty in the U.S. Senate, where the senators from states asked to make compromises were expected to give their support. Increasingly others shared this view.[3] Adams too had some second thoughts. By the summer of 1822 he had concluded that the British had placed so many conditions on any talks as to render a settlement unlikely. Adams's biographer, Samuel Flagg Bemis, also surmised that Adams understood that any compromise in which territory claimed by a state was given up would so raise the issue of states' rights as to ruin his chances for the presidency in 1824.[4] Adams's leadership seemed to falter. He continued to press Richard Rush in London with long instructions that pointed out the advantages of a negotiated boundary line, but he did not give any indication of what that line might have been.[5]

When talks finally opened in London in 1824, a number of questions were linked together. Rush was instructed to obtain American use of the St Lawrence River. This the British, through William Huskisson and Stratford Canning, were prepared to allow, but in exchange for a compromise on the New Brunswick–Maine boundary that provided for an all-season road to Quebec. The foreign secretary, George Canning, was also prepared to make a concession on the old Collins–Valentine line of the forty-fifth parallel between Lower Canada and New York. Moreover, in his instructions to Huskisson and Stratford Canning, the foreign secretary said that British interests could be satisfied by 'a less Southern Line than the one required by our Commissioners' – something other than the line from Mars Hill to the Chaudière River – but he also pointed out that if that line were given up there was no alternative natural frontier before the St John River. 'It must, therefore, be the first object of your endeavors ... to obtain from the United States an acknowledgement of the line demanded by His Majesty's Commissioner,' after which it would be possible to make concessions on matters such as commercial use of the St Lawrence, the Collins–Valentine line, islands in the Detroit River, the Lake of the Woods, and the forty-ninth parallel.[6] Rush, however, was instructed not to link boundary matters in the same treaty as the navigation of the St Lawrence and trade issues. When asked to make a counter-proposal, Rush simply offered to move the talks to Washington. In the end, no negotiated settlement was reached, nor were the steps agreed on for arbitration by a friendly sovereign.[7]

John Quincy Adams was elected president in 1824, albeit in one of the most controversial elections in American history. He called Richard Rush back to the United States to become secretary of the treasury, and in the spring of 1825 sent to London Rufus King, who had previously served as minister to Britain under the president's father, John Adams. Well on in years, King had very uncertain health, and he arrived in England near collapse after a very difficult voyage. The thought that King might be sitting down with British officials to negotiate a compromise boundary was a great worry to some. Colonel Thomas Barclay in New York wrote to Ward Chipman, Jr, with whom he had worked so long on the boundary question: 'I hope too much may not be conceded to these States, still I am led to fear,' he confessed; 'I shall only add your late good father, you, and myself have done our duty; let those who have the matter charged do theirs.'[8] Others agreed. William Huskisson, in a memorandum written later in July 1826, argued that Britain should decline American offers to negotiate on the boundary because the British case was so strong that in a court of law, on the two main issues of the New Brunswick–Maine boundary and the forty-fifth parallel, 'the Verdict in neither case could for a moment be doubtful.' The key to the New Brunswick boundary was what the Treaty of Paris of 1783 meant by 'Atlantic Ocean.' 'It is upon this answer to this question that our claim to the disputed Territory appears to hinge,' he wrote. 'The right understanding of this point is therefore of paramount importance.'[9] Between his difficulties with health and with the foreign secretary, George Canning, King's mission was not a success. The two men had made no progress over the northeastern boundary when King left for New York, having requested to go home.[10]

In the circumstances the president turned in May 1826 to his nation's most experienced diplomat (other than Adams himself), Albert Gallatin, then U.S. minister to France, to lead a special mission to Britain to negotiate a resolution of the boundary and several other problems.[11] Gallatin was well known to the British. He had been Jefferson's brilliant secretary of the treasury and one of the negotiators of the Treaty of Ghent, and as the American minister to Paris and joint negotiator of the so-called Rush–Gallatin Convention with Britain in 1818 he had dealt with commerce, fisheries, and slaves seized in the War of 1812 and helped decide on the forty-ninth parallel as the boundary from the Lake of the Woods to the Rocky Mountains and joint occupancy of the Oregon territory. Surprisingly, perhaps, Gallatin as a young man and recent immigrant to the United States had in 1780 commanded militia troops on Passamaquoddy Bay during the Revolutionary War. More to the point, however, he, John Quincy Adams, and Henry Clay had also negotiated a commercial agreement with Britain in 1815 that was due to expire in 1826. Thus he was a logical person to renew this agreement and to deal with the boundary matters for both the northeast and Oregon as well.[12] Gallatin and his family arrived in London from the United States in August 1826 and settled at 62 Seymour Street. By 1 September he had presented his credentials to King George IV, but with members of the government away from London during the summer it was not until mid-September that correspondence opened about diplomatic questions, and not until mid-October that talks began.[13] Merely the thought that Gallatin would be holding talks about the boundary with the government was a source of grave concern for some. Henry Bliss, a London barrister, wrote to Ward Chipman, Jr, 'The negotiations which are now pending between Mr. Canning and the new American Minister, are the cause of much anxiety to us here, as they must be to all who live, or feel an interest in the Colonies, or even in the Empire, though people here will never be convinced of that.'[14]

Gallatin's first instructions from Secretary of State Henry Clay urged that he attempt a negotiated settlement on the northeast boundary, because there were 'great, if not insuperable difficulties which lie in the way of a settlement of the question in the mode [arbitration] stipulated in that Article [article 5 of the Treaty of Ghent].'[15] However, if the British insisted on arbitration, or if negotiations were unsuccessful, the United States must comply with the treaty's terms. However, just before sailing for England, Gallatin wrote to Clay that his instructions did not give him as much authority as he had expected, and he had specifically urged that talks on the northeastern boundary move to Washington. He suggested that he 'may be safely trusted' to carry out the negotiations himself, and he asked also for some flexibility in arranging for a possible reference to a friendly sovereign.[16] He also queried other matters such as the Oregon boundary, use of the St Lawrence, and trade.

Clay replied in August, amending his original instructions to allow Gallatin to pursue the negotiations and to use his own judgment up to a certain degree. However, as for the placement of the boundary, Clay said, the president was 'especially, not now, prepared to authorize any stipulations, involving a cession of territory belonging to any State in the Union,' nor should Gallatin abandon any claim to use of the St Lawrence or to territory south of the forty-ninth parallel in the west.[17]

If Gallatin could not abandon territory claimed by any state (Maine, Massachusetts, New Hampshire, Vermont, or New York), and if the British could not give up any claim north of the Mars Hill–Chaudière River watershed, there was no room for compromise or serious negotiations. Recognition of this situation did not crystallize until the late summer of 1827. Meanwhile, inconclusive talks began in early 1827. Gallatin found the report of British Agent Ward Chipman, Jr, on the northeastern boundary 'irksome' and that of Commissioner Thomas Barclay 'a tissue of unfounded assertions and glaring sophistry,' although he conceded that the British arguments about the Connecticut River and the forty-fifth parallel were strong.[18]

About the British negotiators, Gallatin was not pleased. They were Charles Grant, a member of Parliament and later first Baron Glenelg, and Henry Unwin Addington, a career diplomat and later permanent undersecretary at the Foreign Office. As for Addington, who had been British chargé d'affaires in Washington in 1823 and then minister to Frankfurt, Gallatin regarded him as 'extremely unmanageable, not from ignorance ... , but because he has imbibed all the prejudices and zeal of the British agents [both Chipman and Barclay, in this case] and provincial authorities on that question.'[19] The American diplomat lamented that Addington seemed to have no inclination to pursue the problem in a detached manner. Perhaps Addington and Grant had been supplied with copies of William Huskisson's long memorandum on the boundary question. In it Huskisson, a member of Parliament who had held numerous government offices, concluded that the Americans' desire to negotiate the northeastern boundary arose out of their recognition of the weakness of their claims. 'The extreme anxiety of the American Government to avoid a reference [arbitration]; the labored arguments which they have used against it; and the very language in which it is deprecated in Mr. Adams' Instructions to Mr. Rush (Instructions never intended for our Inspection) afford a strong presumption that they are conscious of the weakness of their case, if not the bad faith of their Agents upon the principal matters in dispute.'[20]

How Adams's 1826 instructions to Rush got into Huskisson's hands was never explained, but they certainly strengthened the general British belief that the American case was a fabrication and that an objective arbitration would support the British claim. British officials' suspicion about the fate of treaties in the U.S. Senate also persuaded them that arbitration by a friendly sovereign offered a more certain, as well as a more objective, route to a settlement. Thus they felt no urgency to pursue serious negotiations that might involve abandoning claims to specific territory. There was also another consideration. The British political circumstances that had delayed the proceedings of the article-7 commission were in play – Liverpool's stroke in February 1827, the difficulty until April of forming a new government under George Canning, and Canning's own death in August. Perhaps it was just not possible for British diplomats to make decisions in these conditions.

By the end of August Lord Goderich had formed a new government and the same Foreign Office negotiators were in place. Agreements were reached on the continued joint occupation of Oregon, renewal of the commercial convention of 1815, and settlement of the value of slaves taken by the British during the War of 1812 (the issue of liability having been already decided by the arbitration of the tsar of Russia), but the northeastern boundary proved more intractable.[21] On 1 September Grant and Addington reported to Lord Dudley, the foreign secretary, that Gallatin had abandoned any further hope of a negotiated settlement and was prepared to discuss the matter of an arbitration. When he heard later that the Americans had been disappointed at failure to reach a negotiated settlement, Dudley commented that where 'a large mass of territory is claimed by each party with equal tenacity, and what each on his own side considers perfect validity of pretension, negotiations can be undertaken on one principle alone, namely, that of strictly equal concession on both sides.'[22] This was true enough and a shrewd insight, but as Dudley himself noted, this was a difficult position for the Americans to admit.

For most of September 1827 talks went on about how to structure the arbitration. Both Gallatin and President Adams had earlier agreed that the boundary issue had become so complex, and the documents, surveys, and maps produced by the commission so voluminous and contradictory, that no reigning monarch could be expected to deal conscientiously with the matter as a single arbitrator or umpire and still look after domestic duties. Gallatin had raised many of these questions some months earlier in his correspondence with Secretary of State Clay. Even Huskisson, the previous year, had agreed that the question had to be made 'intelligible' before it could be submitted for arbitration.[23] How to simplify this voluminous material? Rather than merely submitting all the material generated by the commission together with the two separate reports of the commissioners, it was decided that each side would draft new briefs, but through a specific process. Within nine months of the ratification of the convention under negotiation, any new evidence on the boundary question acquired since the termination of the commission in 1822 could be exchanged by the two parties. Within fifteen months, the British and American governments would exchange copies of formal first statements. Within twenty-one months, they would exchange replies to the first statements, or definitive statements. Finally, after being checked, the many documents and statements would be presented to the arbitrator. Because of the complicated map problem – no map of the disputed region had been agreed on as being accurate and objective – each side would submit a copy of Mitchell's map (copies of which, it was agreed, had been used by the negotiators in 1782 and 1783), with a line marking what it believed to be the intended boundary.

These provisions, it was hoped, would provide for the arbitrator a manageable problem that could be objectively decided. The arbitrator was to be chosen by mutual agreement after exchange of the ratifications, and it was presumed that he would reach a decision within two years. The arbitrator was also empowered to request specific information if he required it, including the ordering of a new survey of the region in dispute. Although the convention repeated several times that the arbitrator's decision would be 'final and conclusive,' it did not attempt to direct him as to how to proceed to a decision. His only instruction lay in the first article, which invited him to 'investigate and make a decision upon the Points of Difference.'[24] This proved to be a major oversight by the diplomats.

On 29 September Gallatin, Grant, and Addington signed the agreement which became known as the Convention of 1827. Gallatin and his wife and daughter were able to leave England for New York on 8 October.[25] President Adams submitted the three conventions (on trade, Oregon, and arbitration of the northeastern boundary) to the Senate on 11 December, and it approved the arbitration convention in March by a vote of thirty-five to four. The ratifications were exchanged in London on 2 April 1828, setting the arbitral process in motion and requiring, first of all, quick selection of a friendly sovereign.

Gallatin was not sanguine about the outcome of an arbitration. As early as 1826 he had attempted to warn the secretary of state: 'An Umpire, whether he be a King or a Farmer, rarely decides on strict principles of law: he has always a bias to try if possible to split the difference: and, with that bias, he is very apt to consider any previous proposal from either party as a concession that his title was defective, and as justifying a decision on his part that will not displease too much either party, instead of one founded on a strict investigation of the title.'[26] Clay included this statement in correspondence sent to the governor of Maine for information in March 1827. Governor Enoch Lincoln replied on 18 April that Maine and Massachusetts had 'a perfect title' to the lands in dispute and that federal agents had no authority 'to propose any compromise as to [Maine's] boundary.' It was the duty of the federal government to protect Maine's territory, he said. Lincoln sent a similar complaint to Clay in September, and in late October, after signing the convention setting up the arbitration process, Lincoln protested vigorously that Maine's territorial integrity was to be 'subjected to the mercy of a foreign individual' who was likely to 'split the difference,' as Gallatin had warned. 'I cannot but yield to the impulse of saying, most respectfully, that Maine has not been treated as she has endeavored to deserve,' he concluded. This correspondence became public when it was quoted in a report by the state legislature in 1828, and the groundwork was laid for Maine's protest against any award by the arbitration process.[27]

The question of an appropriate arbitrator had vexed the minds of responsible figures since it became apparent that a decision by the commissioners was unlikely. The Americans, particularly Adams, favoured the tsar of Russia, first Alexander, and later Nicholas, although Gallatin had also been instructed in 1826 to propose the president of the republic of Colombia, the king of Prussia, the king of France, the king of Württemberg, or the duke of Saxe Weimar.[28] A year and a half later, on 20 February 1828, William B. Lawrence, American chargé in London, was told to propose the tsar, the king of Denmark, or the king of the Netherlands.[29] Lawrence attempted to sound out opinion in the diplomatic community in London. He learned that it was presumed 'improbable' that the British would agree to the Russian emperor and assumed that the king of the Netherlands, William I, would be unacceptable to the United States. Prince Christoph von Lieven, the Russian ambassador, confided to Lawrence that although the king of the Netherlands was of the highest 'personal character and upright views,' it was a fact that 'after Portugal no one was more likely to be influenced by her [Britain]' than the king of the Netherlands.[30]

Nevertheless, on 17 May the secretary of state wrote to Lawrence that President Adams had 'weighed all the considerations you have suggested respecting the King of the Netherlands' and had concluded that 'they did not seem to him to overrule the confidence he has in the intelligence and personal character of that Monarch.'[31] The British objected to the tsar, in part because of Russian policy towards Turkey. As early as 1823 George Canning had suggested to his cousin Stratford, then minister to the United States, that the American government be sounded out on its willingness to accept King William.[32] While Lawrence was discussing the selection in June with Lord Dudley, the foreign secretary was replaced by Lord Aberdeen, who proposed the emperor of Austria and the king of Sardinia. After a complicated process of balloting on a list of candidates, Lawrence and Aberdeen agreed on William I, king of the Netherlands. Notes to that effect were exchanged on 17 and 18 June 1828.[33]

A minor incident occurred when news of the selection leaked before completion of arrangements for a joint invitation. Chargé Lawrence was blamed, but King William was approached privately by Sir Charles Bagot, by then British ambassador to the Netherlands, and told of the situation. The king had indeed been informed of his selection by the American chargé at The Hague, Christopher Hughes, but he had regarded this as an 'informal notice.' Bagot reported that the king 'assured me that, however disagreeable he might consider jobs of this sort to be in themselves, from the impossibility of satisfying both Parties, he felt greatly flattered at having been selected by the two countries as a Referee in such a matter,' and he took no offence at the official silence surrounding the selection.[34] Bagot and Hughes presented the joint invitations to King William on 21 January 1829, the king responding in a very friendly manner and promising an official reply in a few days.[35]

The exchange of ratifications and the selection of a friendly sovereign as arbitrator set in motion the procedures to assemble the materials and to marshal the arguments on the basis of which the arbitrator was to make his decision. The Americans started early. Secretary of State Henry Clay asked Albert Gallatin, who had given up his post in London when he returned to the United States the previous autumn, to assist in the preparation of the American statements. 'Your familiarity with the subject, and the confidence reposed by the President in you,' wrote Clay, who felt that his own duties precluded his looking after the matter, 'render it desirable to engage your services to assist in making them.'[36] Gallatin willingly agreed, and he responded confidently that 'I have a perfect conviction that the right boundary of the state of Maine, as claimed by the United States, is in strict conformity with the letter of the treaty of 1783 and with the intention of the parties.'[37] Gallatin began immediately collecting maps and documents to support the American claim.

Clay suggested in early March that a second person would be appointed to assist Gallatin, particularly in travelling to New Brunswick and Lower Canada searching for documents that might buttress the American argument, but it was not until mid-May that William Pitt Preble of Maine was appointed to carry out that role. This was a gesture intended to win the State's support and confidence for the arbitration process. Preble had studied at Harvard and practised law from 1811; he helped with the founding of the state of Maine in 1820 and was appointed to its Supreme Court. This opportunity of working with Gallatin marked the beginning of Preble's fourteen-year involvement with the boundary question, during which time he was a passionate defender of Maine's interests. While the appointment seemed prudent, Preble's personality and his fierce advocacy of Maine's largest claims became a serious problem. The historian Robert V. Remini described Preble as 'an incompetent, vain, abrasive hot head, and a self-righteous prig.' It was certainly an appointment that would have echoes for years. Preble received letters of introduction from the British minister to Sir Howard Douglas, lieutenant-governor of New Brunswick, to look for material among the government papers in Fredericton.[38] Preble was to search for documents that showed that British occupation of lands claimed by the United States did not antedate 1783. It was to no avail. Douglas, advised by Chipman and William F. Odell, former British surveyor for the commission and then provincial secretary, did not allow Preble and his assistant to make a blanket search.[39] Preble abandoned a planned trip to Lower Canada, but for reasons of time. On 3 June 1828 he requested copies of specific documents from the British government, which after some delay the British agreed to supply, but in the end it was in Boston, New York, Philadelphia, and Washington that Gallatin and Preble found the documents that they would join with those accumulated by the commission.[40] By 30 December 1828 the two had assembled and made multiple copies of all the new evidence that they intended to exchange, and they then began work on the first statement while waiting for the new British documents.[41]

In American domestic politics 1828 saw the fiercely contested presidential election in which Andrew Jackson defeated John Quincy Adams, who was running for his second term. Jackson rewarded many of his supporters with key diplomatic positions, so Louis McLane replaced James Barbour as American minister in London, and Martin Van Buren succeeded Henry Clay as secretary of state. Before Van Buren took office in the spring of 1829, James A. Hamilton served as acting secretary of state. On 5 March, the day after Jackson's inauguration, Henry Clay visited Hamilton to explain some of the details of the international situation, including the current proceedings concerning the arbitration. Clay pointed out that the selection of the king of the Netherlands had never been submitted to the U.S. Senate for approval, although the Convention of 1827 had been. Clay attempted to explain the delicacy of the situation but left it to the Jackson administration to decide whether to formalize this decision in a convention and submit it to the Senate or simply accept it as things stood. Hamilton reported all of this to Jackson on 9 March, noting that King William was the 'sovereign who was [the] least desirable to this Government to be the arbitrator.'[42]

The new administration made no change in the status of the proceedings and retained Gallatin and Preble to complete American preparations. Jackson appointed Preble American minister to The Hague in November 1829, to replace the chargé, Christopher Hughes, who went to Stockholm; he wanted in place a representative who was expert on the northeastern boundary.[43] With the accumulation of documents, Gallatin began drafting the first statement of the American argument. It is uncertain how much Preble contributed to that document, but clearly he worked with Gallatin in Washington at least periodically during 1829. By 2 July, copies were delivered to the British minister in Washington, and the British first statement went to the American minister in London. The second, or definitive U.S. statement, was delivered on 30 December 1829.[44]

The British were slower than the Americans in gathering the people who were to prepare their arguments for the arbitrator. This may have stemmed from their confidence in the strength of their case and from the fact that they held substantial sections of the disputed territory. Henry Unwin Addington, who was to become the principal author of the British first statement, wrote to Lord Aberdeen on 3 April 1828, submitting his draft of the statement. The issue was of such great importance, he said, that the 'preservation of the Province of New Brunswick' hinged on the outcome.[45] To John Backhouse, undersecretary at the Foreign Office, Addington confided the following week, 'We certainly have the advantage over the Americans of a *de facto* occupation of parts of that territory, & of long standing,' even though such a position did not necessarily bring *de jure* recognition. Nevertheless, 'It appears to *us* that our claim is the valid, the American claim the invalid, one.'[46]

The British began to discuss the question in the summer of 1828. Although they had objected to Americans' looking for new documents, they asked Charles R. Vaughan, the new British minister to the United States, to request copies of various papers from the U.S. State Department. Not surprisingly, in view of Sir Howard Douglas's earlier refusal, the secretary of state did not comply with all the requests.[47] Both William Huskisson and Addington were by then involved. Suggestions surfaced of bringing Douglas back from New Brunswick to give advice. Dr Tiarks was consulted, and he, as well as Douglas, suggested that Ward Chipman, Jr, should be recruited.

'Mr. Chipman is certainly well acquainted with the whole case and there is perhaps no individual *better* qualified to write the statement to be laid before the Arbitrator.'[48] Chipman had in effect grown up with the northeastern boundary question, his father being appointed British agent for the St Croix Commission when he was just nine years old. Like his father, young Chipman also went to Harvard, and he turned aside invitations to remain with his relatives in Massachusetts, returning to New Brunswick, where he was called to the bar in 1808. More important, however, in January 1817 he was appointed British agent jointly with his father under both articles 4 and 5 of the Treaty of Ghent. He did much of the field work, which was less suitable for his father, and it increasingly fell to him to draft the final arguments for the British case in 1820 and 1821. When his father died in 1824, the British government retained him as an authority on the question.[49] In 1827 Chipman began publishing, under the pen name 'Verax,' a series of letters in the *City Gazette* of Saint John that were later printed as a pamphlet; there he restated the British arguments on the northeastern boundary line from Mars Hill west to the Chaudière River watershed. The watershed of the Métis River, which the Americans claimed was the highlands mentioned in the treaty of 1783, divided the water flowing into the St Lawrence merely from that flowing into the Bay of Chaleurs, Chipman emphasized, not from that entering the Atlantic Ocean. Furthermore, he argued, the recently published *Secret Journals* of the old Continental Congress showed that the American negotiators in Paris, having failed to get agreement on the St John River as the boundary, had been instructed to abandon it and accept a boundary further west. Chipman understood this to mean that the Americans thereby gave up the expectation of the boundary's reaching as far north as the St John River, much less extending beyond it. He addressed the 'great power' question head on. Britain's claims rested not on the 'will,' as he put it, to have the territory, nor on the incidental fact of possession, even though Britain did exercise jurisdiction over the territory. It claimed the territory on the basis of its rights as laid down in the treaty of 1783. *Letters on the Boundary Line* developed a clear, well-reasoned argument, and Chipman saw that copies reached England as well as the maritime colonies.[50]

Chipman was an appropriate person to assist in the preparation of the arguments for the king of the Netherlands, and he assured the Foreign Office that he was willing to go to England to help. 'I do not know that I can look forward to gaining reputation or emolument by it,' he wrote. 'But I remember the adage not to look back, when one's hand is to the plough, and I trust I shall be enabled to do my duty to the King's government.'[51] He left New Brunswick in the late summer of 1828, being first 'cast ashore' on the trip across the Bay of Fundy. All his papers and the dispatches that he was taking for Sir Howard Douglas had to be dried out and thus were in deplorable condition. The voyage across the North Atlantic was so rough that Mrs. Chipman had not recovered after a month in England.[52]

Addington agreed that Chipman had extensive knowledge of the details and issues, having worked on the question for years, but he noted: 'His great fault is that he is rather a special pleader than a broad and powerful reasoner, and, as such, is likely to encumber a case with petty details, and not adhere sufficiently to a simple and bold line of argument,' Addington went on, 'Therefore his lucubrations ought to be keenly examined and revised by some able and classical logician of the stamp of Mr. Brougham or Lord Stowell.'[53] In fact, Chipman and Addington were in close correspondence throughout 1828 and 1829 in the assembling of documents and the marshalling of arguments. Addington was asked to draft the British first statement, and comments were then sought from a number of people, including Dr Tiarks, for which Addington was grateful. 'I can hardly speak too highly of his qualifications,' he said. The revised statement went off to the Americans, and Addington and Stratford Canning set to work on the definitive statement. Once again Tiarks made comments, but both Chipman and Douglas had arrived in London in 1828 and also wrote long analyses.[54] Addington found particularly helpful Chipman's assistance on the British versus the American highlands, but Douglas's proposal of 'a whole new argument' did not provide him with material that was immediately useful.[55] Lord Aberdeen thought that Canning, who as a former minister to the United States had also worked on the boundary question, 'thoroughly understands the subject.' Aberdeen wanted him to draft the material for the arbitrator, but the Duke of Wellington regarded the matter as 'too serious for S. Canning.' Canning was enlisted, although along with several others, and he sent his opinions to Aberdeen as well.[56]

While opinions were being sought about the British definitive statement, copies of the American first statement circulated within the government. It was recognized as a powerful and effective argument. Addington's first reaction was that, but for the recently published instructions of the Continental Congress to accept the St John River as the boundary, 'we should be beat out of the Field without redemption.' After a more careful reading he asserted: 'It is a paper of great ability, well condensed and offering as few points of attack as a Statement on so complicated a subject well could,' and he lamented that the American argument was 'much less complicated than ours' and that: 'appearances are all in their favour.'[57] Canning admitted to Aberdeen: 'The Americans have evidently employed a very able hand in drawing up the statement of their case.'[58] Chipman gave a 485-page critique of the American statement, and Douglas sent a long critical analysis. Tiarks noted, 'It is a very able exposition of the American case and shows that the British claim with regard to the North West Angle of Nova Scotia labours under great difficulties,' but he thought unconvincing the arguments devoted to the source of the Connecticut River and the forty-fifth parallel.[59]

One thing was clear, the British second statement would have to be strong. On first reading of the American statement, Addington wrote to Backhouse that the British reply should consist of a detailed rebuttal by Chipman – a 'charge with the bayonet' – while he himself could only occasionally 'throw in a shot from afar.' Altogether Addington was not happy trying to defend this argument. 'Put my foot ... upon a rock, and I am willing to fight like a bull-dog: but I cannot fight up to my neck in a mud bank,' although he added a postscript that these comments should not lead Backhouse to think that 'I believe the American case to be just althou it is strongly put.'[60] After consideration for a week, Addington had reshaped the direction of the British definitive statement. As he told Backhouse, it should be 'concise' and not attempt an elaborate point-by-point refutation of the American statement. The Americans' attempt to base their argument on the French and English boundaries of 1763 had to be explained, although there were 'fatal documents' that were 'fearfully against us,' but the British argument should hinge on the instructions of the Continental Congress in 1779 – that the delegation in Paris would attempt to secure the St John River as the boundary.[61]

Addington's misgivings about the British position, together with his admiration for the American statement, may have undermined government confidence in his suitability to draft the definitive statement. Aberdeen had sent the American statement to Canning in the summer, and on 7 August 1829 Canning replied in measured tones, saying that he wished that the British case were stronger on the New Brunswick–Maine question and raising the likelihood that the arbitrator would attempt 'to oblige both parties whenever he can do so with a tolerable appearance of fairness.'[62] By November, Aberdeen had concluded that Canning was the person to write the definitive statement, over the hesitation of the Duke of Wellington.[63]

The voluminous materials of Addington, Chipman, Douglas, and Tiarks were to serve as Canning's resources. Aberdeen told him that the drafting required a person who was familiar with the issues and could argue persuasively 'so as to produce the most powerful effect.' The statement should be an 'exercise of judgement and discretion, rather than ingenuity and invention; and one in which the scissors may be used, more than the pen.'[64] By late November, Aberdeen, working with Canning, reported to the prime minister, 'The American Case [sic] is going well,' but as late as 27 and 28 December Wellington was sending them copies of his own memoranda on aspects of the boundary question as well as material from Douglas.[65] Aberdeen replied that they had incorporated Wellington's suggestions into the final draft and that the text was going to the printer on the night of 28 December. The definitive statement was completed and delivered by the due date of 2 January 1830.[66] The duke approved.

What were the arguments, so labouriously put together, and with such wide consultation, submitted to the king of the Netherlands? Each side took the text of the Treaty of Paris of 1783 and attempted to show how the two passages describing the northeastern boundary set forth deliberately and unequivocally the line of boundary that they proposed. They then further reinforced the arguments for these lines by references to both historic and recent documents, to the results of the commission surveys, and to Mitchell's map. They appealed also to common sense, to the syntax of the text of the treaty, and to the historical circumstances in which the treaty was negotiated and the War of Independence concluded. The authors of the statements had been carefully selected and assembled by their two governments, and they represented a major effort to obtain the desired results through the arbitration process.

The American first statement, written by Gallatin and Preble, began with an attempt to define the terms 'North West Angle of Nova Scotia' and 'highlands' used in the treaty. They argued, first, that the Northwest Angle was a specific place, just as the highlands referred to were a specific watershed. The Americans posited that 'the intersection of a line drawn due north from the source of the River St. Croix, with the Highlands which divide the rivers that empty themselves into the river St Lawrence from those which fall into the Atlantic Ocean, must be found on the very Highlands thus described.'[67] That intersection also formed the Northwest Angle of Nova Scotia. The Americans attempted to anticipate the British observation that the watershed that they described separated streams emptying into the Bay of Chaleurs and the Gulf of St Lawrence, by arguing that these bays and estuaries were obviously integral with the great ocean and not distinguishable from the Atlantic.[68]

The Americans then undertook an elaborate attempt to show that in both historic colonial charters and legislation, as well as in British treaties with France, the boundary claimed by the United States was the historic working boundary. Although they cited numerous documents, this argument hinged most clearly on the similarity of wording in the Royal Proclamation of 1763, the Quebec Act of 1774, and the treaty of 1783. The proclamation described the boundary as 'passing along the Highlands which divide the rivers that empty themselves into the said River St. Lawrence, from those which fall into the Sea: and, also, along the north coast of the Bay des Chaleurs.' The Quebec Act described the boundary, from east to west, as formed by 'a line from the Bay of Chaleurs, along the Highlands which divide the rivers that empty themselves into the River St. Lawrence from those which fall into the Sea.'[69] The boundaries described in these documents were unmistakably located, the statement said, on the watershed or highlands on the south side of the St Lawrence. The treaty of 1783 declared that the boundary was to be formed 'by a line drawn due north from the source of the St. Croix river [the boundary between old Massachusetts and Nova Scotia] to the Highlands, along the said Highlands which divide those rivers that empty themselves into the river St. Lawrence from those which fall into the Atlantic Ocean.'[70] The Americans declared that the highlands described in the 1783 treaty were the same ones described in the proclamation and the Quebec Act. Much of the British argument challenged the validity of that assumption.

The American first statement discussed the historic colonial boundaries, particularly between Nova Scotia and Massachusetts, citing, among other things, numerous maps of the years from 1763 to 1783, most of them published in London, showing the boundary as claimed by the United States. The statement did not attempt a full rebuttal of the British argument but devoted several pages to undermining the proposition that the highlands referred to in the treaty of 1783 were the ridge of hills extending west from Mars Hill just forty miles north of the source of the St Croix River. Among several objections, the Americans emphasized that streams flowing both north and south from the sides of Mars Hill emptied into the St John River and therefore could in no way conform to the language of the treaty. The statement also pointed out that there was no ridge of highland east of Mars Hill to form the corresponding boundary of Quebec and New Brunswick as described in the documents of 1763 and 1774.[71]

The American statement also put forward arguments for the boundary along the Connecticut River and the forty-fifth parallel to the St Lawrence River. The terms of the treaty of 1783 dealing with the 'northwestern most head' of the Connecticut River were broad, the Americans said. It was understood by these terms that there were several heads to the river, without regard to the size or name of the streams, and the American case admitted that several streams might be considered. The United States claimed Indian Stream as the river intended as the northwesternmost head, largely because it was the most northern and most western of the several tributaries of the Connecticut.[72] The argument for the forty-fifth parallel was more laboured. There the American statement outlined the background of the 1771–4 colonial survey of the forty-fifth parallel, the so-called Collins–Valentine line, proposing that this had been the accepted line for generations and that this was the boundary assumed in 1783. As for the fact that the commission's surveys showed that line to be inaccurate, the statement suggested that these were minor errors and that it was for the arbiter to decide whether any adjustment from the old line was necessary.[73] Although it ended on its weakest note, the statement was generally a powerful rationale for the American claim, as several British commentators observed.

The British first statement began by acknowledging the 'imperfect topographical knowledge' of the country by the negotiators in 1782 and 1783 and by noting that this fact helped to explain the ambiguities and difficulties that had arisen when an effort was made to define the border. The British argued that the American attempt to reconcile the language of the treaty of 1783 with the topography was basically flawed. They took the position that the Bay of Fundy and the Bay of Chaleurs were discrete bodies of water. Therefore, when the treaty of 1783 mentioned the highlands that divided the rivers that emptied into the St Lawrence from the rivers that emptied into the Atlantic Ocean, the treaty could not have been intended to refer to the St John or the Restigouche – these two rivers did not empty into the Atlantic, within the terms of the treaty, but into the Bay of Fundy and the Bay of Chaleurs. 'This is the cardinal point of the whole of this branch of difference between Great Britain and the United States,' the statement said.[74] That being the case, the British statement went on to say, the line due north from the source of the St Croix River could not proceed 145 miles north to the St Lawrence watershed, as the Americans claimed, because such a line crossed both the St John and the Restigouche rivers, whose watersheds could not be included in the words of the treaty. A close reading of the text of the treaty, the British noted, said that the due-north line should be drawn from the source of the St Croix River 'to the Highlands, and along the said Highlands which divide those rivers that empty themselves into the river St. Lawrence from those which fall into the Atlantic Ocean,' which, the British statement argued, meant the first highlands due north from the source of the St Croix. That first highlands was to be found at Mars Hill, and it also began a ridge of land extending west that formed a watershed dividing the St John River on the north and the Penobscot, Kennebec, and Androscoggin rivers on the south. All the southern rivers flowed directly into the Atlantic, the British pointed out, not into the Bay of Fundy. Furthermore, this watershed or highlands, if extended far enough west, reached the watershed of the Chaudière River, which flowed northwest, emptying into the St Lawrence River opposite Quebec City. Therefore these highlands, from Mars Hill west to the Chaudière, fulfilled the provision of the treaty of 1783 by eventually dividing the waters that emptied into the St Lawrence from those that emptied into the Atlantic.[75]

To buttress this argument, the British first statement also referred to the early instructions sent to the American negotiators in Paris, recently published in the *Secret Journals*, urging an eastern U.S. boundary 'along the middle of St. John's River, from its source to its mouth in the Bay of

Fundy.'[76] The British negotiators at Paris did not agree to this proposed boundary, but the instructions from the Continental Congress, the British statement claimed, showed that the Americans harboured no expectations of a boundary line north of the St John River. The British also argued that the colonial charters and instructions to colonial governors were less clear than the Americans had asserted in their attempt to show that the U.S. claim was merely the old colonial boundary between Massachusetts and Nova Scotia. Other boundaries had existed at various times, thus blurring any clear tradition. Furthermore, the British placed great emphasis on the existence of the fief of Madawaska, which dated from a French charter in 1683, eight years before the revised Massachusetts charter, and the Madawaska settlement, dating from the late eighteenth century. The settlement, on both sides of the St John River, persisted down to the present and could not have been conceived to be included within U.S. territory in the negotiations of 1782–3. In short, the British claimed, there had been extensive and continuous occupation of the region for generations.[77]

The British argument then turned to challenge the American claim of a significant highlands on the south bank of the St Lawrence from the Métis River west to the upper Connecticut. The British asserted that the highlands from Mars Hill west to the Chaudière watershed were higher and more mountainous than the highlands further north that the Americans proposed and also that the Mars Hill line was more clearly what had been intended in the topographical terms used in the treaty. In fact, because no complete survey of the contested areas had still been carried out, both sides were dependent on visual observations rather than on scientific information about the details of either of these watersheds.[78]

The claims for the head of the Connecticut River and the forty-fifth parallel were simply put. The British denied that either of the two rivers on which the Americans focused – Hall's Stream or Indian Stream – was relevant. The true head bore the name Connecticut River and carried the largest volume of water. It also continued well past these two tributaries (also well to the east) to Connecticut Lake, and the northwesternmost brook flowing into that lake was the boundary intended in the treaty of 1783. As for the forty-fifth parallel, the Treaty of Ghent provided for an accurate survey of that line, and the commissions had almost completely carried out that task (certainly sufficient to show the errors of the Collins–Valentine line). The Americans had themselves accepted the inaccuracy of the old line. All that remained was for the arbitrator to authorize establishment of the astronomically correct forty-fifth parallel.[79]

The second, or definitive statements, were produced some six months after the first, at the end of December 1829, and they provided both countries with the opportunity to respond and rebut the arguments of the first statements and to develop further their own arguments. The Americans, once again Gallatin and Preble, chose to structure their definitive statement largely as a refutation of the British first statement, whereas the British in some respects simply elaborated on their earlier arguments.

The Americans argued that the British first statement had put forward an interpretation of the treaty based on a presumption of the negotiators' intentions but that it had never proved with any evidence that the Mars Hill line either was specifically intended by the treaty or had any historical existence. The Americans also returned to their reading that the Bay of Fundy and the Bay of Chaleurs were parts of the Atlantic Ocean. They pointed out that almost every stream flowing into the ocean passed through some bay or gulf and that, by the British interpretation, there would be no river emptying directly into the Atlantic. Furthermore, the U.S. definitive statement went on to assert, the negotiators of the treaty of 1783 could not have had any objection to a geographical line crossing such rivers as the St John or tributaries of the Restigouche because they understood that to be the case in the forty-fifth parallel in the north and the thirty-first parallel in the south, where the lines crossed many rivers and streams. The British objection was not sound within the text of the treaty.[80]

As for the reading of the text that implied that due-north line was to stop at the first highlands, the American definitive statement argued that both internal and external evidence made it clear that the line was to run north to the highlands that separated the waters emptying into the St Lawrence and that this intersection was also the Northwest Angle of Nova Scotia.[81] The British reading focused on only one of the two passages in the treaty describing the eastern boundary and misconstrued that. The second passage, the Americans argued, was unmistakable – 'and from its source [the St Croix] directly north to the aforesaid highlands which divide the rivers that fall into the Atlantic Ocean from those which fall into the River St. Lawrence.'[82] The Americans held that this clearly meant a line north to the watershed of the St Lawrence. The Americans also quoted Ward Chipman, Sr, the British agent in the St Croix Commission, as saying that the due-north line chosen would be advantageous to New Brunswick because it would provide 'a greater extent of navigation on the St. John River,' thus clearly acknowledging that the boundary was to cross that river.[83] Only during the negotiations at Ghent in 1814 had New Brunswick or the British government proposed a boundary that was intended to serve military and transportation needs. As for any French claims in the Madawaska area, these would have been superseded by first British jurisdiction and then by the treaty of 1783 itself, nor did occupation after 1783 have any relevance to the question.[84]

In closing the arguments, the American definitive statement returned to the intentions of the negotiators of 1782–3. The 1782 instructions to Governor John Parr of Nova Scotia defined his jurisdiction in the west as running from the St Croix River, and 'by the said river to its source, and by a line drawn due North from thence, to the Southern boundary of our Colony of Quebec'; and the instructions to Governor Frederick Haldimand of Québec in 1782 described the southern boundary of that colony as being 'bounded on the South, by a line from the Bay of Chaleurs along the highland which divide the rivers that empty themselves into the River St. Lawrence from those which fall into the sea, to a point as 45 degrees in Northern latitude, on the Eastern bank of the River Connecticut.'[85] In short, Gallatin and Preble argued that the 1783 northeastern boundary was the same line that had separated the colonies before the Revolution. The British interpretation varied so greatly from these historic boundaries, and from the obvious meaning of the words of the treaty, that it required vastly different language from that which was in the treaty. The Americans also noted that while the fief of Madawaska dated from 1663 (though invalid under British jurisdiction after 1763), the French community of the Madawaska settlements along the St John River had in fact moved there only after 1784, as the result of the loyalist settlement on the lower St John River.[86]

The U.S. definitive statement's discussions of the northwesternmost head of the Connecticut River and the location of the forty-fifth parallel were largely restatements of the earlier arguments. The facts that one of the 'heads' of the river in question bore the name Connecticut River or Main Branch and that it flowed out of the Connecticut Lake were of no vital importance when the text of the treaty acknowledged that there were several possible heads of the river from which the northwesternmost was to be chosen. It was a matter for a discrete decision, because the framers could not have known the topography of the region. As for the forty-fifth parallel, the Americans simply urged acceptance of the old boundary without really justifying it in terms of the treaty of 1783 or the Treaty of Ghent.[87]

The British definitive statement did not attempt a point-by-point refutation of the American arguments. It started by denying that the British government had ever agreed simply to re-establish the old colonial boundary when defining the limits of the new United States, any more than it had been willing to accept the St John River, as proposed by Congress. In short, a completely new boundary line was created in 1783, and the determination of its whereabouts would be the duty of the arbitrator. In these circumstances the references to the Royal Proclamation of 1763 and to the Quebec Act of 1774 were beside the point. The British asserted, however, that the American attempts to erase the distinctions between the Bay of Fundy and the Gulf of St Lawrence were flawed. The treaty of 1783 used those very terms to describe specific places in other parts of the text. Thus the Americans obtained the right to fish in the Gulf of St Lawrence, as well as in the Atlantic. The British also argued that it could hardly have been the intention of the negotiators to give substantial portions of the upper rivers to one country and the lower rivers to the other. Why would the St John and other streams be cut by a boundary line in mid-course? On the contrary, the British argued, the framers tried to assign whole river systems to each country, which was why they used highlands that served as watersheds as reference points.[88]

The British definitive statement also returned to the merits of the Mars Hill line. Mars Hill was clearly the highest point in the eastern boundary area, and although not all the country had been surveyed, it was clear, the definitive statement urged, that a significant highland extended west, forming the watershed for the Penobscot, Kennebec, and Androscoggin rivers on the south and the St John River on the north. Mars Hill was thus the Northwest Angle of Nova Scotia mentioned in the treaty. The Americans themselves, the British argued, referring to the words of Sullivan and Madison, had earlier admitted not knowing where the Northwest Angle was to be found. The American claim north of that point could not be sustained by topography, the terms of the treaty, or logic, they concluded. The Royal Proclamation and the Quebec Act were not relevant. The Americans had specifically rejected both of them as acts against which they rebelled in 1775.[89] Reasserting their claim to the Mars Hill line, the British second statement concluded, 'It has been shown to demonstration, that the northwest angle of Nova Scotia was totally unknown in 1783, that no provincial boundary line had been acknowledged, ascertained, or even existed for any practical purpose, at that time, between the western extremity of Chaleurs Bay, and the Highlands situated at the heads of the Kennebec and Chaudière Rivers, and consequently that the supposed identity between that line and the line now claimed by the United States is a mere illusion, resting on no positive foundation whatever.' The British went on to say that they drew proof of this contention from 'evidence and documents exhibited by the United States themselves,' in both material supplied for the commission and the newly published *Secret Journals.*[90]

The northwesternmost head of the Connecticut River and the forty-fifth parallel received brief treatment. Very simply, the tributaries named by the United States were not the true head of the Connecticut River, even if the Indian Stream had its source further north than any other. Only the brooks running into Connecticut Lake qualified as heads of the river. The accurate survey of the forty-fifth parallel had posed a problem only when the American surveyors discovered that the fortifications under construction at Rouse's Point were actually in British territory. However, this did not in any way diminish the original intention of both the treaty of 1783 and the Treaty of Ghent to establish the boundary along the true forty-fifth parallel.[91]

In March 1831 both Tiarks and William Pitt Adams, a young Foreign Office clerk, were sent to The Hague to serve under Sir Charles Bagot and to check and collate the statements, documents, and maps.[92] Douglas was sent as well, possibly at Wellington's instigation, but in a different capacity. Sir Howard was both a serving army officer (he had been with Wellington in Spain and had also written several military treatises) and lieutenant-governor of New Brunswick. As Aberdeen explained it rather awkwardly to Bagot, Douglas might be of some service to the ambassador because of his knowledge of the boundary area, although he 'entertains some peculiar opinions upon the subject which may not be altogether sound.' Furthermore, Douglas was to have 'no official character whatever, and his stay at the Hague will depend upon the necessity which you may feel to exist for availing yourself of his assistance.'[93] In fact, Backhouse had specifically told Douglas that, according to the terms of the Convention of 1827, 'all personal negotiation or verbal discussion with the Arbiter is precluded,' although Aberdeen thought that Bagot 'should have the advantage of personal communication with you on this important and complicated question.'[94] When

Douglas arrived, all the documents had been checked and the statements were ready to be submitted to the king.

By this time also William Pitt Preble had been in The Hague for over two months, had presented his credentials, and had been joined by Charles Steward Daveis, a lawyer from Portland, Maine, who had been appointed a special confidential agent to convey the completed definitive statement to the Netherlands. Daveis was also to assist Preble, particularly in checking the documents during March 1830 prior to their presentation to the king.[95]

Preble and Gallatin had seemed confident that the American case was impregnable and that all was running smoothly in their favour. Gallatin wrote to Secretary of State Martin Van Buren that the British definitive statement was 'not formidable and does not contain any important or new argument which has not been anticipated in our Second Statement.'[96] The British, in contrast, began to worry about the Americans and the prospects of the arbitral process. Preble had remarked to Tiarks and William Pitt Adams that the Americans intended to publish the arguments of both sides after the decision. Bagot saw this as a manoeuvre to narrow the arbitrator's options and to force him to chose one side or the other. Bagot then began to muse about the alternatives – the possibility that the king might not chose one argument and reject the other, but rather might attempt to resolve the matter 'by some arbitrary decision which may, in his opinion, best reconcile the general interests of the two Parties.'[97] In short, what should the British be prepared to do if the king handed down a reasonable compromise? Aberdeen replied to Bagot that the Convention of 1827 gave the arbiter the right to request more information from either party, the right to order a new survey of the contested region, and, most important, the 'full power to decide the matter in the dispute in any way which he would think would be substantially just to both parties.' Aberdeen said that he had no idea of the American government's thoughts on this question but that Bagot should feel free to tell the king that the British government believed that he had 'full discretion' to decide the question as he saw best.[98] This was a thoughtful anticipation by the British of the possible outcome of the process. The Americans seemed to have no such concerns.[99]

All things considered, the British and the Americans worked together quite well in The Hague in March 1830 checking the documents and the texts. It was no small undertaking. The British alone submitted six wooden chests containing documents and one tin case holding maps. William Pitt Adams reported to the Foreign Office: 'The examination has passed off very satisfactorily, and we have met with a more accommodating spirit on the part of the Yankees than we had been led to expect.' While there had been a quibble by the Americans on the last day about whether the British statements had been delivered on the correct days, Adams was able to say that there had been 'no frivolous objections.'[100] On 1 April 1830, in a modest ceremony, Sir Charles Bagot and William Pitt Preble jointly presented the complete sets of statements, evidence, and maps, both British and American, all carefully collated and checked, to King William.

Chapter Eight

The Award and Its Problems

The king of the Netherlands received the statements and accompanying documents from Sir Charles Bagot and William Pitt Preble on 1 April 1830. King William I, his foreign minister, Baron J.G. Verstolk van Soelen, and the staff of the Foreign Ministry at The Hague were to examine, analyse, and consider the facts and the merits of the two sets of arguments. Both the Americans and the British had admitted that the task would be arduous and very probably thankless, and internal political problems in both the Netherlands and the United States were to impede its acceptance in the next few years.

It was uncertain how the king intended to proceed – how much he would attend to the material himself and how much he would delegate. By late May Preble reported to Washington that the king had left for his summer residence, Het Loo, to work on the statements and documents. Several months later, after talking to the Dutch foreign minister, Preble understood that King William had decided to work on the material by himself without the assistance of the Foreign Ministry. 'I can only assure you the King will investigate the subject thoroughly,' Preble quoted Baron Verstolk, and 'the decision will be his own.'[1] Bagot learned in July that the king had set up a committee to study the boundary question, made up of Baron Verstolk, General Baron Jean de Constant Rebecque, and a third person whose identity Bagot had not yet discovered. The British minister was pleased by these two, both of whom knew English well, but particularly by General Constant, who had been on the staff of the king – then the prince of Orange – with the British army in Spain during the Peninsular campaign in the Napoleonic War.[2]

However, as early as 13 May 1830 Sir Howard Douglas recorded having a conversation with the king on the boundary question – exactly what the undersecretary had warned him in March that he should not do – in which the king revealed considerable familiarity with certain aspects of the matter. As Sir Howard related the interview, King William commented on how strange it was that the question had remained unsettled for forty-seven years. 'Such a boundary as is claimed by the United States was not contemplated at the time [of the negotiation of the Treaty of Paris of 1783],' Douglas assured the king. 'It was first mooted constructively, on some obscurities in the letter of the treaty of 1783, at Ghent, but not absolutely claimed till the census of 1820.'[3] The king paused and then said to Douglas that the British statement seemed to embrace the position of the earlier eighteenth-century regime of colonial New France. Sir Howard replied that those were 'provincial interests' with which the king need not concern himself. 'Those old boundaries were never settled,' he said, thus sweeping aside the American argument that the treaty of 1783 established the U.S. boundary along the lines already understood to mark out Quebec, Nova Scotia, and Massachusetts in 1763 and 1774.

The king and the general went on to talk about the difficulty of a satisfactory decision. Douglas said Britain's desire was for security not territory, to which the king said, 'but this is a question of right.' Sir Howard answered that Britain certainly thought that its case was based on legal rights, but that the king was empowered to decide the issue 'in any way your Majesty may deem consistent with the objects of the arbitration – even should it be by splitting the difference, as was proposed by Mr. Gallaton [sic].' Douglas's notes related the exchange: '"Did Mr. Gallaton propose that?" cried the King eagerly. Yes, sire, and gave offence to the State of Maine by the admission this implied.'[4] However, what Gallatin had uttered as a warning to Clay Douglas asserted as a willing assumption to the king. Douglas was something of a loose cannon, and he was to get himself and Bagot into trouble in the Netherlands in just a few more months. In this instance it would appear that he was already pointing King William in the direction of a compromise settlement. Gallatin's warning to Clay that an arbitrator always attempts to 'split the difference' had become public knowledge, thanks to the report of the Maine legislature in 1828.[5]

Preble had reported to Secretary of State Martin Van Buren that Douglas's arrival at The Hague in early April had caused something of a stir among both the Dutch officials and the British embassy's staff. Bagot was quoted as saying that if Douglas 'should attempt to speak to the King or to any of his Ministers on the subject of the Boundary business he [Bagot] would instantly quit his post,' Preble wrote.[6] The Dutch, he said, resented and commented publicly on the presence of the actual governor of New Brunswick in The Hague, whereas the Americans, Preble said optimistically, had 'nothing to do, but to stand still, in order to stand well.'[7] Sir Howard also began to generate some comment within the Foreign Office when he suggested in June that the king of the Netherlands be urged to order a new survey of the whole northeastern border region with a view to reopening the question of the location of the true St Croix River. Although the identification of that river and the decision about its source had been determined in 1798, there was a body of opinion in New Brunswick that thought that the source of the river chosen was disadvantageous to the province and favoured either a more western source, or a more western river, such as the Penobscot. The Foreign Office consulted Ward Chipman, Jr, who was back in England, and he advised it that his father had correctly discovered the true St Croix River in 1796 and that the work of 1798 could not now be undone.[8] Preble concluded that both Sir Howard and Dr Tiarks would 'accomplish much less than they had hoped.'[9]

If the American minister attempted to keep a discreet distance from the king and the Dutch foreign minister, he did work to keep informed about opinion in the Netherlands concerning the arbitration. People took the choice of King William as arbitrator as a great compliment to the king and were very pleased. The United States occupied a complicated position in the sentiments of the country – the darling of the liberals and reformers, Preble said, who saw it as the example of democratic government, and the anathema of the conservatives, who saw it as the source of greatest threat to the ideology of monarchical forms of government. Even so, Preble concluded that the weight of the American case was such that it would be supported generally. He reported conversations in The Hague where he was assured that the American case would win. In May he quoted one man as saying, 'Depend upon it, Sir, it is impossible the King should decide against you.'[10] Preble's correspondence showed a degree of optimism that was to gradually erode over the course of the summer.

At this point events within the Netherlands took an unexpected turn. Preble had commented in June that 'the people of Belgium are not in the best humor.'[11] It was a shrewd insight. On 25 August 1830 a performance in Brussels of the opera *La Muette de Portici* provided the occasion for a popular uprising of Belgians against the state of the Netherlands, of which they were part. After the lead singer's aria, with the emotive words, 'My country gave me life, I shall give it liberty!,' crowds streamed out into the streets demanding self-government for the Belgian provinces. The Congress of Vienna had united the Protestant, Dutch-speaking northern Netherlands with the Catholic, French-speaking Belgian provinces in 1814 under William VI, prince of Orange, as William I, king of the Netherlands. Though an economic reformer, William was seen by many as too authoritarian and not sensitive to the Catholic preferences of the Belgians.

The agitation in Belgium in late August, also inspired by the July Revolution in France, led to the defection of major elements of the army, and within two months the Dutch were driven from most of Belgium. On 5 October Belgian independence was declared, and William appealed to Britain and the European great powers to assist him and to preserve the international system created by the Congress of Vienna. Because the balance of power in Europe was affected by the fate of the Netherlands, and threatened by the possible growth of French influence in Belgium, the British convened a conference of great powers in London on 4 November 1830 to decide what the Belgians might be permitted to do. When the king turned to Britain for support in the autumn, Sir Charles Bagot was placed in constant close contact with him.[12] Indeed, Bagot had observed several years earlier that while the king had no fondness for Britain, 'he knows just as well as you do that when ever he is in a difficulty he must turn to us in preference to any other power,' and Bagot added ominously, 'so far we may always count upon a sort of predilection in our favour.'[13] In effect, Bagot anticipated the very situation that was unfolding, to the horror of the American minister.

As the British role in the fate of the Low Countries expanded, Preble became very anxious about the extent to which the king was still a free agent to decide the boundary question objectively. As he put it, the fear of French intervention threw the government 'openly into the arms of Great Britain.' Preble was alarmed that 'the British ambassador is privy to, and participates in, all their counsels' and 'is in truth here the most important personage.'[14] These worries were not misplaced. General Constant, who previously had been working on the king's committee to advise him on the boundary arbitration, was sent to London in early August to confer with the Duke of Wellington about the defence of the Belgian frontier, and Baron Verstolk, another member of the committee, pleaded with Bagot to arrange for a loan for the Netherlands government to meet the cash needs of the situation (the best the British government could do was to guarantee a loan of £500,000 to be undertaken by either Baring Brothers bank or the Rothchilds).[15] All of this was managed with utmost secrecy. However, Bagot sent Sir Howard Douglas into Belgium in October to inspect the fortifications along the French frontier, during the course of which Douglas opened talks between the Dutch and Belgian generals to prevent further fighting. News of Douglas's actions became public and were an embarrassment to Bagot. Certainly they illustrated publicly the extent to which the British were involved in the domestic problems of the Netherlands, whatever Britain's role in the upcoming London conference on Belgium might be.[16]

By mid-September 1830 Preble's optimism about the likelihood of the king's supporting the American arguments had evaporated. Opinion among the Court circle in the midst of the rebellion became very anti-democratic, and the United States was one of the most conspicuous representatives of both a successful rebellion and a democratic system, as Preble explained to Van Buren. With U.S. prestige falling and British influence rising, Preble requested a meeting with Baron Verstolk. As discreetly as he could, he asked the foreign minister how the turbulent events in the Netherlands, as well as Britain's changed position, might affect the king's arbitration. Verstolk was reassuring: although the king had chosen to work on the boundary statements by himself, he had devoted a substantial amount of time to the matter during the summer, and the minister said that he was confident that a decision would be made by early January 1831. Verstolk had no knowledge of what decision the king might reach, and he assured Preble that the monarch would 'be influenced by no other motives or considerations, than those of justice and impartiality.'[17] This, of course, was a reply that was to be expected. Preble was still not confident. Although he thought the king an honourable man, and while he noted that many Dutch were still favourably disposed to the United States, he was sure that there were those in the Court circle who would gladly sacrifice American interests to win support from Britain. He heard rumours from his contacts in Dutch society that political expediency might determine the award. 'Their opinions check my confidence – alarm my anxiety,' Preble confessed to Van Buren, 'but my faith in the King's integrity repels their insinuations.'[18] It was a reasonable concern. In the circumstances, how could the king render a decision that could be seen to be just?

Preble would have been even more alarmed if he had known of the deliberations of the London conference. Shortly after it convened in early November, the Tory government of the Duke of Wellington was defeated on a vote in the House of Commons and resigned. It gave way to a Whig government led by Lord Grey and with Lord Palmerston as foreign secretary.[19] Palmerston quickly came to the conclusion that Belgium would have to be given its independence. This might be thought to have made an enemy of King William, but the king was still dependent on British influence to determine the borders of Belgium, to decide the fate of Luxemburg (of which he was the grand duke), to select a new sovereign for Belgium (for which the king's son, William, prince of Orange, was a candidate), and to limit French power. Indeed, the king had sent the prince to London in the autumn in the hope that he might influence events.

In early January 1831, several of these issues came to the surface just as the king was about to announce his decision in the arbitration. On 2 and 3 January, the French ambassador to Britain, Prince Charles Maurice de Talleyrand, suggested that in exchange for withdrawing the name of the duc de Nemours, younger son of King Louis Philippe, from among the candidates for the Belgian throne France be compensated with Belgian territory. This proposition, perceived as a threat, revived, within the next several days (7–11 January), the candidacy of William, prince of Orange.[20] Thus, even without the Belgian provinces, the interests of the king of the Netherlands were still very much dependent on Britain's actions at the London conference.[21]

On 10 January 1831 at 11:30 in the morning King William handed down his long-awaited award. The king had asked both Preble and Bagot to meet with him at the palace at The Hague. With Baron Verstolk in attendance, the king made a short speech, in which he said that it was, as Bagot reported, 'his anxious wish that the decision to which He had arrived upon the question might be as satisfactory to our respective Governments as He believed it to be in strict accordance with a fair spirit of justice, and of the reasonable pretensions of both Parties.' Copies of the decision, signed by the king and the minister of foreign affairs under the great seal of the Netherlands, were then given to both representatives. Sir Charles Bagot, the adept and professional diplomat, made a short speech himself, graciously thanking the king for his labours on behalf of Britain and the United States.[22]

The king had prepared a long statement in the decision in which he analysed all the major arguments put forward by each side, considering in turn each of the three contested sections of the boundary. Of the three, the most difficult and the most important was the Quebec–New

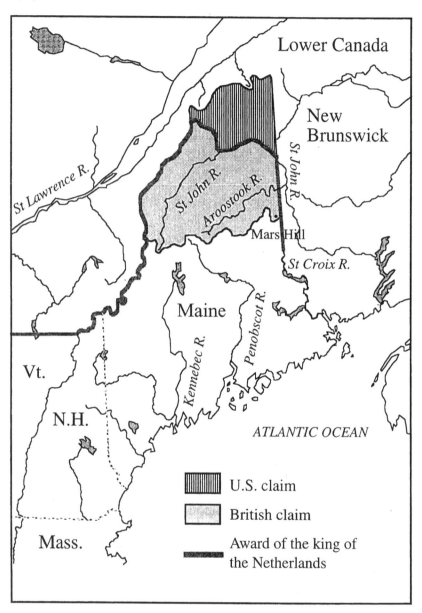

Map 12. Award of the king of the Netherlands (article 5), 1831

Brunswick–Maine boundary. There the king found some force to the argument that the treaty of 1783 had intended simply to duplicate the colonial boundaries of 1763 and 1774. However, the 'specification [in the treaty] does not imply the entire coincidence of boundaries between the two Powers, as settled by the succeeding Article, with the ancient delimitation of British Provinces, whose preservation is not mentioned in the Treaty of 1783.'[23] Thus both the change in wording (from 'sea' to 'Atlantic Ocean') and the failure to state specifically that the new national boundaries would duplicate the old provincial boundaries rendered this argument inconclusive. The king disregarded references to the Northwest Angle of Nova Scotia, concluding that such a specific place had not been known to exist in 1783 and could not in confidence be said to be identified now. Reference to such a place, 'which still remaining itself to be found, cannot lead to the discovery of the line which it is to terminate.'[24] As for the fief of Madawaska or the Madawaska settlements, the king said that their existence was not relevant to the validity of any claims arising out of the treaty of 1783.

Taking into account the insufficiency of any of these arguments to prove conclusively the case of either of the two parties, the king introduced several other considerations. He thought it improbable that the British would have agreed to a boundary north of the St John River that effectively blocked any land communication between New Brunswick and Quebec. Furthermore, he took the point that the treaty may have intended the Bay of Fundy and the Bay of Chaleurs to be discrete bodies of water, rather than parts of the Atlantic Ocean. In any case a line extended from the source of the St Croix due north of the St John River reached highlands that divided waters which fell into the Bay of Fundy from waters that fell into the Bay of Chaleurs – only some miles further north were highlands that divided waters falling into the St Lawrence from waters falling into the Bay of Chaleurs.[25] As for the argument that the boundary was to be found south of the St John River, the king pointed out that the highlands proposed separated the waters falling into the Atlantic (the Penobscot) from the waters falling into the Bay of Fundy (St John) and that 'the verb "divide" appears to require the contiguity of the objects to be "divided"' (the waters falling into the St Lawrence from waters falling into the Atlantic, as mentioned in the treaty), which the Mars Hill line did not provide.

King William therefore declared that 'the arguments adduced on either side, and the documents exhibited in support of them, cannot be considered as sufficiently preponderating to determine a preference in favor of either one of the two lines respectively claimed by the High Interested Parties' and as such 'do not permit us to award either of those two lines to one of the said Parties, without violating the principles of law and equity with regard to the other.'[26] As a result, the king said that it was his opinion that it would be 'suitable to adopt' a boundary drawn due north from the St Croix River, along the middle of the St John River, to the St Francis River, along the middle of the St Francis to its northwesternmost branch (indicated on a map provided), and along the watershed line proposed by the United States until it joined the line proposed by Britain, and thence until it reached the northwesternmost head of the Connecticut River. This was then a compromise line, albeit along the most obvious natural boundary in the region. Of the 12,027 square miles of land in dispute, the king allocated 7,908 square miles (or 5,016,120 acres) to Maine and 4,119 square miles (or 2,626,160 acres) to New Brunswick and Quebec.[27]

The king turned next to the other two questions – first, to the headwaters of the Connecticut River. He pointed out that as early as 1772 one of the tributaries considered by the United States was known by its current name, Hall's Brook, and unlikely to be confused with the larger stream that bore the name Connecticut River. The king therefore decided that the British claim was the correct northwesternmost head of the Connecticut River intended in the treaty of 1783. With the last question, the matter of the forty-fifth parallel from the Connecticut River west to the St Lawrence River, the arbitrator said that inasmuch as the Treaty of Ghent clearly ordered the survey of the forty-fifth parallel, and inasmuch as the old survey was clearly inaccurate, no good purpose would be served by failing to implement the new survey. However, the king took note of the fact that the United States had constructed its fortifications at Rouse's Point in good faith and on the assumption that it was south of the forty-fifth parallel. Therefore the king decided that the boundary should be marked according to the 'observed latitude' but recommended provision to allow American territory to extend to the fort and for a radius of a kilometre around it.[28]

It was a bold statement by the king. Although on the two secondary issues – the head of the Connecticut River and the proper location of the forty-fifth parallel – the award pretty much subscribed to the British claim, it did take into consideration U.S. security needs by making provision for the retention of Fort Montgomery at Rouse's Point. With regard to the main issue of the boundary from the Northwest Angle of Nova Scotia and the 'highlands,' the king declared frankly that none of the arguments and none of the documents could establish the case sufficiently to overturn the arguments of the opposite side.

To some degree the predicament embraced in that conclusion has never been resolved. None of the most objective studies of the northeastern boundary question since then has ever proved the arguments of either side to complete satisfaction. William F. Ganong came closer than anyone else, in his 1901 study of New Brunswick, in demonstrating the validity of the American case by using the findings of the Quebec–New Brunswick Boundary Commission of 1851, which concluded that the region north of the St John River and south of the St Lawrence watershed belonged to the Crown, but not to either province (Ganong's conclusion was that if the territory had not belonged to either province in 1851 it was because prior to 1842 it had, in fact, belonged to the United States).[29] But even Ganong's logic could not dispel the obscurities of the text of the treaty of 1783 or the uncertainties of the many documents and maps.

However, whether the king was wise to propose a compromise, rather than to chose one side or the other, was another matter. How much the rebellion of Belgium and the king's dependence on the British and the other northern powers affected his judgment in these matters is difficult to assess. The evidence is not clear, but it is difficult not to conclude that these circumstances influenced him. Certainly he could not wish to antagonize the British gratuitously in his circumstances, although it seems improbable that an award based on the American arguments would have provoked a vindictive response by the British. Any country that submits to an arbitration has to consider the possibility that the decision will not be in its favour. As for Britain's support of the Netherlands in the crisis, Lord Aberdeen refused to send troops, and Lord Palmerston, when he succeeded Aberdeen at the Foreign Office, although he opposed a French prince on a Belgian throne, was largely responsible for the creation of an independent Belgium. Furthermore, much of this was clear before the award was handed down on 10 January 1831.[30]

Even so, the king broke the provisions of the Convention of 1827 in proposing a compromise boundary line rather than choosing one claim or the other. The British had anticipated this possibility and agreed to accept it. However, in the circumstances the king *appeared* to many as deliberately refusing to make the choice, thus avoiding a decision in favour of the somewhat stronger American argument, and decided instead on a compromise that would be less injurious to British interests and thus less likely to cause resentment in Britain and very possibly injury to the interests of the Netherlands. Whatever the motivation for the compromise proposal, and whatever the merits of this particular compromise, the results could not have been foreseen.

William Pitt Preble was dismayed by the king's decision. Although his optimism over the certainty of a decision favourable to the American case had waned as the events of the summer and autumn had unfolded in the Netherlands, he was still unprepared for, and certainly unwilling to accept, the decision that was given. On 12 January, just two days after the king announced the award, Preble wrote to Baron Verstolk, the foreign minister, with generous compliments to the king, but nevertheless to protest the nature of the decision. The king had, Preble said, 'abandoned altogether the boundaries of the Treaty and substituting [sic] for them a distinct and different line of demarcation.' As a result, 'it becomes the duty of the undersigned, with the most profound respect for the friendly views of the Arbitrator, to enter a protest against the proceeding, as constituting a departure from the powers delivered by the high parties interested, in order that the rights and interests of the United States may not be supposed to be committed by any presumed acquiescence on the part of their representative.'[31] Preble also wrote to Sir Charles Bagot informing him of his letter to Verstolk and his desire to indicate that there was a technical objection to the award and that it could be only formally accepted by the government in Washington.[32] Verstolk made a completely noncommittal reply to Preble, saying that with the announcement of the award the king felt that he had fully discharged his duties in the affair.[33]

Preble wrote to Secretary of State Van Buren, enclosing his correspondence with Verstolk and Bagot, outlining the problems with the award as he saw it and the disastrous circumstances surrounding it. Commenting way beyond his letter to Verstolk, Preble attempted to explain the motivation of the king. In the first place, while the choice of King William as arbitrator had originally been 'exceedingly unfortunate,' the revolutionary events in France and Belgium, and the subsequent dependence of the Netherlands on Britain, 'left to the King of the Netherlands not even the semblance of independence.'[34] Preble had hoped that the king might disqualify himself as the arbitrator in the circumstances, and Preble intended his interview with the foreign minister in September both to signal his unease and to sound out the situation. In this regard Preble felt that Baron Verstolk had deliberately worked 'to lull my apprehensions, and to re-assure my confidence,' in order to keep the king engaged in the arbitration process as a means with which to show 'gratitude' to the British at U.S. expense. Even the newspapers, Preble said, drew the analogy between the king's compromise boundary in North America and the appropriateness of a compromise line in the new boundary between Belgium and the Netherlands to be decided at the London conference. The king's position had been distressing, Preble observed with some understanding, 'and who can answer for his own judgement under such circumstances!' Nevertheless, the nature of the award seemed to Preble to release the United States from 'all further obligation' under the Treaty of Ghent regarding article 5. As for this process just completed, the United States 'are disembarrassed from this miserable measure of Arbitration,' as he put it, 'and are at full liberty to vindicate their rights, and pursue their own measures in their own way.'[35] Preble concluded by saying that the matter would be in the hands of President Jackson, who was in no way committed by Preble's actions. The letter was a biting attack on the king and on Preble's perceived betrayal of U.S. interests.

Preble also wrote to Louis McLane, the American minister to Britain, elaborating somewhat on his criticism of the decision. The compromise line of the St John River had been specifically rejected both at Ghent and in the negotiations prior to the arbitration, as King William should have understood from the documents presented to him. In early February Preble wrote again to Van Buren describing public opinion in the Netherlands about the award and noting that the king had recently been described as 'arbitrateur,' which was understood to have more the meaning of mediator than the title 'Arbitrator' or 'Arbiter,' which had more the meaning of judge. The latter were the terms used in the Convention of 1827. He concluded by saying that current British pressure on Belgium could be seen as being the result of King William's gesture to Britain on the boundary question.[36]

British reaction to the award was much less dramatic and vastly more positive. Indeed, the British had already decided that even if the king were to propose a compromise line they would feel predisposed to accept it. When the award was made on 10 January, Bagot sent a copy back to London with Douglas, but he also wrote privately to Palmerston, praising the king for acting on the whole question in circumstances in which he might have asked for more time. More important, Bagot thought the decision a good one. 'As far as I am a judge of the question,' he wrote, 'it appears to me that we have no reason to be dissatisfied with the decision taken as a whole.' Bagot's opinion was not a superficial one; he had been involved with the boundary question periodically since 1816. As for the United States, Bagot thought that the decision would 'not be altogether unsatisfactory to the Federal Government in America,' and he was certain that Britain's ceding of Rouse's Point would as a matter of national interest compensate the United States for its loss of territory of less importance. Maine, however, would be another matter, and Bagot thought that the decision would 'raise a storm in the district of Maine,' although that rivalry between the two levels of the American political system was something 'with which we have nothing to do.' Shrewdly, Bagot observed that these kinds of federal–state rivalries were the sorts of 'battles perhaps which are destined, someday or other, to dissolve the confederation.'[37] Bagot then went on to anticipate the arguments against the award that the 'Mainites' were likely to put forward in opposition. He was not far wide of the mark.

On 18 January Lord Palmerston sent instructions that the king be generously thanked for his labours at a time when he had many other responsibilities. Palmerston also asked that Bagot convey the British king's pleasure in 'acquiescing on His part in the decision of His Netherlands My.' – a decision that was regarded as just and which transcended the obscurities of the treaty of 1783 by 'a liberal compromise.'[38] It may be presumed that the view of the Foreign Office can be seen in Undersecretary John Backhouse's comments to Stratford Canning, that the king had 'decided in a way that I think we ought to consider very satisfactory – especially in the present irritated state of his mind in respect to this country.'[39] At almost the same time, of course, the Foreign Office learned of Preble's claim that the award did not comply with the request to the king to determine the correct reading of the terms of the treaty of 1783. An opinion from the Crown law officers was requested on 27 January, and on 9 February Herbert Jenner wrote to confirm an earlier conversation in which he had stated that the instructions to the king had been sufficiently specific about the exact things that he was to determine that the king did not have the power properly to suggest alternatives. Therefore, 'the Arbitrator had exceeded the Authority with which he was empowered by the two Countries.' As a result, Jenner concluded, 'a sufficient pretext is afforded to the American Government to object to be bound by the decision of the Arbitrator, if they should be inclined to avail themselves of it.'[40] In May, Jenner and Thomas Denmar sent a more elaborate reply to Palmerston, which drew the same conclusion about the U.S. right to dissent from the award but commented about the compromise. 'This We think, however just and Equitable may have been the reasons, upon which this decision may have been founded, He was not authorized to do.'[41] These opinions answered the question of whether the British government had the right simply to impose the boundary line as devised by the arbitral award independent of the compliance of the United States or the state of Maine.

Something of a debate went on as to what the British government should do. Charles Vaughan kept up a steady correspondence during the spring of 1831 with Palmerston and Backhouse, attempting to inform them about U.S. opinion. By July, Vaughan, then returned to London, reported that President Jackson and his advisers were inclined 'to acquiesce in the decision of the King of the Netherlands, but they stand in awe of remonstrances of Maine & Massachusetts.' It was Vaughan's opinion that Jackson would wait until the next session of Congress and then submit the award to the Senate to let it decide. Although he had been informed of the law officers' opinion, Vaughan thought that the British government ought to press the Americans to accept the award and should appoint commissioners to mark out the boundary.[42]

In any case, Palmerston chose to move slowly on how to approach the United States. On 14 October, he wrote to Charles Bankhead, British chargé d'affaires in Washington, instructing him to give formal notice that the British were prepared to accept the award, even taking into account the objections raised against it. In a second note of the same day, Palmerston laid out more delicate instructions. Bankhead could 'intimate privately' to the secretary of state that the British government would not look on acceptance of the award 'as necessarily precluding the two Govt. from future modification of the terms of the arrangement of that instrument' if it were demonstrated that the boundary line was 'capable of being improved to the mutual convenience and advantage of both Countries.'[43] Bankhead was to take precautions not to be misunderstood and to make it clear that the United States must accept the award as it stood before any such modification could be considered.

All things considered, Palmerston's was a very generous offer and, in a country where the decision-making process was less dependent on the acquiescence of a second tier of state governments, might well have smoothed over any objections that had arisen regarding the manner in which the award was reached. However, in the United States in the 1830s, with as many as five states affected and a large number of others ready to sympathize, not on the boundary matter, but on the relationship of the state governments to the federal government, it was not a practical suggestion. Bankhead sent off a long note to Secretary of State Edward Livingston on 20 December 1831, informing him of the British decision to accept the award, but he waited to see what the Senate might do with the award before raising the possibility of a negotiated adjustment of the boundary line.[44]

If the British were cautious and unsure of how to proceed, the Americans enjoyed no position of advantage either. Preble communicated the results of the award, as soon as it was known, to the government of Maine as well as to the Department of State. He then requested permission to leave The Hague in early March, and by the end of the month this had been granted. Preble thus returned to the United States by 14 July and, ostensibly to see his wife and family home to Portland, travelled immediately to Maine, where he conferred with state officials.[45] Initiative thus passed into the hands of the governments of Maine and Massachusetts. On 27 February the Maine legislature passed a series of resolutions declaring variously that the state of Maine had the authority to exercise its jurisdiction in the territory claimed as far north as the St Lawrence watershed, that the Convention of 1827 violated Maine's sovereign rights, that the arbitrator's decision 'ought not to be considered obligatory upon the Government of the United States,' and that no state could be called on to give up its territory without its consent. Governor Samuel E. Smith wrote to President Jackson conveying these resolutions and commenting that rumours had reached Maine that the arbitrator had made a decision dividing the disputed territory by a compromise line and that the 'boundaries, as designated by treaties [have] been totally disregarded.'[46]

Copies of the text of the award and Preble's protest were forwarded to the Maine government in mid-March, after the official text had arrived in Washington. In reaction, the state legislature adopted a report on 31 March which questioned the independence of the arbitrator, describing the king as being overthrown by the Belgians, deprived of more than half of his kingdom. These events 'reduced him to the former dominions of the Stadtholder' and rendered him no longer king of the Netherlands, but 'only King of Holland.'[47] The legislature objected to his compromise decision and declared that its adoption by the federal government would be 'in violation of the constitutional rights of the State of Maine.'[48] Attitudes hostile to the award were no doubt strengthened by the arrival of William Pitt Preble in July. Preble himself published a pamphlet anonymously later in 1831 in which he argued strongly that the king had been given no authority to depart from the obligation of choosing between the two sets of claims. 'It was not for him to assume the office and attributes of a friendly compounder, governed by no rule or principle but his own discretion,' Preble wrote, and he called attention to the king's 'recommendation' of the proposed compromise boundary rather than the use of the word 'decision.'[49]

In these circumstances and for other reasons as well, the Jackson administration moved slowly. In the culmination of the crisis over the reputation of the wife of the secretary of war, Peggy O'Neal Eaton, Jackson asked his entire cabinet to resign and appointed a new cabinet. In this reshuffling Martin Van Buren became minister to Britain and Edward Livingston secretary of state. All of this took place during the spring and summer of 1831, but by August the new secretary of state began to draft instructions for the new minister. The result was a shrewd and thoughtful analysis of the situation. The United States had grounds for objection to the award, on the basis of both the changed domestic circumstances of the king of the Netherlands and the compromise decision outside the parameters of the instructions to the arbitrator. The first objection was not practical because it would be 'offensive to the monarch who was chosen to decide our difference,' and also it was inadequate, because the extent of the king's dependence on Britain had been known before the award was announced.[50] The only sound basis for an objection was that the award did not answer the questions put to the arbitrator to identify the boundary described in the treaty of 1783. While the United States would be within its rights to object on this issue, Livingston said, there was a problem of international opinion. The United States, having agreed to arbitration, would appear to have rejected the award because it was not favourable. 'This would not be strictly the true, but would be the popular statement,' and such a state of affairs would 'throw a shade of ill faith over the reputation of our Government' which would probably not be diminished 'by the cogency of our legal arguments.'[51]

It was a thoughtful assessment, and it gave rise to the question of whether to accept the award notwithstanding the objections to its process. Maine claimed about four and a half million acres of 'generally bad land,' Livingston asserted, and New Hampshire, about a hundred thousand acres of 'equally bad land.' The award ceded about a million acres, or almost one-third of the total, to Britain. What were the practical consequences? Lower Canada and New Brunswick got a road 'without any consequent loss to us; for in time of war we can always cut off the communication, and, in time of peace, it does us no harm.' For its part, the United States got the fort at Rouse's Point – 'the only military position that can defend the entrance into Lake Champlain, in time of war.' Then there was the larger question of open-ended international controversies. 'The pendency of every question between nations is a positive evil,' the Secretary said; 'its settlement is a positive good.' Negotiations, joint commissions, and now arbitration having failed, what alternatives were left? 'The dispute, then, must be renewed with all its consequences of broils from conflicting establishments in the disputed grounds,' Livingston observed grimly, resulting in 'a border war, ending, sooner or later, in a general one.'[52]

At this point, however, having progressed so logically to this conclusion, the Jackson administration's resolution faltered. On the one hand, Livingston said, 'The President ... is of opinion that, although we are not strictly bound by the award, it is expedient that we should abide by it.'[53] Charles Vaughan reported to Palmerston that 'the President expressed his perfect satisfaction with the decision, where upon its receipt at Washington, it was translated to him.'[54] On the other hand, it was not clear, Livingston observed, 'how far the United States can cede any part of a State,' and Jackson was not willing to 'assume responsibility' for such a decision. His cabinet had advised him to 'report the case to the Senate, and take their advice on the expediency of submitting to the award.'[55] This was an approach that ran counter to the logic of the earlier analysis of the benefits of the award and the probable consequences of its failure. However, the foreign policy of the United States, more than that of most countries, required regard to internal political pressures. Van Buren was instructed to inform the British government of the president's views if the British formally decided to accept the award (which they did on 14 October) and simply to refer the matter back to Washington if they rejected it.

Jackson submitted the award, together with correspondence from Preble and the government of Maine, to the Senate for advice on 7 December 1831. In January the Senate requested more documents from Maine and more diplomatic correspondence. By 21 March the Senate's Foreign Relations Committee adopted a resolution recommending acceptance of the award, over opposition from the senators of the affected states. Furthermore, it was clear that there was insufficient support in

the Senate itself to carry the measure by a two-thirds vote.[56] Deliberations in that chamber were seriously disrupted by the antagonisms
roused throughout the political community by Jackson's tariff bill (the
so-called 'Tariff of Abominations') and the resistance to it in South
Carolina, which led to the 'Nullification Crisis.' In the course of this
political debate, opinions became so polarized as virtually to paralyse
the legislature. Even confirmation of Jackson's appointment of Van
Buren as minister to Britain fell victim to the passions of the day. When
the Senate's vote was tied on the matter, Vice-President John C. Calhoun, president of the Senate and also a forceful advocate of states'
rights from South Carolina, cast the tie-breaking vote against Van
Buren, thus defeating and embarrassing the administration.

In the meantime Jackson discussed the possibility of compensation to
Maine and Massachusetts for the loss of claimed territory. 'The question
of indemnity for territory surrendered is a good one, but a question of
great delicacy arises on the manner of suggesting it to the Senate,' he
said, indicating that the administration must not be seen initiating a
procedure to alienate territory of a state, even though the boundary
claimed had never been established.[57] Secretary of State Livingston
opened confidential talks with Preble, who had returned to Washington
in March 1832 as official agent of the state of Maine, to explore the possibility of compensation to Maine by the transfer of federal lands in the
west in exchange for Maine's surrendering claims of jurisdiction to
lands in the disputed boundary territory. Preble agreed to obtain
authority from the state government to enter into such talks but added
specifically in an *aide-mémoire* that Maine would never 'assent to the
award of the arbiter, and he could not be the channel of any proposition
direct[ed] to that effect.'[58] Despite opposition from one member of the
Maine caucus in Congress, the proposal for an indemnity for land
claimed north of the St John River was discussed and agreed to in principle by the state legislature in a secret session. By the end of March, Livingston was able to report to the president that, while no concrete
propositions had been put forward by either the federal or the state government, Maine seemed willing to consider compensation in western
land in return for agreeing to some kind of compromise settlement,
though not necessarily that of the award. Unfortunately, however, discussion of the idea of 'selling' to the British the northern lands claimed
by Maine got into the newspapers.[59]

In early April, Preble told Livingston that Maine would appoint commissioners to carry out these talks if the federal government did

the same. This was done. Governor Smith informed the president on 10 May that Preble, Reuel Williams, and Nicholas Emery had been appointed to confer with federal authorities on the boundary matters with the hope of arranging an amicable settlement between the United States and Britain.[60] The president appointed Livingston, Secretary of the Treasury, Louis McLane, and Secretary of the Navy, Levi Woodbury, and the two groups held several meetings between 18 May and 2 June.

By early June they had reached the stage where the Maine delegates were prepared to sign an agreement that had several key provisions. The federal government would open new talks with Britain to determine the line designated in the treaty of 1783, but, if that process failed, Maine would agree to 'the establishment of such a new boundary between the dominions of the United States and Great Britain as should be mutually convenient.' In the event, Maine was to be compensated by equivalent territory elsewhere in the country (the Michigan territory was mentioned) – upwards of a million acres. In order to facilitate this arrangement, Maine also agreed to 'release to the United States the right and claim of Maine to jurisdiction over the territory lying north and east of the line designated by the Arbitrer.'[61] This understanding seemed to open the door to enabling the state and federal governments to work in harmony in attempting to reach a new agreement with Britain. On 12 June, however, Livingston wrote to Preble accepting the Maine delegation's request that further talks be suspended until the Senate advised the president about accepting the award of the king of the Netherlands.[62]

The behaviour of the Senate was somewhat baffling. Although its Foreign Relations Committee had recommended acceptance of the award, the Senate itself was not in favour. Henry Clay, once again a Senator from Kentucky, argued that if the arbitrator had not decided the issue the award was not binding and that if the president said that the award was binding Congress as a whole needed to pass legislation to implement it. In any case, it was not for the Senate to decide. However, Clay also took the view that when king William issued the award he was no longer king of the Netherlands, but king only of Holland, and subject to British judgment for the fate of his kingdom. He was not in a position to decide the question objectively and had not done so. Peleg Sprague of Maine asserted that the king had not decided the question submitted to him but had proposed a new boundary. Maine, he said, could not accept this. A resolution supporting acceptance was amended on

16 June in such a way as to nullify it. Daniel Webster proposed an amendment to send the whole matter of the award back to the president for him to decide without the advice of the Senate. This was defeated. A resolution to reject the award was passed on 21 June and then defeated two days later. However, there was not sufficient support in the chamber to pass a resolution accepting the award. On 23 June the Senate passed a resolution advising the president to reopen negotiations with the British.[63]

The British watched events with a mixture of exasperation and dismay. In December 1831 Bankhead had reported to Palmerston that he estimated from speeches by John Holmes of Maine (the former commissioner under article 4) that 'ultimately the Senate will agree to the Award of the King of the Netherlands.'[64] Unfortunately by January 1832 he had second thoughts. 'I fear that some difficulty will be experienced,' he said, and, moreover, 'The President and his Cabinet have no influence in accelerating the passage of the measure through the Senate.'[65] In February, Bankhead worried about the effect of the resolutions passed by the Maine legislature and Preble's presence in Washington as Maine's agent. The British chargé became only superficially aware of the secret talks that began in the spring between delegations from Maine and members of the cabinet. When he asked Livingston about what was happening, he got an evasive reply. Nevertheless, between Maine newspaper accounts and what he heard, Bankhead was not far from the truth. Maine seemed ready to agree to some kind of compromise in exchange for an indemnity, he wrote, and Preble seemed 'to have adopted a course more likely to bring the question to an equitable issue' than when he protested to the king.[66]

In June, with the fate of the award in the Senate still uncertain, Bankhead decided to approach Livingston with the proposition that Palmerston had suggested the previous October – that the British government might be willing to negotiate adjustments to the boundary if the United States first accepted the award. He had hesitated because the Senate seemed so dilatory and because of his anxiety that any overt action by a British representative might compromise the chance of the award's being approved by the Senate. However, he had learned in the previous few days that the Senate was dealing with the award, and presumably he must have known also about the growing interest in Maine, in the Senate, and perhaps in the State Department for new negotiations leading to a compromise line, but starting from something like the boundary set forth in the award. Bankhead gave no indication of Livingston's response to the proposition, other than to say that the secretary of state asked whether or not Bankhead could consider such negotiations before the award had been accepted.[67] While the answer was negative, Livingston must have been encouraged that the British were in fact prepared to consider some adjustment to the king's line.

At this point things began to come apart. By July it became publicly acknowledged that the Senate would not advise the president to accept the award because it had failed to identify the boundary in the treaty of 1783, although the Senate had passed a resolution urging the president to open fresh negotiations for an 'amicable, speedy, and satisfactory conclusion, [of] a question which might otherwise interrupt the harmony which so happily subsists between the two countries.'[68] In retrospect it was a glib and empty gesture. Bankhead wrote immediately to Palmerston, with no doubt genuine 'regret,' to say that the Senate had rejected the award, despite the president's wishes and the Foreign Relations Committee's approval. He ascribed the real cause to Maine's refusal to negotiate with the federal government about an indemnity and the Jackson administration's unwillingness to force an issue of states' rights during an election year.[69] Livingston wrote a long letter to Bankhead some days later, officially informing him of the failure of the award and of the Senate's urging fresh negotiations. Indeed Livingston wrote also to Aaron Vail, the new American chargé in London – Martin Van Buren having returned home to receive the vice-presidential nomination – to inform him of the award's defeat and to ask him to indicate to the British government the president's desire to open talks on the boundary question.[70]

By late August the British minister to the United States, Charles Vaughan, still on leave in England, was asked to comment on the reports of the Senate's action. Vaughan wrote to Backhouse that they must be suspicious of proposals to negotiate a new boundary after the Senate and Maine had rejected an award that was, in Vaughan's words, 'detrimental to Great Britain, & advantageous to them.' Even before talks began, the Senate proposed a demand for U.S. navigation rights on the St John River. He certainly thought that before negotiations began the British government should obtain assurances from the United States that the federal government had the power to conclude an agreement. 'We have a singularly crafty people to deal with,' the minister concluded, with more exasperation than generosity, 'and we are bound therefore to look with some suspicion & distrust upon any proposal made by them.' Vaughan repeated these views to Palmerston during the autumn. But although he could sincerely say, 'I feel all possible anxiety to see this Question of Boundary settled,' his suspicion of the Americans did not allow him much scope to suggest any positive steps.[71]

Caution, suspicion, the fact that the accredited Minister was still on leave, and resentment at the failure of the award all help explain why the British government did nothing during the months after the Senate's action. In late February 1833 Livingston wrote to Aaron Vail that 'we are waiting anxiously for a decision of the British Government to our proposition for the renewal of negotiations on the subject of the North East Boundary.' The United States did not insist on holding the talks in Washington, the secretary said, but was determined to get them started. Vail wrote to Palmerston on 3 April inquiring about the British government's views and assuring him that the United States would be willing to hold the talks in London.[72] Palmerston's hesitation, however, was more governed by his lack of understanding of what the United States expected from the negotiations and his doubts about the American government's ability to obtain ratification of any new treaty in the Senate. By April 1833 Charles Vaughan was back in Washington, however reluctantly, and about to begin a series of long exchanges with first Livingston and then his successor, Louis McLane. Vaughan skilfully held the secretaries at arm's length, assuring them of Britain's desire to settle the question as soon as possible, but inquiring whether 'the President of the United States will possess the power of carrying into full effect his part of any engagement which may be concluded between the Plenipotentiaries of the two Governments.'[73]

If Vaughan saw the confusion and contradictory behaviour of the federal and state governments, as indications of 'a singularly crafty people,' he overestimated the Americans. If he genuinely thought that time was on the Americans' side in this matter, he was wrong. Another opportunity closed even before Vaughan reached the United States. On 4 March 1833 the Maine legislature passed resolutions repealing the authority delegated a year earlier to enable the three delegates to negotiate on Maine's behalf for both a compromise line and indemnity for lands given up. The new resolutions said that any treaty or agreement concerning Maine's boundary would have to be submitted to the people and approved by a majority vote. It was a 'death blow,' one Maine historian wrote, to the negotiation of a compromise boundary line.[74]

With Maine's action in March 1833, if not with the Senate's refusal to advise the president in the previous July, the chain of events set in motion by the Treaty of Ghent in December 1814 to settle the whole of the eastern North American boundary – from Passamaquoddy Bay to the Lake of the Woods – came to an end. It was almost twenty years since the Treaty of Ghent had ended the War of 1812 and seventeen years since the first commissions had met at St Andrews, New Brunswick, in 1816. In truth, the process had stopped the previous summer, but efforts had continued, led by Secretary of State Livingston, to devise a way to obtain Maine's acceptance of some form of compensation for northern lands that the British were less and less willing to cede. When these efforts broke down in March 1833, the process stopped. On 28 December, Charles Bankhead informed the U.S. secretary of state that, because the United States had rejected the boundary proposed by the king of the Netherlands, the British government felt no longer committed to its original acceptance and hereby announced that it 'withdraws its consent' to accept the compromise recommended.[75]

A decade later, when a successful boundary treaty was finally negotiated, former president Andrew Jackson wrote to one of his old confidants, 'I had determined to accept the award made by the King of Holland regardless of the remonstrance of Judge Preble, but my whole cabinet remonstrated against my decision recommending me, as the senate was in session, to lay it before them. I yielded to this recommendation, but sincerely I have regretted it since.'[76]

What can be said about the award by the king of the Netherlands? Certainly, the monarch had exceeded his authority in devising a compromise boundary line that flew so dramatically in the face of the language of the treaty of 1783. As John G. Deane, of the Maine legislature, put it, the king 'found the highlands ... to be in the base of the river St. John,' and Deane concluded, 'No person but a Dutchman who had lived among bogs and dikes could possibly have come to such a result.'[77] Nevertheless, the line proposed by the king, following the St John and the St Francis rivers, was the clearest natural frontier in the region, and, while not mathematically balanced, it did divide the disputed territory in a practical way. As a compromise line, it was not a bad boundary. During the next decade of controversy, this would not be forgotten.

Chapter Nine

Skirmishes on the Frontier

If the diplomatic efforts to salvage some kind of settlement out of the collapse of the arbitration finally trickled to an end in 1833, the 1830s and early 1840s saw serious crises along the frontier between British North America and the United States – perhaps most notably, as this chapter recounts, the *Caroline* affair, the Aroostook crisis, and the McLeod affair. By the early 1840s there was the grave possibility that a third war involving Britain, the United States, and British North America might result from the constant friction along the border, despite the efforts of many responsible authorities.

Apart from the desirability of resolving once and for all the boundary as set forth in the Treaty of Paris of 1783, there were growing tensions resulting from evolving national interests, spreading settlement, and commercial development in parts of the borderlands. Early Loyalist settlement in what became New Brunswick was along the Bay of Fundy coast in places such as St Andrews and Saint John. Given the topography of that coastline, the lower reaches of major rivers, such as the St Croix and the St John, ran from north to south. Loyalist settlement along these rivers eventually brought New Brunswickers into contact with the United States. For the most part, the St Croix Commission had resolved the ambiguity of that boundary in 1798. However, as English New Brunswickers moved north up the St John into settlements at Fredericton, Woodstock, Grand Falls, and several smaller communities, they came ever closer to the disputed boundary area. Furthermore, in the 1780s the French-speaking Acadians, who in the 1760s had been allowed to remain in small settlements along the coast, moved north to an old Indian village on the Madawaska River, a tributary of the St John, some 130 miles from the English-speaking settlements. By 1787 eighty Acadian families had received land grants in this remote region. But if Woodstock was only about ten miles east of the due-north line from the source of the St Croix, and Grand Falls only about two miles east of the due-north line, the Madawaska settlements were at least thirty miles west of the line and thus bound to fall within the territory claimed by the United States. The fact that early settlement in Maine tended to be much further south and along the coast meant that serious pressure from American population did not begin to surface until into the 1820s, whatever the territorial claims based on the treaty of 1783 might be.[1]

Another consideration was Britain's evolving interests in New Brunswick and Upper and Lower Canada. From the end of the War of American Independence until the end of the Napoleonic Wars, New Brunswick had been a principal supplier of timber for the Royal Navy. Britain's interests tended to focus on the security of the east coast settlements. However, both the conflict with the United States in 1812 and the restoration of peace in Europe in 1815 changed its interests. The War of 1812, which proved that the United States could strike at British possessions in North America, demonstrated the military importance of an overland route from New Brunswick to Lower Canada, particularly during winter, when the St Lawrence was frozen. This route was essentially up the St John River to the Madawaska River, across Lake Temiscouata, and over the height of land to Rivière du Loup and the St Lawrence. Britain's determination to protect this route can be seen in Stratford Canning's conclusions of 1824 and 1825. 'The extent of the territory in dispute is not without some degree of interest,' he said, 'but the objects of real importance are to remove the American frontier as much as possible from the line of the St. Lawrence, to open a direct communication between Canada and New Brunswick.'[2]

The Canadian Rebellions of 1837 in the winter of 1837–8 and the 'Aroostook War' in the winter of 1839 drove home the continuing military value of this vital link in time of crisis. Furthermore, as Upper and Lower Canada became increasingly important as suppliers of timber, fur, and agricultural produce, the link took on increasing economic significance as well. Whatever thoughts British diplomats may have had about the border between New Brunswick and Maine in the 1780s, or even in 1814, they could view the undecided boundary only with growing concern in the 1830s and 1840s. As the nineteenth century unfolded, the importance of the Maritime colonies declined, at least in proportion to the expanding Canadas. To secure the route and to protect Upper and Lower Canada became a major priority.[3]

The Canadas, however, were never easy colonies to govern. As Lord Melbourne, the prime minister, wrote to the secretary of war after the rebellions had broken out, 'How these provinces are to be settled with anything like security, I do not see. The French population entirely hostile and ready to rise whenever called upon, the frontier thronged with refugees, the Americans always exciting and ready to assist rebellion, and the English population loyal according to their own fancy, and upon condition that they have their own way in everything.'[4] It was not a straightforward situation.

Britain's status as a great power meant that it could not look at these North American questions in isolation. British foreign policy in the 1830s and early 1840s was very turbulent, thanks in part to the measures implemented by Lord Palmerston as foreign secretary. Particularly relevant was the deterioration of British relations with France late in the 1830s, paralleling a similar breakdown of relations with the United States. Early in 1841 a friend warned the Duke of Wellington from Paris that the French government would exploit any trouble with the United States. 'Any idea of war between England and America would be hailed with great delight, and M. Thiers has already expressed his gratification at such a probability.'[5] Britain had little freedom of action in European international relations.

Britain became the world's leading power in the years after 1815, whereas the United States, even though it emerged from the War of 1812 stronger than before, was still very weak on the international scale. Not surprisingly, Britain did not hesitate to assert its vital strategic interests in the border region, particularly the road from Saint John to Quebec City, as those interests grew. British and New Brunswick officials included substantial parts of the disputed border region within their jurisdiction while acknowledging that a final settlement might surrender some of that land to the United States. As Henry Unwin Addington wrote to the undersecretary at the Foreign Office, 'We certainly have the advantage over the Americans of a *de facto* occupation of parts of that territory, and of long standing,' although he added confidentially, 'but I doubt whether we have a right to argue that such occupation draws along with it the "de jure" as well as the "de facto."'[6] In fact, an assumption of *de jure* occupation is exactly what transpired; British interests were paramount, even if the legalities were uncertain. New Brunswickers were closer to the disputed territory; they did get there first, if only to cross it on their way to Quebec.

Americans from Maine saw this New Brunswick presence as an aggressive attempt to pre-empt American claims to the territory based on the Treaty of 1783 and as an implementation of the notion that possession is nine-tenths of the law. As was shown above, Maine spokesmen argued that the intentions of the negotiators and the wording of the treaty of 1783 clearly meant the northern boundary to run along the crest of the St Lawrence watershed, with all of the land in the St John and Aroostook river valleys, west of the due-north line, within the United States. Therefore they saw the building of the military road, the extension of New Brunswick's political and legal institutions, the construction of army depots and barracks, and the cutting of timber as elements of a conscious and aggressive imperial expansion into the historic territories of Massachusetts and Maine. When the district of Maine separated from Massachusetts and became a state in March 1820, these sentiments had behind them the political institutions then comparable to those of New Brunswick, though less well situated and supported. The result was a border situation increasingly dangerous to peace between Britain and the United States and more and more difficult to resolve.

One of the early acts in 1820 of the very first governor of Maine, William King, was to assert Maine's interest in the border region to the American agent of the commission under the fifth article of the Treaty of Ghent. This action was not lost on the British agent, who noted that the new state would follow boundary matters with greater interest than either Massachusetts or the U.S. federal government. Although Maine authorities did follow closely the events of the next several years, it was not until 1825 that a new governor, Albion K. Parris, sent an agent into the Aroostook area to report on both lumber operations and land settlement expanding west from New Brunswick. Both the Maine and Massachusetts legislatures took steps to grant deeds to American settlers in the region, and by the end of the summer grants of one hundred acres each were made to John Baker and several others along the St John River. Baker had a farm, a sawmill, a gristmill, and a small store and became the centre of the American community. There were Acadians just down river in the Madawaska settlements and a smattering of English New Brunswickers as well – about 1,200 people altogether. Thus by the mid-1820s people from both New Brunswick and Maine (acting under the authority of their governments) were beginning to settle near to each other and sometimes with stormy relations.

The lieutenant-governor of New Brunswick, Sir Howard Douglas, raised the boundary matter with the British minister to the United

States, Sir Charles Vaughan, in the autumn of 1825. The commission under article 5 had failed to reach a decision in 1822, and resolution of the New Brunswick–Maine boundary was being tentatively discussed, prior to the start of the search for an arbitrator.[7] Douglas complained that George W. Coffin and James Irish, land agents for Massachusetts and Maine, respectively, had been offering to draw up deeds for settlers. They had not only claimed the territory north of the St John River to be American, but they had also assured the settlers that it was not necessary for them to fulfil any obligation to train with the New Brunswick militia and that the New Brunswick land grants were not valid.[8] The U.S. secretary of state, Henry Clay, raised these matters with governors Albion K. Parris of Maine and Levi Lincoln of Massachusetts and learned that New Brunswick lumbermen were cutting timber within the United States. Clay told the governors that every effort was being made to negotiate a final boundary settlement but that, 'in the meantime, it is desirable that each party, governed by a spirit of moderation, should refrain from the adoption of any measure which may tend to give inquietude to the other.' Governor Lincoln replied that Massachusetts had no intention to 'embarrass' the federal government in its negotiations.[9] The two states were in effect warned not to cause trouble.

It was perhaps only a matter of time before an incident involving an unsettled claim would lead to a challenge of jurisdiction. When John Baker and several others who had settled on the St John River, together with some Acadians, attempted to celebrate the fourth of July in 1827 by raising a 'liberty pole,' a New Brunswick magistrate, George Morehouse, ordered him to take the flag down. The next day Baker prepared a declaration, signed by a number of neighbours, in which the signatories asserted their rights as American citizens on what they believed to be territory held by deeds issued by the authority of the state of Maine. Baker was again challenged by Morehouse, who demanded to see the declaration. Although those acts had not been authorized by the government of Maine, Baker and several others took their complaints to the state government in Portland.[10]

The New Brunswick government regarded this as an incursion into its territory and Baker's defiance as a threat. The high sheriff of York, Edward W. Miller, was sent to make a quiet arrest, but when it was learned that he had assembled a body of armed men, the lieutenant-governor and the attorney general dispatched a special messenger with orders for him to proceed without his armed posse. The sheriff complied with these specific instructions, but by the time he reached the

Madawaska settlements he had a new party of men. Baker, having returned home, was arrested while in bed during the early hours of 25 September and taken to jail in Fredericton, New Brunswick.[11]

Governor Lincoln then wrote to Sir Howard Douglas asking for information concerning the arrest and warning that such acts appeared to assert New Brunswick's authority in territory where sovereignty had not yet been determined. These gestures, he said, were bound to inflame the passions of Americans who believed those territories to be part of Maine. Douglas's reply did not satisfy Lincoln, who then sent Charles S. Daveis, a Portland lawyer, to speak to Douglas and obtain Baker's release. The governor also wrote to the U.S. secretary of state, who sent a federal agent, Samuel B. Barrell, to Maine and New Brunswick to investigate and use whatever influence could be brought to bear.[12] The secretary complained to Vaughan that undue force had been used on the frontier, that Baker had been arrested in his sleep by forty-five armed men for trivial charges, and that the property of others had been 'carried off to the last Cow' by New Brunswick officials. Vaughan responded that the charges against Baker were serious and his actions a threat to New Brunswick.[13] At the instigation of the U.S. Senate, President Adams commented on Baker's confinement by saying that it was 'incompatible with the mutual understanding existing between the Government of the United States and of Great Britain.' The British minister had made such an assertion on 27 February, and both the president and the secretary of state were quick to deny it.[14]

Neither Daveis nor the secretary of state and the president had any influence in getting Baker's release. Indeed, the American special agent, Samuel B. Barrell, reported to Clay that there had been 'much undue excitement' about Baker. Barrell had talked with Baker several times and concluded that 'there was no occasion for our Government to interfere with the proceedings against him on the part of the authorities of N. Brunswick.'[15] Baker went to trial on 8 May 1828, some eight months after he had been arrested. The trial was presided over by three judges: John Saunders, the chief justice of the province; Ward Chipman, Jr, the British agent for the commissions under articles 4 and 5; and John Murray Bliss. The attorney general acted as prosecutor and entered a charge of conspiracy and sedition by virtue of Baker's raising an American flag in the 'County of York,' New Brunswick; of his proclaiming the region to be part of the United States; and of his obstructing the delivery of the mails. Baker, speaking in his own defence, denied the right of the court to try him. The jury found Baker guilty, and he was fined twenty-five pounds sterling and sentenced to a further two months in jail, although he was so well known in Fredericton that he was allowed to walk freely about the town. Baker was released on 25 October, his fine paid by the state of Maine.[16]

Crown officials effectively asserted their authority from the Aroostook River north and west beyond the St John River into most of the disputed territory, despite the uncertainty of where the boundary would finally run. This practice of assuming authority all along the frontier inescapably strengthened the British position in the region. However, as Maine's foremost historian of the controversy has concluded, these actions 'served only to embitter the people of Maine against their provincial neighbors for a long time.'[17] In 1828, the U.S. government, partly to assert itself in the region and partly to reassure the Maine and Massachusetts governments and the local settlers, built a fortification at Houlton, about four or five miles from the due-north line and about ten miles from Woodstock, New Brunswick, to be garrisoned by 200 men. As well as showing the flag, and providing a local market for farm produce, the soldiers built one of the first roads into the area.[18]

A second incident occurred in 1831. The Maine legislature had authorized the election of representatives from the Madawaska area, south of the St John River. Local settlers met in August to attempt to implement the procedures for town organization and elections. Not only did the Americans in the area participate, but, as the New Brunswick historian James Hannay noted, 'they induced a few of the more ignorant French to cooperate with them.'[19] They were ordered to cease by the local captain of the New Brunswick militia. A second meeting in September to arrange for an election brought further protest and a decision by the New Brunswick government to act once again. The new lieutenant-governor, Sir Archibald Campbell, a tough and autocratic soldier, led a large armed party, which ascended the St John River from Fredericton and searched the area for those who were known to have participated in election affairs. Numerous people fled into the woods, including John Baker, but several were arrested on 26 September and taken back to Fredericton for trial. Three were charged and convicted, with fines of fifty pounds and sentences of three months each. Once again letters from the governor of Maine had no effect, and in view of the U.S. government's ongoing effort to negotiate some kind of settlement with the British government, Secretary of State Livingston urged the governor not to aggravate the situation.[20]

Late in December 1835, officials from Lennoxville in Lower Canada attempted to arrest several people in the Indian Stream settlement in the disputed territory along the upper Connecticut River, between Lower Canada and New Hampshire. After one man was taken into custody, the officials were set upon by an armed party, the prisoner was set free, and at least one of the officials, a magistrate, was injured and taken prisoner himself to Canaan, Vermont.[21] In fact, trouble had been brewing in this area for some years. Earlier in 1832 some residents in the region had proclaimed the 'Republic of Indian Stream,' and they rejected the authority of both New Hampshire and Lower Canada. Both the province and the state subsequently attempted to assert jurisdiction in the area, giving rise to fresh tensions. Anxiety about this incident continued into 1836, when the government of Lower Canada accepted the assurances of the New Hampshire militia that the state would not assert its authority in the region until the boundary was permanently decided. The Connecticut River boundary remained an issue discussed by the British and American governments, however, until 1837.[22]

Another crisis arose in 1837. The Maine government commissioned Ebenezer S. Greely, a land agent, to take a census of people living in 'Penobscot County,' including the northern regions beyond the surveyed townships. On 29 May 1837 Greely was arrested and taken to Woodstock, New Brunswick, but he was subsequently released because he was acting as an official of the state of Maine. However, he was arrested again on 6 June and taken this time to Fredericton and jailed. An appeal from the U.S. president was successful, and by the end of August Greely had been let go. Greely's determination to continue to work in the Madawaska region was a source of anxiety for the federal government, and by September he was arrested again. Not until February 1838 was he released for the third time.[23] As a result of Greely's presence, Lieutenant-Governor Sir John Harvey sent one company of 43rd Regiment to Woodstock and another to Grand Falls, and guns and ammunition were stored in the area to equip 500 militiamen should the need arise.[24] Thus these persisting incidents kept the volatile boundary issue before the public in both New Brunswick and Maine and generated strong feelings of resentment on both sides.

In 1837 a major crisis blew up further west along the frontier that had its origins in the domestic politics of Upper and Lower Canada, but which had consequences that spilled over into the United States for the next five years.[25] Though not directly related to the boundary settlement, these disturbances affected relations between Britain and the United

States and exacerbated the problem of confidence and trust. The 1830s marked the end of a conservative atmosphere in both Europe and America that had prevailed since the Congress of Vienna. A climate for change was generated by the Polish revolt in Russia, the July Revolution in France, and the August uprising in Belgium, all in 1830, and the passage of the great Reform Bill in Britain in 1832. British North America had also been subject to political tension between democratic reformers and conservative oligarchical rule. Colonial governments created in the late eighteenth century had an upper house and an executive council appointed by, and responsible to, the lieutenant-governor. This led in Upper and Lower Canada to growing antagonism between the elected lower house and the governments. As various spokesmen for the legislators defied the governors and their advisers, a crisis developed. Rebellion broke out in Lower Canada in November 1837, and although this was suppressed by crown forces without much difficulty, it led to increased agitation in Upper Canada also. The government in Upper Canada moved to arrest the leading reformers in the legislature on 1 December, and by the sixth the colony was in a state of rebellion, although crown authorities never really lost control. The leaders of the rebellions in the two provinces, Louis-Joseph Papineau in Lower Canada and William Lyon Mackenzie in Upper Canada, together with many of their followers, 'Patriots' and 'Rebels,' respectively, fled across the border into Vermont and New York.[26]

Papineau travelled to New York and then to Paris, while Mackenzie stayed in the border region and made Buffalo, New York, where he was hailed as a hero, his base for a return to Upper Canada. Mackenzie was a Scottish immigrant to Upper Canada who, through the newspapers that he edited, had emerged as a prominent critic of the political establishment of the province (the 'Family Compact'). He was elected to the legislative assembly in 1828, became the first mayor of Toronto in 1834, and emerged as a leader of public discontent. Mackenzie had the support of not only those who had fled with him but also a growing number of enthusiastic New Yorkers. (He promised all who joined him three hundred acres and a hundred dollars when he formed a government in Canada.) Towards the end of December 1837, Mackenzie was able to lead his followers – figures vary from 150 to 700 – across the Niagara River to Navy Island on the Canadian side. This was an excellent site, in swiftly moving water, near Niagara Falls, with steep banks that could be easily defended. Mackenzie had managed to acquire some cannons with which his forces had bombarded some of the farms near Chippawa. The lieutenant-governor of Upper Canada sent 2,500 militia to the area. On 28 December the Rebels hired the forty-six-ton steamer, *Caroline*, out of Buffalo, to move men and supplies from Schlosser, New York, across the river to Navy Island. The Canadian militia investigated and decided that the *Caroline* posed a serious military threat. The following evening, 29 December, a party of seven boats, each crewed by eight men, and led by Commander Andrew Drew of the Royal Navy, set out for Navy Island to destroy the *Caroline*. Finding that the vessel was not at the island, they crossed the river to Schlosser, boarded the ship there, cutting it loose and setting it on fire. In the mêlée several Americans were slashed with cutlasses and others beaten. Amos Durfee was shot, and several people were never accounted for. The *Caroline* itself broke up and sank just before reaching the falls. Commander Drew and his men returned to Chippawa as heroes. It was a classic exercise in nineteenth-century 'gunboat diplomacy' by a great power against a minor power.[27]

The effect in the United States was electric. News of the rebellions themselves had already reached Washington, and President Martin Van Buren, then struggling with a financial panic, had already sent messages to the border governors and federal district attorneys, asking them to take into custody anyone attempting to involve the United States in the conflict. Governor William L. Marcy of New York had downplayed the urgency of the request, and the district attorney was slow in getting to Buffalo. Thus, despite the president's best efforts, Mackenzie's expedition to Navy Island and the *Caroline* affair had occurred and provoked an incident.[28] As this new crisis unfolded, exaggerated accounts spread throughout the country, with stories that over forty Americans had been massacred in their sleep in an attack by British troops. Van Buren learned of the incident as he was about to preside over a dinner party at the White House. He told General Winfield Scott, one of the guests, 'Blood has been shed; you must go with all speed to the Niagara frontier.'[29]

The danger was that the passionate local population would provoke incidents that would make war unavoidable. General Scott's task was to assert federal authority in the region, in the face of inertia by local government officials, and to exercise a calming influence. Existing neutrality legislation was very weak, local authorities were sympathetic with Mackenzie, the state militia was unreliable, and there were almost no army troops available. The U.S. army numbered only 7,834 in 1837, and more than half of its men were engaged in the Seminole War in Florida; the rest were dispersed among some sixty posts and forts throughout the

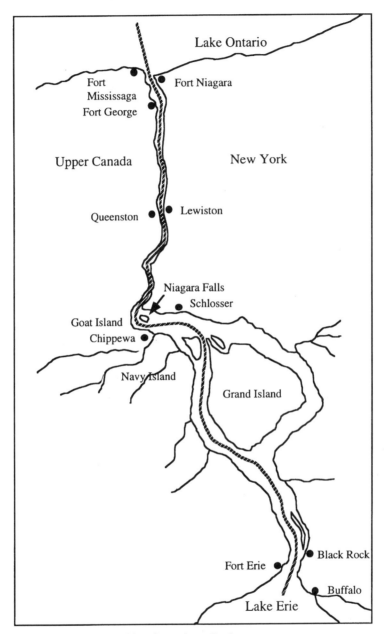

Map 13. The Niagara River boundary: final

country. The garrisons along the northern frontier were, according to one historian, manned by 'the aged and infirm, freeing more able combatants for service elsewhere.'[30] Nevertheless, such was Scott's prestige that, travelling through western New York with Governor Marcy, he was able to have a calming effect, despite sympathy for the Rebels. The president also facilitated the passage by early March 1838 of a new neutrality law that gave the federal government more power to seize weapons and to intervene to prevent filibustering expeditions.[31] On 12 March the secretary of state, John Forsyth, sent the American minister in London, Andrew Stevenson, instructions to protest to the British government against the sinking of the *Caroline* and the injury and damage caused, which he did on 22 May. However, this message was also accompanied by a personal note from Van Buren to Lord Palmerston, delivered by the president's son, assuring the foreign secretary of his good will in the crisis.[32]

The British gradually became convinced that Van Buren genuinely wanted peace and was not hoping to exploit the rebellions as an opportunity to annex British North America. The contrast between President Jackson's lack of action along the Texas frontier in 1836 and Van Buren's efforts and statements concerning the northern frontier was clear to everyone.[33] The prime minister, Lord Melbourne, wrote to Lord John Russell that Van Buren's neutrality proclamation was 'highly satisfactory.'[34] Nevertheless, Palmerston made no serious attempt to accept responsibility for or to acknowledge wrong-doing in the sinking of the *Caroline* or the death and injury caused by Commander Drew's expedition.[35] Palmerston took three weeks to answer Stevenson's protest of 22 May and then merely said that he would give the matter due consideration. He also sent a note to the United States, but unaccountably the British minister failed to deliver it. It was not until 3 September 1841, almost three and a half years later, that Palmerston, in his last moments in office, answered Stevenson's letter.[36]

Neither Palmerston nor Van Buren wanted to allow the rebellions or the *Caroline* matter to jeopardize relations, but American public opinion remained indignant that these questions were never addressed. Thus, all along the frontier, from Vermont west to Detroit, Americans remained hostile to the British regime in Canada, and many people were attracted to revolutionary societies such as the 'Patriots' or the 'Hunters and Chasers of the Eastern Frontier.' In late May 1838, the Canadian river boat *Sir Robert Peel*, travelling between Prescott and Kingston in Upper Canada, was stopped and its passengers were put ashore by fifty men dressed as Indians. The ship was set afire and sunk to the cries of 'Remember the *Caroline*.' It was of little satisfaction that the leader of this outrage was a Canadian, William Johnston, then very much a pirate among the Thousand Islands of eastern Lake Ontario.[37] Governor Marcy called out two companies of New York militia, but without much effect, and General Alexander Macomb, who had succeeded Winfield Scott, minimized the potential danger in these events.[38] Upper Canadian militiamen retaliated by firing on the American steamboat *Telegraph*, while it attempted to dock at Brockville, Upper Canada, on 14 April 1839, and on 16 May the American schooner *G.P. Weeks* was seized at Brockville because it had a cannon on deck.[39]

With membership in the Patriot Hunter societies along the frontier growing to an estimated 200,000, a serious crisis developed by the autumn of 1838. The steamship *United States* sailed on 11 November from Sackett's Harbor on Lake Ontario down the St Lawrence, in company with several other ships picked up at Watertown and Ogdensburg, New York, intending to land a substantial number of Patriot Hunters near Prescott. After some misadventures, two schooners and two other steamboats were seized by U.S. Marshal Nathanael Garrow, but the *United States* landed its contingent on the Canadian shore. British troops and Canadian militiamen almost immediately surrounded them, and after some heavy gunfire in what has been called the Battle of the Windmill, in which between 20 and 40 were killed on both sides, the remaining 140 surrendered. Nine of the Patriots were hanged, the rest sentenced to the penal colony in Van Diemen's Land (Tasmania).[40]

Further skirmishing went on over the next few months, most notably at Windsor on the Detroit River in Upper Canada, but crown forces showed that they could deal effectively, as well as ruthlessly, with these adventurers. General Scott was recalled to the northern frontier to replace the ineffective General Macomb.[41] William Lyon Mackenzie was eventually tried and convicted in New York for violating American neutrality laws in 1839. Though fined only ten dollars and sentenced to eighteen months in jail, Mackenzie remained a hero all along the border and especially in New York.[42]

The Van Buren administration's attempts to discourage American intervention in Canada's political troubles had their costs. His Democratic Party lost in New York in the 1838 elections, and his advisers urged him not to take such a strong stand regarding American neutrality. The consequences were too critical to ignore, however, and on 3 December 1838 the president confronted the issue directly in three long paragraphs in his annual address to Congress. He deplored the fact that Americans had encouraged insurrection in a country with which the United States was at peace, and he emphasized that this was contrary to both domestic and international law. 'The results of these criminal assaults upon the peace and order of a neighboring country have been,' he said, 'as was to be expected, fatally destructive to the misguided or deluded persons engaged in them and highly injurious to those in whose behalf they are professed to have been undertaken.'[43] The president's sentiments were not welcome along the border, where many people saw British colonial regimes as encroaching on U.S. territory along the frontier and repressing the democratically inclined people within their own jurisdictions. Eventually about 2,000 U.S. army troops were stationed from Vermont to Michigan, and American officers assisted British officials in frustrating Patriot Hunter activities. Nevertheless, by the end of the 1830s attitudes along the border, not just in Maine and Massachusetts, were poisoned. While the Rebellions of 1837 and the *Caroline* affair had nothing directly to do with the boundary dispute, they aggravated the boundary crisis and reinforced American anxiety about British aggression.[44]

Even before the rebellions in Upper and Lower Canada had fully run their course, Anglo–Canadian–American relations were threatened along the northeastern frontier once again. The winter of 1839 saw the outbreak of the 'Aroostook War,' or the 'Pork and Beans War.' This crisis brought to a head the rivalries over land and timber cutting that had been growing for years. In late 1838 the Maine legislature had become increasingly concerned about lumbermen, sometimes with licences from New Brunswick, cutting timber in the Aroostook River valley on land claimed by the state. In fact, both Maine and New Brunswick lumbermen cut trees wherever they could throughout this region, and the authorities were often ignored. Thus a very awkward and complicated situation existed in the Aroostook and upper St John River valleys, where proper licensing and clear authority were difficult to establish. National loyalties were not necessarily the first concern of either the settlers or the lumbermen in the region. Nevertheless, the estimate was that some 250 men, with numerous teams of oxen, were engaged in extensive timber operations, each year cutting logs valued at about $100,000. Land agents from both Maine and Massachusetts reported these operations and gave warnings to the 'trespassers.'

A posse of about 200 men, led by agent Rufus McIntire and Bangor lumberman Hastings Strickland, set out in late January 1839, into the Little Madawaska River, a tributary of the Aroostook. McIntire himself and his two assistants were taken prisoner in their sleep by a group of 'trespassers' and taken to Fredericton, where they were placed in the cell previously occupied by John Baker.[45] The posse in turn subsequently arrested about twenty 'trespassers,' including James A. MacLaughlan, the so-called Warden of the Disputed Territory, and sent them back to Bangor, Maine, where MacLaughlan was lodged in the town's best hotel. The early retreat of the Maine posse and the capture of its leader left it open to considerable ridicule and gave rise to bits of doggerel, such as, 'Run, Strickland, run! / Fire, Stover, fire! / Were the last words of McIntire.'[46]

When informed of this clash, Governor John Fairfield sent 300 militia to the Aroostook region, where they built block houses at Fort Hill and Fort Fairfield, and he called up 10,000 more men. He also requested assistance from both Massachusetts and the federal government to 'cooperate with the forces of this State in repelling an invasion of our Territory.'[47] Public opinion in Maine and in much of the nation rallied behind these efforts. The Massachusetts legislature voted its support, and on 2 March Congress authorized the president to raise 50,000 troops and expend as much as ten million dollars if war erupted. Several other states passed resolutions of support also. Fairfield also reminded Van Buren that while Maine was 'Democratic to the backbone,' failure by the government to support the state would be a political disaster.[48]

Lieutenant-Governor Sir John Harvey was supported by public opinion in New Brunswick and Nova Scotia as strong and belligerent as that in Maine. The Nova Scotia legislature, which was in session at the time, voted £100,000 and authorized the raising of 8,000 militiamen. Harvey had earlier sent two companies of regular army troops to the border region, but in this crisis he called out 850 militiamen and placed them in Woodstock. The lieutenant-governor also informed Sir John Colborne, commander-in-chief of British forces in Canada, about the situation, and he quickly sent the 11th Regiment and some artillery to the Temiscouata and Madawaska regions. Lieutenant Colonel Charles Grey thought war over Maine's actions in the disputed territory a strong possibility, though not inevitable. However, as late as March, Sir George Arthur, lieutenant-governor of Upper Canada, concluded, 'I do not see how this can terminate without a *General* war.'[49]

Thus the New Brunswick–Quebec frontier appeared to be on a war footing. All this having been done, Lieutenant-Governor Harvey then eased the situation by releasing McIntire and several others on parole. Governor Fairfield also released MacLaughlan and the others captured by the posse, but not before he had sent troops and military supplies to Bangor. Harvey wrote to both Fairfield and the British minister in Washington, Henry S. Fox. Fox protested to the secretary of state about Maine's 'unjustifiable incursion into a part of the disputed territory' and asserted that all parties well understood that until the boundary lines were finally decided 'all that part of the disputed territory is placed under the exclusive jurisdiction of Her Majesty's Authority.'[50] This statement generated fierce resistance. British forces and New Brunswick officials had gradually extended their authority into these regions, but there had never been an agreement acknowledging a British right in the matter, and both the U.S. and the Maine governments denied Britain and New Brunswick those rights.[51]

The British minister and the U.S. secretary of state, John Forsyth, exchanged notes about the matter and on 27 February 1839 signed an agreement whereby officials in New Brunswick would release all Americans held captive and all Maine militiamen would withdraw from the disputed territory.[52] President Van Buren also prevailed on General Winfield Scott to persuade Maine to accept this arrangement and to ease the situation in New Brunswick. Years later Scott recalled that he told the president, 'If you want *war*, I need only look on in silence. The Maine people will make it for you fast and hot enough. I know them; but if *peace* be your wish, I can give no assurance of success. The difficulties will be formidable.' Van Buren replied, 'Peace with honor,' so Scott set out to achieve just that.[53] Fortunately, despite all the warlike words spoken and printed, in both Maine and New Brunswick, no actual fighting had broken out. Troops from New Brunswick were badly equipped and cautious, while the Maine militia found winter duty in the woods uncomfortable and saw the 'trespassers' engaging in farming and lumbering despite them. Reportedly the only clash was between British and American soldiers drinking together in a tavern in Houlton, Maine, south of the crisis region.[54]

Nevertheless, Scott found the war spirit high as he travelled north through Massachusetts and Maine in early March. Many of his old soldiers from the War of 1812 cheered him on, expecting him to lead U.S. forces against the British once again. Scott had a formidable task in persuading the politicians in Augusta, both Whig and Democrat, to agree to the memorandum signed by Fox and Forsyth. For reasons of political advantage, neither party wanted to appear to weaken on the Aroostook question. Scott took up residence in the governor's mansion and, in daily contact with the leading politicians of both parties, gradually won their confidence. The Maine government felt that the Fox–Forsyth memorandum, which would withdraw the Maine militia from the Aroostook region, did not require a similar withdrawal by the British and even left their troops in the disputed territory. They insisted on some conciliatory gesture by the British.[55]

Fortunately, General Scott and Sir John Harvey enjoyed an acquaintanceship of mutual respect as gentlemen officers that arose out of their meeting on the field during the War of 1812. Scott was able to obtain Harvey's agreement to a statement that satisfied Maine's sense of propriety. The result, Scott reported to the secretary of war, was that 'it is not the intention of the Lieutenant Governor of Her Britannic Majesty's Province of New Brunswick, under the expected renewal of negotiations between the cabinets of London & Washington, on the subject of the said disputed territory, without renewed instructions to that effect from his Government, to seek to take military possession of that territory, or to seek by military force to expel therefrom the armed civil posse or the troops of Maine.'[56] Thus the Maine militia would withdraw voluntarily, although an unarmed civil posse could remain, and New Brunswick's forces would not attempt to remove it. The New Brunswick government seized the timber already cut and placed the proceeds in a 'disputed territory fund' to be distributed to the proper owner after the boundary had been determined. Log booms were built across the Aroostook and Fish rivers to prevent timber that had been cut without authority from being rafted down river to sawmills on the lower St John. One source of irritation for Maine, however, was that the troops sent from Quebec to Temiscouata and Madawaska were not under Harvey's command, and they stayed in the region despite the agreement. New Brunswickers resented the fact that timber cutting had been stopped.[57] However, General Scott had achieved 'Peace with honor' for President Van Buren and for Maine. The British minister, Henry S. Fox, whose dislike of the Americans was sharpened by these incidents, was instructed by Lord Palmerston to 'cultivate the Americans as much as you can,' as Sir Charles Vaughan had done before him, in order to stabilize and improve relations.[58] It must have been unwelcome advice to the minister.

This process eased the Aroostook crisis. Although British troops remained north of the St John River, as well as east of the due-north line, Sir George Arthur felt that British forces had been foolish to give up the disputed territory in the Aroostook valley. The New Brunswick historian W.S. MacNutt concluded that the Maine interests had been successful in ending logging operations along the Aroostook River valley.[59] As a result of the Rebellions of 1837 and the Aroostook crisis, the British held over 11,500 regular army troops in British North America by 1840. The new governor general, Charles Poulett Thomson, later Lord Sydenham, warned Prime Minister Lord Melbourne in late 1839, 'Nothing but the presence of so large a force keeps the Yankees in check, and it must at the least be kept up, if not increased.'[60] (The whole U.S. army numbered only 7,834 at this time.) The Maine militia was ordered home at the end of March. Tradition has it that its men taunted the U.S. army troops stationed in Houlton, who had been ordered to remain in the town during the whole of the crisis.[61]

The prospect that diplomatic negotiations would soon resume to settle the boundary implied in the Scott–Harvey talks became part of the understanding, although this was more of an aspiration than a fact. In 1839 there were no talks under way, and no real prospect that talks could be started with any common agreement from which to proceed. However, the crisis brought on by the Aroostook War, not to mention the *Caroline* affair, brought home the urgency of a settlement. Over the years the disputed territory had become too heavily populated to remain safely in the indeterminate state that had been allowed to exist.

A fresh crisis blew up in 1840 that had the potential to bring about the war between Britain and the United States that people increasingly feared. This crisis was the last legacy of the Rebellions of 1837 in the Canadas and the destruction of the steamer *Caroline*. The British had never acknowledged the death of Amos Durfee and the injuries to other people on the ship to the satisfaction of the U.S. State Department or of the residents of upstate New York. Although on 22 May 1838 the American minister to Britain had raised the issue of British responsibility for the raid and the damages resulting from it, Lord Palmerston had never officially responded to the question. In November 1838 Palmerston had instructed the British minister in Washington to state that the destruction of the ship had been an official act. However, Henry S. Fox, whose dislike of the Americans made it difficult for him to have any but the most minimal dealings with them, had not done so, with the result that a growing sense of grievance festered.[62] Almost three years after the sinking of the *Caroline*, all this unresolved business boiled over in the 'McLeod affair.' This too, like the Rebellions of 1837 themselves, had little overtly to do with the settlement of the boundary but heightened mutual antagonisims, making a boundary settlement still more difficult.[63]

Alexander McLeod was a deputy sheriff from Niagara, Upper Canada, whose duties took him into the United States to monitor the activities of Canadian Patriots and their American supporters. Although McLeod was not a spy, he, and numerous others, were clearly engaged in intelligence activities against William Lyon Mackenzie and his supporters, and it was entirely predictable that these missions were strongly resented in the border regions of New York. McLeod seemed also to have been a person whom it was easy to dislike. He had been involved in some questionable financial matters, and he was having an affair with a woman whose husband lived in the United States. He was alleged to have bragged, both in Canada and in New York, that he had been with the party that sunk the *Caroline*, although that was never proved. His dislike of both the rebels and the Americans, however, was never in question. On 2 September 1840 McLeod was arrested in Manchester, New York, south of Rochester, for participation in the *Caroline* affair, but released for lack of evidence. Shortly afterwards he was again arrested in Niagara Falls but was released because the warrant was made out for Angus McLeod, rather than Alexander.[64] A more prudent man might have stayed away from New York, but McLeod returned to defend himself in a civil suit concerning his misappropriation of funds. The result was that he was arrested in Lewistown on 12 November 1840 on a charge of murder and arson and lodged in the Lockport jail. Several people came forward to testify that he had been in the party that sank the *Caroline* and killed Amos Durfee in December 1837.[65]

That McLeod and several others were ever subject to arrest was a result of the British government's failure to take public responsibility for the famous raid in 1837. By the end of December 1837 the Rebellion had been crushed and Britain was not in a state of war, certainly not with the United States. Could the *Caroline* raid be considered an act of war in these circumstances? If war did not exist, were the invasion and assault an act of brigandage or piracy? Even in a police action, were Crown officials justified in a punitive expedition to sink the *Caroline* when that ship itself had not been involved in hostile actions and, whatever the legality of Mackenzie's seizure of Navy Island, no fatalities had yet resulted? Americans were always quick to take offence at British actions, and the British, especially under foreign secretaries such as George Canning and Lord Palmerston, were not hesitant to scorn American sentiments. In the absence of British acknowledgment of responsibility for the raid,

New Yorkers took the view that the raid was the work of private individuals who carried out capital crimes in the United States and who, if apprehended within the state's jurisdiction, were liable to prosecution.

Crown authorities in Upper Canada were slow to react to McLeod's arrest. Sir George Arthur, lieutenant-governor, was reluctant to commit himself to supporting the deputy sheriff, in view of McLeod's reputation, although a solicitor was employed. Arthur told the new governor general, Lord Sydenham, that he understood that McLeod had not been a part of the *Caroline* expedition but that he had 'from time to time boasted of having played an active part in it,' and Arthur suspected McLeod of attempting to manipulate the situation for his own benefit.[66] Lord Sydenham sent as much as $5,000 in funds from the military budget to help finance McLeod's defence and also requested the assistance of Henry S. Fox in Washington. Fox protested to Secretary of State Forsyth that the destruction of the *Caroline* was a 'publick act' and therefore was a matter for the two national governments, not for the state of New York.[67]

However, this was a delicate issue, because no formal explanation had ever been given the American government in response to the American minister's letter to Palmerston on 22 May 1838. Fox's note of 13 December 1840 was the first acknowledgment of any kind of British responsibility for the raid. Forsyth's reply to Fox explained the difference between state and federal jurisdictions in the American federal system but focused on the argument that no principle of law sanctioned criminal acts, even if carried out in the service of a government. The federal government would not therefore intervene in the criminal proceedings under way in the New York courts.[68] Fox, however, was convinced that the administration's refusal to intervene arose from the president's desire to leave a political hot potato for his newly elected successor, the Whig general William Henry Harrison.

The McLeod affair certainly generated a new Anglo–American crisis. The British Parliament debated the issue in February 1841, and all parties rallied behind the government.[69] Palmerston took a strong stand. He instructed Fox to 'make a formal demand for the release of McLeod' and to tell President Van Buren that 'the British nation will never permit a British subject to be dealt with as the people of New York propose to deal with McLeod, without taking signal revenge upon the offenders.' McLeod's execution would mean 'war immediate and frightful in its character, because it would be a war of retaliation and vengeance.' Fox was to leave Washington 'immediately' if McLeod were executed.[70] Some historians have argued that Palmerston's success in dealing with a Middle East crisis, the Mehemet Ali affair, the previous autumn left him free for the first time to concentrate on American concerns, and they suggest that he was not slow to exploit an opportunity that promised to win applause at home and teach the troublesome Americans a lesson. Fox was instructed to 'demand from the Government of the United States, formally, in the name of the British Government, the immediate release of McLeod.'[71] Palmerston told Stevenson that the president should intervene in the matter, and Stevenson himself reported that he was sure that McLeod's execution would mean war. Palmerston seemed to have both the opposition and the public in Britain behind him on this issue.[72]

Sydenham did not think Palmerston's note to the Americans strong enough – it should have demanded McLeod's immediate release. 'Jonathan' (the derogatory British term for Americans), he wrote home to England, 'will never be fair or just unless he is compelled, but he will always yield if you are firm.'[73] Palmerston agreed with Sydenham. 'With such cunning fellows as these Yankees, it never answers to give way,' he told Lord John Russell, 'because they always keep pushing on their encroachments as far as they are permitted to do so.' Because the Americans were bullies, Palmerston said, 'they will give way when in the wrong, if they are firmly and perseveringly pressed.'[74] Although the complicated details of the case became blurred, there was widespread agreement in Britain that no servant of the Crown could be taken to court in a foreign country for having done his duty. The words *Civis Romanus sum* rang in the air.

In the midst of this growing crisis, William Henry Harrison took over the White House in March 1841. Harrison appointed Daniel Webster, the distinguished lawyer and senator from Massachusetts, as secretary of state, and although Harrison died after only a month in office, his successor, John Tyler, kept Webster in his cabinet.[75] The new secretary of state was more anxious to establish better relations with Britain than his predecessor Forsyth, and he tended to agree with the principle that the British took in the McLeod affair – namely, that an individual could not be tried for acts carried out as the instrument of his government – but Webster was also bound by what he regarded as the Anglo–American legal tradition of a court system independent from control of the executive. In other words, the U.S. executive could not quash proceedings in the courts (especially state courts) any more than the British government could do so in England's lower courts. The case must be allowed to proceed, and the issues would be sorted out by the legal process.[76]

As the case worked its way through the preliminary court proceedings, public opinion became a factor in the United States as well as in Britain. Many Americans seemed to see British indignation at McLeod's arrest as typical great power intimidation of a smaller nation. Certainly opinion along the New York border, not unlike that along the Maine border, saw imperial Britain bullying the United States. Webster tried to get the case taken out of the local court or taken before the U.S. Supreme Court, but without success. Pressure to get New York's governor, William H. Seward, to dismiss the case or to give assurances of a pardon in the event of a conviction met with indignation. The governor did provide military protection during the trial, which was moved from Lockport, in the Niagara area, to Utica, over 180 miles east, in order to secure an impartial jury and more tranquil surroundings.

The state's chief justice had been slated to preside, but when he fell ill he was replaced by a circuit court judge, Philo Gridley. The state's attorney general, Willis Hall, served as prosecutor, and a Utica attorney, Joshua A. Spencer, was the most prominent of several defence lawyers on the case. Webster, himself one of the country's leading lawyers, wished for a stronger defence counsel and arranged for Spencer's appointment as U.S. district attorney in the midst of the case.[77] This move appeared to many to constitute federal intervention in the New York court system, despite Webster's disclaimers to Fox, and provoked some strong complaints from the governor to President Tyler.[78] Nevertheless, Seward did assure the federal government that if McLeod were convicted – which he doubted, on the basis of the evidence – he would intervene and prevent any sentence from being imposed.[79]

The British, who could not be certain how these events would unfold, took an increasingly strident tone. Palmerston responded in both private conversation and official correspondence. On 5 September 1841 Fox conveyed to Webster Palmerson's view that McLeod's conviction and execution would mean 'the heavy Calamity of War,' and Palmerston's successor, Lord Aberdeen, instructed Fox, as Palmerston himself had in February, to 'forthwith quit Washington, and return to his country,' in the event of McLeod's execution.[80] President Tyler told Fox that in such an event he would not be allowed to leave the United States until all efforts to prevent a rupture between the two countries had failed.

When the trial took place in October 1841, the prosecution was unable to establish its case. Although conflicting testimony was presented by both sides, the defence produced a credible witness who said that McLeod had spent the entire night of the *Caroline* raid in his house in Upper Canada, some distance from the scene. The jury needed only a half-hour to return a verdict of not guilty. McLeod was carefully transported back to Upper Canada by way of Lake Champlain, rather than through the Niagara region, so there was no opportunity for vigilante activity.[81]

Even before the McLeod case had ended, still another incident threatened again relations between the United States and British North America. This involved the capture and kidnapping of James W. Grogan in Alburgh, Vermont. Grogan was an American who, together with his father and family, had moved to Lower Canada after the War of 1812. Following the Rebellions of 1837 the Grogans' sympathies were doubted, and, despite the general amnesty to rebels, Crown forces burned their houses and farm buildings and drove them all, adults and children, across the border into Vermont. The younger Grogan, together with friends and family, mounted his own campaign of revenge in 1838, recrossing the border and burning at least four farms himself.[82]

Grogan soon resettled in Lockport, New York, and in the midst of the McLeod affair launched a civil suit in Lower Canada in 1841 for damages and injury caused by provincial authorities. In order to pursue the case, Grogan returned to Alburg, Vermont, a few miles south of the border, where on 19 September he met some British soldiers whom he had known in Lower Canada and proceeded to drink with them in a local tavern. When some concerned friends suggested to him that the soldiers might intend to get him drunk and abduct him, Grogan made his way to his brother-in-law's house, where he intended to spend the night. Some hours after midnight the soldiers burst into the house, shouting threats, and wounding Grogan with their bayonets in the process. They dragged him into the street to cries of 'Why don't you blow his brain out?' and 'Damn you, why don't you shoot him?' Grogan was beaten, thrown in a wagon, taken to Clarenceville, Lower Canada, and placed in jail. However, the acting governor, Sir Richard Jackson, on learning of the circumstances, released Grogan on 4 October and had him transported to the Vermont border.[83]

Before Grogan's release, however, protest meetings took place across Vermont, and the governor wrote to the U.S. secretary of state describing the incident and registering a protest. Acting Secretary of State

Fletcher Webster, Daniel's son, wrote to Henry S. Fox on 28 September urging that Grogan be released and his captors punished for their unlawful invasion of U.S. territory.[84] This looked like another *Caroline* raid, wherein Crown officials had violated U.S. sovereignty and carried out military operations against Americans with impunity. However, both colonial officials, such as Sir Richard Jackson, and the new Tory government in England realized the explosive nature of the borderland and the awkwardness of legal proceedings against a person held in questionable circumstances. The unfortunate example of both the *Caroline* raid and the McLeod trial loomed ominously. The Duke of Wellington thought that the colonial authorities should be investigated, the new governor was urged to avoid similar incidents with the Americans and to apologize to the governor of Vermont, and the foreign secretary wrote to Fox to accept 'any reasonable indemnity.'[85] Grogan had already been released, and Fox never mentioned any indemnity in his discussions with the U.S. State Department, but the speed with which the British government moved to sooth American feelings was an indication of how close it believed war might be between the two nations.

As if simply to add further confusion to the border situation, John Sheridan Hogan from Upper Canada was arrested in Lockport, New York, in March 1842. Hogan had been part of the *Caroline* expedition. A distressed Fox wrote to Lord Aberdeen, 'What could have induced him under these circumstances, and in the present state of things between the Two Countries, to set foot in the United States, I am unable to say.' In the event, Hogan was released because of an error in the warrant, leading Sir Charles Bagot, now the new governor general of British North America, to report with relief to the Colonial Office, 'We have narrowly escaped I think, a serious inconvenience in the affair of Hogan.'[86]

All these incidents, from John Baker's arrest in 1827 to James Grogan's abduction in 1841, showed a steady escalation of tension along the frontier, and although there were trouble spots all the way west to the communities along the Niagara and Detroit rivers, the most serious flash point was the contested borderland between New Brunswick and Maine. Americans saw incidents such as the *Caroline* affair and the Aroostook crisis as examples of aggressive and provocative action by the British. The British in turn perceived events such as the Aroostook crisis and the McLeod affair as examples of American incursions into the disputed territory and insolent provocation. Would another crisis ignite the powder keg? Would Britain and the United States risk war over these stretches of frontier wilderness? Would national pride, conflicting interests, and the murky terms of the treaty of 1783 permit a negotiated settlement? If a crisis blew up in America, what role would France play? There were no clear answers to these questions.

Chapter Ten

Surveys and Struggles

The British government had seen little promise in opening talks to negotiate a revised boundary after the failure by 1833 of the arbitration by the king of the Netherlands in 1830–1, and it was even less hopeful about the proposals for a new joint boundary commission to search still further to find the 'highlands' mentioned in the Treaty of Paris of 1783. However, during the mid- and late 1830s conditions steadily worsened along the frontier, from Maine and New Brunswick to Michigan and southwestern Upper Canada, and talks – or perhaps talks about talks – continued, for all these initiatives failed to yield any concrete results. What did transpire, as the chapter explains, was a new survey for the northeastern boundary by Maine in 1838; one by the British in 1839, with a report in 1840; a flurry of responses in the United States; and a new U.S. government survey later in 1840. As many observers had feared, however, these efforts contributed more to continued discord than to a settlement.[1] Indeed, these precarious attempts to deal with the boundary took place against the backdrop of the McLeod affair, described in chapter 9, which was the last legacy of the Rebellions of 1837 and the sinking of the *Caroline*.

In their objections to the proposals of the king of the Netherlands, Maine's spokesmen argued that the U.S. government had no power, under the constitution, to negotiate away the territory of a sovereign state within the union. While this was a workable legal position, many leaders in Maine were prepared to consider a compromise line that offered Maine some significant concession of land elsewhere in exchange for its abandoning its claim to territory north of the St John River. In early 1836, about two months after the British had formally withdrawn their agreement to accept the Dutch award, the U.S. government came up with a daring proposal. What private talks with Maine spokesmen might have preceded this offer is unknown. Nevertheless, the U.S. secretary of state, John Forsyth, proposed on 29 February that, in view of all the difficulties that had arisen attempting to comply with the terms of the treaty of 1783, a new boundary line be negotiated along the St John River, 'from its source to its mouth.'[2] This proposal would have surrendered the claims of Maine north of the St John River, which had been so objectionable in 1831, but it would have given to Maine the territory from the St Croix and the due-north line east to the St John River. It would have cost New Brunswick several towns, including Woodstock, and the Loyalist centre of St Andrews and taken the boundary right to the provincial capital of Fredericton. It would have retained the major port town of Saint John, on the east bank of the river, but would probably have sacrificed the islands in Passamaquoddy Bay whose possession had been determined in 1817. The British had rejected a similar proposal at the peace negotiations in 1782 and 1783, and not surprisingly they rejected the new one.[3]

If the New Brunswickers and the British felt the Americans keeping up steady pressure to occupy and settle the disputed territory, the authorities in Maine were no less anxious about similar pressures from New Brunswick. By 1831 there were about 3,000 people living between Houlton Plantation in the south and the Madawaska settlements in the north. However, they were so spread out over many square miles of countryside that two British surveyors described the disputed territory as 'a wilderness, where not a human being was to be met with, with the exception of a few settlers upon the Roostuc River ... and a few wandering Indians employed in the chaise, or occasionally, of some American lumberers.' In the mid-1830s, British engineers and surveyors started to look for suitable terrain in the disputed territory for a railway right-of-way from St Andrews to Quebec City. That a permanent railway was likely to be built on land that was still claimed by both sides generated indignant protests in Maine. A note from Washington was, in this case, sufficient to get the British government to intervene and stop work on the railway.[4]

This sort of sparring, like the Rebellions of 1837 that broke out in the autumn, drove home the urgency of a rapid settlement of the situation. On 19 January 1837 the British minister told John Forsyth that the government was prepared to consider the new American proposal for another boundary commission.[5] The shape of the commission and its powers would have to be negotiated, however, and this proved the stumbling block. Lord Palmerston concluded that the American commissioners would inevitably look for the 'highlands' north of the St John River and that this would lead 'not to a settlement but a dispute.' As long as the Americans held that the Bay of Fundy was part of the Atlantic Ocean as mentioned in the treaty of 1783, there was no hope of reaching agreement on the basis of the treaty. Indeed, as Palmerston admitted to Fox, 'If the Bay of Fundy is, for the purposes of the Treaty, to be considered as the Atlantic Ocean, then the Line claimed by the United States is the Line of the Treaty.' However, if the contrary were the case, Palmerston concluded, then the 'highlands' would be found west and south of the St John River. Palmerston grew to feel that only when the Americans were prepared to negotiate a conventional line could the dispute be settled, and then probably by 'an equal division' of the territory, with 'the course of the St John as the Boundary.'[6] The American government was cool to British suggestions about how to structure the proposed commission and where it would be free to explore.[7] No solution for the creation of a joint commission was ever found.

Maine took the initiative while the talks went on. Its legislature passed a resolution declaring that if Congress failed to approve a joint Anglo–American survey, Maine itself would authorize a commission to survey the disputed territory and identify the topography – the 'highlands' – that would satisfy the terms of the treaty of 1783. By 10 September 1838, Governor Edward Kent appointed John G. Deane, Milford P. Norton, and James Irish to explore and survey the line of boundary intended in the historic treaty. The state had commissioned Deane to explore and survey the frontier regions of Maine in 1828 and 1831, and he had also been sent to New Brunswick to keep in contact with the imprisoned John Baker. Although the 1838 season was nearly over, the commissioners and crews set out from Bangor towards the boundary region to the north. One of the commissioners went up the Penobscot River, portaged into the Allagash River, and proceeded thence to the St John. The other two headed up the Penobscot for the Aroostook River, where they parted, one following the Aroostook to its confluence with the St John, east of the due-north line in New Brunswick territory, and the other continuing north to the St John above Grand Falls.[8]

All three parties were to meet on the Grand River, which flowed in a southwesterly direction into the St John. From this river the parties, including the surveyors and workmen, proceeded more or less along the due-north line, until they reached the Métis River flowing north into the St Lawrence River. They had reached the height of land forming the watershed for streams flowing north into the St Lawrence, east into the Restigouche, and south into the St John. This was the watershed explored by the commission under article 5 of the Treaty of Ghent during the seasons of 1817 and 1818, and just as then it convinced these commissioners that they had identified the 'highlands' specified in the treaty. The commissioners then proceeded to explore the region, one party taking astronomical sightings to determine latitude and longitude, one investigating the various streams descending from the 'highlands,' and the last following the ridge of 'highlands' west in order to demonstrate its geographical consistency. Their conclusions were that the ridge of 'highlands' was viable and that about a mile from the Métis River the altitude of the land was more than 500 feet above the level of the St John River, or about 2,300 feet above sea level, the highest point north of the marker at the source of the St Croix River.[9]

John G. Deane reported to Governor Kent in late 1838, 'It is difficult to imagine a more certain and accurate description of boundaries than that contained in the treaty of 1783, or which, with more certainty, can be applied on the earth's surface.' Kent, in his annual message to the legislature in early 1839, announced to the people of his state that the highlands and the Northwest Angle of Nova Scotia, mentioned in the treaty, had been found. This was more or less what the American commissioner and agent had found in the earlier survey.[10]

In the summer of 1838, before the prospect of a joint commission had faded, a remarkable figure put himself forward as the candidate for the American commission. That person was George William Featherstonhaugh, an Englishman who had been living in the United States since 1806. Born in London in 1780, Featherstonhaugh was raised in Scarborough by his mother after his father's death left the family in precarious circumstances. Bright and inquisitive, Featherstonhaugh was well educated in school, but unable to attend university. His desire to make his fortune took him to the United States. By 1808 he had married into the prominent Duane family of New York, and he became a prosperous farmer and entrepreneur (he was a founder of what later became the New York Central Railroad) in the Schenectady area. Featherstonhaugh also cultivated an early interest in science and became an authority on geology. His reputation, based on the publication of several books and numerous articles, led to President Andrew Jackson's appointment of him in 1834 as the first United States geologist, which service took him across much of the Midwest and resulted in several more important publications and reports.[11] It was on the strength of this success that Featherstonhaugh hoped to be appointed to the proposed commission, without regard for his continued British allegiance.

As the possibility of a joint commission melted away in the summer of 1838, Featherstonhaugh talked with Henry S. Fox, the British minister in Washington, about his heading a British commission. Fox warmed to the idea and recommended him to Lord Palmerston, and Featherstonhaugh himself went north to Lower Canada to meet with Lord Durham, the new governor general, and to secure his endorsement for such an appointment.[12] Once in London, he solicited the support of John Backhouse, undersecretary at the Foreign Office, and several other highly placed people, including Sir Charles Vaughan, the former minister to the United States. He conveyed to all of them his views on the boundary matter, and Backhouse was certainly impressed with his arguments in an extensive memorandum and passed them on to Lord Palmerston, who had a long meeting with Featherstonhaugh on 26 March.[13]

Featherstonhaugh had well-developed opinions on the boundary. First, he argued that there had been a mistranslation of the 1621 charter for Nova Scotia granted to the Earl of Stirling, from which he concluded that the Penobscot River was the St Croix intended to form the boundary and that it was to proceed northwest, not north. Featherstonhaugh concluded that north, and subsequently west, of the source of the Penobscot a genuine 'highland' existed that did divide waters flowing into the Atlantic from waters flowing into the St Lawrence. The description of the boundary in the treaty of 1783 should have gone from west to east. He held that the intended boundary could be determined by 'Geological Jurisprudence' and by the 'unerring principle in the Geology of the Country' through which the appropriate highlands would be convincingly revealed. Furthermore, the current problems derived from what Featherstonhaugh regarded as the pro-American bias in the composition of the St Croix Commission, with Colonel Thomas Barclay (an old New York Loyalist), David Howell (from Rhode Island), and Judge Egbert Benson (a New Yorker), and from the fact that Barclay had been 'done brown' by the two Yankees and led to accept the Schoodiac River far to the east of the Penobscot. Finally, Featherstonhaugh asserted that a more scientific, or 'geological,' examination of the topography would start in the west, where the Chaudière flowed into the St Lawrence and the Penobscot drained into the Atlantic.[14]

These views, of course, ignored a great deal of contrary evidence, including the facts that the St Croix River in the treaty was expected to empty into the Bay of Fundy (miles east of Penobscot Bay) and that the British agent at the St Croix Commission, Ward Chipman, had been decisive in identifying the St Croix River through very impressive archaeological work.[15] However, these views coincided with, and reinforced, Lord Palmerston's own opinion that the intended boundary should be far south of the region claimed by the Americans. In fact, as early as 1837 Palmerston had concluded that the boundary recommended by the king of the Netherlands, far from being the satisfactory compromise many in the Foreign Office thought in 1831, was far too generous to the Americans.[16]

The Foreign Office hired Featherstonhaugh to assist on boundary matters by April 1839 and appointed him British commissioner, as it also did a Royal Engineer, Lieutenant-Colonel Richard Zachariah Mudge, who was something of a scientist and a fellow of the Royal Society.[17] The two men were opposites. Featherstonhaugh was eager, passionate, and convinced of his own rightness and of the bad faith of all who disagreed with him, while Mudge, recommended as a 'safe man,' was discreet, of 'high character,' and much more cautious.[18] There had been some concern whether the two could work together. Palmerston wanted them to be equal in rank, but Mudge to be the senior surveyor. Featherstonhaugh's personality was so strong, however, that he dominated all of the commission's activities. After he had been appointed, Featherstonhaugh so bombarded Palmerston with persistent letters that the foreign secretary complained that Featherstonhaugh 'seems to think that I have nothing else in the world to do but to attend to him and his business.'[19]

After some delay, and a trip to Paris to look for documents, Featherstonhaugh and Mudge arrived in New York in late July 1839 and made their way north, stopping in Bangor, Houlton, Woodstock, and Fredricton. By 14 August they reported to Palmerston that they were assembling the crews for their expeditions and that they had consulted with Lieutenant-Governor Sir John Harvey, as well as with Chief Justice Ward Chipman, Jr, and William F. Odell, both of whom had served on the earlier commission. Featherstonhaugh became engrossed in political matters, advising officials in Maine about prudent actions to follow on the boundary question, and intervening in the actions of New Brunswickers in their unsuccessful attack on the Maine militia at Fort Fairfield in early September (part of the aftermath of the 'Aroostook War' of the previous winter).[20] However, instructions from Palmerston, clearly drafted with Featherstonhaugh's advice, gave the commissioners three missions to carry out: explorations of the several ridges from the source of the Chaudière east to Mars Hill, from the source of the Chaudière east-northeast to the Bay of Chaleurs, and along the line proposed by the Americans from the Chaudière to the intersection with the line drawn due north from the source of the St Croix.[21] Featherstonhaugh and Mudge were themselves to undertake the central mission – exploring the country along the southern watershed of the St John River to its source.

This was not an easy task, given both the lateness of the season and the amount of time available. Most of the travel had to be done in canoes or on foot, the woods being too dense to allow horses to be used. The parties ate very well – moose, trout, and partridge being plentiful, together with supplies that had been carried in, including bottles of London porter. However, insects plagued them early on, and the weather became increasingly wet and cold, with the first snow falling by late September. Mudge found it all an ordeal. His canoe overturned at least twice, his chronometer was ruined, and other equipment was lost. Featherstonhaugh described Mudge as becoming completely unkempt, not shaving for the whole expedition, and 'heartily sick of the whole affair.' The old soldier was simply not up to the work. Featherstonhaugh himself stated that the exploration was 'the most arduous service I ever was upon,' but he was so exhilarated by his discoveries that he was able to claim that 'I am in excellent spirits and ready for anything.'[22] This was all to the good, because canoes kept tipping over, causing loss of equipment and supplies and placing the men in jeopardy. While writing to Sir John Harvey, Featherstonhaugh was interrupted by cries that an overturned canoe had been spotted on the lake, only to return to his letter to assure the lieutenant-governor that his assistant and an Indian had been saved.[23]

The expedition left Fredericton on 24 August and proceeded up the St John River by boat. It spent a full day exploring Mars Hill, which Featherstonhaugh calculated to be 1,688 feet high. Further north, he and Mudge conferred with people at Great Falls, and a party under George Wightman was sent east up the Tobique River to explore the terrain between the St John River and the Bay of Chaleurs, and a second party under Hugh Josiah Hansard was sent up the St John with supplies to rendezvous at the upper Allagash River. On 10 September Featherstonhaugh rode on horseback to Fort Fairfield on the Aroostook River, to confer with the American commander there, and the rest of the main party followed the next day.[24] By the end of September, having ascended the Aroostook River and Millinocket Lake, the party arrived at the headwaters of the Allagash River. There it rendezvoused with the supply party under Hansard. Featherstonhaugh was delighted to report to the Foreign Office that he had found an unbroken ridge along the southern St John watershed, which constituted, in his judgment, the 'highlands' described in the treaty of 1783. *'Everything that I had hoped for has been realized!,'* he told John Backhouse. 'I have now personally examined, crossed and recrossed over and over again, so that I can now sit down with my mind somewhat at ease to make you participate in my great satisfaction, by the assurance that all is right, and entirely right, *and no mistake!!!'*[25]

Featherstonhaugh and Mudge had yet to get to the actual source of the St John and the Chaudière rivers. At the end of September the crews were split up. Twenty-two men were dismissed and sent back to Fredericton. Mudge and a small party travelled down the Allagash to the St John, and they were to then ascend the St John and meet Featherstonhaugh and the remainder of the party, who were to make their way west from the Allagash to Baker Lake and the headwaters of the St John River. This endeavour took about two weeks, after which Featherstonhaugh and Mudge and their combined crews made their way, via Lake Etchemin, to Quebec City, where they arrived on 21 October.[26] They reported to Palmerston in triumph that they had accomplished their mission in a little over two months. 'We therefore report to your Lordship the existence of an uninterrupted line of highlands, and a true axis of elevation, holding its course irregularly at some points, from South West to North East, from the head of the Connecticut River to the Great Falls of the River St. John, and which divides the water flowing into the Atlantic Ocean from water flowing into the St. Lawrence.'[27]

Featherstonhaugh also assured Backhouse that he had completely undercut the American claim for the ridge on the north side of the St John as being the 'highlands' in the treaty of 1783, by showing that, in addition to its failure to divide waters flowing into the Atlantic and the St Lawrence, it had a thirty-mile gap (the location of Lake Temiscouata and the portage to the St Lawrence) and was therefore not a continuous line of highlands.[28] Mudge was also convinced that they had established the British claim, but he recognized that the Americans were equally convinced of the merits of their case. In these circumstances, 'A compromise is all that can be effected without going to war,' Mudge confided to his diary.[29] Featherstonhaugh was now confident that the

American claims, particularly concerning the Northwest Angle of Nova Scotia at the watershed of the Métis River, were 'the most inflated humbug that ever flourished in the regions of bombast,' and he assured Lieutenant-Governor Sir John Harvey, 'I shall unbombast Master Jonathan surprisingly.'[30]

Featherstonhaugh returned to England early in 1840, sailing from New York after having conferred with Governor Fairfield on his travels from Fredericton. His son James and Lieutenant W.E. Delves Broughton, of the Royal Engineers, were sent back to the borderlands during the summer of 1840 to complete the details of the survey, particularly the northern 'highlands' identified by the Americans.[31]

Featherstonhaugh devoted himself to preparing the final report of the commission for Palmerston. The report was a devastating attack on the American claims, from the negotiations of the peace treaty in 1783 right up to the survey by the Maine commission in 1838. Mudge and Featherstonhaugh argued that the British had never agreed in 1783 to a boundary that entered the St John watershed, much less one that crossed it. In 1798 the wrong source of the St Croix had been selected, with the result that the due-north line was too far east to strike the major 'highlands' that Featherstonhaugh had identified. In fact, his report recommended that the current source of the St Croix, and the due-north line, be set aside and a new and correct source of the St Croix be fixed at the western end of Schoodiac Lake and a new line extended northwest to the easternmost source of the Chaudière River. The American rejection of the award of the king of the Netherlands surely entitled the British to reject, even at this late date, the award of the St Croix Commission of 1798, the report asserted. The report dismissed contradictory evidence, such as Colonel Bouchette's surveys, as erroneous, and Mitchell's map and the post-1783 maps, as irrelevant. The report turned instead to seventeenth-century maps by the Venetian Coronelli and by the French explorers. Perhaps surprisingly, the report did agree with the American contention that the 1763 and 1774 descriptions of the colonial borders did describe the northern U.S. claim, but it disagreed about what those descriptions meant.[32]

Once the Treaty of Ghent commissions had started their work, the report stated, the Americans had resorted to misrepresentation of fact and mere conjecture to argue for a viable 'highlands' north of the St John River that satisfied the terms of the treaty. In other words, 'the conclusions upon which they have rested the American case, instead of being the legitimate results of practical investigation, are unsubstantial inventions brought forward in the absence of all real investigation; conveying erroneous ideas of the nature of the country; and calculated to mislead, not only their own authorities, but public opinion in the United States and in Europe, as to the merits of this question.'[33] Thus the agents of both the federal government and Maine had deliberately misled the American government and people in the surveys. In contrast, the British claim, the report said, was substantiated by the survey that established a ridge of 'highlands' running from the source of the Connecticut River and the Chaudière River, northeast along the watershed of the St John and the western Penobscot, and along the ridges adjacent to the Aroostook River, to its south. Although the south-flowing St John passed through the landmass, this ridge continued northeast, the report held, into New Brunswick (north of the Miramichi River), to the south bank of the Bay of Chaleurs. The boundary should follow this ridge of 'highlands,' or 'axis of maximum elevation,' northeast until it crossed the line due north from the source of the St Croix, unless that source could be changed and a new due-north line established.[34] It was a bold claim, reasserting in stronger language an even larger claim than that put forward by Ward Chipman, Jr, in 1826.

Featherstonhaugh delivered the report to Palmerston on Saturday evening, 18 April 1840, and the two of them spent the entire Sunday going through it. Palmerston was completely convinced by Featherstonhaugh's arguments. 'It quite knocks over the American claim,' he wrote to the prime minister a week and a half later, 'and I think it sets up ours.' He was certain that the data in the report would undermine the widespread belief in the United States in the justice of that nation's claims. From this point on, Palmerston became an unbending advocate of the British boundary claim, as described by Featherstonhaugh. The survey had been 'absolutely necessary as a foundation for any further proceeding, and it will turn out to have been a great advantage to us.' Some years later, a member of the British consular service with some knowledge of the boundary question, Thomas C. Grattan, wrote that Palmerston, distracted by pressing European crises, had 'adopted somewhat too hastily a plausible but shallow Report' and that his opinion had set the 'tone' for people such as Fox and Sydenham and Crown officials in New Brunswick, who subsequently 'maintained a style of haughty assumption.'[35]

Although they were well pleased with the findings and recommendations in the report, the foreign secretary and the cabinet moved more slowly than Featherstonhaugh preferred.[36] By April, Palmerston was ready to have the report released. Two copies were sent to Secretary of State Forsyth, and the government hoped to persuade the Americans to agree to another arbitration through a single 'umpire,' confident that, given Featherstonhaugh's 'geological' evidence, a complete victory for the British claims was now likely.[37] The Americans were not to be hurried on this matter, the Aroostook War and the McLeod affair disrupting the possibility of quiet talks on these questions. Furthermore, the Americans now were determined to undertake their own unilateral survey of the boundary area.

Not surprisingly, the report of Mudge and Featherstonhaugh stirred up anxiety and resentment in the United States, and its belligerent tone generated an equally truculent response – reports from Maine and Massachusetts, an attack in the *New York Review*, and a book by veteran diplomat Albert Gallatin. The Massachusetts report, drafted by Charles Francis Adams, son of John Quincy Adams, concluded that if the British document were understood 'as in any degree characteristic of the future intentions of Her Majesty's Ministers, it might, indeed, be regarded as indicative of a disposition unfavorable to any pacific settlement whatsoever.'[38] Maine, of course, protested and issued its own report criticizing the recommendations of the British report. Maine also circulated the supportive resolutions passed by Indiana and Alabama.[39]

However, the *New York Review* published the strongest attack on the British document. It singled out Featherstonhaugh as 'the *soi-disant* United States Geologist–British Commissioner,' the former writer of fiction. Having lived in the United States for some thirty years, the *New York Review* pointed out, Featherstonhaugh now 'favors Her Majesty's government with elaborate argument, deduced from ancient charters and other documents, very naturally maintaining the pretensions of his new masters against "the revolted colonies," whose bread he no longer eats, though in doing so he does not deal much more kindly with the arguments of his friends than with those of his enemies.' (The report asserted a claim to an altogether new boundary for the British, rather than providing evidence for the line claimed before the commission or before the king of the Netherlands.) The journal did not hesitate to point out, or to ridicule, the fact that Featherstonhaugh's new boundary line crossed and recrossed rivers and streams, such as the Aroostook, without pretending to follow any watershed or highlands.[40] It was a stinging rebuke. The newspapers joined in, the *Niles' National Register* calling the document a 'weak, one-sided, and we had almost said, insulting report.'[41]

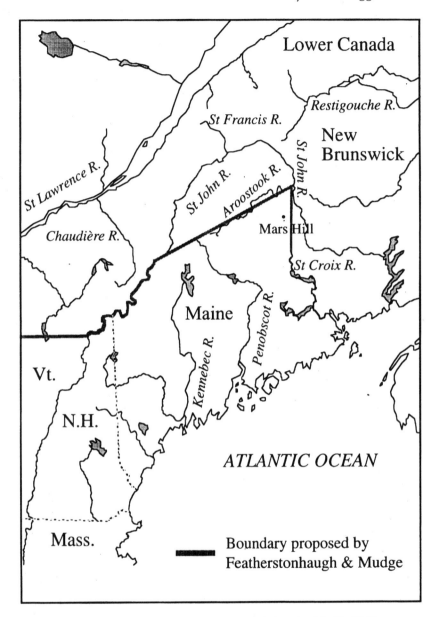

Map 14. Report of the British boundary commission (article 5), 1840

The most distinguished critic of the British report was none other than Albert Gallatin, the retired public servant and diplomat who had helped to draft the American case presented to the king of the Netherlands in 1830. Gallatin was no longer engaged by the government, but he was troubled by the character and tone of the report and by the fact that Palmerston had made it a public document. 'The fact, that the Secretary of State for foreign affairs did lay before the Parliament of Great Britain the report of the late commissioners, affords strong evidence, that that distinguished statesman, amidst his more important and overwhelming avocations, had not found time thoroughly to investigate the merits of the case and to judge for himself.'[42] Given Palmerston's own opinions on the boundary and his involvement in the commission's work, Gallatin was quite wrong in this assumption, but he was determined to state the American position, show up the weaknesses in the British claims, and, perhaps, tweak Palmerston's nose. However, in view of the nature of the report and the recent trend of events, Gallatin was also worried that the document contributed more to the drift towards a possible Anglo–American war than to a peaceful settlement. Gallatin also lamented the fact that neither nation had published the statements presented to the king of the Netherlands, which he considered more accurate and sophisticated than the recent report. Therefore, in a book published in 1840 at his own expense, Gallatin made public for the first time extensive passages from the American arguments that he and Preble had drafted in 1829.[43]

Gallatin reviewed the historic arguments of both parties, concentrating on the reading of the terms of the 1783 treaty, the origins of the notions of the colonial boundaries in 1763 and 1774, and the two sides' different understandings of the meaning of 'highlands' that divided the waters flowing into the St Lawrence from those entering the Atlantic. Gallatin, however, directed much of his essay to an analysis and refutation of the assertions made by Mudge and Featherstonhaugh in their report. The issue of the mistranslation of the 1621 Latin charter to Sir William Alexander was a false one, Gallatin said. The precise translation of the words in question was 'towards the north,' which both the British traditionally and the Americans since the 1760s had taken to mean north, or due north, in practical terms. By no means did it mean 'west' or 'northwest,' as Mudge and Featherstonhaugh had asserted, giving rise to their suggestion of an altogether new hypothetical boundary from the source of the St Croix straight northwest to the source of the

Chaudière (or its tributary, the Metjarmette).[44] Nevertheless, this was a digression.

The heart of the British report was the proposed new boundary. This line did not follow the previously proposed British boundary, which started near Mars Hill and progressed west along the watershed dividing the streams flowing into the St John from those entering the Penobscot and Kennebec rivers. Rather, it started at a point just south of where the Aroostook River crossed the due-north line and progressed along a series of ridges southwest to the source of the Chaudière River. Gallatin pointed out that this line failed for most of its length to divide streams flowing into any of the waters mentioned in the treaty of 1783. Indeed, for much of its length it was wholly within the St John tributaries, which the British maintained did not flow into the Atlantic at all. Thus, Gallatin argued, this line was even less in conformity with the treaty of 1783 than had been the British proposal of 1827 and 1830, and its elevation was no greater than the American line either.

Gallatin was also amazed that the British report recommended opening up the matter of the source of the St Croix River, which had been settled in 1798 by the arbitral decision and a treaty. The terms of the treaty forbade absolutely the reopening of the question. Gallatin concluded that the new proposals were contrived and mischievous, as well as less convincing than the earlier British arguments. 'The authors of the statements [presented to the king of the Netherlands] understood the British case better than the late commissioners [Mudge and Featherstonhaugh].'[45]

Gallatin's little book was sold in the United States, but in November 1840 the author sent a large number of copies to Joshua Bates in London, one of the partners in Baring Brothers bank, in the hope of influencing British thinking. 'It is an appeal to justice and to public opinion,' he wrote, 'the only means, as I believe, by which an ultimate collision may be prevented.'[46] It may be that Gallatin's missive had something of the effect that he desired. Bates wrote back to him in February that the book had 'produced a deep impression in the highest quarters.'[47] Certainly it is likely that the book was read by Lord Ashburton, Bates's partner at the bank, who was soon to become fully engaged in the boundary question, and probably other Tory leaders read it as well.

The book fell into Featherstonhaugh's hands, and he was not pleased; Gallatin was 'a tricky, cunning person, worthy of the country of his adoption,' he assured John Backhouse at the Foreign Office. The volume was full of 'innumerable sophistries,' he said, 'but I promise you I will take the starch out of the whole of them.' Featherstonhaugh boasted about Gallatin that he would 'roast him to rags upon his own spit.'[48] Featherstonhaugh had his followers, but he would have increasing opposition also. Word began to circulate that Featherstonhaugh and his son James had not surveyed all that they claimed either. One of the American surveyors who had met the British party in the woods commented, 'The miserable Report of the British Commissrs. in 1840 was based upon hearsay and a slight examination of the line claimed *only* by them.' It was suggested that 'the Report was made first – a verdict given against our topographical claims – and the evidence attempted to be collected two years after.'[49] A year later, with a change of governments in both London and Washington, Edward Everett, the new American minister, warned Lord Aberdeen, the new foreign secretary, 'against placing too much confidence in the report of Mr. Featherstonhaugh, as it was produced under circumstances, which must detract from the weight of that gentleman's authority.'[50]

The U.S. government had been placed in an awkward position by first the Maine and then the British surveys. In 1840 it was very late in responding to the efforts of these two rival governments. Not until 20 July of that year did Congress authorize a commission to explore and survey the disputed borderland. The following day Secretary of State John Forsyth wrote to Professor James Renwick at Columbia College in New York offering him leadership of the commission. Forsyth also appointed as commissioners Captain Andrew Talcott of Gladensburg, Connecticut, and Professor Parker Cleveland of Bowdoin College in Maine. After Cleveland refused the appointment, Forsyth turned on 18 August to Major James D. Graham at West Point. The commissioners received instructions from Forsyth to form three parties and to explore and survey the topographical features of land formations in a western and southerly direction from the Bay of Chaleurs to the source of the Connecticut River. They were given copies of the recent report of Featherstonhaugh and Mudge and urged to take careful account of these new British claims. They also received the report of the Maine commission and the statements presented to the king of the Netherlands in 1830. In short, the U.S. commission was both to explore on its own and to prepare revised arguments to meet the new claims of both Maine and the British.[51]

Professor Renwick and his party set out from Portland, Maine, in late August and by 3 September had reached Woodstock, New Brunswick, having passed through Bangor, Oldtown, and Houlton, and then they ascended the St John River to Grand Falls by 8 September. Renwick took his party to the north side of the St John and went up the Green River to its source. This was both a historic spot, where Bouchette and Johnson had explored in 1817, and a strategic region, the watershed for streams flowing south to the St John, east to the Restigouche, and north to the St Lawrence. Renwick divided his party into four smaller groups, sending one of them to explore the headwaters of the Restigouche – the Wagansis, the Mempticook, the Grande Fourche, and the Kedgwick – and a second to descend to the Bay of Chaleurs. The third party was to explore the highlands on Green River Mountain, and the fourth was to look after moving supplies to Lake Temiscouata and then explore Lake Tuladi and the streams entering it from the north, which put that group at the headwaters of the Rimouski River flowing north into the St Lawrence.

In his letters to Forsyth in October, Professor Renwick said that his men had really found 'a continuous range, not of highlands, but of mountains, from the North shore of the Bay of Chaleurs, extending around the source of the tributaries of the Restigouche and St. John to the Temiscouata portage.' Renwick told him, although he was not ready to include this in the interim report, that 'when our observations come to be calculated, the height of the peaks will far exceed those actually measured by Messrs. Mudge and Featherstonhaugh on the line they have chosen, while even the gaps where the streams rise will be higher than the summits of the greater part of that line.'[52] However, time and resources were such that a careful survey had to be abandoned in late autumn in favour of more simple explorations. Barometers broke, and the weather closed in with heavy snowfalls, making it difficult to determine altitude and to take accurate astronomical sightings. Renwick was also distressed to see how much better the British astronomical instruments were than his own, when he encountered Lieutenant Broughton and young Featherstonhaugh in the woods, and he decided to buy some French instruments on his own. The shallowness of the streams in late autumn meant that canoes were not practical for carrying supplies, and almost everything had to be packed on men's backs. Fatigue and illness took their toll, and one engineer was seriously injured.[53]

By 6 September, Captain Talcott had led his party up the Connecticut River, where it explored the several sources of that river. The men kept to the edge of those streams flowing north into the Salmon River, clearly in Lower Canada. Talcott thought that he found the true dividing ridge forming the boundary of New Hampshire. On 24 September he turned towards the topographical features of the watersheds of the Chaudiere to the north and the Androscoggin, the Kenebec, and the Penobscot to the south and east. By 23 October the team had reached the Kenebec road, and three days later it was at Lake Etchemin. A heavy snowfall at that moment prevented further advance.[54]

The third party, under Major Graham, was the last to get started. Graham enlisted the services of several fellow officers to work as engineers, and they proceeded to Portland and to Bangor, where he consulted with Professor Renwick. On 13 September, Graham and his party arrived in Houlton Plantation, where he collected equipment and recruited a working crew of chainbearers, instrument carriers, and axemen. Thence the group made its way to the monument erected in 1817 to mark the source of the St Croix River. Men began clearing the undergrowth from the cut in the forest that had marked the due-north line twenty-three years earlier. They established observation sites at various distances to check the accuracy of the 1817 survey, and it was hoped that they would be able to mark carefully the due-north line at least as far as Mars Hill or the Aroostook River. On 13 November a heavy snowfall dumped sixteen inches on the region. Equally difficult, heavy cloud cover made astronomical sightings difficult and intermittent. These winter conditions slowed the men down, but, despite living in army tents and bunks, they got on well. Small stoves kept the tents warm, at least until the fires went out at night, and there was no sickness. On 18 November, the party was opposite Mars Hill, and by mid-December it was overlooking the Aroostook River. However, on 16 December, with two feet of snow on the ground, it closed work for the season.[55]

Although field work by the three parties went on until late November and mid-December, with much still to be done, the urgency of the boundary question necessitated an interim report. Thus, by 6 January 1841, the three commissioners signed a report for President Van Buren outlining the work that they had accomplished. The report took some pains to acknowledge the assistance and courtesy extended to them in New Brunswick by Lieutenant-Governor Sir John Harvey, New Brunswick land agent Lieutenant-Colonel MacLaughlan, and several other soldiers, public officials, and private citizens. They did not spell out firm conclusions in any detail, as Renwick had privately to Secretary of State Forsyth, but they clearly were heading in the direction of reinforcing the now-historic American claim for identification and location of the 'highlands' and the Northwest Angle of Nova Scotia of the treaty of 1783 on the ridge of land forming the watershed beginning with the Métis River, flowing into the St Lawrence, and winding its way west and south to the source of the Connecticut.[56] Indeed, to complete the work, they sent parties out during the summer of 1841.

The final report was submitted over a year later, on 31 March 1842, with the findings of the three commissioners stated succinctly at the end of the document.[57] The St Croix and its source had been solemnly decided by Britain and the United States 'and can not now be disturbed,' and the due-north line could not be altered. The Northwest Angle of Nova Scotia was held to be where the borders of New Brunswick and Maine met the southern border of Quebec along the St Lawrence watershed. The 'highlands' were the watershed that formed a ridge extending from the Gaspé peninsula to the headwaters of the Connecticut River. Finally, the northwestern source of the Connecticut River was Indian Stream.[58] The commissioners based these conclusions on a detailed discussion of the commissions' explorations, the history of the boundary question, and a refutation of Mudge and Featherstonhaugh's assertions. They reasserted the logic of the traditional U.S. claims, but on the basis of exploration and survey that went beyond the work of the commission of 1817–22.

Because the British report had introduced so many new issues and presented such controversial arguments, this new U.S. report attempted to deal specifically with what it had said. The Americans confronted the pugnacity of the British report directly and described it as expressing an 'unfriendly spirit.' Indeed, 'Charges of direct and implied fraud are made, and language is used throughout that is irritating and insulting,' which attitudes, the Americans hoped, did not reflect the 'sentiments of the British nation.'[59] The authors noted that the territory in question was of greater value to British North America than it was to the United States and that British use of the road across the disputed territory to move troops to suppress the recent rebellions was a good illustration of that value. The issue, however, was not need but right, under the terms of the treaty of 1783. If the United States were shown not to have a valid claim, it would cheerfully give up its pretensions, but if the American claim were shown to be valid, 'national honor forbids that this title should be abandoned.'[60]

Mudge and Featherstonhaugh did not establish their case, the American report asserted. They had based much of their argument on documents other than the treaty of 1783 – French and Venetian maps, for instance. They also became diverted by the translation of a seventeenth-century charter for Nova Scotia, which was irrelevant – the common translation was correct, and the terms had been in use for over one hundred years before the treaty of 1783. As for the Northwest Angle of Nova Scotia, the 1783 boundary was premised on the 1763 and 1774 descriptions of the colonial boundaries, and the treaty made no sense when it was presumed to trace an altogether new boundary, as asserted by Mudge and Featherstonhaugh. The British commissioners' position on the 'highlands' was even more obscure, with the eastern end where the Aroostook River crossed the line due north from the source of the St Croix River (just above where the Aroostook entered the St John). The American report asserted that this region was lower in elevation than the northern ridge that it proposed and failed to conform to the language of the treaty of 1783 because it did not divide waters that flowed into the St Lawrence from those that entered the Atlantic. The new British ridge was a watershed for streams flowing into the St John River only. Perhaps even more surprising, the Americans said, this was the third version of a boundary claimed by the British since 1798.[61] In short, the Americans concluded, the arguments and claims of Mudge and Featherstonhaugh were less valid and less convincing than the British case presented to the king of the Netherlands in 1830.

As the surveying parties carried out their work and released their reports in 1840 and 1841, talks went on between the two governments. The two sides were too far apart to make any real progress, however. The Americans seemed to hold their position that any discussions, surveys, or arbitration had to consider the possibility of a boundary north of the St John River. The new British proposal seemed to be an expansion of earlier claims. As Andrew Stevenson had written to Richard Rush in early 1840, even before Featherstonhaugh had drafted his report, the British seemed less willing to reach an accommodation over the dispute. 'One thing (between ourselves) is very certain, Mr. Bull is not getting at all more disposed to yield anything to us in the way of compromise, & our Govt. must keep an eye to the Borders.'[62] Even the talk about a new Anglo–American joint commission was seen as a manoeuvre to create a background for a fresh arbitration. Indeed, one of Lord Palmerston's last dispatches to Fox in Washington before leaving office was to propose a joint commission based in Quebec City, operating under conditions that had their origins in the proposals put forward by Featherstonhaugh, which would explore the disputed territory from west to east beginning at the head of the Connecticut River and which, failing an agreement, would be subject to arbitration by persons named by the kings of Prussia, Sardinia, and Saxony.[63] It is difficult to think what Palmerston intended by this elaborate proposal, but he had been so convinced by Featherstonhaugh's arguments that he increasingly felt that Britain could obtain all of the territory in dispute. Lord Melbourne's Whig government staggered to its end on 28 August. In fact, Fox may never have delivered the proposal to Secretary of State Webster, for the copies in the U.S. State Department came through the dispatches from the American minister in London, Andrew Stevenson. In any case, the Americans were sure to reject it, particularly the proposed arbitration.

What was of more concern, however, was the persistent talk of conflict and war throughout the late 1830s and early 1840s. Although each incident and crisis had been met with deliberate efforts by both governments and by many officials in the troubled regions, many people felt that conflict was inevitable. Palmerston had threatened Stevenson with war over the possible execution of McLeod and had told Backhouse in 1840 that in any encroachments on the border 'force will be repelled with force.'[64] The governor general of British North America, Lord Sydenham, had written to Fox in July 1841 similarly that pressure from Maine along the frontier with New Brunswick would result in an 'almost certainty of collision between them.'[65] Similarly, the *Dublin University Magazine* concluded in the spring of 1841 that 'sooner or later, war we will have.' Citing Featherstonhaugh and Mudge's report as the basis for the British claim, and taking into account the pugnacity that it saw in the Americans, the journal asserted, 'The boundary question will, we much fear, not be settled without a recourse to hostilities.'[66] Americans expected a clash also. Richard Rush had thought that a clash was coming in January 1840 with the crisis of British troop movements north of the St John River, and he seemed to find little to change his mind in the remarks of the Duke of Wellington several months later. He feared a conflict and that 'the war will be bigger, if it comes, and more formidable to England before it ends than has entered into his conceptions, I fancy.'[67]

An impasse seemed to have been reached. The boundary had to be settled, but there was less room for negotiation or compromise by the autumn of 1841 than there had been ten years earlier. All the machinery for settlement – joint commissions, unilateral commissions, arbitration, and negotiation – had been tried and failed. Yet the prospect of continually escalating crises that promised to result eventually in a disastrous conflict that no thoughtful person wanted was too grim to contemplate.

PART THREE

Grasping the Nettle:
1841–1845

Chapter Eleven

Sea Change: Initiative and Compromise

Governments change, and with changes of cabinets and policies it is sometimes possible to initiate a fresh approach to intractable old problems. Something of this sort occurred between 1840 and 1842 in Britain, the United States, and Canada. In November 1840, in the United States, the Jacksonian Democrats, who had been in power since 1829, were defeated, and the first Whig president was elected. Politically this was a move somewhat to the right, away from the frontier-influenced, populist, and chauvinistic Jacksonians, and towards the more eastern-based, commercially oriented Whigs. Practically the situation was less clear when the new president, William Henry Harrison, died in April 1841, after only about a month in office, bringing John Tyler of Virginia to the White House as the first vice-president to succeed a dead president. Tyler had been a states'-rights Democrat who quarrelled with Andrew Jackson and who had very shallow roots in the Whig party. Although he retained Harrison's cabinet, he managed to alienate it on issues of domestic politics, and in September 1841 Henry Clay led a mass resignation.

The one Whig who remained with Tyler was Daniel Webster, the secretary of state, who was committed to a settlement of the many outstanding issues with Britain. Webster was one of the leading lawyers in the country, a famous orator, and also a strikingly handsome man. He was known as both 'the god-like Daniel' and 'black Dan.' First elected to Congress in 1813, and to the Senate in 1827, he emerged as a national political figure as well as the leading spokesman for Massachusetts. When Webster told Tyler that he would stay in the cabinet, Tyler replied, 'Give me your hand on that, and now I will say to you that Henry Clay is a doomed man from this hour.' This was putting the best face on a difficult situation. In fact, Tyler became a president without a party.[1]

In Britain a different, but equally complicated, situation unfolded in 1841. The Whig government of Lord Melbourne, with Lord Palmerston as foreign secretary, lost its majority in the House of Commons over the summer and was succeeded on 30 August by a new Tory government led by Sir Robert Peel, with Lord Aberdeen as foreign secretary. Aberdeen had a long career in government service, beginning as a diplomat in 1803 and ending as prime minister from 1853 to 1855. This was the second time that he served as foreign secretary. In foreign affairs he was unflamboyant, but he strongly believed that conciliation and careful negotiations bore results. As a young diplomat in 1813 Aberdeen had seen the carnage and horror of the battlefield, and, while no pacifist, he was never a chauvinist either. Here too was a conservative government with less of a predisposition to take an aggressive or chauvinistic position on foreign policy matters than its predecessor under Palmerston. The Tories, who inherited crises in Afghanistan and China, as well as along the British North American border, wanted a less volatile foreign policy. Aberdeen saw Britain's greatest danger as coming from a possible war with the United States or France, and past experience had shown that a war with one led to war with both.[2]

It may have been simply a matter of coincidence that brought these two governments to power within a year of each other. The result, however, was an opportunity for two relatively like-minded governments, once the acquittal of McLeod in October had cleared the air, to make a fresh start. The border questions were the most volatile of their mutual problems.

In British North America, as well, things were changing. The Rebellions of 1837 had resulted in the Colonial Office's appointing a new governor general, Lord Durham, to investigate the causes of political unrest and to make recommendations. The so-called Durham Report of 1839 recommended, among other things, the political union of Upper and Lower Canada with a new legislature. It fell to Sir Charles Bagot, as the new governor general from late 1841 to implement many of the changes, as well as to advise on the efforts to resolve the boundary crisis. Bagot, of course, was familiar with the tangled history of the question, having been British minister to the United States from 1816 to 1818 and also having presided over the submission of the British case to King William in 1830 while he was ambassador to the Netherlands. Bagot was appointed governor general in part because he had demonstrated an ability to get along with the Americans during his earlier diplomatic post in Washington.[3] However, the persistent difficulties that he faced with the new Canadian legislature – widespread opposition to the Union and demands by the reformers that the lower house determine the government – led to growing anxiety about the wisdom of continued British colonial involvement in North America, apart from the Maritime provinces. By the spring of 1842 Sir Robert Peel mused to Lord Aberdeen that 'the connection with the Canadas *against their will*, nay, without the cordial co-operation of the predominant party in Canada, is a very onerous one.' The constant unrest in Canada aroused American interest, Peel said, and then left Britain in the unrewarding position of having to defend Canada against the Americans. If the Canadians did not want British rule, 'let us have a friendly separation while there is yet time, rather than recommence a system of bickering and squabbling on petty points, the result of which will be increasing ill humour and alienation.'[4] While these private remarks may have been a long way from official policy, they do reveal that this British government's attitudes towards the North American colonies might not embrace unlimited support.

It was Daniel Webster who made the first effort to search for a way out of the apparent conundrum of further boundary surveys. On 11 May 1841, he asked Francis Calley Gray, a prominent Boston shipping merchant and state politician who was travelling to England, to talk about the boundary with various public figures in London, such as Francis T. Baring, chancellor of the exchequer; Henry Labouchere, president of the Board of Trade; John Backhouse, permanent undersecretary at the Foreign Office; and possibly Lord Palmerston himself. The message that Webster sent was that surveys, commissions, and arbitrations were all costly, time-consuming, and not certain to bear fruitful results. What he suggested was the negotiation of a new compromise boundary line. 'Possibly,' Webster wrote, 'there may be some idea of an *exchange* of territory suggested.' One proposal was that the United States give up its claims to lands north of the St John River and east of the Madawaska River (to accommodate the British need for a military road), in exchange for the narrow strip of land between the due-north line and the St John River north of the Eel River, or possibly Campobello Island or Grand Manan Island.[5] Webster also tried out these ideas on Joshua Bates, a Baring Brothers partner visiting the United States. Bates wrote to the London bank saying that Gray was 'authorized to settle all,' which certainly was not so, but he urged that the partners introduce Gray to all the important people.[6] This initiative may have been premature, because the McLeod trial still clouded Anglo–American relations, certainly in the mind of Lord Palmerston.

Whether Gray talked to Backhouse and Palmerston is uncertain. Certainly there was recognition in England that Webster, perhaps because of his visit there in 1839, was an American politician who was not hostile to Britain and with whom the British could negotiate. By midsummer of 1841, Palmerston was certainly talking about a changed attitude by the governments of Maine and the United States, although he attributed that shift to what he was convinced was the overwhelming evidence in the report of Mudge and Featherstonhaugh.[7]

The Baring Brothers connection proved more fruitful in the end. On 29 August 1841, as Melbourne's Whig government was collapsing, Lord Ashburton, the retired senior partner of the bank, wrote to Sir Robert Peel, just as Queen Victoria was calling Peel to form a new government. Ashburton conveyed to Peel a letter from Webster to Joshua Bates discussing the American political situation and referring to the Gray letter. It did not spell out details, but Ashburton emphasized Webster's point about the precariousness of his position in Tyler's cabinet and the need to move quickly to settle Anglo–American difficulties. Peel's reply was noncommittal but took note of Webster's initiative.[8] Clearly there was a need to do something about these several outstanding issues, particularly once the McLeod affair was over in mid-October. A copy of the *New York Herald* urging a special mission to deal with the crisis was sent to the new foreign secretary, Lord Aberdeen.[9] Both Aberdeen and Peel agreed that Henry S. Fox, the British minister in Washington, was unsuitable for the task. 'He seems terribly imbued with a feeling of hatred of the United States and its institutions,' Peel observed to the foreign secretary, and he queried the most effective means to advance British interests.[10] Fox's failings as a diplomat had become notorious. He would not be the person to handle delicate negotiations with the Americans.

Ashburton was the logical choice. He had first approached Peel about these matters at the onset of the new government and had been offered a post; he had turned it down and was thus available. He was currently giving the government advice on trade and financial issues; his nephew was the new chancellor of the exchequer, and he himself had been president of the Board of Trade in 1834 during Peel's first government and for his services had been created Baron Ashburton in 1835.[11] Furthermore, his American connections made him a unique figure in British public life. Alexander Baring had been born in 1774. As a young man he had lived in the United States representing Baring Brothers bank, and under his leadership the bank became the foremost British investment house dealing in American securities. While in the United States he not only made extensive land purchases in Maine, albeit not in the contested areas, but he also married Anne Bingham, the daughter of the wealthy and politically well-connected Philadelphia Revolutionary, Senator William Bingham. In 1803 Baring had negotiated the financing of the Louisiana Purchase for the Americans; he had opposed the British orders in council that helped generate the War of 1812 and became known as a public figure 'friendly' to the United States. He was on cordial terms with numerous prominent Americans, including Albert Gallatin and Daniel Webster himself.[12] If the Tory government wanted to find a negotiator who enjoyed prestige and respect at home, as well as good will in the United States, it could not have done better than Lord Ashburton.

The foreign secretary approached Ashburton with the offer to lead a special mission to settle the range of issues with the United States, and by 22 December 1841 Ashburton agreed. Although he coyly questioned his own health and his ability, Ashburton was willing to undertake the task because of 'the great importance of the service' and because he had been assured 'the support and entire confidence of my masters.' Certainly the mission was important, but Ashburton's masters would come under such intense political pressure that Ashburton would have cause for second thoughts about the prospects of success. At the moment, however, he was hopeful because he had reason to 'believe the [Tyler] Administration to be well disposed' to a reasonable settlement, although he cautiously added to the head of the British foreign service, 'but my sources of information must necessarily be very imperfect.'[13]

Everyone was delighted. Aberdeen reported to Peel that it was 'a great stroke' that Ashburton agreed, even with a certain amount of 'fear and trembling.' Peel responded similarly, 'I am rejoiced ...'[14] Even the Duke of Wellington, the Tory patriarch and minister without portfolio in Peel's cabinet, assured Aberdeen that he was 'very happy to learn' that Ashburton had agreed to head the mission to the United States, although he was later to have misgivings about the terms of a possible boundary settlement.[15] Later also there was some concern about Ashburton's age – he was sixty-seven – and his restrained manner. The diarist Charles Greville thought him too given to 'vacillation and irresolution' and too old to deal effectively with the aggressive Americans.[16]

The new American minister to Britain, Edward Everett, the former Whig governor of Massachusetts, who was very familiar with the northeastern boundary question, arrived in London in mid-December. Everett reported to Daniel Webster as early as the thirty-first that Aberdeen had told him of Ashburton's appointment. By late January news came back to the British government about the American reaction to the mission. Webster wrote officially to Everett asking him to convey the president's sentiments and saying that Ashburton's 'high character' was 'well known to this Government.' Privately Webster told Everett that, although the appointment was a surprise, as far as he was concerned, 'no selection of a Minister could be more agreeable to me than that of Lord Ashburton.'[17] The former American minister, Richard Rush, described Ashburton in even more glowing terms: 'It would be difficult to determine which was most conspicuous about him,' Rush wrote in his memoirs, 'superior intelligence of mind with skills in affairs, or a uniformly discreet and most conciliating temper to co-operate with the powers of his understanding, in dealing with affairs.'[18]

Fox wrote Aberdeen that the U.S. administration received the announcement 'with much pleasure, as proof of the earnest wish of Her Majesty's Government to terminate as speedily as possible the existing differences.'[19] Privately Fox assured Aberdeen, 'Nothing can possibly be better than the tone and temper in which Mr. Webster has received the announcement of Lord Ashburton's appointment,' although Fox also warned that the U.S. political situation so weakened Webster's position that while he might agree to reasonable compromises with Ashburton he would probably find it difficult to carry them into effect. 'Still,' Fox concluded, 'to have the prime minister a friend rather than an enemy, will I hope count for something.' Fox similarly reported to Aberdeen President Tyler's 'satisfaction' with the special mission and his hope that the negotiations would establish 'the relations of the two countries upon a safe and friendly footing for many years to come.'[20] Newspapers such as the *Niles' National Register* were delighted. It called the appointment a 'friendly gesture,' indicative of the British government's desire to settle the outstanding controversies.[21]

Early in the new year of 1842 Ashburton himself wrote a note to Webster as a courtesy to say that he had been persuaded to undertake this mission. Much of his thirty-five years of public service, Ashburton said, had been devoted to promoting 'peace and harmony between our countries'; he had 'watched with anxiety' each unfolding crisis, fearing that 'through the neglect of some or the malevolence of others [the crisis might] end in a storm, the disastrous consequences of which defy exaggeration.' Therefore, he concluded, he looked forward happily 'to cooperate with you in this good work.'[22] It was a noble statement, in which Ashburton stepped outside the complimentary, noncommittal language of diplomacy and revealed something of that character which had made him such a conspicuous choice as special minister. This indeed would be a different kind of search for the boundary, and a number of people, as this chapter outlines, would seek to influence the proceedings, even before negotiations began in June.

Ashburton wanted to sail for the United States as soon as possible, and the first-class frigate HMS *Warspite* was put at his disposal. Aberdeen also thought it advantageous that he put to sea before Parliament sat and a debate emerged about the merits of negotiations with the Americans. In all this haste, however, difficulties unfolded over the instructions that Ashburton was to have about what would be an acceptable settlement, particularly concerning the northeastern boundary. It may have been that Aberdeen had assured Ashburton, in his original invitation to him, that the government would be satisfied with almost any reasonable settlement that he might be able to obtain. Hence Ashburton's very specific mention to both Aberdeen and Webster of the 'support and *entire* confidence' that he enjoyed from his 'masters,' as he put it.[23]

Aberdeen put together the instructions after Ashburton had left London to join the *Warspite* at Yarmouth Roads. The foreign secretary outlined three acceptable boundaries. The most preferable line represented the extreme British claim and ran from the watershed south of the Aroostook River, southwest to the source of the St John River, and thence to the northwesternmost branch of the headwaters of the Connecticut River. This was essentially the boundary line proposed in the British arguments submitted to the king of the Netherlands. The second was to run along the Aroostook west to the Fish River, then north following that stream to its confluence with the St John River, along that stream to its source, and then to the northwesternmost head of the Connecticut. The third – the greatest compromise that the British would accept – was the line suggested by the king of the Netherlands, which ran from the due-north line along the St John River, up the St Francis River, and then along the watersheds of the St Francis and St John rivers southwest along the height of land to the headwaters of the Connecticut.[24]

The instructions included details for a settlement of the western boundaries also. The last segment of the old 1783 boundary in the Lake Superior region remained to be determined. This border, Aberdeen said, was 'less important than either of those upon which I have addressed you.' Here there were two problems. The first was St George's Island in the St Mary's River at Sault Ste Marie. Aberdeen urged Ashburton to secure the island if he could, although he might cede it in exchange for suitable concessions elsewhere. The second problem concerned the rival claims for the route between Lake Superior and the Lake of the Woods. Aberdeen said that the compromise route of the Pigeon River to the Lake of the Woods, with British possession of the Grand Portage trail along the south side of the Pigeon River, would be preferable, but the portage trail could be abandoned in exchange for a suitable concession either in the Great Lakes region or in the Oregon territory. Two proposals were also described for the Oregon territory. The first was to extend the boundary line from the forty-ninth parallel south down the continental divide to the Snake River, along that stream to the confluence with the Columbia River, and down the Columbia to the Pacific Ocean. British territory would remain west of the Rocky Mountains and north of the Columbia. The second proposal was to extend the forty-ninth parallel to the first tributary of the Columbia, McGillivray's River, and along it to the Columbia, and from the Columbia to the Pacific.[25]

Before these instructions went to Ashburton, Aberdeen showed them to Peel, who in turn gave them to Wellington. Wellington found them most unsatisfactory. He sent a 'protest' to Aberdeen in mid-afternoon of 8 February and wrote again in the evening, enclosing a commentary. Wellington focused his displeasure on the third boundary. He emphasized that communications between the Maritime colonies and Lower Canada were a paramount strategic interest and that the line of the king of the Netherlands put the Americans dangerously close to the best overland road. The duke argued that Britain was in no way bound by this line and that Ashburton should make a major effort to obtain acceptance of the maximum British claim.[26] Aberdeen sent Ashburton a copy of Wellington's memorandum and noted, 'If the Duke's views were adhered to, you would have little chance of success,' but he conceded that Wellington's arguments deserved careful consideration and added rather hopefully that the 'recent investigation [by Mudge and Featherstonhaugh] has improved our position, and must have tended to render the Americans less confident.'[27] Aberdeen also showed the instructions and Wellington's comments to the colonial secretary, Lord Stanley, who agreed with the duke about the security of the military road linking Lower Canada with the Maritimes. Stanley also asked whether it was worth initiating these talks unless there were some assurances that the state of Maine could not subvert them, and he urged that the instructions to Ashburton be brought before the cabinet.[28]

As a result of the subsequent discussion in cabinet, Aberdeen warned Ashburton that the final instructions would be delayed and that he should not make any comment regarding the boundary until then.[29] At the request of cabinet, Aberdeen asked the opinion of four experts with both administrative and military experience serving in British North America. However, Sir James Kempt, Sir Howard Douglas, Lord Seaton, and Sir George Murray, all soldiers and former lieutenant-governors, each returned slightly different concerns over Ashburton's instructions and the security of communications between the Maritime colonies and Canada. Aberdeen also found correspondence from Lord Palmerston in 1833 and 1835 in which the St John River was proposed as a compromise line. The result of the varied recommendations, and Palmerston's offer of the St John River, allowed Aberdeen, as he thought, to deal with the misgivings of Wellington and others in new instructions. As one historian has noted, 'It was a bold business to defy the greatest soldier of the age on a question of security,' but Ashburton was given the means to allow the negotiation to begin.[30]

On 31 March the foreign secretary sent new instructions to Ashburton outlining in more specific terms what would be acceptable to the British government. He described the land route between New Brunswick and Lower Canada along the St John River, the Madawaska River, and Lake Temiscouata, and he emphasized that 'it is deemed essential that this line should be preserved.' To secure this route the American border could not be allowed north of the St John and east of the Madawaska River, nor could it be located on the watershed separating the St John and the St Francis rivers from the streams flowing into the St Lawrence River, as suggested by the king of the Netherlands. In short, while the king's line might be acceptable in the east (the St John River, but not north of it), it would have to be improved upon in the upper St Francis watershed, which came within thirty miles of Quebec City. 'It thus very materially interferes with the freedom and security of our communications,' Lord Aberdeen stressed. In order to obtain American compliance with this reduction of the territory proposed by the king of the Netherlands, Aberdeen suggested concessions to the Americans on Rouse's Point and the old (and incorrect) survey line of the forty-fifth parallel and the headwaters of the Connecticut River. The findings of the report by Mudge and Featherstonhaugh were also to be kept before the Americans.[31]

Peel also raised the possibility of a financial indemnity for Maine, if it came to that, and Aberdeen mentioned this in his private letter to Ashburton, along with the suggestion that the Americans might also be allowed to float timber down the St John River. As if to anticipate that Ashburton might find the new conditions unattractive to the Maine spokesmen, Aberdeen stated that he was sure that the state had a senator or congressman or agent in Washington 'who probably might act in concert with Webster, and may ensure the acceptance of the terms agreed upon with him.' The foreign secretary presumed that Ashburton 'must have some means, therefore, of carrying that State with you in the negotiations with the General Government.'[32] Was this a pious hope or a subtle suggestion to use secret service funds and some covert activity to obtain compliance?

Ashburton received the first hint that problems had emerged within the British government when the original instructions arrived while he was waiting for favourable winds to allow the *Warspite* to put to sea. After reading the memorandum of the Duke of Wellington, which Aberdeen enclosed, Ashburton responded by saying that he was 'little likely to satisfy him [the duke] on the Boundary question by anything I can do.'[33] When the 31 March instructions arrived, Ashburton, by then in Washington, replied with two official dispatches and one private letter. In the official dispatch devoted to the boundary question, he attempted to explain the complicated U.S. political situation (both the federal–state problem and the momentary weakness of the presidency) and how these conditions stood to influence any settlement. American general opinion, Ashburton observed, supported Maine and Massachusetts in their territorial claims, but it also recognized the ambiguities of the boundary situation and accepted, more or less, the line of the king of the Netherlands as a reasonable compromise by an objective outsider. However, Ashburton feared that if Britain, after having taken the initiative for a settlement on the basis of compromise, came forward now with a final offer that substantially reduced the territory awarded to the United States by the king, which both Maine and the Senate had previously rejected, 'the consequence could not fail to be that the Union would indignantly take part with Maine, and we should pass for a Power having trifled with and insulted the country.'[34] Privately, Ashburton wrote to Aberdeen, 'If you had read to me your present instructions before I had left London I should have ventured under such circumstances to give an opinion that it was inexpedient to send this mission.' Ashburton attempted to be as hopeful as he could, and he did not want to rule out a possible settlement. As for the merits of the defence of the line of communication from New Brunswick to Lower Canada, Ashburton considered the Madawaska settlements south of the St John River and directly west of the due-north line more important than the highlands west of the St Francis River. Therefore he asked Aberdeen for clarification about which area the government regarded as more important. In his private note, Ashburton closed with the warning that he was 'strongly impressed with the dangers of letting the soldiers have their own way in this matter.'[35]

Aberdeen seemed a bit taken aback by Ashburton's reaction to the March instructions. He replied, 'I do not quite understand why you feel yourself so much crippled by the modifications of your original instructions.' Aberdeen pointed out that the king of the Netherlands' line had been the extreme concession that the government had been prepared to accept in February, and this had not changed. However, while Wellington and several others had wanted to improve the line west of the St Francis River, overlooking Quebec, Ashburton himself had become preoccupied with the improvement of the line south of the St John River in the Madawaska settlements. Madawaska, Aberdeen noted, 'may be a desirable object; but I should apprehend it would be found equally difficult to obtain, as the territory to which I refer [west of the St Francis River].' Aberdeen thought the lands in the Madawaska settlements 'much more valuable' to Maine and the Americans. Fixing the boundary on the upper St John and St Francis rivers, 'within sight of Quebec, would scarcely be tolerated in this country.'[36] Four days later he wrote to Ashburton more specifically that, of the two variations of the line drawn by the king of the Netherlands, the changes west of the St Francis River were 'preferable.'[37] All things considered, Aberdeen said that Wellington had been very tenacious in his views about the maximum British claims, and only the contradictory recommendations by the four military experts had persuaded him to compromise. 'You have little notion of the difficulties I have had in obtaining for you the powers you actually have,' Aberdeen emphasized.[38]

The final instructions were sent out on 26 May 1842, offering the clarification requested by Ashburton in April. They made mention of the first two boundary proposals of February. The British government regarded the boundary line proposed by the king of the Netherlands as a basis for negotiation, 'subject to such modifications as may suit the interest and convenience of both [parties].' It placed the highest priority on the area west of the St Francis and north of the St John rivers. Failing an American willingness to agree to this arrangement, Ashburton was authorized to propose a boundary that placed the Madawaska settlements, between the Aroostook and Fish rivers, within British territory. Concessions in return for either of these plans could be acceptance of the Americans' right to float timber and other products down the St John River or acceptance of the old forty-fifth parallel between New York and Lower Canada, which would allow numerous American settlers and the fortification at Rouse's Point to remain in the United States, or of any equivalent American proposal that Ashburton thought reasonable. The government rejected the idea of ceding the 'narrow strip' between the due north line and the St John River.[39] The islands of Grand Manan and Campobello, raised in the previous summer by Webster, were not mentioned. By 29 June, Ashburton was able to reply that these instructions were 'perfectly sufficient for my purpose' and that he understood that his powers would allow him to stay within the limits of the British claim, if not likely to allow him to strive for all that he had hoped to obtain.[40]

Ashburton was returning to the United States for the first time in many years, and he was impressed with, though not enamoured of, the country. He spelled out for Aberdeen the many problems that it faced with its chaotic finances and distinctive form of government. 'To the common observer it might be a matter of doubt how this confederation can hold together another year – bankrupt finances – bad administration & jobbing in every department – a loose ill conceived mass of conflicting interests, in short apparently nothing for the eye of confidence to rest upon,' he reported. 'Yet with all these disadvantages I believe that the energy & power of the country would be found to be immense in the case of war and that the jarring elements would unite for the purpose.' Ashburton advised 'conciliation,' or in somewhat more flamboyant language, 'humour the Wild Beast, and [it is] my humble opinion that it may easily be done.'[41] This was certainly advice that was congenial to the foreign secretary. Peel had earlier written to Aberdeen that 'we *must* come to an agreement on the boundary,' and the foreign secretary expanded on that sentiment to Ashburton, saying that 'the importance of a successful result is so great, as almost to justify any sacrifice compatible with the safety of our N. American Provinces.'[42] Ministers' concerns about the importance of a settlement with the United States may have

affected their reactions to the problems that Sir Charles Bagot was finding in working with the Canadian legislature and the need for sacrifices
to guarantee the security of the military road connecting Canada with
New Brunswick.[43]

The previous summer Webster had urged new talks on the basis of a
compromise boundary. This was a sensible idea, although Webster and
the U.S. government were not exactly free agents in the matter. Maine
had declared, through its members in Congress and through legislation,
that the federal government did not have the constitutional authority to
give up the territory of any state without its permission. The key then
was to get Maine's permission – a daunting prospect, given its seemingly
unswerving demand for the full territorial claim well north of the St
John River along the 'highlands' of the St Lawrence watershed. Webster
pursued several methods in the search for Maine's compliance with a
compromise settlement.

About a month after Webster's own initiative, a Maine politician,
newspaper publisher, and entrepreneur, Francis O.J. Smith, approached
him with a plan. Smith was a successful Portland lawyer who had served
as a Democrat in both houses of the Maine legislature, as well as in Congress. By the end of the 1830s he owned an interest in several newspapers, including the *Augusta Age*, the *Augusta Patriot*, and the *Portland
Eastern Argus*. He was also a partner with Samuel F.B. Morse in creating
an international telegraph system, through which he made a fortune.
Smith had written to President Martin Van Buren in 1838 with a boundary proposal, but without generating a response. In May 1841 he conferred with Webster in Washington and found him more receptive.
Later he wrote to the secretary of state that the problem was not
between the British and American governments, but 'with the people of
Maine and the people of the British provinces.' Previous efforts had
been directed 'at the wrong end of the dispute,' he said. Smith proposed that steps be taken to 'prepare public sentiment in Maine for a
compromise of the matter through a conventional line' and that this
compromise be based on both an exchange of land and on financial
compensation. Smith proposed to manage the practicalities of his plan,
and he suggested $3,500 and travelling expenses for doing it. He also
pointed out that this would be much less expensive (as well as much
quicker and more certain of success) than renewed surveys, not to mention a resort to arms.[44]

With Webster's approval and an advance of $500 from the President's secret service funds, Smith proceeded to write three articles, over the pen name 'Agricola,' under the title 'Northeastern Boundary – Why Not Settle It?' These appeared in the *Portland Christian Mirror* on 18 November and 2 December 1841 and 3 January 1842. 'Agricola' argued that the people of Maine should ask the state government to seek a compromise settlement on the boundary, in which Maine recognized Britain's need for a secure military road in exchange for the U.S. right of navigation of the St John River through British territory; he also urged federal compensation for the expenses incurred by the state in the defence of its claims during the Aroostook War and earlier and for the value of any territory given up. The articles had an impact. The *Portland Eastern Argus* reprinted them, and, while perhaps not surprising in view of Smith's interests, this showed the support of Maine's leading Democratic newspaper. Papers such as the *Portland Advertiser* and the *Bangor Whig* began to express sympathetic views, and several national papers reprinted these articles. Webster himself wrote editorials for the *National Intelligencer* in Washington.[45]

Smith also travelled throughout Maine talking to politicians and prominent people about a compromise settlement. His previous political experience, as well as his many commercial enterprises, opened doors for him in various levels of Maine society and gave him access to many people. By late November 1841 Smith told Webster that, through his meetings and correspondence with people in Maine from both political parties, great progress was being made in moving 'our people toward the necessary preliminaries of a satisfactory compromise of the dispute.' Smith thought that if one or two people in each county could be employed to keep the discussion about a compromise settlement before the public, in order to keep pressure on the legislature, Maine could be counted on to come to an agreement. He thought that two or three thousand dollars would be sufficient to bring this plan into operation. It is not clear whether Webster authorized the expenditure of funds for this purpose.[46]

Webster also wrote directly to the outgoing Whig governor of Maine, Edward Kent, in late 1841, reporting that no progress had been made on the boundary question over the past year. 'The interest of both parties undoubtedly requires a compromise,' he observed, querying whether Britain might 'pay for the land north of the [St John] river' and whether navigation of the St John or the transfer of the 'narrow strip' might be a consideration. Certainly Kent publicly stated his willingness to compromise: 'Maine for the sake of the peace and quiet of the country ... might forbear to enforce her extreme rights pending negotiations.' A subsequent 'Report of the Land Agent of the State of Maine,' released on 31 December 1841, said that Maine should accept 'the settlement of a new boundary line in reciprocal terms,' those possible terms being navigation, some contiguous territory, and some other 'equitable' form of 'recompense.'[47] This was a major step.

Webster got unsolicited assistance from another source also. The Harvard historian Jared Sparks, editor of *The Diplomatic Correspondence of the American Revolution, The Writings of George Washington*, and *The Works of Benjamin Franklin*, and later president of Harvard, conveyed to Webster the results of his researches in England and France on the treaty of 1783. Initially, Sparks wrote to Webster on 7 June 1841 sending a copy of William Faden's 1783 map, which he had purchased in London. This map had been produced after the Preliminary Articles of Peace had been signed and was used by members of Parliament when the definitive Treaty of Paris was debated in Parliament in 1783. Sparks pointed out that the boundary marked on the Faden map was 'precisely as claimed by the United States,' and he noted that in debates over the treaty, in which it was complained that too much territory had been ceded to the Americans, neither Lord Shelburne nor Richard Oswald spoke out to say that the boundary marked on the map was incorrect. Indeed, the Faden map went through several printings without change, suggesting to Sparks that the MPs and the public regarded the boundary indicated to be accurate, if controversial.[48]

Sparks's findings and conclusions would hardly have been surprising to Webster, reassuring as they may have been about the merits of the American claims. The whole American case was built on historical evidence and logic of this kind. However, seven months later, when news of the Ashburton mission to the United States became public, Sparks wrote again to Webster, telling him of a more disturbing discovery that he had made in Europe. Clearly Sparks had been reluctant to reveal this information, or he would have done so in his first letter. Nevertheless, the prospect of actual negotiations pushed him to come forward. He reported to Webster that while working in the Archives Nationales in Paris he had found a letter from Benjamin Franklin, one of the American negotiators in Paris, to the comte de Vergennes, the French foreign minister, written on 6 December 1782, just a few days after the Preliminary Articles of Peace had been signed. Franklin said that he was sending Vergennes a copy of a map with the boundary between the United States and British North America 'marked with a strong red line.' Sparks said that he then went to the map collection in the French archives, where he found a map of North America that seemed to him to resemble the one referred to by Franklin. To his amazement, the northeastern boundary on this map, marked with a 'strong red line,' was well south of the St John River and even south of Mars Hill. This boundary conformed much more closely to that claimed by the British, except to further the British claim in the area north and west of the St Croix River. Sparks was clearly distressed at uncovering evidence that, as he thought, undercut the claims of Maine and Massachusetts, and he pointed out that there was no 'positive proof, that this map is actually the one marked by Franklin,' although that was clearly the conclusion that he drew. Sparks enclosed for Webster a contemporary map on which he drew the boundary as he remembered it from the French archive.[49]

Sparks's findings, discouraging as they might have appeared, were useful information for Webster. They reinforced some discoveries that Webster had made himself. As early as 1838 Webster had been told by the British consul in New York about a Mitchell map that had belonged to Baron von Steuben, which had a boundary marked along the Maine–New Brunswick frontier that conformed to the British claim. This document, however interesting, had no official standing and in no way constituted a treaty map. It had merely been owned by a prominent member of the Revolutionary War generation. Nevertheless, Webster bought it for $200 and then sold it to Charles S. Daveis. Daveis had been the author of a report in 1828 on New Brunswick activity in the disputed territory and a strong defender of Maine's interests. He also served as an agent for Maine in Washington. However, in 1842 Webster bought back the von Steuben map from Daveis, who had himself come to support a compromise settlement. Eventually, both maps were given to Sparks, with instructions to show the maps in confidence to key figures in Maine and Massachusetts, not so much to convince anyone of the merits of the British claims as to warn those people prepared to hold out for the full northern claims of Maine and Massachusetts that eventual public knowledge of these maps, and probably of other similar ones, would seriously undermine the credibility of the American claims. At least $250 was paid to Sparks from the secret service fund. In short, Webster hoped that knowledge of these maps would encourage the two states to agree to a compromise before the strength of the American claims was weakened.[50]

Webster also enlisted several other prominent Maine spokesmen in supporting a compromise boundary. Peleg Sprague, a former congressman and senator from Maine and currently a federal judge in Massachusetts, received $250 from secret service funds to go to Augusta in the spring of 1842 to use his influence with members of the Maine government and legislature. Similarly, Albert Smith was sent on two trips to Augusta, Portland, and Boston to promote the idea of a compromise settlement. Smith, a recent Congressman and former federal marshal, was paid $600, also from secret service funds. Webster himself travelled to Boston in May to confer with Governor Davis of Massachusetts.[51]

Webster employed all these measures to shape public opinion and build support for the negotiation of a compromise boundary. The failure of the arbitration of the king of the Netherlands haunted these negotiations and demonstrated that, in the absence of agreement by Maine and Massachusetts, the Senate was unlikely to ratify any permanent settlement of the Maine boundary. It was clear that Webster would have to get some kind of formal agreement if he were to proceed successfully. He had already been in contact with the governors, but, as soon as Ashburton was settled in Washington in early April, Webster asked him if he were authorized to negotiate a compromise boundary. Obtaining a positive response, Webster wrote to both John Fairfield, recently re-elected Democratic governor of Maine, and John Davis, the Whig governor of Massachusetts, on 11 April.[52]

Webster's letters were models of both warning and persuasion. Previous administrations had attempted to negotiate a new joint commission, Webster said, to resurvey the boundary and, in the event of failure to agree, to establish machinery for another arbitration by a friendly sovereign, as the two countries were committed to doing under the Treaty of Ghent. Webster was fully aware of strong opposition in Maine to placing the fate of the boundary in the hands of a foreign arbitrator, so this warning would have generated anxiety. Webster also mentioned the unilateral surveys that were then under way, pointing out that the federal survey had been in the field for two seasons at an expense of $100,000 and had at least another season of work (both Maine and the British had surveys under way also). The result of these surveys, Webster said, was likely to be another joint commission, which might order its own survey of the disputed territory. Webster was not hopeful about a commission's reaching an agreement, and an arbitrator might order still another survey.

In short, Webster warned, a new commission might take seven or eight years at the least and substantial amounts of money and still might not yield a satisfactory result. Fortunately, Ashburton was empowered by his government, Webster reported, to negotiate a conventional line, or compromise boundary, and therein lay the most speedy, economical, and satisfactory solution – a compromise based on such 'mutual considerations and equivalents as may be thought just and equitable.' The key word here was 'equivalents.' A compromise based on the idea that Maine would give up territory north of the St John River for some 'equivalent' territory in New Brunswick was the prospect that made compromise attractive. However, before the U.S. government felt that it could proceed in this sensible direction, it needed the participation and cooperation of Maine and Massachusetts in the form of two commissions 'empowered to confer with authorities of this Government upon a Conventional line, or line by agreement, with its terms, conditions and equivalents, with an understanding that no such line will be agreed to [between Webster and Ashburton] without the assent of such commissioners.' The president, Webster said, asked that the two governors quickly recall their legislatures to authorize and appoint such commissions.[53]

As unusual as this plan might have appeared – Ashburton was startled by the thought of including state commissions or delegations in the negotiations at some level – it was a splendid device.[54] Furthermore, the preparatory work that Webster had undertaken – in Francis O.J. Smith's newspaper campaign, Sparks's circulation of the maps unfavourable to the American claims, and Smith and Sprague's lobbying – had created a climate that allowed public sentiment and politicians of both parties to support this method of reaching a compromise solution.

Governor Fairfield consulted with others as to whether he should convene the legislature as requested. He certainly came under pressure from those enlisted to support a compromise settlement, such as Professor James Renwick, who wrote that the alternative to a settlement was a war that would serve neither Maine nor the nation. Webster travelled north in mid-May to Massachusetts and Maine to add his weight to the proposals, and Sparks showed Fairfield his maps. Ashburton feared Fairfield's opposition, but eventually the governor recalled the legislature.[55]

The Maine legislature met on 18 May to discuss Webster's proposals. By 25 May the House had voted 177 to 11 in favour, and the Senate 29 to 0. The legislature elected two Democrats, Judge William Pitt Preble, joint author of the U.S. case submitted to the king of the Netherlands, and Edward Kavanagh, a Maine politician and former minister to Portugal (later governor of Maine), and two Whigs, Edward Kent, a former governor, and John Otis, a member of the legislature and later congressman. Sir Charles Bagot reported to Ashburton that, while he knew little about the other members of the delegation, Preble had been his diplomatic 'colleague' at The Hague. 'I found him a tenacious and difficult man to deal with,' Bagot confessed, 'but I am told that he now professes great anxiety for an amicable adjustment, though not, as I suspect without large concessions on our part.'[56] Thomas C. Grattan, the British consul in Boston, had also served at The Hague and Brussels, and he knew Preble in 1830 and 1831. He described Preble as being 'well-known' for his 'obstinacy of character and fixed opinions on the matter' of the boundary. The other commissioners were 'in mortal fear of his [Preble's] stern and uncompromising character,' Grattan observed.[57]

The governor of Massachusetts, John Davis, replied to Webster that he had the power to appoint the commissioners and therefore had no need to convene the legislature. He named Abbott Lawrence, a Boston merchant and a Whig; Charles Allen, a Whig member of the legislature; and John Mills, a Springfield lawyer and a Democrat. All three had been members of a Massachusetts–Connecticut boundary commission in 1826, and Lawrence was to have a further career as American minister to Britain from 1849 to 1852. Webster admitted to Davis that 'the boundary is infinitely the most difficult' of the many issues before the negotiators, and for this reason he intended to confer with the governor when he next went to Boston.[58]

The Maine and Massachusetts commissioners met in Boston on 7 June to discuss their objectives at the negotiations. Led by Preble, they also called on Grattan in Boston and discussed the boundary question, about which the consul was well informed. Indeed, they so valued his advice that they invited him to go with them to Washington to assist in the negotiations.[59] For reasons of protocol, Grattan demurred, but the following day he concluded that he might 'do a service' by at least 'acting as a check on Judge Preble's dogmatic obstinacy.' They all travelled together to New York, where they met with Professor James Renwick. A Columbia College instructor, Renwick had led the current U.S. commission on the boundary. He showed the delegation one of the maps marked with the British boundary claims that had several weeks earlier been confidentially exhibited to a secret committee of the Maine legislature. Preble was 'outraged' that Webster would have given the map to Renwick to use with the commissions, and he threatened to return to Maine, resign from the commission, and denounce Webster 'as a traitor.' Renwick quickly left, and Preble was persuaded to continue to Washington, but Webster's 'feeler' had nearly terminated the Maine commission. The delegates arrived in Washington on 12 June and booked into Fuller's Hotel. Grattan also stayed at the hotel with them, but he reported his unusual mission to Ashburton and Aberdeen, warning the latter that Preble must be 'humoured.' The Massachusetts delegation reached Washington on 13 June, and the two commissions met with Webster at one o'clock at the State Department in cordial and promising circumstances. The Americans were ready to begin talks on the boundary by 17 June.[60]

If Webster was compelled to obtain the participation of the representatives of Maine and Massachusetts in any boundary decision, Ashburton, perhaps because he was not a professional diplomat and despite the complications concerning his instructions, was also moved to consult with various interested parties in British North America in approaching the negotiations. As soon as he arrived in the United States, Ashburton wrote to Sir Charles Bagot, the new governor general of Canada, asking advice on boundary matters, particularly on the issues surrounding the questions of the head of the Connecticut River and the regions west of Lake Superior. This was a sensible consultation because of Bagot's long involvement with the boundary question. Bagot replied by sending a messenger with a memorandum and numerous documents and maps on the New Hampshire–New York section of the border. Ashburton was delighted and suggested that the author of the memorandum, Mr A. Wells, be sent to Washington to work with him. Bagot complied, and Wells, who had worked for the boundary commission in 1818, was sent to advise Ashburton until late July.[61]

Similarly, on 28 April Ashburton wrote to Sir William Colebrook, the lieutenant-governor of New Brunswick, outlining his mission and asking advice on the northeastern boundary, particularly on possible concessions to the United States, such as the area between the St John River and the due-north line, the 'narrow strip,' the navigation of the St John River, and Campobello Island. Colebrook had already taken the liberty of sending to Ashburton, through Fox in Washington, the reports of the Maine land agent of 31 December 1841 and of New Brunswick's 'Warden of the Disputed Territory' of 8 April 1842. The Maine report raised the matter of the cession of the 'narrow strip' and the navigation of the St John River, while the New Brunswick report reasserted the several British proposals that placed the boundary well south of the line of the king of the Netherlands. After reading this material, Ashburton asked specifically for more information about the Madawaska settlements south of the St John and also if Colebrook would send someone 'to assist me with local knowledge.'[62] Colebrook responded by sending a delegation made up of James A. MacLaughlan, author of the New Brunswick report; Alfred Reade, his son-in-law and private secretary; Charles Simonds, Speaker of the legislature; and Sir John Caldwell, former receiver general of Lower Canada and a prominent Grand Falls lumberman and land speculator who had good contacts with the Maine and New Brunswick legislatures.[63] Well before serious talks with the Americans began, Ashburton realized that the 'narrow strip,' along the west bank of the St John, including Woodstock, would not be an acceptable 'equivalent' to be exchanged with the Americans.[64]

Ashburton received advice from several other people as well. The British consul in Boston, Thomas C. Grattan, came to Washington at the invitation of the Maine and Massachusetts commissioners. Ashburton was 'much pleased' by Grattan's initiative and reportedly urged him to stay as long as he could. The consul saw his delicate role as that of a mediator. 'I strove to reconcile their conflicting notions, and bring them all to bear upon a favourable construction of the English claims,' he later wrote. Sometimes he was successful, sometimes not, but he did not attempt to 'dispute' with the commissioners. Grattan also wrote to Bagot and Aberdeen, offering information and opinions. However, Grattan's relations with Ashburton became increasingly strained.[65] Ashburton also got assistance, particularly on the western boundary, in the form of maps, documents, and advice, from Anthony Barclay, former British commissioner under articles 6 and 7 of the Treaty of Ghent. Barclay had continued to reside in the United States after the termination of the commissions and became British consul in New York in 1842. In view of his father's long service to the Crown on several commissions, Barclay certainly could speak with authority on many aspects of the border question.[66] Given all these consultants, as well as Aberdeen's final instructions, by mid-June Ashburton was also ready to begin the negotiations on the boundary, supported by an entourage of interested parties that was as large, if not as powerful, as that of the Americans.

Chapter Twelve

The Webster–Ashburton Negotiations

Lord Ashburton's arrival in the United States had met with widespread approval. He landed at Annapolis, Maryland, on 4 April 1842, after fifty-two days at sea, the *Warspite* having been driven by storms well south of its anticipated landfall at New York. Two days later he presented his credentials to President John Tyler at the White House. In reply to Ashburton's address, the president expressed 'high gratification' that the British government should send a special mission to resolve issues with the United States, and he was confident that it would facilitate the 're-establishment of the most friendly feeling between the two nations.'[1] Ashburton settled into a furnished house off Lafayette Square, arranged by Webster. He brought with him a large entourage, consisting of Humphrey St John Mildmay, his son-in-law and partner in Baring Brothers, as secretary to the mission, and Frederick Bruce, future minister to the United States, and a Mr Shedding, as private secretaries. In addition were five upper servants, three servants in livery, a carriage, horses, and lots of luggage. Lady Ashburton, despite the opportunity to revisit her homeland, was not well enough to take such an extended trip.[2]

Newspapers such as the *New York Herald* and *Niles' Register* were enthusiastic about Ashburton and confident in the prospects of the mission. The *National Intelligencer* commented that Ashburton's special mission was an indication of the 'earnestness' of the British government, and the paper was 'full of hope and even of expectation' that the negotiations would 'bring about an amicable and satisfactory settlement of the questions in dispute between the two nations.'[3] Joshua Bates was told by a New York friend that there was widespread 'hope entertained that Ashburton's mission will attain the objects desired and peaceful adjustment of all the points of entanglement,' although the fragility of the Tyler administration was acknowledged; Bates and Baring Brothers heard much the same from other U.S. correspondents.[4] Philip Hone, the New York businessman and socialite, who also doubted the capacities of the Tyler government, welcomed the Ashburton mission. He thought the sending of 'so distinguished a man' was 'strong proof of the desire on the part of the British government to preserve friendly relations, if possible, with this country.' Daniel Webster had assured him, fairly accurately as it turned out, that they would reach a settlement by September. Webster told an English friend that 'a pair of more friendly negotiators never put their heads together.'[5]

Not surprisingly, the sceptics were found among those with a stake in the boundary issue. Maine senator Reuel Williams wrote to Governor Fairfield in late February that he was afraid that 'in the adjustment of the complicated questions with England we may find some of our rights sacrificed for the attainment of others or to preserve peace.' After conferring with Webster, following Ashburton's arrival, he was still suspicious.[6] Another of the governor's correspondents was doubtful about the whole process. 'Ashburton is a shrewd man & I fear is playing a dual game,' confided Nathan Clifford from Washington. He was sure that Ashburton intended to insist on a division of the territory, offering only navigation of the St John River or an indemnity. Nobody believes 'that he intends an exchange of territory.' As for support in Washington, 'I have no confidence in Webster, he is corrupt,' Clifford concluded.[7]

Whatever the misgivings, the most informed praise for the Ashburton mission came from a man who had devoted many years to the settlement of the boundary dispute and who also knew Ashburton personally, Albert Gallatin, now eighty-two and retired in New York. Gallatin saw Ashburton as perfect for the task and the British government as well intentioned. 'To all who know you it [the mission] affords a decisive proof of the sincere wish, on the part of your Gov't., to attempt a settlement of our differences as far as practicable,' the older diplomat wrote. He went on to praise any effort 'to prevent an unnatural and, on both sides, absurd and disgraceful war.' Gallatin attempted to warn Ashburton of the unusual circumstances of American politics at the moment. The administration had good intentions but had no secure political base. In the situation he said, 'I hope that higher motives will prevail over too sensitive or local feelings.' It was a prudent warning from someone with years of experience in American politics. Gallatin closed by saying that for the previous twenty years he had worked for peace and that this was his greatest consolation. 'May God prosper your efforts and enable you to consummate the holy work,' he concluded.[8]

Ashburton could have no doubts about the good wishes for, and perils confronting, his task, which occupies this chapter. His responsibilities involved boundaries in the northeast, west of Lake Superior, and in the jointly occupied Oregon territory, and a number of other issues between Britain and the United States, including unresolved aspects of the *Caroline* and the McLeod affairs.

The Americans – both Webster and the commissions from Maine and Massachusetts – were ready by 17 June 1842 to begin negotiations on the northeastern boundary. Ashburton was embarrassed because the final commentary on his instructions, which he had requested from Aberdeen and which were being sent by steamer, did not arrive in Washington for another week and a half. Webster became anxious during this time over Ashburton's apparent reluctance. The Englishman 'appears to me, certainly,' Webster wrote to Edward Everett in London, 'to be under restraint not heretofore apparently felt by him.'[9] Privately Webster wrote much the same to Everett but added that Aberdeen should be made aware of this and that as promising a moment for general negotiations might not come again for another fifty years.[10] Ashburton saw significant restrictions of his powers in the second set of instructions, and of course when Webster noticed his discomforture Ashburton was waiting for final clarification of those instructions. Ashburton was also aware, as he reported to Aberdeen, 'that Webster has discovered some evidence, known at present to nobody, but favourable to our claim, and that he is using it with the Commissioners.' Sent on 14 June, this observation came just days after Ashburton's first talks with Thomas C. Grattan, the British consul from Boston who had accompanied the state commissioners to Washington. It is reasonable to assume that he learned of this from Grattan, but did Grattan explain to him in detail the map with the British boundary marked on it that he had seen in Renwick's hands in New York the previous week? If so, it would partially explain Ashburton's willingness to make an expansive claim before he received Aberdeen's final comments on his instructions.[11]

On 13 June Ashburton wrote Webster a long letter discussing the boundary in fairly general terms. Essentially he said that Britain had serious historic claims but that, because none of the earlier attempts to settle the boundary had been successful, only a reasonable compromise or another arbitration remained. However, he did venture that the land in question was generally of such poor quality that, but for Britain's need for a road connecting New Brunswick with the Canadas, it would have abandoned claims to the region years ago.[12]

Ashburton had still not heard from Aberdeen, but he began talks with Webster on Saturday the eighteenth. He agreed to Webster's request that he draft a formal set of proposals, which he sent to Webster on 21 June, the following Tuesday. This was a carefully worded statement. Like Shakespeare's Henry V, Ashburton professed to no diplomatic skills and as a plain simple man claimed to lay all his cards on the table without cunning. In fact, he was still playing for time, but his earlier talks with Webster made it awkward to begin with elaborate maximum claims. Ashburton stated that quite beyond Britain's actual rights to the region in dispute, its two reasonable claims in the area hinged on its need to secure a safe road linking the several provinces and its need to secure for the Crown the loyal British subjects in the Madawaska settlements. In order to facilitate these two claims, Ashburton proposed a boundary that proceeded from the source of the St Croix River up the due north line to one of the tributaries of the St John River (probably the Aroostook and the Little Madawaska rivers), then west to the Fish River, and north along that stream to the St John River. This proposed boundary line would have placed the French-speaking Madawaska settlements on the south bank of the St John River within British territory. Ashburton did not describe the proposed boundary further west, clearly waiting for more specific instructions from London. Although he stated that the land ceded to the United States, presumably south of the Aroostook, was more fertile than that retained by Britain, Ashburton offered three concessions in exchange for his claims – first, that the old Collins–Valentine survey line of the forty-fifth parallel be accepted as the permanent boundary (thus confirming for the United States the fortifications at Rouse's Point); second, that Britain accept the American claim for the head of the Connecticut River; and third, that Maine lumber and forest products receive free navigation on the St John River.[13]

These proposals came as a blow to the commissioners of both states, who were also shown Ashburton's letter and the red-line map of Professor Sparks. Although the British government had announced that it was prepared to negotiate on the basis of reasonable compromise, and despite Ashburton's protests that he was not entering the diplomatic exercise of submitting extreme claims as bargaining positions, he had proposed a boundary that went well south of the St John River, a circumstance that, for Maine and Massachusetts, made this offer less acceptable than the line of the king of the Netherlands. Furthermore, he had offered Maine no substantial concessions, and no territorial equivalents at all.

It was in this context that Webster wrote his two urgent messages to Everett in London on 28 June, the following week. 'The truth is,' Webster concluded, 'Lord Ashburton is not left free.' As a result, especially after all the private talks between them, 'Our movement, for the last ten days, if any has been made, has been rather backward.'[14] Former president John Quincy Adams, then a congressman from Massachusetts and no stranger to the boundary questions, talked with Abbott Lawrence, one of the Massachusetts commissioners. Lawrence told him that things were not going very well. Ashburton 'had recently received instructions from home, and had intimated that they tied him up far beyond those he had brought with him; and even that if they had prescribed them to him before he left home, he would not have accepted the missions.' However, in the actual negotiations, Lawrence said, both Ashburton and the Maine commissioners were 'tenacious upon trifles.' The 'Clouds are thickening round us,' Adams concluded gloomily.[15] President Tyler requested a meeting with Ashburton and worked his southern charm on the diplomat. After flattering Ashburton about his unique role and opportunity, the president asked forcefully, 'If you cannot settle them [the boundary questions], what man in England can?' Ashburton, moved by Tyler's urgency, replied, 'Well! well! Mr President, we must try again.'[16]

Perhaps not surprisingly, the Maine delegation was indignant. It wrote to Webster on 29 June that the governor and legislature had been prepared to satisfy Britain's need for a road to link its provinces in exchange for 'such equivalents as might be mutually satisfactory.' Ashburton, however, had proposed a boundary line that went way beyond the need to secure a road, had attempted to extend the line south of the St John River, and had not offered any important 'equivalent' in exchange (meaning land rather than the proposed trade concession, which the Maine delegation held was actually of as much benefit to New Brunswick as to Maine). The territorial concessions offered by Ashburton, it noted, were all to the benefit of other states. The Maine commissioners found it distressing that Ashburton, in his remarks about plain dealing, had presented these proposals as Britain's final offer, rather than as a bargaining position, which was interpreted as an ultimatum. 'In this state of things,' the delegation wrote, 'it becomes a bounden duty on the part of the Undersigned to say to you, that if the yielding and relinquishing on the part of the State of Maine, of any portion of Territory, however small, on the South side of the St John be with her Britannic Majesty's Government a sine qua non to be an amicable settlement of the boundary of Maine, the mission of the Commissioners is ended.'[17] This too sounded like an ultimatum.

The Maine spokesmen then gave a short refutation of Ashburton's arguments, pointed out the equivalents that might have been offered to Maine from New Brunswick (Grand Manan and Campobello Island or the 'narrow strip'), and then put forward their own proposal for a compromise boundary, as devised with the Massachusetts commissioners. This boundary would proceed up the due-north line to the St John River, west along the river to a point three miles west of the Madawaska River, then by a straight line to Long Lake, then west by a straight line to a point where the St Francis River exits Lake Pohenagamook, and then south and west along the watershed to the Connecticut River.[18] This boundary was a variation of the line suggested by the king of the Netherlands. The commissioners knew that the military road actually ran on the north bank of the St John River and followed the Madawaska valley to the Temiscouata portage and thence towards Rivière du Loup, which flowed into the St Lawrence. Therefore, they reasoned, the British had no need for land south of the St John River or west of the Madawaska. However, from the British point of view, such a boundary would place the Americans dangerously close to the road for military purposes – closer in fact than the king of the Netherlands had allowed.

It is difficult to say what the commissioners found to be more objectionable – Ashburton's proposal to move south of the St John River in the Madawaska settlements or his failure to offer adequate equivalents. As for the claim to the Madawaska settlements, Webster contributed to Ashburton's expectations there. A willingness to relinquish claims to the Madawaska region was implied in Webster's letter to Francis Calley Gray, of 11 May 1841, to be shown to numerous people in England (possibly Ashburton himself), and the cession was specifically mentioned as late as 25 April 1842 in Webster's letter to Edward Everett.[19] It would seem that the U.S. cession of Madawaska was discussed and assured in the early talks between Webster and Ashburton in April, before the state commissioners arrived in Washington. If Grattan did tell Ashburton about the map that he saw Renwick show the Maine delegation, that also may have inadvertently reinforced Ashburton's determination to secure the Madawaska region for New Brunswick. Still more positively, Ashburton, commenting later on talks between Everett and Aberdeen, in which

U.S. willingness to cede Madawaska had been assured, wrote, 'So Webster promised me also, but when it came to the point he joined the Maine people in wondering that we should ever have thought of coming south of the St John and pronouncing it impossible.'[20] Grattan later wrote that Ashburton said that his instructions specifically claimed the settlements, which was only partially true. Grattan said that he urged Ashburton to have the instructions changed, and he wrote himself to Aberdeen to say that the commissioners' response to a claim for the Madawaska settlements south of the St John River 'would instantly and unanimously break it [the negotiation] up.'[21]

As the Maine commissioners were writing their critique of the British proposal, Ashburton received his final instructions from Aberdeen and replied that these were 'sufficient.' Privately, Ashburton wrote Aberdeen that the U.S. political situation was so unsettled that he probably would not be able to do all that he had hoped. In the official correspondence of the same date he had said that it would not be possible to deal with the Oregon question. Although he had not yet received from Webster a reply to his boundary proposal, Ashburton had perceived the determination of the Maine and Massachusetts commissioners to reject any boundary line south of the St John River. As early as 29 June he concluded, 'I shall probably give up after a little fight my cherished Madawaska Settlements.' It was clear to him that the commissioners were 'doggedly resolved not to let us over the St John, and that they would break off [talks] on that point.' Britain, he felt, was in a weak position on this issue because Palmerston had earlier proposed the St John River to the Americans. Nevertheless, he was optimistic that Aberdeen's military advisers could be satisfied.[22]

Meanwhile, Washington's notorious summer heat and humidity were taking their toll on Ashburton's stamina and good humour. He complained to Aberdeen and asked Webster on 1 July to get him 'released' from the agony. 'I contrive to crawl about in this heat by day & pass my nights in a sleepless fever,' he wrote. 'In short, I shall positively not outlive this affair if it is to be much prolonged.'[23] He urged Webster to push the state commissioners to respond. There was no need. Webster had the long letter of the Maine commissioners, and he evidently passed it to Ashburton that same day. Although he could hardly have been surprised, as his pessimistic remarks to Aberdeen a few days earlier suggest, Ashburton reacted strongly to the reply of the Maine delegation. He found neither the arguments nor the tone agreeable, he reported to Webster, and he complained specifically of 'the Master's hand,' refer-

ring presumably to the influence of Judge Preble. Nevertheless, Ashburton had that day a productive talk with Edward Kavanagh, one of the
Maine commissioners, and thought him a 'sensible liberal man.' Ashburton also suggested a meeting with Webster that evening.[24]

Whatever discussions the two diplomats might have had earlier, on
8 July Webster formally replied to Ashburton's earlier proposal. He
began with a brilliant legal reading of the terms of the treaty of 1783,
showing with great clarity the Americans' rationale for their maximum
claims. That Webster was one of the great lawyers of the early nineteenth century was conspicuously demonstrated in the letters. However,
as freely admitted, the objective in the talks was not to prove a case, but
to arrive at a mutually agreeable compromise. With this Webster agreed,
but the British claim to the Madawaska settlements south of the St John
River seemed to him not a claim based on workable compromise or
need, when clearly in his judgment the river itself made the best compromise boundary. Were Ashburton at liberty to cede territory such as
the 'narrow strip,' he might be able to take a more accommodating attitude towards the Madawaska claim. 'But, in the present posture of
things,' Webster wrote, 'I cannot hold out the expectation to your Lordship that any thing south of the river can be yielded.' He asserted that
the establishment of American sovereignty would not be a burden to the
French-speaking Acadians in the region.[25]

Webster then proposed a boundary, drawing in large measure on the
line suggested by the Maine commissioners in their letter to him the
previous week. It would extend up the due-north line to the St John
River, then west to a point three miles beyond the confluence of the
Madawaska River, then by a straight line to Long Lake, thence by a
straight line to the point where the St Francis River flows out of Lake
Pohenagamook, and finally along the watershed dividing streams entering the St Lawrence from those flowing south and east. The line along
the watershed was to extend southwest to the headwaters of the Connecticut River.[26] Webster also mentioned the equivalents proposed by
Ashburton in his letter of 21 June, but he again took very much the
views expressed by the Maine commissioners as to their value.

Ashburton replied promptly on the following Monday, 11 July,
expressing some dismay at Webster's analysis of the terms of the treaty
of 1783 and the basis of American claims. Ashburton was certainly a very
shrewd and successful banker, but of course he was no lawyer and could
not attempt to compete with Webster in this sort of argument. Even so,
he attacked the Maine commissioners' letter of 29 June for saying that

the only real task in determining the true boundary was to identify the Northwest Angle of Nova Scotia and then propose a new boundary line west of the Madawaska River – what Ashburton called, rather facetiously, an entirely new Northwest Angle. He then turned to several pronouncements of Madison, Jefferson, Sullivan, and the king of the Netherlands that the Northwest Angle could not be identified. Ashburton skilfully fell back on the proposition that the basis for this negotiation was practical compromise rather than historic claims. 'Our immediate business is with the compromise of what is not otherwise to be settled, and argument and controversy, far from assisting to that end, have more generally a tendency to irritate and excite.' Thus Ashburton, while not in Webster's league as a legal advocate, was able to avoid Webster where the American was strongest and keep the discussion focused on the contemporary problem of the impasse and the need to make a reasonable compromise. Furthermore, Ashburton urged that subsequent negotiations be done in person. 'I always thought this part of our duty better performed by conference than by correspondence.'

Ashburton did mention two more important substantive points. As for the 'narrow strip' between the due-north line and the west bank of the St John River, which had been mentioned by both the Maine commissioners and Webster, Ashburton said, 'This strip I have not power to give up,' not to mention the preferences of the Loyalists living in that region. However, he did intimate that he would abandon his claim to the Madawaska settlements on the south bank of the St John, which had so alarmed the Maine delegation. 'Perceiving from your note, as well as from personal conversation that concession on this point is insisted upon, I might be disposed to consider whether my anxious desire to arrive at a friendly settlement would not justify me in yielding, however reluctantly, if the latter part of your proposals did not, if finally persevered in, forbid all hope of any settlement whatever.' In other words, Ashburton would consider abandoning the claims south of the St John if the Americans would be more reasonable about the proposed boundary west of the Madawaska. Ashburton pointed out that this boundary outlined by both Webster and the Maine commissioners abandoned Webster's 'own principle of maintaining the great river as the best boundary.' Furthermore, acceptance of the proposed boundary would be much more disadvantageous to Britain than the king of the Netherlands' line, while by contrast he had offered the Americans genuine concessions elsewhere. Once again he urged that further negotiations be done in person.[27]

Ashburton's decision to give up his claims to the Madawaska settlements seemed to be a turning point. Grattan later thought that this concession allowed the negotiations to move 'with a suddenness that seemed almost magical,' although tension and uncertainty persisted for another two weeks before a decisive breakthrough took place. During this time Ashburton, however, felt increasingly disillusioned. 'Preble has got the deputation in his hand and is as yet obstinate and unmanageable,' he complained to Aberdeen. Ashburton's confidence in the secretary of state was deteriorating also. 'My real difficulty is with Webster who yields and promises everything, but when it comes to execution is so weak and timid and irresolute that he is frightened by everybody and at last does nothing.' A somber Ashburton lamented that he had been 'too sanguine in my expectations.'[28]

The secretary of state met several times during the week of 11 July with Ashburton and the state commissioners, and by Friday the fifteenth he sent the Maine delegation a letter together with a new proposal. The line that he described was clearly the fruit of serious bargaining, but Webster said merely that he had 'reason to believe' that Ashburton 'would agree' to such a border. He attempted to assure the commissioners that the proposed boundary ceded to Maine was the largest portion of the contested region, though not quite as much as had been awarded by the king of the Netherlands. Army engineers had told him that they were the least fertile and the most mountainous lands of the disputed territory. The proposed agreement would confer great benefits on the United States – Indian Stream as the northwestern source of the Connecticut River and the old forty-fifth parallel boundary of 1774 between Lower Canada and New Hampshire, Vermont, and New York (including also the fortifications at Rouse's Point). As well, Maine and Massachusetts would obtain the right to float forest products down the St John River through New Brunswick, as offered by Ashburton earlier, and each would receive an indemnity from the U.S. government of $125,000, plus expenses incurred during the Aroostook War and the state survey.[29]

The proposed boundary would extend up the existing due-north line to the St John River, west along the middle of the river to the St Francis River, northwest along that stream to Lake Pohenagamook, from there southwest by a straight line to the northwest branch of the St John, and from there by a straight line to the southwest branch of the St John. It would then follow this stream to its source at the Metjarmette Portage and thence the highlands to the headwaters of the Connecticut.[30] This proposal conformed in large measure to the boundary suggested by the king of the Netherlands, but, as urged in Aberdeen's instructions to Ashburton, it moved the western Maine boundary fifteen to thirty miles east, off the crest of the hills overlooking Quebec City and the St Lawrence. Of the 12,027 square miles of territory in dispute, the United States was allocated 7,015 square miles (or 4,489,600 acres) and Britain 5,012 square miles (or 3,207,680 acres). Although the United States was confirmed in its title to 2,003 square miles more than Britain, this settlement provided the Americans with 893 square miles less than had been proposed by the king of the Netherlands in 1831.[31]

The commissioners replied the next day, Saturday 16 July, in a very strongly worded rejection of Webster's proposal. With an increasingly sharp edge to their language, they attacked Ashburton's proposal of 11 July, singling out the deficiencies in his concessions and his references to the points made by the king of the Netherlands. They returned also to one of the arguments of the American claim, based on the similarities of language, and presumably on the intent, of the boundaries described in the Royal Proclamation of 1763, the Quebec Act of 1774, and the Treaty of Paris of 1783, dismissing the distinction made by the British that the Bay of Fundy and the Bay of Chaleurs did not constitute the Atlantic as intended in the treaty.[32]

At this point a second period of crisis in the negotiations began. The Maine commissioners had been willing to abandon claims to the substantial region north of the St John River in order to facilitate the road connecting Lower Canada with New Brunswick, but they saw no reason to give up claims to the St John's northwestern tributaries. For this they had expected territorial concessions, such as the 'narrow strip,' or Grand Manan, or Campobello. In fact the New Brunswickers and the British government were even less willing to consider giving up territory than was Maine or Massachusetts – they had ruled out these possible territorial concessions before the talks began. Ashburton could offer only lands to the west, and while they might be valuable to other states and the U.S. government, they constituted no 'equivalent' concession for the territory that Maine was asked to abandon. Accordingly the Maine and Massachusetts commissioners requested, through the secretary of state, a meeting with Ashburton on Tuesday morning, 19 July.[33] Whatever transpired in these talks is lost to us, for the existing papers and documents say nothing. However, before the end of that week the two states' commissioners had come around.

On Wednesday, the Massachusetts commissioners wrote to Webster that, even though the boundary proposed was 'not all, which might have been hoped for, in view of the strength of the American claim,' they were well aware of both the history of the controversy and the immense difficulties in the current negotiations, not to mention the need for a speedy settlement. They expressed clear understanding of the realities of international relations when they said that they were 'aware that the Government and people of the United States desire to preserve peace and friendly relations with other nations, so long as they can be maintained with honor, by concessions which, not a just policy alone, but that which is liberal and magnanimous, may require.' They accepted the proposed settlement, but with several conditions – free transportation on the St John River for all products of the soil, not just forest products, and monetary compensation of $150,000, rather than $125,000, for the abandoned territory. The two states were also to share the $14,893 from the fund created from the timber cut in the disputed territory, largely in the Aroostook River valley.[34]

The Maine commissioners wrote to Webster on Friday 22 July. Theirs was a grudging letter, rehearsing the story of the negotiations, with Maine's willingness to accommodate the military road and their dismay at the British refusal to consider territorial equivalents for what Maine was expected to abandon. They stated once again their conviction that the terms of the treaty of 1783 were perfectly clear and realizable and that the territory that they were abandoning to Britain was far more valuable than anyone had been prepared to admit, yet they noted that a more generous settlement with Britain did not seem possible. Therefore, in view of the prolonged and costly history of the border dispute and the urgings of the president and the secretary of state, they wrote to 'give the assent of the State to such Conventional line, with the terms, conditions, and equivalents herein mentioned.'[35]

So the decision was made. After years of disagreement, negotiation, commissions, surveys, international arbitration, border skirmishes, bluff, and intimidation – the impasse had been broken. The search for the northeastern boundary was over. Thanks largely to Webster, Maine and Massachusetts had been persuaded to accept a boundary that was substantially more modest than their long-held claims. Thanks to Aberdeen, Peel, and Ashburton, Britain stepped back from the confrontational approach of Palmerston and with greater calm and flexibility was able to obtain a better boundary than that proposed by the king of the Netherlands in 1831 or Palmerston himself in 1833. The constant and long-standing irritant was removed, and the spectre of war driven away. It was a decisive moment in the history of relations between Britain, its North American colonies, and the United States.

These letters may have taken some time in preparation, during which period Preble went back to Maine, the least satisfied of any of the participants. In any case Webster did not formally convey to Ashburton the news of the agreement of the two delegations until 27 July, the following week. The British envoy quickly wrote to Aberdeen, 'It is with much satisfaction that I have the honor of informing your Lordship that I have at last settled the terms of the Convention of Boundaries.'[36] As for those terms, Ashburton was well satisfied to have improved the king of the Netherlands' line around the northwestern tributaries of the St John River. The new lines from Lake Pohenagamook to the Metjarmette Portage moved the boundary from the summit of the watershed to a point at least fifty miles from Quebec. 'I am well pleased that we end by driving the enemy off that Crest of Highlands so much coveted by the War Office,' he wrote to Aberdeen privately.[37] Ashburton had acquiesced in the further concession of agricultural products as well as forest products entitled to free navigation on the St John, and his New Brunswick advisers had assured him that northern Maine was not likely to grow very much agricultural produce, so that this was more symbolic than practical. Privately, Ashburton also assured Aberdeen that no mention had been made of a payment of money by Britain. As for the state commissions, Ashburton said that the Maine delegates 'were most difficult to deal with.' He had met with them and had feared for a while that the whole negotiation could collapse, but 'at last Preble yielded and after signing he went off to his Wilds in Maine as sulky as a Bear.' With a certain exhaustion, as well as satisfaction, Ashburton concluded that 'no better terms were obtainable.'[38] This was unquestionably true. At a formal dinner, given by Webster on Saturday evening, 23 July, Ashburton and Webster gave toasts to 'Brother Jonathan' and 'John Bull.' President Tyler made some generous remarks about the commissioners from Maine and Massachusetts but then concluded with a toast to Webster and Ashburton, saying, 'Blessed are the peace-makers.'[39]

The northeastern boundary was not the only border issue intended to be resolved by Ashburton on his special mission to the United States. In the far west the boundary remained undecided between the United States and British North America in what was known as the Oregon territory. Although the status of this region had been discussed on numerous occasions, a temporary expedient had been devised by Albert

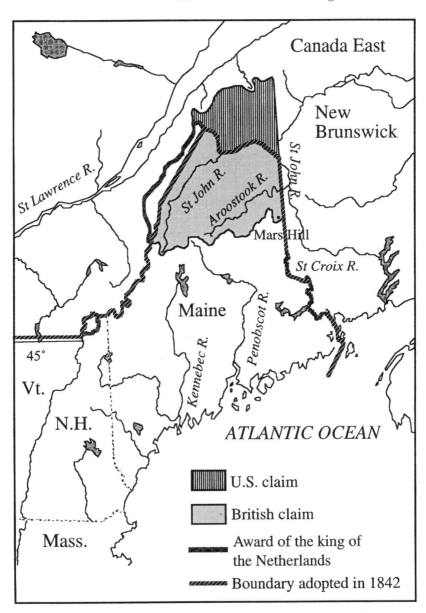

Map 15. Webster–Ashburton Treaty boundary (articles 4 and 5), 1842

Gallatin and Richard Rush for the United States and Henry Goulburn and Frederick J. Robinson for the British in 1818 – joint occupation of the territory by the citizens and subjects of both countries, without prejudice to the conflicting claims to the region. This arrangement had been renewed from time to time, but it was expected that Ashburton would attempt to resolve this issue during his talks with Webster. The Oregon question, however, proved almost as intractable as the northeastern boundary, with a long history of competing claims, many rival interest groups, and not a little national pride involved. The complexity of this question, on top of all the other, more pressing problems confronting the two nations, rendered it mutually agreeable to delete Oregon from their discussions, as Ashburton reported to Aberdeen by as early as 29 June.[40]

The other remaining undecided boundary was that border first described in the treaty of 1783 extending from Sault Ste Marie across Lake Superior and overland to the Lake of the Woods. The commission for article 7 of the Treaty of Ghent, under Peter B. Porter and Anthony Barclay, had been unable to reach an agreement by 1827. Although the Treaty of Ghent had made provision for arbitration by a friendly sovereign, no serious step had been taken in that direction. The last mention of the matter arose in a letter from Secretary of State John Forsyth to British Minister Henry S. Fox in 1839, and that initiative was never taken up.[41] As a result, Ashburton's instructions in the spring of 1842 empowered him to settle this western boundary as well as the others.

Clearly, in their numerous private talks together, Ashburton and Daniel Webster raised the questions involved in this series of problems and examined the reports and maps produced by the commission under article 7. Ashburton had assistance on this matter from Sir Charles Bagot and also 'much useful advice' from Anthony Barclay, then living in New York. On 16 July 1842, with the northeastern boundary still undecided, Ashburton wrote to Webster proposing a solution for this more westerly region. First, and as Barclay had appeared to have been ready to do in 1827, Ashburton offered to give up claims to St George's, or Sugar Island, in the St Mary's River at the Sault. This would give the Americans 25,920 acres of what were held to be quite fertile land, albeit in a region where the population was still very sparse and land abundant. Second, Ashburton proposed to accept the Pigeon River route west to Rainy Lake as the boundary (the northwesternmost point of the Lake of the Woods having been informally agreed on in 1826). However, while Ashburton's description of the proposed boundary line west was very general, he specifically placed it for eight miles on the south side of the Pigeon River west from Lake Superior along the old portage trail. In exchange for these two large British concessions, Ashburton asked that British subjects be permitted by right to use a western channel in American waters in northern Lake St Clair, which was more navigable for entry to the St Clair River. He also asked that they be allowed to use the southern channel in U.S. waters around Barnhart's Island in the St Lawrence River near the Long Sault rapids.[42]

The boundary that Ashburton described and the special privileges that he requested seemed in many ways both generous and reasonable, but they incorporated exactly the disputed points that had led to the failure of the commission under article 7 in 1827. The Americans then had been quite prepared to accept the Pigeon River route as the border intended in the treaty of 1783. Their claim for the Kaministiquia River–Dog Lake route had been very much a counter-claim to meet the British demand for the St Louis River–Vermillion River route well to the south. The British had been ready to compromise on the Pigeon River route, but only if the border extended to the eight-mile portage trail on the south bank of the Pigeon River. Porter had insisted that as commissioner he had the power only to decide what had been intended in the treaty of 1783 and none to agree to matters of convenience, such as the portage trail, which required proper diplomatic powers. Similarly, the British would have waived their claim to St George's Island in the St Mary's River at the Sault in 1827 if the Americans had been willing to write into the final report that British subjects had the right to use the channels in American water between Barnhart's Island and the south shore of the St Lawrence. Porter had again claimed that he did not have authority to act in this matter; the Barnhart's Island region had been already decided by the commission under article 6 and was thereby closed, and he could not make agreements guaranteeing such rights in any case.[43]

Fortunately, in this regard, both Ashburton and Webster had been specifically empowered to devise a mutually agreeable boundary, or conventional line, and to commit their countries to such decisions in order to facilitate a broad settlement. Webster consulted with an old Mackinac Island fur trader, Robert Stuart, as well as former commission officials Joseph Delafield and James Ferguson, who assured the secretary that the Pigeon River was the true 'Long Lake,' that St George's Island was valuable, and that much of the rest of the region was 'one waste of rock and water.'[44]

On 27 July, Webster replied to Ashburton's letter. He announced the agreement of the Maine and Massachusetts commissions and the specific terms for the northeastern boundary but also spoke to the Great Lakes border as well. Webster accepted the boundary through the St Mary's River, including St George's Island on the American side of the border, and the Pigeon River route from Lake Superior, south of Hunter Island, to the Lake of the Woods. However, he stipulated that the boundary run along the Pigeon River itself, although he agreed 'that all the usual portages along the line from Lake Superior to the Lake of the Woods, and also Grand Portage ... shall be free and open to the use of the subjects and citizens of both countries.' Similarly he agreed to the British use of the American channels at Barnhart's Island and Lake St Clair, and he asked for the same privileges for Americans in the Detroit River in using the Canadian channel when passing Bois Blanc Island.[45] The boundary of some 758.8 miles was marked out and signed on the maps made by David Thompson for the commission in 1826. Only provisions for final surveying and marking needed to be made.

The series of crises in trilateral relations that prompted the Ashburton mission ran well beyond the several boundary disputes, as crucial as they were. In the minds of mid-nineteenth-century Britons and Americans several of the other issues may in fact have seemed more important. Although the McLeod trial had ended satisfactorily, the United States still had to pass legislation that would convince the British government that the U.S. government had the powers to protect agents of another country from the reach of municipal courts. The Americans, for their part, had still not received what they regarded as an adequate explanation from the British government, not to mention apology or indemnity, for the aggressive military raid into the United States in 1837 that resulted in the destruction of the steamer *Caroline* and the death of at least one person. The slavery issue, always close to the surface in mid-nineteenth-century affairs, constituted a major area of antagonism also. The Americans were resentful that the British authorities had in November 1841 freed the slaves on board an American brig, the *Creole,* that put into Nassau in the Bahamas as the result of a mutiny. The British themselves wanted American cooperation in stopping the slave trade off the coast of Africa. Related to several of these issues was the matter of extradition of suspected criminals for violations of the law in the other country. Could the exchange of fugitives be arranged without violating political rights or aggravating the slavery question? Finally, impressment, a ghost from the Royal Navy's practices during the Napoleonic Wars, refused to be laid to rest.

Legislation to empower the U.S. government to assume jurisdiction in situations where the accused had been acting in the service of another government was urged by President Tyler in his annual address to Congress in December 1841. The bill was introduced in the spring of 1842. Attitudes towards the measure, called the 'McLeod law,' tended to divide along party lies, the Democrats opposing the bill and the Whigs supporting it. Southerners of both parties were cautious about the possibility of foreign abolitionists being exempted from prosecution by southern state courts. Debate in Congress surfaced after Ashburton's arrival in the United States, and clearly his presence made the bill's passage more likely. In the end the Senate voted its approval on 8 July, and the House on 27 July.[46]

The *Caroline* business demanded more ingenuity by the diplomats. The Americans had from time to time since 1837 asked the British for an explanation for the sinking of the *Caroline*, and Palmerston's note of August 1841 had hardly put the matter to rest. Aberdeen, in his original instructions of 8 February 1842, gave Ashburton minimal guidance on the question. He simply said that there appeared no good reason why a reply had not been given to the queries of the Americans but that the action by Crown officials in Upper Canada was justified.[47] Ashburton and Webster discussed the matter, but nothing was put to paper until after the boundary questions had been decided. On 27 July, Webster sent Ashburton a short note in which he said that while the action of the *Caroline* itself might be legally questionable, the raid that resulted in her destruction was clearly a violation of American sovereignty and dignity. He further emphasized that 'to this day, no atonement, or even apology, has been made by Her Majesty's Government.'[48] Webster felt that American honour required some formal acknowledgment by Britain.

Ashburton replied with a long, skilful letter the following day. He affirmed Britain's devotion to the principles of international law involved in the sanctity of sovereignty, but he dwelt also on the right of self-defence. He then recalled the bare details of the events leading up to the incident itself – concluding that the actions taken by Crown agents – the militia – had been justified in the circumstances. However, Ashburton also stated that it was 'to be regretted ... that some explanation and apology for this occurrence was not immediately made; this with a frank explanation of the necessity of the case probably would have prevented much of the exasperation and of the subsequent complaints and recriminations to which it gave rise.' This was as close as a great power need come in taking responsibility for an armed incursion into the territory of a lesser power in the nineteenth century. Ashburton then closed the note with his own complaint that it was still possible in the United States for private people to be held for prosecution by the state courts for deeds carried out under the commission of a foreign power, although legislation to remedy that situation had just passed the Senate the previous day.[49] The question of indemnity for the destruction of property or the loss of life was not raised. Webster and Tyler accepted Ashburton's letter as an apology and a statement that Britain intended no disrespect through the incursion. It was a tribute to Ashburton's skill as a diplomat that such a deliberately ambiguous letter should have been so accepted.[50]

As with the *Caroline* affair, the slavery question proved to be an intractable problem for Webster and Ashburton. By the 1840s any public issue touching slavery, even remotely, found powerful opposition from southern congressmen and senators, generally from the White House, and often from the executive departments. While a northerner himself, Webster had little room in which to manoeuvre in dealing with slavery matters that came before him. However, circumstances did not allow him to ignore these issues. The most pressing crisis was southern U.S. reaction to the freeing of slaves on board the *Creole* by British authorities in the Bahamas. For southern pro-slavery advocates the example of the *Creole* – that slaves could obtain their freedom while under transportation by overthrowing the ship's crew and sailing to a British port – was tantamount to an incitement to a slave revolt. This was a greater potential problem than it might first appear because the movement of slaves from the old slave states of Virginia and the Carolinas to the new cotton fields of Alabama and Mississippi involved transportation by ship either along the coast through the Florida Straits or into the Atlantic and through the Bahama Strait (or Northeast Providence Channel), and then west around Florida.

Although both Webster and Edward Everett in London sent letters and appeals demanding restitution, the British insisted that slaves were free when they touched British soil. Ashburton's instructions did not give him any authority to commit Britain on matters arising out of the *Creole* situation, but the issue was so pressing among southern U.S. politicians that he knew that he could not avoid making some response. Once again Ashburton proved to be an able diplomat. In a letter to

Webster on 6 August, he attempted to reassure pro-slavery interests. First, he cautiously said that the specific grievances surrounding the *Creole* case would best be dealt with in London and that the abolition of slavery in the British Empire precluded any appeal for the return of slaves once they had reached British jurisdiction. However, British authorities had no justification to interfere with ships operating under the laws of their own nations, making innocent passage through international waters or driven by chance into British waters. In the end, he took it on his own responsibility to assure Webster that 'there shall be no officious interference with American vessels driven by accident or violence into those ports.'[51] President Tyler was shown the original copy of the letter and made a number of suggestions, to Ashburton's irritation, but which were incorporated into the final version nevertheless. In the end, the Americans recognized that this letter marked the extent to which Ashburton could go on this issue.[52]

Closely related to the *Creole* case, but with pressure coming from the British rather than the Americans, was the question of obtaining American assistance in suppressing the African slave trade by some means of preventing slavers from falsely flying the American flag in order to obtain immunity from British intervention. Britain had emerged since 1807 as the leading force in the anti-slavery movement, and British public opinion strongly endorsed the government's steps to end the international slave trade. Britain's naval supremacy put it in a position to make impossible the continued transportation of Africans to the slave markets in North and South America and the West Indies. Indeed, the United States was a serious obstacle to these ambitions, and many of the most formidable British critics of that nation were those who exploited the contradiction between the self-proclaimed land of freedom and the actual land of slavery. The United States had refused in 1841 to sign the Quintuple Treaty legalizing search-and-visit privileges and, through a hostile publication by Lewis Cass, now the American minister to France, had contributed to the decision of the French Chamber of Deputies to postpone ratification of the treaty. Southerners saw British efforts to stop the African slave trade as a first step in a campaign against slavery itself, even though the U.S. constitution had banned the importation of slaves after 1808. The British proposal for dealing with the situation was to obtain American agreement to stop ships on the high seas flying the American flag to determine whether the ships were actually from the United States. Northerners objected to this practice because it was a procedure that was too reminiscent of impressment, which had been such a volatile issue in the years leading up to the War of 1812, and also because the search-and-visit practice would serve to reinforce Britain's maritime supremacy.[53]

After months of correspondence on the subject, support formed around the proposal to have U.S. navy vessels sail in company with the Royal Navy so that the American authorities would challenge suspicious ships flying the American flag, and the British, ships flying other flags. Webster attempted to sound out Aberdeen through Everett, in London, on a suggestion along those lines in late April. The idea of joint cruising, for which Tyler also claimed credit, was supported by both the British and the Americans by August. The United States agreed to station ships, which would cumulatively amount to eighty guns, off the West African coast to cooperate with British cruisers in the suppression of the slave trade. Originally the agreement to do this was to have formed a separate convention, but at the last minute it became part of the boundary treaty, as articles 8 and 9.[54]

A partially related issue was that of impressment. Webster worked very hard in discussions with Ashburton to get the British to agree to abandon the practice of claiming the right in time of war to press into service all able-bodied British subjects, even if found on American ships or claiming American citizenship (the British maintained further that a British subject could not change his citizenship). Both Ashburton and Aberdeen regarded impressment as a crude and obsolete method of maintaining crews for the Royal Navy. However, the Admiralty refused to agree formally never to use impressment again in time of war. Webster had to be content with Ashburton's private assurance that impressment was not likely ever to be employed again.[55]

The remaining issue to be settled was extradition of fugitives from the justice systems of Britain and the United States. In practical terms, the border between British North America and the United States was so 'transparent' that it was a simple matter for robbers to find a safe haven on the other side of the boundary and thus enjoy their wrongful gains. Extradition clauses had been written into the Jay–Grenville Treaty of 1794, but when these provisions lapsed no new extradition treaty was negotiated. The current situation was clearly unhealthy and unsatisfactory to authorities on both sides of the border. The slavery issue, however, once again entered the negotiations. The Americans wanted mutiny included in the list of extraditable offences, in order to protect slave owners against the recurrence of events like the *Creole* incident. The British, for their part, opposed returning fugitive slaves, even though those people might be in violation of the law of various American states.[56] The result was a restricted list of common felonies that had the least possible political implications – murder, assault to commit murder, piracy, arson, robbery, forgery, and the manufacture of forged paper or documents.[57]

So, at last, all the issues for which a settlement was possible were pulled together. Articles 1–7 dealt with boundary provisions and mutual concessions, articles 8 and 9, with joint cruising, and article 10, with extradition. The *Caroline* incident, the *Creole* incident, and impressment were dealt with in duly noted correspondence between Webster and Ashburton. The power of the U.S. government to protect the agents of foreign governments was settled through legislation passed by Congress in July 1842. All this effort had been terribly exhausting. In the midst of the *Creole* discussions, Ashburton wrote to Webster rejoicing in cooler weather and concluding, 'I really believe that if yesterday's [temperature] had continued I should not have lived to sign any treaty with you, which is now the great object, as it is likely to be the fifth act of my life.'[58]

Ashburton reported to Aberdeen as soon as all the details were in place. 'I have much satisfaction in informing your Lordship that my tedious negotiation for the settlement of the Boundaries between Her Majesty's Dominions and the United States of America is at last closed.' Of all the difficulties, Ashburton had already fully informed the foreign secretary. He hoped that the results would receive the queen's 'approbation,' and he was confident that the terms had 'secur[ed] the interests of the Colonies,' especially because the continued unrest along the border, he was certain, 'could not have been suffered long to continue without endangering the maintenance of peace.'[59] Privately he told Aberdeen that the whole treaty almost came apart the previous day over the *Creole* notes, when Tyler sent a 'querulous foolish letter' to Webster objecting to the language in Ashburton's letter. The changes were made at the last minute. Webster, whom Ashburton had strongly criticized from time to time, 'behaved well & liberally throughout.'[60]

Maine's remaining commissioners, Kent and Otis, dined alone with Ashburton in late July and for the first time found him 'very pleasant and yielding.' Webster's own immediate sentiments are unknown, although six months later he told Jared Sparks that it had been a 'great stroke' to get the agreement of Maine and Massachusetts. Tyler wrote to Webster on 8 August, during completion of all the preparations, saying that 'the affair [was] settled with England, and we shall have cause for unmixed joy.'[61] It was indeed a moment for joy, and compliments were exchanged all round. On Tuesday, 9 August, the treaty was signed at ten o'clock in the morning at the White House, with President Tyler and his cabinet looking on.

The Webster–Ashburton Treaty was a monumental accomplishment for all parties and a major step in normalizing relations between British North America and the United States along 2,540 miles on the eastern half of the continent. A workable and lasting boundary was created. For the United States this treaty in 1842 was the most complex, far reaching, and important yet signed in time of peace. But if the search for the boundary was finally over, it was by no means the end of the Webster–Ashburton Treaty.

Chapter Thirteen

Storm over the Treaty

Lord Ashburton felt that the completed treaty met with widespread satisfaction in the United States, and he was fêted during the remainder of
his visit. He stayed in Washington for about another week, during which
time the final versions of the text were worked out. John Tyler graciously
gave him a farewell dinner on Wednesday, 17 August, and then he
thought it best to leave Washington while the treaty was being considered by the Senate. His son-in-law, Humphrey St J. Mildmay, and his secretaries, Frederick Bruce and Mr Shedding, travelled north to Niagara
Falls and to see Sir Charles Bagot in Kingston.[1]

Ashburton himself visited Philadelphia, Boston, and New York. In
Boston he was asked to speak at Faneuil Hall, he was made an honorary
member of the American Peace Society as a result of the treaty, and he
was presented at a Phi Beta Kappa dinner in Cambridge. A song was
written in his honour, two lines of which were: 'O'er the Lion and Eagle
now hovers the Dove; / To-day there's a banquet of national love.'[2] In
New York, where Ashburton spent about a week, he had an opportunity
to meet with Albert Gallatin. Several dinners were arranged by both private people and groups of merchants, of which the most notable took
place at Astor House on 1 September. Distinguished New Yorkers presided, and speeches were given by several people, including Senator
George Evans of Maine, Captain Lord John Hay of HMS *Warspite*, Thomas C. Grattan, the British consul in Boston and raconteur, and Ashburton himself. Philip Hone, who attended the event, recorded in his diary
that Ashburton's remarks were 'plain and sensible, and [were] made
eloquent by the warmth of his feelings, and his extreme sensibility to the
kindness which he has received in this country.' Queen Victoria was
toasted cheerfully enough, Hone reported, but the reciprocal toast to

President Tyler met with 'dead silence' from a room filled with New York Whigs.[3] The following evening, when Ashburton and a party of naval officers attended a play, the orchestra played 'God Save the Queen' and 'Rule Britannia,' after which the crowd gave three cheers for the diplomat.

On Saturday, 3 September, Ashburton joined the *Warspite* while large crowds turned out to see him off. Cannon salutes were exchanged between the *Warspite* and the USS *North Carolina*, the seventy-four-gun receiving ship off the Brooklyn Naval Yard. Commodore Matthew Calbraith Perry, who would later open trade between the United States and Japan, paid a courtesy call on the British ship, where toasts were made. The *Warspite* broke out the American flag when the commodore left, fired a twenty-one gun salute, and got under way, flanked by two steamships. It was a scene of Anglo–American good will unequalled since the departure of Sir Charles Bagot as British minister in 1818.[4]

In British North America and in Britain also, the first reactions to the treaty settlement were positive. Sir Charles Bagot responded to Ashburton's announcement of 9 August with warm praise. 'I congratulate you with all my heart,' he wrote, saying that the treaty would remove, 'I trust forever, the two most considerable sources of irritation and misunderstanding between us and our neighbours.' He was sure that the document would be well received at home. Later in the month, after reading the text of the treaty, he said appreciatively that the concessions won in the channels of the St Lawrence River were much appreciated in Upper Canada.[5] Bagot also wrote to the secretary for war and colonies, Lord Stanley, 'Thank God however, the point is settled at last.' He thought that 'almost any settlement was desirable so far as these Provinces were concerned.'[6] In England, Lord Aberdeen informed Sir Robert Peel of the outlines of the northeastern boundary settlement following receipt of Ashburton's early message. 'It is a great matter to have obtained anything better than the line of the king of the Netherlands, in its most important part,' he told the prime minister, adding that the British concessions in more distant parts of the boundary were 'of little consequence.'[7] The Duke of Wellington noted with pleasure, 'We shall settle our affairs in North America.'[8]

News of the treaty reached Britain by late August and was reported on the twenty-third in such London newspapers as the *Morning Chronicle*. Charles Greville noted in his diary on 11 September: 'There is a very general feeling of satisfaction at the termination of the boundary dispute with the Americans,' although he recognized that Lord Palmerston would be certain to object.[9] Ashburton arrived at Spithead on 23 or 24 September to more naval salutes, and early the next week he was invited to London to confer with the foreign secretary, who also commented that, while the treaty was initially 'either well or silently received,' it had more recently come under attack from Palmerston and the *Morning Chronicle*.[10] In both countries, a shadow began to creep over the treaty that never entirely lifted.

Even as the treaty was being signed, the controversy started to unfold. After the documents were signed on Tuesday, 9 August 1842, Webster revealed to Ashburton the maps that Jared Sparks and others had shown to members of the Maine and Massachusetts governments and to the state commissioners and very shortly would show to members of the Senate. These maps, acquired by Webster or produced by Sparks, showed a northeastern boundary that was well south of the American boundary claim and tended to reinforce, if not exceed, the British claim. These maps had no official standing, of course, but they suggested that in the aftermath of the War of Independence there had been several alternative views of what the 1783 boundary settlement had been.

Ashburton wrote the same day to Aberdeen saying that Webster had shown him the maps after he had signed the treaty. Ashburton made two quite remarkable assertions about the documents. 'This extraordinary evidence places this [British] case beyond all possible doubt,' he wrote, and although eventually both he and Aberdeen took the view, quite correctly, that these maps could not be seriously linked to the treaty of 1783, he seemed clearly convinced of their validity at the time. Ashburton also added, in his note to Aberdeen, that 'if I had known it before I *agreed* to sign I should have asked your orders, not withstanding the manner of my becoming acquainted with it.'[11]

This does raise the question of whether Ashburton had previously known about the maps and their contents. On 8 June, Thomas C. Grattan had been witness in New York to Preble's blow-up over maps shown by Professor James Renwick to the Maine commissioners. Within days Grattan met with Ashburton in Washington, and by 14 June Ashburton reported to Aberdeen that he had 'reason to suspect' that Webster was using 'some evidence, known at present to nobody, but favourable to our claim.'[12] Thus it is reasonable to conclude that Ashburton had some sense of the maps, through this channel, if not the specific details.

Furthermore, Ashburton opened a second whole line of historical controversy when he raised the point with Aberdeen in his 9 August letter by acknowledging that he had used British secret service money to help finance Jared Sparks's trips to speak with the governors of Maine and Massachusetts, and he noted that, in the absence of these visits, 'Maine would never have yielded.'[13] It is reasonable to assume that Ashburton had a clear understanding of the kind of material that Sparks used to persuade the two state governments to agree to a compromise settlement, even if he had not actually seen it himself. Having helped to finance the process of attempting to influence those states through Sparks, he could hardly have felt himself deceived by Webster.

Although the extent of Ashburton's involvement in, and knowledge of, these affairs would not become known until generations later, when Aberdeen's private papers in the British Museum were opened to the public, it could be inferred from Thomas C. Grattan's memoirs, published in 1851. Ashburton certainly understood full well the influence that the maps had. 'The truth is that *probably* but for this discovery [of the red-line maps] there would have been no treaty,' he told John Wilson Croker some months later, although he also said to Croker much of what he had written to Aberdeen – namely, that 'if the secret had been known to me earlier I could not have signed it.'[14] Ashburton's protests read like statements for the record, rather than candid accounts of his sentiments.

President Tyler sent the treaty to the Senate for approval on 11 August 1842. The original separate conventions, dealing with boundaries, the slave trade, and extradition, had by this time been redrafted to form a single comprehensive document. Webster had the previous day sent to the chairman of the Senate's Foreign Relations Committee several parcels of documents to assist the committee in reaching a decision to approve the treaty, including the so-called red-line maps. The treaty was quickly reported out of the committee by its chairman, William C. Rives of Virginia, on 15 August for debate and approval in the Senate. The debates were held in secret session so that Rives could present to the chamber the controversial maps. Once again the purpose was not to convince the legislators of the possible merits of the British case so much as to persuade them that the alternatives to a compromise boundary were not very promising. The introduction of the maps led to a fierce argument about the merits of various maps and opened the door to eventual public knowledge of Webster's use of the maps to win the compliance of the representatives from Maine and Massachusetts.

However, in the Senate itself several people spoke passionately. Levi

Woodbury of New Hampshire argued that the maps were not very help-ful and that the Senate should be guided by other considerations. The Missouri Democrat, Thomas Hart Benton, attacked the treaty and the use of the maps. Benton was a prominent Jacksonian Democrat, anglo-phobe, and expansionist, who would take a larger role in the agitation over the Oregon territory in 1845 and 1846. He may have involved him-self in this question as much to frustrate Webster and Tyler for political reasons as to defend U.S. claims along the Maine border. As for Maine's consent, Benton said that U.S. territorial limits were the concern of the federal rather than the state governments, thus challenging the guiding principle of the previous ten years. He described the decision on 17 June to negotiate a conventional line as 'black Friday,' and he claimed that the treaty was a 'solemn bamboozlement.' As for the maps, Benton recounted that he had been shown maps by Thomas Jefferson years ear-lier that had the American claim marked on them. When Jefferson's map was brought to the Senate chamber, however, it showed a boundary that supported the British claim, to the dismay of Benton, who then denounced Webster for behaving discreditably by not showing Ashbur-ton the Sparks maps.[15] John C. Calhoun of South Carolina pointed out that the Senate had followed Maine's wishes in 1831 by rejecting the award of the king of the Netherlands and that the Senate would be fool-ish now not to accept a boundary settlement that Maine had accepted.

One powerful opponent of the treaty was Maine Senator Reuel Wil-liams, who argued that his state had agreed to a compromise settlement with the understanding that it would give up part of its claims in exchange for equivalent land concessions by New Brunswick. However, as the talks proceeded it became clear that Ashburton had no authority to make any equivalent territorial concessions from contiguous New Brunswick land. The resulting boundary agreement was not what Maine had been led to believe might be the result of a compromise settlement. Williams urged that the president be instructed to take possession of the disputed territory immediately.[16] James Buchanan, a Democrat from Pennsylvania, and within two years secretary of state himself, echoed Williams's arguments – that Ashburton had not been able to exchange land for land – and he also emphasized that the abandonment of Maine's claims meant the surrender of lands fought for by the nation's forefathers. Those very territories would be used by the British as mili-tary positions against the United States, he assured the Senate.[17] Out-side the Senate, Governor Fairfield was also dissatisfied. While unwilling to criticize the Maine delegation at the talks, he wrote, 'For myself, I can truly say that I am deeply disappointed,' and he was unsparing in his criticism of the British government and its 'unyielding and grasping spirit.'[18]

The treaty came to a vote on Saturday, 20 August 1842, and passed comfortably by a margin of thirty-nine to nine, well in excess of the two-thirds' majority required for a treaty. Of the two Maine senators, Williams, a Democrat, voted against, and George Evans, a Whig, voted for. By the end of the month the Senate had voted to make public the debates that had been conducted in secrecy, so that gradually the exact terms of the treaty, as well as the information about the various maps used by Webster, Sparks, and others, became public knowledge.[19]

The opinions of major figures were mixed. Andrew Jackson had condemned the treaty and hoped that the Senate would reject it. He felt that it was 'not only disgraceful, but humiliating to our national character and humbling us in dust and ashes,' and that it compared very poorly to the award of the king of the Netherlands that had been rejected during his term of office.[20] John Quincy Adams congratulated Webster on the treaty and its ratification by the Senate. Webster replied that he was 'glad to have it off his shoulders,' and he wrote to a friend, in some exhaustion, that 'the treaty is done! and I am almost done too.' Webster departed for his home, Marshfield, as soon as Congress adjourned, much to the disgust of the work-driven Adams. Webster also paid tribute to President Tyler. 'Your steady support and confidence, your anxious and intelligent attention to what was in progress, and your obliging and pleasant intercourse, both with the British minister and the commissioners of the States, have given every possible facility to my agency in this important transaction.'[21]

Newspaper reaction to the treaty had been mixed. Judge Preble's arrival back in Maine in late July gave rise to speculation that the boundary provision would not be entirely to Maine's satisfaction. But with news of the outlines of the treaty, stronger opinions were expressed. The *Augusta Age* said on 12 August that the settlement was 'a disastrous one,' even taking into account its many strengths. The newspaper concluded, however, that there was no alternative. The *Kennebec Journal* thought that the treaty would be rejected by the Senate, although the *Portland Eastern Argus* said that if the rest of the nation thought that Maine should 'make the sacrifice, she would do it.'[22] To generate more open support, Webster drafted some editorials for the *National Intelligencer,* published on 23 August. Although focused largely on the history of the controversy and the process of negotiation, the editorial said, 'National honor has been maintained' and descent into war avoided.[23]

Things looked different on a more personal level. Commissioner Edward Kent wrote to his colleague Edward Kavanagh on his return to Bangor, Maine, that he was 'highly gratified to find so general and hearty approval of our proceedings by the sober, discrete & honest men of the State.'[24] T.W. Ward, the Baring Brothers agent in Boston, wrote to the London office that although politicians from both parties would attempt to 'embarrass the government,' they would not want to have to deal with these matters themselves. The treaty would be ratified, he said confidently, and there was a general feeling that 'the country is greatly indebted to Ashburton.'[25] Webster's turn for praise came when he too was guest of honour at Faneuil Hall in Boston on 30 September. To a packed assembly, Mayor Jonathan Chapman told of the great achievement of the treaty. Philip Hone also recorded that Webster gave detailed accounts of the negotiations of the treaty and its merits to small dinner parties.[26]

News of the treaty arrived in Britain before Ashburton returned in late September. Very probably even before he saw the text of the treaty, Palmerston was preparing his opposition to it. On 24 August he wrote to Lord John Russell, singling out 'the remarkable change' that had occurred in the attitude of the government of Maine 'owing to the new light thrown upon the question by the Report of Messrs. Mudge and Featherstonhaugh.'[27] However, Palmerston seemed to expect a complete collapse of the American claims, not merely their willingness to settle for a compromise. Charles Greville understood that Palmerston would feel obliged to attack the treaty along with other aspects of Aberdeen's foreign policy. Visiting Broadlands, Palmerston's country home, on 17 September, Greville recorded his host's complaints that, as in all Tory foreign policy matters, '*we give up everything*,' and he said that there was no difficulty in obtaining settlements if Britain simply gave in to all demands. In the current treaty negotiations, Palmerston thought, 'we have been overreached by the Americans,' and Ashburton himself had an 'American bias' and a deficiency of 'character.' As far as Palmerston was concerned, territorial concessions should never have been made because Britain had 'already *proved* our right to the disputed land' since the arbitration by the king of the Netherlands, 'which clearly establishes our rights.' This was a theme that Palmerston would develop over the next six months and which Greville noticed appeared almost word for word in the *Morning Chronicle* in the next few days.[28]

The *Chronicle* took the view that Mudge and Featherstonhaugh's report had irrefutably established the correctness of the British claims and that any retreat from the boundary proposed there was gratuitous. Ashburton had been 'bullied, or bamboozled, or both,' and the paper described the treaty as 'Lord Ashburton's capitulation' – a phrase that stuck.[29] 'The motto of the Government in foreign affairs seems to be "Give way,"' Palmerston wrote to Lord Minto, and he further asserted that 'Ashburton's treaty is very discreditable to the negotiators who concluded it, and to the Government who sanctioned it.' He argued that Ashburton had been 'outwitted' and had given up to the Americans weapons that they would later use against Britain.[30] In late September, Palmerston also complained to Lord John Russell, who had assumed the leadership of the Whigs after the fall of the Melbourne government, declaring, 'Never was there imbecility like that of Ashburton.' Ashburton had been a strong critic of Palmerston's policies during the Mehemet Ali crisis in 1840 and 1841, and Palmerston hit back at Ashburton with a vengeance, calling him 'a half Yankee,' who was willing to betray the national interest for business reasons. He said that he understood that 'the Duke of Wellington is angry at the cession of Rouse's Point, and well he may be.'[31] For his part, Ashburton was convinced that Featherstonhaugh's arguments and the survey in 1839 were the main reasons for Palmerston's violent objection to a boundary that was an improvement on the one that he would have accepted in the 1830s.[32]

Melbourne wrote to Russell on 7 October, 'Every one who is acquainted with or has considered the subject seems to me to have come to your opinion, that the arrangement made by Ashburton is a bad one, and that we ought to have had, and might have had, better terms.' Nevertheless, he agreed with Russell that unless unusual circumstances emerged they should 'state the objections to the treaty strongly' but not attempt to have it rejected by Parliament. Melbourne was sure that Palmerston would 'concur' in this plan.[33] Palmerston would not. In fact, the Whigs were slightly embarrassed by Palmerston's increasingly intemperate attacks on both Ashburton and the terms of the treaty. Just as Melbourne was writing to Russell, Charles Greville noted that 'Palmerston has certainly not acted wisely as one of the Leaders of his Party.' Greville thought that he should have taken public opinion and the views of his friends into account before presuming such a stance. Russell, Greville recorded, 'thought at first that we had conceded too much, but on further examination he changed his opinion, and he now thinks the settlement on the whole a good one.' The public approved of the treaty, Greville concluded, and wanted good relations with the United States. The following day, however, he recorded that Russell had changed his mind about the treaty again.[34]

Charles Arbuthnot passed on to Sir Robert Peel the comments of that Whig stalwart Lord Grey, who referred to 'vituperative' articles in the *Morning Chronicle* presumed to have been written by Palmerston. 'How he could make up his mind to attack an arrangement certainly preferable to that to which we would have agreed in 1831, it is for him to consider, but to me such attacks from such a quarter create only feelings of disapprobation and disgust.' Grey was 'thankful to have the question settled.'[35] Many of his own party agreed. Clearly, even Palmerston's colleagues did not understand the extent to which he had been influenced by Featherstonhaugh's theories. Lord Fitzwilliam complained to Russell about the carping over the treaty. 'It is really very foolish to attack the Government upon the good they do as well as upon the evil and still more to endeavour to rouse anti-American feeling in the country.'[36] To the surprise of both Aberdeen and Peel, Featherstonhaugh made a speech praising the treaty to the Cornwall Polytechnic Society in Falmouth.[37]

Parliament was not in session during the autumn and would not sit again until the new year, and so public discussion of the treaty took place in the newspapers. Palmerston strongly influenced the opinions expressed in several papers, writing letters and directives that were sometimes edited and sometimes published whole. Of these papers the most prominent were the *Morning Chronicle*, the *Morning Herald*, and the *Globe*. Through this medium the treaty became known as a 'wretchedly bad arrangement' and a 'needless, gratuitous, and imbecile surrender.' Perhaps most damaging of all was the phrase 'Lord Ashburton's capitulation,' which was repeated endlessly. The Tory government responded through *The Times*, attacking Palmerston, who was described as a tiresome dinner companion who insisted on boring the whole table. *The Times* noted how humiliating it must have been for Palmerston to witness Aberdeen's successful foreign policy in China, Afghanistan, and the United States.[38]

The government seemed a bit embarrassed by the criticism of the treaty. When Ashburton returned to England in late September, Aberdeen noted the growing opposition to the treaty led by Palmerston in the *Morning Chronicle* and the *Globe*. The foreign secretary told Ashburton that he was 'perfectly satisfied' with the treaty and that the resolutions of a variety of difficulties with the United States 'far outweigh in my mind the value of any additional extent of Pine Swamp.' Nevertheless, Aberdeen, perhaps taking a lead from Ashburton's own letter of 9 August saying that knowledge of the Sparks maps might have strengthened the arguments for holding more territory, lamented the abandonment of the upper St John River and commented, 'I think it probably might have been obtained by perseverance,' which would have had a powerful effect on British public opinion.[39] Ashburton, of course, was also convinced, as he said to Aberdeen, that no better territorial arrangements could have been negotiated (at least not without equivalent cessions of land in New Brunswick).

Nuances of this government dissatisfaction emerged in the correspondence about how to honour Ashburton for his services. He was offered a step up in the peerage, from baron to viscount, together with the Order of the Bath. Ashburton declined the Order of the Bath and indicated that he would accept an earldom – a further advancement in the peerage. Aberdeen privately told Peel that an 'earldom alone would appear more disproportioned to his merits, all things considered.'[40] Peel agreed, and he also thought that the maps were bound to become general knowledge and that the public would inevitably conclude that better terms might have been obtained. The prime minister attempted to explain to Ashburton that the government could not appear to be too 'exulting' in its satisfaction over the treaty. It was pleased, on the one hand, but 'still we cannot deny that we have made concessions,' on the other hand. It was impossible not to 'compare what we relinquished with what we retained.'[41] In the background, though not mentioned to Ashburton, lurked the possible effect of the map question. Ashburton, mortified by the government's guarded endorsement of his work, refused all honours.

Peel's anxiety about the maps was not misplaced. News of the secret Senate debates became public in the United States late in the year and reached England in January 1843. The result was a new and more powerful attack on Ashburton and the treaty. Featherstonhaugh, who had supported the treaty in the autumn, but who was nevertheless turned down for the appointment to lead the British party to mark the new boundary, published privately an attack on the treaty entitled *Observations upon the Treaty of Washington Signed 9th August 1842*. He too was convinced that the map that Sparks found in Paris showed the true boundary and that the Americans knew that they did not have 'the slightest shadow of right to any part of the territory which they have been disputing with Great Britain for near fifty years.'[42] Charles Greville noted that the news of the red-line maps had caused a 'great sensation' and that 'people cry lustily against Webster for having taken us in' – a sentiment that was never quite to disappear – but Greville added with some insight, 'I do not think with much reason.'[43] Ashburton too commented on the public indignation over Webster's failure to inform him of the red-line maps, but he admitted that, in the absence of the use of the maps with the state commissioners and the Senate, 'there would have been no treaty.'[44]

However, the government intended to be better able to defend itself by the time that Parliament opened, and to do that it authorized some research of its own. Sir Henry Lytton Bulwer, a diplomat and later Palmerston's biographer, was sent to Paris to examine the maps in the Archives Nationales. At first, as Peel confessed to Croker, he found only two maps, each of which 'follows exactly with a crimson line, the boundary claimed by the United States!!' Peel wondered if Sparks could have been so mischievous as to have made up the whole business, but eventually both Franklin's letter and the map described by Sparks were found.[45] However, the red-line map in question, once identified, was hardly an overwhelming piece of evidence for the British claim. Although the boundary was well to the south, 'There is not on this map,' Bulwer reported, 'any writing signifying why it was thus marked, nor do I know of any clue thereto, except the letter of Dr. Franklin ... should be considered to furnish such.'[46] Thus no serious conclusions could be drawn from the map.

Meanwhile, a more remarkable discovery was made. Ashburton, who was a trustee of the British Museum, learned that a map from the collection of King George III had been transferred in 1839 from the museum to the Foreign Office. A search for this map was made by the Foreign Office, and it was found to be in the possession of George W. Featherstonhaugh, in his capacity of agent for the preparation of documents for the Ashburton mission. Featherstonhaugh had withheld this document, which proved to be a Mitchell map with a number of markings on it, including a very distinguishable red line marking out a boundary much as claimed by the Americans, particularly in Maine–New Brunswick and between Lake Superior and the Lake of the Woods. Of special interest was a hand-written inscription, 'Boundary as described by Mr. Oswald,' in four separate places along the line. It transpired that this map had been brought to the attention of the foreign secretary, Lord Palmerston, in 1839, by Antonio Panizzi, keeper of printed books at the British Museum, and Palmerston had requisitioned it for the Foreign Office. There it had been used by Featherstonhaugh in his researches and the preparation of his report, after which it remained in his hands. This map from the king's collection appeared to be a more authoritative description of the boundary than any others yet discovered.[47]

Charles Greville recounted for his diary an incident concerning hidden maps well before the public was aware of either the red-line maps or King George's map. An official from the State Paper Office, Charles Lemon, told Greville that in the spring of 1842 he had been working for the government preparing maps and documents for use in the boundary settlement. Lemon remembered that 'there was an Old map of N. America, which had been lying neglected and tossed about the office for the last twenty-five years, and he determined to examine this map.' Lemon found the map, on which he discovered both red lines and pencil lines, and he concluded that this was 'the original map (supposed to be lost, for it never could be found), which was used for marking and settling the Boundary question.' Lemon informed the Foreign Office, which had the document examined by James Arrowsmith, head of the firm of map makers and a fellow of the Royal Geographical Society, and several others. The red lines were deemed to be of considerable age, and the pencil marks more recent. Copies were then made of the map to be rushed to Ashburton in the United States by dispatch, while the map itself was held to be 'of such importance that they ordered it to be instantly locked up and that nobody should have access to it.' Greville concluded, in the wake of the recent treaty, that knowledge of this map had been crucial to the settlement.[48]

Ashburton's discovery of the King George map, as it became known, had several implications. First, it seemed to turn around the situation where the Americans had a map that proved the British case but was covered up by the secretary of state in a most ungentlemanly way. Now the British had a map that appeared to prove the American case, but it had been covered up by the treaty's most bitter critic, Lord Palmerston, when he was foreign secretary. Who were the gentlemen now? In practical terms, the discovery of the King George map protected the treaty, Ashburton, and the government from Palmerston's violent accusations of betrayal or incompetence. The revelation of the map in Britain had something of the same effect there that Webster had anticipated with the circulation of the red-line maps in the United States; the King

George map demonstrated that there was evidence that gave credence, though not proof, to the American case. The discovery of the map and its circumstances also put Palmerston on the defensive. He was now seen to have hidden evidence that supported the claims of the other side.[49]

Palmerston had an opportunity to attack the treaty and Ashburton publicly when Parliament opened. He spoke for over three hours on 21 March 1843, criticizing Ashburton, his American connections, his American-born wife, and his public speeches while in the United States. In the end Palmerston's vitriol brought discredit on himself rather than on the treaty or Ashburton.[50] Although both Palmerston in the Commons and Lord Macauley in the House of Lords spoke in opposition to the treaty, it received a strong defence also. The young Benjamin Disraeli gave a very knowledgeable speech, indicating that he had read a copy of the Franklin letter and looked at copies of the controversial maps from the French archives, as well as the King George map. Sir Howard Douglas, the former lieutenant-governor of New Brunswick who had played a major role in the boundary dispute from 1824 to 1831, supported the treaty and said that, if it represented any British surrender, such capitulation had taken place when Palmerston was foreign secretary and the Americans had been allowed to settle in, and fortify, territory that he had earlier defended.[51]

The most powerful, and insightful, statements about the treaty, however, came from the prime minister himself. Sir Robert Peel outlined the long history of the boundary controversy, pointing out the opportunities that Palmerston had had to settle it and the actual state of crisis in 1841 when Palmerston left office. He said that his own government had sent someone to Paris (Bulwer) who had found a William Faden map of 1783 and a map from *Bew's Journal* of 1783 reporting on the debate over the treaty in Parliament. Both maps had boundaries marked that conformed to the American claim. On further inquiry in Paris the government finally found a map by M. d'Anville published in 1746 and marked with a bold red line that appeared to be the map described by Jared Sparks. However, 'we can trace no indication of connection between it and the dispatch of Dr. Franklin,' he emphasized. 'To say that they were connected is a mere unfounded inference.' This was the most profound public statement yet made about the relevance of the French maps to the boundary settlement. Peel then went on to describe to the House the King George map. It was a Mitchell map with the boundary conforming to the American claim marked out with the accompanying inscription, 'as described by Mr. Oswald,' he said. Peel argued that the boundary marked on the King George map settled the matter no more than the so-called red-line maps in the French archives. He asserted decisively that 'nothing can be more fallacious than founding a claim upon contemporary maps, unless you can also prove that they were adopted by the negotiators.' This was the crucial point, particularly with the King George map. Inasmuch as no maps registered what had finally been agreed on, they proved nothing.[52]

Peel also berated Palmerston's charges that Britain had needlessly accepted a compromise, when allowing the question to go to arbitration, especially with the red-line maps as evidence, would have resulted in winning the entire claim along the New Brunswick border. The maps, showing a variety of boundaries, would not have given clear direction to an arbiter. Peel then fired a parting shot at Palmerston. George Canning and Lord Aberdeen had looked for documents in Paris, even if not completely successfully, and no blame in this matter should attach to them. 'If blame should fall upon anyone, it should fall upon those who have been conducting these negotiations for years' – meaning Palmerston during most of the 1830s. Finally, Peel pointed out that while Palmerston had criticized Webster for not showing the red-line map to Lord Ashburton before the negotiations, Palmerston himself had concealed the King George map. 'That map was in the possession of the noble Lord,' Peel pointed out, 'but he did not communicate its contents to Mr. Webster.'[53] Opposition to the treaty melted away. Palmerston even apologized for calling Ashburton 'half Yankee.' Charles Greville commented to his diary that Palmerston's 'Anti-Ashburton philippic' was very able, but it made his friends uncomfortable and immediately prompted 'votes of thanks' to Ashburton in Parliament. Even so, the Duke of Wellington 'regretted the motion of thanks altogether' and said that the government had not been consulted in it.[54]

In the House of Lords the independent radical Lord Brougham moved a vote of thanks to Ashburton that was passed unanimously. The motion expressed the approval of the Lords and 'rejoice[d] in the terms, alike advantageous and honourable to both parties,' and it praised the 'high sense of ability with which the Lord Ashburton ... executed his commission.' After all the accusations, these were more than flowery compliments. Several weeks later the Commons passed a similar resolution by 238 to 96. *The Times* wrote that this should end the matter of the boundary, the maps, the treaty, and Ashburton's capitulation. Lord Palmerston, *The Times* thought, would have to swallow the fact that he had been abandoned by his colleagues.[55]

Ashburton wrote to Webster in the spring of 1842 to assure him 'that the discoveries here [of the King George map] are quite recent, and were wholly unknown to me when I was at Washington.' This was no doubt true, but Ashburton's soothing suggestion that 'the map question now fortunately only interests historians,' was more hopeful than accurate. Ashburton thought that the controversy on both sides of the Atlantic was an indication that the settlement was balanced and fair – 'so much so,' he said, 'that critics are at a loss to determine which of us had the advantage in the scramble for the swamps on the St. John.'[56] Years later, however, the matter of the King George map still troubled him. He told Edward Everett that if he had seen the map 'he would not have gone to America' – a signal admission of concern about its possible impact on the whole question. Indeed, Everett concluded that if both the red-line maps in the United States and the King George map in England had been known to the public, 'neither party would have given way.'[57] This was probably an accurate assessment, even taking into consideration the prospect of possible conflict as a result of continued disagreement over the boundary.

In the United States public acceptance of the treaty became increasingly general. Professor Sparks, not an uninterested party to be sure, wrote a favourable article in the *North American Review*. In April 1843 Albert Gallatin gave a talk at the New York Historical Society with Daniel Webster as the guest of honour. The eighty-two-year-old Gallatin was unable to present his own paper to the large crowd, and it was read by the grandson of John Jay. Gallatin had just uncovered still another copy of Mitchell's map, traceable to the Paris peace talks at the end of the American Revolution. This map had belonged to John Jay, one of the American negotiators, and had been in the possession of the Jay family. The map had a boundary marked on it favourable to the U.S. claim, with the inscription 'Mr. Oswald's line' (referring to Richard Oswald, one of the British negotiators in 1782) in Jay's handwriting. However, in its eastern extremity the boundary line marked ran along the St John River before proceeding north to the watershed of the St Lawrence River. Gallatin observed that the St John had been rejected by the British government fairly early in the negotiations, so this was understood not to have been the boundary finally agreed on. Gallatin expressed confidence that the Webster–Ashburton Treaty would establish peace and good relations between Britain and the United States for years to come, and he noted significantly that compromise 'in treaties as in private contracts, is necessary for the preservation of mutual confidence and sincere friendly relations between nations or individuals.' In the published version of the talk, he added that controversial maps should be recognized only as 'historical or supplementary documents.'[58]

Webster resigned from Tyler's cabinet on 8 May 1843 and returned briefly to private life. His public presence and his identification with the Whig party were such that he was soon called back to public service. The Massachusetts legislature returned him to the Senate in 1845, and he was once again plunged into the turbulent national politics of the era. During his career Webster had made many enemies, as well as friends, and when he spoke in the late 1840s in the Senate about compromise and moderation in dealing with the Oregon and Texas questions, Democrats and expansionists accused him of wanting to sacrifice American claims in the west in the way that he had in the northeast. This provoked Webster to lash out at his accusers by name.

One of them, Congressman Charles I. Ingersoll, a Democrat from Pennsylvania, occupied the powerful position of chairman of the House Foreign Affairs Committee. Ingersoll claimed that Webster, while secretary of state, had attempted to coerce New York Governor William H. Seward into releasing Alexander McLeod from jail before his famous trial in October 1841. Webster was able to demonstrate that there was no basis for these charges, but he refused to make peace with Ingersoll, and so the congressman came forward with new charges that Webster had used secret service funds improperly, that he had attempted to bribe the press, and that he owed the government (the secret service fund) $2,290 for monies unaccounted for. Ingersoll sought the retroactive impeachment of then Senator Webster for these alleged activities four years earlier as secretary of state. A select committee of five was appointed by the House to investigate.[59]

Ingersoll brought charges that involved specific disbursement of funds, thus revealing that he had been given access to recent confidential State Department records. That in itself raised questions among the Whig members of Congress about whether Ingersoll had violated the law, but that protest could not draw attention away from the select committee's activities. The most prominent witness was former president John Tyler, who assured the committee that he had known about, and had authorized, the use of secret service fund monies. Tyler thought that Webster had been the proper person to handle the allocation of funds in view of the international nature of the boundary dispute. Tyler said that when he had become president 'the peace of the country was most seriously threatened.' Both the McLeod affair and the Maine boundary crisis had created circumstances that could have easily led to war with Britain. Something had to be done. A reasonable negotiation with Britain was obstructed by the passions in Maine, where 'political parties in that State had not marshaled themselves against each other,' Tyler noted, 'but rather vied with each other in the effort to go farthest in the assertion of the territorial rights of that State.' The president put $15,000 from the secret service fund in Webster's hands to try to give the administration a voice in the public discourse in Maine. The administration 'wanted merely to be heard and understood,' and the proposed newspaper campaign was the most effective way to achieve this, Tyler said.[60]

Francis O.J. Smith also testified and explained the origins of his proposal to Webster in May and June 1841 to write articles for Maine newspapers that would encourage discussion about a compromise settlement. With Webster's agreement, Smith had prepared three articles for the *Christian Mirror* entitled 'Northeastern Boundary – Why Not Settle It?' under the pen name 'Agricola.' These articles had appeared between November 1841 and February 1842 and subsequently been reprinted in other newspapers in Maine and elsewhere. In them Smith had urged that a compromise boundary settlement might have more benefits for Maine than arbitration and would be less risky. The pieces were taken seriously and, together with Smith's talks with people in Maine, did promote discussion about compromise. However, no laws were broken, nor was the political process corrupted, Smith said.[61]

Edward Stubbs, the disbursing clerk of the State Department, also testified, giving information about the complicated financial arrangements involved in Webster's activities. Secret service funds had been properly disbursed to various people performing services, and correct vouchers had been submitted. Before he left office in May 1843, Webster had returned unexpended monies, but he did not have vouchers for $2,290. He was asked by the department to provide the vouchers or the money, both of which he was able to do before the Tyler administration left office in March 1845. In the end, Webster had paid the department $1,050 on 1 February 1845, settling the debt that he owed.[62]

All three charges against Webster were laid to rest by the testimony of Tyler, Smith, and Stubbs. The committee voted four to one that there was no evidence of wrong doing by Webster. Though exonerated, Webster, like Lord Ashburton, had been the subject of abuse and held up to public scrutiny for his efforts to settle the boundary. However, even if use of the secret service money to promote the idea of a compromise settlement was legal, there were eyebrows raised. Was it proper, even if legal, to use such funds to shape domestic public opinion, albeit on a foreign relations matter? This, together with the then-public knowledge of Webster's use of the red-line maps, gave credence to the view that Webster had been devious and perhaps unscrupulous in obtaining Maine's agreement to the treaty settlement. The discovery of the King George map in London and of John Jay's map in New York led many people in the United States, and particularly in Maine, to believe that the United States had needlessly compromised on the boundary at the moment when convincing new evidence appeared to prove its case. Thus, despite widespread relief that the boundary crisis was over, and general agreement about the merits of the boundary line itself, the Webster–Ashburton Treaty, and the manner in which it was negotiated, remained under the shadow that began to form at the moment of its signing.

Thus the search for the boundary ended in compromise rather than in fulfilment of the precise terms of the Treaty of Paris of 1783. From the islands in Passamaquoddy Bay, through the due-north line and the St John River valley between New Brunswick and Maine, through the awkward meridian separating New York and Quebec, through the water channels and portage routes, to the remote reaches of the Pigeon River and the Lake of the Woods – over two thousand five hundred miles from the sea – a mixture of needs and political expediency shaped the final decisions. The great surveying expeditions of four boundary commissions between 1816 and 1826 resulted in the exploration and mapping of extensive portions of the wilderness frontier, but they had contributed to actual agreements for only parts of the whole boundary. The 1831 proposal of the king of the Netherlands, though rejected at the time, had in many respects led the way on the eastern frontier. Eventually substantial persuasive efforts had to be exerted on many of the interested parties. Britain was too much the leading world power to be forced to accept the full American claims, but the United States, despite its domestic turbulence and apparent disorganization, was too valuable a source of raw materials for British industry, too good a customer for British goods, and too much an influence in international affairs to be dismissed with scorn and given an ultimatum. Although the United States has more commonly been seen as aggressive and expansionist in the early nineteenth century, it was British claims that expanded steadily in those years.[63] Arguably, the Barclays and the Chipmans, those two Loyalist families, rescued a very weak British case and, by consistent efforts over forty years, and with skilful lawyerly arguments, presented a serious alternative to the American claims. The promotion of the British arguments reached a climax in the provocative joint efforts of Palmerston and George W. Featherstonhaugh in 1840 and 1841.

Leading a new government in London in 1841, Sir Robert Peel, Lord Aberdeen, and Lord Ashburton understood that less aggressive British demands were essential to ending the steadily escalating crisis with the United States. New president John Tyler and Secretary of State Daniel Webster also understood that a more cautious and innovative procedure was needed to avoid conflict with Britain and to protect national, as opposed to local, interests. After years of preparation, a way opened in 1842. Lord Ashburton wrote to Webster after the arguments in Parliament about the treaty and the maps, and he concluded, 'the treaty was a good and wise measure, and good and wise because it was fair.'[64] After all the failures and the many crises, this was a reasonable judgment.

Of course, the debate over the merits of the boundary settlement has continued right up to modern times. The criticism and accusation of betrayal of both local and national interests have been paralleled by praise of the arrangements as a testimonial to common sense and good will – a demonstration that nations can live together and resolve their difficulties. The contradiction of these two traditions seemed to trouble no one; the respective advocates ignored each other. But the search for the boundary was no small feat. Both sides had wanted more land than was obtainable, and many people were convinced that they had an iron-clad case for all the land that they claimed. Firmness and fortitude, the patriots had claimed, were all that were required, in defence of national honour. The price, however, was too high, the risk too great, the danger too ominous for sensible people to contemplate. The description of Daniel Webster's diplomacy as a cautious 'balancing [of] the nation's priorities with its means of enforcement' might serve as a useful commentary on the policies of both the United States and Britain.[65] If politics is the art of the possible, the boundary determined in the Webster–Ashburton Treaty was a most politically sensible settlement.

The last one hundred and fifty years have seen fantastic change around the world – war, revolution, the emergence and disappearance of nations, untold misery and human suffering, and, of course, the periodic change of national boundaries. Consider, for example, the many transformations of the German or Russian boundaries, the last of which took place only a decade ago. The Canadian–American boundary, how-ever, has held, and it remains a tribute to all who had a part in the quest for it and the making of it – 'a good and wise measure.' The search for the boundary ended with gradual acceptance of the reality that peace and harmony with one's neighbours were worth more than miles of wilderness.[66] The process through which the boundary was finally deter-mined established a tradition in Canadian–American relations that emphasized the settlement of disputes through negotiation and inter-national law, not by force. It is a legacy that continues today in such permanent bodies as the International Joint Commission and the dispute-settlement mechanisms set up under the Canada–United States and the North American free trade agreements.

Notes

Abbreviations

AHR	*American Historical Review*
BECHS	Buffalo and Erie County Historical Society, Buffalo
BL	British Library, London
CHR	*Canadian Historical Review*
CO	Colonial Office Papers, PRO, London
DAB	*Dictionary of American Biography*, ed. James Truslow Adams. 21 vols. (New York: Charles Scribner's Sons, 1940–74).
DCB	*Dictionary of Canadian Biography*, ed. George W. Brown et al. 14 vols. (Toronto: University of Toronto Press, 1966–98).
DCUSCR	William R. Manning, ed., *Diplomatic Correspondence of the United States: Canadian Relations, 1784–1860* (Washington, DC: Carnegie Endowment for International Peace, 1940)
DNB	*Dictionary of National Biography*, ed. Sir Leslie Stephen and Sir Sidney Lee. 21 vols. (Oxford: Oxford University Press, 1917–73).
FO	Foreign Office Papers, PRO, London
HBC Archives	Hudson's Bay Company Archives, Winnipeg
LC	Library of Congress, Washington, DC
Maine HS	Maine Historical Society, Portland
Mass HS	Massachusetts Historical Society, Boston
MHS	Minnesota Historical Society, St Paul
MVHR	*Mississippi Valley Historical Review*
NA	National Archives, Washington, DC
NAC	National Archives of Canada, Ottawa
NBM	New Brunswick Museum, Saint John
NEQ	*New England Quartely*

PRO   Public Record Office, London
RG   Record Group, Department of State, NA

Preface

1 Sir Robert Falconer, Watson Chair Lectures, 1925, in Falconer, *The United States as a Neighbour, from a Canadian Point of View* (London: Cambridge University Press, 1925), 38.
2 P.E. Corbett, *The Settlement of Canadian–American Disputes: A Critical Study of Methods and Results* (New Haven, Conn.: Yale University Press, 1937), 3.
3 Hugh Llewellyn Keenleyside and Gerald S. Brown, *Canada and the United States: Some Aspects of Their Historical Relations* (New York: Alfred A. Knopf, 1952), 137.
4 Sir Francis Hincks, 'The Boundaries Formerly in Dispute between Great Britain and the United States' (Montreal: John Lovall, 1885), 4–5.
5 Robert McElroy and Thomas Riggs, eds., *The Unfortified Boundary: A Diary of the First Survey of the Canadian Boundary Line from St. Regis to Lake of the Woods by Major Joseph Delafield, American Agent under Articles VI and VII of the Treaty of Ghent* (New York: private, 1943), 10.
6 Lord Ashburton to Daniel Webster, 28 April 1843, in James W. McIntyre, ed., *The Writings and Speeches of Daniel Webster* (Boston, Little, Brown, 1903), 18:190.

Chapter 1. Introduction: Working out a Method, 1783–1814

1 Lord Byron described Baring less flatteringly in *Don Juan,*

> Who holds the balance of the world? Who reign
>   O'er congress, whether royalist or liberal?
> Who rouse the shirtless patriot of Spain
>   (That make old Europe's journals squeak and gibber all).
> Who keep the world, both old and new, in pain
>   Or pleasure? Who make politics run glibber all?
> The shade of Buonaparte's double daring? –
> Jew Rothschild, and his fellow-Christian, Baring.

Quotations from Philip Ziegler, *The Sixth Great Power: A History of One of the Greats of All Banking Families, The House of Barings, 1762–1929* (New York: Alfred A. Knopf, 1988), 85 and 96–7.
2 Definitive Treaty of Peace, signed at Paris, 3 Sept. 1783, in Hunter Miller, ed., *Treaties and Other International Acts of the United States of America* (Washington,

DC: Government Printing Office, 1931), 2: 152–3. Article 2 repeats part of the description, after taking the boundary line from along the Florida border into the Atlantic. It reads: 'East, by a Line to be drawn along the Middle of the River St. Croix, from its Mouth in the Bay of Fundy to its Source; and from its Source directly North to the aforesaid Highlands, which divide the Rivers that fall into the Atlantic, from those which fall into the River St. Lawrence; comprehending all Islands within twenty Leagues of any Part of the Shores of the United States, & lying between Lines to be drawn due East from the Points where the aforesaid Boundaries between Nova Scotia on the one Part and East Florida on the other, shall respectively touch the Bay of Fundy and the Atlantic Ocean, excepting such Islands as now are or heretofore have been within the Limits of the said Province of Nova Scotia.

3 For a complete discussion of these issues, see Clarence W. Alvord, *The Mississippi Valley in British Politics* (Cleveland: Arthur H. Clark, 1917); T.P. Abernathy, *Western Lands and the American Revolution* (New Haven, Conn.: Yale University Press, 1937); Richard Van Alstyne, *Empire and Independence* (New York: John Wiley and Sons, 1965); and J. Leitch Wright, Jr, *Britain and the American Frontier, 1783–1815* (Athens: University of Georgia Press, 1975).

4 For an overview of the diplomatic problems of the War of Independence, see Samuel Flagg Bemis, *The Diplomacy of the American Revolution*, 3rd ed. (Bloomington: Indiana University Press, 1957); and William C. Stinchcombe, *The American Revolution and the French Alliance* (Syracuse, NY: Syracuse University Press, 1969). The most comprehensive study of the peace negotiations is Richard B. Morris, *The Peacemakers: The Great Powers and American Independence* (New York: Harper and Row, 1965).

5 Particularly good in explaining Shelburne's intentions in the peace negotiations is Vincent T. Harlow, *The Foundation of the Second British Empire: Discovery and Revolution* (New York: Longmans, Green, 1952); also see Van Alstyne, *Empire and Independence*, 206–27.

6 See John Cannon, *The Fox–North Coalition: Crisis of the Constitution, 1782–84* (Cambridge: Cambridge University Press, 1969).

7 Spain still held Louisiana and had recaptured Florida during the war. The Spanish dominated much of the region south of the Ohio River, and the French proposals would have consolidated Spain's position in most of the Mississippi valley as well as along the whole coast of the Gulf of Mexico.

8 The seven forts along the border were Dutchman's Point and Pointe-au-Fer (commanding the northern portion of Lake Champlain), Oswegatchie (on the south bank of the St Lawrence River), Oswego (on the eastern end of Lake Ontario, commanding the Mohawk–Hudson River route into New York), Niagara (at the western end of Lake Ontario and on the east bank of

the Niagara River), Detroit (on the Detroit River), and Michilimackinac (on the Straits of Mackinac between Lake Huron and Lake Michigan). Also see Wright, *Britain and the American Frontier,* 15–49.

9 See Samuel Flagg Bemis, *Jay's Treaty: A Study in Commerce and Diplomacy* (New Haven, Conn.: Yale Univeristy Press, 1923); and Jerald A. Combs, *The Jay Treaty: Political Battleground of the Founding Fathers* (Berkeley: University of California Press, 1970).

10 See Governor John Parr to Sir Guy Carleton, 25 July and 15 Aug. 1783, in W.O. Raymond, ed., *The Winslow Papers* (Saint John: New Brunswick Historical Society, 1901), 110 and 123–33; John Hancock to John Parr, 12 Nov. 1784, John Parr to John Hancock, 7 Dec. 1784, and Thomas Carleton to John Hancock, 21 June 1785, in Mary A. Giunta, ed., *The Emerging Nation: A Documentary History of the Foreign Relations of the United States under the Articles of Confederation, 1780–1789* (Washington, DC: National Historical Publications and Records Commission, 1996), 2: 894–5 and 901; John Jay to Congress, 21 April 1785, and John Jay to John Adams, 3 Aug. 1785, in Manning, ed., *DCUSCR,* 1: 5–14; and W.S. MacNutt, *The Atlantic Provinces: The Emergence of Colonial Society, 1712–1857* (Toronto: McClelland and Stewart, 1965), 127–8. Also see James Hannay, *History of New Brunswick* (Saint John: John A. Bowes, 1909), 242–66; and Edgar Crosby Smith, 'Our Eastern Boundary; The St. Croix River Controversy,' in Louis Clinton Hatch, ed., *Maine: A History* (New York: American Historical Society, 1919), 1: 89–91.

11 George Washington to Congress, 9 and 18 Feb. 1790, and Report of a Committee to the United States Senate, 9 March 1790, in Manning, ed., *DCUSCR,* 1: 41–4. For observations on the first use of an arbitration commission in modern times, see John Bassett Moore, ed., *International Adjudications Ancient and Modern: Modern Series* (New York: Oxford University Press, 1929), 1: x. The Jay–Grenville Treaty also provided for two other mixed commissions to determine debts that antedated and debts that arose out of (Loyalist claims) the War of Independence. The claims of Massachusetts to the territory as far east as the Magaguadavic generated anxiety in Loyalist settlements such as St Andrews.

12 See 'Thomas Barclay,' in *DCB,* 6: 33–6; and also Lord Grenville to Thomas Barclay, March 1796, in George Lockhart Rives, ed., *Selections from the Correspondence of Thomas Barclay: Formerly British Consul General at New York* (New York: Harper & Brothers, 1894), 46–7. Phineas Bond, the British chargé d'affaires and consul in Philadelphia, had hoped for the appointment as British commissioner. See Joanne Loewe Neel, *Phineas Bond: A Study in Anglo-American Relations, 1786–1812* (Philadelphia: University of Pennsylvania Press, 1968), 143.

13 See 'David Howell,' in *DAB,* 9: 301; and 'Egbert Benson' in ibid., 2: 204. For a brief description of the Americans, see W.S. MacNutt, *New Brunswick, A His-*

tory: 1784–1867 (Toronto: Macmillan, 1963), 124–5. For the documents concerning the setting up of the commission and the preliminary meeting, see Moore, ed., *International Adjudications*, 1: 10–20.

14 John Bassett Moore, *History and Digest of the International Arbitrations to Which the United States Has Been a Party* (Washington, DC: Government Printing Office, 1898), 1: 7–15; and Thomas Barclay to Lord Grenville, 30 Aug. 1796, in Rives, ed., *Thomas Barclay*, 56–60.

15 See 'Ward Chipman, Sr.,' in *DCB*, 6: 135–44; Edward Grey, 'Ward Chipman, Loyalist,' *Massachusetts Historical Society Proceedings* 54 (1922), 331–53; and Duke of Kent to Thomas Carleton, 10 June 1796, in Raymond, ed., *Winslow Papers*, 421–2. Some in New Brunswick and Nova Scotia seem to have held that Barclay and Chipman had ties that were too close to the United States and that they were not to be trusted with local interests. MacNutt, *New Brunswick*, 125.

16 See 'James Sullivan,' in *DAB*, 18: 190–1.

17 Moore, *International Arbitrations*, 1: 40–59, and 2: 395–6. Also see 'Edward Winslow,' in *DCB*, 5: 865–9. Winslow wrote to a friend that the appointments rescued Chipman and himself from 'slipping into obscurity and despair,' following their resettlement in New Brunswick. He correctly predicted that the work would reflect so well on Chipman that he would be given higher responsibilities. Edward Winslow to Jonathan Sewall, 14 Jan. 1797, in Raymond, ed., *Winslow Papers*, 709–10.

18 Moore, ed., *International Adjudications*, 1: 40–53. For the best description of the work of the commission, see R.D. and J.I. Tallman, 'The Diplomatic Search for the St. Croix River, 1796–1798,' *Acadiensis* 1 (spring 1972), 59–71. Also see Henry S. Burrage, *Maine in the Northeastern Boundary Controversy* (Portland: Printed for the State, 1919), 42–67; and Bradford Perkins, *The First Rapprochement: England and the United States, 1795–1805* (Berkeley: University of California Press, 1967), 48–52. The British consul in Philadelphia was convinced that the American claim for the Magaguadavic River was based solely on the assertions in Sullivan's book. Phineas Bond to Thomas Barclay, 27 July 1796, in Rives, ed., *Thomas Barclay*, 52–4.

19 Moore, ed., *International Adjudications*, 1: 63–80; and L.F.S. Upton, *Micmacs and Colonists: Indian–White Relations in the Maritimes, 1713–1867* (Vancouver: University of British Columbia Press, 1979), 99–101. Also see John Jay to James Sullivan, 28 July 1797, in Henry P. Johnston, ed., *The Correspondence and Public Papers of John Jay* (1890; reprint, New York: Burt Franklin, 1970), 4: 228–9.

20 See Arguments of Mr. Sullivan, Mr. Sullivan's Rejoinder, Mr. Sullivan's Observations, and Mr. Sullivan's Remarks, including the depositions of Captain Nicholas Awawas, one of the Indians, in Moore, ed., *International Adjudica-*

tions, 1: 83–165, 335–513; 2: 149–219, 261–311, and 333–59. Because there was not time to make a complete survey of all the streams entering Passamaquoddy Bay, Sullivan agreed to accept the results of a British survey made in 1772 for several key areas. This led Barclay to regard Sullivan as a 'fool' because the survey favoured the British argument; he sent his 'congratulations' to Chipman. Col. Thomas Barclay to Ward Chipman, 4 May 1797, cited in Tallman and Tallman, 'The Diplomatic Search for the St. Croix River,' 68. Secretary of State Pickering thought Sullivan's arguments entirely convincing. See Timothy Pickering to James Sullivan, 15 April 1797, in Manning, ed., *DCUSCR*, 1: 103–7.

21 See Mr. Chipman's Statement, Mr. Chipman's Supplemental Argument, Mr. Chipman's Postscript, Mr. Chipman's Reply, and Deliberations on the Award, in Moore, ed., *International Adjudications*, 1: 169–330; 2: 3–145, 223–58, 315–29, and 359–73; and particularly Benson's report, in 2: 376–8.

22 See Tallman and Tallman, 'The Diplomatic Search for the St. Croix River, 68–70; and MacNutt, *The Atlantic Provinces*, 127. Chipman also received advice and suggestions from such people as William King, a former undersecretary for the American colonies and then colonial agent for New Brunswick, and Jonathan Odell, a New Jersey Loyalist and then provincial secretary for New Brunswick. William Knox to Ward Chipman, 2 Feb. 1797, and Jonathan Odell to Ward Chipman, 24 March 1798, in F-134–3 and 4, Ganong Collection, NBM. Barclay complained that Chipman was left to his own resources while Sullivan had assistance from an impressive staff. Thomas Barclay to Lord Grenville, 24 Oct. 1796, in Rives, ed., *Thomas Barclay*, 65–8.

23 Ward Chipman to Sir Thomas Carleton, 12 Aug. 1796, in F-134–7, Ganong Collection, NBM. For a skilful analysis of the two arguments, see David Demeritt, 'Representing the "True" St. Croix: Knowledge and Power in the Partition of the Northeast,' *William and Mary Quarterly*, 3rd series, 54 (July 1997), 515–48. Demeritt notes that Indians provided testimony to support the agent's arguments, whatever interests that the Indians themselves might have had were not a feature of the final settlement. Ibid., 545.

24 Sullivan was worried before the commissioners met that Benson would concede to the British everything up to the Penobscot River. See James Sullivan to Timothy Pickering, Secretary of State, 29 Sept. 1798, in Thomas C. Amory, *The Life of James Sullivan: With Selections from his Writings* (Boston: Phillips, Samson, 1858), 1: 329–31; and Chipman to Robert Liston, 23 Oct. 1798, in Rives, ed., *Thomas Barclay*, 87–9. The British consul in Philadelphia, Phineas Bond, turned over to Barclay and Chipman the valuable materials that he had collected on the question of which river might be the St Croix. Neel, *Phineas Bond*, 142–3.

25 Chipman to William Knox, 1 Dec. 1798, F-134-10, Ganong Collection, NBM; and Sullivan to Timothy Pickering, 25 Oct. 1798, Sullivan to Howell, 24 Oct. 1798, and Robert Liston to Chipman, 23 Oct. 1798, in Moore, ed., *International Adjudications*, 2: 367–71.

26 Chipman to Robert Liston, 23 Oct. 1798, and Robert Liston to Chipman, 23 Oct. 1798, in Rives, ed., *Thomas Barclay*, 87–90; Moore, *International Arbitrations*, 1: 27–8; and Henry S. Burrage, 'The St. Croix Commission, 1796–98,' *Maine Historical Society Collections* (1895), 241–51. The cost of the commission's work was not insignificant. Commissioners received £1,000 per year, and the final expenses by late 1798 came to U.S.$19,803.92, with more to be spent on surveying and marking the boundary. Moore, ed., *International Adjudications*, 2: 385–91.

27 Timothy Pickering to Sullivan, 30 Oct. 1798, in Manning, ed., *DCUSCR*, 2: 144.

28 Barclay to Lord Grenville, 10 Nov. 1798, in Rives, ed., *Thomas Barclay*, 90–4.

29 Sir John Wentworth to Winslow, 24 Dec. 1798, and Winslow to Edward G. Lutwyche, c. early 1799, in Raymond, ed., *Winslow Papers*, 434–6. Raymond, himself a student of the New Brunswick boundary question, observed that this comment by Winslow indicated agreement with Ward Chipman that the due-north line from the source of the St Croix River was then expected to extend north of the St John to reach the highlands indicated in the treaty of 1783; ibid. Whatever the implications of the due-north line, one historian of the St Croix River, Guy Murchie, concluded that Champlain's 1612 map of the region was perfectly clear, delineating the three major rivers, the settlement on St Croix Island (Dochet Island), and the tributaries of the Chiputneticook branch of the Schoodiac River in the shape of a cross. Guy Murchie, *Saint Croix: The Sentinel River* (New York: Duell, Sloan and Pearce, 1947), 172–4.

30 Amory, *James Sullivan*, 1: 325.

31 For a detailed analysis of the relationship of the fur trade, British strategy, and the western boundary, see Samuel Flagg Bemis, 'Jay's Treaty and the Northwest Boundary Gap,' *AHR* 27 (April 1922), 465–84.

32 Rufus King to James Madison, 13 May 1803, in Manning, ed., *DCUSCR*, 1: 555–8; and Perkins, *The First Rapprochement*, 142–4.

33 Rufus King to James Madison, 9 Dec. 1803, James Madison to James Monroe, 14 Feb. 1804, and James Monroe to James Madison, 3 June 1804, in Manning, ed., *DCUSCR*, 1: 562–3, 167–8, and 563–5; Alexander Winchell, 'Minnesota's Northern Boundary,' in *Minnesota Historical Society Collections*, 8 (1898), 193–9; and Perkins, *The First Rapprochement*, 144–9. On learning that Moose, Dudley, and Frederick islands were to be ceded to the United States,

the prominent Saint John Loyalist George Leonard led a protest. See George Leonard to the President of H.M. Council, 17 June 1806, George Leonard to Anthony Merry (British Minister to the United States), 20 Aug. 1806, and Winslow to Lord Sheffield, 28 Aug. 1806, in Raymond, *Winslow Papers*, 553–4, 557, and 562.

34 James Monroe and William Pinkney to James Madison, 3 Jan. and 25 April 1807, in Manning, ed., *DCUSCR*, 1: 585–98; and Winchell, 'Minnesota's Northern Boundary,' 193–9. The best discussion of these failed negotiations is found in A.L. Burt, *The United States, Great Britain and British North America: From the Revolution to the Establishment of Peace after the War of 1812* (New Haven, Conn.: Yale University Press, 1940), 185–206. The ambiguity about ownership of the islands in Passamaquoddy Bay encouraged a great deal of smuggling.

35 For a very useful account of these events, see Reginald Horsman, *Matthew Elliott, British Indian Agent* (Detroit: Wayne State University, 1964); and Reginald Horsman, 'British Indian Policy in the Northwest, 1807–1812, *MVHR* 45 (1958), 51–66. Also see Julius W. Pratt, *The Expansionists of 1812* (New York: Macmillan, 1925), 17–59; and Julius W. Pratt, 'Fur Trade Strategy and the American Left Flank in the War of 1812,' *AHR* 40 (Jan. 1935), 246–73.

36 Lord Liverpool to James Stephens, 24 March 1814, cited in Bradford Perkins, *Castlereagh and Adams: England and the United States, 1812–1823* (Berkeley: University of California Press, 1964), 65–6.

37 Lord Castlereagh to Secretary of State, 4 Nov. 1813, cited in Donald R. Hickey, *The War of 1812: A Forgotten Conflict* (Urbana: University of Illinois Press, 1989), 285.

38 Tentative suggestions for peace talks started almost as soon as the war began. However, the United States responded to the Russian invitation for mediation in 1813 by sending James A. Bayard and Albert Gallatin to St Petersburg to join the American minister there, John Quincy Adams. The British rejected the Russian offer, but the foreign secretary, Lord Castlereagh, wrote to President James Madison proposing talks in Gothenburg, Sweden. Madison responded positively and sent Henry Clay and Jonathan Russell to join them. In the meantime France was defeated, Napoleon abdicated, and the war in Europe ended. With peace in Europe, however fragile, the talks shifted to Ghent, which was more convenient than Gothenburg.

39 See 'John Quincy Adams,' in *DAB*, 1: 84–93; and Samuel Flagg Bemis, *John Quincy Adams and the Foundations of American Foreign Policy* (New York: Alfred A. Knopf, 1950), 196–220.

40 See 'Albert Gallatin,' in *DAB*, 7: 103–9; and Raymond Walters, Jr, *Albert Gallatin: Jeffersonian Financier and Diplomat* (New York: Macmillan, 1957), 13 and

276–88. Gallatin's original appointment was turned down by the Senate because he was then still officially secretary of the treasury. However, Madison resubmitted his name when talks were arranged in Ghent, and the second appointment was confirmed.

41 See 'James A. Bayard,' in *DAB*, 2: 64–6.

42 See 'Henry Clay,' in ibid., 4: 173–9; and Robert V. Remini, *Henry Clay: Statesman for the Union* (New York: W.W. Norton, 1991), 94–122. The first three commissioners had been authorized to open talks under the invitation of the tsar of Russia. Clay and Russell were added to the delegation when Castlereagh approached Madison about talks in Gothenburg and later Ghent.

43 See 'Jonathan Russell,' in *DAB*, 16: 245. Russell served as minister to Sweden and Norway from 1814 to 1818 but returned home to the United States. He was elected to Congress in 1820 and became a bitter critic of John Quincy Adams. To discredit Adams among western Americans he published letters from Adams on the Mississippi question at Ghent. Adams obtained copies of the original letters from the State Department and showed that Russell had fabricated serious changes in the text. Russell's credibility was completely destroyed as a result.

44 See 'James Lord Gambier,' in *DNB*, 20: 393–5.

45 See 'Henry Goulburn,' in ibid., 22: 283–4; and Brian Jenkins, *Henry Goulburn, 1784–1856: A Political Biography* (Montreal: McGill-Queen's University Press, 1996), 56–81. Goulburn had focused on colonial affairs as undersecretary while his chief was devoted to the war effort. This meant that Goulburn was particularly well informed about British North America, as well as committed to a favourable peace treaty.

46 See 'William Adams,' in *DNB*, 1: 109.

47 Several useful discussions of the peace negotiations at Ghent are Frank A. Updyke, *The Diplomacy of the War of 1812* (Baltimore: Johns Hopkins University Press, 1915), Fred L. Engelman, *The Peace of Christmas Eve* (London: Rupert Hart-Davis, 1962), Perkins, *Castlereagh and Adams*, and Hickey, *The War of 1812*. A Canadian perspective can be obtained from Pierre Berton, *Flames across the Border, 1813–1814* (Toronto: McClelland and Stewart, 1981), 401–19.

48 Commissioners Extraordinary and Plenipotentiary of the United States for treating of peace with Great Britain, to the Secretary of State, 12 Aug. 1814, and Protocols of Conferences held with the British Commissioners, 8 and 9 Aug. 1914, in *American State Papers, Foreign Relations* (Washington, DC: Gales and Seaton, 1832), 3: 70–9; and Castlereagh to His Majesty's Commissioners appointed to negotiate at Ghent, 28 July 1814, in Charles W. Vane, Marquess of Londonderry, ed., *Correspondence, Despatches, and Other Papers, of Viscount*

Castlereagh, Second Marquess of Londonderry (London: William Shoberl, 1852),
10: 67–72. On 19 August the British said that they would accept the line of
the Treaty of Greenville (1794) through Ohio from Lake Erie to the Ohio
River as the eastern boundary of the Indian state. Lord Gambier, Henry
Goulburn, and William Adams to the United States Ministers, 19 Aug. 1814,
in Manning, ed., *DCUSCR*, 1: 632–40. British determination to control the
region from the Appalachian Mountains to the Mississippi River and from
the Great Lakes to the Gulf of Mexico surfaced repeatedly in the years from
1763 to 1815 and can be seen in the military operations in the northwest and
at New Orleans. See Wright, *Britain and the American Frontier 1783–1815*,
passim; Charles M. Gates, 'The West in American Diplomacy, 1812–1815,'
MVHR 26 (1939–40), 499–510; and Pratt, 'The American Left Flank in 1812,'
246–73.
49 Adams later commented that the British demands were 'arrogant, overbearing, and offensive' and that the Americans had been weak and ineffective;
Diary, Friday, 19 Aug. 1814, and Wed., 12 Oct. 1814, in Charles Francis
Adams, ed., *Memoirs of John Quincy Adams* (1874–7; reprint, New York: AMS
Press, 1970), 3: 20 and 51.
50 Adams to James Monroe, 5 Sept. 1815, in Manning, ed., *DCUSCR*, 1: 647–52;
Friday, 19 Aug. 1814, in Adams, ed., *Memoirs of John Quincy Adams*, 3: 19.
Hickey estimates that there were over 100,000 white settlers and about
20,000 Indians in the territory. He also concluded that the amount of territory involved was about 250,000 square miles and 15 per cent of the United
States, not the 30 per cent claimed by the American commissioners. Hickey,
The War of 1812, 290.
51 Adams, James A. Bayard, Henry Clay, Jonathan Russell, and Albert Gallatin,
to the British Ministers, 24 Aug. 1814, in Manning, ed., *DCUSCR*, 1: 636–41.
52 Albert Gallatin to James Monroe, 20 Aug. 1814, in ibid., 1: 634–6; and Goulburn to Castlereagh, 26 Aug. 1814, in Arthur R. Wellesley, Duke of Wellington, ed., *Supplementary Despatches, Correspondence and Memoranda of Field
Marshal Arthur Duke of Wellington, K.G.* (London: John Murray, 1862), 9: 193–
4. Clay wrote privately to James Monroe, 'The prospect of peace has van-
ished,' and he asked Goulburn to prepare his passport a few days later. Clay
to Monroe, 19 Aug. 1814, in James F. Hopkins and Mary W.M. Hargreaves,
eds., *Papers of Henry Clay* (Lexington: University of Kentucky Press, 1959), 1:
968. On 27 August, Adams talked to the other American commissioners
about returning to St Petersburg. Diary, Saturday, 27 Aug. 1814, in Adams,
ed., *Memoirs of John Quincy Adams*, 3: 23. Bayard was convinced that the
ground work was being 'laid of a protracted war.' Bayard to Levett Harris, 28
Aug. 1814, in Elizabeth Donnan, ed., *Papers of James A. Bayard, American His-*

torical Association, Annual Report, 1913 (Washington, DC: Government Printing Office, 1915), 2: 327.

53 Lord Gambier, Henry Goulburn, and William Adams to the United States Ministers, 4 Sept. 1814, and John Quincy Adams to James Monroe, 5 Sept. 1814, in Manning, ed., *DCUSCR*, 1: 647–52. The British commissioners said privately to the Americans, 'their only objective to be security to Canada.' Memorandum of Conferences, Saturday, 27 Sept. 1814, in Donnan, ed., *Papers of James A. Bayard*, 338.

54 John Quincy Adams, James A. Bayard, Henry Clay, and Albert Gallatin, to the British Ministers, 9 Sept. 1814, in Manning, ed., *DCUSCR*, 1: 653–9. Although the original instructions to the American commissioners on 23 June 1813 and 28 January 1814 urged the acquisition of Canada, the American delegation, having not yet had an opportunity to state its own peace demands, had not revealed that the annexation of Canada had been encouraged by the American government. James Monroe to Albert Gallatin, John Quincy Adams, and James A. Bayard, 23 June 1813, and James Monroe to John Quincy Adams, James A. Bayard, Henry Clay, and Jonathan Russell, 28 Jan. 1814, in ibid., 213 and 217. Also see Perkins, *Castlereagh and Adams*, 111–15.

55 For the quotation, see Lord Gambier, Henry Goulburn, and William Adams to the United States Ministers, 19 Sept. 1814, in Manning, ed., *DCUSCR*, 1: 660–3. Also see Jenkins, *Henry Goulburn*, 85–6.

56 John Quincy Adams, James A. Bayard, Henry Clay, Jonathan Russell, and Albert Gallatin, to the British Ministers, 25 Sept. 1814, Lord Gambier, Henry Goulburn, and William Adams, to the American Ministers, 8 Oct. 1814, and John Quincy Adams, James A. Bayard, Henry Clay, Jonathan Russell, and Albert Gallatin, to the British Ministers, 13 Oct. 1814, in Manning, ed., *DCUSCR*, 1: 663–78; and Lord Bathurst to the Commissioners at Ghent, 5 Oct. 1814, in Vane, ed., *Correspondence ... of Viscount Castlereagh*, 10: 148–9. Also see Engelman, *Peace of Christmas Eve*, 186–8.

57 Lord Gambier, Henry Goulburn, and William Adams, to the United States Ministers, 21 Oct. 1814, in Manning, ed., *DCUSCR*, 1: 681–4; and Lord Bathurst to the Commissioners at Ghent, 18 Oct. 1814, in Vane, ed., *Correspondence ... of Viscount Castlereagh*, 10: 168–70. Clay was convinced that the British would abandon *uti possidetis* also but would hold firm on the islands in Passamaquoddy Bay and the route to Quebec. See Clay to Monroe, 26 Oct. 1814, in Hopkins and Hargreaves, eds., *Papers of Henry Clay*, 1: 995.

58 Col. Sir H. Torrens to General Sir George Murray, 14 April 1814, in Wellesley, ed., *Supplementary Despatches*, 9: 58.

59 Liverpool to Castlereagh, 4 Nov. 1814, and Liverpool to Wellington, 13 Nov.

1814, in Charles Duke Younge, *The Life and Administration of Robert Banks, Second Earl of Liverpool, K.G.* (London: Macmillan, 1868), 3: 58–62; and Wellington to Liverpool, 9 and 18 Nov. 1814, in Wellesley, ed., *Supplementary Despatches*, 9: 424–6 and 435–7. Wellington confided to a fellow officer, 'I have told the Ministers repeatedly that naval superiority on the lakes is a sine qua non of success in war on the frontier of Canada, even if our object should be solely defensive.' Wellington to Lt. Gen. Sir George Murray, 22 Dec. 1814, in Lt. Col. Gurwood, ed., *The Despatches of Field Marshal the Duke of Wellington* (London: John Murray, 1838), 12: 224. Also see Dudley Mills, 'The Duke of Wellington and the Peace Negotiations at Ghent in 1814,' *CHR* 2 (March 1921), 19–32. Goulburn observed to Bathurst, 'If we had either burnt Baltimore or held Plattsburg, I believe we should have had peace on the terms which you have sent to us in a month at latest. As things appear to be going in America, the result of our negotiation may be very different.' Goulburn to Lord Bathurst, 21 Oct. 1814, in Wellesley, ed., *Supplementary Despatches*, 9: 366.

60 Perkins, *Castlereagh and Adams*, 69 and 91. As early as 28 August, Castlereagh questioned making an issue over territory. 'The substance of the question is, are we prepared to continue the war for territorial arrangements; and , if not, is this the best time to make our peace.' Castlereagh to Liverpool, 28 Aug. 1814, in Vane, ed., *Correspondence ... of Viscount Castlereagh*, 10: 100–2. Several historians have concluded that the British commissioners took the instructions from Liverpool and Castlereagh in too literal a sense and thus presented a much more demanding position at the opening stages of the talks. See Perkins, *Castlereagh and Adams*, 67–99; and C.T. Bartlett, *Castlereagh* (New York: Charles Scribner's Sons, 1966), 236–8. However, the British continued military operations as late as November, December, and January in Spanish Florida and New Orleans, with the hope, Wright has argued, of detaching New Orleans and Louisiana and the entire west bank of the Mississippi River and linking up with Lord Selkirk's settlers along the Red River, south of Lake Winnipeg – all of this notwithstanding the terms of the Treaty of Ghent. Wright, *Britain and the North American Frontier*, 175–85.

61 John Quincy Adams, James A. Bayard, Henry Clay, Jonathan Russell, and Albert Gallatin, to the British Ministers, 10 Nov. 1814, and Projet of Treaty of Peace submitted by the United States Ministers to the British Ministers at Ghent, with the alterations proposed by the British Ministers, in Manning, ed., *DCUSCR*, 1: 686–700; and Perkins, *Castlereagh and Adams*, 123–6. Adams noted on the British reception of the *projet*, 'All the difficulties to the conclusion of a peace appear to be now so nearly removed, that my colleagues all consider it certain. I think it myself probable.' Diary, Sunday, 27 Nov. 1814,

in Adams, ed., *Memoirs of John Quincy Adams*, 3: 70. Lord Liverpool outlined numerous of Britain's problems to Castlereagh and then concluded, 'Under such circumstances it has appeared to us desirable to bring the American war, if possible, to a conclusion.' Liverpool to Castlereagh, 18 Nov. 1814, in Younge, *Life of Lord Liverpool*, 2: 72–3.

62 Adams et al. to the British Ministers, 10 Nov. 1814, and Projet of Treaty, in Manning, ed., *DCUSCR*, 1: 686–700. The British, by insisting on a two-person instead of the three-person commission, had in legal terms substituted a joint commission for a mixed commission. For a brief discussion, see Diary, Thursday, 1 Dec. 1814, in Adams, ed., *Memoirs of John Quincy Adams*, 3: 83.

63 For the definitive text of the Treaty of Ghent, see Miller, ed., *Treaties*, 2: 574–84.

64 John Quincy Adams, James A. Bayard, Henry Clay, Jonathan Russell, and Albert Gallatin, to James Monroe, 25 Dec. 1814, in Manning, ed., *DCUSCR*, 1: 705–8; Diary, Saturday, 24 Dec. 1814, in Adams, ed., *Memoirs of John Quincy Adams*, 3: 126. Although Adams had a few days earlier agreed with Clay that 'the peace would be bad enough,' on the day of the signing he gave thanks that the treaty had been completed and prayed that it would be for the best interests of the United States. Sunday, 11 Dec., and Monday, 24 Dec. 1814, ibid., 104 and 127. Bayard wrote to his cousin that the treaty was 'as favorable as could be expected under existing circumstances.' Bayard to Andrew Bayard, 24 Dec. 1814, in Donnan, ed., *Papers of James A. Bayard*, 364. Clay commented to Monroe in lukewarm fashion that the treaty 'cannot be pronounced very unfavorable. We lose no territory, I think no honor.' Clay to Monroe, 25 Dec. 1814, in Hopkins and Hargreaves, eds., *Papers of Henry Clay*, 1: 1007.

Chapter 2. Article 4: Islands in the Bay

1 Holmes to Monroe, 20 Oct. 1816, Box 3, Northeastern Boundary, RG 76, NA.

2 Chipman himself expressed the same concern about the Americans and seemed to conclude that it was unlikely that the commission would reach an agreement. Even before the commissioners met, he warned that 'our efforts must therefore be principally directed to the making of such a statement of the grounds of our rights, as may secure a favorable decision of the umpire to whom the questions respecting them will probably be ultimately referred.' Wentworth to Chipman, 28 Feb. 1816, and Chipman to Wentworth, 18 March 1816, F-24-11, Hazen Collection, Chipman Papers, NBM.

3 See 'John Holmes' in *DAB*, 5: 166–7.

4 See 'James T. Austin' in ibid., 1: 433–4.

5 Lord Bathurst to Barclay, 25 June 1815, FO 5/108, PRO; and Lord Castlereagh to Thomas Barclay, 4 Sept. 1815, in Rives, ed., *Thomas Barclay*, 356 and 365–9.

6 Holmes to Richard Rush, Acting Secretary of State, 20 Oct. 1817, in *British and Foreign State Papers, 1816–1817* (London: James Ridgway and Sons, 1838), 4: 805–6.

7 Cited in Moore, *International Arbitrations*, 1: 52. For preliminary activity, see Rives, ed., *Thomas Barclay*, 356.

8 Journal of the Commission under the Fourth Article of the Treaty of Ghent, 23 and 24 Sept. 1816, Northeastern Boundary, RG 76, NA; and Moore, *International Arbitrations*, 1: 53. Ward Chipman thought highly of his son, who graduated from Harvard in 1805 and was admitted to the New Brunswick bar in 1808. 'He is mild and I think gentlemanlike in his manner and deportment, very industrious, but ambitious to understand and to excel in whatever he undertakes,' the father wrote to his friend Edward Winslow. 'Should he hereafter have a field for exertion I doubt not he will do well.' The young man did not disappoint his father. Raymond, ed., *Winslow Papers*, 542.

9 Journal of ... the Fourth Article, 24 Sept. 1816, Northeastern Boundary, RG 76, NA.

10 Moore, *International Arbitrations*, 1: 58–9.

11 Chipman to Sir ..., 18 March 1816, Chipman Papers, MG 23 D 1, NAC.

12 Miller, ed., *Treaties*, 2: 151.

13 Moore, *International Arbitration*, 1: 50.

14 Barclay to Castlereagh, 10 Aug. 1816, in Rives, ed., *Thomas Barclay*, 371.

15 Moore, *International Arbitrations*, 1: 51.

16 Barclay to Castlereagh, 12 Aug. 1816, FO 5/116, PRO; Castlereagh to Barclay, 1 Jan. 1817, and Barclay to William Hamilton, 11 Jan. 1818, FO 5/125, PRO.

17 Austin to Monroe, 8 Feb. 1817, Box 3, Northeastern Boundary, RG 76, NA. Also see Edgar Crosby Smith, 'Our Eastern Boundary; The St. Croix River Controversy,' in Hatch, ed., *Maine, A History*, 1: 100–2.

18 Barclay to Castlereagh, 5 June 1817, FO 5/125, PRO.

19 Journal of ... Fourth Article, 9–12 June 1817, Northeastern Boundary, RG 76, NA.

20 Barclay to Castlereagh, 5 June 1817, FO 5/125, PRO.

21 Austin to Adams, 22 Sept. 1817, Box 3, Northeastern Boundary, RG 76, NA.

22 Holmes to Richard Rush, Acting Secretary of State, 26 June and 27 Aug. 1817, Box 3, Northeastern Boundary, RG 76, NA. Barclay informed Charles Bagot, British minister to the United States, of Holmes's situation. Bagot felt

that there was nothing that he could properly say to the secretary of state, but he noted that if he learned that instructions had been sent to the American agent to bring the arguments to a speedy conclusion he would give similar advice to the British agent. Bagot commented, 'It is much to be wished that you & Mr. Holmes should conclude the business, & that the delay necessarily attending the appointment of a New Commissioner should if possible be avoided.' Bagot to Barclay, 10 Sept. 1817, Vol. 17, Bagot Papers, MG 24 A 13, NAC. Adams did send such instructions to Austin on 29 Sept., but without Bagot's knowledge. Adams to Austin, 29 Sept. 1817, Domestic Letters, M 40 (roll 15), RG 59, NA.

23 Journal of ... Fourth Article, 25–30 Sept. and 1–8 Oct. 1817, Northeastern Boundary, RG 76, NA; and Austin to Adams, 22 Sept. 1817, Box 3, ibid.

24 Holmes to Adams, 2 Oct. 1817, and Austin to Adams, 2 and 3 Oct. 1817, Box 3, ibid. Also see Adams to Austin, 29 Sept. 1817, Domestic Letters, M 40 (roll 15), RG 59, NA. Bagot was a well-placed young diplomat, related by marriage to the Wellesleys and a protégé of George Canning's. He was remarkably successful in establishing good relations with the Americans after the War of 1812, and he was rewarded with a knighthood on his return to England in 1819. Bagot's diplomatic career was further involved with the boundary question while he served as British ambassador to the Netherlands during the attempted arbitration and as governor general of British North America during the Webster–Ashburton negotiations. See William H. Masterson, *Tories and Democrats: British Diplomats in Pre-Jacksonian America* (College Station: Texas A&M University Press, 1985), 171–95.

25 Barclay to Castlereagh, 25 Oct. 1817, FO 5/125, PRO; and Rives, ed., *Thomas Barclay*, 388–95.

26 ibid.

27 Austin to Adams, 11 Oct. 1817, Box 3, Northeastern Boundary, RG 76, NA.

28 Holmes to Adams, 14 Oct. 1817, ibid.

29 Barclay and Holmes to Castlereagh, 24 Nov. 1817, and Castlereagh to Barclay, 13 Jan. 1818, FO 5/125, PRO; Holmes to Adams, 24 Nov. 1817, Box 3, Northeastern Boundary, RG 76, NA; and Annual Message to Congress, 2 Dec. 1817, in James D. Richardson, ed., *A Compilation of the Messages and Papers of the Presidents* (New York: Bureau of National Literature, 1897), 2: 581. Also see *American State Papers: Foreign Relations*, 4: 171. Bagot wrote to Barclay that he thought the settlement 'completely satisfactory.' Bagot to Barclay, 6 Dec. 1817, Vol. 12, Bagot Papers, MG 24 A 13, NAC.

30 Boston, *Gazette*, 1 Dec. 1817, p. 1.

31 Adams to Bagot, 6 Dec. 1817, Notes to Foreign Ministers in the U.S., M 38 (roll 2), RG 59, NA; Bagot to Lt. Gen. Sir John Sherbrooke and Lord Dal-

housie, 9 Dec. 1817, and Charles Bagot to Sherbrooke, 13 May 1818, Vol. 1, Bagot Papers, MG 24 A 13, NAC; Bagot to Adams, 25 May 1818, Box 3, Northeastern Boundary, RG 76, NA; and John Rurgins and forty-two citizens of Eastport to Captain R. Gibbons, 27 June 1818, CB. DOC., NBM.

32 Wentworth to Chipman, 28 Feb. 1816, and Chipman to Wentworth, 18 March 1816, Chipman Papers, MG 23 D 1, NAC. See 'Sir John Wentworth' in *DCB*, 5: 848–51.

33 William F. Ganong, 'A Monograph of the Evolution of the Boundaries of the Province of New Brunswick,' in *Transactions of the Royal Society of Canada*, Second Series, 7 (May 1901), Section II, 294–5.

34 Burt, *United States, Great Britain and British North America*, 423.

35 Barclay to Castlereagh, 25 Oct. 1817, FO 5/125, PRO; and Ganong, 'Boundaries,' 295. For comments on the difficulties of this decision, see James B. Stephens, *Boundary Making: A Handbook for Statesmen, Treaty Editors, and Boundary Commissioners* (Washington, DC: Carnegie Endowment for International Peace, 1945), 144–5.

Chapter 3. Article 5: Highlands and the Source of the St Croix

1 Rev. William O. Raymond, *The River St. John: Its Physical Features, Legends and History from 1604 to 1784* (1910: reprint, Sackville: *Tribune Press*, 1943), 1–5; and Richard W. Judd, *Aroostook: A Century of Logging in Northern Maine* (Orono: University of Maine Press, 1989), 1–3 and 15.

2 See 'Cornelius P. Van Ness' in *National Cyclopedia of American Biography*, 8: 316. Although he was popular as governor, fortune turned against him when he sought a seat in the U.S. Senate. Embittered by this defeat, he moved to New York City, broke with John Quincy Adams, and supported Andrew Jackson. For his loyalty to Jackson he was made U.S. minister to Spain. Some years later President John Tyler gave him the plum patronage appointment of collector of customs for the Port of New York.

3 See 'William C. Bradley' in *DAB*, 1: 576. Commissioner Holmes had suggested to James Monroe that Colonel Austin would like to be appointed agent for the commission under the fifth article, as well as agent under the fourth. Nothing more was heard of this suggestion. Holmes to Monroe, 20 Oct. 1816, Box 3, Northeast Boundary, RG 79, NA. The British minister reported to the Foreign Office that Bradley was 'one of the ablest topographical engineers in the country.' Bagot to Edward Cooke, 10 March 1817, FO 5/125, PRO.

4 Two of Bouchette's books were relevant to the work of the commissions and make his appointment as surveyor logical. They were *A topographical descrip-*

tion of the province of Lower Canada, with remarks upon Upper Canada, and on the relative connection of both provinces with the United States of America (London: W. Faden, 1815) and The British dominions in North America; or a topographical description of the provinces of Lower and Upper Canada ... (London: Longman, Rees, Orme, Brown, and Green, 1832), 2 vols. See 'Joseph Bouchette' in DCB, 7: 95–8.

5 'John Johnson' in National Cyclopedia of American Biography, 17: 290–1; Abby Maria Hemenway, 'John Johnson,' Vermont Historical Magazine 1 (1867), 596–9; and Colin Campbell to William F. Odell, 29 July 1843, F-32-16, Odell Collection, NBM.

6 Barclay to Castlereagh, 2 and 25 June 1817, FO 5/125, PRO; and Journal of ... the Fifth Article, 4–11 June 1817, FO 303/8, PRO.

7 Journal of ... the Fifth Article, 11 June 1817, FO 303/8, PRO; and Instructions to the Surveyors of the U.S. Northern Boundary Line, c. June 1817, U.S. Treaty Series, RG 76, NA.

8 Instructions to Surveyors, n.d., c. June 1817, NE Boundary Papers II, Mass HS.

9 Journal of Colin Campbell, 10 July 1817, Box 6, ibid.

10 Colin Campbell to Ward Chipman, 20 May 1820, Box 2, ibid.; William C. Bradley, expenses, 1819, Box 3, ibid.; and William C. Bradley to John Quincy Adams, 18 Jan. 1819, U.S. Treaty Series, RG 76, NA.

11 Joseph Bouchette, Report to Commissioners under the Fifth Article of the Treaty of Ghent, 21 May 1818, and John Johnson to W.C. Bradley, Agent in the part of the United States under the Fifth Article of the Treaty of Ghent, 22 May 1818, Vol. 55, Boundary Commission, MG 23 D 1, NAC.

12 'S.T.' referred to Samuel Titcomb, a surveyor in 1797 who marked the source of the St Croix River. Journal of Colin Campbell, 31 July 1817, Box 7, NE Boundary Papers II, Mass HS; and Field Book of Joseph Bouchette [31 July 1817], A-266, Odell Collection, NBM.

13 Journal of Colin Campbell, 30 July 1817, Box 7, NE Boundary Papers II, Mass HS.

14 Bouchette, Report, 21 May 1818, and Johnson to Bradley, 22 May 1818, Vol. 55, Boundary Commission, MG 23 D1, NAC.

15 Field Book of Joseph Bouchette, 2 Aug. 1817, A-266, Odell Collection, NBM; and Bouchette, Report, 21 May 1818, and Johnson to Bradley, 22 May 1818, Vol. 55, Boundary Commission, MG 23 D 1, NAC.

16 Cairnes to Ward Chipman, Jr., 4 Aug. 1817, Vol. 52, Boundary Commission, MG 23 D 1, NAC.

17 Bouchette to Chipman, 20 July and 4 Aug. 1817, ibid.

18 Unfortunately Cairnes was wrong about the likelihood of the Americans'

producing memoirs about their explorations. No American diaries or memoirs of these surveys exist. Cairnes to Ward Chipman, Jr., 4 Aug. and 14 Sept. 1817, ibid.

19 Cairnes to Ward Chipman, Jr., 14 Sept. 1817, ibid.

20 Cairnes to Ward Chipman, Jr., 18 and 28 Aug. 1817, ibid.

21 Journal of Colin Campbell, 12 Aug. 1817, Box 7, NE Boundary Papers II, Mass HS.

22 Journal of ... the Fifth Article, 21 May 1818, FO 303/8, PRO.

23 Bouchette, Report, 21 May 1818, and Johnson to Bradley, 22 May 1818, Vol. 55, Boundary Commission, MG 23, D 1, NAC.

24 Peter Fisher, *The First History of New Brunswick* (1825; reprint, Woodstock: Larsen's Printing, 1980), 40–1.

25 Montgomery Cairns to Ward Chipman, Jr., 25 Sept. 1817, Vol. 52, Boundary Commission, MG 23 D 1, NAC.

26 Bouchette, Report, 21 May 1818, and Johnson to Bradley, 22 May 1818, Vol. 55, Boundary Commission, MG 23 D 1, NAC.

27 Bouchette to Chipman, 11 Oct. 1817, Vol. 52, Boundary Commission, MG 23 D 1, NAC.

28 The passage in curved brackets was in a footnote in the original letter. Cairnes to Ward Chipman, Jr., 25 Sept. 1817, ibid.

29 Bouchette to Chipman, 11 Oct. 1817, ibid.

30 Barclay to Chipman, 8 Nov. 1817, F-32-1, Odell Collection, NBM; and Rives, ed., *Thomas Barclay*, 396.

31 Barclay to Chipman, 6 Dec. 1817, in Rives, ed., *Thomas Barclay*, 398–9.

32 Barclay to Castlereagh, 1 Jan. 1818, FO 5/136, PRO. The version of this letter published by Rives is significantly stronger. The key sentence reads, 'It appears they both [Bouchette and Johnson] consider this Stream to comport with the description of the second Article of the Treaty of 1783.' Very probably this text contains Barclay's original draft and the letter actually sent to Castlereagh a less assertively phrased reconsideration. Rives, ed., *Thomas Barclay*, 400.

33 Barclay and Van Ness, Agreement of Commission regarding meeting, 27 March 1818, Box 6, NE Boundary Papers II, Mass HS.

34 Barclay to J.P. Morier, 14 June 1815, FO 5/111, and Barclay to Castlereagh, 28 Oct. 1816, FO 5/116, PRO; Barclay to Chipman, 8 Nov. 1817, F-32-1, Odell Collection, NBM; and Henry Goulburn to Barclay, 14 March 1817, in Rives, ed., *Thomas Barclay*, 374.

35 See Barclay to J.P. Morier, 14 June 1815, FO 5/111, PRO. Bouchette, though passionately pro-British, was a French Canadian and perhaps did not fit in

with the English, Loyalist, New Brunswick and Nova Scotia group that made up both the British commission staff and the surveying party.

36 MacNutt, *New Brunswick, A History*, 209; and Burrage, *Maine in the Northeastern Boundary Controversy*, 101–2. Colin Campbell had first used the expression 'gulled,' to describe Bouchette's views on the boundary line north of the St John River, in a letter to William Odell in 1843. See Campbell to Odell, 29 July 1843, F-32-16, Odell Collection, NBM.

37 In 1815 Bouchette had described the southern boundary of Lower Canada: a 'ridge generally denominated the Land's Height, dividing the waters that fall into the Saint Lawrence from those taking a direction towards the Atlantic ocean, and along whose summit is supposed to run the boundary line between the territories of Great Britain and the United States of America. This chain commences upon the eastern branch of the Connecticut river, takes a north-easterly course, and terminates near Cape Rosier in the gulf of Saint Lawrence.' Bouchette, *A Topographical Description of the Province of Lower Canada*, 25–6.

38 Barclay to Castlereagh, 1 Jan. 1818, F-32-1, Odell Collection, NBM; and Rives, ed., *Thomas Barclay*, 400–2. Several years later Bouchette changed his mind. He wrote in his capacity as surveyor general of Quebec to the lieutenant-governor of Lower Canada that the American claims in and north of the St John River valley were inflated and wrong, and he agreed with the view of the British agent that the ridge extending from the Chaudière River in the west to Mars Hill in the east constituted the boundary intended in the treaty of 1783. See 'Report No. 1, 24 Dec. 1821, from Joseph Bouchette, Surveyor General of Quebec, to Colonel John Ready, Civil Secretary, regarding the boundary dispute with the United States,' New Brunswick Boundary Disputes: Reports, Publications, RS 915, F 13746, Provincial Archives of New Brunswick (hereafter PANB), Fredericton.

39 See 'William F. Odell' in *DCB*, 7: 657–9.

40 Odell to Chipman, 3 Feb. 1818, and Lord Bathurst to Lieutenant Governor George S. Smyth, 26 Feb. 1818, F-32-3, Odell Collection, NBM.

41 Ward Chipman, Agent, Memorial respecting the survey, 23 May 1818, Box 6, NE Boundary II, Mass HS.

42 Chipman to Goulburn, 27 March 1818, Vol. 53, Boundary Commission, MG 23 D 1, NAC.

43 William C. Bradley, Agent, Memorial respecting the survey, 23 May 1818, Box 6, NE Boundary II, Mass HS; and Journal of ... the Fifth Article, 23 May 1818, FO 303/8. PRO.

44 Barclay to Castlereagh, 23 May 1818, FO 5/136, PRO. Barclay also concluded

in May 1818 that the Americans were prepared, because of the expense of the commissions, to negotiate a more convenient boundary. This of course did not materialize. Barclay to Chipman, 19 May 1818, F-134-6, Ganong Collection, NBM.

45 Journal of Colin Campbell, 17–18 and 21–29 June 1818, Vol. 31, Boundary Commission I, MG 23 D 1, NAC; and Barclay to Castlereagh, 5 June 1817, in Rives, ed., *Thomas Barclay*, 378–80.

46 William F. Odell, Report of work for 1818, Vol. 55, Boundary Commission, MG 23, D 1, NAC.

47 Ibid.; and James White, 'Boundary Disputes and Treaties,' in Adam Short and Arthur G. Doughty, eds., *Canada and Its Provinces* (Toronto: Glasgow, Brook, 1914), 8: 787.

48 Colin Campbell, Report, 1 Nov. 1818, Vol. 55, Boundary Commission, MG 23 D 1, NAC.

49 William F. Odell, Report of work for 1818, ibid.

50 John Johnson, in Appendix 56, *Statement of the United States, of the case referred, in pursuance of the Convention of 29th Sept., 1827, Between the Said United States and Great Britain, to His Majesty, The King of the Netherlands, For His Decision Thereon* (Washington, DC: printed but not published at the Office of the United States Telegraph, 1829), *Evidence*, 407–10 (hereafter *North-East Boundary, Evidence*).

51 William F. Odell, Report of work for 1818, Vol. 55, Boundary Commission, MG 23 D1, NAC.

52 John Johnson, in Appendix 56, *North-East Boundary, Evidence*, 409–10.

53 Chipman to Barclay, 28 Dec. 1818, FO 5/145, PRO.

54 Journal of ... the Fifth Article, 3–25 May 1819, NE Boundary Papers II, Mass HS.

55 Odell to Ward Chipman, Jr., 25 July 1819, F-32-4, Odell Collection, NBM.

56 William F. Odell, Report to Commissioners, n.d., Vol. 53, Boundary Commission, MG 23 D1, NAC.

57 Colin Campbell, Report, May 1820, Vol. 54, Boundary Commission, MG 23 D 1, NAC; and Colin Campbell in Appendix 56, *North-East Boundary, Evidence*, 412.

58 Alden Partridge, in Appendix 56, *North-East Boundary, Evidence*, 413.

59 Barclay to Castlereagh, 12 June 1820, FO 5/153, PRO.

60 Odell Journal, 1–15 July 1820, F-34-2, Odell Collection, NBM.

61 N.H. Loring, in Appendix 56, *North-East Boundary, Evidence*, 416–17 and 423.

62 See Appendix 56, ibid., 417–22; and Odell Journal, 2–30 Sept. 1820, F-34-2, Odell Collection, NBM.

63 See Appendix 56, *North-East Boundary, Evidence*, 417–21; and Odell Journal, 2–11 Oct. 1820, F-34-2, Odell Collection, NBM.

64 Journal of ... the Fifth Article, 25 Nov. 1820, FO 303/8, PRO.

65 Ibid., 14 May–9 June 1821.

Chapter 4. Article 5: The Forty-Fifth Parallel, the Connecticut, and Deadlock

1 For an account of the 1770s survey of the Quebec–New York border, see Don W. Thomson, *Men and Meridians: The History of Surveying and Mapping in Canada* (Ottawa: Queen's Printer, 1966), 1: 252.

2 Barclay to Castlereagh, 5 June 1817, FO 5/125, PRO.

3 John Ogilvy to Thompson, 18 Jan. 1817, Box 31, Northern Boundary, RG 76, NA.

4 Van Ness to Monroe, 14 Feb. 1817, Box 6, Northeastern Boundary, RG 76, NA; and Ellicott to the President, March 1817, Reel 2, Ellicott Papers, LC.

5 Barclay to Castlereagh, 5 June 1817, FO 5/125, PRO.

6 Barclay to Commissioners under the 6th and 7th Articles, 14 July 1817, Box 31, Northern Boundary, RG 76, NA.

7 Correspondence from Bouchette to the Foreign Office suggests that Commissioner Ogilvy was as dissatisfied with Bouchette as Barclay had been. See Bouchette to William Hamilton, 23 April 1817, FO 5/125, PRO; and Goulburn to Barclay, 14 March 1817, in Rives, ed., *Thomas Barclay*, 378.

8 See 'Johannes Ludwig Tiarks' in *DCB*, 2: 865–6.

9 See 'Andrew Ellicott' in *DAB*, 3: 89–90; and John C. Green, *American Science in the Age of Jefferson* (Ames: Iowa State University Press, 1984), 134–43.

10 See 'Ferdinand Rudolph Hassler' in *DAB*, 2: 385–6; Florian Cajori, *The Chequered Career of Ferdinand Rudolph Hassler* (Boston: Christopher Publishing House, 1929), 59–69; and Adams to Van Ness, 27 April 1818, and Adams to Hassler, 27 April 1818, Domestic Letters, RG 59, M 40 (roll 15), NA.

11 Barclay to Castlereagh, 2 Sept. 1817, FO 5/125, PRO; Bradley to Adams, 8 April 1818, Box 6, Northern Boundary, RG 76, NA. Also see Report of D.P. Adams, 3 June 1818, Box 31, Northern Boundary, RG 76, NA.

12 Barclay to Castlereagh, 25 June 1818, FO 5/136, PRO.

13 Tiarks to Barclay, 5 Nov. 1817, and Tiarks to Sir Joseph Banks, n.d., winter 1818, Vol. 1, Tiarks Papers, MG 24 H 64, NAC.

14 Bradley to Adams, 18 May 1818, Box 6, Northeastern Boundary, RG 76, NA.

15 Rough minutes of meeting at St Regis, 12 June 1818, Box 6, North East Boundary Papers II, Mass HS.

16 Tiarks to Barclay, 4 Aug. 1818, and Tiarks to ——— [Ward Chipman], 6 Aug.

1818, Vol. 1, Tiarks Papers, MG 24 H 64, NAC; Delafield Diary, 24 July 1818, in McElroy and Riggs, eds., *Unfortified Boundary*, 204; and Cajori, *Chequered Career*, 94–102.

17 Tiarks to Barclay, 15 Oct. 1818, in Barclay to Bagot, 23 Oct. 1818, Vol. 17, Bagot Papers, MG 24 A 13, NAC.
18 Barclay to Bagot, 23 Oct. 1818, ibid.
19 Bagot to Barclay, 28 Oct. 1818, ibid.; Bagot to Adams, 31 Oct. 1818, Vol. 14, ibid.; Barclay to Planta, 26 Oct. and 3 Nov. 1818, FO 5/136, PRO; and Bagot to Castlereagh, 2 Nov. 1818, in Vane, ed., *Correspondence ... of Viscount Castlereagh*, 12: 69–70. British forces burned the fortifications that they had built along the Mississippi rather than turning them over to the United States at the end of the War of 1812.
20 Bradley to Adams, 2 Nov. 1818, Box 6, Northeastern Boundary, RG 76, NA.
21 See Joseph Bouchette, Surveyor General, to Hon. Thomas Dunn, President of Lower Canada, 22 Jan. 1807, Box 8, North East Boundary Papers II, Mass HS; and S. Williams to Major Roberdeau, 6 July 1816, Reel 2, Ellicott Papers, LC. As early as 1807 Bouchette suspected some error in the old line.
22 Barclay to Castlereagh, 28 May 1819, FO 5/145, PRO.
23 Tiarks to Planta, 28 Nov. 1818, Vol. 1, Tiarks Papers, MG 24 H 64, NAC.
24 Planta to Barclay, 13 Jan. and 10 March 1819, FO 5/145, PRO.
25 Van Ness to Adams, 20 May 1819, Box 6, Northeastern Boundary, RG 76, NA. For a more sympathetic view of Hassler, see Cajori, *Chequered Career*, 102–4.
26 Adams to Van Ness, 27 May 1819, Domestic Letters, RG 59, M 40 (reel 15), NA. Also see Adams to Ellicott, 27 May 1819, and Adams to Major Thayer, 27 May 1819, ibid. For Tiarks's observations on Hassler's request for more money, see Tiarks to Planta, 7 June 1819, and Tiarks to Banks, 8 June 1819, Vol. 1, Tiarks Papers, MG 24 H 64, NAC.
27 Van Ness to Adams, 16 July 1819, Box 6, Northeastern Boundary, RG 76, NA.
28 Barclay to Castlereagh, 28 May 1819, FO 5/145, NAC. Also see Tiarks to Barclay, 4 July 1819, Vol. 1, Tiarks Papers, MG 24 H 64, NAC; and Barclay to Stratford Canning, 18 May 1819, and Stratford Canning to Barclay, 21 May 1819, FO 5/158, PRO. Reacting to a British complaint, Commissioner Van Ness pointed out to Adams that the original delay had occurred in 1817, when most of a summer was lost while the party waited for the British astronomer to arrive from England. Van Ness to Adams, 11 July 1818, Box 6, Northeastern Boundary, RG 76, NA.
29 Ellicott to Sara [Ellicott], 31 July 1819, Reel 2, Ellicott Papers, LC.
30 Ibid.
31 Tiarks to Barclay, 1 Aug. 1819, Vol. 1, Tiarks Papers, MG 24 H 64, NAC; and Barclay to Castlereagh, 30 Aug. 1819, FO 5/145, PRO.

32 Barclay to Castlereagh, 30 Aug. 1819, FO 5/145, PRO.

33 Bradley to Commissioners under the Fifth Article, 16 May 1820, Vol. 56, Boundary Commission Records, Chipman Papers, MG 23 D 1, NAC; Barclay to Van Ness, 21 Aug. 1820, FO 5/164, PRO; and Griffin [Ellicott] to ————, 28 Aug. 1820, Reel 2, Ellicott Papers, LC.

34 W.C. [Ward Chipman] to Goulburn, 24 June 1820, Box 7, Barclay Papers, Maine HS.

35 Bradley to Adams, 25 July 1821, Box 6, Northeastern Boundary, RG 76, NA. Ferdinand Hassler provided the government with an essay on geocentric latitude. See F.R. Hassler, 'Upon the Geocentric Latitude,' 3 May 1819, box 1, North East Boundary Papers II, Mass HS.

36 Daniel Doan, *Indian Stream Republic: Setting a New England Frontier, 1785–1842* (Hanover, NH: University Press of New England, 1997), 60–5 and 81–2.

37 Report of T. Carlisle in Appendix 56, *North-East Boundary, Evidence*, 424.

38 Tiarks Journal, Nov. 1820 (written on birch bark), Vol. 3, Tiarks Papers, MG 24 H 64, NAC.

39 For a description of the preparations of the maps in this area, see Tiarks to Chipman, 9 March 1821, Vol. 53, Boundary Commission Records, Chipman Papers, MG 23 D 1, NAC. Also see Doan, *Indian Stream Republic*, 96–9.

40 Bradley to Adams, 16 Oct. 1821, Box 6, Northeastern Boundary, RG 76, NA.

41 Barclay to Castlereagh, 12 Aug. 1816, FO 5/116, PRO.

42 Barclay to Castlereagh, 2 Sept. 1817, FO 5/125, PRO; and Barclay to Castlereagh, 4 Dec. 1818, FO 5/136, PRO.

43 Barclay to Castlereagh, 12 June 1820, FO 5/153, PRO.

44 Barclay to Castlereagh, 28 Feb. 1818, FO 5/136, PRO. Ward Chipman certainly thought that the negotiation of a new compromise boundary for which there would be no controversy about disputed landmarks was a good idea. It would also cost less than the survey procedure then being employed. See Chipman to Goulburn, 27 March 1818, Vol. 53, Boundary Commission Records, MG 23 D 1, NAC.

45 Van Ness to Adams, 1 and 4 April 1820, Box 6, Northeastern Boundary, RG 76, NA.

46 See Accounts of C.P. Van Ness, Box 6, Northeastern Boundary, RG 76, NA; and Accounts of William C. Bradley, 20 May 1819, Box 3, NE Boundary Papers II, Mass HS. In late 1820 Secretary of State John Quincy Adams sent the accounts of the commissions to Congress. These figures would seem to indicate that the commission for article 5 had cost $116,037.41 1/2 between 1816 and 1820. See *American State Papers: Foreign Relations*, 5: 50–69.

47 Van Ness to Adams, 6 Jan. 1821, Box 6, Northeastern Boundary, RG 76, NA.

48 Ward Chipman exclaimed to Henry Goulburn at the Foreign Office his own

'alarm, and I may add distress at the enormous expense that attends the Surveys.' Chipman to Goulburn, 27 March 1818, Vol. 53, Boundary Commission Records, MG 23 D 1, NAC.

49 Memorials concerning the North West Angle of Nova Scotia and the Northwesternmost Head of the Connecticut River to be ascertained and determined by the Commissioners under the Fifth Article of the Treaty of Ghent ... , Ward Chipman, 8 June 1821, FO 303/17, PRO.

50 To the Honorable the Commissioners Appointed Pursuant to the Fifth Article of the Treaty concluded at Ghent ... , William C. Bradley, 8 June 1821, FO 303/18, PRO.

51 Journal of ... the Fifth Article, 1–14 June 1821, Northeastern Boundary Papers, Mass HS.

52 Chipman to Goulburn, 15 Aug. 1821, Vol. 53, Boundary Commission Records, MG 23 D1, NAC.

53 Bradley to Adams, 16 Oct. 1821, Box 6, Northeastern Boundary, RG 76, NA. Bradley also complained about the additional work caused by the realization that no decision would be reached by the board and that all the official documents would have to be copied out in duplicate for the arbitrator to use in an eventual decision. Bradley to Adams, 4 Oct. 1821, F-40-1, Hazen Collection, Chipman Papers, NBM.

54 Bradley to Adams, 16 Oct. 1821, Box 6, Northeastern Boundary, RG 76, NA.

55 Ibid. Also see Memorandum by Thomas Barclay, 4 Oct. 1821, Memorandum by C.P. Van Ness, 4 Oct. 1821, and Van Ness to Barclay, 10 Nov. 1821, Vol. 54, Boundary Commission Records, MG 23 D 1, NAC; and John Francis Sprague, 'The North Eastern Boundary Controversy, 1783–1842,' in Hatch, ed., *Maine: A History*, 1: 249.

56 Barclay to Londonderry, 3 Oct. 1821, FO 5/164. Also see Van Ness to Adams, 20 Nov. 1821, Box 6, Northeastern Boundary, RG 76, NA.

57 See Mr. Sullivan's Rejoinder, 14 June 1798, in Moore, ed., *International Adjudications*, 1: 358–9. Views of this nature were expressed by American officials from time to time. One statement that served to undercut a consistently strong position on the usefulness of the terms of the treaty of 1783 was made by Thomas Jefferson to Congress in 1803 while negotiations for a boundary settlement were under way. He said that the boundary terms in the treaty 'were too imperfectly described to be susceptible of execution.' Thomas Jefferson, Annual Message to Congress, 17 Oct. 1803, in Richardson, ed., *Messages and Papers of the Presidents*, 1: 347.

58 Report of the British Commissioner, in Appendix no. 53, *North-East Boundary, Evidence*, 371–2.

59 Ibid., 375.

60 Ibid., 374–6.

61 Ibid., 377.

62 Ibid., 378–80.

63 Report of C.P. Von Ness, in Appendix no. 54, *North-East Boundary, Evidence,* 381–2.

64 Ibid., 383–6.

65 Ibid., 388–9.

66 Ibid., 390–1.

67 Ibid., 393–4.

68 Ibid., 395–9. Also see Doan, *Indian Stream Republic,* 99–100.

69 Report of C.P. Van Ness, in Appendix no. 54, *North-East Boundary, Evidence,* 380.

70 Ganong, 'Boundaries,' Section II, 7: 328.

71 Barclay to Londonderry, 6 Oct. 1821, FO 5/164, PRO; and Canning to Londonderry, 5 Nov. 1821, FO 5/159, PRO. Stratford Canning was a younger cousin of George Canning's, and while he benefited from his kinsman's influence, he enjoyed a successful diplomatic career on his own merits, eventually being created Viscount Stratford de Redcliffe. In 1820 he succeeded Bagot as British minister in Washington, where he had a sometimes-stormy relationship with John Quincy Adams. Masterson, *Tories and Democrats,* 196–222.

72 Adams to Rush, 5 Jan. 1822, Diplomatic Instructions, All Countries, RG 59, M 77 (roll 4), NA.

73 Barclay to Chipman, 16 April 1822, and Chipman to Nathaniel Atcheson and Thomas Bonner, 19 April 1822, F-30-18 and 23, Hazen Collection, Chipman Papers, NBM. Barclay left London early because his wife fell seriously ill in New York. The younger Chipman remained in England until the spring of 1823.

74 Barclay to Londonderry, 11 July 1822, FO 5/170, PRO, and United States, Continental Congress, *Secret Journals of the acts and proceedings of Congress from the first meeting thereof to the dissolution of the Confederation,* 4 vols (Boston: Thomas B. Wait, 1820–1).

75 Ibid. Ward Chipman gave similar advice to the governor general the following year. See Chipman to Dalhousie, 27 Dec. 1823, F-101–10, Hugh T. Hazen Collection, NBM.

76 See Barclay to Castlereagh, 1 Jan. 1818, FO 5/136, PRO. In 1817 and 1818, the old Collins–Valentine line of the forty-fifth parallel was presumed to be generally accurate, and the British were prepared to accept the fact that the two forts on Lake Champlain were in the hands of the Americans. Britain's steady shift of position on this question and on the northeastern boundary shows a significant escalation of its expectations of what might be achieved through the resolution of the boundary as a result of the survey and the commissions.

Chapter 5. Article 6: The St Lawrence and the Great Lakes

1 Porter to President James Madison, 27 Nov. 1815, Box 1, Northern Boundary, RG 76, NA; and Moore, *International Arbitrations*, 1: 163.

2 John J. Bigsby, *The Shoe and Canoe, or Pictures of Travel in the Canadas* (London: Chapman and Hall, 1850), 1: 255. Also see 'Peter Buell Porter' in *DAB*, 15: 99–100.

3 Ogilvy to Castlereagh, 1 Nov. 1816, FO 5/116, PRO.

4 See 'John Ogilvy,' in *DCB*, 5: 635–6; and William A. Bird, 'Reminiscences of the Boundary Survey between the United States and British Provinces,' in *Publications of the Buffalo Historical Society* (Buffalo: Peter Paul Book Company, 1896), 4: 12.

5 Delafield Diary, 26 June 1818, in McElroy and Riggs, eds., *Unfortified Boundary*, 189–90.

6 Report of Commissioners Ogilvy and Porter, 18 Nov. 1816, FO 5/116, PRO.

7 Sewell Diary, 13 May 1817, Sewell Papers, MG 24 B 169, NAC.

8 See 'Stephen Sewell,' in *DCB*, 6: 700–2.

9 Sewell Diary, 18–20 May 1817, Sewell Papers, MG 24 B 169, NAC.

10 Minutes of the Proceedings of the Commissioners under the 6th and 7th Articles, 23–9 May 1817, Barclay Papers, MG 24 B 175, NAC. William A. Bird, of Troy, New York, was appointed assistant surveyor, and Major Joseph Delafield, of New York, served as secretary to the American agent.

11 See 'David Thompson,' in *DCB*, 8: 878–84; and David Thompson Journal, March 1817, Box 9, Barclay Papers, Maine HS. Dr Elliot Coues described Thompson as 'the greatest geographer of his day in British America,' and J.B. Tyrrell, editor of *David Thompson's Narrative*, called him the 'greatest practical land geographer who ever lived.' Elliott Coues, ed., *New Light on the Early History of the Greater Northwest: The Manuscript Journals of Alexander Henry and David Thompson* (1897; reprint, Minneapolis: Ross & Haines, 1965), 1: xxii; and J.B. Tyrrell, cited in Victor G. Hopwood, ed., *David Thompson: Travels in Western North America, 1784–1812* (Toronto: Macmillan, 1977), 5. A copy of Thompson's famous map of 'The North West Territory of the Province of Canada' can be seen on display at the Ontario Archives in Toronto. None of the published documents or the biographical materials on Thompson attempts to examine his important work with the commissions. For the quotation, see Adams to Porter, 6 March 1819, E-49-1, Porter Papers, Buffalo and Erie County Historical Society, Buffalo (hereafter BECHS).

12 Sewell Diary, 21 May to 4 June 1817, Sewell Papers, MG 24 B 169, NAC; Delafield Diary, 25 June 1817, in McElroy and Riggs, eds., *Unfortified Boundary*, 146; and Bird, 'Reminiscences of the Boundary Survey,' 4.

13 Rush to Hawkins, 22 March 1817, Box 1 Northern Boundary, RG 76, NA.

14 Hawkins to Board of Commissioners under Articles 6 and 7, 29 May 1817, ibid.

15 Rush to President, 22 June 1817, ibid.

16 Porter to Rush, 15 Aug. 1817, ibid.; Adams to Hawkins, 5 May 1818, Domestic Letters, M 40 (roll 15), RG 59, NA; and Delafield Diary, 2 Aug. 1817, in McElroy and Riggs, eds., *Unfortified Boundary*, 160–1. Hawkins continued to complain about this decision, and correspondence went back and forth for about a year. This whole question has been very skilfully analysed by Michael F. Scheuer, who makes the point that the decision to give the commissioners the primary role in deciding how the surveys should be carried out was crucial in giving them room to reach a settlement between themselves – essentially a political rather than a judicial decision. Scheuer also sees this precedent as important for the success of subsequent Anglo–American joint commissions. See Michael F. Scheuer, 'Peter Buell Porter and the Development of the Joint Commission Approach to Diplomacy in the North Atlantic Triangle,' *American Review of Canadian Studies* 12 (1982), 65–73. Bird described Hawkins as something of a troublemaker, causing alarm to the settlers as well as difficulty for General Porter. Delafield kept on good terms with Hawkins even after he had succeeded him as agent. See Bird, 'Reminiscences of the Boundary Survey,' 11–12; and McElroy and Riggs eds., *Unfortified Boundary*, 38–41.

17 Sewell Diary, 1 June – 15 July 1817, Sewell Papers, MG 24 B 169, NAC.

18 Delafield Diary, 3 May – 16 Aug. 1817, in McElroy and Riggs, eds., *Unfortified Boundary*, 135–62.

19 Sewell Diary, 17–31 July 1817, Sewell Papers, MG 24 B 69, NAC; Delafield Diary, 31 July – 2 Aug. 1817, in McElroy and Riggs, eds., *Unfortified Boundary*, 159–61; and Journal of the Commission under Articles 6 and 7, 3 June – 8 Aug. 1817, FO 303/29, PRO. Porter also entertained the president at Niagara, but it is not clear that anything about the boundary was discussed, other than the Hawkins affair. Monroe travelled as far west as Detroit. See W.P. Casson, *James Monroe* (Chapel Hill: University of North Carolina Press, 1946), 289–90.

20 See copies of letter from David Thompson to Sir Robert Peel, Lord Stanley, and William E. Gladstone, summer 1840, in L.J. Burpee, 'Some Letters of David Thompson,' *CHR* 4 (June 1923), 116–17.

21 Journal of ... Articles 6 and 7, 27–8 Oct. 1817, FO 303/29, PRO; Minutes of the Commissioners under the 6th & 7th Articles, 29 Oct. 1817, Barclay Papers, MG 24, B 175, NAC; and Delafield Diary, 25 Sept. – 4 Nov. 1817, in McElroy and Riggs, eds., *Unfortified Boundary*, 173–8.

22 Porter to Adams, 3 Nov. 1817, Box 1, Northern Boundary, RG 76, NA.

23 Barclay to Sewell, 3 Dec. 1817, Box 31, Northern Boundary, RG 76, NA.

24 See Thomas Barclay to Commissioners under Articles 6 & 7, 14 July 1817, and Van Ness to Commissioners under Articles 6 & 7, 4 Aug. 1817, Box 31, Northern Boundary, RG 76, NA.

25 Journal of ... Articles 6 and 7, 1 June 1818, FO 303/29, PRO. Also see Bagot to Castlereagh, 9 Nov. 1817, FO 5/123, PRO; Planta to Ogilvy, 9 Dec. 1817, and Planta to Hale, 9 Dec. 1817, FO 5/125, PRO; and Bird, 'Reminiscences of the Boundary Survey,' 13. Hale had been appointed by Sherbrooke in the late summer of 1817, but concern then arose as to whether a commission under the great seal of the Canadas would be sufficient or whether the letter of commission should come directly from His Majesty's Government, as was finally done. See Bagot to Adams, 24 Sept. 1817, Vol. 14, Bagot Papers, MG 24 A 13, NAC.

26 Ogilvy to Castlereagh, 5 May 1818, FO 5/130, PRO.

27 Reports of the location of the forty-fifth parallel were completed during the course of the summer. See Report by Thompson, 24 June 1818, Reports by David P. Adams, 3 July and 4 Nov. 1818, Box 31, Northern Boundary, RG 76, NA; and Tiarks to Barclay, 13 Aug. 1818, Vol. 1, Tiarks Papers, MG 24 H 64, NAC. Also see Resolutions of the Commissioners meeting in Burlington, Vermont, 15 May 1818, Box 6, NE Boundary Papers II, Mass. HS.

28 Porter to Adams, 8 Dec. 1818, Box 1, Northern Boundary, RG 76, NA.

29 Fraser to Porter, 19 Sept. 1818, and Adams to Porter, 11 Nov. 1818, E-33, Porter Papers, BECHS; Ogilvy to Castlereagh, 10 Oct. 1818, FO 5/136, NA. For the final meeting of the year at Montreal, see Minutes of the Proceedings of the Commissioners under Articles 6 & 7, 1 Oct. 1818, Barclay Papers, MG 24 B 195, NAC.

30 Delafield Diary, 8 June – 21 Sept. 1818, in McElroy and Riggs, eds., *Unfortified Boundary*, 185–215; Fraser to Porter, 19 July 1819, E-28, Porter Papers, BECHS; and Scheuer, 'Peter Buell Porter, 65–73.

31 See Adams to Porter, 6 March 1819, E-49-1, Porter Papers, BECHS.

32 Delafield Diary, 26 Aug. 1817 and 16 June 1818, in McElroy and Riggs, eds., *Unfortified Boundary*, 164–5 and 222–4. General Porter's older brother, Judge Augustus Porter, owned the land next to the falls along the American side of the river, and he maintained a bridge across the river to Goat Island.

33 Adams to Porter, 6 Jan. 1819, Alex Stevenson to John Ogilvy, 1 Feb. 1819, and Sewell to Ogilvy, 24 March 1819, Box 31, Northern Boundary, RG 76, NA. Also see Minutes of the Commissioners under Articles 6 & 7, 4 June 1819, Barclay Papers, MG 24 B 175, NAC.

34 Delafield Diary, 20 Aug. 1819, in McElroy and Riggs, eds., *Unfortified Boundary*, 261.

35 Porter to Adams, 30 Sept. 1819, Box 1, Northern Boundary, RG 76, NA. The British agent also informed the Foreign Office on his return to Quebec. See Hale to Planta, 17 Oct. 1819, FO 5/145, PRO. Dr Bigsby described Ogilvy's symptoms, saying that he suffered from 'utter prostration' and for several days before his death lay in a 'lethargic state.' Porter, he said, came down with a fever in the marshes at the eastern end of Lake Erie, and David Thompson was ill for twenty-one days, suffering from 'high fever and delirium,' from which he did not fully recover until the following winter. Bigsby called the illnesses 'ague or bilious remittent fever.' The area around Lake Erie was always unhealthy, he wrote, but 1819 was an exceptionally bad year. Bigsby, *Shoe and Canoe*, 1: 250–2.

36 Porter to Adams, 30 Sept. 1819, Box 1, Northern Boundary, RG 76, NA.

37 Fraser to Porter, 22 Aug. 1819, E-77, and 30 Aug. 1819, E-79, Porter Papers, BECHS. Also see Thompson to John Macauly, 24 Oct. 1839, in 'Remarks on the Maps from St. Regis to Sault Ste. Marie,' *Papers and Records of the Ontario Historical Society*, 1 (1899), 120.

38 Hale to Porter, 19 Oct. 1819, E-83, Porter Papers, BECHS.

39 Barclay to Castlereagh, 11 Oct. 1819, FO 5/145, PRO; and Hale to Barclay, 21 Feb. 1820, Box 7, Barclay Papers, Maine HS.

40 Bigsby, *Shoe and Canoe*, 1: 253; Castlereagh to Anthony Barclay, 10 Jan. 1820, FO 5/153, PRO; and Journal of ... Articles 6 and 7, 3 June 1820, FO 303/29, PRO. Barclay was British consul in New York from 1842 to 1856. He died in Hartford, Connecticut, on 21 March 1877.

41 Anthony Barclay to Porter, 2 May 1820, Box 31, Northern Boundary, RG 76, NA; Anthony Barclay to Planta, 20 June 1820, FO 5/153, PRO; and Hale to Porter, 2 May 1820, E-93-1, Porter Papers, BECHS. Colonel Hale had urged the appointment of a physician in the aftermath of the disastrous 1819 season. Hale to Porter, 19 Oct. 1819, E-83, Porter Papers, BECHS.

42 See 'John Jeremiah Bigsby,' in *DCB*, 7: 72–3; and Henry R. Schoolcraft, *Personal Memoirs of a Residence of Thirty Years with the Indian Tribes on the American Frontiers: With Brief Notices of Passing Events, Facts, and Opinions, A.D. 1812 to A.D. 1842* (Philadelphia: Lippincott, Grambo, 1851), 182. Bigsby and Schoolcraft corresponded for some years on scientific matters.

43 Adams to Delafield, 19 May 1820, Domestic Letters, M 40 (roll 16), RG 59, NA.

44 Porter to Adams, 2 Dec. 1820, Box 1, Northern Boundary, RG 76, NA; and Schoolcraft, *Personal Memoirs*, 183. Delafield received his appointment as agent in March 1821. See Delafield to Adams, 14 March 1821, Box 1, Northern Boundary, RG 76, NA. Also see 'Joseph Delafield' in *The Cyclopedia of American Biography*, 11: 28–9; and McElroy and Riggs, eds., *Unfortified Bound-*

ary, 34–8 and 42–7. For comments about the geological interests of both
Delafield and Bigsby, see John C. Green and John G. Burke, 'The Science of
Minerals in the Age of Jefferson,' *Transactions of the American Philosophical
Society* 68: 4 (July 1978), 65 and 108.

45 See *American State Papers; Foreign Relations*, 5: 50–68. The total expense of the
commissions under articles 6 and 7 is difficult to estimate. At an annual cost
of over $40,000, it may have been a total expenditure by 1827 of as much as a
half-million dollars. Also see Adams to Porter, 19 March 1819, E-50, and
Delafield to Porter, 5 Jan. 1820, E-84-2, Porter Papers, BECHS.

46 See Adams to Rush, 22 March 1821, in Manning, ed., *DCUSCR*, 2: 4–5; and
Porter to Adams, 2 Aug. 1821, Box 1, Northern Boundary, RG 76, NA.
Delafield appears to have been paid $1,000 per year, much less than the Brit-
ish agent, who was still receiving £1,000 sterling, or about $4,444. Also see
Delafield to Porter, 27 Jan. 1821, E-107-2, and Porter to Anthony Barclay,
9 April 1821, E-113-2, Porter Papers, BECHS.

47 See Porter to Adams, 24 March 1820, Box 1, Northern Boundary, RG 76, NA;
Anthony Barclay to Castlereagh, 27 March 1820, FO 5/153; Porter to Hale,
28 March 1820, Box VII, Barclay Papers, Maine HS; and Bigsby, *Shoe and
Canoe*, 1: 246–7 and 253.

48 Memorial of John Hale, 3 June 1820, Box 31, Northern Boundary, RG 76,
NA; and Bigsby, *Shoe and Canoe*, 1: 253–60.

49 Journal of ... Articles 6 and 7, 2–5 June 1820, FO 303/29, PRO.

50 Delafield Diary, 2–17 July 1820, in McElroy and Riggs, eds., *Unfortified Boundary*, 277–80; Harlan Hatcher, *Lake Erie* (Indianapolis: Bobbs-Merrill, 1945),
107–10; and Alex R. Gilpin, *The Territory of Michigan, 1805–1837* (East Lansing: Michigan State University Press, 1970), 69–138. The steamboat *Walk in
the Water*, built in 1818, was the first on Lake Erie. The ship was large at the
time, at 135 feet in length and 330 tons' burden, and had two fifteen-foot
paddles; she could carry sixty passengers comfortably and, at an average
speed of six knots, could make the trip from Buffalo to Mackinac Island and
back in fourteen days. Lord and Lady Selkirk were among the first passengers. The ship was lost on a sandbar twelve miles from Buffalo on 30 Oct.
1821.

51 Bigsby, *Shoe and Canoe*, 1: 257–8, 261–3, and 335.

52 Anthony Barclay to Castlereagh, 9 Nov. 1820, FO 5/153, NA.

53 Bigsby, *Shoe and Canoe*, 1: 296–8. Delafield worried that several of the sick
men appeared to have the same kind of fever that killed Colonel Ogilvy the
previous year. Delafield Diary, 10 and 11 Aug. 1820, in McElroy and Riggs,
eds., *Unfortified Boundary*, 292–3.

54 David Thompson to John Macauly, 24 Oct. 1836, in Thompson 'Remarks on

the Maps from St. Regis to Sault Ste. Marie,' 121; Bigsby to Anthony Barclay, 4, 11, and 21 July 1820, Box 7, Barclay Papers, Maine HS; Joseph E and Estelle L. Bayliss, in collaboration with Milo M. Quaife, *River of Destiny: The Saint Marys* (Detroit: Wayne State University Press, 1955), 69–70; and Bigsby, *Shoe and Canoe*, 2: 126. Bigsby described approvingly the Indians whom he saw along the Lake Huron shore. 'I was delighted with the well-fed, good-humoured looks of these red men; and I made favourable comparisons between them and the Glasgow weavers.' Ibid., 2: 97. The name of the British ship, *Confiance*, was not inconsequential. While the ship itself had been captured from the Americans in 1814 and renamed, the name chosen was that of the British flagship that had surrendered to the Americans at the Battle of Plattsburg on Lake Champlain. Defiance and bravado, if not arrogance.

55 Delafield Diary, 10–29 Sept. 1820, in McElroy and Riggs, eds., *Unfortified Boundary*, 307–20; and Fred Landon, *Lake Huron* (Indianapolis: Bobbs-Merrill, 1944), 196–9.

56 Delafield Diary, May – Oct. 1820, in McElroy and Riggs, eds., *Unfortified Boundary*, 266–322, quotation from 297; and Fraser to Porter, 13 June 1820, E-95, Porter Papers, BECHS.

57 Delafield Diary, 17 Sept. and 21–23 Sept. 1820, in McElroy and Riggs, eds., *Unfortified Boundary*, 311–12 and 314–17.

58 Delafield Diary, 10 Sept. 1820, ibid., 307–8.

59 Anthony Barclay to Castlereagh, 9 Nov. 1820, FO 5/153, PRO.

60 Ibid.

61 Anthony Barclay to Londonderry, 27 June 1821, CO 6/5, PRO.

62 David Thompson Journals, 1821, Vols. 17–19, Tyrrell Papers, Vol. 1, MG 30 D 49, NAC; and Delafield to Porter, 31 May 1821, E-117-4, and Porter to Anthony Barclay, 30 July 1821, E-120-1, Porter Papers, BECHS.

63 See Journal of ... Articles 6 and 7, 5 Dec. 1821, FO 303/29, PRO; and Memorandum from Porter, n.d, c. 28 Jan. 1822, Box 1, Northern Boundary, RG 76, NA; Delafield to Board of Commissioners, 21 Nov. 1821, cited in McElroy and Riggs, eds., *Unfortified Boundary*, 51–2; and Thompson, 'Remarks on the Maps from St. Regis to Sault Ste. Marie,' 117–18. Thompson's memoir is particularly useful in explaining the decisions for the allocation of islands in the St Lawrence River, for which he came in for some criticism.

64 See Porter to Adams, 17 Dec. 1821, Box 1, Northern Boundary, RG 76, NA; Anthony Barclay to Canning, 18 Dec. 1821, FO 5/170, PRO; and Journal of ... Articles 6 and 7, 3 Jan. 1822, FO 303/29, PRO; Hale to Board of Commissioners, 12 Dec. 1821, E-125-11, and Delafield to Board of Commissioners, 13 Dec. 1821, E-125-12, Porter Papers, BECHS. Delafield presumed that part of Barclay's determination to hold the three islands, or to obtain a guarantee

that they would not be fortified, arose from British desire to build a naval base at or near Amherstburg. In that event the three small islands would dominate the entrance to the naval base. Delafield to Adams, 18 Dec. 1821, Box 1, Northern Boundary, RG 76, NA.

65 Canning to Londonderry, 1 Jan. 1822, and Canning to Londonderry, 8 Feb. 1822, FO 5/166, PRO. Also see Canning to Anthony Barclay, 1 Jan. and 2 Feb. 1822, Box 8, Barclay Papers, Maine HS.

66 Adams to Rush, 5 Jan. 1822, Diplomatic Instructions, All Countries, M 77 (roll 4), RG 59, NA. Adams had conveyed much the same view to Canning. Canning to Anthony Barclay, 12 Jan. 1822, Box 8, Barclay Papers, Maine HS.

67 See Journal of ... Articles 6 and 7, 29 Jan. 1822, FO 303/29, PRO; Anthony Barclay to Londonderry, 9 Feb. 1822, FO 5/170, PRO; and Porter to Adams, 9 Feb. 1822, Box 1, Northern Boundary, RG 76, NA.

68 Anthony Barclay to Londonderry, 18 Jan. and 9 Feb. 1822,, FO 5/170, PRO.

69 Canning to Anthony Barclay, 2 Feb. 1822, Box 8, Barclay Papers, Maine HS; and Dalhousie to Anthony Barclay, 23 Feb. 1822, FO 5/170, PRO. Dalhousie also said to Canning that the islands were 'altogether unimportant' if they were not fortified. Dalhousie to Canning, 22 Feb. 1822, FO 5/167, PRO.

70 Certainly provocative incidents between soldiers and civilians of both countries took place along the border, particularly in the area of the Detroit River, in such a way as to encourage mutual suspicion. See, for example, Monroe to Bagot, 14 Aug. 1816, in Manning, ed., *DCUSCR*, 1: 251–2.

71 Londonderry to Anthony Barclay, 9 March 1822, FO 5/170, PRO; Foreign Office to Canning, 9 March 1822, FO 5/165, PRO; and Canning to Anthony Barclay, 22 April 1822, Box 8, Barclay Papers, Maine HS. For an analysis of this particular boundary problem, see Michael F. Scheuer, 'Deadlock: Charting the Canadian–American Boundary on the Detroit River,' *Michigan History* 67 (1983), 24–31.

72 Canning to Londonderry, 29 April 1822, FO 5/167, PRO. For further comments, see also Canning to Londonderry, 8 May 1822, FO 5/168, PRO.

73 Anthony Barclay to Londonderry, 19 June 1822, FO 5/170, PRO; Porter to Adams, 21 June 1822, Box 1, Northern Boundary, RG 76, PRO; and Journal of ... Articles 6 and 7, 18 June 1822, FO 303/29, PRO. There was no sinister reason for Porter's changing the date of the meeting. He simply wanted to attend a board meeting of the New York Canal Commissioners to determine the western terminus for the Erie Canal, which was a matter of great material interest to him. See Porter to Anthony Barclay, 12 May 1822, Box 8, Barclay Papers, Maine HS. For the text of the decision, see Declaration of the Commissioners under Article 6 of the Treaty of Ghent (Document 33), signed at Utica, New York, 18 June 1822, in Miller, ed., *Treaties*, 3: 65–9.

74 See Planta to Anthony Barclay, 19 March 1823, and Barclay to George Canning, 24 Feb. 1824, FO 5/187, PRO; and H. George Classen, *Thrust and Counterthrust: The Genesis of the Canada–United States Boundary* (Chicago: Rand McNally, 1965), 101–2. This portion of the boundary was 955.9 miles long.

Chapter 6. Article 7: From Lake Superior to the Lake of the Woods

1 Miller, ed., *Treaties*, 2: 153.
2 Anthony Barclay to Planta, 21 Jan. 1822, FO 5/170, PRO.
3 Porter to Adams, 12 Feb. 1822, Box 1, Northern Boundary, RG 76, NA. Porter had earlier described the region beyond Lake Superior as 'a country which is, comparatively, of little importance.' Porter to Adams, 2 Dec. 1820, ibid.
4 Bigsby to Anthony Barclay, 27 June 1823, Box 8, Barclay Papers, Maine HS.
5 Bigsby, *Shoe and Canoe*, 2: 255.
6 Porter to Adams, 12 Feb. 1822, Box 1, Northern Boundary, RG 76, NA.
7 Delafield to John Adams, 24 July 1822, ibid.
8 See Mentor L. Williams, ed., *Schoolcraft's Narrative of Travels through the Northwestern Regions of the United States extending from Detroit through the Great Chain of American Lakes to the Sources of the Mississippi River in the Year 1820* (1821; reprint, East Lansing: Michigan State University Press, 1992), 176.
9 Delafield to Porter, 20 April 1822, E-138-2, Porter Papers, BECHS.
10 Delafield to Adams, 24 July 1822, Box 1, Northern Boundary, RG 76, NA.
11 Journal of the Board of Commissioners under Article 7, 18 June 1822, FO 303/29, PRO.
12 See Delafield to Porter, 20 April 1822, E-138-2, and Delafield to Stuart (Mackinac Island), 6 June 1822, E-139-1, Porter Papers, BECHS; and Ferguson to Porter, 20 Aug. 1822 (from Arrow Lake), Box 1, Northern Boundary, RG 76, NA. George W. Whistler's sister Sara married James Abbott, a prosperous merchant and postmaster of Detroit. Abbott, the son of an English fur trader, was well connected in Upper Canada through both his father and his three sisters, who married militia officers on the opposite side of the Detroit River. George's son, born in 1834 after George had left the army, James Abbott McNeill Whistler, became the famous artist. 'George W. Whistler,' *Appleton's Cyclopaedia of American Biography*, 6: 463–4.
13 Ferguson to Porter, 20 Aug. 1822, E-142, and 23 Sept. 1822, E-142-3, Porter Papers, BECHS; and Delafield Diary, 22 May – 30 June 1823, in McElroy and Riggs, eds., *Unfortified Boundary*, 368–73 and 412; William A. Bird, 'Reminiscences of the Boundary Survey between the United States and British Prov-

inces,' 5; Grace Lee Nute, *Lake Superior* (Indianapolis: Bobbs-Merrill Company, 1944), 37–92; and William E. Lass, *Minnesota's Boundary with Canada: Its Evolution since 1783* (St Paul: Minnesota Historical Society Press, 1980), 38.

14 International Boundary Commission (IBC), *Joint Report upon the Survey and Demarcation of the Boundary between the United States and Canada from the Northwesternmost Point of Lake of the Woods to Lake Superior* (Washington, DC: Government Printing Office, 1931), 213; and Bigsby, *Shoe and Canoe*, 2: 36.

15 David Lavender, *The Fist in the Wilderness* (Albuquerque: University of New Mexico Press, 1964), 246–8. Selkirk was sued in both Canada and the United States for his actions. While passing through Detroit in 1818 he was served a summons. It was partly because of Selkirk's actions at Fond du Lac that Governor Lewis Cass led an expedition through that region in the summer of 1820. The ostensible mission was to discover the source of the Mississippi, but the assertion of U.S. sovereignty in the Lake Superior area and the hope of impressing and winning the loyalty of the Native people were also part of the objective. Cass returned west in 1826, with much the same purpose, to negotiate the Treaty of Fond du Lac. See Williams, ed., *Schoolcraft's Narrative Journal of Travels*; and Thomas L. McKenney, *Sketches of a Tour to the Lakes, Of the Character and Custom of the Chippeway Indians and of Incidents Connected with the Treaty of Fond du Lac* (1827; reprint, Minneapolis: Ross & Haines, 1959).

16 Bigsby, *Shoe and Canoe*, 2: 206 and 266; and Survey of the Thompson Journals in Vol. 1, Tyrrell Papers, MG 30 D 49, NAC.

17 Delafield to Adams, 24 Sept. 1822, Box 1, Northern Boundary, RG 76, NA.

18 Bird, 'Reminiscences of the Boundary Survey,' 5–6; and Schoolcraft, *Personal Memoirs*, 176.

19 Bigsby, *Shoe and Canoe*, 2: 230–2; Delafield Diary, 6 July 1813, in McElroy and Riggs, eds., *Unfortified Boundary*, 400–1; and Bryan Eddington, 'The Great Hall at Old Fort William,' *Beaver* 312 (summer 1981), 38–42.

20 Bird, 'Reminiscences of the Boundary Survey,' 5–6.

21 Anthony Barclay to George Canning, 19 May 1823, FO 5/187, PRO. The British agent, John Hale, had some doubts about the time needed to complete the work and queried whether Thompson was not simply generating employment for himself. See John Hale to Anthony Barclay, 7 April 1823, Box 8, Barclay Papers, Maine HS.

22 Dr. John J. Bigsby to Anthony Barclay, 13 May 1823, Box 8, Barclay Papers, Maine HS. When Bigsby left Quebec City with Hale in April, they were still under winter conditions, and they travelled over half of the trip to Kingston by sleigh. Bigsby, *Shoe and Canoe*, 2: 36–46.

23 Henry Putney Beers, *The Western Military Frontier, 1815–1846* (1935; reprint, Philadelphia: Porcupine Press, 1975), 46–7; Lavender, *The Fist in the Wilderness*, 306–7 and 373–4; and Schoolcraft, *Personal Memoirs*, 87–93. During the Mexican crisis, Fort Brady was closed in 1846, which was possible after the Webster–Ashburton Treaty had settled the eastern Canadian–American boundary.

24 Bigsby, *Shoe and Canoe*, 2: 124–8; Delafield Diary, 9 June 1823, in McElroy and Riggs, eds., *Unfortified Boundary*, 370; Mentor, ed., *Schoolcraft's Narrative Journal of Travels*, 16 and 468; Bayliss and Bayliss, with Quaife, *River of Destiny*, 54–72; and Graham A. MacDonald, 'Commerce, Civility and Old Sault Ste. Marie,' *Beaver* 312 (winter 1981), 52–9. Schoolcraft, in the course of his duties at the Sault, achieved great acclaim as an author, explorer, linguist, and anthropologist, specializing in Native people. He married Johnston's daughter Jane, who had travelled to Ireland and England. His first impression of the Anglo–Irishman was, 'It is refreshing to find a person who, in reference to this language, knows the difference between the conjugation of a verb and the declension of a noun.' Schoolcraft, *Personal Memoirs*, 100.

25 Bigsby, *Shoe and Canoe*, 2: 124–30.

26 Ibid., 57–81, 124–8, and 186–8.

27 Ibid., 256, 271, 302, and maps. William Keating gave different spellings for the Indian words. Thus Lake of the Sand Islands was rendered Pekwaonga Osagaagan, and Lake of the Woods, Metekoka Osagaagan. William H. Keating, *Narrative of an Expedition to the Source of St. Peter's River, Lake Winnepeek, Lake of the Woods, Etc., Performed in the Year 1823, By Order of the Hon. J.C. Calhoun, Secretary of War, Under the Command of Stephen H. Long, U.S.T.E.* (1824; reprint, Minneapolis: Ross & Haines, 1959), 106.

28 Bigsby, *Shoe and Canoe*, 2: 286–307; and J.B. Tyrrell, ed., *David Thompson's Narrative of His Explorations in Western America, 1784–1812* (Toronto: Champlain Society, 1916), 12: 288.

29 Bigsby to Anthony Barclay, 28 July 1823, Box 8, Barclay Papers, Maine HS.

30 Bigsby, *Shoe and Canoe*, 2: 230; and Guide to the Thompson Journals, Vol. I, Tyrrell Papers, MG 30 D 49, NAC.

31 Bigsby to Anthony Barclay, 24 Nov. 1823, Box 8, Barclay Papers, Maine HS.

32 Delafield Diary, 18 May – 23 June, in McElroy and Riggs, eds., *Unfortified Boundary*, 368–72.

33 Delafield Diary, 8 – 15 July 1823, in ibid., 402–7.

34 Delafield Diary, 3 May – 31 July 1823, in ibid., 375–428; and Bigsby, *Shoe and Canoe*, 2: 260.

35 William Keating, travelling with Major Long through the Lake of the Woods

and Rainy River some weeks after the American surveyors, met the British party and talked in some detail with Bigsby and with Native people. Keating wrote, 'We had heard from the Indians that the boundary line had been run to Rat Portage, and were therefore anxious to find it out.' He asserted elsewhere that at Rat Portage was probably the northwesternmost point. Keating, *Narrative of an Expedition to the Source of St. Peter's River,* 102–3.

36 Delafield Diary, 8 Aug. 1823, in McElroy and Riggs, eds., *Unfortified Boundary,* 434; and Louis Erdrich, ed., *The Falcon: A Narrative of the Captivity and Adventures of John Tanner* (New York: Penguin Books, 1994), 276–7. In the summer of 1823, Major Stephen H. Long was sent on an expedition that took him up the Minnesota River (then called the St Peter's River) to the Red River and north to Lake Winnipeg and then back south through the Winnipeg River into the Lake of the Woods and the canoe route east to Fort William. Although he followed closely in the tracks of the American surveying party of that summer, he was several weeks behind it and never met it. However, he and his party did meet the British surveyors. He also talked with John Tanner at the Rainy Lake post where Delafield had seen him. Long offered to take Tanner with him and did so as far as Fort William, but Tanner's weak physical condition and his family troubles prevented his accompanying Long back to the settled parts of the United States at that time. See Lucile M. Kane, June D. Holmquist, and Carolyn Gilman, eds., *The Northern Expeditions of Stephen H. Long: The Journals of 1817 and 1823 and Related Documents* (St Paul: Minnesota Historical Society Press, 1978), 204–29; Keating, *Narrative of an Expedition to the Source of St. Peter's River,* 113–16; and Dr. John McLoughlin, 1 Sept. 1823, Post Journals, Lac la Pluie, 1823–24, B.105/a/9, HBC Archives.

37 Delafield Diary, 27 July 1823, in McElroy and Riggs, eds., *Unfortified Boundary,* 422; and Bigsby, *Shoe and Canoe,* 2: 273. Bigsby wrote that McGillivray pointed out the American agent on the opposite shore fishing and then said, 'He is fishing for a dinner. If he catches nothing he will not dine.' Nevertheless, McGillivray reported to the Hudson's Bay Company that the American Fur Company did pose a serious threat to its operations in the Lac la Pluie district. As for the surveys themselves, Dr John McLoughlin, McGillivray's predecessor, worried that they created a 'disagreeable state of uncertainty' for the company's interests in the district. Simon McGillivray, Jr., Post Reports, Lac la Pluie, 1824–1825, B.105/e/4, and Dr. John McLoughlin, Post Reports, Lac la Pluie, 1822–23, B.105/e/2, HBC Archives.

38 Delafield Diary, 1 Aug. – 24 Oct. 1823, in McElroy and Riggs, eds., *Unfortified Boundary,* 428–62, quotation from 430; and Schoolcraft, *Personal Memoirs,* 183.

39 Porter to Adams, 20 Oct. 1823, Box 1, Northern Boundary, RG 76, NA. Por-

ter said much the same thing to Commissioner Barclay. He also suggested a meeting of the board in January in Albany, where the commissioners could meet with the agents and surveyors. Porter to Anthony Barclay, 15 Oct. 1823, Box 8, Barclay Papers, Maine HS.

40 Porter to Adams, 20 Oct. 1823, Box 1, Northern Boundary, RG 76, NA.

41 Delafield to Adams, 28 Nov. 1823, ibid. Ferguson had also learned of the interest in the St Louis River route from both Thompson and the fur trader John Charles Sayer, but like Delafield he seemed to think that the inspiration for this interest came from Schoolcraft's book rather than knowledge of the earlier trade routes in the region. Ferguson was reinforced in his own understanding of the primacy of the Grand Portage route from what he had been told by Indians at Fort William. See Ferguson to Porter, 23 Sept. 1822, E-142-3, and 20 Jan. 1823, E-150, Porter Papers, BECHS.

42 Delafield to Adams, 9 Oct. 1823, Box 1, Northern Boundary, RG 76, NA.

43 Report of Mr. Thompson, 20 Feb. 1824, Box 31, ibid. Bigsby mentioned in his book, published some years later, that he had an old French map that showed 'Pigeon Bay' extending fifty or sixty miles west from Lake Superior. Bigsby, *Shoe and Canoe*, 2: 234.

44 Journal of ... Article 7, 21 Feb. 1824, Box 1, Northern Boundary, RG 76, NA; and Report of the Agent of His Britannic Majesty, 21 Feb. 1824, Box 31, ibid. For commentary on this meeting, see Hon. William E. Culkin, 'Northern Minnesota Boundary Surveys in 1822 to 1826, Under the Treaty of Ghent,' *Minnesota Historical Society Collections*, 15 (1915), 380–1.

45 Porter to Adams, 26 Feb. 1824, Box 1, Northern Boundary, RG 76, NA.

46 Anthony Barclay to George Canning, 10 March 1824, FO 5/192, PRO. Barclay also pointed out to Canning an alternative northwestern point on the lake, although it was not much more favourable to British fur trade interests. Simon McGillivray warned the Hudson's Bay Company that fur operations in the Lac la Pluie district would be 'reduced to nothing' by American control of the Lake of the Woods as far north as Rat Portage. Simon McGillivray, Jr., Post Reports, Lac la Pluie, 1824–25, B.105/e/4, HBC Archives.

47 See Guide to the Thompson Journals, Vol. I, Tyrrell Papers, MG 30 D 49, NAC. Thompson had also hoped to explore Caribou Island in Lake Superior to determine whether it might be Isle Philipeaux but was warned against it by Lieutenant Henry W. Bayfield of the Royal Navy, who had made a survey of the lake himself. Rather than risking the reefs around the island, Bayfield suggested, Thompson should consult his (Bayfield's) notes, copies of which he duly sent on. See Bayfield to Thompson, 15 July and 10 Oct. 1824, Box 31, Northern Boundary, RG 76, NA.

48 Report of J. Ferguson, 20 Feb. 1824, Box 9, Barclay Papers, Maine HS; and IBC, *Joint Report*, 216–18.

49 See Simon McGillivray, Post Reports, Lac la Pluie, 1823–24, B.105/e/3, Simon McGillivray, Post Reports, Lac la Pluie, 1824–25, B.105/e/4, and J.D. Cameron, Post Reports, Lac la Pluie, 1824–25, B.105/e/5, HBC Archives.

50 Memorial by Joseph Delafield, 25 Oct. 1824, Box 31, Northern Boundary, RG 76, NA; and Journal of ... Article 7, 28 Oct. 1824, FO 303/29, PRO.

51 Anthony Barclay to George Canning, 28 Oct. 1824, FO 5/187, PRO.

52 Porter to Adams, 10 Nov. 1824, Box 1, Northern Boundary, RG 76, NA. Although Simon McGillivray, the Hudson's Bay Company factor at Rainy Lake, talked about the Fond du Lac route to Lake Superior, he clearly assumed that the old Grand Portage route to Rainy Lake would be recognized as the border. 'We conceive they [the American fur traders] have a right of Territory and Trade all South of the Old Canoe Track from the Grand Portage of Lake Superior to portage du Rat in the Lake of the Woods.' Simon McGillivray, Jr., Post Reports, Lac la Pluie, 1824–25, B.105/e/4, HBC Archives.

53 Delafield to Adams, 17 Nov. 1824, Box 1, Northern Boundary, RG 76, NA.

54 Garry to Lord Bathurst, 30 Oct. 1824, FO 5/187, PRO; John H. Pelly to George Canning, 24 Nov. 1824, London Correspondence with all Government Departments, 1813–25, A 8/1, HBC Archives; and 'Diary of Nicholas Garry,' *Transactions of the Royal Society of Canada*, Series II (1912), 128. Six months later, Pelly wrote to the foreign secretary to ask about the status of the boundary in the Lake of the Woods. He was told that Dr Tiarks had been sent out to make a scientific calculation of the position of the northwesternmost corner of the lake. See [John H.] Pelly to George Canning, 25 May 1815, and Planta to John H. Pelly, 27 May 1825, London Correspondence with all Government Departments, 1813–25, A 8/1, HBC Archives.

55 Planta to Anthony Barclay, 11 Dec. 1824, FO 5/187, PRO. As Planta put it, 'Unless observations be made for this express purpose [finding the northwesternmost point of the Lake of the Woods that would facilitate British passage from Rainy River to the Winnipeg River], and not for surveying the Lake generally, as appears to have been the case hitherto, it seems almost impossible, from the nature of the Country, to avoid Error [i.e., passage through American territory].'

56 Henry Rolleston to Anthony Barclay, 18 Dec. 1824, and Memorandum of Dr. Tiarks, FO 5/187, PRO.

57 Planta to Anthony Barclay, 12 Feb. 1825, FO 5/200, PRO.

58 Anthony Barclay to Joseph Planta, 14 and 23 Feb. 1825, ibid.

59 Planta to Tiarks, and Planta to Anthony Barclay, 2 April 1825, ibid. For

instructions to Barclay, see Henry Rolleston to Anthony Barclay, 10 May 1825, Box 8, Barclay Papers, Maine HS.

60 Anthony Barclay to Planta, 16 May 1825, FO 5/200, PRO. IBC, *Joint Report*, says that Ferdinand Hassler accompanied Tiarks and Barclay on this expedition west, but this is not confirmed by any of the official papers or in the biographical material about Hassler. Although it would have been prudent for the United States to have sent an astronomer to accompany Tiarks on this mission, the opinion that the U.S. government then had about Hassler makes him an unlikely candidate. See IBC, *Joint Report*, 218; and Lass, *Minnesota's Boundary with Canada*, 48. For some commentary on Tiarks's work, see Whittemore S. Boggs, *International Boundaries: A Study of Boundary Functions and Problems* (New York: Columbia University Press, 1940), 49.

61 Culkin, 'Northern Minnesota Boundary Survey,' 380–2.

62 IBC, *Joint Report*, 218–19. Only Alexander N. Winchell seems to have pointed out that Angle Inlet, identified by Tiarks as the northwesternmost point of the Lake of the Woods, is nowhere near the true northwestern extremity of the lake. A modern map of the lake will reveal that point to be considerably further north and west – probably in Indian Bay in Shoal Lake, near where Winnipeg obtains its water supply. A boundary reaching to such a point would still have given the Hudson's Bay Company unobstructed passage through the Lake of the Woods to Rat Portage and the Winnipeg River, although it would have presented the United States with a larger and slightly more awkward Northwest Angle than the present one. Nonetheless, it is a puzzle that the vast western arms of the Lake of the Woods appeared to be unknown to so experienced an explorer as Thompson. Winchell, 'Minnesota's Northern Boundary,' 211–12.

63 Anthony Barclay to Planta, 5 Oct. 1825, FO 5/200, PRO.

64 The Report of J.L. Tiarks, Astronomer on the part of His Britannic Majesty under the Sixth and Seventh Articles of the Treaty of Ghent, on his Astronomical Observations for ascertaining the northwestern point of the Lake of the Woods, 18 Nov. 1815, sent to Donald Fraser, E-161, Porter Papers, BECHS.

65 Anthony Barclay to Planta, 7 Nov. 1825, FO 5/200, PRO; and Tiarks to Planta, 9 Jan. 1826, Vol. 1, Tiarks Papers, MG 24 H64, NAC.

66 Henry Rolleston to Anthony Barclay, 7 Jan. 1826, Box 9, Barclay Papers, Maine HS.

67 Porter to Clay, 16 Nov. 1825, Box 1, Northern Boundary, RG 76, NA. Porter certainly knew about Tiarks's mission, and he requested a copy of Tiarks's report from Barclay. See Peter B. Porter to Anthony Barclay, 31 Dec. 1825, Box 8, Barclay Papers, Maine HS. Delafield also reported the expedition of

Barclay and Tiarks, but like Porter he was preoccupied with the likelihood of British claims for the Fond du Lac–St. Louis River route to the interior. Delafield to Clay, 23 Sept. 1825, in James F. Hopkins, ed., *The Papers of Henry Clay* (Lexington: University Press of Kentucky, 1972), 4: 677.

68 Journal of ... Article 7, 1 and 2 Nov. 1825, FO 303/29, PRO.

69 Porter to Clay, 16 Nov. 1825, Box 1, Northern Boundary, RG 76, NA.

70 Anthony Barclay to George Canning, 27 Feb. 1826, FO 5/215, PRO.

71 Planta to Anthony Barclay, 8 March 1826, ibid.

72 Anthony Barclay to Porter, 25 April 1826, and Porter to Clay, 15 May and 28 Aug. 1826, Box 1, Northern Boundary, RG 76, NA; and Memorandum by Joseph Planta, and minute by H.U. Addington, 18 Sept. 1826, FO 5/215, PRO.

73 Clay to the President of the U. States, 25 Sept. 1826, Unofficial letters of Henry Clay, E 870, Domestic Letters, M 40 (roll 19), RG 59, NA. Porter was also authorized to locate the forty-ninth parallel as far west as the Red River, carrying into effect the boundary as decided under the Convention of 1818. Clay to Porter, 22 Oct. 1826, ibid.

74 See Anthony Barclay to Planta, 27 and 31 Oct. 1826, FO 5/215, PRO.

75 Joseph Delafield complained that Thompson had completed the maps supporting British interests (the St Mary's River, the St Louis River route, and the Lake of the Woods) but had neglected his other assignments (the Pigeon River – Rainy River route and the Kamanistiquia route). Delafield to Porter, 23 April 1826, E-162-7, and 7 June 1826, E-163-12, Porter Papers, BECHS. Also see Delafield to Clay, 25 May 1826, in James F. Hopkins and Mary W.V. Hargreaves, eds., *The Papers of Henry Clay* (Lexington: University of Kentucky Press, 1973), 5: 395–6.

76 George Canning to Anthony Barclay, 17 June 1826, and Planta to Anthony Barclay, 17 June 1826, FO 5/209, PRO; and Clay to Porter, 22 Oct. 1816, Domestic Letters, M 40, RG 59, NA.

77 Journal of ... Article 7, 5–11 Oct. 1826, FO 303/29, PRO.

78 Porter to Clay, 16 Oct. 1826, Box 1, Northern Boundary, RG 76, NA. General Porter had written to Clay as recently as 8 Oct. assuring him that as a result of conversations with Barclay on the boundary he anticipated 'an amicable & speedy result.' Porter to Clay, 8 Oct. 1826, in Hopkins and Hargreaves, eds., *Papers of Henry Clay*, 5: 764. However, both Clay and Adams agreed to the reference to London. Clay to Porter, 22 Oct. 1826, Domestic Letters, M 40, RG 59, NA.

79 Anthony Barclay to Planta, 28 Oct. 1826, FO 5/215, PRO. After his letter of 28 Oct. was written, Barclay approached Porter with still another compromise. This was to agree to the Pigeon River as the border, but to provide a

guarantee that the old portage route on land could be used by the citizens of both countries. Porter replied that his commission did not give him diplomatic powers to negotiate a boundary other than that which was described in the treaty of 1783. Only a separate treaty negotiation could accomplish such a diplomatic compromise. Anthony Barclay to Planta, 1 Nov. 1826, FO 5/215, PRO. For the American views, see Porter to Clay, 16 Oct. 1826 and 2 Nov. 1826 (Private), and Delafield to Clay, 28 Oct. 1826, Box 1, Northern Boundary, RG 76, NA. Also see Journal of ... Article 7, 23 Oct. 1826, FO 303/29, PRO. Clay passed on to Porter the president's willingness both to continue the board for another season and to authorize the placement of monuments at the most northwestern point of the Lake of the Woods and where the forty-ninth parallel crossed the Red River. Clay to Porter, 22 Oct. 1826, Domestic Letters, M 40, RG 59, NA.

80 See Vaughan to Clay, 23 Oct. 1826, and Porter to Clay, 2 Nov. 1826, in Hopkins and Hargreaves, eds., *Papers of Henry Clay*, 5: 817 and 860; Clay to Vaughan, 15 Nov. 1826, Notes to Foreign Ministers in the U.S., M 38 (roll 3), RG 59, NA; and Vaughan to George Canning, 20 Nov. 1826, and Vaughan to Anthony Barclay, 20 Nov. 1826, FO 5/213, PRO.

81 Adams, Annual Message, 5 Dec. 1826, in Richardson, ed., *Messages and Papers of the Presidents*, 3: 922.

82 See Porter to Clay, 31 Oct. 1826, Box 1, Northern Boundary, RG 76, NA; Clay to Porter, 4 Nov. 1826, Domestic Letters, M 40 (roll 19), RG 59, NA; and Porter to Anthony Barclay, 20 April 1827, Anthony Barclay to Planta, 8 May 1827, and Foreign Office to Anthony Barclay, 5 July 1827, FO 5/240, PRO.

83 Planta to Anthony Barclay, 8 Jan. 1827, FO 5/240, PRO.

84 Gallatin and Addington had dinner with Canning on 28 July, twelve days before he died. Addington reported that Canning had a 'ghastliness of feature, and dejection of air' that prompted the advice from the guests that Canning get away from his duties and take a holiday. Clearly no serious discussion of the boundary was attempted. Henry Unwin Addington to Stratford Canning, 9 Aug. 1827, in Arthur Aspinall, ed., *The Formation of Canning's Ministry, Feb. to Aug. 1827* (London: Royal Historical Society, 1937), 279.

85 Anthony Barclay to Planta, 4 April 1827, FO 5/240, PRO.

86 Foreign Office to Anthony Barclay, 5 July 1827, ibid.

87 The board of commissioners was to have met in March 1827, but Barclay had not by then received instructions on the basis of his inquiries about room for compromise on the contentious issues. Only after receiving Undersecretary Planta's note of 5 July 1827 was Barclay able to schedule the Oct. meeting. See Delafield to Clay, 22 March 1827, in Mary W.M. Hargreaves and James F.

Hopkins, eds., *The Papers of Henry Clay* (Lexington: University Press of Kentucky, 1981), 6: 342.

88 Anthony Barclay to Porter, 13 Sept. 1827, FO 5/240, PRO; and Delafield to Clay, 22 Sept. 1827, Box 1, Northern Boundary, RG 76, NA. Also see Planta to Anthony Barclay, 8 Jan. 1827, FO 5/240, PRO; and Porter to Clay, 27 Feb. 1827, Delafield to Clay, 22 March 1827, and Porter to Clay, 20 April 1827, Box 1, Northern Boundary, RG 76, NA.

89 Delafield to Clay, 6 April 1827, Box 1, Northern Boundary, RG 76, NA.

90 See Journal of ... Article 7, 23–27 Oct. 1827, FO 303/29, PRO; and the reports of the British and American commissioners in 'Boundary Between the United States and Great Britain, Message from the President of the United States, 3 July 1838,' Doc. No. 451, House Doc., Vol. 11, 25th Congress, 2nd Session. For comments on the unsatisfactory closing of the commission, see Porter to Clay, 26 and 30 Oct. 1827, in Hargreaves and Hopkins, eds., *Papers of Henry Clay*, 6: 1189, 1208–9, and 1238–9. Porter was still more upset about Barclay's separate report, completed after the last meeting of the board in December. On 21 March 1828, Porter wrote to Clay setting forth his objections to many of the assertions of both Barclay and David Thompson. He queried whether he should also issue his own supplementary report. See Porter to Clay, 21 March 1828, in Robert Seager II, ed., *The Papers of Henry Clay* (Lexington: University Press of Kentucky, 1982), 7: 176–9.

91 Delafield to Porter, 30 Dec. 1827, E-168, 8 Jan. 1812, E-171, and 31 Jan. 1828, E-172, Porter Papers, BECHS.

92 Lieutenant Whistler, who had been the principal American draftsman, published, on the basis of his work, a series of eight maps of the Great Lakes boundary region through the Washington printer Gales and Seaton in 1828. See Seymour I. Schwartz and Ralph E. Ehrenburg, *The Mapping of America* (New York: Harry N. Abrams, 1980), 252.

93 Forsyth to Fox, 29 July 1839, in Manning, ed., *DCUSCR*, 4: 89–90; and Fox to Palmerston, 10 Aug. 1839, FO 5/332, PRO.

Chapter 7. Preparing for Arbitration

1 Diary, 22 Nov. 1821, in Adams, ed., *Memoirs of John Quincy Adams*, 5: 407.

2 28 Oct. 1822, ibid., 6: 91.

3 See Barclay to Londonderry, 11 July 1822, FO 5/170; and William Huskisson to Duke of Wellington, 30 July 1824, Vol. 13, Huskisson Papers, Add. Mss. 38,746, BL.

4 See Diary, 1 July 1822, in Adams, ed., *Memoirs of John Quincy Adams*, 6: 41. 'To this [negotiation] the British Government have agreed, but with a notifica-

tion that they are not disposed to yield upon the point made by their Commissioner on this article as they had with regard to the sixth [the islands in the Detroit River] – which seems almost equivalent to saying that it is useless to negotiate.' Also see Bemis, *John Quincy Adams*, 473.

5 See for example, Adams to Rush, 25 June 1823, *American State Papers: Foreign Affairs*, 5: 523–7.

6 F.O. [George Canning] to Huskisson and Stratford Canning, 31 May 1824, Instructions on Negotiations, FO 5/199, PRO. Surprisingly, in the light of these instructions, some in the government thought that Canning was 'inclined to undervalue the New Brunswick territory' and that he needed stiffening. G. Baillie to Sir Howard Douglas, 6 Nov. 1824, Vol. 2, Douglas Papers, MG 24 A 3, NAC. Huskisson did look for room to negotiate. In July 1824 he asked Wellington to order a report to be made on the military significance of Rouse's Point in order to determine whether it was actually as valuable as various colonial officials had said or whether other areas such as the New Brunswick frontier were more important. Huskisson to Wellington, 30 July 1824, Vol. 13, Huskisson Papers, Add. Mss. 38,746, BL.

7 Bemis, *John Quincy Adams*, 474–6. For comments on the failure to reach an agreement, see George Canning to Charles R. Vaughan, 2 June 1825, FO 5/199, PRO.

8 Barclay to Ward Chipman, Jr., 24 April 1826, Vol. 52, Chipman Papers, MG 23 D 1, NAC. Also see G. Baillie to Sir Howard Douglas, 16 Dec. 1825, Vol. 2, Douglas Papers, MG 24 A 3, NAC. 'As to the Boundary Line I do not know how it will be settled. The Commissioners recommended that we should on no account give up the point, but at the same time they say that we mustn't return Rouse's Point which gives us Command of Lake Champlain in the event of a War. Mr. Canning thinks that a reference to a third Power is not tempting and in my poor opinion negotiations with the Americans less so. The Engineer Officers further recommend the completion of a good Military Road between Fredericton & Quebec forthwith, and I therefore do not see how we can possibly give up the point in dispute. Indeed I would almost as soon permit them [the Americans] to take possession of St. James Park.' In short, no compromise and give up nothing.

9 William Huskisson, 'Memorandum of Important questions pending,' 15 July 1826, Vol. 33, Huskisson Papers, Add. Mss. 38,766, BL.

10 As late as 20 April 1826, Canning wrote to King to inquire whether he had powers to resume negotiations on the boundary. George Canning to King, 20 April 1826, FO 5/220, PRO. King's instructions from Secretary of State Clay contained no mention of the northeastern boundary. See Clay to King, 10 May 1825, in Hopkins, ed., *Papers of Henry Clay*, 4: 340–54. Some

thought King a most effective minister right up to his return to the United States. 'Unfortunately, the present American Minister is the most esteemed and the best received of all the envoys from that Country, and has no doubt been selected to obtain from Administration what no other person could.' Bliss to Ward Chipman Jr., 11 June 1826, Vol. 5, Chipman Papers, MG 23 D 1, NAC.

11 Clay to Gallatin, 2 and 5 May 1826, Diplomatic Instructions, All Countries, M 77 (roll 6), RG 59, NA; and Beckles Willson, *America's Ambassadors to England (1785–1928): A Narrative of Anglo–American Diplomatic Relations* (1928; reprint, Freeport, NY: Books for Libraries Press, 1969), 165–79.

12 See Walters, *Albert Gallatin*, passim. Gallatin was born in Geneva in 1761 into a prosperous and well-connected family, but he left in 1780 to seek his fortune in the United States. Within a decade he achieved considerable prominence in the country as a politician supporting the Jeffersonian Republicans. His rather aristocratic origins made him an exceptional American representative in Europe from 1814 to 1830. The British regarded him with some suspicion but respected his abilities.

13 Walters, *Albert Gallatin*, 332–5.

14 Bliss to Ward Chipman Jr., 5 Oct. 1826, Reel C-1180, Chipman Papers, MG 23 D 1, NAC.

15 Clay to Gallatin, 19 June 1826, Diplomatic Instructions, All Countries, M 77 (roll 6), RG 59, NA.

16 Gallatin to Clay, 29 June 1826, in Hopkins and Hargreaves, eds., *Papers of Henry Clay*, 5: 508–16.

17 Clay to Gallatin, 8 Aug. 1826, Diplomatic Instructions, All Countries, M 77 (roll 6), RG 59, NA. Clay used very much the same language in correspondence with President Adams. See Adams to Clay, 5 July 1826, and Clay to Adams, 25 July 1826, in Hopkins and Hargreaves, eds., *Papers of Henry Clay*, 5: 521 and 567.

18 Gallatin to Clay, 30 Jan. 1827, in Henry Adams, ed., *The Writings of Albert Gallatin* (Philadelphia: J.B. Lippencott, 1879), 2: 357.

19 Gallatin to Clay, 6 March 1827, in ibid., 2: 361–2. Both Merk and Perkins noted that Addington was increasingly aggressive and expansionist in dealing with the northeastern and Oregon boundaries. Perkins concluded that Addington was essentially a 'subordinate' whose role was to represent the interests of his superiors to the fullest, not that of a diplomat who might negotiate a bold compromise. See 'Henry Unwin Addington,' in *DNB*, 1: 121; Frederick Merk, *The Oregon Question: Essays in Anglo–American Diplomacy and Politics* (Cambridge, Mass.: Harvard University Press, 1967), 156–8 and 197–204; and Bradford Perkins, ed., *Youthful America: Selections from Henry*

Unwin Addington's Residence in the United States of America, 1822, 23, 24, 25 (Berkeley: University of California Press, 1960), 5–8.

20 William Huskisson, 'Memorandum of Important questions pending,' 15 July 1826, Vol. 33, Huskisson Papers, Add. Mss. 38,766, BL. Huskisson was president of the Board of Trade in Lord Liverpool's government and was colonial secretary from August 1827 in the governments of Lord Goderich and later the Duke of Wellington.

21 Two other conventions were signed on 6 Aug. 1827.

22 Dudley to Vaughan, 5 June 1828, FO 5/235, PRO. Dudley did express willingness to reopen negotiations if the Americans would agree to equal concessions. Also see Charles Grant and H.U. Addington to Lord Dudley, 1 Sept. 1827, FO 5/230, PRO. Spokesmen for Maine continued to assert a claim for possession of the whole of the disputed territory right up to the St Lawrence watershed. See Maine, *January Session, 1828, Doc. No. 13, Report of the Joint Select Committee of the Senate and House of Representatives of the State of Maine, In relation to the North-Eastern Boundary of the State* (Portland: Thomas Todd, 1828).

23 See Gallatin to Clay, 21 March 1827, and Gallatin to Clay, 13 Sept. 1826, in Adams, ed., *Writings of Gallatin*, 2: 369–70 and 324. For Adams's views, see Adams, ed., *Memoirs of John Quincy Adams*, 5: 407. Even the text of the convention noted that the reports and documents of the commission under the fifth article were such that it was 'unprobable that any Sovereign or State should be willing or able to undertake the office of investigating and arbitrating upon them.' Miller, *Treaties*, 3: 320. For a short history of the arbitration, see Francis M. Carroll, 'Kings and Crises: Arbitrating the Canadian-American Boundary Dispute, and the Belgian Crisis, 1830–31,' *NEQ* 73 (June 2000).

24 Miller, *Treaties*, 3: 320–3.

25 See Grant and Addington to Dudley, 29 Sept. 1827, FO 5/230, PRO; Gallatin to Clay, 21 Sept. 1827, in Adams, ed., *Writings of Gallatin*, 2: 388–9; and Walters, *Albert Gallatin*, 339–41. Of the four who voted against the convention, John Chandler and Albion K. Parris were from Maine, Levi Woodbridge was from New Hampshire, and William Smith was from South Carolina – an ominous portent. See Bemis, *John Quincy Adams*, 477.

26 Gallatin to Clay, 30 Oct. 1826, in Manning, ed., *DCUSCR*, 2: 524.

27 Clay to Lincoln, 27 March 1827, Lincoln to Clay, 18 April and 3 Sept. 1827, Clay to Lincoln, 30 Oct. 1827, and Lincoln to Clay, 16 Nov. 1827, in Hargreaves and Hopkins, eds., *Papers of Henry Clay*, 6: 363–4, 459–60, 994–5, 1205–6, and 1272–3; and Maine, *Jan. Session, 1828, Doc. No. 13, Report of the Joint Select Committee of the Senate and House of Representatives of the State of Maine,*

In Relation to the North-Eastern Boundary of the State, 32–3. Also see Geraldine Tidd Scott, *Ties of Common Blood: A History of Maine's Northeast Boundary Dispute with Great Britain, 1783–1842* (Bowie: Heritage Books, 1992), 56–7.

28 See the original instructions to Albert Gallatin at the beginning of his mission, Clay to Gallatin, 19 June 1826, Diplomatic Instructions, All Countries, M 77 (roll 16), RG 59, NA.

29 For Adams's views as early as 22 Nov. 1821, see Adams, ed., *Memoirs of John Quincy Adams,* 5: 407. Clay to Lawrence, 20 Feb. 1828, in Manning, ed., *DCUSCR,* 2: 147. Also see notes in Miller, *Treaties,* 3: 357–8.

30 Lawrence to Clay, 29 March 1828, in Manning, ed., *DCUSCR,* 2: 693–4.

31 Clay to Lawrence, 17 May 1828, in ibid., 2: 174.

32 See George Canning to Stratford Canning, 17 March 1823, FO 5/174, PRO. It is surprising that the United States agreed to consider the king of the Netherlands in view of his country's dependence on Britain during and after the Congress of Vienna, which united Holland with the old Spanish Netherlands under Stadtholder William of Orange, who became King William I of the Netherlands. See J.C. Westerman, *The Netherlands and the United States: Their Relations in the Beginning of the Nineteenth Century* (The Hague: Martinus Nijhoff 1935), 63–81.

33 For a full description of the whole process of selection, see Lawrence to Clay, 14 and 22 June 1828, in Manning, ed., *DCUSCR,* 2: 728 and 736–40. Sir Charles Bagot, British ambassador to the Netherlands, had reported to George Canning several years before that William I had no love for the British. Despite his kinship ties, various British honours, and some time on Wellingston's staff, 'he hates the King of England as he hates poison,' Bagot observed, but William also knew that in a crisis he had to depend on Britain, and therefore 'we may always count upon a sort of predilection in our favour.' Bagot to George Canning, 4 April 1826, in Josceline Bagot, ed., *George Canning and His Friends* (London: John Murray, 1909), 2: 343. This passage is quoted more fully in chapter 8, below, p. 175.

34 Aberdeen to Bagot, 5 Aug. 1828, and Bagot to Aberdeen, 12 Aug. 1828, Vol. 48, Aberdeen Papers, Add. Mss. 43,086, BL.

35 See Hughes to Secretary of State, 8 and 21 Jan. 1829, Dispatches from US Ministers, Netherlands, M 42 (roll 12), RG 59, NA.

36 Clay to Gallatin, 9 Feb. 1828, Box 18, Northeastern Boundary, RG 76, NA.

37 Gallatin to Clay, 18 Feb. 1828, ibid.

38 Clay to Gallatin, 8 March 1828, ibid.; Clay to Preble, c. 19 May 1828, Preble Papers, LC; and Vaughan to Douglas, 22 May 1828, and Vaughan to Dudley, 28 May 1828, FO 5/237, PRO; Robert V. Remini, *Andrew Jackson and the Course of American Democracy, 1833–1845* (New York: Harper and Row, 1984),

3: 195; and Cornelius A. Van Minnen, *American Diplomats in the Netherlands, 1815–50* (New York: St Martin's Press, 1993), 68–9. Also see 'William Pitt Preble,' in *DAB*, 15: 184–5.

39 Douglas to Huskisson, 7 July 1828, FO 5/255, PRO. The British did not at all approve of this attempt to find new evidence to be incorporated into the argument for the arbitrator. What they had in mind as permissible 'new evidence' that was to be exchanged within six months of the ratifications was material that had come to light after the closing of the commission and up to the convention of 1827. The under secretary at the Foreign Office wrote to H.U. Addington that Sir Howard Douglas had suspected the Americans of attempting 'some underhanded proceeding' in asking to search for documents. The Foreign Office was uncertain how to deal with the question. Backhouse to Addington, 14 Aug. 1828, FO 5/253, PRO. However, eventually it too would search for new documents. See Addington to Backhouse, 22 Aug. 1828, ibid.

40 See Daniel Brent to Preble, 27 Sept. 1828, Gallatin to Clay, 25 Oct. 1828, and Gallatin and Preble to Clay, 27 and 29 Dec. 1828, Box 18, Northeastern Boundary, RG 76, NA. A long correspondence between the new American minister in London, James Barbour, and Lord Aberdeen developed about what were admissible documents. It continued until June 1829, after which Barbour returned to the United States, and it reveals that the two men had very little regard for each other. See Barbour to Aberdeen, 7 Nov. 1828, FO 303/35, PRO.

41 See 'Report upon the conditions of our Foreign Relations made to President Jackson,' in James A. Hamilton, *Reminiscences of James A. Hamilton; or, Men and Events, at Home and Abroad, During Three Quarters of a Century* (New York: Charles Scribner, 1869), 590.

42 Hamilton, *Reminiscences*, 116; and Hamilton to Secretary of State, 9 March 1829, Box 18, Northeastern Boundary, RG 76, NA.

43 Preble was appointed in late 1829, although Cornelius P. Van Ness, the former commissioner under the fifth article, had been approached. Christopher Hughes, the chargé at The Hague, had expected to get the appointment, but as a Virginian he was deemed unsuitable for a position that so directly affected the interests of the border states, and so he was sent to Stockholm instead. In any case, King William let it be known that he was not pleased that the United States had failed for several years to send a permanent accredited diplomat. Jackson's biographer Remini has noted that this appointment was also made in the hope of strengthening the fortunes of the Democratic Party in New England, but without consultation with Albert Gallatin, who might have warned the administration of Preble's abrasive quali-

ties. Hamilton, *Reminiscences*, 108; Van Minnen, *American Diplomats in the Netherlands*, 61–7; Van Buren to Hughes, 29 May 1829, Diplomatic Dispatches, All Countries, M 77 (roll 7), RG 59, NA; Van Buren to Preble, 2 Nov. 1829, Diplomatic Instructions, M 77 (roll 8), RG 59, NA; and Remini, *Andrew Jackson*, 3: 195. Also see Vaughan to Aberdeen, 4 June 1829, FO 5/249, PRO. For the British view of all this, see Bagot to Aberdeen, 9 June 1829, Vol 48, Aberdeen Papers, Add. Mss. 43,086, BL.

44 See 'Report,' in Hamilton, *Reminiscences*, 510. Several historians have argued that the American case was poorly prepared (Gallatin had failed to inquire at the British Museum and thereby missed the King George map with marking that would later prove so controversial) and badly argued, although the British officials preparing the opposing case were very impressed and worried by it. See Walters, *Albert Gallatin*, 343; and Bemis, *John Quincy Adams*, 478.

45 Addington to Aberdeen, 3 April 1828, FO 5/253, PRO.

46 Addington to Backhouse, 11 April 1828, ibid.

47 Vaughan to Dudley, 20 June 1828, and Vaughan to Aberdeen, 30 April 1828, Boundary Papers, British, 1827–28, FO 303/35, PRO. As late as 8 Jan. 1829, Aberdeen was asking Vaughan to send copies of various American public documents. Aberdeen to Vaughan, 8 Jan. 1829, Vol. 63, Aberdeen Papers, Add. Mss. 43,121, BL.

48 Tiarks to Backhouse, 18 Aug. 1828, Tiarks Papers, Vol. 1, MG 24 H 64, NAC. Sir Howard Douglas was also talked about as the person to prepare the British statement. See F.C. Gray to Ward Chipman Jr., 30 June 1828, Chipman Papers, Vol. 52, MG 23 D 1, NAC. For Douglas's urging of Chipman's participation, see Sir Howard Douglas to Sir George Murray (Colonial Office), 25 Sept. 1828, CO 188/38, PRO.

49 See 'Ward Chipman,' in *DCB*, 8: 149–53. Ward Chipman, Jr, was elected to the New Brunswick House of Assembly in 1815 and was chosen Speaker in 1820. He was made a judge of the Supreme Court of New Brunswick in 1824 and was appointed to the legislative council on his father's death. In 1834 Chipman became chief justice of the province. He was a conservative jurist and remained a pillar of the governing oligarchy of New Brunswick.

50 'Verax' (Ward Chipman, Jr) *Letters on the Boundary Line, First Published in The City Gazette* (Saint John: Alexander McLeod, 1828), 3–30; and *Secret Journals of the Acts and Proceedings of Congress*. In a letter to Henry Rolleston at the Foreign Office, Chipman revealed that he had written the letters to counter the influence of publications in Maine, and he sent copies to Rolleston. Ward Chipman, Jr., to Rolleston, 28 Jan. 1828, FO 5/253, PRO.

51 Ward Chipman, Jr., to Rolleston, 30 July 1828, FO 5/253, PRO.

52 Ward Chipman, Jr., to Robert W. Hay, 3 Nov. 1828, CO 6/6, PRO.

53 Addington to Backhouse, 22 Aug. 1828, FO 5/253, PRO.

54 Douglas to Sir George Murray, 5 Jan. 1829, and Douglas to Robert W. Hay, 21 May 1829, CO 6/7, PRO. Sir James Willoughby Gordon, having been involved with the St Croix Commission in 1796–8, was asked to assist Tiarks in the preparation of maps for the king of the Netherlands. See Gordon to Lord Grey of Howick, 26 Sept. 1842, Vol. I, Grey Papers, MG 24 A 10, NAC. Anthony Barclay travelled to London in the summer of 1828, delivered some maps and documents to the Foreign Office, and had an interview with Aberdeen, but he seems to have had no significant role in the preparation of the British case. See Anthony Barclay to Backhouse, 22 July 1828, and 8 and 19 Aug. 1828, FO 5/240, PRO.

55 Addington to Aberdeen, 4 May 1829, FO 5/253, PRO. For examples of the Addington–Chipman collaboration, see Addington to Ward Chipman, Jr., 6, 10, 17, 21, and 23 Dec. 1828, Vol. 52, Chipman Papers, MG 23 D 1, NAC. Chipman received praise from Addington through Aberdeen and wrote back, 'It may perhaps be satisfactory to you if I take this occasion to express to you what I feel, our entire satisfaction with your conduct and bearing towards me in this matter. I am particularly obliged by the flattering terms in which you have mentioned me to Aberdeen.' Chipman returned to New Brunswick in July 1829 with thanks and praise from Aberdeen as well. Ward Chipman, Jr. to Addington, 30 March 1829, and Aberdeen to Ward Chipman, Jr., 5 July 1829, ibid. Also see Addington to Ward Chipman, Jr., 31 March and 19 April 1829, ibid.

56 Stratford Canning to Aberdeen, 7 Aug. 1829, FO 5/253, PRO; and Muriel E. Chamberlain, *Lord Aberdeen: A Political Biography* (London: Longman, 1983), 246. Canning's biographer asserted that he had a major role in the preparation of the definitive statement. See Stanley Lane-Poole, *The Life of the Right Honourable Stratford Canning, Viscount Stratford de Redcliffe* (London: Longmans, Green, 1888), 2: 337.

57 Addington to Backhouse, 8 and 17 Sept. 1829, FO 5/253, PRO.

58 Stratford Canning to Aberdeen, 15 Sept. 1829, ibid.

59 Ward Chipman, Jr., to Aberdeen, 26 Sept. 1829, FO 5/254, PRO; Douglas to Aberdeen, 23 Sept. 1829, FO 5/253, PRO; and Tiarks to Backhouse, 25 Aug. 1829, ibid.

60 Addington to Backhouse, 8 Sept. 1829, FO 5/253, PRO.

61 Addington to Backhouse, 17 Sept. 1829, ibid.

62 Stratford Canning to Aberdeen, 7 Aug. 1829, FO 352/23, PRO.

63 Aberdeen to Wellington, 20 Oct. 1829, and Wellington to Aberdeen, 21 Oct. 1829, Vol. 20, Aberdeen Papers, Add. Mss. 43,058, BL.

64 Aberdeen to Stratford Canning, 3 Nov. 1829, FO 352/23, PRO.

65 Aberdeen to Wellington, 22 Nov. 1829, Vol. 20, Aberdeen Papers, Add. Mss. 43, 058, BL.

66 Aberdeen to Wellington, 28 and 29 Dec. 1829, and Wellington to Aberdeen, 27 and 28 Dec. 1829, ibid. Canning had attempted to incorporate the opinions of several people, particularly Douglas, into the text, but he held to his own line of argument about the Northwest Angle of Nova Scotia. 'Sir H.D.'s opinion may, after all, be right & mine wrong, or it may turn out that his proposed attention is more in form than in substance. But in any case I hold it to be a duty which, I owe to the interests of the question, to state this much.' Stratford Canning to Aberdeen, 30 Dec. 1830, FO 5/253, PRO. For Wellington's comment, see Aberdeen to Stratford Canning, 25 Dec. 1829, FO 352/23, FO.

67 *North-East Boundary, Evidence,* 9.

68 Ibid., 10–13.

69 Ibid., 25.

70 Ibid., 25.

71 Ibid., 27–37.

72 Ibid., 37–41.

73 Ibid., 41–5.

74 Britain, *First Statement on the part of Great Britain, according to the provisions of The Convention concluded between Great Britain and the United States, on the 29th Sept., 1827, for regulating the Reference to Arbitration of the Disputed Points of Boundary under the Fifth Article of the Treaty of Ghent* (n.p., n.d. [Foreign Office, c. 12 July 1829]), 10–12.

75 Ibid., 11–16, 19–23, and 29–33.

76 Ibid., 17–23.

77 Ibid., 25–9. Huskisson had argued in his earliest memoranda on the subject that British subjects had occupied the disputed territory since at least 1783, if not, as in the case of the Madawaska settlements, since 1763. William Huskisson, Memorandum, 1 May 1828, FO 5/255, PRO.

78 Britain, *First Statement,* 29–33.

79 Ibid., 35–40.

80 United States, *Definitive Statement on the Part of The United States, of the case referred, in pursuance of the Convention of 29th Sept., 1827, between the said States and Great Britain, to His Majesty the King of the Netherlands, for His Decision Thereon* (Washington: Printed at the Office of the United States' Telegraph, 1829 [Printed but not published]), 2–3 and 5–23.

81 Ibid., 24–6.

82 Ibid., 63–7.

83 Ibid., 58–9.

84 Ibid., 28–34.

85 Ibid., 75.

86 Ibid., 72–82.

87 Ibid., 82–7.

88 Britain, *Second Statement on the part of Great Britain, According to the Provisions of The Convention concluded between Great Britain and the United States, on the 29th Sept., 1827, for regulating the Reference to Arbitration of the Disputed Points of Boundary under the Fifth Article of the Treaty of Ghent* (n.p., n.d. [Foreign Office, c. 1829]), 3–20.

89 Ibid., 21–30.

90 Ibid., 33.

91 Ibid., 34–41.

92 Backhouse to Adams and Tiarks, 10 March 1830, and Adams and Tiarks to Backhouse, 17 March 1830, FO 5/255, PRO. Adams was subsequently posted to Washington, after which he had a series of minor diplomatic posts. He was assassinated while serving as British consul general in Peru in 1852. C.R. Middleton, *The Administration of British Foreign Policy, 1782–1846* (Durham, NC: Duke University Press, 1977), 261.

93 Aberdeen to Bagot, 25 March 1830, Vol. 48, Aberdeen Papers, Add. Mss. 43,036, BL; Backhouse to Bagot, 23 March 1830, FO 37/168, PRO. Stratford Canning had speculated on this very issue in August. See Stratford Canning to Aberdeen, 7 Aug. 1829, FO 352/23, PRO.

94 Backhouse to Douglas, 8 March 1830, FO 5/255, PRO.

95 Adams to Backhouse, 2 April 1839, ibid.; and Preble to Van Buren, 30 Nov. 1829 and 30 Jan. 1830, Box 18, Northeastern Boundary, RG 76, NA. Also see Bagot to Aberdeen, 26 Jan. 1830, FO 37/169, PRO.

96 Gallatin to Van Buren, 26 Jan. 1830, Box 18, Northeastern Boundary, RG 76, NA.

97 Bagot to Aberdeen, 19 March 1830, Vol. 48, Aberdeen Papers, Add. Mss. 43,086, BL. Also see Adams and Tiarks to Backhouse, 19 March 1830, FO 5/255, PRO.

98 Aberdeen to Bagot, 25 March 1830, Vol. 48, Aberdeen Papers, Add. Mss. 43,036, BL.

99 As early as 1826, Gallatin had warned Clay, at a time when it seemed possible to negotiate a compromise boundary line, that an arbitrator was likely to seek some kind of compromise and would 'try if possible to split the difference.' Albert Gallatin to Henry Clay, 30 Oct. 1826, in Manning, ed., *DCUSCR*, 2: 524.

100 Tiarks and Adams to Backhouse, 1 April 1830, Vol. 1, Tiarks Papers, MG 24
 H 64, NAC; and Adams to Backhouse, 2 April 1830, FO 5/255, PRO. Also
 see Aberdeen to Bagot, 5 March 1830, FO 37/168, and Bagot to Aberdeen,
 1 April 1830, FO 37/169, PRO.

Chapter 8. The Award and Its Problems

1 Preble to Van Buren, 27 May 1830 and 14 Sept. 1830, Despatches from US
 Ministers, Netherlands, Roll 13, M 42, RG 59, NA. For a discussion of the circumstances of the king's arbitration, see Carroll, 'Kings and Crises.'
2 Bagot to Aberdeen, 13 July 1830, Vol. 49, Aberdeen Papers, Add. Mss. 43,087,
 BL.
3 W.S. Fullom, *The Life of General Sir Howard Douglass* (London: John Murray,
 1863), 295. One commentator has said that Douglass had 'slyly dropped into
 the royal ear a few well-chosen words as to Gallatin's supposed readiness to
 "split the difference."' Classen, *Thrust and Counterthrust*, 26.
4 Fullom, *Sir Howard Douglass*, 296–7. For the complaints by the governor of
 Maine concerning Gallatin's remark to the secretary of state, see Lincoln to
 Clay, 16 Nov. 1827, in Hargreaves and Hopkins, eds., *Papers of Henry Clay*, 6:
 1272.
5 Gallatin had warned Clay in October 1826 about the perils of arbitration,
 and a copy of his letter had been sent to the governor of Maine on 27 March
 1827; the critical passage from the letter was quoted in a report of the Maine
 legislature published in January 1828. See Gallatin to Clay, 30 Oct. 1827, in
 Manning, ed., *DCUSCR*, 2: 524; Clay to Lincoln, 27 March 1827, in Hargreaves and Hopkins, eds., *Papers of Henry Clay*, 6: 363–5; and Maine, *Jan. Session, 1828, Doc. No. 13, Report of the Joint Select Committee of the Senate and House
 of Representatives of the State of Maine, In Relation to the North-Eastern Boundary of
 the State*, 32–3.
6 Preble to Van Buren, 7 April 1830, Despatches from US Ministers, Netherlands, M 42 (roll 13), RG 59, NA.
7 Preble to Van Buren, 17 May 1830, ibid.
8 See Backhouse to Ward Chipman, Jr., 22 June 1830, and Ward Chipman, Jr.,
 to Backhouse, 1 July 1830, FO 5/254; and Backhouse to R.W. Hay [Colonial
 Office], 23 June 1830, FO 5/264, PRO.
9 Preble to Van Buren, 15 June 1830, Despatches from US Ministers, Netherlands, M 42 (roll 13), RG 59, NA.
10 Preble to Van Buren, 27 May 1830, and 14 Sept. 1830, ibid.; William Pitt Preble to Stephen Thacher, 1 June 1830, Preble Papers, LC; and Van Minnen,
 American Diplomats in the Netherlands, 69–71.

11 Preble to Van Buren, 15 June 1830, Despatches from US Ministers, Netherlands, M 42 (roll 13), RG 59, NA.

12 Bagot to George Villiers, 23 Sept. 1825, cited in G.P. de T. Glazebrook, *Sir Charles Bagot in Canada: A Study in British Colonial Government* (Oxford: Oxford University Press, 1929), 11. For the international context of this situation, see E.H. Kossman, *The Low Countries, 1780–1940* (Oxford: Clarendon Press, 1978), 103–60; and G.W.T. Omond, 'Belgium, 1830–1839,' in Sir H.W. Ward and G.P. Gooch, eds., *The Cambridge History of British Foreign Policy, 1783–1919* (Cambridge: Cambridge University Press, 1923), 2: 124–5. A good analysis of the Belgian rebellion from the point of view of British foreign policy can be found in Chamberlain, *Lord Aberdeen*, 242–6.

13 Bagot to George Canning, 4 April 1826, in Bagot, ed., *George Canning and His Friends*, 2: 343.

14 Preble to Van Buren, 14 Sept. 1830, Despatches from US Ministers, Netherlands, M 42 (roll 13), RG 59, NA. Even during the previous year, the British government had discussed the need to advise the king of the Netherlands about his domestic political problems. See Wellington to Aberdeen, 24 Nov. 1829, Vol. 20, Aberdeen Papers, Add. Mss. 43,058, BL.

15 Bagot to Aberdeen, 7, 13, and 28 Aug. 1830 and 1 and 21 Sept. 1830, and Aberdeen to Bagot, 10 Aug., 7 Sept., and 15 Oct. 1830, Vol. 49, Aberdeen Papers, Add. Mss. 43,087, BL.

16 See Fullom, *Sir Howard Douglass*, 298–304; and Bagot to Aberdeen, 6 and 8 Nov. 1830, Vol. 49, Aberdeen Papers, Add. Mss. 43,087, BL. 'I am in that state of rage and vexation in which it is, I believe, very imprudent to write a letter,' Bagot declared to Aberdeen, revealing his attitude towards Douglas on this occasion. Bagot also reported that the king had not been pleased with the reports of the work of the London conference. Bagot to Aberdeen, 9 Nov. 1830, FO 37/171, PRO.

17 Preble to Van Buren, 14 Sept. 1830, Despatches from US Ministers, Netherlands, M 42 (roll 13), RG 59, NA.

18 Ibid.

19 Sir Llewellyn Woodward, *The Age of Reform, 1815–1870* (Oxford: Clarendon Press, 1962), 76–9.

20 For an account of Britain and these European events, see Kenneth Bourne, *Palmerston: The Early Years, 1784–1841* (New York: Macmillan, 1982), 322–37; Sir Charles Webster, *The Foreign Policy of Palmerston, 1830–1841* (London: G. Bell & Sons, 1951), 1: 109–25; and Jasper Ridley, *Lord Palmerston* (London: Granada Publishing, 1972), 176–91.

21 The great powers decided in Nov. 1830 that Belgium and the Netherlands should be separated, on the condition of Belgium's perpetual neutrality, and

the details were worked out by 20 Jan. 1831, just ten days after the king announced his decision in the arbitration. The Belgians accepted the Jan. protocol, and they also agreed to Prince Leopold of Saxe-Coburg-Saalfield as their king. William refused to sign the accord and sent troops back into Belgium in Aug. only to have them driven out by the French in a serious crisis. The Belgian crisis remained unresolved until the Dutch finally agreed to the settlement in 1839.

In the meantime, Belgian relations with Britain were cemented by the accession to the throne of Victoria, Leopold's niece, in 1837. Leopold had worked for almost ten years to arrange her marriage to his brother's son Albert of Saxe-Coburg, which finally took place in 1840.

Leopold himself had been married to Charlotte, only child of the Prince Regent (later George IV); she died in 1817 during the delivery of their first child, a stillborn son. In the ensuing rush to produce an heir, her uncle Edward, Duke of Kent, wedded Leopold's sister, Victoria of Saxe-Coburg, widowed princess of Leiningen. She gave birth to their only child, Victoria, on 24 May 1819, eight months before her husband's death.

Leopold had turned down the throne of newly independent Greece in 1830 because he thought its system of government insufficiently democratic. During his long reign in Belgium (1831–65) he became renowned as an international arbiter and earned the sobriquet 'Juge du Paix de l'Europe.'

22 Bagot to Palmerston, 11 Jan. 1831 (copy), Vol. 198, Aberdeen Papers, Add. Mss. 43, 236, BL.

23 Moore, *International Arbitrations*, 1: 129.

24 Ibid., 1: 130–1.

25 Ibid., 1: 132.

26 Ibid., 1: 133.

27 Ibid., 1: 134 and 136–7.

28 Ibid., 1: 135–6. For commentary on the award in the context of other arbitrations, see A.O. Cukwurah, *The Settlement of Boundary Disputes in International Law* (Manchester: University of Manchester Press, 1967), 175–8.

29 William F. Ganong, 'A Monograph of the Evolution of the Boundaries of the Province of New Brunswick,' 411.

30 See Bourne, *Palmerston: The Early Years*, 334.

31 Preble to Baron Verstolk, 12 Jan. 1831, Despatches from US Ministers, Netherlands, M 42 (roll 13), RG 59, NA.

32 Preble to Bagot, 15 Jan. 1831, and Bagot to Preble, 17 Jan. 1831, ibid; and Van Minnen, *American Diplomats in the Netherlands*, 72–3.

33 Baron Verstolk to Preble, 30 Jan. 1831, Despatches from U.S. Ministers, Netherlands, M 42 (roll 13), RG 59, NA.

34 Preble to Van Buren, 16 Jan. 1831, ibid.

35 Ibid. As late as 8 March these messages had still not reached Van Buren and the president. Jackson complained to McLane in London and, fearing problems over the boundary question, urged him to stay on as minister there. Andrew Jackson to Louis McLane, 8 March 1831, in John Spencer Bassett, ed., *Correspondence of Andrew Jackson* (Washington, DC: Carnegie Institution of Washington, 1929), 4: 247; and Scott, *Ties of Common Blood*, 76–7.

36 Preble to McLane, 25 June 1831, and Preble to Van Buren, 5 Feb. 1831, Despatches from US Ministers, Netherlands, M 42 (roll 13), RG 59, NA. In his discussion of boundary problems, A.O. Cukwurah concluded that both governments must have contemplated some kind of compromise award by the arbitrator. '[I]t must be observed that documents relating to this settlement strongly suggest that the parties were essentially asking the King of the Netherlands to dictate a compromise that they had been unable to reach themselves.' Cukwurah, *The Settlement of Boundary Disputes in International Law*, 201–2.

37 Bagot to Palmerston, 11 Jan. 1831 (copy), Vol. 198, Aberdeen Papers, Add. Mss. 43,236, BL.

38 Palmerston to Bagot, 18 Jan. 1831, Vol. 50, Palmerston Papers, Add. Mss. 48,466, BL.

39 Backhouse to Stratford Canning, 15 Jan. 1831, FO 352/23 PRO.

40 Herbert Jenner to Foreign Office, 9 Feb. 1831, in Clive Parry, ed., *Law Officers' Opinions to the Foreign Office, 1793–1860* (Westmead: Gregg International Publishing, 1970), 3: 350–6.

41 Herbert Jenner and Thomas Denmar to Palmerston, 18 May 1831, ibid., 3: 354–63. The governing passage in the Treaty of Ghent, article 4, read that the friendly Sovereign 'shall be requested to decide on the differences which may be stated in the said report or reports [of the commissioners].' Miller, ed., *Treaties*, 2: 577.

42 Vaughan to Backhouse, 20 July 1831, FO 5/265, PRO.

43 Palmerston to Bankhead, Numbers 2 and 3, 14 Oct. 1831, FO 5/266, PRO.

44 Bankhead to Livingston, 20 Dec. 1831, Notes from the British Legation, M 50 (roll 16), RG 59, NA.

45 See Preble to Van Buren, 3 March 1831, and Preble to Jackson, 14 July 1831, Despatches from US Ministers, Netherlands, M 42 (roll 13), RG 59, NA; and Van Buren to Preble, 17 March 1831, Diplomatic Instructions, M 77(roll 8), RG 59, NA.

46 John G. Deane to Van Buren, 27 Feb. 1831, and Smith to Jackson, 2 March 1831, Box 19, Northeastern Boundary, RG 76, NA. Also see Sprague, 'The

North Eastern Boundary Controversy, 1783–1842,' in Hatch, ed., *Maine: A History*, 1: 267–9.

47 Cited in Burrage, *Maine in the Northeastern Boundary Controversy*, 165.

48 Governor Samuel E. Smith to Van Buren, 26 March 1831, and Smith to Jackson, 23 June 1831, Box 19, Northeastern Boundary, RG 76, NA.

49 [William Pitt Preble], 'The Decision of the King of the Netherlands considered in reference to the rights of The United States and of the State of Maine' (Portland: Thomas Todd, 1831), 3 and 8. Burrage and Jones both claim this pamphlet to be the work of Preble, and lines in the text repeat phrases that appeared in Preble's correspondence. See Burrage, *Maine in the Northeastern Boundary Controversy*, 174; John Spencer Bassett, 'Martin Van Buren,' in Samuel Flagg Bemis, ed., *The American Secretaries of State and Their Diplomacy* (1928; reprint, New York: Cooper Square Publishers, 1963), 4: 191–4; and Howard Jones, *To the Webster–Ashburton Treaty: A Study in Anglo–American Relations, 1783–1843* (Chapel Hill: University of North Carolina, 1977), 16.

50 Livingston to Van Buren, 1 Aug. 1831, Diplomatic Instructions, Great Britain, M 77 (roll 73), RG 59, NA.

51 Ibid.

52 Ibid. Jackson himself wrote to Van Buren a few days later, saying that he had met with Preble to discuss the award. Jackson felt that the United States would have to wait for Britain to make the first public gesture towards accepting the award. He thought that Van Buren could suggest this discreetly to the British. Jackson to Van Buren, 10 Aug. 1831, in Bassett, ed., *Correspondence of Andrew Jackson*, 4: 330.

53 Livingston to Van Buren, 1 Aug. 1831, Diplomatic Instructions, Great Britain, M 77 (roll 73), RG 59, NA.

54 Vaughan to Palmerston, 20 April 1831, CO 6/9, PRO.

55 Livingston to Van Buren, 1 Aug. 1831, Diplomatic Instructions, Great Britain, M 77 (roll 73), RG 59, NA.

56 Maine and Massachusetts sent this view to Congress. See Maine, *Resolutions of the Legislature of the State of Maine, respecting the advice of the King of the Netherlands, in relation to the North Eastern Boundary* (Portland: Thomas Todd, 1832), and Massachusetts, *Senate ... No. 5, Report of the Committee on Public Lands, on the subject of the North Eastern Boundary* (Boston: Dutton and Wentworth, 1832). For comment, see Bankhead to Palmerston, 13 July 1832, CO 6/10, PRO. Bankhead reported, 'I am sure that the President and his Cabinet regret this decision on the part of the Senate.'

57 Jackson to Livingston, 10 Nov. 1831, in Bassett, ed., *Correspondence of Andrew Jackson*, 4: 371. About the same time Jackson wrote to Van Buren to say that

the situation was awkward, and U.S. good faith seemed questioned, but that his advisers assured him that the Senate would eventually accept the award rather than risking possible conflict with Britain. Jackson to Van Buren, 14 Nov. 1831, ibid., 373–4.

58 Memorandum by Livingston and William Pitt Preble, 15 Feb. 1832, Box 19 Northeastern Boundary, RG 76, NA.

59 Livingston to Jackson, 29 March 1832, Diplomatic Instructions, Special Missions, M 77 (roll 152), RG 59, NA. Also see Francis Rawle, 'Edward Livingston,' in Bemis, ed., *American Secretaries of State and Their Diplomacy*, 4: 225–7; Burrage, *Maine in the Northeastern Boundary Controversy*, 194–204; and Scott, *Ties of Common Blood*, 78–80. The editor of the *Portland Advertiser* was put in jail briefly for being in contempt of the legislature for publishing information about the debates in the secret session.

60 Preble to Livingston, 7 April 1832, and Smith to Jackson, 10 May 1832, Box 19, Northeastern Boundary, RG 76, NA.

61 Protocol, signed by William Pitt Preble, Reuel Williams, and Nicholas Emery, n.d. (c. 30 June 1832), Diplomatic Instructions, Special Missions, M 77 (roll 152), RG 59, NA.

62 Livingston to Preble, 12 June 1832, ibid.

63 See Miller, *Treaties*, 3: 376–7; Burrage, *Maine in the Northeastern Boundary Controversy*, 206–11; and Scott, *Ties of Common Blood*, 78–81.

64 Bankhead to Palmerston, 20 Dec. 1831, FO 5/266, PRO.

65 Bankhead to Palmerston, 20 Jan. 1832, FO 5/272, PRO.

66 Bankhead to Palmerston, 12 March 1832, and 29 March 1832, ibid.

67 Bankhead to Palmerston, 13 June 1832, FO 5/273, PRO.

68 Miller, *Treaties*, 3: 377–8.

69 Bankhead to Palmerston, 13 July 1832, FO 5/273, PRO.

70 Livingston to Bankhead, 20 July 1832, Diplomatic Instructions, Special Missions, M 50 (roll 152), RG 59, NA; Bankhead to Livingston, 21 July 1832, Notes from the British Legation, M 50 (roll 15), RG 59, NA; and Livingston to Vail, 21 July 1832, Diplomatic Instructions, Great Britain, M 77 (roll 73), RG 59, NA.

71 Vaughan to Backhouse, 23 Aug. 1832, and Vaughan to Palmerston, 20 Sept. 1832, FO 5/279, PRO. Vaughan had also told Lord Palmerston that 'secure communication' between the Maritimes and the Canadas was the 'one essential point' of any settlement, and he wrote to Lord Goderich that the desire for navigation of the St John River was a key reason for the rejection of the award of the king of the Netherlands. Vaughan to Palmerston, 30 July 1832, and Vaughan to Goderich, 7 Feb. 1833, in John A. Doyle, ed., 'The Papers of Charles R. Vaughan, 1825–1835,' *AHR* 7 (April 1902), 302–5. William Odell

wrote to the lieutenant-governor of New Brunswick in October to urge that in any negotiations with the Americans the British not agree to a boundary as far north as the St John River or to the use of the lower St John. See Odell to Major General Sir Archibald Campbell, 20 Oct. 1832, F-32-10, Odell Collection, NBM.

72 Livingston to Vail, 26 Feb. 1833, Diplomatic Instructions, Great Britain, M 77 (roll 73), RG 59, NA; and Vail to Palmerston, 3 April 1833, FO 5/287, PRO.

73 Vaughan to Livingston, 14 April 1833 and 11 May 1833, and Vaughan to McLane, 31 May 1833 and 6 June 1833, Notes from the British Legation, M 50 (roll 17), RG 59, NA.

74 Vaughan to Palmerston, 4 July 1833, Vol. 85, Aberdeen Papers, Add. Mss. 43,123, BL; and Burrage, *Maine in the Northeastern Boundary Controversy*, 216. As late as July 1833 Vaughan was still considering a conventional line that would give both parties what they needed in the disputed territory.

75 Bankhead to Forsyth, 28 Dec. 1835, in Manning, ed., *DCUSCR*, 2: 991–5. Also see Palmerston, minute, 24 June 1835, and Palmerston to Lord Glenelg, 22 July 1835, FO 5/305, PRO.

76 Jackson to Francis P. Blair, 7 Aug. 1842, in Bassett, ed., *Correspondence of Andrew Jackson*, 6: 162. When a new set of negotiations was starting in 1842, Edward Everett, the American minister to Britain, recounted to Daniel Webster, then secretary of state, a version of this story. Everett had been told by Jackson's secretary of state that 'General Jackson thought he ought at once to have issued his proclamation declaring the award of the King of the Netherlands final, and that he always afterward regretted he had not.' Everett added that this was 'the only occasion in his [Jackson's] life, on which he had allowed himself to be overruled,' and it was the 'one where he ought to have been particularly tenacious.' Edward Everett to Daniel Webster, 21 Jan. 1842, in Kenneth Shewmaker, ed., *The Papers of Daniel Webster: Diplomatic Papers, 1841–1843* (Hanover, NH: University Press of New England, 1983), 1: 493.

77 Deane to Van Buren, 28 Feb. 1831, Box 18, Northeastern Boundary, RG 76, NA. For a later view of the arbitration from the perspective of Maine, see Sprague, 'The North Eastern Boundary Controversy,' in Hatch, ed., *Maine: A History*, 257–8.

Chapter 9. Skirmishes on the Frontier

1 MacNutt, *New Brunswick: A History*, 1–93.

2 Memorandum in the Canning Papers, FO 350/59, cited in Kenneth Bourne, *Britain and the Balance of Power in North America, 1815–1909* (London: Longmans, 1967), 59. There was a second overland road mapped by Sir James Kempt. This road went up the Restigouche River and its tributary, the Mata-

pediac River, and thence to the Métis on the St Lawrence. It was longer and more remote but had the one advantage of being further from any land claimed by the Americans. However, the route to Quebec along the St John River valley and the Temiscouata portage had been developed since at least 1800, and New Brunswickers had petitioned the British government to secure such a route during the negotiations at Ghent in 1814. Ibid., 44–5; Dugald Campbell to Edward Winslow, 14 July 1800, in Raymond, ed., *Winslow Papers*, 454.

3 Albert B. Corey, *The Crisis of 1830–1842 in Canadian–American Relations* (New Haven, Conn.: Yale University Press, 1941), 159; and Thomas LeDuc, 'The Maine Frontier and the Northeastern Boundary Controversy,' *AHR* 53 (Oct. 1947), 31–3. British attitudes towards the military road between New Brunswick and Lower Canada are discussed in Bourne, *Britain and the Balance of Power in North America*, 43–6 and 59–60.

4 Melbourne to Howick, 2 Jan. 1839, cited in Philip Ziegler, *Melbourne: A Biography of William Lamb, 2nd Viscount Melbourne* (New York: Alfred A. Knopf, 1976), 281.

5 Raikes to Wellington, 11 Feb. 1841, in Harriet Raikes, ed., *Private Correspondence of Thomas Raikes with the Duke of Wellington and Other Distinguished Contemporaries* (London: Richard Bentley, 1861), 246–8. Also see Bourne, *Palmerston: The Early Years*, 550–620; and Ridley, *Lord Palmerston*, 225–355.

6 Addington to Backhouse, 11 April 1828 (private), FO 5/253, PRO.

7 Burrage, *Maine in the Northeastern Boundary Controversy*, 118 and 123–5; and Richard W. Judd, 'The Aroostook War,' in Richard W. Judd, Edwin A. Churchill, and Joel W. Eastman, eds., *Maine: The Pine Tree State from Prehistory to the Present* (Orono: University of Maine Press, 1995), 348.

8 Vaughan to Clay, 15 Nov. 1825 and 2 Dec. 1825, in Manning, ed., *DCUSCR*, 2: 492–5; and Clay to Vaughan, 25 Nov. 1825 and 18 Jan. 1826, in ibid., 2: 70–3.

9 Clay to Lincoln, 15 Dec. 1825, and Lincoln to Clay, 22 Dec. 1825, in ibid., 2: 72–3. Also see Clay to Lincoln, 13 May 1826, Box 20, Northeastern Boundary, RG 76, NA; and Clay to Vaughan, 23 June 1826, Notes to Foreign Ministers in the U.S., M 38 (roll 3), RG 59, NA, in which Clay points out how cooperative the states have been; and Clay to Lincoln, 27 March 1827, in Hargreaves and Hopkins, eds., *Papers of Henry Clay*, 6: 363–4, in which Clay points out how restrained the New Brunswick authorities have been.

10 Sprague, 'The North Eastern Boundary Controversy, 1783–1842,' in Hatch, ed., *Maine: A History*, 1: 259–61; and John Francis Sprague, *The North Eastern Boundary Controversy and the Aroostook War* (Dover, Maine: The Observer Press, 1910), 29–31. Sprague also says that Morehouse was active in 'harassing' American settlers in the region from the Aroostook to the St John rivers – seizing produce and timber and issuing summonses for trespass. Also

see Scott, *Ties of Common Blood*, 40–52; and James Morton Callahan, *American Foreign Policy in Canadian Relations* (1937; reprint, New York: Cooper Square Publishers, 1967), 145–7.

11 Hannay, *History of New Brunswick*, 2: 425–8. Hannay notes that Sheriff Miller had earlier been involved in questionable practices to invalidate elections in York County. For detailed correspondence about the Baker affair, see Executive Council Records, Boundaries, RS 8, F 6772, Provincial Archives of New Brunswick; and for Foreign Office opinion on Baker, Greely, and other disturbances along the Maine–New Brunswick frontier, see 'American North-Eastern Boundary,' April 1939, in Kenneth Bourne and D. Cameron Watt, eds., *British Documents on Foreign Affairs: Reports and Papers from the Foreign Office Confidential Print*, Series C, *North America, 1837–1914* (Frederick, Md.: University Publications of America, 1986), *McLeod and Maine, 1837–1842*, 1: 38–70.

12 See Lincoln to Clay, 3 Sept. 1827, Clay to Vaughan, 14 Sept. 1827, Clay to Barrell, 19 Nov. 1827, and Clay to Vaughan, 29 Feb. 1828, in Manning, ed., *DCUSCR*, 2: 136–63.

13 Clay to Vaughan, 17 Nov. 1827, in Hargreaves and Hopkins, eds., *Papers of Henry Clay*, 6: 1299–1300, and also see Clay to Lincoln, 27 Nov. 1827, in ibid., 6: 1321–3.

14 Adams to the United States Senate, 3 March 1828, in Manning, ed., *DCUSCR*, 2: 163–4; and Vaughan to Clay, 27 Feb. 1828, and Clay to Vaughan, 17 March 1828, in ibid., 2: 684–7 and 167–2. Also see Douglas to Vaughan, 4 Oct. 1827, ibid., 2: 652–3. Even before the Baker arrest came to Governor Lincoln's attention, he was writing to Clay informing him of incursions of New Brunswick officials into areas where Maine felt its claims could not be challenged. See Lincoln to Clay, 3 Sept. 1827, in Hargreaves and Hopkins, eds., *Papers of Henry Clay*, 6: 994; and Scott, *Ties of Common Blood*, 52–8.

15 Barrell to Clay, 9 Dec. 1827 and 22 Jan. 1828, in Manning, ed., *DCUSCR*, 2: 664–5 and 682. Also see Lincoln to Clay, 18 April 1828, in Robert Seager II, ed., *Papers of Henry Clay* (Lexington: University of Kentucky Press, 1982), 7: 232.

16 Burrage, *Maine in the Northeastern Boundary Controversy*, 150; Sprague, 'The North Eastern Boundary Controversy,' in Hatch, ed., *Maine: A History*, 261–4; and Scott, *Ties of Common Blood*, 52–8 and 61–6. Also see Barrell to Clay, 11 Feb. 1828, in Manning, ed., *DCUSCR*, 2: 148–60.

17 For an account of the trial, see Douglas to Vaughan, 12 May 1828, in Manning, ed., *DCUSCR*, 2: 715–24; and Burrage, *Maine in the Northeastern Boundary Controversy*, 150.

18 Judd, *Aroostook*, 27.

19 Hannay, *History of New Brunswick*, 2: 16–17.

20 Burrage, *Maine in the Northeastern Boundary Controversy*, 175–89; and Calla-

han, *American Foreign Policy in Canadian Relations*, 150–1. Also see Hannay, *History of New Brunswick*, 2: 15, for a description of Campbell as the 'most unfit man' to be made governor of a growing colony. Campbell had almost as much trouble with the people and legislature of New Brunswick as he did with the Americans in the disputed territory. Hannay routinely referred to Campbell as 'this old military tyrant.' Also see Livingston to Bankhead, 17 Oct. 1831, McLane to Vaughan, 21 Dec. 1833, and Bankhead to Livingston, 25 Nov. 1831, in Manning, ed., *DCUSCR*, 2: 232–4, 251–3, and 884–5. It would appear that Baker was content, after all this disruption, to live under the British flag. Although he had the option under the Webster–Ashburton Treaty of selling out and moving south of the St John River into the jurisdiction of Maine, he chose to live out his life in New Brunswick, a British subject. See Classen, *Thrust and Counterthrust*, 88.

21 See Bankhead to Forsyth, 18 Feb. 1836, and Forsyth to Fox, 12 Jan. 1837, in Manning, ed., *DCUSCR*, 3: 363–76 and 8–22.

22 See R.L. Reid, 'The Indian Stream Territory: An Episode of the North-East Boundary Dispute,' *Transactions of the Royal Society of Canada*, third series, Section II, 34 (May 1940), 143–71; Roger Hamilton Brown, *The Struggle for the Indian Stream Territory* (Cleveland: Western Reserve University Press, 1955), 49–94; Classen, *Thrust and Counterthrust*, 35–42; and Doan, *Indian Stream Republic*, 185–247.

23 See Forsyth to Stevenson, 12 July and 28 Sept. 1837, Stevenson to Palmerston, 10 Aug. 1837, Stevenson to Forsyth, 21 Aug. 1837, and Stevenson to Palmerston, 18 Nov. 1837, in Manning, ed., *DCUSCR*, 3: 27–31, and 397–404. Burrage, *Maine in the Northeastern Boundary Controversy*, 224–8. Sprague notes that the anxiety of New Brunswick authorities arose partly over distribution of surplus government revenues in the U.S. Treasury. Having paid off the national debt, the federal government was collecting more tax money than it was spending. This money was to be distributed to the state governments in proportion to their number of representatives in Congress, as determined by population, but in New Brunswick this was seen as a bribe. Sprague, *North Eastern Boundary*, 38; and Glyndon G. Van Deusen, *The Jacksonian Era, 1828–1848* (New York: Harper and Row, 1959), 106–7.

24 Hannay, *History of New Brunswick*, 2: 50; Sprague, 'The North Eastern Boundary Controversy,' 265–7; Callahan, *American Foreign Policy in Canadian Relations*, 185–8; and Scott, *Ties of Common Blood*, 97–108. Of interest vis-à-vis for this episode is the correspondence of the lieutenant-governor during 1837. See Sir John Harvey's Letter Book, 1837, F-198, Ganong Collection, NBM. For detailed correspondence about the Greely affair, see Executive Records, Boundaries, RS 8, F 6772, Provincial Archives of New Brunswick.

25 On the very eve of the Rebellions, Fox reported to Palmerston the urgency that President Van Buren felt 'lest some new obstacle may any day arise, – either through hostile collision on the frontier, or by the passing of an angry resolution in Congress, – which shall render it difficult for either Government, to accede with a good grace to such terms of friendly agreement, as may otherwise be yet within their reach.' It was a prophetic observation. Fox to Palmerston, 24 Nov. 1837, FO 5/314, PRO.

26 See Corey, *Crisis of 1830–1842 in Canadian–American Relations*, 7–29. Several books examine the Rebellions specifically. See Edwin C. Guillet, *The Lives and Times of the Patriots* (Toronto: University of Toronto Press, 1968); Joseph Schull, *Rebellion: The Rising in French Canada* (Toronto: Macmillan, 1971); and William Kilbourn, *Firebrand: William Lyon Mackenzie and the Rebellion in Upper Canada* (Toronto: Clarke, Irwin, 1956). Papineau's activities in the United States were less spectacular than those of Mackenzie, but they were not insignificant. For a good account of those who fled from Lower Canada, see John Duffy and H. Nicholas Muller, 'The Great Wolf Hunt: The Popular Response in Vermont to the *Patriote* Uprising of 1837,' *Journal of American Studies* 8 (1974), 153–69. A discussion of both the theoretical problems giving rise to the Rebellions and also the American dimension is in William P. Shortridge, 'The Canadian–American Frontier during the Rebellions of 1837–1838,' *CHR* 7 (March 1926), 13–26; and Orrin Edward Tiffany, 'The Relations of the United States to the Rebellion of 1837–1838,' *Buffalo Historical Society Publications* 8: 7–147.

27 Kenneth R. Stevens, *Border Diplomacy: The* Caroline *and McLeod Affairs in Anglo–American–Canadian Relations, 1837–1842* (Tuscaloosa: University of Alabama Press, 1989), 10–14; and Howard Jones, 'The *Caroline* Affair,' *Historian* 38 (May 1976), 485–502.

28 James C. Curtis, *The Fox at Bay: Martin Van Buren and the Presidency, 1837–1841* (Lexington: University Press of Kentucky, 1970), 172–3. Also see Fox to Palmerston, 13 Dec. 1837, FO 97/12, PRO. Fox recognized that whatever the president might do, a rebellion in British North America would find much support in the United States.

29 Winfield Scott, *Memoirs of Lieut.-General Scott, LL.D., Written by Himself* (New York: Sheldon, 1864), 1: 307. Fox informed Sir Francis Bond Head that the president had ordered the U.S. marshal in Buffalo to 'proceed *at all risks* to do his duty, in arresting such persons who have transgressed the law.' Fox to Sir Francis Bond Head, 4 Jan. 1838, FO 97/12, PRO. However, Fox pressed the U.S. government hard, calling Mackenzie's forces 'piratical invaders' and pointing out the Americans involved, including 'General' Rensselaer Van Rensselaer. Fox to Forsyth, 4 Jan. 1838, Notes from the British Legation,

M 50 (roll 19), RG 59, NA. Not all Americans were sympathetic. Philip Hone thought 'this unjustifiable violation of neutrality on the part of our citizens very naturally excites the vengeance of the loyalists,' who in turn sank the *Caroline*, but he recognized that destroying the vessel in a New York port, rather than seizing it in Canadian waters, would jeopardize good relations. Hone regarded the 'patriots' as 'pirates' and their commander, Rensselaer, as a 'humbug.' Diary, 4 and 19 Jan. 1838, in Allan Nevins, ed., *Diary of Philip Hone, 1828–1851* (1927; reprint, New York: Kraus Reprint Co., 1969), 296–8.

30 Curtis, *The Fox at Bay*, 171; and C.P. Stacey, 'A Private Report of General Winfield Scott on the Border Situation in 1839,' *CHR* 11 (Dec. 1940), 407. Others argue that the effective strength of the army was actually about 5,000 men, with half of these in Florida and the remainder spread among the sixty military posts. In 1838 the British had 4,500 regular army troops in Upper and Lower Canada, and by 1839 they had some 10,500, including two battalions of guards. Bourne, *Britain and the Balance of Power in North America*, 79 and 99.

31 See Ivor D. Spencer, *The Victor and the Spoils: A Life of William L. Marcy* (Providence, RI: Brown University Press, 1959), 105–7. Scott's task was made more difficult by the fact that his nephew, Orrin Scott, was prominent among the Hunters lodges. Oscar A. Kinchen, *The Rise and Fall of the Patriot Hunters* (New York: Bookman Associates, 1956), 37.

32 Forsyth to Stevenson, 12 March 1838, and Stevenson to Palmerston, 22 May 1838, in Manning, ed., *DCUSCR*, 3: 48–51 and 449–66. Also see Van Buren to Lord Palmerston, 16 May 1838, cited in Curtis, *The Fox at Bay*, 177–8; Alvin Laroy Duckett, *John Forsyth: Political Tactician* (Athens: University of Georgia Press, 1962), 208–9; Beckles Willson, *America's Ambassadors to England*, 216–17.

33 Palmerston asked Fox as early as 13 and 19 Jan. 1838 to express to the American government the thanks of the British government for the 'friendly spirit evinced on this occasion [the Rebellions] toward Gt. Britain,' which he also referred to as 'piratical invasions.' Palmerston to Fox, 13 and 19 Jan. 1838, Vol. 69, Palmerston Papers, Add. Mss. 48,495, BL. Lieutenant-Colonel Charles Grey, sent to Washington by Lord Durham, wrote to his father, Lord Grey, 'On the whole I cannot but think the American Government is disposed to cooperate fairly,' and he also reported that British and American boats were patrolling jointly, looking for Patriots among the Thousand Islands in Lake Ontario. Charles Grey to Lord Grey, 17 June and 15 July 1838, Vol. 2, MG 24 A 10, Grey Papers, NAC. For similar comments in his journal, see William Ormsby, ed., *Crisis in the Canadas, 1838–1839: The Grey Journals and Letters* (Toronto: Macmillan, 1964), 36–47. Governor General Sir

John Colborne wrote to Sir George Arthur that despite rumours he did not think war likely. Sir John Colborne to Sir George Arthur, 11 May 1838, in Charles R. Sanderson, ed., *The Arthur Papers* (Toronto: University of Toronto Press, 1957), 1: 118–19.

34 Melbourne to Russell, 8 Dec. 1838, in Lloyd C. Sanders, ed., *Lord Melbourne's Papers* (London: Longmans, Green, 1889), 441. Melbourne clearly understood the awkward position in which the U.S. government found itself. He suggested to Palmerston that some special arrangements be negotiated and special considerations made. 'I am aware also that we do not abstain so far from the same sort of conduct as to enable us to complain with a very good grace ... I think we should have great regard and make great allowance for the situation of the American government and particularly that we should if possible abstain from any violation of their territory.' Palmerston acted with forbearance, but he would not have liked Melbourne's advice. Melbourne to Palmerston, 15 Dec. 1838, cited in Ziegler, *Melbourne*, 286–7.

35 Palmerston to Stevenson, 6 June 1838, in Manning, ed., *DCUSCR*, 3: 469; and Reginald C. Stuart, *United States Expansionism and British North America, 1775– 1871* (Chapel Hill: University of North Carolina Press, 1988), 133. Commander Drew received no reprimand or criticism from either the government or the navy and eventually rose to the rank of admiral. The militia commander at Chippawa, Allan MacNab, Drew's superior, was given a knighthood almost immediately, in March 1838.

36 Jones, *To the Webster–Ashburton Treaty*, 29. Lord Rokeby wrote to Thomas Raikes that 'America has shown very friendly feelings on this business.' Rokeby to Raikes, 18 Feb. 1838, in Raikes, ed., *Private Correspondence of Thomas Raikes*, 78.

37 Stevens, *Border Diplomacy*, 37–8. For a useful study of these secret societies, see Kinchen, *The Rise and Fall of the Patriot Hunters*, passim, especially 39. Also see Guillet, *Life and Times of the Patriots*, 178–87; and Spencer, *The Victor and the Spoils*, 106–7.

38 Curtis, *The Fox at Bay*, 179.

39 Stevens, *Border Diplomacy*, 38; and Paul A. Varg, *United States Foreign Relations, 1820–1860* (East Lansing: Michigan State University Press, 1979), 99–101.

40 Kinchen, *Rise and Fall of the Patriot Hunters*, 69–78. President Van Buren sent personal appeals to Palmerston to treat Canadian prisoners with 'mercy.' He pointed out that leniency would to an 'eminent degree ... strengthen the hand of our well disposed citizens on the frontier' and, although this was not mentioned, of the president as well. Martin Van Buren to Andrew Stevenson, 1839, n.d., Vol. 14, Stevenson Papers, LC.

41 Stevens, *Border Diplomacy*, 39–41; and Kinchen, *Rise and Fall of the Patriot Hunt-*

ers, 79–86. British intelligence in Canada reported that the Patriotes had been supported by the French and Russian governments, as well as the American. Intelligence Report, by Stewart Derbyshire, 30 July 1839, FO 97/18, PRO; and Fox to Palmerston, 20 Aug. 1839, FO 5/333, PRO.

42 Kilbourn, *Firebrand*, 209–11; and Stevens, *Border Diplomacy*, 45–6. The British minister was quite surprised that any American court would convict Mackenzie, but he also suspected that Mackenzie would be allowed to escape. Fox to Palmerston, 4 July 1839, FO 5/332, PRO.

43 Second Annual Message, 3 Dec. 1838, in Richardson, *Messages and Papers of the Presidents*, 4: 1702–4. General Scott was even more forceful in his denunciation of the criminality of Patriot Hunter activities. For a vivid condemnation, see Stacey, 'A Private Report of General Winfield Scott on the Border Situation in 1839,' 411–14. An interesting British view of the United States during this crisis is to be found in a letter by Lord Durham's aide, Charles Grey, who was sent on a special mission to talk to President Van Buren. Charles Grey to Lord Grey, 17 June 1838, Vol. 2, Grey Papers, MG 24 A 10, NAC. American authorities attempted to co-operate with Crown forces in Upper and Lower Canada, as late as 1842, supplying them with intelligence about 'Patriot' activities in the United States. This information often got a mixed reception. See Aberdeen to Fox, 31 March 1842, FO 5/376, PRO.

44 Stuart, *United States Expansionism and British North America*, 137.

45 Israel Washburn, *The North-Eastern Boundary* (Portland: Maine Historical Society, 1881), 73–6. An American in Fredericton at the time, Colonel Ebenezer Webster, who attempted to obtain the release of McIntire and his assistants, was also arrested and put in jail. Graeme Wynn has shown that New Brunswick lumbermen had throughout the 1820s and 1830s cut timber more or less in defiance of the regulations that deputy surveyors attempted to impose in order to protect Crown lands and Crown timber. That these lumbermen should also cut freely in the disputed territory is therefore not surprising. By 1836 two 'Restook' lumber companies had been incorporated in New Brunswick with the intention of cutting timber in the disputed territory along the Aroostook River. See Graeme Wynn, 'Administration in Adversity: The Deputy Surveyors and Control of New Brunswick Crown Forests before 1844,' *Acadiensis* 7 (autumn 1977), 55–65; Judd, *Aroostook*, 1–33; and T.C.L. Ketchum, *A Short History of Carleton County New Brunswick* (1922; reprint, Woodstock: Larsen's Printing, 1981), 35–8; and Scott, *Ties of Common Blood*, 136–47.

46 Esther Clark Wright, *The Saint John River* (Toronto: McClelland & Stewart, 1949), 228–9.

47 Howard Jones, 'Anglophobia and the Aroostook War,' *NEQ* 48 (Dec. 1975), 525; and Washburn, *The North-Eastern Boundary*, 76–9.

48 Sprague, *North Eastern Boundary*, 65; and Sprague, 'The North Eastern Boundary Controversy,' 271–4. For a detailed analysis of public opinion in Maine, see David Lowenthal, 'The Maine Press and the Aroostook War,' *CHR* 32 (Dec. 1951), 315–36; and Jones, 'Anglophobia and the Aroostook War,' 519–39. There were some dissenting voices. The Boston banker T.W. Ward wrote to Baring Brothers in London, 'I wish the governor of Maine were at the north pole and a regiment of our politicians with him.' T.W. Ward to Baring Brothers & Co., 24 Feb. 1839, Vol. 29, Baring Papers, MG 24, D 21, NAC. Philip Hone noted how the 'rumors of war on the northeastern boundary' had aggravated the financial crisis in the country. He referred derisively to the 'loafer loyalists' and the 'loafer patriots,' and he understood that Daniel Webster might be sent to England to negotiate a settlement. Diary, 21 Feb., 22 March, and 15 and 26 April 1838, in Nevins, ed., *Diary of Philip Hone*, 382–3, 385, and 389–91. Also see J. Chris Arndt, 'Maine in the Northeastern Boundary Controversy: States Rights in Antebellum New England,' *NEQ* 62 (June 1989), 215–18.

49 Colborne to Arthur, 23 Feb. 1839, Arthur to Col. J.F. Love, 6 March 1839, and Sir George Arthur to Colborne, 28 March 1839, in Sanderson, ed., *Arthur Papers*, 2: 51, 75, and 93–4; Charles Grey to Lord Grey, 26 Feb. and 13 March 1839, in Ormsby, ed., *Crisis in the Canadas*, 192–7; and Hannay, *History of New Brunswick*, 2: 52. Colborne had been lieutenant-governor of Upper Canada and was briefly governor general of British North America as well as commander-in-chief.

50 Fox to Forsyth, 23 Feb. 1839, in Manning, ed., *DCUSCR*, 3: 482–3. Sir John Harvey may also have been influenced to release McIntire and the others by Jonathan P. Rogers, a former attorney general of Maine, who had been sent by Governor Fairfield to obtain the release of the Americans. Washburn, *North-Eastern Boundary*, 76.

51 The propriety or otherwise of Fox's claims gave rise to an interesting discussion within the Foreign Office. H.U. Addington, who had drafted the British first statement for the king of the Netherlands, wrote to the undersecretary that while it was true that 'we have undoubtedly heretofore virtually exercised, or rather half-exercised, jurisdiction in the settled parts of the disputed lands, ... that exercise was but tacit, and never clearly allowed although silently acquiesced in, by the Americans, if even that.' Even this acquiescence was predicated on the assumption that the boundary would be settled under the provisions of the Treaty of Ghent. Addington concluded, 'It is quite clear that we cannot maintain, even in arguments, the broad Claim asserted by Mr.

Fox.' Addington to Backhouse, 30 March 1839, FO 5/340, PRO. Also see Hugh Murray to Backhouse, 1 April 1839, ibid. Palmerston conveyed a version of these opinions to Stevenson. See Stevenson to Forsyth, 5 April 1839, Despatches from U.S. Ministers, Great Britain, M3 (roll 42), RG 59, NA; and Willson, *America's Ambassadors to England*, 220–2.

52 Memorandum signed by Forsyth and Fox, 27 Feb. 1839, in Manning, ed., *DCUSCR*, 3: 65–6. For a detailed account of the confrontation along the frontier, see Scott, *Ties of Common Blood*, 148–63.

53 Scott, *Memoirs*, 2: 334.

54 There were two accidental deaths among the Maine militia. One man died of measles, another in a shooting accident. Lowenthal, 'The Maine Press and the Aroostook War,' 333; and Scott, *Ties of Common Blood*, 163–87.

55 *Niles' National Register*, 2 March 1839, 1–2, and 9 March 1839, 17–18. Governor Fairfield eventually agreed to an accommodation, but he was very sensitive to the political ramifications of any apparent backing down in favour of the British. In that event, 'God only knows what the result would be politically,' he warned President Van Buren, a fellow Democrat. Curtis, *The Fox at Bay*, 184–5. Paul Varg has shown that there was considerable opposition in Massachusetts to being dragged into a conflict by the actions of Maine, despite an interest in the disputed territory. See Paul Varg, *New England and Foreign Relations, 1789–1850* (Hanover, NH: University Press of New England, 1983), 137–40.

56 Scott to Harvey, 21 March 1839, in Manning, ed., *DCUSCR*, 3: 106–13. As early as 11 March, Harvey had given instructions to forces under his command to keep to the fringes of the disputed territory, such as north of the St John River, and to avoid any clash with Maine militia. Harvey to Col. C.B. Goldie, 11 March 1839, Vol. 1, Harvey Papers, MG 24 A 17, NAC. Also see Scott, *Memoirs*, 2: 338–52. Both Scott and Harvey were heroes of the War of 1812; they had fought opposite each other and held each other in high regard. In his memoirs, Scott recounts an incident in which Harvey had strayed close to U.S. lines and he prevented a soldier from shooting Harvey at close range. After the war they had also exchanged friendly letters. Fox later concluded that Scott was 'one of the best of the Americans.' Fox to Harvey, 12 April 1839, FO 97/15, PRO. Harvey referred to Scott as 'my friend.' See Harvey to Marquis of Normanby, 23 April 1839, ibid. Both Normanby and Palmerston agreed with Harvey's actions, and the foreign secretary sent his approval. Palmerston to Backhouse, Minute, 16 May 1839, FO 5/341, PRO; and Lord Normanby to Harvey, 16 May 1839, in Sanderson, ed., *Arthur Papers*, 2:176–7.

57 Jones, *To the Webster–Ashburton Treaty*, 38; Scott, *Ties of Common Blood*, 263–65;

Judd, *Aroostook*, 33–6; and MacNutt, *New Brunswick*, 269–73. MacNutt shows
that the agreement was strained from time to time. A large barracks and supply depot were built at Temiscouata in apparent violation of the agreement,
and a group of disgruntled New Brunswick lumbermen made an armed
'demonstration' before Fort Fairfield. Nevertheless, the agreement held.
Palmerston wrote to Fox that he was pleased with the agreement and the
arrangements that had been made, but he did drop the militant warning
that if the forces of Maine attempted to occupy the disputed territory 'they
must be expelled by force of arms, let the consequences be what they may.'
Palmerston to Fox, 8 April 1839, FO 97/19, PRO.
58 Palmerston to Fox, 8 April 1839, FO 97/19, PRO. General Scott, for all his
good efforts, was not universally admired. Within the army he was known by
the double-edged nickname 'Old Fuss and Feathers.' The Baring Brothers
agent in Boston, T.W. Ward, commented similarly that he was 'an upright,
second rate, gentlemanly soldier, with a good deal of vanity, & egotism – &
not a sound man – & yet of pure character & right purpose.' Ward to Messrs.
Baring Brothers & Co., 21 Feb. 1841, Vol. 32, Baring Brothers Papers, MG 24
D 21, NAC. By the same token, Sir John Harvey came under increasing criticism from both the foreign secretary, Lord Palmerston, and the governor
general, Lord Sydenham. See Palmerston to Russell, minute, 16 July 1840,
FO 5/356, PRO; and Sydenham to Russell, 24 Nov. 1840, in Paul Knaplund,
ed., *Letters from Lord Sydenham, Governor General of Canada, 1839–1841, to Lord
John Russell* (London: George Allen & Unwin, Ltd., 1931), 101. Fox, the
nephew of Charles James Fox, owed his appointment to political influence.
He was most unhappy in the United States, and Aberdeen eventually
brought him home. Former president Andrew Jackson urged Vaughan,
before he left for London, to tell Queen Victoria that the boundary must be
settled or it would lead to war, despite the desires of the two governments to
maintain peace. See Jackson to Major William B. Lewis, 29 May 1839, in Bassett, ed., *Correspondence of Andrew Jackson*, 6: 16.
59 Arthur to Thomson [possibly Lord Sydenham], 7 April 1840, in Sanderson,
ed., *Arthur Papers*, 3: 11; and MacNutt, *New Brunswick*, 269. The very fact that
the American flag was flown at Fort Fairfield was provocative to some British
subjects. See George W. Featherstonhaugh to Harvey, 23 Oct. 1839, Vol. 4,
Harvey Papers, MG 24 A 17, NAC. By the autumn, Fox was also pessimistic
about the situation in Maine and worried that a clash was almost inevitable.
Fox to Palmerston, 13 Nov. 1839, FO 5/334, PRO. The following winter, a
new crisis threatened: authorities in Maine complained that the stability of
the situation was jeopardized when fresh British troops moved into the
Temiscouata region. Richard Rush wrote to Andrew Stevenson in London

that this was 'stirring news' and that 'the storm is before us,' clearly expecting hostilities to break out. Rush to Stevenson, 24 Jan. 1840, Vol. 17, Stevenson Papers, LC. Senator Reuel Williams told Fairfield that he thought that 'the British authorities are trifling with us' and later concluded that these actions made clear to the public the aggressive intentions of the British. Williams to Fairfield, 10 and 21 Jan. 1840, Fairfield Papers, LC. Other Maine politicians in Washington feared that the administration was unwilling to protect the state's interests. Congressman Albert Smith wrote to the governor that President Van Buren was as 'cold as an *icicle* on the boundary question.' Smith to Fairfield, 8 Jan. 1840, ibid. Secretary of State Forsyth wrote to the British minister about these reports and was told that a small number of troops had simply been rotated. Forsyth to Fox, 16 Jan. 1840, and Fox to Forsyth, 26 Jan. 1840, FO 97/16, PRO.

However, regular incidents such as this convinced the British that the Americans were always pushing and probing. Palmerston, talking to John Backhouse, said that along the boundary 'force will be met with force.' Palmerston to Backhouse, Minute, 16 Feb. 1840, FO 5/355, PRO. Aberdeen, who would be foreign secretary again within six months, admitted that British relations with the United States were 'worse than ever,' for which he held Palmerston responsible, but he did not believe that events would result in war. Aberdeen to Princess Lieven, 24 April 1840, in E. Jones Parry, ed., *The Correspondence of Lord Aberdeen and Princess Lieven, 1832–1854* (London: Royal Historical Society, 1938), 1:138–9. Daniel Webster was quoted in the press as believing that the crisis would not escalate into open fighting. *Niles' National Register,* 23 March 1839, 53.

60 Thomson to Melbourne, 12 Dec. 1839, in Sanders, ed., *Lord Melbourne's Papers,* 447.

61 *Niles' National Register,* 20 April 1839, 113; Lowenthal, 'The Maine Press and the Aroostook War,' 333. Although the Aroostook crisis eased in 1840, Charles Poulett Thomson, the new governor general, took a much more forceful stance towards the United States. More troops were sent to the Temiscouata area under his orders, and he roundly criticized Lieutenant-Governor Harvey in New Brunswick for making any agreements with the Maine authorities. The Yankees were moving into the Aroostook and the St John valleys, building roads, and setting up block houses. By early 1841 Thomson, by then Lord Sydenham, concluded that this was the time for 'compelling a settlement. The Americans are utterly unprepared for war and *cannot* engage in it whilst we never were so well prepared on this side, which they know full well.' See numerous letters in Knaplund, *Letters from Lord Sydenham,* 52–3, 72, 101–2, and 123. Palmerston also kept up steady pressure

on the Americans. See Palmerston to Fox, 19 July 1841, Vol. 69, Palmerston Papers, Add. Mss. 48,495, BL.

62 Corey, *The Crisis of 1830–1842 in Canadian–American Relations*, 130–1.

63 The most recent and thorough account is in Stevens, *Border Diplomacy*, passim. Also see Alastair Watt, 'The Case of Alexander McLeod,' *CHR* 12 (June 1931), 145–67.

64 Alexander McLeod was said to have resembled his brother Angus, and Angus was known to have been a member of the *Caroline* raid. Given the inflamed passions along the border, the people of the Niagara region may have been just as pleased to convict the brother, or they may have hoped that Angus would have submitted himself to the New York courts rather than see Alexander hanged.

65 Stevens, *Border Diplomacy*, 71–89.

66 Arthur to Sydenham, 11 Jan. 1841, in Sanderson, ed., *Arthur Papers*, 3: 237–8.

67 Fox to Forsyth, 13 and 29 Dec. 1840, Notes from the British Legation, M 50 (roll 20), RG 59, NA; Sydenham to Russell, 10 April and 25 May 1841, in Knaplund, ed., *Letters from Lord Sydenham*, 133 and 138; and Howard Jones and Donald A. Rakestraw, *Prologue to Manifest Destiny: Anglo–American Relations in the 1840s* (Wilmington, Del.: Scholarly Resources, 1997), 53–8 and 177–8.

68 Forsyth to Fox, 26 Dec. 1840, FO 97/16, PRO. Also see Duckett, *John Forsyth, Political Tactician*, 209–10.

69 See Stevenson to Forsyth, 9 Feb. 1841, in Manning, ed., *DCUSCR*, 3: 611–12.

70 Palmerston to Fox, 9 Feb. 1841, Vol. 79, Palmerston Papers, Add. Mss. 48,495, BL. Kenneth Bourne had concluded that at least some of this was a gesture, that Palmerston knew that McLeod had an alibi, and that there was little likelihood of war on this issue. Bourne, *Palmerston: The Early Years*, 636–7.

71 Fox to Webster, 12 March 1841, in Shewmaker, ed., *Papers of Daniel Webster, Diplomatic Papers*, 1: 41–4; and Wilbur Devereux Jones, *The American Problem in British Diplomacy, 1841–1861* (London: Macmillan, 1974), 2.

72 See Stevenson to Webster, 9 March 1841, in Manning, ed., *DCUSCR*, 3: 614–15; and Willson, *America's Ambassadors to England*, 224–6. Stevenson also sent instructions to Commodore Isaac Hull in the Mediterranean to safeguard his squadron by taking them past the Straits of Gibraltar, lest they be bottled up in the event of war. Palmerston related to Henry S. Fox that he had told Stevenson in private conversation that McLeod's execution would mean war. Bourne, *Britain and the Balance of Power in North America*, 86. About the same time, early March, Joshua Bates, a partner in Baring Brothers, wrote to Ashburton's son-in-law assuring him that there was 'not the slightest fear of war.' The new U.S. administration would take care of everything. Bates to

Humphrey St. J. Mildmay, 10 March 1841, Vol. 10, Baring Brothers Papers, MG 24 D 21, NAC.

73 Sydenham to Russell, 25 May 1841, in Knaplund, ed., *Letters from Lord Sydenham*, 138–9.

74 Palmerston to Russell, 19 Jan. 1841, cited in Herbert C.F. Bell, *Lord Palmerston* (London: Longmans, Green and Co., 1936), 1: 253. Some historians argue that Palmerston used strong language with the Americans but followed a very cautious policy. See ibid., 248–54; and Bourne, *Palmerston: The Early Years*, 587. In fact, some Englishmen were prepared to admit that there was a case to be made for the American position, as Charles Greville, no admirer of American institutions, outlined in his diary. 'Yesterday Lord Lyndhurst was at the [Privy] Council Office, talking over this matter with Jenner and Littledale, and He said it was very questionable if the Americans had not right on their side; and that he thought, in a similar case here, we should be obliged to try the man, and if convicted, nothing but a pardon could save him. These opinions, casting such serious doubts on the question of right, are at least enough to restrain indignation and beget caution.' Diary, 12 March 1841, in Lytton Strachey and Roger Fulford, eds., *The Greville Memoirs, 1814–1860* (London: Macmillan, 1939), 4: 364–5.

75 In the summer of 1841, President Tyler, who was more of a renegade Democrat than a Whig, vetoed the attempt by Congress to charter a new central bank. The rechartering of a central bank had been a major Whig principle, and the president's veto provoked the resignation of all of Harrison's Whig appointees to the cabinet, except Webster. The result was that Tyler was a president without a party, and Webster, though still a Whig, was in a most precarious position.

76 Webster to Fox, 24 April 1841, in Shewmaker, ed., *Papers of Daniel Webster, Diplomatic Papers*, 1: 136–46. Tyler later recounted that at his first cabinet meeting he was confronted with a strongly worded note from Fox concerning the McLeod case. Lyon G. Tyler, ed., *The Letters and Times of the Tylers* (1884; reprint, New York: DaCapo Press, 1970), 2: 206. For an account of Webster's role in the McLeod affair, see George E. Carter, 'Daniel Webster and the Canadian Rebellions of 1837–1838,' *Canadian Historical Association Historical Papers* (1970), 120–31. The governor general of Canada, Lord Sydenham, did not expect much difference between the Democrat and Whig administrations in the United States. 'All parties are equally disposed to play the rogue,' he confidently assured Lord John Russell. Sydenham to Russell, 20 Dec. 1840, in Knaplund, ed., *Letters from Lord Sydenham*, 109. Fox told Palmerston much the same. Webster would be even more weak and irresolute in dealing with the Maine government than Forsyth. See Fox to Palmer-

ston, 8 Aug. 1841, FO 5/362, PRO. Sir George Arthur, in contrast, concluded that the new administration would be more friendly. See Arthur to Col. G.A. Wetherall, 8 March 1841, in Sanderson, ed., *Arthur Papers*, 3: 369.

77 See Webster to Spencer, 16 and 19 April 1841, in Shewmaker, ed., *Papers of Daniel Webster, Diplomatic Papers*, 1: 57–8; and Jones and Rakestraw, *Prologue to Manifest Destiny*, 57–61.

78 For this correspondence, see Shewmaker, ed., *Papers of Daniel Webster, Diplomatic Papers*, 1: 68–72 and 77–94.

79 See Seward to R.M. Blatchford, 23 March 1846, in C.H. Van Tyne, ed., *The Letters of Daniel Webster* (New York: McClure, Phillips and Company, 1902), 315. Webster also enlisted the assistance of the U.S. attorney general, John J. Crittenden, who travelled to the border region to advise McLeod's counsel and to Albany to consult with Governor Seward. Crittenden may have been paid as much as $1,000 in connection with his trip to New York and the defence of McLeod. See Webster to John J. Crittenden, 15 March 1841, in Shewmaker, ed., *Papers of Daniel Webster, Diplomatic Papers*, 1: 45–8 and 637. Also see Glyndon G. Van Dusen, *William Henry Seward* (New York: Oxford University Press, 1967), 77–8.

80 Palmerston to Fox, 18 Aug. 1841, Vol. 79, Palmerston Papers, Add. Mss. 48,495, BL (Palmerston left office less than ten days later, 27 August); and Fox to Webster, 5 Sept. 1841, in Manning, ed. *DCUSCR*, 3: 673. Webster rather facetiously replied to Fox, repeating the minister's phrase, that 'it would be unbecoming either Government to utter threats of war.' Webster to Fox, 20 Sept. 1841, ibid., 3: 150–1.

81 Stevens, *Border Diplomacy*, 143–55. McLeod was given a pension of £200 by the British government in 1855. Moore, *International Arbitrations*, 1: 398.

82 Stevens, *Border Diplomacy*, 55–6 and 138–9.

83 Sworn Deposition of James W. Grogan, 13 Oct. 1841, in Shewmaker, ed., *Papers of Daniel Webster, Diplomatic Papers*, 1: 153–7.

84 Fletcher Webster to Fox, 28 Sept. 1841, in Manning, ed., *DCUSCR*, 3: 155. Also see Charles Davis and William Barron to Daniel Webster, 16 Oct. 1841, in Shewmaker, ed., *Papers of Daniel Webster, Diplomatic Papers*, 1: 158–60.

85 Cited in Stevens, *Border Diplomacy*, 141–2.

86 Fox to Aberdeen, 11 March 1842, FO 5/377, PRO; and Bagot to Lord Stanley, 24 March 1842, Vol. 7, Bagot Papers, MG 24 A 13, NAC. As if to tempt fate further, Colonel Allan MacNab, under whose orders the *Caroline* expedition had set out, passed through the United States to board ship for England. Although he travelled under the name of Colonel Johnstone, Bagot was appalled at the risk that he took. See Corey, *Crisis of 1830–1842 in Canadian–American Relations*, 179–80.

Chapter 10. Surveys and Struggles

1 See, for example, Sir Charles R. Vaughan's letter to the secretary of state in early 1834 rejecting a proposed new joint commission. He asked 'whether there is any reasonable probability that a fresh local survey, to be made in the manner suggested, would afford a solution of the remaining Problem,' and he asserted that 'no such Highlands can be found in that particular Meridian ... [north of Mars Hill].' Vaughan to McLane, 10 Feb. 1834, in Manning, ed., *DCUSCR*, 2: 946–50.

2 Forsyth to Charles Bankhead, 29 Feb. 1836, in ibid., 3: 4–6. Also see Eugene I. McCormac, 'John Forsyth,' in Bemis, ed., *The American Secretaries of State and Their Diplomacy*, 4: 330–2.

3 Charles Bankhead to Forsyth, 4 March 1836, and also Stevenson to Forsyth, 22 Feb. 1836, in Manning, ed., *DCUSCR*, 3: 376–7 and 381–2.

4 Judd, *Aroostook*, 6–9; R.Z. Mudge and G.W. Featherstonhaugh, *Report of the British Commissioners Appointed to Survey the Territory in Dispute Between Great Britain and the United States of America, on the Northeastern Boundary of the United States, April 16th, 1840* (London: T.R. Harrison, 1840), 7–8; Forsyth to Fox, 23 March 1837, and Fox to Forsyth, 24 Aug. 1837, in Manning, ed., *DCUSCR*, 3: 23–6 and 400–1; and Harvey to the Secretary of the Saint Andrews Rail Road Association, 24 July 1837, Sir John Harvey Letter Book, 1837, F-198, Ganong Collection, NBM.

5 Fox to Forsyth, 10 June 1837, in Manning, ed., *DCUSCR*, 3: 410–14.

6 Palmerston to Fox, 19 Nov. 1837, FO 97/19, PRO. Fox agreed with Palmerston. See Fox to Palmerston, 4 May 1838, FO 5/323, and the following year, Fox to Harvey, 11 July 1839, FO 97/16, PRO. Advice about a boundary settlement in these circumstances was solicited from the lieutenant-governor of New Brunswick. See Harvey to Fox, 2 Nov. 1838, Sir John Harvey Letter Book, 1838, A-154, NBM.

7 Forsyth to Fox, 27 April 1838, in Manning, ed., *DCUSCR*, 3: 53–4; and also Fox to Palmerston, 5 April 1838, FO 5/322, PRO.

8 *Niles' National Register*, 15 Sept. 1838, 34; Burrage, *Maine in the Northeastern Boundary Controversy*, 247–50; and Scott, *Ties of Common Blood*, 60, 64–7, 82–4, and 111–13. Also see Maine, *January Session, 1828, Document No. 13. Report of the Joint Select Committee of the Senate and House of Representatives of the State of Maine, in Relation to the North-Eastern Boundary of the State.*

9 Burrage, *Maine in the Northeastern Boundary Controversy*, 247–50; and *Niles' National Register*, 10 Nov. 1838, 162.

10 Burrage, *Maine in the Northeastern Boundary Controversy*, 251; and *State of Maine to the Senate and House of Representatives. Edward Kent, Council Chambers,*

2 January 1839 (n.p., n.d.). The governor had also expanded the state militia to its highest level ever, 43,896 men. Scott, *Ties of Common Blood*, 112.

11 Edmond Berkeley and Dorothy Smith Berkeley, *George William Featherstonhaugh: The First U.S. Geologist* (Tuscaloosa: University of Alabama Press, 1988), passim. Featherstonhaugh was also something of a social climber, which is not irrelevant to this subject, inasmuch as securing territory for Britain and resolving the troublesome boundary question might well result in some reward from the government. In the end, Featherstonhaugh was given a consulate in Le Havre, where he served with distinction. As late as the spring of 1839 Palmerston was still pressing the Americans for a joint survey of the disputed territory. See Palmerston to Fox, 6 April 1839, Vol. 69, Palmerston Papers, Add. Mss. 48,495, BL.

12 Fox to Palmerston, 12 Jan. 1839, FO 5/331, PRO; Journal, 11 and 13 Sept. 1838, Reel 10, Featherstonhaugh Papers, MHS; and Berkeley and Berkeley, *Featherstonhaugh*, 207–17.

13 Featherstonhaugh to Backhouse, 12 March 1839, and Memorandum by John Backhouse, 15 March 1839, FO 97/15, PRO; G.W. Featherstonhaugh, 'Memoir serving to explain the case of the territory in dispute with the State of Maine,' in Bourne and Watt, eds., *Foreign Office Confidential Print ... McLeod and Maine, 1837–1842*, 75–82; Journal, 26 March 1839, Reel 10, Featherstonhaugh Papers, MHS; and Berkeley and Berkeley, *Featherstonhaugh*, 218.

14 Featherstonhaugh, 'Memoir,' 75–82; and Berkeley and Berkeley, *Featherstonhaugh*, 205. Henry Unwin Addington, who had helped to draft the British case for the king of the Netherlands, was shown some of Featherstonhaugh's propositions. His response to Backhouse was cautious: 'The idea is ingenious and I dare say the description of the lay of the land is correct: but that is not the point for us to build our point upon. The point is what was the intention of the framers of the Treaty of 1783 with reference to the former boundaries of the respective Provinces, and particularly on Canada: And the foundation stone of *our* whole question is, Did those framers include the St. John in the class of Atlantic Rivers, or did they not? Twist and turn the matter as you will, to this it must come, first and last: and all the discussions and fresh surveys in the world will never advance you one step until this fundamental point is settled.' Addington did not think the idea of a new survey very good because it simply delayed possible negotiations. Addington to Backhouse, 9 April 1839, FO 5/340, PRO.

15 Berkeley and Berkeley, *Featherstonhaugh*, 218–25; and Featherstonhaugh to Backhouse, 3 April 1839, FO 5/340, PRO. As early as 1826, the argument had circulated in London that the St Croix Commission had identified the

wrong river in 1798 and that the Penobscot River, considerably further west, had been the St Croix River intended in the treaty of 1783. This claim, like later ones, ignored Ward Chipman's archaeological research identifying the ancient settlements of De Mont and ascribed the selection of the Schoodiac River to shrewd negotiating by the Americans. See [Anon.], *Consideration of the Claims and Conduct of the United States Respecting their North Eastern Boundary, and of the Value of the British Colonies in North America* (London: John Hatchard and Son, Piccadilly, 1826), 6–27.

16 Lord Palmerston, Minute on the Boundary to Colonial Office, Sept. 1837, FO 5/320, PRO.

17 Palmerston to Backhouse, 8 April 1839, FO 5/340, PRO.

18 Sir Harry Verney to Backhouse, 26 April 1839, ibid.; and Backhouse to Palmerston, 8 May 1839, FO 97/15, PRO.

19 Palmerston to Backhouse, 11 June 1839, and Memorandum on Boundary Commission, by Lord Palmerston, 10 June 1839, FO 97/15, PRO. On his appointment, Featherstonhaugh in his journal 'thank[ed] God for an opportunity of being useful to my Country, and of distinguishing myself.' Journal, 13 April 1839, Reel 10, Featherstonhaugh Papers, MHS.

20 Accompanying Featherstonhaugh and Mudge were their personal servants, three Royal Engineers, and Featherstonhaugh's son James, who was hired in New York. See Featherstonhaugh and Mudge to Palmerston, 4 Sept. 1839, FO 97/15, PRO; Featherstonhaugh to Harvey, 8 Sept. 1839, Vol. 4, Harvey Papers, MS 24 A 17, NAC. Fox did not have much confidence in Featherstonhaugh's influence on Governor Fairfield or in the governor's reliability. Fox to Thomson [possibly Lord Sydenham], 29 Jan. 1840, in Sanderson, ed., *Arthur Papers*, 2: 399. Featherstonhaugh was delighted at his reception by Sir John Harvey and particularly that Chipman and Odell were impressed with his theory of the boundary. He recorded that they had 'declared before Sir John that if my views could be carried out, the British case would be triumphant.' Featherstonhaugh Journal, 10 Aug. 1839, in Alec McEwen, ed., *In Search of the Highlands: Mapping the Canada–Maine Boundary, 1839* (Fredricton: Acadiensis Press, 1988), 17–18. Also see Scott, *Ties of Common Blood*, 247–50.

21 Palmerston to Featherstonhaugh and Mudge, 9 July 1839, FO 97/15, PRO; and Suggestion on Boundary Question, Lord Lansdowne, n.d., c. July 1893, FO 5/343, PRO.

22 Featherstonhaugh to Backhouse, 4 Sept. 1839, FO 97/15, PRO; and Featherstonhaugh to Harvey, 28 Sept. 1839, Vol. 4, Harvey Papers, MG 24 A 17, NAC. By the end of their expedition, Mudge recorded that Featherstonhaugh was also exhausted. See the Featherstonhaugh and Mudge journals in McEwan, ed., *In Search of the Highlands*, passim.

23 Featherstonhaugh to Harvey, 28 Sept. 1839, Vol. 4, Harvey Papers, MG 24 A 17, NAC.
24 Featherstonhaugh Journal, 24 Aug.–11 Sept. 1839, in McEwan, ed., *In Search of the Highlands*, 22–34.
25 Featherstonhaugh to Backhouse, 28 Sept. 1839, FO 97/15, PRO.
26 Featherstonhaugh Journal, 30 Sept.–21 Oct. 1839, in McEwan, ed., *In Search of the Highlands*, 53–71.
27 Featherstonhaugh and Mudge to Palmerston, 22 Oct. 1839, FO 97/15, PRO. Mudge left Quebec City for New York, while Featherstonhaugh sailed for the Métis River on the St Lawrence and then made his way south to its source. It was this watershed that the Americans claimed as the highlands that divided the waters flowing into the St Lawrence from those draining into the Atlantic and that thus constituted the Northwest Angle of Nova Scotia. Featherstonhaugh calculated that its height was a mere 290 feet. In fact, this location was later measured to be 1,300 feet above sea level. How Featherstonhaugh could have been so much in error is difficult to understand. Featherstonhaugh then made his way back to the St Lawrence and took the Grand Portage–Temiscouata route to the St John River and Fredericton, which he reached by mid-November. See Featherstonhaugh Journal, 22 Oct.–16 Nov. 1839, in McEwan, ed., *In Search of the Highlands*, 73–81; and International Boundary Commission, *Joint Report upon the Survey and Demarcation of the Boundary Between the United States and Canada From the source of the St. Croix River to the St. Lawrence River*, 292.
28 Featherstonhaugh to Backhouse, 22 Oct. 1839, FO 97/15, PRO.
29 Mudge Journal, 15 Oct. 1839, in McEwan, ed., *In Search of the Highlands*, 103.
30 Featherstonhaugh to Harvey, 13 Nov. 1839, Vol. 4, Harvey Papers, MG 24 A 17, NAC. Featherstonhaugh was fond of using such terms to talk about Americans. Earlier in the year he had written to Backhouse, 'will it not then be singularly hard if we cannot find time to unbombast the impudence of the matchless Jonathan?' See Featherstonhaugh to Backhouse, 1 May 1839, FO 97/15, PRO.
31 See [Lord Palmerston] to James D. Featherstonhaugh and Lt. W.E. Delves Broughton, 1 June 1840, FO 97/15, PRO. These latter two men arrived in Halifax on 17 July and carried out their work during the summer and autumn, often with great difficulty. They even had a mutiny of workers, but they were able to compile the data that Featherstonhaugh wanted for a supplement to the report that he and Mudge were preparing. Featherstonhaugh felt fully vindicated by the result. See W.E.D. Broughton to Palmerston, 29 July 1840, W.E.D. Broughton and James D. Featherstonhaugh to Palmerston, 27 Oct. 1840, and Featherstonhaugh to Backhouse, 20 Nov. 1840, FO 97/15,

PRO. They were sent out again in 1841. Palmerston to W.E.D. Broughton and James D. Featherstonhaugh, 3 May 1841, and W.E.D. Broughton to Aberdeen, 17 Nov. 1841, FO 97/15, PRO; and *Supplementary Reports Relating to The Boundary between the British Possessions in North America and the United States of America under the Treaty of 1783*, originally published by Parliament in London, 1842, in the *British Parliamentary Papers, United States of America* (Shannon: Irish University Press, 1972), 11, passim.

32 Mudge and Featherstonhaugh, *Report of the British Commissioners*, 9–52.
33 Ibid., 53–7. While Featherstonhaugh was making these accusations about the American surveys, his son was in the northern region hoping to substantiate Featherstonhaugh's presumptions about the topography in that region. See the comments of Richard D. Cutts to John Fairfield, 20 Oct. 1840, Fairfield Papers, LC. While Featherstonhaugh was still working for the U.S. government, Henry R. Schoolcraft had some doubts about the reliability and honesty of his work. Featherstonhaugh asked him for the best map of the upper Mississippi River, which he had not visited, so as to include the details in a map that he was making. 'Why undertake to make a map of part of the country which he did not see?,' Schoolcraft queried in his journal. Schoolcraft, *Personal Memoirs*, 539.
34 Mudge and Featherstonhaugh, *Report of the British Commissioners*, 40 and 56–7. Ward Chipman, Jr, had re-entered the debate about the boundary with the publication of a small book that made public much of the material prepared a decade earlier for the king of the Netherlands. He asserted that the Americans' failure to get agreement on the St John River in 1782 marked a turning point in the negotiations. The boundary agreed on was south of the St John watershed and ran along the ridge, or highlands, that had an eastern terminus at Mars Hill. This had been made confusing by British willingness to accept the St Croix River rather than the more logical Penobscot or Kennebec rivers as the coastal starting point for the boundary. [Ward Chipman, Jr] *Remarks upon the Disputed Points of Boundary under the Fifth Article of the Treaty of Ghent, principally compiled from the Statements Laid by The Government of Great Britain before the King of the Netherlands, Arbiter* (Saint John: D.A. Cameron, 1839).
35 Palmerston to Melbourne, 22 April 1840, in Sanders, ed., *Lord Melbourne's Papers*, 458–9; and Thomas Colley Grattan, *Civilized America* (London: Bradbury and Evans, 1859), 1: 359–61. Backhouse told Mudge of his 'satisfaction' with the report and observed that it 'must dispel the existing illusions respecting American rights in the Disputed Territory,' although Backhouse did not have much regard for American capabilities to reason. Backhouse to Mudge, 17 May 1840, FO 97/15, PRO. Sydenham expressed a note of cau-

tion to Sir George Arthur, saying, 'I think well of the Maine question, if Palmerston does not hold his head too high in consequence of Mudge's report which gives us more than we asked.' [C.P.] Thomson to Arthur, 30 June 1840, in Sanderson, ed., *Arthur Papers*, 3: 90.

36 Featherstonhaugh to Harvey, 29 April 1840, Vol. 5, Harvey Papers, MG 24 A 17, NAC. Featherstonhaugh also reported that Palmerston complimented him profusely on the report.

37 See Palmerston to Backhouse, 19 April 1840, FO 97/15, PRO; Palmerston to Fox, 27 April 1840, FO 5/347, PRO; and Palmerston to Fox, 3 June 1840, in Bourne and Watt, eds., *Foreign Office Confidential Print ... McLeod and Maine, 1837–1842*, 83–4.

38 Massachusetts House Document, No. 44, *Report of the select committee [of Massachusetts] on the message of the Governor transmitting the resolutions of Maine and Indiana in regard to the northeastern boundary* (n.p., 1841), 2.

39 Maine, *Report of the Committee on the North-Eastern Boundary* (n.p.: Severence and Dorr, 1841); and Maryland, *Report of the Select Committee to whom were referred Resolutions of the States of Maine, Indiana and Ohio, in relation to the North-Eastern Boundary* (Annapolis: William McNair, 1841).

40 'The History of the Negotiations in reference to the Eastern and Northeastern Boundaries of the United States,' *New York Review* (Jan. 1841), 1–2 and 48–50.

41 *Niles' National Register*, 12 Sept. 1840, 25–31. Thomas C. Grattan, British consul in Boston, wrote to Palmerston that Americans were prepared to make a reasonable settlement of the boundary question but that the Mudge and Featherstonhaugh's report had been 'decidedly injurious to the continuance of the amicable feeling thus evidenced.' See Thomas C. Grattan to Lord Palmerston, 29 March 1841, in Bourne and Watt, eds., *Foreign Office Confidential Print ... McLeod and Maine, 1837–1842*, 146–9. Also see the critique of the report by E. Cushing of Boston, 10 Oct. 1840, in ibid., 83–5. For the comments of one of the few historians to consider Mudge and Featherstonhaugh's survey, see Scott, *Ties of Common Blood*, 265–7.

42 Albert Gallatin, *The Right of the United States of America to the North-Eastern Boundary Claimed by Them* (1840; reprint, New York: Books for Libraries Press, 1970), ix.

43 Walters, *Albert Gallatin*, 373.

44 Gallatin, *The Right of the United States*, 140–2.

45 Ibid., 150–62.

46 Gallatin to Bates, 28 Nov. 1840, cited in Walters, *Albert Gallatin*, 374.

47 Bates to Gallatin, 3 Feb. 1841, cited in ibid.

48 Featherstonhaugh to Backhouse, 21 Dec. 1840, FO 97/15, PRO. Featherstonhaugh also wrote to Ward Chipman, Jr, for advice and information to

assist him in writing a refutation of Gallatin's book. He wanted to know, among other things, when the Americans had claimed land north of the St John River, convinced as many were that this claim was as recent as 1820. Chipman replied that the U.S. claim antedated the War of 1812, and he conceded that 'unfortunately ... it seemed to be taken for granted [in New Brunswick] ... that the due North line was to cross the St. John before it reached Highlands, so that I fear an investigation into the point of time when the American claims originated will not turn to our advantage.' Featherstonhaugh to Ward Chipman, Jr., April 1841, and Ward Chipman, Jr., to Featherstonhaugh, 10 May 1841, Vol. 52, Reel C-1185, Chipman Papers, MG 23 D 1, NAC. Featherstonhaugh's book was *Historical Sketch of the Negotiations at Paris in 1782, from Inedited Documents; with remarks on Mr. Albert Gallatin's 'Right of the United States of America to the North-eastern Boundary Claimed by Them'* (London, 1842).

49 Richard D. Cutts to John Fairfield, 20 Oct. 1841, John Fairfield Papers, LC.

50 Everett to Webster, 15 Dec. 1841, in Shewmaker, ed., *The Papers of Daniel Webster, Diplomatic Papers,* 1: 167.

51 Forsyth to Renwick, Talcott, and Cleveland, 21 July 1840, Domestic Letters, M 40 (roll 29), RG 59, NA. Also see Forsyth to Renwick and Cleveland, 29 July 1840, Forsyth to Reuel Williams, 5 Aug. 1840, and Forsyth to Graham, 18 Aug. 1840, ibid. Featherstonhaugh despised Renwick, thought highly of Graham, and presumed Talcott to be a 'fair man,' but he was certain their mission was the 'mystifying and muddling of things still more,' and he urged his son James to keep an eye on them. George W. Featherstonhaugh to Sir John Harvey, 27 Sept. 1840, Vol. 5, Harvey Papers, MG 24 A 17, NAC. Secretary of War Joel R. Poinsett had started a limited survey of the Moosehead Lake area as early as 1838. Scott, *Ties of Common Blood,* 113–15.

52 Renwick to Forsyth, 20 Oct. 1840, Box 19, Northeastern Boundary, RG 76, NA.

53 'Report of the Commissioners appointed by the President of the United States under the act of Congress of 20th July, 1840 ...,' cited in Richardson, ed., *Messages and Papers of the Presidents,* 5: 1847–50.

54 Ibid., 5: 1851–2. Also see Renwick to Forsyth, 1 Aug. 1840, and Talcott to Forsyth, 19 Oct. 1840 and 1 Nov. 1840, Box 19, Northeastern Boundary, RG 76, NA. Featherstonhaugh reacted strongly to newspaper accounts that Renwick had discovered a range of mountains from the Bay of Chaleurs to the source of the St John. He regarded Renwick as an imposter who had no scientific or technical training. The fact that Renwick taught at Columbia College in New York was of no consequence to him, because he regarded the institution as merely a big school for boys. Featherstonhaugh to Backhouse, 23 Dec. 1840, FO 97/15, PRO.

55 Graham to Forsyth, 10 Dec. 1840, Box 19, Northeastern Boundary, RG 76, NA; Graham to Forsyth, 14 Dec. 1840, Box 29, ibid.; and 'Report of the Commissioners appointed 20th July, 1840,' cited in Richardson, ed., *Messages and Papers of the Presidents*, 5: 1852–5.

56 'Report of the Commissioners appointed 20th July, 1840,' cited in Richardson, ed., *Messages and Papers of the Presidents*, 5: 1846–56. Also see Renwick to Webster, 16 Aug. 1841 (Rivière de Loup, Lower Canada), and Graham to Webster, 8 Oct. 1841 (camp near Tobique, New Brunswick), Box 19 Northeastern Boundary, RG 76, NA.

57 See Renwick to Webster, 31 March 1842, and 'Report of the Commissioners appointed by the President of the United States for the purpose of surveying and exploring the boundary line between the States of Maine and New Hampshire and the British Provinces,' cited in Richardson, ed., *Messages and Papers of the Presidents*, 5: 1965–2003. For a discussion of the preparation of the report, see Renwick to Webster, 8 Jan. and 4 March 1842, Box 20, Northeastern Boundary, RG 76 NA. Although the report was submitted in March 1842, the surveying parties went out again in the spring of that year until called back by Webster at the end of June. See Webster to Talcott, 30 June 1842, Domestic Letters, M 40 (roll 30), RG 59, NA; and Renwick to Webster, 3 and 19 July 1842, Box 20, Northeastern Boundary, RG 76, NA.

58 'Report of the Commissioners ... British Provinces,' in Richardson, ed., *Messages and Papers of the Presidents*, 5: 1994.

59 Ibid., 5: 1978.

60 Ibid., 5: 1978.

61 Ibid., 5: 1991.

62 Stevenson to Rush, 28 Feb. 1840, Vol. 40, Stevenson Papers, LC.

63 Palmerston to Fox, 24 April 1841, in Manning, ed., *DCUSCR*, 3: 678–80. In March 1841 the British consul in Boston told Palmerston that the Americans were not persuaded by Mudge and Featherstonhaugh's report and were not likely to acquiesce in an unfavourable arbitration award. He was sure that they would accept a financial settlement and urged Palmerston to consider that solution. T.C. Grattan to Palmerston, 29 March 1841, FO 97/15, PRO.

64 Palmerston to Backhouse, Minute, 16 Feb. 1840, FO 5/355, PRO.

65 Sydenham to Fox, 13 July 1841, FO 5/362, PRO. Also see the accompanying correspondence of Fox to Palmerston, saying much the same, and Colonel A. Murray to Palmerston, warning of an inevitable U.S. attack on the British provinces. Fox to Palmerston, 13 July 1841, FO 5/361; and Murray to Palmerston, 14 Jan. 1841, FO 97/15, PRO.

66 'England and her Foreign Relations,' *Dublin University Magazine* 17 (April 1841), 511–12.

67 Rush to Stevenson, 8 April 1840, Vol. 19, Stevenson Papers, LC.

Chapter 11. Sea Change: Initiative and Compromise

1 Tyler, *The Letters and Times of the Tylers*, 2: 122; Claude M. Fuess, *Daniel Webster* (Boston: Little, Brown, 1930), 2: 99; and Irving Bartlett, *Daniel Webster* (New York: W.W. Norton, 1978), 3–11. Remini concludes that Webster and Tyler developed a very close working relationship and that Tyler came to depend on Webster to a great extent. Robert V. Remini, *Daniel Webster: The Man and His Time* (New York: W.W. Norton, 1997), 530 and 545–6.

2 Woodward, *The Age of Reform*, 109–12; Chamberlain, *Lord Aberdeen: A Political Biography*, 8; Norman Gash, *Sir Robert Peel: The Life of Sir Robert Peel after 1830* (London: Longmans, 1972), 249–88; and Kenneth Bourne, *The Foreign Policy of Victorian England, 1830–1902* (Oxford: Clarendon Press, 1970), 47–55. Thomas Raikes wrote to the Duke of Wellington from Paris in early 1841 that if British relations with the United States continued to deteriorate, as official correspondence indicated, there was no predicting what the French would do, but they would take advantage of the situation. Wellington agreed, saying that the 'American affair is more full of difficulties' and concluding that this situation would stimulate France. Raikes to Wellington, 11 Feb. 1841, and Wellington to Raikes, 12 March 1841, in Raikes, ed., *Private Correspondence of Thomas Raikes with The Duke of Wellington*, 247 and 266.

3 Glazebrook, *Sir Charles Bagot in Canada*, 1–32; and J.M.S. Careless, *The Union of the Canadas: The Growth of Canadian Institutions, 1841–1857* (Toronto: McClelland and Stewart, 1967), 1–19 and 58–74. Lord Stanley instructed Bagot, among other things, to 'allay irritation' and to encourage 'mutual good understanding' between Canada and the United States, while all the time protecting Canada and forwarding the interests of the Crown. See Stanley to Bagot, 8 Oct. 1841, cited in Glazebrook, *Sir Charles Bagot in Canada*, 125–9.

4 Charles Stuart Parker, ed., *Sir Robert Peel, from His Private Papers* (London: John Murray, 1899), 3: 379–89. The previous Whig government had also been anxious about political events in British North America. The prime minister thought that if Sydenham 'fails in the Union, all is up,' and 'those who sent him too.' Melbourne to Russell, 28 Dec. 1839, in Sanders, ed., *Lord Melbourne's Papers*, 446.

5 Webster to Francis Calley Gray, 11 May 1841, in Shewmaker, ed., *Papers of Daniel Webster: Diplomatic Papers*, 1: 73–5. As a senator from Massachusetts, Webster had not been prominent in the boundary agitation. Governor Everett had sought his advice in 1838, and Webster had himself looked to Judge

Joseph Story for opinions. See Everett to Webster, 14 April 1838, and Webster to [Joseph Story], 12 May 1838, in Charles M. Wiltse and Harold D. Moser, eds., *The Papers of Daniel Webster, Correspondence, Volume 4, 1835–1839* (Hanover, NH: University Press of New England, 1980), 287–8 and 298–9. Webster had held these sorts of views about the boundary for some time. Over a year earlier he had written, 'Two men of sense, with a map before them could sit down in London or Washington, and agree on a line, in an hour, that would well enough suit the convenience of both parties.' Further surveys, he said, aggravated the problem rather than solved it. See Webster to Nicholas Biddle, 9 Feb. [1840], ibid., 4: 10–11.

6 Bates to Baring Brothers & Co., 1 May 1841, Vol. 10, Baring Papers, MG 24 D 21, NAC. Webster, while a senator, had in early 1839 put forward a plan for new negotiations with Britain over the boundary. Of the several proposals that he outlined, the most promising was thought to be the negotiation of a new 'conventional line,' which would entail compromise by both sides ('England will not gratuitously, yield her pretensions; & something must be yielded by us'). Webster also urged that both the governor of Maine and the Maine delegation in Congress be consulted in order to determine in advance what Maine would accept. See 'A Scheme for the Settlement of the Northeastern Boundary,' c. April 1839, in Van Tyne, ed., *Letters of Daniel Webster*, 215–18. Paul Varg makes the point that Webster understood and spoke for those New England commercial interests that held peace with Britain to be essential for the continued prosperity of the country. Webster's willingness to consider some form of compromise on the boundary, rather than holding to a determined nationalist position, would make sense in that context. Paul Varg, *New England and Foreign Relations*, 215–18.

7 See 'P' to Colonial Office, 28 Aug. 1841, FO 5/374, PRO. 'It is evident the facts which have been brought out by the Survey now going on must have had a strong effect on the minds of the men of the United States, however little the Americans may be disposed to acknowledge the correctness of the Report.' Remini, *Daniel Webster: The Man and His Time*, 519. Webster had visited England in 1839, partially financed by Baring Brothers bank, for which he was legal counsel in the United States. While it was essentially a pleasure trip, Webster met numerous public figures, such as the Duke of Wellington, Sir Robert Peel, and Lord Ashburton, and attempted to improve the British image of the United States. Webster had offered to go to England in early 1839 to negotiate a settlement, but the Van Buren administration had not taken up his proposal. See Memorandum of Proposal for Special Mission to England, 10 March [1839], and Daniel Webster to Nicholas Biddle, 29 March 1839, in Wiltse and Moser, ed., *The Papers of Daniel Webster: Correspon-*

dence, 4: 350–4; and Bartlett, *Daniel Webster*, 156–61. The English historian Peter Parish has commented that Webster was one of the few American political figures respected and admired by the British. See Kenneth E. Shewmaker, ed., *Daniel Webster: 'The Completest Man'* (Hanover, NH: University Press of New England, 1990), xxiii.

8 Ashburton to Peel, 29 Aug. 1841, and Peel to Ashburton, 3 Sept. 1841, Vols. 306 and 307, Peel Papers, Add. Mss. 40,486, BL.

9 *New York Herald*, 15 Oct. 1841, Vol. 23, Aberdeen Papers, Add. Mss. 43,061, BL.

10 Peel to Aberdeen, 17 Nov. 1841, ibid. Aberdeen later wrote that Fox, 'although not without ability, did nothing. He passed his time in bed, and was so detested by every member of the U.S. Government that they had no communication with him, except as it was absolutely indispensable.' Lord Aberdeen to Lord Clarendon, 5 Nov. 1854, cited in Jones, *The American Problem in British Diplomacy*, 17–18.

11 See, for example, Peel to Ashburton, 17 Nov. 1841, and Ashburton to Peel, 21 and 22 Nov. 1841, Vol. 315, Peel Papers, Add. Mss. 40,495, BL.

12 Unfortunately there is no biography of Ashburton, but something of his life can be derived from two books on his bank. See Ralph W. Hidy, *The House of Baring in American Trade and Finance: English Merchant Bankers at Work, 1763–1861* (Cambridge, Mass.: Harvard University Press, 1949), 28–48; and Ziegler, *The Sixth Great Power*, 45–99.

13 Ashburton to Aberdeen, 22 Dec. 1841, Vol. 85, Aberdeen Papers, Add. Mss. 43,123, BL.

14 Aberdeen to Peel, 23 Dec. 1841, and Peel to Aberdeen, 24 Dec. 1841, Vol. 23, Aberdeen Papers, Add. Mss. 43,061, BL.

15 Wellington to Aberdeen, 29 Dec. 1841, Vol. 22, Aberdeen Papers, Add. Mss. 43,060, BL.

16 Diary, 8 Jan. 1842, in Strachey and Fulford, eds., *Greville Memoirs*, 5: 1. Lord William Russell in Vienna disliked the tone of the Peel government, its 'concessions in America' among other things. He thought that Britain's world position was seen to be in decline. Lord William Russell to Lord John Russell, 9 Jan. 1842, in G.P. Gooch, ed., *The Later Correspondence of Lord John Russell, 1840–1878* (London: Longmans, Green, 1925), 1: 52. The inspector general of troops in Canada, John Macaulay, thought that Ashburton would 'come out & make offers of great concessions – Jonathan will take advantage of these offers but will not assent in toto.' Macaulay was sure that the United States would strike at Britain when the opportunity presented itself. 'I fear war sooner or later is inevitable.' Macaulay to Arthur, 20 April 1842, in Sanderson, ed., *Arthur Papers*, 3: 490.

17 Webster to Everett, 29 Jan. 1842, in Manning, ed., *DCUSCR*, 3: 158–9; and
    Webster to Everett, 29 Jan. 1842 (private), in Shewmaker, ed., *Papers of Daniel
    Webster, Diplomatic Papers*, 1: 496–7. After meeting Ashburton in early January,
    Edward Everett was surprised to discover how unfamiliar he was with the
    details of the boundary question. But then Everett was himself a Massachu-
    setts man and as former governor had been thrust into the midst of the
    boundary crisis in 1839. George J. Gill, 'Edward Everett and the Northeastern
    Boundary Controversy,' *NEQ* 42 (June 1969), 203; and Willson, *America's
    Ambassadors to England*, 229–32. Everett had a distinguished career in both
    public service and academe. He had been a professor of Greek at Harvard
    when elected to Congress in 1825 and to the governorship in 1836; he served
    as minister to Britain from 1841 to 1845, after which he served as president of
    Harvard until he was appointed secretary of state in 1852; he later served
    briefly in the Senate from Massachusetts and also ran unsuccessfully as a can-
    didate for the vice-presidency in 1860. See 'Edward Everett,' in *DAB*, 6: 223–6.
18 Richard Rush, *A Residence at the Court of London* (London: Richard Bentley,
    1845), 267.
19 Everett to Webster, 31 Dec. 1841, in Shewmaker, ed., *Papers of Daniel Webster,
    Diplomatic Papers*, 1: 173–5; and Fox to Aberdeen, 28 Jan. 1842, FO 5/377,
    PRO. Early in 1841, just before the Whig administration took office in Wash-
    ington, the governor of Maine urged Webster to see to the appointment of a
    northerner, preferably from Maine, as minister to Britain. Edward Everett, as
    note 17 above showed, was well qualified. See Edward Kent to Webster, 17 Feb.
    1841, in Shewmaker, ed., *Papers of Daniel Webster, Diplomatic Papers*, 1: 34–6.
20 Fox to Aberdeen, 29 Jan. 1842, Vol. 85, Aberdeen Papers, Add. Mss. 43,123,
    BL; and Fox to Aberdeen, 28 Jan. and 25 Feb. 1842, FO 5/377, PRO.
21 *Niles' National Register*, 29 Jan. 1842, 337.
22 Ashburton to Webster, 2 Jan. 1842, in Shewmaker, ed., *Papers of Daniel Webster,
    Diplomatic Papers*, 1: 486–8. Lady Ashburton also wrote to Webster, reporting
    a successful visit to the family's country house by Everett. She said that her
    husband had been appointed because he was in England 'the person most
    zealous in the cause of America, & most sanguine as to the possibility of set-
    tling the long pending differences between the two countries.' Lady Ashbur-
    ton to Webster, 12 Jan. 1842, ibid., 1: 490.
23 Ashburton to Aberdeen, 22 Dec. 1841, Vol. 85, Aberdeen Papers, Add. Mss.
    43,123, BL; and Ashburton to Webster, 2 Jan. 1842, in Shewmaker, ed., *Papers
    of Daniel Webster, Diplomatic Papers*, 1: 487. Also see Ephraim Douglass Adams,
    'Lord Ashburton and the Treaty of Washington,' *AHR* 17 (July 1912), 67.
    Adams suggested that Ashburton was initially provided with a mere outline
    of instructions.

24 Aberdeen to Ashburton, 8 Feb. 1842, FO 5/378, PRO.

25 Ibid.

26 Wellington to Aberdeen, 8 Feb. 1842, 3:00 p.m. and evening, and Memorandum on Ashburton's Instructions from the Duke of Wellington, 8 Feb. 1842, Vols. 2 and 85, Aberdeen Papers, Add. Mss. 43,030 and 43,123, BL.

27 Aberdeen to Ashburton, 9 Feb. 1842, Vol. 85, Add. Mss. 43,123, BL.

28 Lord Stanley, Memorandum on Instructions to Lord Ashburton, 11 Feb. 1842, Vol. 34, Add. Mss. 43,072, BL.

29 In the words of one historian, 'Aberdeen was plainly out of tune with his colleagues and, not for the first time, he sent a private letter with his instructions which came very close to modifying them.' Chamberlain, *Lord Aberdeen: A Political Biography*, 323.

30 Aberdeen to Ashburton, 3 March 1842, Vol. 85, Aberdeen Papers, Add. Mss. 43,123, BL; Aberdeen to Wellington, 22 March 1842, Wellington to Aberdeen, 22 March 1842, and Aberdeen to Peel, and enclosures, 26 March 1842, Vols. 22 and 24, Add. Mss. 43,060 and 43,062, ibid. As for the different opinions of the four experts, Sir George Murray and Lord Seaton (formerly Sir John Colborne) supported protecting the existing road along the St John River, while Sir James Kempt and Sir Howard Douglas advocated a northern route by way of the Bay of Chaleurs and the Restigouche River, beyond the current pressure of the Americans. They all agreed that the Americans should be kept south of the St John River. See Kempt to Aberdeen, 1 March 1842, Murray to Aberdeen, 6 March 1842, Douglas to Aberdeen, 7 March 1842, and Seaton to Aberdeen, 9 March 1842, in Aberdeen to Ashburton, 1 April 1842, FO 5/378, PRO. Copies of Palmerston's proposals can be found in Aberdeen's papers. See, for example, Vaughan to Palmerson, 4 July 1833, and Palmerston to Bankhead, 30 Oct. 1835, Vol. 85, Aberdeen Papers, Add. Mss. 43,123, BL. Also see Algernon Cecil, *British Foreign Secretaries, 1807–1916: Personality and Policy* (1927; reprint, Port Washington, NY: Kennikat Press, 1971), 122–3; Jones, *The American Problem in British Diplomacy*, 24–5; Wilbur Devereux Jones, 'Lord Ashburton and the Maine Boundary Negotiations,' *MVHR* 40 (Dec. 1953), 480–2; and Bourne, *The Foreign Policy of Victorian England*, 105–6.

31 Aberdeen to Ashburton, 31 March 1842, FO 5/378, PRO.

32 Aberdeen to Ashburton, 1 April 1842, Vol. 85, Aberdeen Papers, Add. Mss. 43,123, BL.

33 Ashburton to Aberdeen, 10 Feb. 1842, ibid.

34 Ashburton to Aberdeen, 25 April 1842, FO 5/379, PRO.

35 Ashburton to Aberdeen, 26 April 1842, Vol. 85, Aberdeen Papers, Add. Mss. 43,123, BL.

36 Aberdeen to Ashburton, 16 May 1842, ibid.

37 Aberdeen to Ashburton, 20 May 1842, ibid.

38 Aberdeen to Ashburton, 16 May 1842, ibid. Aberdeen attempted to make clear to the Duke of Wellington that while British territorial interests would be protected there were larger considerations at stake. 'The matter is now become invested with considerations of the greatest political importance,' Aberdeen emphasized, 'involving the probability, or rather the certainty of war at no distant period with the United States, in the event of Lord Ashburton's failure.' Aberdeen to Wellington, 22 May 1842, Vol. 22, Add. Mss. 43,060, BL.

39 Aberdeen to Ashburton, 26 May 1842, FO 5/378, PRO. The accompanying private correspondence, based on consultation with the Duke of Wellington, simply restated the official instructions and placed the priority for any territorial improvement of the king of the Netherlands' line in the upper St John–St Francis region. Aberdeen to Ashburton, 26 May 1842, Vol. 85, Aberdeen Papers, Add. Mss. 43,123, BL.

40 Ashburton to Aberdeen, 29 June 1842, FO 5/379, PRO.

41 Ashburton to Aberdeen, 29 May 1842, Vol. 85, Aberdeen Papers, Add. Mss. 43,123, BL.

42 Aberdeen to Ashburton, 2 July 1842, ibid.

43 Peel to Aberdeen, 16 May 1842, in Parker, ed., *Sir Robert Peel*, 3: 388–9.

44 Smith to Webster, 7 June 1841, in Shewmaker, ed., *Papers of Daniel Webster, Diplomatic Papers*, 1: 94–6. Also see Smith to Van Buren, 1 Dec. 1937, in Frederick Merk, *Fruits of Propaganda in the Tyler Administration* (Cambridge, Mass.: Harvard University Press, 1971), 131–8. Merk had reservations about Smith, but Varg described him as someone with 'ability' who played a 'constructive role in the negotiations.' See Varg, *New England and Foreign Relations*, 147–8; and Scott, *Ties of Common Blood*, 278–82.

45 Jones and Rakestraw, *Prologue to Manifest Destiny*, 101–2. For reprints of the Smith articles, see Merk, *Fruits of Propaganda*, 158–72. Also see Burrage, *Maine in the Northeastern Boundary Controversy*, 321; and Richard N. Current, 'Webster's Propaganda and the Ashburton Treaty,' *MVHR* 34 (Sept. 1947), 187–93.

46 Smith to Webster, 20 Nov. 1841, in Merk, *Fruits of Propaganda*, 156–7; and Varg, *New England and Foreign Relations*, 148–9.

47 Webster to Kent, 21 Dec. 1841, in Van Tyne, ed., *Letters of Daniel Webster*, 248–9; Edward Kent, cited in J.R. Baldwin, 'The Ashburton–Webster Boundary Settlement,' *Canadian Historical Association, Annual Report* (1938), 124; and Elijah H.L. Hamlin, 'Report of the Land Agent of the State of Maine, 31 Dec. 1841,' cited in Peleg Sprague to Webster, 17 Feb. 1842, in Shewmaker, ed., *Papers of Daniel Webster, Diplomatic Papers*, 1: 516–17.

48 Sparks to Webster, 7 June 1841, Box 19, Northeastern Boundary, RG 76, NA.

49 Sparks to Webster, 15 Feb. 1842, in Shewmaker, ed., *Papers of Daniel Webster, Diplomatic Papers*, 1: 513–16. The so-called red-line map has been a major source of debate among both interested parties and historians ever since 1842. The map that Sparks may have seen, and the likelihood that it was the one mentioned in Franklin's letter, has been the subject of very close analysis. See Lawrence Martin and Samuel Flagg Bemis, 'Franklin's Red-Line Map Was a Mitchell,' *NEQ* 10 (March 1937), 105–11; and Jones, *To the Webster–Ashburton Treaty*, 102–13.

50 Webster to Sparks, 4 and 16 March 1842, in Shewmaker, ed., *Papers of Daniel Webster, Diplomatic Papers*, 1: 523 and 562; and Sparks to Webster, 16 May 1842, Box 20, Northeastern Boundary, RG 76, NA. Webster also instructed Everett in London not to look for any more maps, for fear of upsetting the complicated procedures that he was orchestrating. Webster to Everett, 14 June 1842, in Shewmaker, ed., *Papers of Daniel Webster, Diplomatic Papers*, 1: 580–1. Also see Merk, *Fruits of Propaganda*, 65–6; and Jones and Rakestraw, *Prologue to Manifest Destiny*, 107–11.

51 See Jones and Rakestraw, *Prologue to Manifest Destiny*, 111–12; Merk, *Fruits of Propaganda*, 66–7; Sprague to Webster, 17 Feb. 1842, in Shewmaker, ed., *Papers of Daniel Webster, Diplomatic Papers*, 1: 516–18; and Webster to Mrs. Edward Curtis, 4 May 1842, in Harold D. Moser, ed., *The Papers of Daniel Webster: Correspondence, Volume 5, 1840–1843* (Hanover, NH: University Press of New England, 1982), 203–4. Albert Smith was later appointed to the joint commission to survey the boundary. While Webster recognized astutely that public opinion needed to be shaped, that the expectations of the possibility of acquiring all the territory claimed by Maine were unrealistic, and that desires for war to vindicate U.S. honour were absurd, many people both then and now have questioned the propriety of his methods, particularly his use of the maps and of the secret service funds, in achieving a compromise settlement. He reshaped public opinion, but his methods would come back to haunt him. See Merk, *Fruits of Propaganda*, 39–92; and Current, 'Webster's Propaganda and the Ashburton Treaty,' 187–92.

52 Webster to Fairfield and Davis, 11 April 1842, in Manning, ed., *DCUSCR*, 3: 161–3. Webster had written to Maine Senator Reuel Williams in early February exploring the possible means through which Maine could be consulted in the process of reaching a practical compromise on the boundary. Williams was to discuss this with Governor Fairfield. Williams replied that Maine would consider the procedures suggested by Webster, and he also indicated that 'an exchange of territory and *equivalents*' (emphasis added) might be possible. Williams confided in the governor that he worried that 'we may

394 Notes to pages 260–2

find some of our rights sacrificed for the attainment of others or to preserve peace.' Williams to Fairfield, 28 Feb. 1842, Fairfield Papers, LC. Also see Webster to Williams, 2 Feb. 1842, and Williams to Webster, 12 and 18 Feb. 1842, in Shewmaker, ed., *Papers of Daniel Webster, Diplomatic Papers*, 1: 489–502 and 518–19. For an earlier proposal to obtain some kind of prior agreement on a boundary settlement from the representatives of Maine, see 'A Scheme for the Settlement of the Northeastern Boundary,' c. April 1841, in Van Tyne, ed., *Letters of Daniel Webster*, 215–18.

53 Webster to Fairfield and Davis, 11 April 1842, in Manning, ed., *DCUSCR*, 3: 161–3. Certainly many people in Maine were agreeable to giving up territory north of the St John River, if in exchange the state might 'get back' Grand Manan or Campobello Island or the 'narrow strip.' Williams to Fairfield, 29 May 1842, Fairfield Papers, LC.

54 For Ashburton's views on bringing the Maine and Massachusetts delegations to Washington, see Ashburton to Aberdeen, 26 April 1842, Vol. 85, Aberdeen Papers, Add. Mss. 43,123, BL.

55 Fairfield to Kavanagh, 16 April 1842, in William L. Lucy, 'Some Correspondence of the Maine Commissioners Regarding the Webster–Ashburton Treaty,' *NEQ* 15 (June 1942), 336–7; Renwick to Fairfield, 2 May 1842, Fairfield Papers, LC; Sparks to Webster, 16 May 1842, Box 20, Northeastern Boundary, RG 76, NA; and Ashburton to Aberdeen, 12 May 1842, FO 5/379, PRO.

56 Bagot to Ashburton, 5 June 1842, Vol. 7, Bagot Papers, MG 24 A 13, NAC.

57 Fairfield to Webster, 27 May 1842, in Manning, ed., *DCUSCR*, 3: 720–1; and Thomas Colley Grattan, *Civilized America* (London: Bradbury and Evans, 1859), 1: 364–5. Grattan had done some service for King Leopold of Belgium and was rewarded by Palmerston with the consulate in Boston, where he proved very popular. Ridley, *Lord Palmerston*, 450.

58 Webster to Davis, 16 April 1842, and Davis to Webster, 17 April 1842, in Manning, ed., *DCUSCR*, 3: 163–4 and 701–3; Merk, *Fruits of Propaganda*, 67–9; Jones and Rakestraw, *Prologue to Manifest Destiny*, 115–16; and Preble to Kavanagh, 28 May 1842, in Lucy, 'Some Correspondence,' 338. Lawrence has been described as a practical businessman 'accustomed to look at all questions in their broadest relations,' with much in common with Ashburton. Hamilton Andrews Hill, *Memoir of Abbott Lawrence* (Boston: n.p., 1883), 61–2.

59 John P. Bigelow to Webster, 26 May 1842, and Commissioners from Maine to Webster, 12 June 1842, Box 20, Northeastern Boundary, RG 76, NA

60 Grattan, *Civilized America*, 1: 367; Grattan to Aberdeen, 14 June 1842, Vol. 85, Aberdeen Papers, Add. Mss. 43,123, BL; and Webster to Ashburton, 17 June

1842, in Manning, ed., *DCUSCR*, 3: 169. For a good discussion of the attempts to influence the Maine commissioners, see Wilbur Devereux Jones, 'Lord Ashburton and the Maine Boundary Negotiations,' *MVHR*, 40 (Dec. 1953), 485–6. The New Hampshire legislature passed resolutions asserting the claims of that state to the headwaters of the Connecticut River. Webster received the resolutions and conferred with the New Hampshire members of Congress. Webster to New Hampshire Delegation in Congress, 18 July 1842, Domestic Letters, M 40 (roll 30), RG 59, NA.

61 Ashburton to Bagot, 16 April and 11 May 1842, Vol. 2, Bagot Papers, MG 24 A 13, NAC; Bagot to Ashburton, 5 May and 5 June 1842, Vol. 7, ibid.; and Ashburton to Bagot, 26 July 1842, Vol. 3, ibid.

62 Ashburton to Colebrook, 28 April 1842, FO 5/288, PRO; and Ashburton to Colebrook, 28 April 1842, with extracts from the Report of the Land Agent of Maine, 31 Dec. 1841, and letter from MacLaughlin to Colebrook, 8 April 1842, FO 5/379, PRO.

63 Jones and Rakestraw, *Prologue to Manifest Destiny*, 118. John Quincy Adams recorded that a Judge Swymmer, from Saint John, New Brunswick, was in Washington during the negotiations. Diary, 5 Aug. 1842, in Adams, ed., *Memoirs of John Quincy Adams*, 11: 229. The timber cut by New Brunswickers along the Aroostook River that led to the so-called Aroostook War in 1839 had been destined for Sir John Caldwell's sawmill at Grand Falls. Scott, *Ties of Common Blood*, 126.

64 Ashburton to Aberdeen, 29 May 1842, FO 5/379, PRO.

65 Grattan, *Civilized America*, 1: 367–8. Also see Grattan to Bagot, 21 May 1842, Vol. 2, Bagot Papers, MG 24, A 13, NAC; Grattan to Aberdeen, 14 June and 30 July 1842, and Lord Aberdeen to Lord Ashburton, 2 July 1842, Vol. 85, Aberdeen Papers, Add. Mss. 43,123, BL; and Jones and Rakestraw, *Prologue to Manifest Destiny*, 128.

66 Ashburton to Aberdeen, 9 Aug. 1842, FO 5/380, PRO. Of all these contributors to the British efforts, only Barclay was praised by Ashburton to Aberdeen.

Chapter 12. The Webster–Ashburton Negotiations

1 *National Intelligencer*, 5 and 9 April 1842; and Ashburton to Aberdeen, 8 April 1842, FO 5/379, PRO.

2 Jones and Rakestraw, *Prologue to Manifest Destiny*, 113; and Remini, *Daniel Webster*, 547–8.

3 *National Intelligencer*, 19 April 1842.

4 J. Goodhue to Bates, 14 April 1842, Prime, Ward & King to Messrs. Baring

Brothers & Co., 28 April 1842, and James G. King to Bates, 9 and 14 May 1842, Vol. 87, Baring Papers, MG 24 D 22, NAC.

5 Diary, 5 April 1842, in Nevins, ed., *Diary of Philip Hone*, 594–5; and Webster to John Evelyn Denison, 26 April 1842, in Harold D. Moser, ed., *The Papers of Daniel Webster: Correspondence, Volume 5, 1840–1843* (Hanover, NH: University Press of New England, 1982), 201. Hone thought that Ashburton and Webster would have 'gotten toe to toe' by 5 April, which was a bit premature. Social events got off to an early start. John Quincy Adams recorded in his diary seeing Ashburton at several dinners and other events in Washington. Adams mentioned dinner at the house of Baron Bodisco, the Russian minister, on 13 April, at Webster's on 21 April, at Ashburton's on 17 May (where he had a 'long conversation with Lord Ashburton'), and at the White House on 11 June (where he had another long talk with him). Adams, ed., *Memoirs of John Quincy Adams*, 11: 133, 139, 147, 150, 156, 172, and 174. Ashburton benefited from his earlier experiences in the United States and enjoyed telling people that he had witnessed the debates on the Jay Treaty in 1795. Robert C. Alberts, *The Golden Voyage: The Life and Times of William Bingham, 1752–1804* (Boston: Houghton Mifflin, 1969), 434.

6 Williams to Fairfield, 28 Feb. and 8 April 1842, Fairfield Papers, LC.

7 Clifford to Fairfield, 4 May 1842, ibid. The governor also received correspondence that was more hopeful about both compromise and the Ashburton mission. See H.I. Anderson to Fairfield, 19 April 1842, and John Burnham to Fairfield, 23 April 1842, ibid.

8 Gallatin to Ashburton, 21 April 1842, Vol. 85, Aberdeen Papers, Add. Mss. 43,123, BL.

9 Webster to Everett, 28 June 1842, in Manning, ed., *DCUSCR*, 3: 169–70.

10 Webster to Everett, 28 June 1842, in Shewmaker, ed., *Papers of Daniel Webster, Diplomatic Papers,*1: 592.

11 Lord Ashburton to Lord Aberdeen, 14 June 1842, Vol. 85, Aberdeen Papers, Add. Mss. 43,123, BL; and Grattan, *Civilized America*, 1: 367–8.

12 Ashburton to Webster, 13 June 1842, in Shewmaker, ed., *Papers of Daniel Webster, Diplomatic Papers,* 1: 575–80. Burrage emphasized that Ashburton noted that British denials of the American claims for the Northwest Angle of Nova Scotia north of the St John River date from the talks at Ghent. Burrage, *Maine in the Northeastern Boundary Controversy*, 328–9.

13 Ashburton to Webster, 21 June 1842, in Shewmaker, ed., *Papers of Daniel Webster, Diplomatic Papers,* 1: 582–9. Also see Burrage, *Maine in the Northeastern Boundary Controversy*, 329.

14 Webster also said specifically, 'The boundary business is by no means in a highly promising state, so many obstacles arise, not only between us and

England, but between us and the Commissioners, and the Commissioners of the two States themselves,' and he concluded that if the negotiations failed things would be left 'much worse than they had been found.' Webster to Everett, 28 June 1842, in Manning, ed., *DCUSCR*, 3: 169–70; and Webster to Everett, 28 June 1842, in Shewmaker, ed., *Papers of Daniel Webster, Diplomatic Papers*, 1: 592.

15 Diary, 3 July 1842, in Adams, ed., *Memoirs of John Quincy Adams*, 11: 196.

16 Tyler, *Letters and Times of the Tylers*, 2: 217–18. The president met with both Ashburton and the commissioners from Maine and Massachusetts several times and presumably exercised his charm to keep the negotiations progressing. Lyon G. Tyler, 'President John Tyler and the Ashburton Treaty,' *William and Mary Quarterly* 25 (July, 1916), 3. Abbott Lawrence was presumed to have great influence with Tyler and the other members of the two state delegations. See Hill, *Memoir of Abbott Lawrence*, 62 and 66.

17 William Pitt Preble, Edward Kavanagh, Edward Kent, and John Otis to Webster, 29 June 1842, in Shewmaker, ed., *Papers of Daniel Webster, Diplomatic Papers*, 1: 595–603. The Maine commissioners were supported by correspondents from home. See John Anderson to Edward Kavanagh, 6 July 1842, in William L. Lucy, 'Some Correspondence of the Maine Commissioners Regarding the Webster–Ashburton Treaty,' 341.

18 Preble et al. to Webster, 29 June, in Shewmaker, ed., *Papers of Daniel Webster, Diplomatic Papers*, 1: 595–603.

19 See Webster to Gray, 11 May 1841, and Webster to Everett, 25 April 1842, ibid., 1: 73–5 and 539–42.

20 Ashburton to Aberdeen, 13 July 1842, Vol. 85, Aberdeen Papers, Add. Mss. 43,123, BL.

21 Grattan, *Civilized America*, 1: 372; and Grattan to Aberdeen, 14 June 1842, Vol. 85, Aberdeen Papers, Add. Mss. 43,123, BL.

22 Ashburton to Aberdeen, 29 June 1842, Vol. 85, Aberdeen Papers, Add. Mss. 43, 123, BL.

23 Ashburton to Webster, 1 July 1842, in Shewmaker, ed., *Papers of Daniel Webster, Diplomatic Papers*, 1: 604.

24 Ashburton to Webster, c. 2 July 1842, in ibid., 1: 604–5.

25 Webster to Ashburton, 8 July 1842, in ibid., 1: 605–11. Tyler later claimed to have consulted with Webster and made 'corrections' from time to time and occasionally shown drafts to the cabinet. See John Tyler to Robert Tyler, 29 Aug. 1858, in Tyler, *Letters and Times of the Tylers*, 2: 242.

26 Webster to Ashburton, 8 July 1842, in Shewmaker, ed., *Papers of Daniel Webster, Diplomatic Papers*, 1: 611–13.

27 Ashburton to Webster, 11 July 1842, ibid., 1: 613–20. E.D. Adams emphasized

that Ashburton had encouraged informal, face-to-face negotiations, in part, one concludes, because of Webster's skill as a lawyer. Ephraim Douglass Adams, 'Lord Ashburton and the Treaty of Washington,' 780.

28 Grattan, *Civilized America*, 1: 377; and Ashburton to Aberdeen, 13 July 1842, Vol. 85, Aberdeen Papers, Add. Mss. 43,123, BL. John Quincy Adams began to hear rumours that the negotiations were now moving along favourably. Diary, 19 July 1842, in Adams, ed., *Memoirs of John Quincy Adams*, 11: 203.

29 Commissioners from Maine and Massachusetts to Daniel Webster, 12 and 13 July 1842, and Daniel Webster to Commissioners from Maine and Massachusetts, 13 July 1842, Box 22, Northeastern Boundary, RG 76, NA; Webster to William Pitt Preble, Edward Kavanagh, Edward Kent, and John Otis, 15 July 1842, in Shewmaker, ed., *Papers of Daniel Webster, Diplomatic Papers*, 1: 620–3. Webster met with the New Hampshire congressional delegation on about 19 or 20 July, at which time there had already been informal agreement on Hall's Stream as the northwestern head of the Connecticut River. This would also have been New Hampshire's claim. See Webster to New Hampshire Delegation in Congress, 18 July 1842, Domestic Letters, M 40 (roll 30), RG 59, NA. For observations on the quality of land north of the St John River and the military value of Rouse's Point, see George W. Coffin, Levi Bradley, and Elijah L. Hamlin to Webster, 3 June 1842, and Captain A. Talcott to Webster, 6 July 1842, Box 20, Northeastern Boundary, RG 76, NA; and General Winfield Scott to President John Tyler, 1 July 1842, Box 22, ibid. Scott said that Rouse's Point was 'superior to any other [fortification] south of it – that is within our line.'

30 William Pitt Preble, Edward Kavanagh, Edward Kent, and John Otis to Webster, 16 July 1842, in Shewmaker, ed., *Papers of Daniel Webster, Diplomatic Papers*, 1: 623–4.

31 For the breakdown of the areas disbursed, see ibid., 620–1. The distance from the source of the St Croix River via the St John River and the highlands to Halls Stream was 515.9 miles.

32 Ibid., 627–37.

33 Webster to Commissioners of Maine and Massachusetts, 18 July 1842, Box 20, Northeastern Boundary, RG 76, NA; Webster to Ashburton, 18 July 1842, and Ashburton to Webster, 18 July 1842, in Manning, ed., *DCUSCR*, 3: 181 and 755. Burrage said that at one point Ashburton showed part of his instructions to the commissioners to convince them that he had no powers to give up land or islands belonging to New Brunswick. Burrage, *Maine in the Northeastern Boundary Controversy*, 358–9.

34 Abbott Lawrence, John Mills, and Charles Allen to Webster, 20 July 1842, in Manning, ed., *DCUSCR*, 3: 756–8; and Miller, ed., *Treaties*, 4: 433. The trans-

fer of funds to Maine and Massachusetts did not actually take place until 1847. Also see Clyde Augustus Duniway, 'Daniel Webster,' in Bemis, ed., *American Secretaries of State and Their Diplomacy*, 5: 25–6.

35 Edward Kavanagh, Edward Kent, John Otis, and William Pitt Preble to Webster, 22 July 1842, in Shewmaker, ed., *Papers of Daniel Webster, Diplomatic Papers*, 1: 638–45.

36 Ashburton to Aberdeen, 28 July 1842, FO 5/380, PRO; and Preble to Webster, 22 July 1842, Box 20, Northeastern Boundary, RG 76, NA. John Quincy Adams recorded a conversation with James A. MacLaughlan from the New Brunswick delegation on 22 July. He said that MacLaughlan joked about the possibility of Britain's ceding the narrow strip between the St John River and the due-north line to the United States. One can infer that MacLaughlan was either totally uninformed about the negotiations or was attempting to assess Adams's reaction to such a proposition. Diary, 23 July 1842, in Adams, ed., *Memoirs of John Quincy Adams*, 11: 216.

37 Ashburton to Aberdeen, 28 July 1842 (private), Vol. 85, Aberdeen Papers, Add. Mss. 43,123, BL.

38 Ibid. Kavanagh returned to Maine early also, but Otis and Kent remained to look after the details of drafting the boundary provision in its final form. Kent commented to Kavanagh, seemingly as a reassurance, 'The navigation clause will, I think, secure all we required, giving both parties where the river is the dividing line equal rights in the whole breadth, & to us the right to run freely with our lumber ... to [and] from the seaport at the mouth.' Edward Kent to Edward Kavanagh, 29 July 1842, in Lucy, 'Some Correspondence of the Maine Commissioners Regarding the Webster–Ashburton Treaty,' 342.

39 Diary, Tuesday, 2 Aug. 1842, in Nevins, ed., *Diary of Philip Hone*, 614. There was a growing sense that a treaty would be signed shortly. Philip Hone observed, 'The ugliest knot is now said to be disentangled. Ibid., 613. However, John Quincy Adams reported that expansionists in other parts of the country were indignant that the United States had not acquired all the territory claimed. Diary, 24 July 1842, in Adams, ed., *Memoirs of John Quincy Adams*, 11: 217.

40 Ashburton to Aberdeen, 29 June 1842, FO 5/379, PRO.

41 Forsyth to Fox, 29 July 1839, in Manning, ed., *DCUSCR*, 3: 89–90.

42 Ashburton to Webster, 16 July 1842, in Shewmaker, ed., *Papers of Daniel Webster, Diplomatic Papers*, 1: 624–7. It is sometimes argued that Ashburton, by agreeing to place the boundary at the Pigeon River, lost for Canada the rich iron deposits of northeastern Minnesota. Thomas LeDuc has examined this claim, showing that only the Vermillion Range and the eastern tip of the Mesabi Range came within the region claimed by the British, leaving the

richer sections of the Mesabi Range and all of the Cuyuna Range well within the American side. Furthermore, LeDuc made a strong case that the iron deposits were not known either by the commissioners in 1827 or by the negotiators in 1842. See Thomas LeDuc, 'The Webster–Ashburton Treaty and the Minnesota Iron Ranges,' *Journal of American History* 51 (1964), 476–81.

43 Ashburton was later described as 'wily' for his proposals about the boundary from Lake Superior to the Lake of the Woods. See Alexander Winchell, 'Minnesota's Northern Boundary,' *Minnesota Historical Society Collections* 8 (1898), 207.

44 Cited in Lass, *Minnesota's Boundary with Canada*, 68. Webster on 15 July asked for U.S. right of passage through the Canadian channel past Bois Blanc Island, probably on the advice of Delafield and Ferguson. Webster to Ashburton, 25 July 1842, and Ashburton to Webster, 29 July 1842, in Manning, ed., *DCUSCR*, 3: 182 and 772.

45 Webster to Ashburton, 27 July 1842, in Shewmaker, ed., *Papers of Daniel Webster, Diplomatic Papers*, 1: 645–9.

46 Stevens, *Border Diplomacy*, 160–4.

47 Aberdeen to Ashburton, 8 Feb. 1842, FO 5/378, PRO.

48 Webster to Ashburton, 27 July 1842, in Shewmaker, ed., *Papers of Daniel Webster, Diplomatic Papers*, 1: 650. For details about the drafting of the legislation, see ibid., 705–9.

49 Lord Ashburton to Daniel Webster, 28 July 1842, in ibid., 651–6; and Lord Ashburton to Lord Aberdeen, 28 July 1842, FO 5/380, PRO. For Webster's long discussion of the international law dimensions of the *Caroline* affair, see Daniel Webster to Lord Ashburton, 1 Aug. 1842, on Shewmaker, ed., *Papers of Daniel Webster, Diplomatic Papers*, 1: 658–5; and John Bassett Moore, *A Digest of International Law* (Washington, DC: Government Printing Office, 1906), 2: 409–14.

50 Stevens, *Border Diplomacy*, 164–5. Also see the discussion in Wilbur Devereux Jones, *Lord Aberdeen and the Americas* (Athens: University of Georgia Press, 1958), 14–15; and Ashburton to Aberdeen, 9 Aug. 1842, FO 5/380, PRO.

51 Ashburton to Webster, 6 Aug. 1842, in Shewmaker, ed., *Papers of Daniel Webster, Diplomatic Papers*, 1: 669–71.

52 Tyler to Webster, 7 Aug. 1842, and Webster to Ashburton, 8 Aug. 1842, ibid., 1: 671–3. Ashburton had asked Webster his opinion on the early drafts of the letter. Ashburton to Webster, 31 July 1842, ibid., 1: 657–8. Also see Lord Ashburton to Lord Aberdeen, 9 Aug. 1842, FO 5/380, PRO. In 1853 an Anglo–American claims commission did compensate the slave owners in the *Creole* incident some $110,000. Joshua Bates, the American living in England and a

partner in Baring Brothers, was the umpire. For a discussion of the award, see Moore, *Digest of International Law,* 2: 351–5; and Jones and Rakestraw, *Prologue to Manifest Destiny,* 142–4.

53 The Quintuple Treaty had been negotiated in late 1841 by Britain, France, Austria, Prussia, and Russia, with the object of allowing Royal Navy ships to stop vessels at sea in order to apprehend slavers. Cass's attack was unsigned, but the authorship became quickly known. The treaty roused anti-British sentiment in France. Palmerston's newspaper attacks on Aberdeen and the French foreign minister also contributed to French displeasure. Jones and Rakestraw, *Prologue to Manifest Destiny,* 72–81; and Roger Bullen, *Palmerston, Guizot and the Collapse of the Entente Cordiale* (London: Athlone Press, 1974), 28–33. Former governor and explorer Lewis Cass was a Michigan Democrat appointed by Van Buren but kept at his post by Tyler. He may have made his statements on the slavery question in the hope of winning southern support for his bid for the presidency.

54 Ashburton to Aberdeen, 6 Aug. 1842, FO 5/380, PRO; Webster to Everett, 26 April 1842, in Shewmaker, ed., *Papers of Daniel Webster, Diplomatic Papers,* 1: 543–4; Tyler, *Letters and Times of the Tylers,* 2: 219–20; Jones and Rakestraw, *Prologue to Manifest Destiny,* 139–42; and Chamberlain, *Lord Aberdeen: A Political Biography,* 313. A version of joint cruising had been tried in the 1830s, and it was again suggested in the 1840s by two U.S. naval officers.

55 See Webster to Ashburton, 8 Aug. 1842, in Shewmaker, ed., *Papers of Daniel Webster, Diplomatic Papers,* 1: 673–9; Ashburton to Webster, 9 Aug. 1842, and Ashburton to Aberdeen, 9 Aug. 1842, FO 5/380, PRO. Aberdeen wrote, 'I regret to say that there are obstacles in the way of adopting the scheme suggested by your Lordship, which at the present moment appear to Her Majesty's Government insurmountable.' Among those reasons were the right to insist on the loyalty of all British subjects without regard to the realities of emigration. See Aberdeen to Ashburton, 3 June 1842, FO 5/378, ibid.

56 Proposed Clause by Webster on Extradition of Criminals, c. 28 April 1842, and Ashburton to Aberdeen, 3 June 1842, FO 5/379, PRO; and Aberdeen to Ashburton, 3 June 1842 (private), Vol. 85, Aberdeen Papers, Add. Mss. 43,123, BL.

57 Lord Ashburton to Lord Aberdeen, 25 April 1842, FO 5/379; Lord Ashburton to Daniel Webster, 9 Aug. 1842, FO 5/390, PRO; Corey, *The Crisis of 1830–1842 in Canadian–American Relations,* 169–79; and Jones and Rakestraw, *Prologue to Manifest Destiny,* 143.

58 Ashburton to Webster, 31 July 1842, in Van Tyne, ed., *Letters of Daniel Webster,* 272–3.

59 Ashburton to Aberdeen, 9 Aug. 1842, FO 5/380, PRO.
60 Ashburton to Aberdeen, 9 Aug. 1842 (private), Vol. 85, Aberdeen Papers,
   Add. Mss. 43,123, BL. Ashburton also wrote to Sir Charles Bagot saying that
   the boundary and extradition questions had been settled. 'The work has
   been tough but we are all in great humor, and I trust my Masters at home will
   be satisfied.' Ashburton to Bagot, 9 Aug. 1842, Vol. 3, Bagot Papers, MG 24 A
   13, NAC.
61 Edward Kent to Edward Kavanagh, 29 July 1842, in Lucy, 'Some Correspondence of the Maine Commissioners Regarding the Webster–Ashburton
   Treaty,' 342–3; Webster to Sparks, 1 March 1843, cited in Fuess, *Daniel Webster*, 2: 111; and Tyler to Webster, 8 Aug. 1842, in Shewmaker, ed., *Papers of
   Daniel Webster, Diplomatic Papers*, 1: 679.

Chapter 13. Storm over the Treaty

 1 Ashburton to Webster, 16 Aug. 1842, and Webster to Ashburton, 16 Aug.
   1842, Manning, ed., *DCUSCR*, 3: 189 and 782; and Ashburton to Bagot,
   14 Aug. 1842, Vol. 3, Bagot Papers, MG 24 A 13, NAC; Bagot to Ashburton,
   25 Aug. 1842, Vol. 8, ibid.; and Ashburton to Aberdeen, 31 Aug. 1842,
   FO 5/380, PRO.
 2 Jones, *To the Webster–Ashburton Treaty*, 166–8. The *National Intelligencer* said
   that the treaty 'reflects the highest credit on those who have conducted the
   negotiations, and gives the fullest assurance that the National honor has
   been maintained.' As for Ashburton, the paper said that 'a wiser or better
   choice could not have been made.' *National Intelligencer*, 23 Aug. 1842. For
   similar sentiments, see *Niles' National Register*, 24 Aug. 1842.
 3 Hone diary, 2 Sept. 1842, in Nevins, ed., *Diary of Philip Hone*, 618; Prime,
   Ward, & King to Messrs. Baring Brothers & Co., 25 Aug. 1842, Vol. 82, Baring Brothers Papers, MG 24, D 21, NAC; and Walters, *Albert Gallatin*, 374.
   Ashburton wrote a genial farewell to Webster before sailing, and he was
   reported to Webster as having praised the secretary warmly. See Ashburton
   to Webster, 3 Sept. 1842, and Jacob Harvey to Webster, 27 Sept. 1842, in
   Harold D. Moser, ed., *The Papers of Daniel Webster: Correspondence, Volume 5,
   1840–1843* (Hanover, NH: University Press of New England, 1982), 241 and
   244.
 4 Jones, *To the Webster–Ashburton Treaty*, 169. Edward Everett in London gave
   great praise to both Ashburton and Webster for completion of the treaty, particularly for the 'control of the negotiations' that Webster had exercised over
   the various American participants. He also spoke out publicly about the merits of the treaty. See Everett to Webster, 31 Aug. 1842, cited in Varg, *New*

England and Foreign Relations, 151; and Speech to the Agricultural Society at
Waltham, 26 Sept. 1842, in Edward Everett, ed., *Orations and Speeches on Various Occasions by Edward Everett* (Boston: Little, Brown, 1865), 2: 442–3.

5 Bagot to Ashburton, 17 and 25 Aug. 1842, Vol. 8, Bagot Papers, MG 24 A 13,
NAC.

6 Bagot to Stanley, 28 Aug. 1842, ibid. H.U. Addington, undersecretary at the
Foreign Office, wrote to Bagot that the treaty ought to 'lighten your labours.'
He thought that it was 'a good thing done' and generally approved across
the country. Addington to Bagot, 3 Oct. 1842, Vol. 3, ibid.

7 Aberdeen to Peel, 15 Aug. 1842, Vol. 24, Aberdeen Papers, Add. Mss. 43,062,
BL.

8 Wellington to Raikes, 6 Sept. 1842, in Raikes, ed., *Private Correspondence of
Thomas Raikes with the Duke of Wellington,* 301.

9 Diary, 11 Sept. 1842, in Strachey and Fulford, eds., *Greville Memoirs,* 5: 32–3.
Morning Chronicle, 23 Aug. 1842.

10 Aberdeen to Ashburton, 26 and 27 Sept. 1842, Vols. 85 and 24, Aberdeen
Papers, Add. Mss. 43,123 and 43,062, BL.

11 Ashburton to Aberdeen (private and confidential), 9 Aug. 1842, Vol. 85
Aberdeen Papers, Add. Mss. 43,123, BL. The *Morning Chronicle* was openly
hostile by 19 Sept. 1842.

12 Ashburton to Aberdeen, 14 June 1842, Vol. 85, Aberdeen Papers, Add. Mss.
43,123, BL. Grattan later wrote to Aberdeen that he had never heard of the
Sparks maps until after the treaty was ratified by the Senate, but he also mentioned the incident in New York with Professor Renwick. It would seem that
Grattan had a clear notion of what was happening, even if he was missing
some of the details. See Grattan to Aberdeen, 31 Dec. 1842, ibid.

13 Ashburton to Aberdeen (private and confidential), 9 Aug. 1842, ibid.

14 Ashburton to Croker, 7 Feb. 1843, in Bernard Pool, ed., *The Croker Papers,
1808–1857* (London: R.T. Batsford, Ltd., 1967), 187. Howard Jones comes to
a different conclusion, taking Ashburton at his word in saying that he had
not been aware of the maps until after signing the treaty. Jones's arguments
are well reasoned. The documents being so incomplete, the whole truth can
never be fully known. See Howard Jones, 'Daniel Webster: The Diplomatist,'
in Shewmaker, ed., *Daniel Webster: 'The Completest Man,'* 213–16.

15 Jones, *To the Webster–Ashburton Treaty,* 163–4; and Merk, *Fruits of Propaganda,*
78.

16 Burrage, *Maine in the Northeastern Boundary Controversy,* 346–8. Reuel Williams wrote to Governor Fairfield that the treaty had been ratified and that
he would be disappointed if the people of Maine approved of it. 'The rights
of Maine have been sacrificed by the indiscretion of the Commissioners at

Ghent, the aversion of all administrations to encounter responsibility & the deceitful assertions as to the powers of Lord Ashburton & the necessity that the Maine Comrs. should be untramelled.' Williams to Fairfield, 21 Aug. 1842, Fairfield Papers, LC.

17 Burrage, *Maine in the Northeastern Boundary Controversy*, 350–1; and Duniway, 'Daniel Webster,' in Bemis, ed., *American Secretaries of State and Their Diplomacy*, 5: 44–5.

18 Scott, *Ties of Common Blood*, 290.

19 Merk, *Fruits of Propaganda*, 78–9.

20 Jackson to Blair, 7 Aug. 1842, in Bassett, ed., *Correspondence of Andrew Jackson*, 6: 162. The date of Jackson's letter would suggest that he had confidential information about the boundary clauses before the final treaty was signed.

21 Diary, 24 Aug. and 6 Sept. 1842, in Adams, ed., *Memoirs of John Quincy Adams*, 11: 243 and 249; Webster to Mrs. James W. Paige, 23 Aug. 1842, in Fletcher Webster, ed., *The Private Correspondence of Daniel Webster* (Boston: Little, Brown and Company, 1857), 2: 146; and Webster to Tyler, 24 Aug. 1842, in Shewmaker, ed., *The Papers of Daniel Webster: Diplomatic Papers*, 1: 695.

22 Cited in Burrage, *Maine in the Northeastern Boundary Controversy*, 354–7.

23 'Editorial: The Treaty of Washington,' 22 Aug. 1842, in Shewmaker, ed., *Papers of Daniel Webster: Diplomatic Papers*, 1: 693–5.

24 Kent to Kavanagh, 16 Aug. 1842, in Lucy, 'Some Correspondence of the Maine Commissioners Regarding the Webster–Ashburton Treaty,' 345.

25 Ward to Messrs. Baring Brothers & Co., 16 Aug. 1842, Vol. 33, Baring Brothers Papers, MG 24 D 21, NAC.

26 Fuess, *Daniel Webster*, 2: 119–20; Bartell, *Daniel Webster*, 181–2; and Diary, 5 Nov. 1842, in Nevins, ed., *Diary of Philip Hone*, 628–9.

27 Palmerston to Russell, 24 Aug. 1842, Vol. 24, Aberdeen Papers, Add. Mss. 43,062, BL.

28 Diary, 17 and 24 Sept. 1842, in Strachey and Fulford, eds., *Greville Memoirs*, 5: 34–5.

29 *Morning Chronicle*, 19 and 24 Sept. 1842.

30 Cited in Hon. Evelyn Ashley, *The Life and Correspondence of Henry John Temple, Viscount Palmerston* (London: Richard Bentley & Sons, 1879), 1: 423.

31 Palmerston to Russell, Sept. 1842, in Gooch, ed., *The Later Correspondence of Lord John Russell*, 1: 59; and Bell, *Lord Palmerston*, 1: 334. Bell noted also that the weakness of the anti-slavery provisions of the treaty partially explained the vehemence of Palmerston's attacks. Ibid., 333. Ashburton attempted to anticipate criticism of the treaty by inviting both John Wilson Croker and George W. Featherstonhaugh to discuss the provisions that had been worked out. Berkeley and Berkeley, *Featherstonhaugh*, 256–7. The charge that Ashbur-

ton benefited from the settlement is a subtle one. The lands in Maine that he had acquired years earlier were not within the disputed territory, although it could certainly be argued that he and Baring Brothers stood to gain from more stable and improved Anglo–American relations. For this argument, see Arndt, 'Maine in the Northeastern Boundary Controversy: States' Rights in Antebellum New England,' 220.

32 Ashburton to Aberdeen, 27 Jan. 1843, Vol. 85, Aberdeen Papers, Add. Mss. 43,123, BL.

33 Melbourne to Russell, 7 Oct. 1842, in Sanders, ed., *Lord Melbourne's Papers*, 515–16.

34 Russell, who clearly had no understanding of the difficulty of obtaining the acquiescence of Maine, Massachusetts, and the Senate in reaching a settlement, told Greville that he thought that the negotiations could have been better handled by Aberdeen and Everett in London. Diary, 4 and 5 Oct. 1842, in Strachey and Fulford, eds., *Greville Memoirs*, 5: 38–40.

35 Arbuthnot to Peel, in Parker, ed., *Sir Robert Peel*, 3: 387. Sir James Willoughby Gordon, who had assisted in the preparation of the British case for the king of the Netherlands, told Lord Howick that the treaty was 'favourable' to British interests. Gordon to Howick, 26 Sept. 1842, Vol. 1, Grey Papers, MG 24 A 10, NAC.

36 Fitzwilliam to Russell, 3 Nov. 1842, in Gooch, ed., *The Later Correspondence of Lord John Russell*, 1: 61.

37 Aberdeen to Peel, 13 Oct. 1842, and Peel to Aberdeen, 15 Oct. 1842, Vol. 24, Aberdeen Papers, Add. Mss. 43,123, BL; and Berkeley and Berkeley, *Featherstonhaugh*, 256.

38 Jones, *To the Webster–Ashburton Treaty*, 169–73. Ashburton wrote to Webster early in the new year to say that despite Palmerston's complaints the public was quite satisfied with the settlement. 'Nobody of common sense cares much about the precise position of Lake Pohenagemook.' The most important reality was that peace had been preserved, he said. Ashburton to Webster, 2 Jan. 1843, in McIntyre, ed., *Writings and Speeches of Daniel Webster*, 18: 162–3.

39 Aberdeen to Ashburton, 26 Sept. 1842, Vol. 85, Aberdeen Papers, Add. Mss. 43,123, BL.

40 Aberdeen to Peel, 28 Sept. 1842, Vol. 24, Aberdeen Papers, Add. Mss. 43,062, BL. Despite what he said to Peel, Aberdeen attempted to flatter Ashburton by writing, 'When I recollect our situation with respect to the United States this time last year, & compare it with our present position, in any opinion a Dukedom would not be disproportionate to the service performed.' Nevertheless, the government, Wellington, and Queen Victoria agreed that a vis-

406 Notes to pages 296–7

countcy and the red ribbon of the Order of the Bath were sufficient honours at the moment. Aberdeen to Ashburton, 26 Oct. 1842, Vol. 85, Add. Mss. 43, 123, ibid.

41 Peel to Ashburton, 16 and 22 Oct. 1842, Vol. 337, Peel Papers, Add. Mss. 40,517, BL. Peel and Aberdeen had recognized that the eventual revelation of the red-line maps would cool enthusiasm for the treaty in Britain. See Aberdeen to Peel, 25 Aug. 1842, Vol. 24, Aberdeen Papers, Add. Mss. 43,062, BL.

42 G.W. Featherstonhaugh, *Observations upon the Treaty of Washington, signed August 9, 1842* (London: John W. Parker, 1843), 103; Berkeley and Berkeley, *Featherstonhaugh*, 256–63; and Featherstonhaugh to Addington, 5 Dec. 1842, and Addington to Featherstonhaugh, 7 and 13 Dec. 1842, FO 97/15, PRO. Featherstonhaugh seemed oblivious to the animosity that his report in 1840 had caused in the United States and the extent to which his appointment would be politically inexpedient. Colin Campbell, the British assistant surveyor under article 5, reacted very strongly to the treaty, to Ashburton, and to several others. 'I cannot reflect with any degree of Patience upon the manner in which our Government has been humbugged from the *first* to the *last* upon the Boundary Question,' he said. Furthermore, he made the extravagant allegation that there had been an 'American interest' at work in the British camp, that Ashburton had profited from the settlement, and that even Sir Howard Douglas had sold out by supporting the treaty. See Campbell to Odell, 29 July 1843, F-32-16, Odell Collection, NBM. David Thompson, British surveyor under articles 6 and 7, reacted similarly. Writing his memoirs in the 1850s, he strongly condemned both the original treaty of 1783 and the final decision in 1842, saying that Ashburton had been 'outwitted' by Webster 'both in New Brunswick, and the interior of Canada.' Tyrrell, ed., *David Thompson's Narrative*, 175–7. Bemis, just as strong a critic of Webster and the treaty, argued that Thompson's long connections with the fur trade made him an interested party and a biased critic on the boundary question. See Bemis, 'Jay's Treaty and the Northwest Boundary Gap,' 480–2.

43 Diary, 9 Feb. 1843, in Strachey and Fulford, eds., *Greville Memoirs*, 5: 81.

44 Ashburton to Croker, 7 Feb. 1843, in Pool, ed., *Croker Papers*, 187.

45 Peel to Croker, 23 Feb. 1843, in Louis J. Jennings, ed., *The Correspondence and Diaries of the Late Right Honorable John Wilson Croker* (New York: Charles Scribner's Sons, 1884), 2: 402–3. Peel also pointed out that Stratford Canning had searched the French archives in 1826, while preparing the British case for the arbitration, and had found nothing.

46 Cited in Lord Edmond Fitzmaurice, *Life of William, Earl of Shelburne* (London: Macmillan, 1876), 3: 325.

47 See A. Panizzi to Palmerston, 1 April 1839, and Foreign Office to The Trust-
   ees of the British Museum, 1 April 1839, FO 5/340, PRO; Miller, ed., *Treaties*,
   3: 328–53, and 4: 403–13; Everett to Webster, 31 March 1843, in Shewmaker,
   ed., *Papers of Daniel Webster: Diplomatic Correspondence*, 1: 787–93; Gill, 'Edward
   Everett and the Northeastern Boundary Controversy,' 211–12; and Jones, *To
   the Webster–Ashburton Treaty*, 109–10.

48 Diary, 11 Sept. 1842, in Strachey and Fulford, eds., *Greville Memoirs*, 5:
   33–4.

49 Everett wrote to Webster with some amazement about the revelation of the
   King George map in Parliament. He said that Peel outlined the treaty negotiations in a speech 'characterized by candor and fairness,' which eventually
   focused on the map question. Peel then described the map in some detail
   and dismissed it and the other maps as 'indecisive.' 'If the discovery of Mr.
   Sparks' Map at Paris was a Singular incident,' Everett commented, 'the
   bringing to light of Mr. Oswald's at London is much more singular.' Everett
   later saw the map and was much impressed with it. He also talked to both
   Ashburton and Aberdeen and was assured that they knew nothing about the
   map until a few days previously. He further noted that the London newspapers had not reported its significance. Everett to Aberdeen, 27 March 1843,
   Vol. 85, Aberdeen Papers, Add. Mss. 43,123, BL; and Everett to Webster,
   28 and 31 March 1843, Despatches from U.S. Ministers, Great Britain, M 30
   (roll 46), RG 59, NA.

50 Ridley, *Lord Palmerston*, 391–2; and Bell, *Lord Palmerston*, 1: 335–6.

51 Burrage, *Maine in the Northeastern Boundary Controversy*, 368–71.

52 'Treaty of Washington,' 21 March 1843, in Robert Peel, *The Speeches of the Late
   Right Honourable Sir Robert Peel, Bart., Delivered in the House of Commons* (London: George Routledge, 1853), 4: 213–31, specifically 229. Hunter Miller
   made much the same point as Peel ninety years later in his discussion of the
   map controversy. 'It was very natural that the possessor of a copy of Mitchell's Map should, after the changes of 1783 in political geography, make
   some attempt to indicate those changes on his map; and unless we know
   something more about a "red line" drawn on a copy of Mitchell's Map than
   that it *is* a red line on such a copy, its historical significance is nil.' Miller, ed.,
   Treaties, 3: 348–9.

53 'Treaty of Washington,' 21 March 1843, in Peel, *Speeches of Sir Robert Peel*, 4:
   229. In replying to Everett's report of Peel's speech, Webster said that it dealt
   with the map issue 'in a very handsome way' and that Peel had exhibited
   'manliness and independence, becoming his character, and honorable to his
   feelings.' Webster to Everett, 25 April 1843, in Shewmaker, ed., *Papers of
   Daniel Webster: Diplomatic Papers*, 1: 794.

54 Cited in Strachey and Fulford, eds., *Greville Memoirs*, 5: 85–6.

55 Jones, *To the Webster–Ashburton Treaty*, 176; and 'Treaty of Washington – Lord Ashburton,' 2 May 1843, in Peel, *Speeches of Sir Robert Peel*, 4: 240–5.

56 Ashburton to Webster, 28 April 1843, in McIntyre, ed., *Writings and Speeches of Daniel Webster*, 18: 190–1. The conversation between Charles Greville and Charles Lemon would suggest that the Foreign Office sent Ashburton a reproduction of the King George map while he was in the United States. Greville's statement in his diary might be called 'hearsay evidence.' Diary, 11 Sept. 1842, in Strachey and Fulford, eds., *Greville Memoirs*, 5: 33–4.

57 Everett to Webster, 3 April 1845, in Charles M. Wiltse, ed., *The Papers of Daniel Webster: Correspondence*, Volume 6, *1844–1849* (Hanover, NH: University Press of New England, 1984), 82. In reporting Ashburton's views to Webster, Everett also commented on Palmerston. Everett did not hold it against Palmerston that he did not reveal the King George map, but the persistent attack on the treaty was another matter. Such conduct was 'not an honorable course,' in Everett's judgment. Ashburton later wrote much the same to the chairman of the Senate's Foreign Relations Committee. 'I was wholly ignorant of the existence of the British Museum map until I returned from America ... and ... myself discovered the existence of this map as enquiries at the Museum of which I am a Trustee.' Ashburton to William Cabell Rives, 26 Aug. 1844, cited in Jones, 'Daniel Webster: The Diplomatist,' in Shewmaker, ed., *Daniel Webster: 'The Completest Man'*, 212. As late at 1845, Ashburton dismissed the Madawaska settlement as a mere 'straggling village' and asserted that the territory acquired east of Quebec City was of much greater importance. Hansard, cited in Jones, 'Lord Ashburton and the Maine Boundary Negotiations,' 490. Also see Duniway, 'Daniel Webster,' in Bemis, ed., *American Secretaries of State and Their Diplomacy*, 5: 43–50.

58 Walters, *Albert Gallatin*, 374–5.

59 Fuess, *Daniel Webster*, 2: 390–3; Bartlett, *Daniel Webster*, 190–3; and Remini, *Daniel Webster*, 610–17.

60 Official Misconduct of the Late Secretary of State, 9 June 1846, U.S. Congress, House Report No. 684, 29th Congress, 1st Session, 9–10. The quarrel between Ingersoll and Webster became very personal. For examples of the language used, as well as an analysis of the incident, see Howard Jones, 'The Attempt to Impeach Daniel Webster,' *Capitol Studies* 3 (fall 1975), 31–44.

61 Jones, 'Attempt,' 11–35.

62 Ibid., 37–8.

63 Keenleyside and Brown have called attention to how Canadian historians, particularly those from the Loyalist tradition, have described the Americans as 'antagonistic, threatening, and bombastic' and the British as prepared to

'sacrifice Canadian interests' for the sake of good relations with the United States. More recently, Stewart has shown that to Americans, Britain and Canada often looked very threatening in the early years of the republic. 'Upper Canada extended like a dagger into the heart of the Old Northwest,' he pointed out, and all the pressure for concessions along the border were seen as a challenge to U.S. survival. See Keenleyside and Brown, *Canada and the United States*, 151–2; and Gordon T. Stewart, *The American Response to Canada since 1776* (East Lansing: Michigan State University Press, 1992), 26–31. Richard Judd has recently made a very good case for the 'distinctive binational lumber economy,' as he calls it, that grew out of the boundary settlement. Lumbermen, sawmill operators, and capital moved easily back and forth across the border once the Webster–Ashburton Treaty opened the way. The Reciprocity Treaty of 1854 allowed lumber cut in sawmills in New Brunswick to enter the United States duty free, and, when that treaty expired, Congress passed legislation in 1866, the Pike Act, that allowed lumber cut originally in Maine to enter the United States duty free. Furthermore, New Brunswick and Maine provided many of the lumbermen and loggers who later in the century formed the backbone of the industry as it moved west to the Great Lakes states and the Pacific northwest. Judd, *Aroostook*, 39–47.

64 Ashburton to Webster, 28 April 1843, in McIntyre, ed., *Writings and Speeches of Daniel Webster*, 18: 190.

65 Jones, *To the Webster–Ashburton Treaty*, xvi. For an examination of the Canadian discussion about the boundary settlement, see Francis M. Carroll, 'The Passionate Canadians: The Historical Debate about the Eastern Canadian–American Boundary,' *NEQ* 70 (March 1997), 83–101. The boundary negotiations that Remini began by describing as 'creative statesmanship' ended, he concluded, as 'a stunning diplomatic triumph.' Remini, *Daniel Webster*, 538 and 564.

66 Writing in the midst of the Second World War, Robert McElroy and Thomas Riggs celebrated the lessons of the boundary settlement by emphasizing what Britain, Canada, and the United States 'escaped by the right use of reason' and that this experience 'should help them and others to be as wise in the future as these two have been in the past.' McElroy and Riggs, eds., *Unfortified Boundary*, 129. Scott's conclusion has been that, although both sides were sufficiently provoked to go to war over the Maine–New Brunswick dispute, kinship ties, intermingling, and commerce had produced, too much of a community for that to happen. Scott, *Ties of Common Blood*, 293–4. Judd concluded that the Webster–Ashburton Treaty 'prevented a third Anglo–American war.' Judd, *Aroostook*, 22.

Sources

Manuscript Materials

Canada

Manitoba Archives, Hudson's Bay Company (HBC) Archives, Winnipeg
  London Correspondence with all Government Department, 1813–1825
  Post Journals, Lac la Pluie, 1817–1828
  Post Reports, Lac la Pluie, 1823–1825
National Archives of Canada (NAC), Ottawa
  Sir Charles Bagot Papers, MG 24, A 13
  Anthony Barclay Papers, MG, 24, B 175
  Baring Brothers and Company, MG 24, D 21
  Boundary Commission Papers, MG 23, D 1
  Ward Chipman Papers, MG 23, D 1
  Sir Howard Douglas Papers, MG 24, A 3
  Charles Grey Papers, MG 24, A 10
  Sir John Harvey Papers, MG 24, A17
  Stephen Sewell Papers, MG 24, B 169
  David Thompson Journals, J.B. Tyrrell Papers, MG 30, D 49
  Johann Tiarks Papers, MG 24, H 64
  J.B. Tyrrell Papers, MG 30, D 49
New Brunswick Museum (NBM), Saint John
  William F. Ganong Collection, F-134–137 and F-198
  Sir John Harvey Letter Book, 1838, A-154
  Hugh T. Hazen Collection, F-101
  Hugh T. Hazen Collection, Chipman Papers, F-14, F-24–40
  Odell Family Collection, F-32–34 and A-266

Provincial Archives of New Brunswick (PANB), Fredericton
  Border Disputes, Maps, F 49
  Executive Council Records, Boundaries, F 6772, F 6673, and F 1697
  New Brunswick Boundary Disputes: Reports, Publications, F 13746
  William Odell Papers, F 368

Great Britain and Northern Ireland

British Library (BL), London
  Lord Aberdeen Papers, Ad.Mss. 43,086–236
  William Huskisson Papers, Ad.Mss. 38,746–66
  Lord Palmerston Papers, Ad.Mss. 48495.
  Sir Robert Peel Papers, Ad. Mss. 40,486 and 40,495.
Public Record Office (PRO), London
  Colonial Office:
  C.O. 6/   General Correspondence, British North America
  C.O. 188/   Original Correspondence, New Brunswick
  Foreign Office:
  F.O. 5/   General Correspondence, United States of America
  F.O. 37/   General Correspondence, Holland and Netherlands
  F.O. 97/   Supplement to General Correspondence
  F.O. 303/   Archives of Commissions
  F.O. 352/   Stratford Canning Papers
Public Record Office of Northern Ireland, Belfast
  Lord Castlereagh Papers

United States

Buffalo and Erie County Historical Society (BECHS), Buffalo
  Peter B. Porter Papers
Library of Congress (LC), Washington, DC
  Andrew Ellicott Papers
  John Fairfield Papers
  William Pitt Preble Papers
  Andrew Stevenson Papers
Maine Historical Society (Maine HS), Portland
  Thomas Barclay Papers
Massachusetts Historical Society (Mass HS), Boston
  North East Boundary Papers

Minnesota Historical Society (MHS), St Paul
    George W. Featherstonhaugh Papers
National Archives (NA), Washington, DC
    Records Relating to International Boundaries, Record Group 76:
    Northeast Boundary
    Northern Boundary
    State Department Records, Record Group 59:
    Diplomatic Instructions, All Countries
    Diplomatic Instructions, Great Britain
    Diplomatic Instructions, Special Missions
    Dispatches from US Ministers, Netherlands
    Domestic Letters
    Notes from the British Legation
    Notes to Foreign Ministers in the U.S.

Official Publications

Great Britain

Bourne, Kenneth, and D. Cameron Watt, eds. *British Documents on Foreign Affairs: Reports and Papers from the Foreign Office Confidential Print, Series C, North America, 1837–1914.* Vol 1. *McLeod and Maine, 1837–1842.* Frederick, Md.: University Publications of America, 1986.
British and Foreign State Papers, 1816–1817. Vol. 6. London: James Ridgway and Sons, 1836.
First Statement on the part of Great Britain, according to the provisions of The Convention concluded between Great Britain and the United States, on the 29th September, 1827, for regulating the Reference to Arbitration of Disputed Points of Boundary under the Fifth Article of the Treaty of Ghent. N.p., n.d. [Foreign Office, c. 12 July 1829].
Mudge, R.Z., and G.W. Featherstonhaugh, *Report of the British Commissioners Appointed to Survey the Territory in Dispute, between Great Britain and the United States of America on the Northeastern Boundary of the United States.* Originally published by Parliament in London, T.R. Harrison, 1840, in the *British Parliamentary Papers, United States of America.* Reprint, Shannon: Irish University Press, 1972. Vol. 11.
Parry, Clive, ed. *Law Officers' Opinions to the Foreign Office, 1793–1860.* Vol. 3. Westmead: Gregg International Publishing, Limited, 1970.
Second Statement on the Part of Great Britain, According to the Provisions of The Convention concluded between Great Britain and the United States, on the 29th September,

1827, for regulating the Reference to Arbitration of the Disputed Points of Boundary under the Fifth Article of the Treaty of Ghent. N.p., n.d. [Foreign Office, c. 1829].

Supplementary Reports Relating to The Boundary between the British Possessions in North America and the United States of America under the Treaty of 1783. Originally published by Parliament in London, 1842, in the *British Parliamentary Papers, United States of America.* Reprint, Shannon: Irish University Press, 1972, Vol. 11.

United States

American State Papers: Foreign Relations. Washington, DC: Gales and Seaton, 1834.

Definitive Statement on the Part of the United States of the case referred, in pursuance of the Convention of 29th September 1827, between the said States and Great Britain, to His Majesty the King of the Netherlands, for His Decision Thereon. Washington, DC: Printed at the Office of the United States' Telegraph, 1829 [printed but not published].

Giunta, Mary A., ed. *The Emerging Nation: A Documentary History of the Foreign Relations of the United States under the Articles of Confederation, 1780–1789.* 3 vols. Washington, DC: National Historical Publications and Records Commission, 1996.

International Boundary Commission. *Joint Report upon the Survey and Demarcation of the Boundary between the United States and Canada from the Northwesternmost Point of Lake of the Woods to Lake Superior.* Washington, DC: Government Printing Office, 1931.

– *Joint Report upon the Survey and Demarcation of the Boundary Between the United States and Canada From the Source of the St. Croix River to the St. Lawrence River.* Washington, DC: Government Printing Office, 1925.

Manning, William R., ed. *Diplomatic Correspondence of the United States: Canadian Relations, 1784–1860.* Vols. 1–3. Washington, DC: Carnegie Endowment for International Peace, 1940–43.

Miller, David Hunter, ed. *Treaties and Other International Acts of the United States Government, 1776–1863.* Vols. 2 and 3. Washington, DC: Government Printing Office, 1931.

Moore, John Bassett. *Digest of International Law.* Vol. 2. Washington: DC: Government Printing Office, 1906.

– *History and Digest of the International Arbitrations to which the United States has been a Party.* Vol. 1. Washington, DC: Government Printing Office, 1898.

– ed. *International Adjudications Ancient and Modern: Modern Series.* Vol. 1. New York: Oxford University Press, 1929.

Richardson, James D., ed. *A Compilation of the Messages and Papers of the Presidents.* Vol. 2. New York: Bureau of National Literature, 1897.

State of Maine. [John G. Deane] *Document No. 13. January Session, 1828, Report of the Select Committee of the Senate and House or Representatives of the State of Maine, In Relation to the North-Eastern Boundary of the State.* Portland: Thomas Todd, 1828.

– *Report of the Committee on the North-Eastern Boundary.* N.p. Severence & Dorr, 1841.

– *Resolutions of the Legislature of the State of Maine, respecting the advice of the King of the Netherlands, in relation to the North Eastern Boundary.* Portland: Thomas Todd, 1932.

– *State of Maine to the Senate and House of Representatives. Edward Kent, Council Chambers, 2 January 1839.* N.p., n.d.

State of Maryland. *Report of The Select Committee to whom were referred Resolutions of the State of Maine, Indiana, and Ohio, in relation to the North-Eastern Boundary.* Annapolis: William McNair, 1841.

State of Massachusetts. *Senate ... No. 5, Report of the committee on Public Lands, on the subject of the North Eastern Boundary.* Boston: Dutton and Wentworth, 1832.

– House Document No. 44, *Report of the joint select committee [of Massachusetts] on the message of the Governor transmitting the resolutions of Maine and Indiana in regard to the northeastern boundary.* N.p., 1841.

Statement of the United States, of the case referred, in pursuance of the Convention of 29th September, 1827, Between the Said United States and Great Britain, to His Majesty, The King of the Netherlands, For His Decision Thereon. Washington, DC: printed but not published at the Office of the United States Telegraph, 1829. Evidence.

United States, Continental Congress. *Secret Journals of the acts and proceedings of Congress from the first meeting thereof to the dissolution of the Confederation.* 4 vols. Boston: Thomas B. Wait, 1820–21.

U.S. Congress. House Document Number 451, 25th Congress, 2nd Session, Vol. 11.

– House Report Number 684, 'Official Misconduct of the Late Secretary of State, 9 June 1846.' 29th Congress, 1st Session.

Memoirs, Diaries, and Letters

Aberdeen, Earl of. *The Correspondence of Lord Aberdeen and Princess Lieven, 1832–1854.* Ed. E. Jones Parry. Vol. 1. London: Royal Historical Society, 1938.

Adams, John Quincy. *Memoirs of John Quincy Adams.* Edited by Charles Francis Adams. Vols. 3–6. Philadelphia: J.B. Lippencott, 1875.

Addington, Henry Unwin. *Youthful America: Selections from Henry Unwin Adding-*

ton's Residence in the United States of America, 1822, 23, 24, 25. Ed. Bradford Perkins. Berkeley: University of California Press, 1950.

Arthur, Sir George. *The Arthur Papers: Being the Canadian Papers, Mainly Confidential, Private, and Demi-Official of Sir George Arthur, C.C.H., Last Lieutenant-Governor of Upper Canada.* Ed. Charles R. Sanderson. Vol. 1. Toronto: University of Toronto Press, 1959.

Barclay, Thomas. *Selections from the Correspondence of Thomas Barclay: Formerly British Consul General at New York.* Ed. George Lockhart Rives. New York: Harper & Brothers, 1894.

Bayard, James A. *Papers of James A. Bayard.* Ed. Elizabeth Donnan. In Vol. 2, American Historical Associations, *Annual Report, 1913.* Washington, DC: Government Printing Office, 1815.

Bigsby, John J. *The Shoe and Canoe, or Pictures of Travel in the Canadas.* 2 vols. London: Chapman and Hall, 1850.

Bird, William A. 'Reminiscences of the Boundary Survey between the United States and British Provinces.' *Publications of the Buffalo Historical Society.* Vol. 4. Buffalo: Peter Paul Book Company, 1896.

Canning, George. *The Formation of Canning's Ministry, February to August 1827.* Ed. Arthur Aspinall. London: Royal Historical Society, 1937.

– *George Canning and His Friends* Ed. Josceline Bagot. Vol. 2 London: John Murray, 1909.

Castlereagh, Viscount. *Correspondence, Despatches, and Other Papers of Viscount Castlereagh, Second Marquess of Londonderry.* Ed. Charles W. Vane, Marquess of Londonderry. Vol. 10. London: William Shoberl, 1852.

Clay, Henry. *The Papers of Henry Clay.* Ed. James F. Hopkins and Mary W.M. Hargreaves. Vol. 1. Lexington: University of Kentucky Press, 1959.

– *The Papers of Henry Clay.* Ed. James F. Hopkins. Vol. 4. Lexington: University Press of Kentucky, 1972.

– *The Papers of Henry Clay.* Ed. James F. Hopkins and Mary W.V. Hargreaves. Vol. 5. Lexington: University Press of Kentucky, 1973.

– *The Papers of Henry Clay.* Ed. Mary W.M. Hargreaves and James F. Hopkins. Vol. 6. Lexington: University Press of Kentucky, 1981.

– *The Papers of Henry Clay.* Ed. Robert Seager, II. Vol. 7. Lexington: The University Press of Kentucky, 1982.

Croker, John Wilson. *The Correspondence and Diaries of the Late Right Honorable John Wilson Croker.* Ed. Louis J. Jennings. Vol. 2. New York: Charles Scribner's Sons, 1884.

– *The Croker Papers, 1808–1857.* Ed. Bernard Pool. London: R.T. Batsford, Ltd., 1967.

Delafield, Joseph. *The Unfortified Boundary: A Diary of the first survey of the Cana-*

dian Boundary Line from St. Regis to Lake of the Woods by Major Joseph Delafield, American Agent under Articles VI and VII of the Treaty of Ghent. Ed. Robert McElroy and Thomas Riggs. New York: privately printed, 1943.

Everett, Edward. *Orations and Speeches on Various Occasions by Edward Everett.* Vol. 2. Boston: Little Brown, 1865.

Featherstonhaugh, George W. *In Search of the Highlands: Mapping the Canada-Maine Boundary, 1839.* Ed. Alec McEwen. Fredericton: Acadiensis Press, 1988.

Gallatin, Albert. *The Writings of Albert Gallatin.* Ed. Henry Adams. Vol. 2. Philadelphia: J.B. Lippencott, 1879.

Garry, Nicholas. 'Diary of Nicholas Garry.' *Transactions of the Royal Society of Canada,* Series II, 1912.

Grattan, Thomas Colley. *Civilized America.* Vol. 1. London: Bradbury and Evans, 1859.

Grey, Lt.-Col. Charles. *Crisis in the Canadas, 1838–1839: The Grey Journals and Letters.* Ed. William Ormsby. Toronto: Macmillan, 1964.

Greville, Charles. *The Greville Memoirs, 1814–1860.* Ed. Lytton Strachey and Roger Fulford. Vols. 4 and 5. London: Macmillan, 1938.

Hamilton, James A. *Reminiscences of James A. Hamilton: or, Men and Events, at Home and Abroad, During Three Quarters of a Century.* New York: Charles Scribner, 1869.

Hone, Philip. *The Diary of Philip Hone, 1828–1851.* Ed. Allan Nevins. 1927. Reprint, New York: Kraus Reprint, 1969.

Jackson, Andrew. *Correspondence of Andrew Jackson.* Ed. John Spencer Bassett. Vol. 4. Washington, D.C., Carnegie Institution of Washington, 1829.

Jay, John. *The Correspondence and Public Papers of John Jay.* Ed. Henry P. Johnston. Vol. 4. 1890. Reprint, New York: Burt Franklin, 1970.

Keating, William H. *Narrative of an Expedition to the Source of St. Peter's River, Lake Winnepeek, Lake of the Woods, Etc., Performed in the Year 1823, By Order of the Hon. J.C. Calhoun, Secretary of War, Under the Command of Stephen H. Long, U.S.T.E.* 1824. Reprint, Minneapolis: Ross & Haines, 1959.

Lawrence, Abbott. *Memoir of Abbott Lawrence.* Ed. Hamilton Andres Hill. Boston: n.p., 1883.

Long, Stephen H. *The Northern Expeditions of Stephen H. Long: The Journals of 1817 and 1823 and Related Documents.* Ed. Lucile M. Kane, June D. Holmquist, and Carolyn Gilman. St Paul: Minnesota Historical Society Press, 1978.

McKenney, Thomas L. *Sketches of a Tour to the Lakes, Of the Character and Custom of the Chippeway Indians and of Incidents Connected with the Treaty of Fond du Lac.* 1927. Reprint, Minneapolis: Ross & Haines, 1959.

Melbourne, Viscount. *Lord Melbourne's Papers.* Ed. Lloyd C. Sanders. London: Longmans, Green, 1889.

Palmerston, Viscount. *The Life and Correspondence of Henry John Temple, Viscount Lord Palmerston.* Ed. Hon. Evelyn Ashley. Vol. 1. London: Richard Bentley & Sons, 1879.

Peel, Sir Robert. *The Speeches of the Late Right Honourable Sir Robert Peel, Bart., Delivered in the House of Commons.* Vol. 4. London: George Routledge and Co., 1853.

– *Sir Robert Peel, from His Private Papers.* Ed. Charles Stuart Parker. London: John Murray, 1899.

Rush, Richard. *A Residence at the Court of London.* London: Richard Bentley, 1845.

Russell, Lord John. *The Later Correspondence of Lord John Russell, 1840–1878.* Ed. G.P. Gooch. Vol. 1. London: Longmans, Green, 1925.

Schoolcraft, Henry R. *Personal Memoirs of a Residence of Thirty Years with the Indian Tribes on the American Frontiers: With Brief Notices of Passing Events, Facts, and Opinions, A.D. 1812 to A.D. 1842.* Philadelphia: Lippincott, Grambo, 1851.

– *Schoolcraft's Narrative of Travels through the Northwestern Regions of the United States extending from Detroit through the Great Chain of American Lakes to the Sources of the Mississippi River in the Year 1820.* Ed. Mentor L. Williams. East Lansing: Michigan State University Press, 1992.

Scott, Winfield. *Memoirs of Lieut.-General Scott, LL.D., Written by Himself.* New York: Sheldon, 1864. 2 vols.

– 'A Private Report of General Winfield Scott on the Border Situation in 1839.' Ed. C.P. Stacey. *Canadian Historical Review* 21 (Dec. 1940).

Sullivan, James. *The Life of James Sullivan: With Selections from His Writings.* Thomas C. Amory. Vol. 1. Boston: Philips, Samson, 1858.

Sydenham, Baron. *Letters from Lord Sydenham, Governor-General of Canada, 1839–1841, To Lord John Russell.* Ed. Paul Knaplund. London: George Allen & Unwin, 1931.

Tanner, John. *The Falcon: A Narrative of the Captivity and Adventures of John Tanner.* Ed. Louis Erdrich. New York: Penguin Books, 1994.

Thompson, David. *David Thompson: Travels in Western North America, 1784–1812.* Ed. Victor G. Hopwood. Toronto: Macmillan, 1977.

– *David Thompson's Narrative of His Explorations in Western America, 1784–1912.* Ed. J.B. Tyrrell. Vol. 12. Toronto: Champlain Society, 1916.

– *New Light on the Early History of the Greater Northwest: The Manuscript Journals of Alexander Henry and David Thompson.* Ed. Elliott Coues. Vol. 1. 1897. Reprint. Minneapolis: Ross & Haines, 1965.

– 'Remarks on the Maps from St. Regis to Sault Ste. Marie.' *Papers and Records of the Ontario Historical Society* Vol. 1. 117–21. 1899.

Tyler, John. *The Letters and Times of the Tylers.* Ed. Lyon G. Tyler. Vol 2. 1884. Reprint. New York: DaCapo Press, 1970.

Vaughan, Sir Charles R. 'The Papers of Sir Charles R. Vaughan, 1825–1835.' Ed. John A. Doyle. *American Historical Review* 7 (Jan., April 1902), 304–29, 500–33.

Webster, Daniel. *The Letters of Daniel Webster.* Ed. C.H. Van Tyne. New York: McClure, Phillips, 1902.

– *The Papers of Daniel Webster: Correspondence.* Vol. 4. *1835–1839.* Ed. Charles M. Wiltse and Harold D. Moser. Hanover, NH: University Press of New England, 1980.

– *The Papers of Daniel Webster: Correspondence.* Vol. 5. *1840–1843.* Ed. Harold D. Moser. Hanover, NH: University Press of New England, 1982.

– *The Papers of Daniel Webster: Correspondence.* Vol. 6. *1844–1849.* Ed. Charles M. Wiltse. Hanover, NH: University Press of New England, 1984.

– *The Papers of Daniel Webster: Diplomatic Papers, 1841–1843.* Ed. Kenneth Shewmaker. Vol. 1. Hanover, NH: University Press of New England, 1983.

– *The Private Correspondence of Daniel Webster.* Ed. Fletcher Webster. Vol. 2. Boston: Little, Brown, 1857.

– *The Writings and Speeches of Daniel Webster.* Ed. James W. McIntyre. Vol. 18. Boston: Little, Brown, 1903.

Wellington, Duke of. *The Despatches of Field Marshal the Duke of Wellington.* Ed. Col. Gurwood. Vol. 2. London: John Murray, 1838.

– *Private Correspondence of Thomas Raikes with The Duke of Wellington and Other Distinguished Contemporaries.* Ed. Harriet Raikes. London: Richard Bentley, 1861.

– *Supplementary Despatches, Correspondence, and Memoranda of Field Marshal Arthur Duke of Wellington, K.G.* Ed. Arthur R. Wellesley, Duke of Wellington. Vol. 9. London: John Murray, 1862.

Winslow, Edward. *The Winslow Papers.* Ed. W.O. Raymond. Saint John: New Brunswick Historical Society, 1901.

Pamphlets and Contemporary Writings

[Anon.] *Consideration of the Claims and Conduct of the United States Respecting Their North Eastern Boundary, and of the Value of the British Colonies in North America.* London: John Hatchard and Son, 1826.

Bouchette, Joseph. *The British Dominions in North America: Or a Topographical Description of the Provinces of Lower and Upper Canada ...* 2 vols. London: Longman, Rees, Orme, Brown, and Green, 1832.

– *A Topographical Description of the Province of Lower Canada, with Remarks upon Upper Canada, and on the Relative Connection of Both Provinces with the United States of America.* London: W. Faden, 1815.

[Chipman, Ward, Jr.] *Remarks upon the Disputed Points of Boundary under the Fifth Article of the Treaty of Ghent, Principally Compiled from the Statements Laid by the*

Government of Great Britain before the King of the Netherlands, as Arbiter. Saint John: D.A. Cameron, 1938.

Featherstonhaugh, George W. *Historical Sketch of the Negotiations at Paris in 1782, from Inedited Documents; with Remarks on Mr. Albert Gallatin's 'Right of the United States of America to the North-eastern Boundary Claimed by Them.'* London, n.p., 1842.

– *Observations upon the Treaty of Washington, Signed August 9, 1842.* London: John W. Parker, 1843.

Gallatin, Albert. *The Right of the United States of America to the North-Eastern Boundary Claimed by Them.* 1840. Reprint, New York: Books for Libraries Press, 1970.

Hincks, Sir Francis. 'The Boundaries Formerly in Dispute between Great Britain and the United States.' Montreal: John Lovall, 1885.

'The History of the Negotiations in Reference to the Eastern and Northeastern Boundaries of the United States.' *New York Review* (Jan. 1841), 3–53.

[Preble, William Pitt.] 'The Decision of the King of the Netherlands Considered in Reference to the Rights of the United States and the State of Maine.' Portland: Thomas Todd, 1831.

'Verax' [Ward Chipman, Jr]. *Letters on the Boundary Line, First Published in the City Gazette.* Saint John: Alexander M'Leod, 1828.

Newspapers and Periodicals

Dublin University Magazine
Eastern Argus (Portland, ME)
Gazette (Boston, MA)
Morning Chronicle (London)
National Intelligencer (Washington, DC)
New York Herald
Niles' National Register (Baltimore, MD)
The Times (London)

Later Works

Abernathy, T.P. *Western Lands and the American Revolution.* 1937. Reprint, New York: Russell & Russell, 1937.

Adams, Ephraim Douglass. 'Lord Ashburton and the Treaty of Washington.' *American Historical Review* 17 (July, 1912), 764–82.

Adams, James Truslow, ed. *Dictionary of American Biography.* 21 vols. New York: Charles Scribner's Sons, 1940–74.

Alberts, Robert C. *The Golden Voyage: The Life and Times of William Bingham, 1752–1804*. Boston: Houghton Mifflin, 1969.

Allen, H.C. *Great Britain and the United States: A History of Anglo–American Relations (1783–1952)*. New York: St Martin's Press, 1955.

Alvord, Clarence W. *The Mississippi Valley in British Politics*. 2 vols. Cleveland: Arthur H. Clark Company, 1917.

Arndt, J. Chris. 'Maine in the Northeastern Boundary Controversy: States' Rights in Antebellum New England.' *New England Quarterly* 62 (June 1989), 205–23.

Baldwin, J.R. 'The Ashburton–Webster Boundary Settlement.' *Canadian Historical Association, Annual Report* (1938), 121–33.

Bartlett, C.T. *Castlereagh*. New York: Charles Scribner's Sons, 1966.

Bartlett, Irving. *Daniel Webster*. New York: W.W. Norton, 1978.

Bassett, John Spencer. 'Martin Van Buren.' In *The American Secretaries of State and Their Diplomacy*, ed. Samuel Flagg Bemis. Vol. 4. 1928. Reprint, New York: Cooper Square Publications, 1963.

Bayliss, Joseph E., and Estelle L., in collaboration with Milo M. Quaife. *River of Destiny: The Saint Marys*. Detroit: Wayne State University Press, 1955.

Beers, Henry Putney. *The Western Military Frontier, 1815–1846*. 1935. Reprint, Philadelphia: Porcupine Press, 1975.

Bell, Herbert C.F. *Lord Palmerston*. 1936. 2 vols. Reprint, London: Frank Cass, 1966.

Bemis, Samuel Flagg. *The Diplomacy of the American Revolution*. 3rd ed. Bloomington: University of Indiana Press, 1957.

– *Jay's Treaty: A Study in Commerce and Diplomacy*. New Haven, Conn.: Yale University Press, 1923.

– 'Jay's Treaty and the Northwest Boundary Gap.' *American Historical Review* 27 (April 1922), 465–84.

– *John Quincy Adams and the Foundations of American Foreign Policy*. New York: Alfred A. Knopf, 1949.

Berkeley, Edmond, and Dorothy Smith Berkeley. *George William Featherstonhaugh: The First U.S. Geologist*. Tuscaloosa: University of Alabama Press, 1988.

Berton, Pierre. *Flames across the Border, 1813–1814*. Toronto: McClelland and Stewart, 1981.

Boggs, Whittemore S. *International Boundaries: A Study of Boundary Functions and Problems*. New York: Columbia University Press, 1940.

Bourne, Kenneth *Britain and the Balance of Power in North America, 1815–1909*. London: Longmans, 1967.

– *The Foreign Policy of Victorian England, 1830–1902*. Oxford: Clarendon, 1970.

– *Palmerston: The Early Years, 1784–1841*. New York: Macmillan, 1982.

Brown, George W., et al., eds. *Dictionary of Canadian Biography.* 14 vols. Toronto: University of Toronto Press, 1966–98.

Brown, Roger Hamilton. *The Struggle for the Indian Stream Territory.* Cleveland: Western Reserve University Press, 1955.

Bullen, Roger. *Palmerston, Guizot and the Collapse of the Entente Cordiale.* London: Athlone Press, 1974.

Burpee, L.J. 'Some Letters of David Thompson.' *Canadian Historical Review* 4 (1923), 105–26.

Burrage, Henry S. *Maine in the Northeastern Boundary Controversy.* Portland: Printed for the State, 1919.

– 'The St. Croix Commission, 1796–98.' *Maine Historical Society Collection.* 1895. 225–51.

Burt, Alfred L. *The United States, Great Britain and British North America: From the Revolution to the Establishment of Peace after the War of 1812.* New Haven, Conn.: Yale University Press, 1940.

Cajori, Florian. *The Chequered Career of Ferdinand Rudolph Hassler.* Boston: Christopher Publishing House, 1929.

Callahan, James Morton. *American Foreign Policy in Canadian Relations.* 1937. Reprint, New York: Cooper Square Publishers, 1967.

Cannon, John. *The Fox–North Coalition: Crisis of the Constitution, 1782–84.* Cambridge: Cambridge University Press, 1969.

Careless, J.M.S. *The Union of the Canadas: The Growth of Canadian Institutions, 1841–1857.* Toronto: McClelland and Stewart, 1967.

Carroll, Francis M. 'Kings and Crises: Arbitrating the Canadian-American Boundary Dispute, and the Belgian Crisis, 1830–31.' *New England Quarterly* 73 (June 2000), 179–201.

– 'The Passionate Canadians: The Historical Debate about the Eastern Canadian–American Boundary.' *New England Quarterly* 70 (March 1997), 83–101.

Carter, George E. 'Daniel Webster and the Canadian Rebellions of 1837–1838.' *Canadian Historical Association Historical Papers* (1970), 120–31.

Casson, W.P. *James Monroe.* Chapel Hill: University of North Carolina Press, 1946.

Cecil, Algernon. *British Foreign Secretaries, 1807–1916: Studies in Personality and Policy.* 1927. Reprint, Port Washington, NY: Kennikat Press, 1971.

Chamberlain, Muriel E. *Lord Aberdeen: A Political Biography.* London: Longman, 1983.

Classen, H. George. *Thrust and Counterthrust: The Genesis of the Canada-United States Boundary.* Chicago: Rand McNally, 1965.

Combs, Jerald A. *The Jay Treaty: Political Battleground of the Founding Fathers.* Berkeley: University of California Press, 1970.

Corbett, P.E. *The Settlement of Canadian–American Disputes: A Critical Study of Meth-*

ods and Results. New Haven, Conn.: Yale University Press, 1937.

Corey, Albert B. *The Crisis of 1830–1842 in Canadian–American Relations.* New Haven, Conn.: Yale University Press, 1941.

Cukwurah, A.O. *The Settlement of Boundary Disputes in International Law.* Manchester: University of Manchester, 1967.

Culkin, Hon. William E. 'Northern Minnesota Boundary Survey in 1822 to 1826.' *Minnesota Historical Society Collections* 15 (1915), 379–92.

Current, Richard N. 'Webster's Propaganda and the Ashburton Treaty.' *Mississippi Valley Historical Review* 34 (Sept. 1947), 187–200.

Curtis, James C. *The Fox at Bay: Martin Van Buren and the Presidency, 1837–1841.* Lexington: University Press of Kentucky, 1970.

Demeritt, David. 'Representing the "True" St. Croix: Knowledge and Power in the Partition of the Northeast.' *William and Mary Quarterly,* 3rd Series, 54 (July 1997), 515–48.

Doan, Daniel. *Indian Stream Republic: Setting a New England Frontier, 1785–1842.* Hanover, NH: University Press of New England, 1997.

Duckett, Alvin Laroy. *John Forsyth: Political Tactician.* Athens: University of Georgia Press, 1962.

Duffy, John, and H. Nicholas Muller. 'The Great Wolf Hunt: The Popular Response in Vermont to the *Patriote* Uprising of 1837.' *Journal of American Studies* 8 (1974), 153–69.

Duniway, Clyde Augustus. 'Daniel Webster.' In Samual Flagg Bemis, ed., *The American Secretaries of State and Their Diplomacy.* Vol. 5. 1928. Reprint, New York: Cooper Square Publishers, 1963.

Eddington, Bryan. 'The Great Hall at Old Fort William.' *The Beaver* 312 (summer 1981), 38–42.

Engleman, Fred L. *The Peace of Christmas Eve.* London: Rupert Hart-Davis, 1962.

Falconer, Sir Robert. *The United States as a Neighbour from a Canadian Point of View.* London: Cambridge University Press, 1925.

Fisher, Peter. *The First History of New Brunswick.* 1925. Reprint, Woodstock, NB: Larsen's Printing, 1980.

Fitzmaurice, Lord Edmond. *Life of William, Earl of Shelburne.* Vol. 3. London: Macmillan and Co., 1876.

Fuess, Claude M. *Daniel Webster.* Boston: Little, Brown, 1930.

Fullom, W.S. *The Life of General Sir Howard Douglass.* London: John Murray, 1863.

Ganong, William F. 'A Monograph of the Evolution of the Boundaries of the Province of New Brunswick.' *Transactions of the Royal Society of Canada,* Second Series 7 (May 1901), Section II, 139–449.

Gash, Norman. *Sir Robert Peel: The Life of Sir Robert Peel after 1830.* London: Longmans, 1972.

Gates, Charles M. 'The West in American Diplomacy, 1812–1815.' *Mississippi Valley Historical Review* 26 (1939–40), 499–510.

Gill, George J. 'Edward Everett and the Northeastern Boundary Controversy.' *New England Quarterly* 42 (June 1969), 201–13.

Gilpin, Alex R *The Territory of Michigan, 1805–1837.* East Lansing: Michigan State University Press, 1970.

Glazebrook, G.P. deT. *Sir Charles Bagot in Canada: A Study in British Colonial Government.* Oxford: Oxford University Press, 1929.

Green, John C. *American Science in the Age of Jefferson.* Ames: Iowa State University Press, 1984.

Green, John C., and John G. Burke. 'The Science of Minerals in the Age of Jefferson.' *Transactions of the American Philosophical Society* 68 no. 4 (July 1978), 5–109.

Grey, Edmond. 'Ward Chipman, Loyalist.' *Massachusetts Historical Society Proceedings* 54 (1922), 330–53.

Guillet, Edwin C. *The Lives and Times of the Patriots.* Toronto: University of Toronto Press, 1968.

Hannay, James. *History of New Brunswick.* 2 vols. Saint John: John A. Bowes, 1909.

Harlow, Vincent T. *The Foundation of the Second British Empire: Discovery and Revolution.* New York: Longmans, Green, 1952.

Hatcher, Harlan. *Lake Erie.* Indianapolis: Bobbs-Merrill, 1945.

Hemenway, Abby Maria. 'John Johnson.' *Vermont Historical Magazine* 1 (1867), 596–9.

Hickey, Donald R. *The War of 1812: A Forgotten Conflict.* Urbana: University of Illinois Press, 1989.

Hidy, Ralph W. *The House of Baring in American Trade and Finance: English Merchant Bankers at Work, 1763–1861.* Cambridge: Harvard University Press, 1949.

Horsman, Reginald. 'British Indian Policy in the Northwest, 1807–1812.' *Mississippi Valley Historical Review* 45 (1958), 51–66.

– *Matthew Elliott, British Indian Agent.* Detroit: Wayne State University Press, 1964.

James, Stephens B. *Boundary Making: A Handbook for Statesmen, Treaty Editors, and Boundary Commissioners.* Washington, DC: Carnegie Endowment for International Peace, 1945.

Jenkins, Brian. *Henry Goulburn, 1784–1856: A Political Biography.* Montreal: McGill-Queen's University Press, 1996.

Jones, Howard. 'Anglophobia and the Aroostook War.' *New England Quarterly* 48 (Dec. 1975), 519–39.

– 'The Attempt to Impeach Daniel Webster.' *Capitol Studies* 3 (Fall 1975), 31–44.

- 'The *Caroline* Affair.' *Historian* 38 (May 1976), 485–502.
- *To the Webster–Ashburton Treaty: A Study in Anglo–American Relations, 1783–1843.* Chapel Hill: University of North Carolina Press, 1977.

Jones, Howard, and Donald A. Rakestraw. *Prologue to Manifest Destiny: Anglo–American Relations in the 1840s.* Wilmington, Del.: Scholarly Resources, 1997.

Jones, Wilbur Devereux. *The American Problem in British Diplomacy, 1841–1861.* London: Macmillan, 1974.

- *Lord Aberdeen and the Americas.* Athens: University of Georgia Press, 1958.
- 'Lord Ashburton and the Maine Boundary Negotiations.' *Mississippi Valley Historical Review* 40 (Dec. 1953), 477–90.

Judd, Richard W. *Aroostook: A Century of Logging in Northern Maine.* Orono: The University of Maine Press, 1989.

- 'The Aroostook War.' In Richard W. Judd, Edwin A. Churchill, and Joel W. Eastman, eds., *Maine: The Pine Tree State from Prehistory to the Present.* Orono: University of Maine Press, 1995.

Keenleyside, Hugh L., and Gerald S. Brown. *Canada and the United States: Some Aspects of Their Historical Relations.* New York: Alfred A. Knopf, 1952.

Ketchum, T.C.L. *A Short History of Carleton County New Brunswick.* 1922. Reprint, Woodstock: Larsen's Printing, 1981.

Kilbourn, William. *Firebrand: William Lyon Mackenzie and the Rebellion in Upper Canada.* Toronto: Clarke, Irwin, 1956.

Kinchen, Oscar A. *The Rise and Fall of the Patriot Hunters.* New York: Bookman Associates, 1956.

Kossman, E.H. *The Low Countries, 1780–1940.* Oxford: Oxford University Press, 1978.

Landon, Fred. *Lake Huron.* Indianapolis: Bobbs-Merrill, 1944.

Lane-Poole, Stanley. *The Life of the Right Honourable Stratford Canning, Viscount Stratford de Redcliffe.* 2 vols. London: Longmans, Green, 1888.

Lass, William E. *Minnesota's Boundary with Canada: Its Evolution since 1783.* St Paul: Minnesota Historical Society Press, 1980.

Lavender, David. *The Fist in the Wilderness.* Albuquerque: University of New Mexico Press, 1964.

LeDuc, Thomas. 'The Maine Frontier and the Northeastern Boundary Controversy.' *American Historical Review* 53 (Oct. 1947), 30–41.

- 'The Webster–Ashburton Treaty and the Minnesota Iron Ranges.' *Journal of American History* 51 (1964), 476–81.

Lowenthal, David. 'The Maine Press and the Aroostook War.' *Canadian Historical Review* 32 (Dec. 1951), 315–36.

Lucy, William L. 'Some Correspondence of the Maine Commissioners Regarding the Webster–Ashburton Treaty.' *New England Quarterly* 15 (June 1942), 332–48.

McCormac, Eugene Irving. 'John Forsyth.' In Samuel Flagg Bemis, ed., *The

American Secretaries of State and Their Diplomacy. Vol. 4. 1928. Reprint, New York: Cooper Square Publishers, 1963.

MacDonald, Graham A. 'Commerce, Civility and Old Sault Ste. Marie.' *The Beaver* 312 (winter 1981), 52–9.

MacNutt, W.S. *The Atlantic Provinces: The Emergence of Colonial Society, 1712–1857.* Toronto: McClelland and Stewart, 1965.

– *New Brunswick: A History, 1784–1867.* Toronto: Macmillan, 1963.

Martin, Lawrence, and Samuel Flagg Bemis. 'Franklin's Red-Line Map Was a Mitchell.' *New England Quarterly* 10 (March 1937), 105–11.

Masterson, William H. *Tories and Democrats: British Diplomats in Pre-Jacksonian America.* College Station: Texas A&M University Press, 1985.

Merk, Frederick. *Fruits of Propaganda in the Tyler Administration.* Cambridge, Mass.: Harvard University Press, 1971.

– *The Oregon Question: Essays in Anglo–American Diplomacy and Politics.* Cambridge, Mass.: Harvard University Press, 1967.

Middleton, Charles Ronald. *The Administration of British Foreign Policy, 1782–1846.* Durham, NC: Duke University Press, 1977.

Mills, Dudley A. 'British Diplomacy and Canada: The Ashburton Treaty.' *United Empire: The Royal Colonial Institute Journal, New Series* 2 (Oct. 1911), 684–712.

– 'The Duke of Wellington and the Peace Negotiations at Ghent in 1814.' *Canadian Historical Review* 2 (March 1921), 19–32.

Morris, Richard B. *The Peacemakers: The Great Powers and American Independence.* New York: Harper and Row, 1965.

Mulligan, Rev. William Orr. 'Sir Charles Bagot and Canadian Boundary Questions.' *Canadian Historical Association, Report.* 1936, 40–52.

Murchie, Guy. *Saint Croix: The Sentinel River.* New York: Duell, Sloan and Pearce, 1947.

Neel, Joanne Loewe. *Phineas Bond: A Study in Anglo–American Relations, 1786–1812.* Philadelphia: University of Pennsylvania Press, 1968.

Nute, Grace Lee. *Lake Superior.* Indianapolis: Bobbs-Merrill, 1944.

Omond, G.W.T. 'Belgium, 1830–1839.' In Sir H.W. Ward and G.P. Gooch, eds., *The Cambridge History of British Foreign Policy, 1783–1919.* Vol. 2. Cambridge: Cambridge University Press, 1923.

Perkins, Bradford. *Castlereagh and Adams: England and the United States, 1812–1823.* Berkeley: University of California Press, 1964.

– *The First Rapprochement: England and the United States, 1795–1805.* Berkeley: University of California Press, 1967.

Pratt, Julius. *The Expansionists of 1812.* New York: Macmillan, 1925.

– 'Fur Trade Strategy and the American Left Flank in the War of 1812.' *American Historical Review* 40 (Jan. 1935), 247–73.

Rawle, Francis. 'Edward Livingston.' In Samuel Flagg Bemis, ed., *The American*

Secretaries of State and Their Diplomacy. Vol. 4. 1928. Reprint, New York: Cooper Square Publishers, 1963.

Raymond, Rev. William O. *The River St. John: Its Physical Features, Legends and History from 1604 to 1784.* 1910. Reprint, Sackville, NB: Tribune Press, 1943.

Reeves, Jesse S. *American Diplomacy under Tyler and Polk.* Baltimore, Md.: Johns Hopkins University Press, 1907.

Reid, R.L. 'The Indian Stream Territory: An Episode of the North-East Boundary Dispute.' *Transactions of the Royal Society of Canada,* third series, 34 no. 2 (May 1940), 143–71.

Remini, Robert V. *Andrew Jackson and the Course of American Democracy, 1833–1845.* Vol. 3. New York: Harper and Row, 1984.

– *Daniel Webster: The Man and His Time.* New York: W.W. Norton, 1997.

– *Henry Clay: Statesman for the Union.* New York: W.W. Norton, 1991.

Ridley, Jasper. *Lord Palmerston.* London: Granada Publishing, 1972.

Scheuer, Michael F. 'Deadlock: Charting the Canadian–American Boundary on the Detroit River.' *Michigan History* 67 (1983), 24–30.

– 'From the St. Lawrence to Lake Superior: The Anglo–American Joint Commission of 1816–1822 and the Charting of the Canadian–American Boundary.' Master of arts thesis, Carleton University, 1980.

– 'Peter Buell Porter and the Development of the Joint Commission Approach to Diplomacy in the North Atlantic Triangle.' *American Review of Canadian Studies* 12 (1982), 65–73.

Schull, Joseph. *Rebellion: The Rising in French Canada.* Toronto: Macmillan, 1971.

Schwartz, Seymour I., and Ralph E. Ehrenburg. *The Mapping of America.* New York: Harry N. Abrams, 1980.

Scott, Geraldine Tidd. *Ties of Common Blood: A History of Maine's Northeast Boundary Dispute with Great Britain, 1783–1842.* Bowie, Md.: Heritage Books, 1992.

Shewmaker, Kenneth, ed. *Daniel Webster: 'The Completest Man.'* Hanover, NH: University Press of New England, 1990.

Shortridge, William P. 'The Canadian–American Frontier during the Rebellions of 1838–1838.' *Canadian Historical Review* 7 (March 1926), 13–26.

Smith, Edgar Crosby. 'Our Eastern Boundary: The St. Croix River Controversy.' In Louis Clinton Hatch, ed., *Maine, a History.* Vol. 1. New York: The American Historical Society, 1919.

Spencer, Ivor D. *The Victor and the Spoils: A Life of William L. Marcy.* Providence, RI: Brown University Press, 1959.

Sprague, John Francis. *The North Eastern Boundary Controversy and the Aroostook War.* Dover, Maine: Observer Press, 1910.

– 'The North Eastern Boundary Controversy, 1783–1842.' In Lous Clinton Hatch, ed., *Maine, a History.* Vol. 1. New York: American Historical Society, 1919.

Stacy, C.P. 'A Private Report of General Winfield Scott on the Border Situation in 1839.' *Canadian Historical Review* 21 (Dec. 1940), 407–14.

Stephen, Sir Leslie, and Sir Sidney Lee, eds. *The Dictionary of National Biography.* 21 vols. Oxford: Oxford University Press, 1917–73.

Stevens, Kenneth R. *Border Diplomacy: The Caroline and McLeod Affairs in Anglo–American-Canadian Relations, 1837–1842.* Tuscaloosa: University of Alabama Press, 1989.

Stewart, Gordon T. *The American Response to Canada since 1776.* East Lansing: Michigan State University Press, 1992.

Stinchcombe, William C. *The American Revolution and the French Alliance.* Syracuse, NY: Syracuse University Press, 1969.

Stuart, Reginald C. *United States Expansionism and British North America, 1775–1871.* Chapel Hill: University of North Carolina Press, 1988.

Tallman, R.D., and J.I. Tallman. 'The Diplomatic Search for the St. Croix River, 1796–1798.' *Acadiensis* 1 (spring 1972), 59–71.

Thomson, Don W. *Men and Meridians: The History of Surveying and Mapping in Canada.* Vol. 1. Ottawa: Queen's Printer, 1966.

Tiffany, Orrin Edward. 'The Relations of the United States to the Rebellion of 1837–1838.' *Buffalo Historical Society Publication* 8 (1905), 7–147.

Tyler, Lyon G. 'President John Tyler and the Ashburton Treaty.' *William and Mary Quarterly* 25 (July 1916), 1–8.

Updyke, Frank A. *The Diplomacy of the War of 1812.* Baltimore, Md.: Johns Hopkins Press, 1915.

Upton, L.F.S. *Micmacs and Colonists: Indian–White Relations in the Maritimes, 1713–1867.* Vancouver: University of British Columbia Press, 1979.

Van Alstyne, Richard W. *Empire and Independence: The International History of the American Revolution.* New York: John Wiley & Sons, 1967.

Van Deusen, Glyndon G. *The Jacksonian Era, 1828–1848.* New York: Harper and Row, 1959.

– *William Henry Seward.* New York: Oxford University Press, 1967.

Van Minnen, Cornelius A. *American Diplomats in the Netherlands, 1815–1850.* New York: St Martin's Press, 1993.

Varg, Paul A. *New England and Foreign Relations, 1790–1850.* Hanover, NH: University Press of New England, 1983.

– *United States Foreign Relations, 1820–1869.* East Lansing: Michigan State University Press, 1979.

Wait, James T., ed. *National Cyclopedia of American Biography.* 59 vols. New York: J.T. Wait, 1892–1971.

Walters, Raymond, Jr. *Albert Gallatin: Jeffersonian Financier and Diplomat.* New York: Macmillan, 1957.

Ward, Sir H.W., and G.P. Gooch, eds. *The Cambridge History of British Foreign Policy, 1783–1919.* Vol. 2. Cambridge: Cambridge University Press, 1923.

Washburn, Israel *The North-East Boundary.* Portland: Maine Historical Society, 1881.

Watt, Alastair. 'The Case of Alexander McLeod.' *Canadian Historical Review* 12 (June 1931), 145–67.

Wayland, Francis Fry. *Andrew Stevenson: Democrat and Diplomat, 1785–1857.* Philadelphia: University of Pennsylvania Press, 1949.

Webster, Sir Charles. *The Foreign Policy of Palmerston, 1830–1841.* Vol. 1. London: G. Bell, 1951.

Westerman, J.C. *The Netherlands and the United States: Their Relations in the Nineteenth Century.* The Hague: Martinus Nijhoff. 1935.

White, James. 'Boundary Disputes and Treaties.' In Adam Short and Arthur G. Doughty, eds., *Canada and Its Provinces.* Vol. 8. Toronto: Glasgow, Brook, 1914.

Willson, Beckles. *America's Ambassadors to England (1785–1928): A Narrative of Anglo–American Diplomatic Relations.* 1928. Reprint, Freeport, NY: Books for Libraries Press, 1969.

Winchell, Alexander N. 'Minnesota's Northern Boundary.' *Minnesota Historical Society Collections* 8 (1898), 185–212.

Wise, Donald A. 'Surveying and Mapping the International Border in Northeast Maine: 1817–1818.' *Surveying and Mapping* 40 (1980), 419–27.

Woodward, Sir Llewellyn. *The Age of Reform, 1815–1870.* Oxford: Oxford University Press, 1962.

Wright, Esther Clark. *The Saint John River.* Toronto: McClelland & Stewart, 1949.

Wright, J. Leitch, Jr. *Britain and the American Frontier, 1783–1815.* Athens: University of Georgia Press, 1975.

Wynn, Graeme. 'Administration in Adversity: The Deputy Surveyors and Control of New Brunswick Crown Forests before 1844.' *Acadiensis* 7 (autumn 1977), 49–65.

Younge, Charles Duke. *The Life and Administration of Robert Banks, Second Earl of Liverpool, K.G.* Vol. 2. London: Macmillan, 1868.

Ziegler, Philip. *Melbourne: A Biography of William Lamb, 2nd Viscount Melbourne.* New York: Alfred A. Knopf, 1976.

– *The Sixth Great Power: A History of One of the Greatest of all Banking Families, The House of Barings, 1762–1929.* New York: Alfred A. Knopf, 1988.

Index

Aberdeen, 4th earl of, 3–4, 157, 234, 244–5, 248, 262–3, 267, 353n, 404n; foreign secretary, 155; preparations of British case, 161; on Douglas going to The Hague, 169; crisis in Belgium, 181; instructions on McLeod, 216, 218; returned as foreign secretary, 244–5; on political difficulties in Canada, 245; instructions to Ashburton, 249–54, 389n, 392n; warned about moment of opportunity, 266; informed of talks by Ashburton, 273–4; improvement in Anglo–American relations, 275–6, 375n; on *Caroline* and *Creole*, 281, 284; reactions to Webster–Ashburton Treaty, 288–90, 401n; on honours for Ashburton, 295–6, 405n; map question, 300, 406n; willing to work for peace, 305

Acadians, 39, 48, 195, 199, 271

Adams, Charles Francis, 230

Adams, David P., 72, 98–9, 102; resignation, 103

Adams, Ephraim Douglas: on Ashburton's instructions, 390n; on negotiations, 398n

Adams, John, 89, 93, 149; testimony for St Croix Commission, 15

Adams, John Quincy, 83, 101, 151–2, 230, 322n, 328n, 395n, 399n; biography, 22; peace negotiations, 24, 30, 318n, 319n; secretary of state, 41; told of talks on islands, 43; transfer of islands, 44; forty-fifth parallel, 73, 75; hired Ellicott, 77; advised to attempt negotiation, 92; president, 96, 138; death of Ogilvy, 104; appointed Delafield, 106–7; expenses of commission, 107; islands in Detroit River, 114; on British gesture, 115; informed of surveys from Lake Superior to Lake of the Woods, 119, 123, 130; disagreements on article-7 commission, 131, 134; agreement to locate forty-ninth parallel, 138; boundary in annual message, 141; offer to negotiate eastern boundary, 147–8, 151–2, 348–9n; election of 1824, 149–50; submitted arbitration convention to Senate, 153, 351n; suggested king of Netherlands, 155; defeated in 1828, 157; on Baker